Manufacturing Planning and Control Systems

Manufacturing Planning and Control Systems

Thomas E. Vollmann

Boston University

William L. Berry

University of Iowa

D. Clay Whybark

Indiana University

DOW JONES-IRWIN
Homewood, Illinois 60430

In memory of Oliver W. Wight;
Professor, Teacher and Friend.
He moved the ball.

A classroom edition of this book is available through Richard D. Irwin, Inc.

ISBN 0-87094-452-5

Library of Congress Catalog Card No. 83–70917

Printed in the United States of America

1 2 3 4 5 6 7 8 9 0 MP 1 0 9 8 7 6 5 4

Preface

Along with countless other people, we started this book with the basic belief that we could write a book that would be useful for practicing managers and also valuable as a classroom text. We retain this belief. Over the years, we have worked with numerous practitioners in seminars, consulting, and research, so our viewpoint on manufacturing planning and control spans both theory and practice.

We first address the fundamentals of materials requirements planning that are found in good practice. The book then moves on to some of the more advanced material that could be incorporated as enhancements to these systems. These materials are also of interest to those with more of a theoretical background. The distinguishing feature of this book, however, is that the theory is not abstract and nonapplicable. We believe that the insights provided will be of use to many academics as they continue to perform research work in manufacturing planning and control.

Early in our writing, our contacts with manufacturing executives and consultants convinced us that we did have a message for the practicing manager. The criticisms of many of them both motivated us and led us to improvements in the material. We especially appreciate the early encouragement of Joe Orlicky, Ollie Wight, Walt Goddard, Tom Wallace, Don Hall, and Mike Glavin. The book also benefited from careful readings by Andre Martin, Professor Bob Fetter, and several anonymous reviewers.

Dean Schuyler Otteson of the Indiana University Business School, Deans Harry Hanson and Derek Abell of IMEDE, Dean Heinz Thanheiser of INSEAD, Dean Henry Morgan of Boston University, and Dean Emmett Vaughan at the University of Iowa all provided support and encouragement for the project.

Several students reviewed parts of the material and made comments after they got their grades, and our graduate students suffered through early drafts and were quick to be helpful. Many typists labored with our collectively poor handwriting. Chief among these were Gail Spiese, Brigit Chevalier, John Fulnecky, Diane Breitenbach, Barb Thomson, Jean Skog, and Michele Nativel. We would like to acknowledge Bill Tallon's help with the material and Col. P. J. Egan's support. To all of these and many more we owe our thanks.

Thomas E. Vollmann
William L. Berry
D. Clay Whybark

Contents

1

Manufacturing planning and control

The central focus of this book is on solving the managerial problems associated with controlling flows of material and inventory levels in manufacturing/distribution systems. Manufacturing planning and control (MPC) encompasses both the solution to particular problems (e.g., in what order to process a set of jobs on a machine to improve some performance measure) and the linkages among problem areas (e.g., how improved component part planning could provide a set of jobs at the machine that would further improve the performance). In each aspect of manufacturing planning and control, we see some or all of the following:

- Key issues: What are the key problem areas?
- Framework: How do these problems relate to other parts of the MPC system?
- Technical considerations: What techniques or systems are useful in solving the problems?
- Managerial considerations: What organizational, managerial or technical changes are necessary to create an effective system?
- Data base: What is the underlying data base to support the systems?
- Examples: How have effective systems been implemented in leading edge firms?

Each of the chapters in the first part of this book is organized around these issues, while the latter part of the book provides technical depth and advanced concepts to enhance a basic operational MPC system. The material in the chapters reflects the substantial progress that has occured in the field of manufacturing planning and control over the last two decades. This progress includes the development of a professional body of knowledge, an attendant development of MPC professionals, the development of computer software that is transplantable between firms, and an increasing application of MPC systems and software in small as well as large firms.

The primary benefit achieved through better manufacturing planning and control is in the reduction of what we call "organizational slack." Organizational slack is manifested in excess inventories, excess capacity, excess labor costs, overtime costs, long manfacturing lead times, poor delivery promise performance, fewer new products with longer development cycles, and a lack of responsiveness to changes in the business environment. Hence, a primary payoff from MPC systems is in reducing organizational slack. This payoff can be measured in terms of improved output per man-hour, reduced overtime, reduced inventory investment, reduced obsolescence, improved inventory turnover, lower purchasing costs, reduced distribution costs, improved customer service levels, and the internal generation of capital investment funds. Specific examples of such gains include:

1. *The Tennant Company*, in a two-year period with its MPC system in place, witnessed the following changes in performances:
   a. Purchased material inventory reduced by 42 percent ($3,129,000).
   b. Production rate increased by 66 percent.
   c. Assembly efficiency increased from 45 percent to 85 percent.
   d. Delivery promises met increased from 60 percent to 90 percent.
2. *Steelcase Inc.* put in a new MPC system to better integrate purchasing with manufacturing and found:
   a. The percentage of past due purchase orders dropped from 35 to 3.2 percent.
   b. In a two-year period, sales rose 58 percent, while purchased part inventories rose by 12 percent.
   c. During the same period, purchasing cost reduction program savings increased from $500,000 per year to $5 million per year.
   d. During a period of severe nationwide shortages, Steelcase had no vendor lead times over five weeks.
   e. In a sharp economic downturn, Steelcase was able to control inventories and maintain profits.
   f. The purchasing manager stated, "Vendor lead times are virtually irrelevant to Steelcase."
3. *Kumera OY* implemented an MPC system in six months during a period of heavy competitive pressure and:
   a. Tripled their gross margin.
   b. Increased inventory turnover from 5 to 10 times per year.

   c. Eliminated late delivery penalties.
   d. With the funds generated, installed modern, numerically controlled equipment which provided them with a distinct competitive advantage.
4. *Black & Decker* cut work in process in half and cut the average shop lead time from 6 to 2.9 weeks during a period of sales growth.
5. *Elliott Company, Division of Carrier Corporation,* improved its performance against customer promise dates by 50 percent while reducing inventory by 23 percent and increasing sales by 32 percent.
6. *Toyota Motor Company* attributes much of their success to their MPC system which is tailored to the Japanese industrial environment. The firm has the highest labor productivity of any automobile company. Moreover, its turnover of working assets is 10 times that of U.S. and Western European producers.

We turn now to a framework for manufacturing planning and control. The MPC framework structures the individual activities into an integrated whole. Thereafter we will look at selected problems associated with material flows and see how a generalized MPC system has been developed that is consistent with both the general framework and the specific problems.

A FRAMEWORK FOR MANUFACTURING PLANNING AND CONTROL

We noted above that the field of manufacturing planning and control is concerned with both specific problems and techniques for their solution, as well as with the linkages or interactions among particular problem areas. It is these interactions that are of interest to us in this section.

In any firm, manufacturing planning and control encompasses three distinct activities or phases. The first activity is establishment of the overall direction for the firm, with the resulting management plan stated in manufacturing terms, such as end items or product options. The manufacturing plan must be consistent with the company's direction and the plans for other departments of the firm. The second MPC activity is the detailed planning of material flows and capacity to support the overall plans. The third and final MPC activity is the execution of these plans in terms of detailed shop scheduling and purchasing actions.

Overall direction

Overall direction is provided by a game plan that links and coordinates the various departments (e.g., marketing, finance, engineering) of the company. The game plan is the responsibility of top management. It should be at all times consistent with strategic plans, departmental budgets, and the manufacturing plans for production output.

The overall direction phase of manufacturing planning and control includes the estimation of demand for the products sold by the firm. It is also necessary to estimate any additional demand for manufacturing capacity that comes from spare part sales, interplant or intercompany transfers, and branch warehouse requirements. In addition to forecasting the total demand, it is also necessary to manage the consumption (transformation) of the forecast by actual customer orders. That is, one must deal with order entry, customer order promising, and order backlog as these actual orders replace forecast information.

End item planning and customer order entry are where detailed tradeoffs are made between marketing and manufacturing. On one hand it is desirable to provide enough stability so that manufacturing can reasonably be held responsible for meeting plans. On the other hand, it is worthwhile to provide sufficient flexibility so that the company can respond competitively to actual customer needs.

Detailed material and capacity planning

The planning of detailed component and raw material needs to support the manufacturing plan can be quite complex. For many firms, this involves the creation of detailed plans for tens or even hundreds of thousands of individual parts.

Detailed capacity planning is the establishment of the individual capacity plans for each machine group, based upon the detailed material plan. Included are the capacity needs for the work already in process as well as the capacity requirements of anticipated orders for all parts.

Execution

Execution of the detailed material and capacity plans involves the scheduling of machine and other work centers. In the factory, this scheduling must reflect such routine events as starting and completing orders for parts, and any problem conditions such as breakdowns or absenteeism. It is usually necessary to update these schedules at least once per day in factories with complex manufacturing processes for producing parts and components.

An analogous detailed schedule is required for purchased parts. In essence, purchasing is the procurement of outside-work-center capacity. It must be planned and scheduled well to minimize the overall cost to the final customers. Good purchasing systems typically separate the procurement activity from routine order release and order follow-up. Procurement is a highly professional job which involves contracting for vendor capacity and establishment of ground rules for order release and order follow-up.

Some firms have used the execution phase to encompass other critical activities. For example, the Elliott Company mentioned above uses a direct analog of shop floor scheduling to plan and control their engineering and drafting activities.

A final activity tied to execution is the measurement of actual results. As products are manufactured, the rate of production and timing of specific completion can be compared to plans. As shipments are made to customers, measures of actual customer service can be obtained. As capacity is used, it too can be compared to plans.

This three-phase framework for material planning and control is supported by a widely applied set of MPC systems and software. The systems are designed to help solve the many problems that arise in managing the flows of material. We will return to a description of these systems after first looking at material flow problems in some detail, seeing the interactions among problems, techniques, and supporting data bases.

MATERIAL FLOWS

A flow of materials occurs in any production or logistics process which procures raw materials, produces components, creates products for selling, and moves them to consumers. An entire spectrum of interrelated management problems arises in this overall flow, and systems must be created to deal with these problems on a routine basis. Furthermore, an accurate data base is required to use the system for routine decision making.

The production/logistics process

Figure 1.1 relates several issues to the flow of materials that is typical for many firms. In the bottom portion, we see a physical flow beginning with purchased raw materials and component parts coming from vendors into inventories. Raw materials are transformed into component parts through machining and other fabrication steps. Component parts are removed from inventory and assembled into finished goods. Finished goods inventories are shipped directly to consumers or by movement through distribution centers and field warehouses. This flow is quite universal, but the specific differences between firms must be taken into account in the detailed design of MPC systems.

One key difference between firms is often seen in the fabrication stage. Some companies have a *job shop* approach, where parts are routed to work centers depending on the production steps required. Other firms have a *flow shop* approach, where one or a few products travel through a set of fabrication activities specially arranged for the particular products. In the latter extreme, we have repetitive manufacturing (e.g., automobiles) and process industries (e.g., chemical plants) in which no significant stoppage in the flow of materials is evidenced, and flow rate becomes the critical decision. The job shop is more flexible in terms of the products that can be

FIGURE 1.1 Material flows, management problems, decision-making techniques, and supporting data base.

Stage	A	B	C	D	E	F	G	H	I	J
Example management problems	How to monitor vendor performance	How to maintain accurate raw material records	How to schedule component item production	How to determine component item requirements	How to schedule final assembly	How to estimate end-item demand for each product	How to route trucks	How much and when to order	How to choose transportation modes	How to select warehouse locations
Techniques and systems	Vendor scheduling procedures	Cycle counting techniques	Shop-floor control systems	Material requirements planning (MRP) systems	Master production scheduling (MPS) systems	Exponential smoothing forecasting procedures	Vehicle scheduling techniques	Independent demand-based inventory procedures	Inventory/transportation trade-off techniques	Warehouse location techniques
Database elements	Purchase orders	Inventory records	Part routings	Bills of material	Open customer orders	Sales order history	Shipping costs	Safety stocks	Transportation costs	Customer ordering patterns

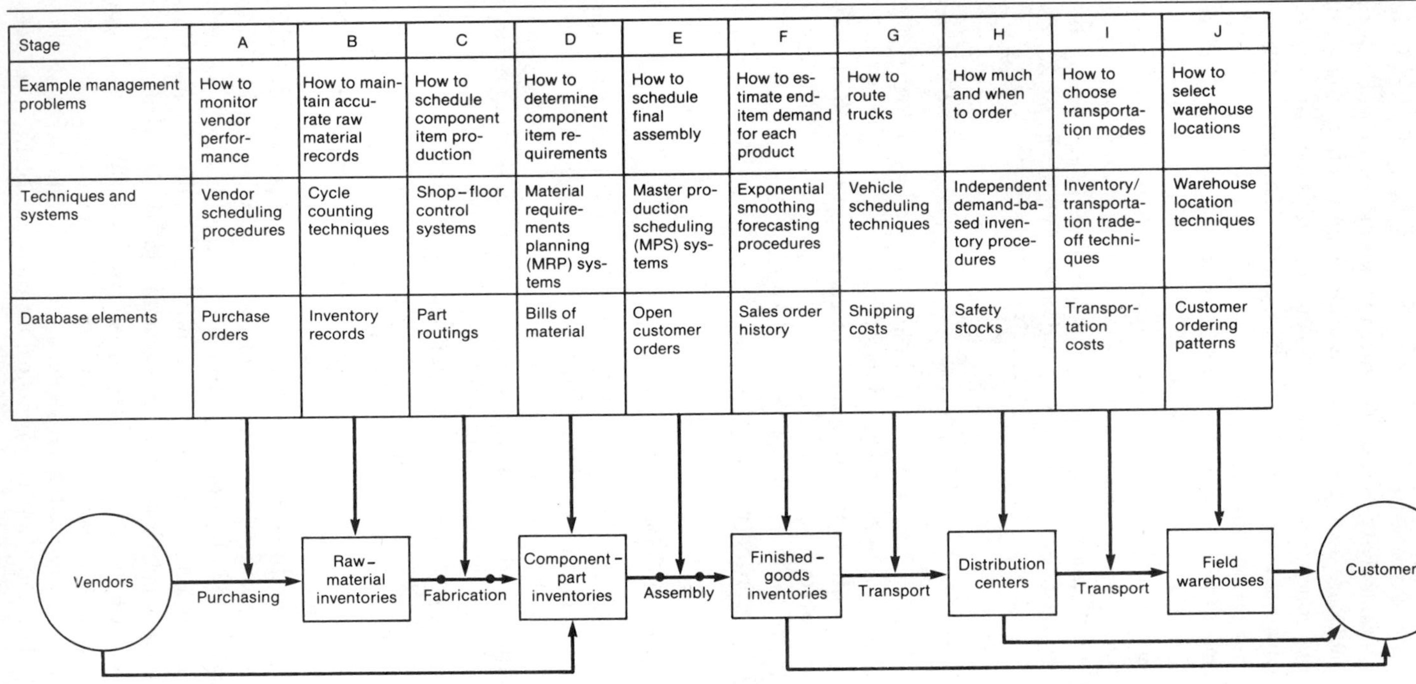

produced, while the flow shop offers efficiencies from specially designed equipment and fast through-put times. But both have flows of material that require scheduling. Thus, even though there may be different emphases, criteria, and problem complexity, the fundamental management questions are still there.

Manufacturing companies can also be distinguished by those that manufacture each customer order on a unique basis (make to order), those that assemble a wide variety of finished goods from a smaller set of standardized options (assemble to order), and those that produce goods for inventory (make to stock). In the latter case, finished goods inventories are used to separate the assembly process from customer orders. The assemble-to-order firm, on the other hand, needs to carefully integrate actual customer orders with option planning and final assembly.

Still another distinction between manufacturing firms has to do with the complexity of component part fabrication and assembly. Some firms do little internal fabrication, purchasing most of their component parts prior to assembly. Others, with extensive machining and other conversion processes, have significantly more complex component part fabrication activities. Similarly, vast differences exist in the complexity of finished goods assembly. Some firms make relatively few products with dozens of component parts; others assemble hundreds of end items made from thousands of component parts. These differences, in turn, lead to differences in the details of the MPC systems required by the firms.

Combinations of all sorts can exist in the complexity of fabrication and assembly. Consider, for example, the differences between a make-to-stock furniture manufacturer and a make-to-order transmission/drive train manufacturer. The furniture manufacturer purchases logs, boards, other raw materials, and component parts such as hinges, drawer pulls, etc. Wood parts are cut from boards and transformed into component parts by a few fairly standard machining steps. Component parts such as tops, sides, legs, etc. are assembled into a large variety of finished goods and thereafter stained and packed. Trucks deliver furniture to warehouses and furniture dealers who sell to final customers. Component fabrication is relatively straightforward, but the assembly scheduling is quite complex in this company.

A somewhat different situation is faced by the company that makes a wide range of heavy-duty transmissions and other drive train equipment for vehicles such as tractors and farm machinery. In this case, final assembly tends to be straightforward, but the number of component fabrication steps can be very large, the machinery utilized is quite expensive (and therefore important to utilize effectively), and the company does not build to stock. The furniture manufacturer has many people committed to the assembly stage—this means that an even flow of material becomes important. The drive train manufacturer does not have the same relative need to smooth the assembly work flow, but is more concerned with a flow of material that provides high utilization of the machine tools for component part fabrication. The systems these companies employ cover the same general material flow problems, but specific design features support their different needs.

Management problems

The top row of Figure 1.1 depicts sample managerial problems that relate to the various stages of production/logistics. For each of these stages (coded A through J in Figure 1.1) several critical questions exist. (We have provided one example for each stage.) Figure 1.1 also shows examples of decision-making techniques and systems that have been designed to solve these problems, and the data base elements that must be maintained to provide the correct input for the techniques and systems. We discuss the questions that face management at each of these stages next.

The first stage, A, depicted in Figure 1.1, relates to the purchase of needed raw material and component parts. Some key management problems to be resolved at this stage include how to select vendors, what approaches should be taken to coordinate vendor activities with production needs, and how to monitor and control vendor performance.

Stage B is concerned with raw material inventories. Included are the managerial questions of how to determine desired inventory levels, proper procedures for physical control over raw materials, and the appropriate record-keeping systems for a particular firm.

Stage C is the conversion of raw materials into fabricated component parts. In many firms, this is the most critical step in production. Key managerial problems include the approach to scheduling each fabrication step for each component part, determining the overall level of fabrication activities, and utilizing work center capacities effectively.

Stage D, component part inventories, is directly linked to stage C. This is because the replenishment of component part inventories places requirements on component part fabrication (or upon vendors for vendor requirements). Some key managerial issues concerning component part inventories are: how to plan and release replenishment orders, how large a batch to produce (lot size) for replenishment, and how to maintain physical control of the inventories.

Stage E is the assembly of component parts into finished goods. Managerial problems at this stage include setting the overall output rate for the manufacturing facility, determining the build schedule for individual end items or options, firming up the final assembly schedule, and monitoring actual performance.

Stage F, finished goods inventories, is linked to assembly in that any difference between desired and actual finished goods inventory levels is a potential source of demand for replenishment orders on assembly. Critical management problems include how to forecast end item demand, ways of accomplishing the customer contact functions of order entry and order promising, setting of safety stocks, and how to establish desired finished goods inventory levels.

Stage G is the outbound transportation of finished goods inventories to the physical distribution system. Managerial issues here include whether to use a private fleet or common carrier, the frequency of distribution center replenishment, the approach to be taken in preparing actual truck and freight schedules, and the integration of product distribution with finished goods inventory level determination.

Stage H, distribution centers, may not be used for all products or even exist in a particular firm. Key managerial questions include whether to have distribution centers, how many to have, where they should be located, the desired distribution center inventory levels, and the approach used for inventory replenishment.

Stage I is the transportation of goods from distribution centers to field warehouses. Managerial questions include the choice of transportation mode, scheduling of replenishment shipments, whether to ship directly to customers, and whether transhipping between field warehouses is to be utilized.

The last stage, J, shown in Figure 1.1, is field warehouses. Managerial questions include whether to utilize this form of physical distribution, analysis of public versus private warehouses, which items to hold and not to hold in these facilities, the approach used for replenishment, and the desired inventory levels.

It should be clear that all of the stages in Figure 1.1 are related, and that the managerial issues are similarly related. Answers to questions at any stage need to be examined in terms of their influence on preceding and succeeding stages. Since the importance and complexity of and emphases on the different stages varies from company to company and industry to industry, the MPC systems can be expected to vary. There has been an acceleration of systems and techniques to help answer managerial questions at each of the stages. They are not all found in all firms, however, since the needs of the firms vary. The application of these techniques in successful companies has been most sharply focused on those stages which are key to the success of the firm.

Techniques and systems

We turn our attention here to the discussion of the techniques, systems, and procedures that have been developed to help solve each of the managerial problems listed in Figure 1.1. Some of these problems are infrequent, such as determining how many distribution centers to have and where to place them. The majority of the problems faced in production and inventory management, however, recur, and the need is to create a routine approach, system, or "decision rule" for handling these problems. Perhaps the most basic cornerstone to improved management of material flows is "doing the routine things routinely." Examples of routine problems include component part planning, transaction processing, establishing priorities for unfinished work (open orders) in the fabrication shop, starting the assembly process by launching an assembly order, and determining the replenishment order to be shipped to a particular warehouse.

There has been some lively discussion among production and inventory management experts on the extent to which decisions about these routine problems can be automated, that is, put on a computer. The key point is not whether or not they can be automated, but rather that the vast majority of these routine decisions should be made in a very predictable way, guided by tightly defined and consistent policies. These policies should lead to specific procedures that could either be manually or computer supported.

This system or decision rule sets the guidelines for detailed execution of the decisions. The managerial issues are how to design the system, provide the data, set the decision rules, implement the system, monitor performance, and make improvements. Improvement usually comes from better techniques, from better integration of the material flow with the organization, and from better (more accurate and more pertinent) data.

Tightly defined systems for guiding routine decision making are very important in providing the linkages among the managerial problems shown in Figure 1.1. This is so because the predictability that arises leads to a phenomenon called *system transparency*. Simply stated, when the decisions that will be made at any stage of the material flow are clearly defined, that area becomes *transparent* to the other stages (subsystems), that is, the response or decision that will be made based on any set of input conditions is readily apparent. For example, a change in the bills of materials at stage D will result in a change in the part routings at stage C for a specific item on a specific date.

An interesting aspect of the various techniques and systems shown in Figure 1.1 for stages A through J is a similarity of certain problems. For example, certain stages are concerned with *scheduling* (A, C, E, G, and I). The techniques that are useful for scheduling in one of these stages are often of interest in another. Moreover, the scheduling done in one stage creates a set of conditions for previous and subsequent stages. We then see the need for integrated scheduling.

Another common problem is the control of inventory levels. Stages B, D, F, H and J all are concerned with inventories. As with scheduling, inventory techniques, systems, and procedures have multiple applications. Moreover, there is critical interaction between the inventory levels and the scheduling stages that replenish and deplete these inventories.

This book is largely devoted to the design of systems to routinely control the material flow process depicted in Figure 1.1. The decision systems necessarily have to be tailored to differing company environments, but in almost every situation there is a basic core of building blocks required. Our intent in the first part of this book is to describe these building blocks, show how they can be linked together for differing companies, illustrate their application in many actual company environments, consider how they are implemented, and assess the resulting costs and benefits to the organizations. The theory and concepts for more advanced system design are presented in the second part of the book.

The data base

Each technique or system relies on certain basic information, examples of which are shown in Figure 1.1. For example, a machine scheduling system for a large job shop needs data for each part to be produced, including some or all of the following: the steps or routing required for fabrication, the expected time for each fabrication step, the due date, the expected time to complete remaining steps, the estimated labor for each step, the quantity to be completed at each step, and each shop order associated with each part.

The data base elements shown in Figure 1.1 are representative of those necessary to support the techniques and systems. Many problems in manufacturing planning and control are not analytically complex; instead, their complexity derives from the enormity of the underlying data base required to properly support routine decision-making systems. It is not unusual, for example, for a firm to require 5 million individual pieces of data to be accurately maintained and accessed to support a component part planning system.

It is not enough to have well-formulated systems. They must be driven with data that are appropriate, consistent, and accurate. The data elements must be the same in all applications. For example, if the record for part 1234 indicates that 120 are on hand, this number should be found to be correct if a physical count were made and should be the same in the customer service information system, the finance system, the manufacturing system, etc. Accurate data require rigorous procedures for their maintenance and for the transactions which update those data. For many firms, the achievement of this data base integrity will require profound changes in day-to-day operations. The management of data, like any other company resource, might necessitate major changes in thinking, habits, and procedures.

The importance of information integrity, even in this brief overview, suggests that the notion of data base integration should be mentioned. A modern manufacturing planning and control system virtually requires that the data elements be maintained in an integrated data base, with common definitions of terms, procedures for processing detailed transactions, clear assignment of organizational responsibility for each data base subsection, and a companywide commitment to maintain the integrity of each data base element. The payoffs achieved with good MPC systems derive largely from a substitution of information for organizational slacks. For example, rather than relying upon high levels of physical inventory to avoid coordination decisions, decisions can be based on data about inventory. These data indicate not only what is in inventory, but what are the planned withdrawals, and the replenishment schedules. To substitute information for inventory, it is necessary to have *high-quality information*. Many chapters in this book deal explicitly with the creation of appropriate data bases and their management. Firms that implement state-of-the-art MPC systems typically find that the day-to-day job becomes management *by* the data base and management *of* the data base.

MANUFACTURING PLANNING AND CONTROL SYSTEMS

Having now looked at the spectrum of material flow problems, their interrelationships, some techniques for dealing with these problems, and the underlying necessary data base, we return to the general approach to MPC systems that has evolved. We will see how it is consistent with the three-phase framework, show how specific material flow problems can be treated with the system, present some key issues for adapting the general system to a specific firm, and consider how the system can be implemented.

The system and the framework

Figure 1.2 is a simplified schematic of a modern MPC system. This diagram shows the skeletal framework for the systems described in subsequent chapters. The full system includes other data inputs, system modules, and feedback connections. Figure 1.2 is divided into three parts. The top third or *front end*, is the set of activities and systems for overall direction setting. This phase establishes the company objectives for manufacturing planning and control. Demand planning encompasses forecasting customer/end product demand, order entry, order promising, accomodating interplant and intercompany demand, and spare parts requirements. In essence, all activities of the business that place demands on manufacturing capacity are coordinated in demand planning. Production planning is that activity which provides the production input to the company game plan and determines the manufacturing role in this agreed-upon strategic plan. The master production schedule (MPS) is the disaggregated version of the production plan. That is, the MPS is a statement to manufacturing of which end items or product options they will build in the future. The MPS must sum up to the production plan.

The middle third, or *engine*, in Figure 1.2 is the set of systems for accomplishing the detailed material and capacity planning. The master production schedule feeds directly into material requirements planning (MRP). MRP determines (explodes) the period-by-period (time-phased) plans for all component parts and raw materials required to produce all the products in the MPS. This material plan can thereafter be utilized in the detailed capacity

FIGURE 1.2 Manufacturing planning and control system (simplified)

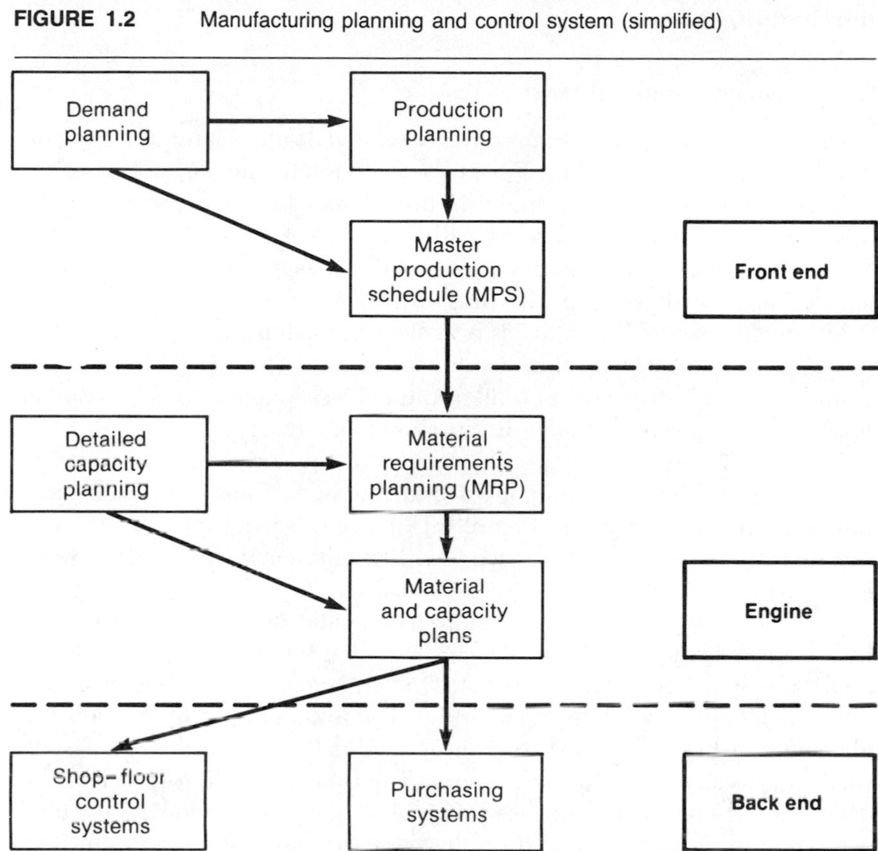

planning systems to compute labor or machine center capacity required to manufacture all the component parts.

The bottom third, or *back end*, of Figure 1.2 depicts the execution systems. Shop floor control systems establish priorities for all shop orders at each work center so that the orders can be properly scheduled. Purchasing systems provide detailed planning information for vendor scheduling. This information relates to existing purchase orders as well as to planned purchase orders.

For each of the subsystems from master production scheduling down through to the back end systems shown in Figure 1.2, computer hardware and software firms have produced packaged software products that provide information support for the activity. Moreover, the software is integrated to follow the framework. That is, the MPS produces the right input to MRP, which, in turn, provides the information to drive the shop floor control and purchasing systems.

The system and material flows

The system outlined in Figure 1.2 is related to the material flows and problems we discussed earlier. For example, the front end part of Figure 1.2 is addressed to the latter stages shown in Figure 1.1, those concerned with finishing the product and dealing with the market. Note, however, that some of the necessary activities (such as the management of spare parts demand) are not shown explicitly in Figure 1.1.

The engine part of Figure 1.2 is primarily associated with the determination of component item requirements, depicted as stage D in Figure 1.1. Again, Figure 1.1 does not show all of the necessary activities. The issue of capacity planning, for instance, is not shown in Figure 1.1.

The back end part of Figure 1.2 deals with the early stages of material flow, those dealing with component and purchased item scheduling and control (stages A through C in Figure 1.1). Stage C is largely concerned with shop floor control systems, and stage A with purchasing systems, both execution activities of a firm.

Figure 1.1 lists an example of a supporting data base element for each of the systems/techniques that are shown. We noted the need for integration of the data base earlier in our discussion. One of the primary reasons that most professionals today view manufacturing planning and control through the framework of Figure 1.2 is that an integrated data base can be established which is consistent with this framework. The front end data base drives the MRP system. The MRP data base provides the information for the detailed material plans. These plans, in turn, drive the capacity planning system. The data base of detailed material and capacity plans drives the back end systems (shop floor and purchasing), which, in turn, have their own data bases.

We see then, that Figure 1.2 is an overall system that is built upon an integrated data base and an integrated set of systems. The result is an integrated approach to dealing with material flow problems. Moreover, the approach shown in Figure 1.2 is now the way leading authorities *think* about MPC systems, and the way that software packages are conceived and designed. The result forms an important base for professional development in this field.

The system and the individual firm

The activities shown in Figure 1.2 are necessarily performed in *every* manufacturing firm, whether large or small. However, the emphasis given to each of the activities depends strongly on the attributes of the company. The importance of the approach presented in Figure 1.2 is that a consistent set of

MPC system modules can ensure that detailed decision making is completely and constantly synchronized with the overall game plan.

It is extremely important *not* to give the impression that all one needs to do is go out and buy the complete set of computer packages depicted in Figure 1.2. That is simply not the case. Computer hardware and software are the easiest aspects of implementing an MPC system. The complexity and changes required in day-to-day operations to drive the system with accurate data bases are much more profound. Even more significant are the changes in methods, habits, and attitudes of the people involved. New ways of *thinking* about their jobs are required.

The implementation of an advanced MPC system can easily represent the most profound change in operations a firm will ever experience. Moreover, each firm has certain unique features that must be considered in the design of its MPC system. One set of unique characteristics concerns the management policies relating to performance measures and response. For example, how does management measure and evaluate customer service, inventory investment, and productivity? Are there specific goals stated for these? How responsive should the system be to the dynamics of the marketplace? To deal with responsiveness, most leading-edge firms have established explicit procedures and time frames for when and how changes to the master production schedule can be made, who makes the changes, how changes are reviewed, and appeal processes. Thus, the responsiveness trade-off gets explicit management attention.

Certain unique attributes of each firm influence the way that each of the systems shown in Figure 1.2 is designed and implemented. For some firms, it is necessary to include distribution systems. Others require a multiple factory approach. Some have a much greater need for extensive supplier networks than others. Also, depending upon the products produced, the firm may be more of a job shop than a flow shop, or vice versa. The company may be in the make-to-order business and necessarily need to effectively integrate the engineering and drafting activities with the MPC system. An assemble-to-order firm, on the other hand, needs a very strong linkage of customer order date promising with manufacturing. The make-to-stock firm may have a greater interest in inventory turnover. The nature of the competitive environment is also important. Some firms compete on the basis of price and/or fast deliveries for stable products. Others are constantly bringing out new products. Products are in different stages of the product life cycle. The MPC system has to be designed to support the market posture of the specific firm in question.

The critical point is that although the basic approach shown in Figure 1.2 applies to any manufacturing firm, it is necessary for the system to be tailored to the specific needs of the firm, which can change over time. Tailoring includes both the degree of development and detail of the individual systems, as well as the sequence for implementing each of the individual systems. In many subsequent chapters, we will show how companies in different kinds of businesses have produced different systems. We also will show that some systems are viewed as more critical in some firms than in others.

Implementing the system

For most firms, successful implementation of a state-of-the-art MPC system brings about profound changes. People do their day-to-day jobs differently and have new ways of thinking about their jobs and how these relate to other jobs. It is not at all easy. There is no exact formula for success, but there are several critical aspects that we can see as important. Thus, we now will present an overview of some of the major dimensions of implementation.

One key to successful implementation is goal setting. It is imperative that performance measures relate to the implementation of the MPC system. Specific targets must be set and evaluated. The manager who implements one of the MPC system modules should be rewarded. Moreover, after implementation, managerial performance evaluation should not be based on any measure that conflicts with MPC system performance goals.

A second key to implementation is organizational design. The need is to create an organizational structure consistent with MPC system activities and interfunctional integration. Senior management's attention must be directed toward the MPC system. Organizational changes in some firms consist primarily of changing attitudes and goals. In other firms, formal changes in the organization are required to achieve the desired results. We find that more and more successful firms are implementing a "materials management" form of organization specifically to facilitate MPC system implementation and operation. The objectives of such organizations are to provide an appropriate level of management for each of the goal-setting, detail-planning, and execution activities, and to assign data base responsibility. Finally, organizational design has to be viewed in light of the goal-setting process. As explicit MPC goals are set and modified, it is to be expected that changes in the organization must occur.

A third key to successful implementation is the proper design and use of project teams. A basic feature of good project team design is to have representation from all groups that will later use the system to do their jobs (the "user" groups). Another is to put the *best* people on the project teams—those whom the user groups can least afford to do without. A sure way to undermine the success of the project is to assign implementation responsibility to the newest or least-qualified person or make the assignment *in addition to* the person's other responsibilities. It is critical to find some way to release the project team members from other responsibilities. Leadership of the project team is also important. Overall leadership must *not* be assigned to system design staff groups or technical computer personnel. They should be used only for certain specific aspects, such as computer programming. Finally, proper project team design also requires that the team report to the appropriate management level in the firm. The interdisciplinary nature of MPC systems requires a high level of reporting to implement those key features that cross many functions.

Another key to implementation implicit in every phase of the project is education. It is necessary for people at all levels of the company to know how the system works, who will process certain kinds of transactions, and how their own jobs will be changed as a result of the MPC system.

The final key to success is monitoring the MPC system implementation process itself. It is necessary to periodically audit actual results in relation to plans, look for roadblocks to success, measure costs and benefits, and reestablish directions.

ORGANIZATION OF THE BOOK

In this final section we provide a brief road map of the remainder of the book. The first part of the book is devoted to the fundamental attributes of an integrated manufacturing planning and control (MPC) system. The perspective is integrative, providing an understanding of each of the basic modules of an MPC system, their interrelationships, the need for data base support, and how these systems have been implemented. The second half of the book provides support material of a more technical nature to better understand the detailed design or enhancement of specific subsystems. The organization that is followed in the majority of the chapters is presented next, followed by our logic for the specific topic sequence of the book.

Chapter organization

The approach taken in most of the chapters is closely related to the issues summarized in the framework of Figure 1.1. We start with a statement of the managerial objective of the system module to be discussed. We list the key topics around which the chapter is organized. We then show how the topic area fits within the overall MPC framework shown in Figure 1.2 and provide references to other parts of the book and a description of any special objectives, constraints, or concerns that apply to the area. Thereafter, we present the systems and techniques that are most important to the module. Many of these are illustrated with examples taken from successfully operating systems.

For many of the system modules, we provide an important section on living with the system. In such sections, we provide information on conditions that must be met to ensure successful use of the system, organizational actions required, and ways to use the information provided by the system to improve performance.

We also identify the data base which must be developed and maintained to support the systems and integrate them into the MPC framework. In most chapters, we illustrate the use of the systems for routine decision making with actual company examples. These examples are quite extensive, reflecting our concern for improved practice. The chapters close with a summary of key points in the form of principles appropriate to the topic.

The chapters are relatively independent although some key vocabulary and concepts appear in the early chapters, and each chapter in the second part of the book depends somewhat on the material from its equivalent fundamental chapter in the first part. Although there is some building to a comprehensive system definition that follows the chapter sequence, it is not essential that the chapters be read in order. We have tried to provide maximum flexibility in this regard. The next section describes the logic of the chapter order and suggests alternatives for different purposes.

Topical sequence

One way that the chapters could have been sequenced is suggested by Figure 1.2. That is, we could present the chapters in a hierarchical order proceeding from overall direction to detailed material planning to shop-floor control and purchasing. In fact, we have not chosen this alternative. We are most concerned with clearly presenting concepts that can be used to improve manufacturing performance. Although conceptually appealing, the hierarchical approach is not consistent with our observations on how best to present the material for ease of understanding or on implementation practice. It has been our experience that most topics in the front end are easier to understand after studying more simple concepts. We have found, also, that most firms do not start MPC system implementation with the overall direction phase. Rather, they typically start with detailed material planning, then implement shop floor control, then detailed capacity planning, and only then turn to the tasks of master production scheduling and production planning.

We have chosen to follow that basic sequence. It permits us to develop some fundamental concepts in a context where understanding is easier and which parallels implementation practice. Consequently, we start with three chapters devoted to the engine. Chapter 2 deals with the detailed planning of component parts. The next chapter deals with two critical MPC system issues: the integrity of the information (data base) and using the system in a dynamic environment. Chapter 4 treats detailed capacity planning.

The next two chapters deal with the back end, or execution, systems. Chapter 5 is devoted to shop floor control and Chapter 6 to purchasing. After describing how detailed plans are put into action, we turn to the front end. Chapters 7 and 8 deal with master production scheduling. Chapter 9 treats production planning, and Chapter 10 is concerned with demand management.

Successful implementation of MPC systems necessitates strong managerial leadership, and we devote an entire chapter to this topic. Thus, Chapter 11 is concerned with implementation and organization change as a central focus, rather than as one topic in the study of individual material flow problem areas.

With the set of chapters that comprise the first half of the book, we have presented the overall manufacturing planning and control system. The balance of the book is devoted to supporting technical and theoretical material. These materials amplify many of the ideas presented in Chapters 2 to 11, they make more explicit some of the key trade-offs in manufacturing planning and control, and they present a base of knowledge for the person who wants to be a professional in manufacturing planning and control.

The sequence of Chapters 12 to 19 parallels that in the first part of the book:

Chapter	*Topics*
12	Advanced Concepts in Material Requirements Planning
13	Advanced Concepts in Scheduling
14	Project Planning and Control
15	Aggregate Capacity Analysis
16	Forecasting Systems
17	Independent Demand Inventory Management
18	Advanced Independent Demand Systems
19	Logistics
20	Other MPC Approaches
Appendix	Example Certification Examination Questions

There are many ways that one can proceed through the book. The choice depends to some extent on the interest of the reader. For someone desiring an understanding of a modern manufacturing planning and control system, we suggest reading Chapters 1 through 11 in sequence, following with the latter chapters that correspond to individual interests. If one is interested in selected aspects of manufacturing planning and control, we suggest reading at least Chapter 2 before moving on to the area(s) of interest. For students in a production planning and control course, the sequence might be basic to advanced chapters for each topic (e.g., Chapters 2, 3 and 12 followed by Chapters 4, 5, 13, and 14, etc.).

Another group is those readers interested in becoming certified in a professional society. They will be interested in the certification examination of the American Production and Inventory Control Society (APICS) or the National Association of Purchasing Management (NAPM), for example. The example certification exam questions in the Appendix will be useful to them.

The chapter references for the various modules of the APICS exam are indicated below:

Examination modules	*Chapters*
Master Planning	7, 8, 9, 10, 14, 15, 16
Material Requirements Planning	2, 3, 4, 12, 17
Capacity Management	2, 3, 4, 5, 9, 15
Inventory Management	3, 10, 15, 17, 18, 19
Production Activity Control	2, 3, 4, 5, 13

Although each certification examination emphasizes certain areas, the overall interest of professional societies is to foster professionalism. This means that all of the topical materials are relevant. For example, although Chapter 11, Implementation, is not included on any of the APICS examination modules, it should perhaps be on *all* of them. A similar argument holds for Chapter 20.

In closing this first chapter, we would like to make one further point. A large amount of personal experience has gone into this text. We have visited many companies and talked with thousands of people about manufacturing planning and control. We are extremely enthusiastic about the potential for MPC systems, and we hope that our enthusiasm is shared by the readers of the book. Installing an MPC system and seeing the results can be one of the most significant and professionally rewarding activities of one's professional life!

REFERENCES

Buffa, E. S., and J. G. Miller. *Production-Inventory Systems: Planning and Control.* 3d ed. Homewood, Ill.: Richard D. Irwin, 1979.

Davis, E. W. "ROA Chart Worksheet," *UVA-OM-300*, and "Return on Assets Problems," *UVA-OM-273R*, Darden School, University of Virginia, Charlottesville, Va, 1981.

Holstein, W. K. "Production Planning and Control Integrated." *Harvard Business Review*, May/June, 1968.

Johnson, G. A. *APICS Bibliography.* Falls Church, Va.: American Production and Inventory Control Society, 1981.

Mabert, V. A., and C. L. Moodie. *Production Planning, Scheduling, and Inventory Control: Concepts, Techniques, and Systems.* Atlanta: Institute of Industrial Engineering, Monograph Series, 1982.

Mather, Hal F. "Manufacturing Control in Perspective." *Production and Inventory Management*, 4th Quarter 1976.

Plossl, G. W. *Manufacturing Control—The Last Frontier for Profits.* Reston, Va.: Reston Publishing, 1973.

Schultz, T. "MRP to BRP: The Journey of the 80's." *Production and Inventory Management Review and APICS News*, October 1981, pp. 29–32.

Wagner, H. M. "The Design of Production and Inventory Systems for Multi-Facility and Multi-Warehouse Components." *Operations Research*, 22, no. 2 (March/April 1974).

Wallace, T. F. *APICS Dictionary*. 4th ed. Falls Church, Va.: American Production and Inventory Control Society, 1980.

Wight, O. W. "Tools for Profit." *Datamation*, October 1980, pp. 93–96.

———. *Production and Inventory Management in the Computer Age*. Boston: Cahners Books International, 1974.

2

Material requirements planning

This chapter deals with material requirements planning (MRP), the central activity in material planning and control (MPC). It is such a key activity that we start the detailed exposition of MPC systems with its description. The managerial objectives of MRP are to provide "the right part at the right time" to meet the schedules for completed products. To do this, MRP provides *formal* plans for each part number, whether raw material, component, or finished good. Accomplishing these plans without excess inventory, overtime, labor, or other resources, is also important. Therefore, the MRP system ensures that the planning is integrated; that is, that the correct number of components for each end item, raw materials for each component, and so on is planned for each part number.

Chapter 2 is organized around the following six topics:

- Material requirements planning in manufacturing planning and control: Where does MRP fit in the overall MPC system framework and how is it related to other MPC modules?
- Record processing: What is the basic MRP record and how is it produced?
- Technical issues: What are the additional technical details and supporting systems of which one should be aware?
- Using the MRP system: Who uses the system, how, and how is the exact match between MRP records and physical reality maintained?

- The MRP data base: What are the computer files that support MRP?
- Manual MRP systems: How can the MRP concepts be applied without a computer?

Important related concepts are found in Chapters 3 and 12. Chapter 3 deals with the basic data needs and dynamics of MRP systems. Chapter 12 describes advanced concepts in MRP.

MATERIAL REQUIREMENTS PLANNING IN MANUFACTURING PLANNING AND CONTROL

Figure 2.1 is our general model of a manufacturing planning and control (MPC) system. Several supporting activities are shown for the front end, engine, and back end of the system. The front end section of the MPC system produces the master production schedule (MPS). The back end, or execution, systems deal with detailed scheduling of the factory and with managing materials coming from vendor plants.

Material requirements planning is the central system in the engine portion of Figure 2.1. It has the primary purpose of taking a period-by-period (time-phased) set of master production schedule requirements and producing a resultant time-phased set of component/raw material requirements.

In addition to master production schedule inputs, MRP has two other basic inputs. A bill of material shows, for each part number, what other part numbers are required as direct components. For example, for an automobile, it could show five wheels required (four plus the spare). For each wheel, the bill of materials could be a hub, tire, valve stem, etc. The second basic input to MRP is inventory status. To know how many wheels to make for a given number of cars, it is necessary to know how many are on hand, how many of those are already allocated to existing needs, and how many have already been ordered.

The MRP data make it possible to construct a time-phased requirement record for any part number. The data can also be used as input to the detailed capacity planning modules.

The MRP system serves a central role in material planning and control. It acts as a translator of the overall plans for production into the detailed individual steps necessary to accomplish those plans. It provides information for developing capacity plans, and it links to the systems that actually get the production accomplished. Because of this key linking role and the central nature of the MRP process and records, we have chosen to describe MRP early in the book. Moreover, the MRP process is where many companies have chosen to start the development of their formal MPC systems.

RECORD PROCESSING

In this section, we present the MRP procedures starting with the basic MRP record, its terminology, timing conventions, and construction. We

FIGURE 2.1 Manufacturing planning and control system

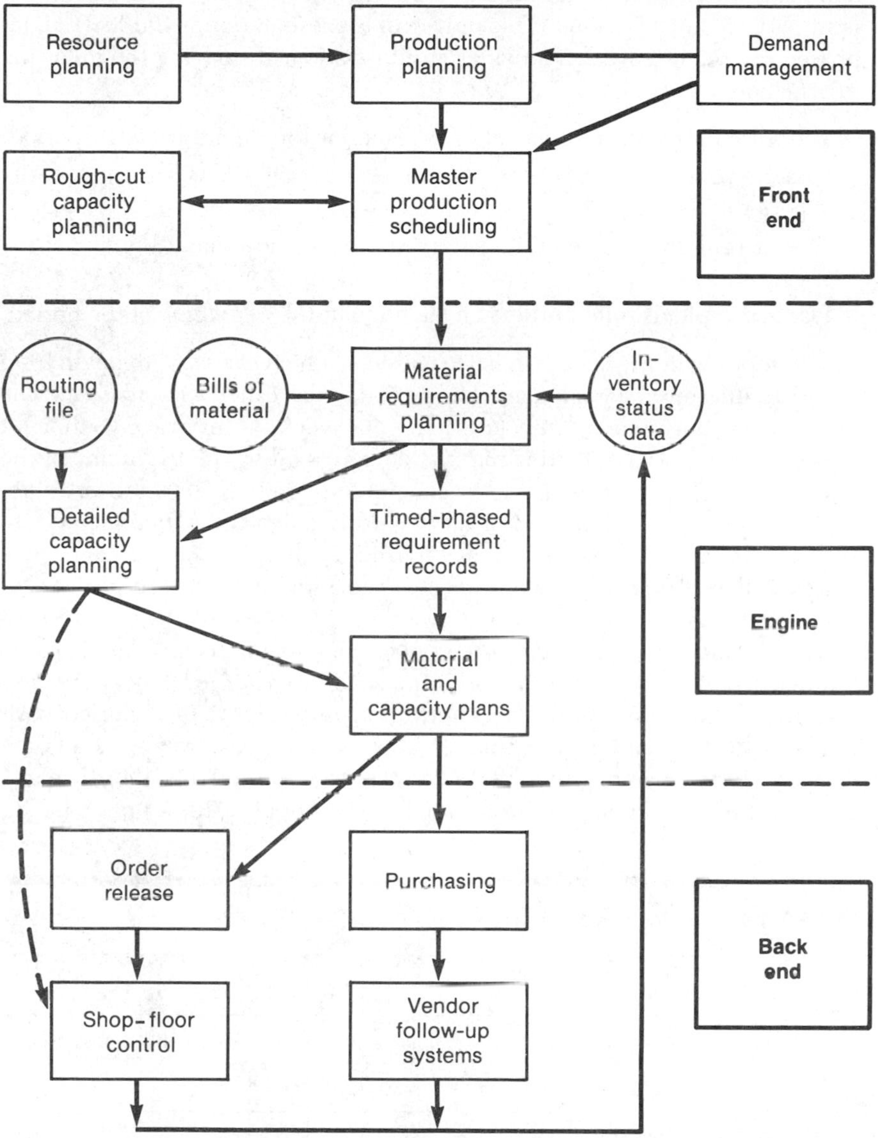

then turn to an example which illustrates the need to coordinate the planning of component parts with end item planning. We examine several aspects of this coordination and the relationships that must be accounted for. We then look at linking the MRP records to reflect all the required relationships. We intend to show clearly how each MRP record can be managed independently while the *system* keeps them coordinated.

The basic MRP record

At the heart of the MPC system is a universal representation of the status and plans for any single item (part number), whether raw material, component part, or finished good. This universal representation is the MRP time-phased record. Figure 2.2 provides an illustration, displaying the following information:

The anticipated future usage of or demand for the item during the period.

Existing replenishment orders for the item due in at the *beginning* of the period.

The current and projected inventory status for the item at the *end* of the period.

Planned replenishment orders for the item at the *beginning* of the period.

The top row in Figure 2.2 indicates periods which can vary in length from a day to a quarter or even longer. The period is also called a *time bucket*. The most widely used time bucket or period is one week. A timing convention for developing the MRP record is that the current time is the beginning of the first period. The initial available balance of four units is shown prior to period 1. The number of periods in the record is called the *planning horizon*. In the simplified example shown as Figure 2.2, the planning horizon is five periods. The planning horizon indicates the number of future periods for which plans are made.

The second row, Gross Requirements, is a statement of the anticipated future usage of or demand for the item. The gross requirements are *time phased*, which means they are stated on a unique period-by-period basis rather than aggregated or averaged. That is, the gross requirements are stated as 10 in period 2, 40 in period 4, and 10 in period 5, rather than as a total requirement of 60 or as an average requirement of 12 per period. This

FIGURE 2.2 The basic MRP record

Period		1	2	3	4	5
Gross requirements			10		40	10
Scheduled receipts		50				
Projected available balance	4	54	44	44	4	44
Planned order releases					50	
Lead time = 1 period Lot size = 50						

method of presentation allows for special orders, seasonality, and periods of no anticipated usage to be explicitly taken into account. A gross requirement in a particular period signifies that a demand is anticipated during that period which will be unsatisfied unless the item is *available* during that period. Availability is achieved by having the item in inventory, or by receiving either an existing replenishment order or a planned replenishment order in time to satisfy the gross requirement.

Another timing convention comes from the question of availability. The convention we use is that the item must be available at the *beginning* of the time bucket in which it is required. That means that plans must be made so that any replenishment order will be in inventory at the beginning of the period in which the gross requirement for that order occurs.

The Scheduled Receipt row describes the status of any open orders (work in process or existing replenishment orders) for the item. This row shows the quantities that have already been ordered and when we expect them to be completed. Scheduled receipts result from previously made ordering decisions and represent a source of the item to meet gross requirements. For example, the gross requirements of 10 in period 2 cannot be satisfied by the 4 units presently available. The scheduled receipt of 50, due in period 1, will be used to satisfy the gross requirement in period 2 if things go according to plan. Scheduled receipts represent a commitment. For an order in the factory, necessary materials have been committed to the order, and capacity at work centers will be required to complete it. For a purchased item, similar commitments have been made to a vendor. The timing convention used for showing scheduled receipts is also at the *beginning* of the period. That is, the order is shown in the period during which the item must be available to satisfy a gross requirement.

The next row in Figure 2.2 is called Projected Available Balance. The timing convention in this row is the *end* of the period. That is, the row is the projected balance *after* replenishment orders have been received and gross requirements have been satisfied. For this reason, the projected available balance row has an extra time bucket shown at the beginning. This bucket shows the balance *at the present time*. That is, in Figure 2.2, the beginning available balance is four units. The quantity shown in period 1 is the projected balance at the *end* of period 1. This means that the projected available balance shown at the end of a period is available to meet gross requirements in the next (and succeeding) periods. For example, the 54 units shown as the projected available balance at the end of period 1 result from the addition of the 50 units scheduled to be received in period 1 to the beginning balance of 4 units. The gross requirement of 10 units in period 2 reduces the projected balance to 44 units at the end of period 2. The term projected *available* balance is used instead of projected *on-hand* balance for a very specific reason. Units of the item might be on hand physically but not available to meet gross requirements because they are already promised or allocated for some other purpose.

The Planned Order Release row is determined directly from the projected available balance row. Whenever the projected available balance would show a quantity insufficient to satisfy gross requirements (a negative quantity), additional material must be planned for. This is done by creating a *planned order release* in time to keep the projected available balance from becoming negative. For example, in Figure 2.2, the projected available balance at the end of period 4 is four units. This is not sufficient to meet the gross requirement of 10 units in period 5. Since the lead time is one week, the MRP system creates a planned order at the beginning of week 4 providing a *lead time offset* of one week. As we have used a lot size of 50 units, the projected available balance at the end of week 5 is 44 units. Another way that this logic is explained is to note that the balance for the end of period 4 (4 units) is the beginning inventory for period 5 during which there is a gross requirement of 10 units. The difference between the available inventory of 4 and the gross requirement of 10 is a *net requirement* of 6 units in period 5. Thus, an order for at least six units must be planned for period 4 to avoid a shortage in period 5.

The MRP system produces the planned order release data in response to the gross requirement, scheduled receipt, and projected available data. When a planned order is created for the most immediate or current period, it is in the *action bucket.* A quantity in the action bucket means that some action is needed now to avoid a future problem. The action is to release the order, which converts it to a scheduled receipt.

The planned order releases are *not* shown in the scheduled receipt row because they have not yet been released for production or purchasing. No material has been committed to their manufacture. The planned order is analogous to an entry on a Christmas list, since the list is comprised of plans. A scheduled receipt is like an order that has been mailed to a catalog firm to send someone on the list a particular gift for Christmas, since a commitment has been made. Like Christmas lists versus mailed orders, planned orders are much easier to change then scheduled receipts. There are many advantages to not converting planned orders into scheduled receipts any earlier than necessary.

The basic MRP record just described provides the correct information on each part in the system. Linking these single part records together is essential in managing the flow of parts needed for a single product or customer. Key elements for linking the records are the bill of materials, the explosion process (using inventory and scheduled receipt information), and lead time off-setting. We consider each of these before turning to how the records are linked into a system.

An example bill of materials. Figure 2.3 shows a snow shovel, which is end item part number 1605. The complete snow shovel is assembled (using four rivets and two nails) from the top handle assembly, scoop assembly, scoop-shaft connector, and shaft. The top handle assembly, in turn, is created by combining the welded top handle bracket assembly with the wooden

FIGURE 2.3 1605 snow shovel shown with component parts and assemblies

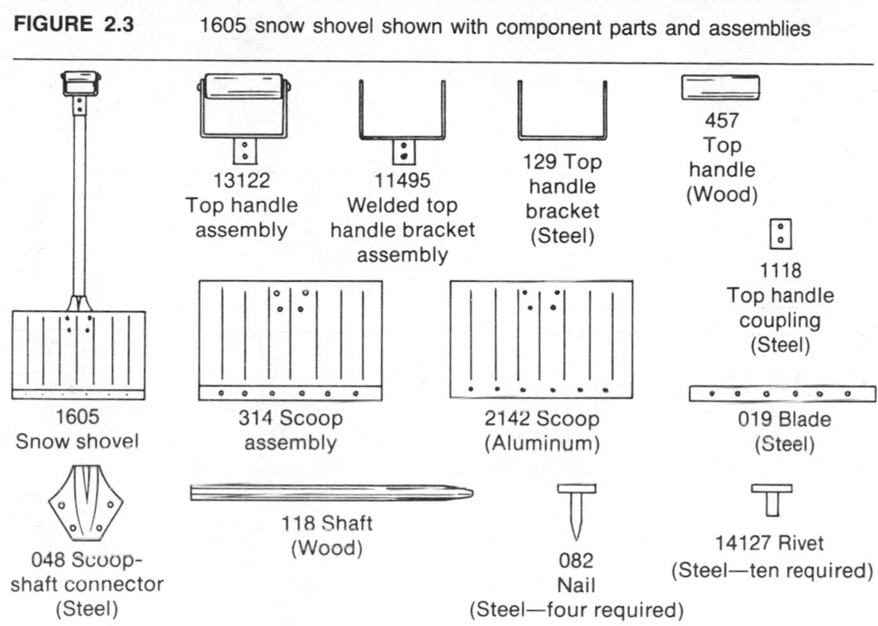

handle using two nails. The welded top handle bracket assembly is created by welding the top handle coupling to the top handle bracket. In a similar way, the scoop assembly is created by combining the aluminum scoop with the steel blade using six rivets.

Explaining even this simple assembly process is a cumbersome task. Moreover, diagrams such as Figure 2.3 get more complicated as the number of subassemblies, components, and parts used increase, or as they are used in increasingly more places (e.g., rivets and nails). Two techniques which get at this problem nicely are the *product structure diagram* and the *indented bill of materials* (BOM) which are shown in Figure 2.4. Both provide the detailed information of Figure 2.3, but the indented BOM has the added advantage of being easily printed by a computer.

Note that both the product structure diagram and the indented BOM show exactly what goes into what instead of being just a parts list. For example, to make one 13122 top handle assembly, we see by the product structure diagram that one 457 top handle, two 082 nails, and one 11495 bracket assembly are needed. The same information is shown in the indented BOM; the three required parts are indented and shown, one level beneath the 13122. Note also that one does *not* need a top handle bracket (129) or a top handle coupling (1118) to produce a top handle assembly (13122). These are only needed to produce a bracket assembly (11495). In essence, the top handle assembly does not care *how* a bracket assembly is made, only that it is made. The making of the bracket assembly is a separate problem.

FIGURE 2.4 Product structure diagram

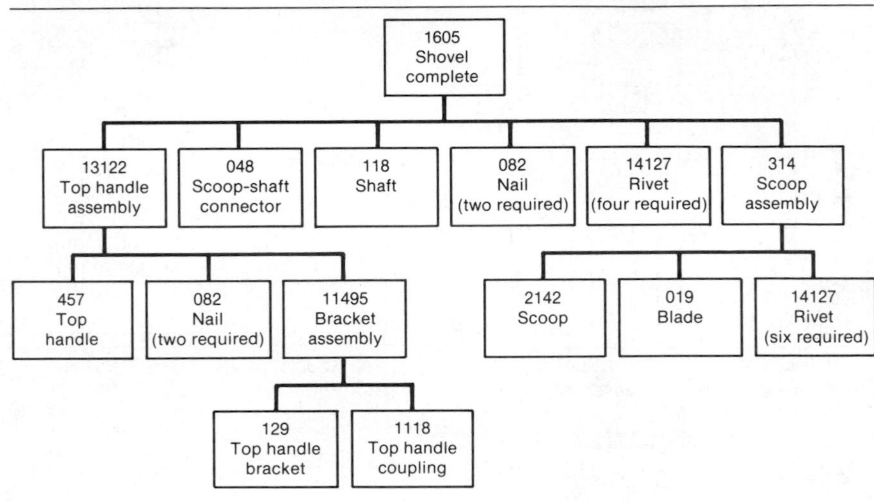

Indented bill of materials (BOM)

1605 Snow Shovel

13122 Top Handle Assembly (1 required)
  457 Top Handle (1 required)
  082 Nail (2 required)
  11495 Bracket Assembly (1 required)
    129 Top Handle Bracket (1 required)
    1118 Top Handle Coupling (1 required)

048 Scoop-Shaft Connector (1 required)
118 Shaft (1 required)
082 Nail (2 required)
14127 Rivet (4 required)
314 Scoop Assembly
  2142 Scoop (1 required)
  019 Blade (1 required)
  14127 Rivet (6 required)

Before leaving our brief discussion of bills of material, it is important to stress that the bill of material used to support MRP may be different from other company perceptions of a bill of materials. The BOM to support MRP must be consistent with the way the product is manufactured. For example, if we are making red automobiles, the part numbers should be for red doors. If green automobiles are desired, the part numbers must be for green doors. Also, if we change to a different set of subassemblies, the indentations on the indented BOM should change as well. Engineering and accounting may well not care what color the parts are or what the manufacturing sequence is.

Gross to net explosion. *Explosion* is the process of translating product requirements into component part requirements, taking existing inventories and scheduled receipts into account. Thus, explosion may be viewed as the process of determining, for *any* part number, the quantities of *all* components needed to satisfy its requirements, and continuing this process for *every* part number until all purchased and/or raw material requirements are exactly calculated.

The gross to net explosion process means that, as explosion takes place, only the component part requirements net of any inventory are considered. In this way, only the *necessary* requirements are linked through the system. Although this may seem like an obvious goal, the product structure can make determination of net requirements more difficult than it seems. To illustrate, let us return to the snow shovel example.

Suppose the company wanted to produce 100 snow shovels and we were responsible for making the 13122 top handle assembly. We are given current inventory and scheduled receipt information from which the gross requirements and net requirements for each component of the top handle can be calculated. This is shown in Figure 2.5.

The gross and net requirements shown in Figure 2.5 may not correspond to what one feels they should be. It might at the outset seem that since one top handle coupling (1118) is used per shovel, the gross requirements should be 100 and the net requirement 46, instead of the 48 and zero that are shown. To produce 100 shovels means we need (have a demand for) 100 top handle assemblies (part 13122). Twenty-five of these 100 can come from inventory, resulting in a net requirement of 75. As we need to make only 75 top handle assemblies, we need 75 top handles and bracket assemblies. This 75 is the *gross* requirement for parts 457 and 11495 (as indicated by the circled numbers in Figure 2.5). Since 2 nails (part 082) are used per top handle assembly, the gross requirement for 082 is 150. The 25 units of top handle assembly inventory contain some implicit inventories of handles, brackets, and nails which the gross to net process takes into account. Looking on down, we see that there are 27 units of the bracket assembly in inventory, so the net requirement is for 48. This becomes the gross require-

FIGURE 2.5 Gross and net requirements calculation for the snow shovel

Part description	*Part number*	*Inventory*	*Scheduled receipts*	*Gross requirements*	*Net requirements*
Top handle assembly	13122	25	—	100	(75)
Top handle	457	22	25	(75)	28
Nail (2 required)	082	4	50	150	96
Bracket assembly	11495	27	—	(75)	(48)
Top handle bracket	129	15	—	(48)	33
Top handle coupling	1118	39	15	(48)	—

ment for the bracket and coupling. Since there are 39 top handle couplings in inventory and 15 scheduled for receipt, there is *no* net requirement for part 1118.

The gross to net relationship is a key element of MRP systems. It not only provides the basis for the calculation of the appropriate quantities, but it also serves as the communication link between part numbers. It is the basis for the concept of *dependent demand,* that is, the "demand" (gross requirements) for top handles depends upon the net requirements for top handle assemblies. To correctly do the calculations, the bill of material, inventory, and scheduled receipt data are all necessary. With these data, the dependent demand can be exactly calculated. It need not be forecast. On the other hand, some *independent demand* items, such as the snow shovel, are subject to demands from outside the firm. The need for snow shovels will have to be forecast. The concept of dependent demand is often called the fundamental principle of MRP. It provides the way to remove uncertainty from the requirement calculations.

Lead time off setting. The gross to net explosion tells us how many of each subassembly and component part are needed to support a desired finished product quantity. What it does not do, however, is tell us *when* each of the components and subassemblies is needed. Referring back to Figures 2.3 and 2.4, it is clear that the top handle bracket and top handle coupling need to be welded together before the wooden top handle is attached. These relationships are known as *precedent relationships.* They indicate the order in which things must be done.

In addition to precedent relationships, the determination of when to schedule each component part also depends upon how long it takes to produce the part, i.e., the lead time. Perhaps the top handle bracket (129) can be fabricated in one day, while the top handle coupling (1118) takes two weeks. If so, it would be advantageous to start making the coupling before the bracket, since they are both needed at the same time to make a bracket assembly.

Despite the fact that the need to take lead time differences into account may seem obvious, many systems for component part manufacturing ignore them. For example, most furniture manufacturers base production on what is called a *cutting.* In the cutting approach, if a lot of 100 chairs were to be assembled, then 100 of each part (with appropriate multiples) are started at the same time. Figure 2.6 is a Gantt chart (time-oriented bar chart) showing how this cutting approach would be applied to the snow shovel example. (Note that the processing times are shown on the chart.)

Figure 2.6 shows clearly that the cutting approach, which starts all parts as soon as possible, will lead to unnecessary work-in-process inventories. For example, the top handle bracket (129) does not need to be started until the end of day 9, since it must wait for the coupling (1118) before it can be put into its assembly (11495), and part 1118 takes 10 days. In the cutting

FIGURE 2.6 Gantt chart for cutting approach to snow shovel problem (front or earliest start schedule)

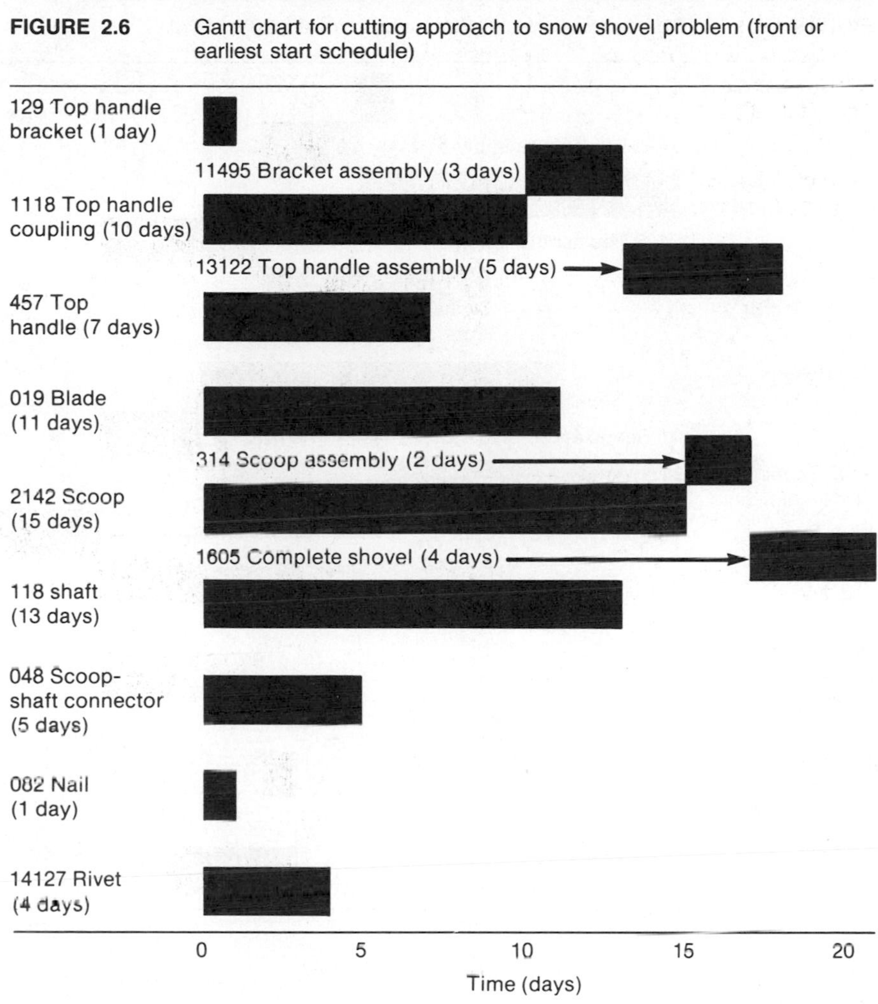

approach, parts are scheduled earlier than need be. This results from using the *front schedule* logic, i.e., scheduling as early as possible.

What should be done is to *back schedule*, i.e., start each item as late as possible. Figure 2.7 provides a back schedule for the snow shovel example. The schedules for parts 1118, 11495, 13122, and 1605 do not change, since they in essence form a critical path. All of the other parts, however, are scheduled later in this approach than in the front scheduling approach. A substantial savings in work-in-process inventory is obtained by this shift of dates.

Back scheduling has several obvious advantages. It will reduce work-in-process, postpone the commitment of raw materials to specific products,

FIGURE 2.7 Back schedule based Gantt chart (latest start)

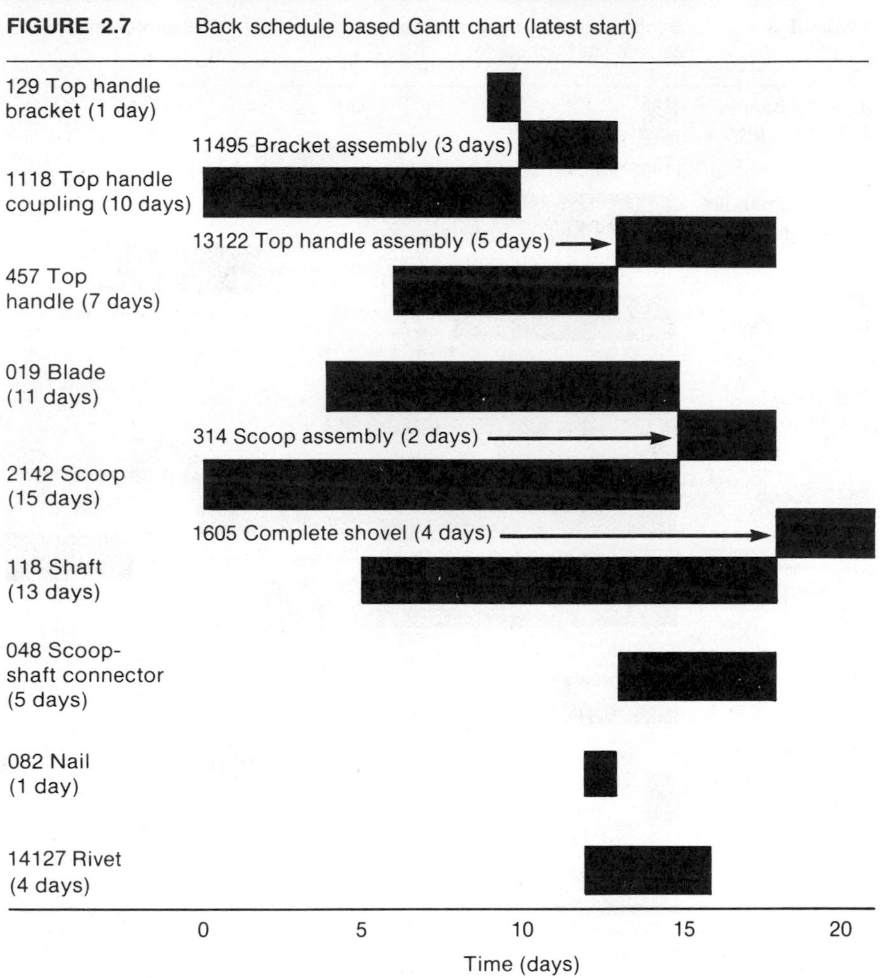

and minimize storage time of completed components. Implementing the back schedule approach, however, requires a system. The system must have accurate BOM data and lead time estimates, some way to ensure that all component parts are started at the right times, and some means of tracking components and subassemblies to make sure that they are all completed according to plans. The cutting approach is much simpler, since all component parts are started at the same time and left in the pipeline until needed.

We want to show how MRP achieves the benefits of the back scheduling approach *and* can perform the gross to net explosion. In fact, the combination of back schedules and gross to net explosion is the heart of MRP. We turn now to linking the basic MRP records to see how MRP achieves these goals.

Linking the MRP records

Figure 2.8 shows the linked set of individual time-phased MRP records for the top handle assembly of the snow shovel. We have already used the first five periods of the 082 nail record shown in Figure 2.8 as the basic record description in Figure 2.2. To see how that record fits into the whole, we will start with the snow shovels themselves. We said that 100 snow shovels were going to be made, and now we see the timing. That is, the gross requirements row shows the total need of 100 time phased as 20 in week, 2,

FIGURE 2.8 MRP records for the snow shovel top handle assembly

			Week									
			1	2	3	4	5	6	7	8	9	10
13122 Top handle assembly Lead time = 2	Gross requirements			20		10		20	5		35	10
	Scheduled receipts											
	Projected available balance	25	25	5	5	0	0	0	0	0	0	0
	Planned order releases			5		20	5		35	10		
457 Top handle Lead time = 2	Gross requirements			5		20	5		35	10		
	Scheduled receipts				25							
	Projected available balance	22	22	17	42	22	17	17	0	0	0	0
	Planned order releases						18	10				
082 Nail (2 required) Lead time = 1 Lot size = 50	Gross requirements			10		40	10		70	20		
	Scheduled receipts		50									
	Projected available balance	4	54	44	44	4	44	44	24	4	4	4
	Planned order releases					50		50				
11495 Bracket assembly Lead time = 2	Gross requirements			5		20	5		35	10		
	Scheduled receipts											
	Projected available balance	27	27	22	22	2	0	0	0	0	0	0
	Planned order releases				3		35	10				
129 Top handle bracket Lead time = 1	Gross requirements				3		35	10				
	Scheduled receipts											
	Projected available balance	15	15	15	12	12	0	0	0	0	0	0
	Planned order releases					23	10					
1118 Top handle coupling Lead time = 3 Safety stock = 20	Gross requirements				3		35	10				
	Scheduled receipts			15								
	Projected available balance	39	39	54	51	51	20	20	20	20	20	20
	Planned order releases			4	10							

10 in week 4, 20 in week 6, 5 in week 7, 35 in week 9, and 10 in week 10. Since each snow shovel takes a top handle assembly, the gross requirements row for the top handle assembly shows when shovel assembly is to begin. Note that the total planned orders for the top handle assembly is the net requirement of 75 that we calculated before in the gross to net calculations of Figure 2.5.

The lead time for the top handle assembly is two weeks, calculated as the five days processing time shown in Figure 2.6 plus five days for paperwork. The lead times for each of the other records is similarly calculated; one week five days) of paperwork time is added to the processing time and the total rounded to the nearest five-day week. The current inventories and scheduled receipts for each part are those shown in Figure 2.5. The scheduled receipts are shown in the appropriate periods. Using the two-week lead time and recognizing a net requirement of five units in week 4 for the top handle assembly, we see the need to plan an order for week 2 of five units.

This planned order release of five units in week 2 becomes a gross requirement in week 2 for the top handles as shown by the circles in Figure 2.8. Note also that the gross requirements for the nails and brackets in period 2 derive from this same planned order release (with two nails per top handle assembly). Thus, the communication between records is the dependent demand that we saw illustrated before in the gross to net calculations of Figure 2.5.

The remaining planned order releases for the top handle assembly exactly meet the net requirements in the remaining periods, offset for the lead time. The ordering policy used for these items is called *lot-for-lot* lot sizing. An exception to the lot-for-lot procedure is the ordering of nails, which is done in lots of 50. In the case of the nails, the total planned orders will not necessarily add up to the net requirements.

Another part for which there is a discrepancy between the planned orders and the net requirements calculated in Figure 2.5 is the top handle coupling. For this part, a safety stock of 20 units is desired. This means the planned order logic will schedule a planned order release to prevent the projected available balance from going below the safety stock level of 20 units. For the top handle couplings this means a total of 4 units must be planned for period 2 and 10 for period 3 to maintain the 20-unit safety stock.

The one element we have yet to clearly show is the back scheduling effect. We saw before that it would be desirable to delay the start of the top handle bracket (part 129) relative to the top handle coupling (part 1118). The MRP records show that the start of the first planned order for part 129 is not until week 4, two weeks after the first planned order for part 1118. Both of these planned orders are to satisfy a gross requirement of 35 derived from the planned order for the bracket assembly in week 5. We see then that the orders are back scheduled. This relationship can be more complicated than our example, since the planned order release timing depends on the safety stock and inventory levels, as well as the lead times. The MRP system, however, coordinates all of that information and determines the appropriate planned order release dates.

At this point, we see fully the linking of the MRP time-phased records. The planned order release row for the top handle assembly (13122) becomes (with the appropriate multiplier) the gross requirement row for each of its components (parts 457, 082, and 11495) and they are linked together. Once all the gross requirement data are available for a particular record, the individual record processing logic is applied and the planned order releases for the part are passed down as gross requirements to its components, following the product structure (BOM) on a level-by-level basis. In some cases, parts will receive their requirements from more than one source (common parts), as is true for the nails and rivets in the snow shovel. In these cases, the gross requirements will reflect needs from more than one planned order release source. Again, the system accounts for this, and incorporates it into the gross to net logic.

We see that the MRP records take proper account of gross to netting. They also incorporate the back scheduling concept, and allow for explicit timings, desired lot sizing procedures, safety stocks, and part commonality. What is of even more importance, however, is independence of the part number planning. With the MRP approach, it is not necessary for the person planning for snow shovels to explicitly coordinate his or her planning with the planning of the component parts. The MRP system accomplishes the coordination. Whatever is done to the MRP record for the snow shovels will result in a set of planned orders that the system will correctly pass down as gross requirements to its components. This means that plans for each part number can be developed independently of the product structures, and the plans at each level will be communicated correctly to the other levels.

So far, we have looked only at the construction of MRP records in the system. It is important to stress that the system is *forward looking*. The records lay out anticipated *future* actions to accomplish product manufacturing objectives. Therefore, it is a proactive system. Problems can be anticipated before they create crises. Since MRP must function in a dynamic world, the system must help managers to be responsive to the problems. Some of the additional technical aspects necessary to make this happen are described next.

TECHNICAL ISSUES

In this section, we briefly introduce some of the technical issues to be considered in the design of MRP systems. The intent is to provide a basic understanding of several additional facets of MRP systems so that we can then facilitate the use of the systems.

Processing frequency

Thus far we have looked only at the static construction of the MRP records and how they are linked together. Since conditions change and new information is received, the records must be brought up-to-date so that plans can be adjusted to reflect these changes. This means processing the MRP records anew, incorporating the current information. Two issues are involved in the processing decision; how frequently should the records be processed, and whether all the records should be processed at the same time.

When all of the records are processed in one computer run, it is called *regeneration*. This signifies that *all* part number records are completely reconstructed each time the records are processed. An alternative is *net change* processing, which means that only those records which are affected by the new or changed information are reconstructed. The key issue raised by contrasting regeneration and net change is the frequency of processing. Let us now consider this issue in more detail.

The appropriate frequency for processing the MRP time-phased records is dependent upon the firm, its products, and its operations. The most common current practice is for weekly processing using regeneration. But some firms regenerate every two weeks or even monthly, while others process all the MRP time-phased records twice per week or even more often.

The prime motivation for less frequent processing is the computational cost. This can be especially high with regeneration, since a new record is created for every active part number in the product structure file at each processing. The computational time required, however, varies considerably from company to company, depending upon the computer approach used, the amount of part numbers, the complexity of product structures, and other factors. For companies using regeneration, typically 8 to 24 hours of central processing unit (CPU) time are required. For example, at the Hill-Rom Company in Batesville, Indiana, regeneration for approximately 13,000 active part numbers is done over each weekend and requires approximately 16 hours of computer (CPU) time on an IBM 370-145.

The problem with processing less frequently is that the portrayal of component status and needs expressed in the records becomes increasingly out-of-date and inaccurate. There are both anticipated and unanticipated causes for this decrease in accuracy. As the anticipated scheduled receipts are received and requirements satisfied, the inventory balances change. As unanticipated scrap, requirement changes, stock corrections, or other such transactions occur, they will cause inaccuracies if they are not reflected in all the time-phased records that are influenced by the transactions. The changes in one record are linked to other time-phased records as planned order releases become gross requirements for lower level components. Thus, some change transactions may cascade throughout the product structure. If these transactions are not reflected in the time-phased records early enough, the result could be material shortages.

More frequent processing of the MRP records increases computer costs but results in fewer unpleasant surprises. When the records reflecting the changes are produced, appropriate actions will be indicated to compensate for the changes. Responding to actual events less frequently can increase the magnitude of compensation required. As the inaccuracies increase in number and magnitude, the system's representation of physical reality is less useful. Thus, to manage effectively, there is a need to keep the records synchronized with actuality.

A logical response to the pressure for more frequent processing is to reduce the amount of calculation required by processing only the records affected by the changes. This net change approach only creates a new part number record when a transaction makes the present component plan inaccurate. Although this could be done as the transaction occurs, the typical approach is to accumulate all the transactions in a day and process them overnight.

The argument for the net change approach is that it can reduce computer time enough to make daily or more frequent processing possible. In companies where this can be done, there is the added advantage of smoothing the computational requirements over the week. On the other hand, daily processing of part of the records could lead to even greater overall computational cost than weekly regeneration. Since only part of the records are reviewed at each processing, the need for very accurate computer records and transaction processing procedures is obvious. Some net change users do an occasional regeneration to clean up all of the records.

The question of processing frequency is important, as we have pointed out. The need for frequent processing must be assessed by each company in light of the computational costs, the rapidity of the decline in record accuracy, and the complexity of their products. The possibility of using net change to increase the processing frequency also must be carefully evaluated. For product structures with a large portion of common parts, very flat structures, firms with few products, or when changes affect a large portion of the part numbers, the advantages of net change tend to be less significant.

Lot sizing

In the snow shovel example of Figure 2.8, we illustrated a fixed lot size (50 units for the nails) and the lot-for-lot procedure. The lot size of 50 for the nails could have been someone's estimate of a good lot size or the result of calculation. The time-phased information can be used in combination with economic, physical, vendor, and other data to develop lot sizes that conform to organizational needs. One might reach the conclusion, for the top handle (1118) in Figure 2.8, that it is undesirable to set up the equipment for *only* 4 parts in week 2, and again for 10 parts in week 3, and so combine the two orders. The time-phased record permits the development of such *discrete* lot sizes that will exactly satisfy the net requirements for one or more periods.

Several formal procedures have been developed for lot sizing the time-phased requirements. The basic trade-off usually involves elimination of one or more setups at the expense of carrying inventory longer. In many cases, the discrete lot sizes that are possible with MRP are more appealing than the fixed lot sizes that could be used. Compare the residual inventory, in week 10, of the nails with that of the bracket assemblies in Figure 2.8, for example.

The lot-for-lot technique seems at first glance to be somewhat too simple-minded since it does not consider any of the economic trade-offs or physical factors. Recall, however, that batching planned orders at one level will increase the gross requirements at the next level in the product structure. So larger lot sizing near the end item level of the bill of materials cascades down through all levels. Thus, it turns out that lot-for-lot is better than one might expect in actual practice, particularly at the intermediate levels in the bill of materials. This is especially the case when a product structure has many levels, and the cascading effect becomes greatly magnified. This cascading effect can be mitigated to some extent for components and raw materials that are very common. When this is the case, again lot sizing may be appropriate. As a consequence, many firms employ lot sizing primarily at the end item and basic component levels, while intermediate subassemblies are planned on a lot-for-lot basis.

Safety stock and safety lead time

Carrying out detailed component plans is sometimes facilitated by the inclusion of *safety stocks* and/or *safety lead times* in the MRP records. Safety stock is a buffer of stock above and beyond that needed to satisfy the gross requirements. This is illustrated in Figure 2.8 by incorporating safety stock for the top handle coupling. Safety lead time is a procedure whereby shop orders or purchase orders are released and scheduled to arrive one or more periods before necessary to satisfy the gross requirements.

We have seen that safety stocks can be easily incorporated into MRP time-phased records. They are merely included in the analysis so that the projected available balance does not fall below the safety stock level instead of zero. To incorporate safety lead time, orders are issued (planned) earlier and are scheduled (planned) to be received into inventory before the time that the MRP logic would indicate it was necessary. Figure 2.9 shows the top handle bracket from Figure 2.8 being planned with a one-week safety lead time. Notice that *both* the planned releases and planned receipt date are changed. Safety lead time is not just inflated lead time.

Both safety stock and safety lead time are used in practice, and there is no structural reason why both cannot be used simultaneously. However, both

FIGURE 2.9 MRP record with safety lead time

			1	2	3	4	5	6	7	8	9	10
Part 129	Gross requirements				3		35	10				
Top handle bracket lead time = 1	Scheduled receipts											
Lot-for-lot	Projected available balance	15	15	15	12	35	10	0	0	0	0	0
Safety lead time = 1	Planned order releases				23	10						

are hedges that to some extent result in indicating that orders should be released (launched) or that they need to be received when, in fact, this is not strictly true. To use safety stocks and safety lead times effectively, the influence of the techniques on plans must be well understood. If it is not well understood, the wrong orders can be sent to the factory, meaning that workers are trying to get out part A because of safety lead time or safety stock when, in fact, part B will be required to meet a customer order, so it would be better to have them working on that.

Safety stock tends to be used in MRP systems where uncertainty about quantities is the problem, e.g., where some small amount of scrap, spare part demand, or other unplanned usage is a frequent occurrence. Safety lead time, on the other hand, tends to be used when the major uncertainty is in the timing rather than the quantity. For example, if a firm buys from a vendor who often misses delivery dates, safety lead time may provide better results than safety stock. This is particularly true when the planned orders from higher-level parts have been lot sized and safety stock would not cover the requirements. Bringing an order in early, on the other hand, will cover the requirements, since the order size was originally based on the requirement.

Low-level coding

If we refer once again to Figure 2.4 we see that the nails (part 082) and rivets (part 14127) are common parts. The planned order row for completed shovels would be passed down as one part of the gross requirements for both of these parts. But there are additional sources of requirements for the nail (part 082)—from the top handle assembly (13122), and for rivets (14127) from the scoop assembly (314). If we process the time-phased record for either of these common parts before all their gross requirements have been accumulated, the computations will all have to be redone. In Figure 2.8, for example, the record for part 082 only includes the requirements passed down from the top handle assembly and not those from the completed snow shovels.

The way this problem is handled is to assign *low-level code numbers* to each part in the product structure or the indented BOM. By convention, the top or final assembly level is denoted as level zero. In our example, the snow shovel would have a low-level code of 0. All immediate component part numbers of this part (13122, 048, 118, 082, 14127, and 314 in Figure 2.4) are given the low-level code number 1. Then the next level down (part numbers 457, 082, 11495, 2142, 019, and 14127) are low-level coded 2. Note that the two common parts (nails and rivets) have just been recoded as level 2, indicating that they are used lower in the product structure. The higher the level codes, the lower in the product structure the part is used. Consequently, the last level code assigned to a part would indicate the lowest level of usage and is the level code retained for that part. We finish the example when part numbers 129 and 1118 are coded level 3. The level code assigned to any part number is based on the part's usage in all products manufactured by the organization.

Once low-level codes are established, MRP record processing proceeds from one level code to the next, starting at level code 0. This ensures that all gross requirements have been passed down to a part before its MRP record is processed. The result is planning of component parts coordinated with the needs of all higher-level part numbers. Within a level, the MRP record processing is typically done in part number sequence.

Pegging

Pegging relates all the gross requirements for a part to all the planned order releases that created the requirements. The pegging records contain the specific part number or numbers of the sources of all gross requirements. At level 0, for example, the pegging records might contain the specific customer orders that are to be satisfied by the gross requirements in the end item time-phased records. For lower-level part numbers, the gross requirements are most often pegged to planned orders of higher level items, but might also be pegged to customer orders if the part is sold as a service part.

Pegging information can be used to go up through the MRP records from a raw material gross requirement to some future customer order. In this sense, it is the reverse of the explosion process. Pegging is sometimes compared to where-used data. Where-used data, however, indicate for *each* part number, the part numbers of all items on which the part is used. Pegging, on the other hand, is a *selective* where-used file. Pegging shows only the specific part numbers that produce the specific gross requirements in each time period. Thus, the pegging information can be used to trace the impact of a material problem all the way up to the order it would affect.

Firm planned orders

The logic that was used to illustrate the construction of an MRP record for an individual part number is automatically applied for every processed part number. The result is a series of planned order releases for each part number. If changes have taken place since the last time the record was processed, the planned order releases can be very different from one record-processing cycle to the next. Since the planned orders are passed down as gross requirements to the next level, the differences can cascade throughout the product structure.

One device for preventing this cascading down through the product structure is to create a *firm planned order* (FPO). FPO, as the name implies, is a planned order that the MRP system *does not* automatically change when conditions change. To change either the quantity or timing of a firm planned order, a managerial action is required. This means that the trade-offs in making the change can be evaluated before authorization.

The FPO provides a means for temporarily overriding the system to provide stability or to solve problems. For example, if the changes are coming about because of scrap losses on open orders, the possibility of absorbing those variations with safety stock can be evaluated. If a more rapid delivery of raw material than usual is requested, say by using air freight, to meet a special need, the lead time can be reduced for that one order, and an FPO means the system will not use the normal lead time offset from the net requirement for that order.

Service parts

Service part demand must be included in the MRP record if the material requirements are not to be understated. The service part demand is typically based on a forecast and is added directly into the gross requirements for the part. From the MRP system point of view, the service part demand is simply another source of gross requirements for a part, and the sources of all gross requirements are maintained through pegging records. The low-level code for a part used exclusively for service would be zero. If it is used as a component part as well, the low-level code would be determined the same way as for any other part.

As actual service part needs occur, it is to be expected that demand variations will arise. These can be partially buffered with safety stocks, inventories specifically allocated to service part usage, or by creative use of the MRP system. By careful examination of pegging records, expected shortage conditions for manufacturing part requirements can sometimes be satisfied from available service parts. Conversely, critical service part requirements can perhaps be met with orders destined for higher-level items. Only one safety stock inventory is needed to buffer uncertainties from both sources, however.

Planning horizon

In Figure 2.8, the first planned order for top handle assemblies occurs in week 2 to meet the gross requirement in period 4 of 10 units. This planned order of 5 units in week 2 results in a corresponding gross requirement in that week for the bracket assembly (part 11495). This gross requirement is satisfied from the existing inventory of part 11495. But a different circumstance occurs if we trace the gross requirements for 35 top handle assemblies in week 9.

The net requirement for 35 units in week 9 becomes a planned order release in week 7. This, in turn, becomes a gross requirement for 35 bracket assemblies (part 11495) in week 7 and a planned order release in week 5. This passes down to the top handle coupling (part 1118), which creates a planned order release for four units in week 2. This means that the *cumulative lead time* for the top handle assembly is seven weeks (from release of the coupling order in week 2 to receipt of the top handle assemblies in week 9).

The cascading of lead times means that the effective length or visibility of the planning horizon is shortened as one moves down the product structure. This is sometimes referred to as loss of low-level visibility. The 10-week planning horizon for the top handle assembly results in a 6-week planning horizon with only 3 weeks of planned order releases for the coupling. The only way to compensate for this is to extend the planning horizon for the items at the top of the bill of material. It is not uncommon to find one to two years as the planning horizon for MRP systems.

Scheduled receipts versus planned order releases

A true understanding of MRP requires knowledge of certain key differences between a scheduled receipt and a planned order. We noted one such difference before: the scheduled receipt represents a commitment whereas the planned order is only a plan—the former is much more difficult to change than the latter. A scheduled receipt for a purchased item means that a purchase order, which is a formal commitment, has been prepared. Similarly, a scheduled receipt for a manufactured item means there is an open shop order. Raw materials and component parts have *already* been specifically committed to that order and are no longer available for other needs. One major result of this distinction, which can be seen in Figure 2.8, is that planned order releases explode to gross requirements for components, but scheduled receipts (the open orders) do not.

A related issue is seen from the following question: Where would a scheduled receipt for the top handle assembly (13122) in Figure 2.8 of say 20 units in week 2, be reflected in the records for the component parts (457, 082, and

11495)? The answer is nowhere! Scheduled receipts are not reflected in the current records for component parts. For that scheduled receipt to exist, the component parts would have already been assigned to the shop order representing the scheduled receipt for part 13122 and removed from the available balances of the components. As far as MRP is concerned, the 20 part 457s, 40 part 082s, and 20 part 11495s do not exist! They are on their way to becoming 20 part 13122s. It is the 13122 record which controls this process, not the component records.

So far we have examined the basic MRP system and some key technical details. Let us now turn to the *use* of the system: Who does what; how is it done; and what transactions need to be processed?

USING THE MRP SYSTEM

In this section we discuss the critical aspects of using the MRP system to ensure that the MRP system records are exactly synchronized with the physical flows of material.

The MRP planner

The persons most directly involved with the MRP system outputs are planners. They are typically in the production planning, inventory control, and purchasing departments. The planners have the responsibility for making the detailed decisions that keep the material moving through the plant to achieve the shipment of final products. Their range of discretion is carefully limited; i.e., without higher authorization, they cannot change plans for end items that are destined for customers. It is, however, their actions that are reflected in the MRP records. Well-trained, high-quality MRP planners are essential to effective use of the MRP system.

Computerized MRP systems often encompass tens of thousands of part numbers. The system produces a set of coordinated MRP time-phased records for each part number. As a consequence, planners are generally organized around logical groupings of parts, such as metal parts, wood parts, purchased electronic parts, West Coast distribution center, etc. Even so, it would not be an effective use of the planners' time to review each record every time the records are processed. At any time, many would require no action, so the planner only wants to review and interpret those records which require action.

The primary actions taken by an MRP planner are:

1. Release orders, i.e., launch purchase or shop orders when indicated by the system.
2. Reschedule the due dates of existing open orders when desirable.
3. Analyze and update system planning factors for the part numbers under his or her control. This would involve such things as changing lot sizes, lead times, scrap allowances, or safety stocks.

4. Reconcile errors or inconsistencies and try to eliminate root causes of these errors.
5. Find key problem areas that require action now to prevent future crises.
6. Use the system to solve critical material shortage problems so that the actions can be captured in the records for the next processing. This means the planner works *within* the formal MRP rules, *not* by informal methods.
7. Indicate where further system enhancements (outputs, diagnostics, etc.) would make the planner's job easier.

Order launching. Order launching is the process of releasing orders to the shop or to vendors (purchase orders). This process is prompted by MRP when a planned order release is in the current time period, the action bucket. The action converts the planned order into a scheduled receipt in a time period that reflects the lead time offset. Order launching is the opening of shop and purchase orders; closing these orders occurs when the scheduled receipts are received into stockrooms. At that time, a transaction must be processed so as to increase the on-hand inventory and eliminate the scheduled receipt. Procedures for opening and closing shop orders have to be carefully defined so that all transactions are properly processed.

The orders indicated by MRP as ready for launching are a function of lot sizing procedures and safety stock, as well as timing. We saw this in our examples where we worked with lot-for-lot approaches and fixed lot sizes. In Figure 2.8, a key responsibility of the planner is to manage with awareness of the implications of these effects. For example, not *all* of a fixed lot may be necessary to cover a requirement, or a planned order that is solely for replenishment of safety stock may be in the action bucket.

When an order is launched, it is sometimes necessary to include a shrinkage allowance for scrap and other process yield situations. The typical approach is to allow some percentage for yield losses which will increase the shop order quantity above the net amount required. To effect good control over open orders, the *total* amount, including the allowance, should be shown on the shop order, and the scheduled receipt should be reduced as actual yield losses occur during production.

Allocation and availability checking. A concept closely related to order launching is that of allocation. An important step prior to order launching involves an availability check for the necessary component or components. From the snow shovel example, if we want to assemble 20 of the top handle assembly (13122) in period 4, the availability check would be whether sufficient components (20 of part 457, 40 of part 082, and 20 of part 11495) are available. If not, the shop order for 20 top handle assemblies (13122) should not be launched, because it cannot be executed without component parts. The planner role is key here, as well. The best course of action might be to release a partial order. The planner should evaluate that possibility.

What most MRP systems do is to first check component availability for any order that a planner desires to launch. If sufficient quantities of each component are available, the shop order can be created. If the order is created, then the system allocates the necessary quantities to the particular shop order. (Shop orders are assigned by the computer, in numerical sequence.) The allocation means that this amount is mortgaged to the particular shop order and is, therefore, not available for any other shop order. Thus, the amounts shown in Figure 2.8 as projected available balances may not be the same as the physical inventory balance. The physical inventory balance could be larger, with the difference representing allocations to specific shop orders that have been released, but for which the component parts have not been removed from inventory.

Creation of the shop order requires more than availability checking and allocation. In addition, *picking tickets* are typically created and sent to the stockroom. The picking ticket calls for a specified amount of some part number to be removed from some inventory location, on some shop order, to be delivered to a particular department or location. When the picking ticket has been satisfied (inventory moved), the allocation is removed and the on-hand balance is reduced accordingly.

Availability checking, allocation, and physical stock picking are a type of double-entry bookkeeping. The result is that the quantity physically on hand should match what the records indicate is available plus what is allocated. If not, corrective action must be taken. The resulting accuracy facilitates inventory counting and other procedures for maintaining data integrity.

Exception codes

Exception codes in MRP systems are used "to separate the vital few from the trivial many." In most systems, if the manufacturing process is under control and the MRP system is functioning correctly, exception coding typically means that only 10 to 20 percent of the part numbers will require planner review at each processing cycle. Exception codes are in two general categories. The first is checking the input data accuracy. Included are checks for dates beyond the planning horizon, quantities larger or smaller than check figures, nonvalid part numbers, or any other desired check for incongruity. The second category of exception codes directly support the MRP planning activity. Included are the following kinds of exception (action) messages or diagnostics:

1. Part numbers for which a planned order is now in the most immediate time period (the action bucket). It is also possible to report any planned orders two to three periods out to check lead times, on-hand balances, and other factors while there is some time to respond, if necessary.
2. Open order diagnostics when the present timing and/or amount for a scheduled receipt is not satisfactory. Such a message might indicate that an open order exists that is not necessary to cover any of the requirements in the planning horizon. This message might suggest order cancellation. Such a message might be caused by an engineering change

which substituted some new part for the one in question. The most common type of open order diagnostic is to show scheduled receipts that are timed to arrive either too late or too early, and should, therefore, have their due dates revised to reflect proper priorities in the factory. An example of this is seen with each of the three scheduled receipts in Figure 2.8. The 457 top handle open order of 25 could be delayed one week. A one-week delay is also indicated for the 082 nail scheduled receipt. For part 1118, the top handle coupling, the scheduled receipt of 15 could be delayed from week 2 until week 5. Another open order exception code is to flag any past-due scheduled receipt (scheduled to have been received in previous periods, but for which no receipt transaction has been processed). MRP systems assume that a past-due scheduled receipt will be received in the immediate time bucket.

3. A third general type of exception message indicates problem areas for production management; in essence, situations where level-zero quantities cannot be satisfied unless the present planning factors used in MRP are changed. One such exception code indicates that a requirement has been offset into a past period, and subsequently added to any requirement in the first or most immediate time bucket. This condition means that an order should have been placed in the past. Since it was not, the lead times through the various production item levels need to be compressed to meet the end item schedule. A similar diagnostic indicates that the allocations exceed the on-hand inventory—a condition directly analogous to overdrawing a checking account. Unless more inventory is received soon, the firm will not be able to honor all pick tickets that have been issued, and there may be a material shortage in the factory.

Bottom-up replanning

Bottom-up replanning is the process of using the pegging data to solve material shortage problems. It is best seen through an example. Let us return again to Figure 2.8, concentrating on the top handle assembly and the nails (parts 13122 and 082). Let us suppose that the scheduled receipt of 50 nails arrives on Wednesday of week 1. On Thursday, quality control checks them and finds the vendor sent the wrong size. This means only 4 of the 10 gross requirement in week 2 can be satisfied. By pegging this gross requirement up to its parent planned order (5 units of 13122 in period 2), it can be seen that only 7 of the gross requirement for 10 units in week 4 can be satisfied (the 5 on hand plus 2 made from 4 nails). This, in turn, means that only seven snow shovels can be assembled in week 4.

The pegging analysis shows that 3 of the 10 top handle assemblies cannot be available without taking some special actions. If none are taken, the planned assembly dates for the snow shovels should reflect only seven units in week 4, with the additional three scheduled for week 5. This should be done if some means is not found to overcome the shortfall in nails. The change is necessary because the 10 snow shovels now scheduled for assembly in week 4 also explode to other parts—parts that will not be needed if only 7 snow shovels are to be assembled.

There may, however, be a critical customer requirement for 10 snow shovels to be assembled during week 4. Solving the problem with bottom-up replanning might involve one of the following alternatives (staying *within* the MRP system, as planners must do):

1. Issue an immediate order to the vendor for six nails (the minimum requirement), securing a promised lead time of two days instead of the usual one week. This will create a scheduled receipt for six in week 2.
2. Order more nails for the beginning of week 3, and negotiate a reduction in lead time of one week for the fabrication of this one batch of part 13122, from two weeks to one week. The planned order release for five would be placed in week 3 and be converted to a firm planned order, so it would not change when the record is processed again. The negotiation for a one-week lead time might involve letting the people concerned start work earlier than week 3 on the two part 13122s for which material already exists, and a reduction in the one-week paperwork time that was included in the lead times.
3. Negotiate a one-week lead time reduction for the assembly of the snow shovels, place a firm planned order for 10 in week 5, which will result in a gross requirement for 10 top handle assemblies in period 5 instead of period 4.

Thus, we see the solution to a material shortage problem might be made by compressing lead times throughout the product structure using the system bottom-up replanning. The planners work within the system using firm planned orders and net requirements to develop workable (but not standard) production schedules. The creativity they use in solving problems will be reflected in the part records at the next MRP processing cycle. All the implications of planner actions will be correctly coordinated throughout the product structure.

It is important to note that the resolution of problems cannot *always* involve reduced lead time and/or partial lots. Further, none of these actions comes for free. In some cases, customer needs will have to be delayed or partial shipments made. Pegging and bottom-up replanning will provide advance warning of these problems so that customers can take appropriate actions.

An MRP system output

Figure 2.10 is an MRP time-phased record for 1 part number out of a total of 13,000 in one manufacturing company. The header information includes the date the report was run, part number and descriptions, planner code number, buyer code number (for purchased parts), the unit of measure for this part number (pieces, pounds, etc.), rejected parts that have yet to receive disposition by quality control, safety stocks, shrinkage allowance for

FIGURE 2.10 Example MRP record

MATERIAL STATUS-PRODUCTION SCHEDULE

DATE- 01/21

* * * * * * *PART NUMBER* * * * * * * NONJEK OPTY SSV LAM PP UPHL	DESCRIPTION	PLNR CODE	BYR COE	U/M	REJECT QUANTITY	SAFETY STOCK	SHRINKG ALLOWNE	LEAD TIME	FAMILY DATA
USTR040	3/16 x 7/8 MR P & C STL STRAP	01	9	LFT		497	1	08	

* ORDER POLICY AND LOT SIZE DATA *

YTD SCRAP	* * * * USAGE * * * * LAST YR	YTD	POLICY CODE	STANDARD QUANTITY	PERIODS TO COMB.	MINIMUM QTY	MAXIMUM QTY	MULTIPLE QTY	MIN ORD POINT
			3		04				

	PAST DUE	563 01/22	564 01/29	565 02/05	566 02/12	567 02/19	568 02/26	569 03/05	570 03/12	571 03/19	572 03/26	573 04/02
REQUIREMENTS	495			483				516				
SCHEDULED RECEIPTS												
PLANNED RECEIPTS							491					337
AVAILABLE ON-HAND	1,500	508	508	25	25	25	516					337
PLANNED ORDERS	491			337				334				

	574 04/09	575 04/16	576 04/23	577 04/30	578 05/07	579 05/14	580 05/21	581 05/28	582 06/04	583 06/11	584 06/18	585 06/25
REQUIREMENTS	337				334							
SCHEDULED RECEIPTS												
PLANNED RECEIPTS				334								
AVAILABLE				334								
PLANNED ORDERS												

	VACATION		586 07/16	587 07/23	588 07/30	589-592 08/06	593-596 09/03	597-600 10/01	601-604 10/29	605-608 11/26	609-612 12/24	
REQUIREMENTS												
SCHEDULED RECEIPTS												
PLANNED RECEIPTS												
AVAILABLE												
PLANNED ORDERS												

* * * * * * * *EXCEPTION MESSAGES* * * * * * * *

PLANNED ORDER OF 491 FOR M-WK 568 OFFSET INTO A PAST PERIOD BY 03 PERIODS

* * * * * * * *PEGGING DATA (ALLOC)* * * * * * * *

790116 455 JN25220

* * * * * * * *PEGGING DATA (REQMT)* * * * * * * *

790205 483 F 17144 790305 516 F 19938 790409 337 F 17144

790507 334 F 19938

anticipated scrap loss, lead time, family data (what other parts are very similar to this one), the year-to-date scrap, usage last year, year-to-date usage, and order policy/lot size data. The policy code of 3 for this part means that the order policy is a *period order quantity* (POQ). In this case, the "periods to comb." = 4, means that each order should combine four periods of net requirements.

The first time bucket is "past due." After that, weekly time buckets are presented for the first 28 weeks of data; thereafter, 24 weeks of data are lumped into 4-week buckets. In the computer itself, all data are kept in exact days, with the printouts prepared in summary format for one- and four-week buckets. The company maintains a manufacturing calendar; in this example, the first week is 563 (also shown as 1/22), and the last week is 612.

In this report, safety stock is subtracted from the on-hand balance (except in the past-due bucket). Thus, the exception message indicating that a planned order for 491 should have been issued three periods ago creates no major problem, since the planner noted that this amount is less than the safety stock. This report shows the use of safety lead time. *Planned* receipts are given a specific row in the report and are scheduled one week ahead of the actual need date. For example, the 337-unit planned order of week 565 is a planned receipt in week 573, although it is not needed until week 574.

The final data on the report is the pegging data section which ties specific requirements to the part numbers from which those requirements came. For example, in week 565 (shop order No. 790305), the requirement for 483 derives from part number F17144. MRP records are printed at this company only for those part numbers for which exception messages exist.

THE MRP DATA BASE

To install and derive maximum benefit from a material planning and control system, a large integrated data base is usually required. The computer hardware and software design aspects of common data bases are beyond the scope of this book. Their importance in MPC systems compels us to briefly identify the primary files and communication links that are required. In this section, we treat the data files that would usually be required to support the engine of the MPC system in Figure 2.1. We make no claim that the following approach is optimal, or that one might not group the data in different ways. Rather, our objective is to illustrate one way the data might be supplied and to identify the elements needed. The enormity of the overall data base even for small firms is awesome, but the data needs exist *even if there is no formal system*, as long as people are manufacturing products.

The item master file

The data on an individual part are often contained in two files. The information that remains the same (or nearly so) from period to period is found in the *item master file*, while the information on part status is found in the subordinate file. The item master file typically contains all the data needed to completely describe each part number. These data are used for MRP, purchasing, cost accounting, and other company functions. The objective is to hold, in one file, all of the static data that describe the attributes of individual part numbers. Included are part number, name, low-level code, unit of measure, engineering change number, drawing reference, release date, planner code, order policy code, lead time, safety stock, standard costs, and linkages to other data files such as routing, where used, bill of material, etc.

The subordinate item master file. A subordinate item master file is often used for changing or dynamic data about individual part numbers. Included are current allocations and the shop order number to which each allocation is tied, time-phased scheduled receipts and associated order numbers, time-phased gross requirements, planned orders, firm planned orders, pegging data, and linkages to the item master file.

The bill of material file. The bill of material file is typically established on a *single level* basis, with each part number linked only to the part numbers of the immediate components required to produce it. That is, the linkages are to one level farther down in the product structure only. By successively linking the part numbers, a full bill of material for each part can be developed from the individual single-level linkings. The data elements held in this file usually include the component part numbers required to make each individual part, number of each required, units of measure, engineering change numbers, effectivity dates, active/inactive coding, and where-used information.

The location file. The location file keeps track of the set of exact physical storage locations for each part number. This can be a highly dynamic file since the data elements usually include departments, rows, bays, tiers, quantities, units of measure, in dates, original quantities, date of last activity, etc.

The calendar file. The calendar file is used to convert from the shop day calendar used by the firm to a day/date/year calendar. The file also provides for phenomena such as annual vacations and holidays.

Open order files. An entire set of files is maintained to support the scheduled receipts (open orders) in the MRP system. These involve both purchase orders and shop orders. For the purchase orders, one needs open purchase orders, open quotations, a vendor master file, vendor performance data, alternate sources, and price/quantity information. Another set of records needs to be maintained to support shop orders in the factory. Included are data files describing open orders, routings, work centers, employees, shifts, tooling, and labor/performance reporting.

Other file linkages. This brief review of data elements shows the enormity of data acquisition, storage, and the subsequent file maintenance required for an effective MRP system. In addition to the data files needed for the engine, many other data files are necessary to flesh out the entire MPC system. Among them are files for forecasting, capacity planning, production scheduling, cost accounting, budgeting, order entry, shop-floor control, distribution, invoicing, payroll, job standards, and engineering.

MANUAL MRP SYSTEMS

After reviewing the list of required data elements, one might reasonably conclude that MRP is only for the large company with sophisticated computer systems. This is often the case, but a few companies have been able to achieve many of the MRP benefits by using MRP approaches in manual systems. Moreover, a new group of less expensive, less complex computer systems is increasingly being used by the smaller firms. Here we will review two manual examples. In both cases, after the manual systems were adopted, it became cost effective to computerize the system. The cost of the computer aspects of MRP continues to decrease. In fact, the significant cost is that of converting company operations over to an MRP-based approach, not the cost of the computer. In both of the following companies, manual MRP was a useful intermediate step in the conversion process.

Dataram

The Dataram company is a manufacturer of high-speed computer core memory units and components used to increase the memory size of a computer's central processing unit. The firm's sales grew from $2.7 million to $10.7 million over a four-year period. At that time, Dataram's products were divided into four major categories: cores, stacks, modules, and systems. Cores are small, doughnut-shaped magnetic storage components. Stacks consist of thousands of cores wired together in grids to form the basis for the storage and transfer of electrical impulses. Modules are assemblies of stacks integrated with timing and control circuits, as well as address and data registers. Systems consist of various numbers of memory modules combined in a chassis with optional internal power-supply units.

The manual production planning and inventory control system at Dataram was based on extensive use of ABC analysis. The company had a total of 1,860 purchased items, and any item representing an expected weekly cost-volume of more than $40 was classified as an A item. The 1,600 B and C purchased components were controlled with a bin reserve system. No formal inventory records were kept, but purchase orders were placed when the inventory reached the reserve quantity. The total investment in B and C items was approximately $250,000. The 260 A items were planned and controlled with a manual MRP system. In this system, an end item production schedule was prepared once per quarter, using six-month buckets. This schedule was used for MRP explosion, with net requirements for modules passed down as gross requirements for both stacks and separately purchased

A parts, and as net requirements for stacks passed down as gross requirements to A purchased parts.

Neither chassis systems nor cores were formally considered in the MRP system. Chassis systems are made to order and use available modules, stacks, and purchased parts. Sufficient cores are manufactured to provide a five-to-seven-week buffer inventory.

When the sales were in the range of $5 million per year, the manual system at Dataram represented a reasonable trade-off between the costs of a production control system and its benefits. However, as the firm's rapid growth continued, several significant problems arose:

1. The six-month time bucket meant that all requirements were due in at the beginning of the six-month period—unless scheduled on a separate basis.
2. There were only two people who really understood how the system worked, and they were increasingly becoming involved in other manufacturing problem areas.
3. The analysis of when an item should move from A status to B or C (and vice-versa) was very cumbersome.
4. The impact of any changes in end item build schedules was difficult to assess in terms of projected component availabilities.

As a result, Dataram installed an IBM System 34 computer and implemented the IBM MAPICS software for MRP. The implementation process was facilitated by the experience the company had built up with the manual system. It took about one year to install the new MRP system. The key problems in the change related to transaction processing for all systems and the procedural reform necessary to use the formal system.

Ethan Allen Furniture Company

The Ethan Allen manual method for detailed component scheduling is based upon MRP logic which utilizes product structures to create demand dependency, lead time offsetting, and gross to netting. The Ethan Allen approach is to establish the assembly date and then prepare a back schedule or Gantt chart of the form shown in Figure 2.7. The parts are scheduled according to their individual lead times to be ready for final assembly. For MRP planning purposes, Ethan Allen incorporates a one-week safety lead time to allow parts to be exactly counted and prepared for final assembly. When the firm changed to a back schedule based approach from a cutting approach, an immediate reduction of 15 to 20 percent in the work-in-process inventory and lead times was achieved in the plants that were converted. (Old ways die hard, however, and though the benefits of back scheduling were clearly demonstrated, one otherwise well-run factory took eight years to convert to the new system.)

The manual MRP-like system is satisfactory for Ethan Allen furniture factories for two basic reasons. First, although a bill of materials for most items would show indentations of several levels, in fact, subassemblies tend to be phantoms. That is, they are not stored. For example, drawers are not stored. They are produced when the end item is produced, being assembled at the same time from basic components. Thus, there is no need for gross to netting on a level-by-level explosion basis. End item needs are multiplied by the number of components per end item, and gross to netting is performed only against component inventories. The second reason that this approach works well for the company is there is very little commonality among parts and no spare parts requirements. Therefore, component parts generally do not receive gross requirements from more than one source.

Manual MRP systems are still in use at many Ethan Allen factories. However, as was true for Dataram, growth makes the management of these manual systems cumbersome. Ethan Allen now has several computerized MRP systems installed and expects to continue the installation of these systems in other factories as their own knowledge increases, as growth dictates, and as the ever-decreasing costs of computers make these conversions more attractive.

CONCLUDING PRINCIPLES

Chapter 2 provides an understanding of the MRP approach to planning. It includes a description of the basic technique and some of the technical issues, as well as how MRP systems are used in practice. MRP, with its time-phased approach to planning, is a basic building-block concept for materials planning and control systems. Later, we will see other applications of the time-phased record. The basic ideas of MRP apply in those situations, too. We see the most important concepts or principles of this chapter as follows:

- Effective use of an MRP system allows development of a forward-looking (planning) approach to managing material flows.
- The MRP system provides a coordinated set of linked product relationships, thereby permitting decision making by individual part number.
- All decisions made to solve problems must be done within the system, and the transactions must be processed to reflect the resultant changes.
- Effective use of exception messages allows focusing attention on the "vital few," not on the "trivial many."
- The system records must reflect the physical reality of the factory if they are to be useful.
- The logical concepts upon which MRP is based apply whether the system is manual or computer based.

REFERENCES

Cox, James F., and Richard R. Jesse, Jr. "An Application of MRP to Higher Education." *Decision Sciences* 12, no. 2 (April 1981), pp. 240–60.

Cox, B. "The Message of MRP." *Phillips Administration Review*, December 1980, pp. 42–54.

Davis, E. W. *Case Studies in Material Requirements Planning.* Falls Church, Va.: American Production and Inventory Control Society, 1978.

Material Requirements Planning Reprints. Falls Church, Va.: American Production and Inventory Control Society, 1973.

Miller, J. G. "Fit Production Systems to the Task." *Harvard Business Review*, January/February 1981.

Miller, J. G., and L. G. Sprague. "Behind the Growth in Materials Requirements Planning." *Harvard Business Review*, September/October 1975.

Myers, K. A., R. J. Schonberger, and A. Amsari, "Requirements Planning for Control of Information Resources," *Decision Sciences*, vol. 14, no. 1, January 1983, pp. 19–33.

New, C. *Requirements Planning.* New York: Halsted Press, 1973.

Orlicky, J. *Material Requirements Planning.* New York: McGraw-Hill, 1975.

Plossl, George W., and Oliver W. Wight, *MRP Planning by Computer*. Falls Church, Va.: American Production and Inventory Control Society, 1971.

Steinberg, E., W. B. Lee, and B. M. Khumawala. "MRP Applications in the Space Program." *Journal of Operations Management* 1, no. 2, 1981.

Steinberg, E., B. M. Khumawala, and R. Scarnell. "Requirements Planning Systems in the Health Care Environment." *Journal of Operations Management* 2, no. 4 (August, 1982).

3

System dynamics and information integrity

This chapter is concerned with the maintenance of accurate information in the material planning and control (MPC) data base, given the dynamic changes which occur constantly in the physical flow of materials. The managerial objective is to provide the information necessary to manage the flows of material—to substitute information for inventory and to eliminate other forms of organizational slack. To do so will require high-quality information. This means that the data base elements must reflect the physical reality. Only by keeping the data *in* the system accurate can the outputs *of* the system be truly integrated into day-to-day decision making.

The chapter is organized around the following five topics:

- Integrity of the manufacturing planning and control data base: What are the principles for management *by* a data base and management *of* a data base?
- System dynamics: What is the MRP planner role, how does MRP reflect changing conditions, and why must transactions be processed properly?
- Procedural reform: What are the critical procedures that must be in place to support an effective MRP system?
- Routine auditing: How are transactions audited, errors detected, and corrections made on a routine, timely basis?

- Organizational considerations: How does a firm design, implement, and maintain an integrated data base for MPC systems, and what are the key organizational implications?

The material in Chapter 2 provides an important background for the concepts in this chapter. Chapter 2 covers the basic MRP record, some key technical issues, managerial use of MRP data, and some underlying data base considerations.

INTEGRITY OF THE MPC DATA BASE: MANAGEMENT *BY* AND *OF* A DATA BASE

The users of a truly effective MPC system, including both MRP planners and first-line supervisors, experience changed roles in their day-to-day decision making. It is paramount for them to take the management actions indicated by the formal system and second to ensure that all actions necessary to provide the correct data are performed. That is, when the MPC system indicates that some action is required, it is the *sole* signal for taking action—management exclusively *by* the system and its data base with no informal dictates that override the system. If the system is to provide proper signals for action, procedures for entering transactions into the data base and responsibilities for doing so without fail must be developed—management *of* the data base. For this change in managerial perspective to take place, several key principles must be followed. Although we present them couched largely in the terminology and examples of MRP, they clearly apply to all of the MPC system modules.

The data base must reflect reality. The objective here is to always have an exact match between what is physically true and the data base representation of the physical entity, viz the data entity. This means that if the inventory balance in a part record indicates that 27 pieces of the part are on hand, then a physical count of that part must yield 27. It also means that if the location file indicates that the 27 pieces are in location N-7, then that is where the 27 pieces must be found, and nowhere else. If a bill of material says three pieces are required for some assembly, there must be three pieces required. If a scheduled receipt indicates that 35 pieces are being worked on in the shop, one can similarly verify that count through physical audit. If someone scraps one or more of these pieces, the system (data base) needs to be informed so that the real number of pieces is always reflected. Similarly, the location of the scheduled receipt, work completed, work remaining, due date, etc. all have to be reflected accurately in the system.

A strong principle that comes from experience is that any action, no matter how worthy it may seem, that comes at the expense of data integrity, must be avoided. The costs of ignoring this principle are very high indeed, including complete collapse of the system. It is more important to strive for the goal of an exact match between the data entity and physical reality than to try to determine what is "good enough." Bankers spend dollars to count pennies in order to realize this concept.

Data base transactions must be processed rapidly. For the system to constantly mirror reality, it is necessary for changes to be processed rapidly as well as accurately. If a scheduled receipt is received and put into stock, the open shop order must be closed out and the on-hand balance increased quickly. Many successful firms require that the data base reflect these transactions within a 24-hour period. Similar speed is required for the processing of customer orders, shipments, orders placed with vendors, receipts from vendors, and any adjustments necessary because of scrap or inventory losses. The longer the time lag between actual physical change and concomitant change in the data base, the less the data base reflects reality—thereby creating a need for informal systems to find out the truth. For example, in a large service center for distribution of structural steel, this principle has been violated. Inventory transactions are batched and processed by the computer on a time availability basis. As a consequence, the inventory clerks maintain a separate card file to know what is really going on. Their need to know on a daily basis leads them to circumvent the system to find out.

Data base maintenance must be tightly controlled. There is a critical distinction between *access* to data which can be available to many users and authority to *change* a given data element. This distinction must be carefully maintained. If the data base is truly to be managed, then specific individuals must have sole authority to make changes in specific data elements and similarly be held responsible for the accuracy of those data. This implies that data accuracy be made a specific part of many job descriptions, and that organizational changes be made to ensure proper data maintenance. A good case in point is the bill of materials file, which traditionally has been managed by the engineering department. The principles of data base accuracy and rapid response to change clearly apply to changes to bills of material. This means that bill of material changes cannot be constrained by antiquated procedures, and that nonengineering uses of the bill of materials must be accommodated. In some companies, these dictates have resulted in maintenance activity for the bill of materials data base being separated from the engineering department and assigned to a materials management group.

All of the data files that are required to support an MPC system have to be tightly controlled. This means organizational assignment of authority to make data base changes. Other areas where reorganization is often dictated by data base maintenance considerations include the functions involving customer order entry, delivery date promising, receipt of purchased parts, quality assurance reporting, and so on.

User actions must be integrated with data base transactions. To achieve data base integrity and to maintain this integrity at high levels, it is desirable to achieve a high degree of congruence between the job actually performed by users and the data which those users provide to the system. If the data collection is simply an added burden to one's job, the chances for mistakes are much greater than if the job performance itself relies upon accurate data. For example, if it can be demonstrated to a first line supervisor that his or her job is actually easier if he or she enters data correctly, higher quality data input should result. To the extent that the transaction reporting on individual orders (scheduled receipts) is integrated with payroll, variance accounting, movements from work in process to finished goods, etc., there are increased pressures for data accuracy.

The system must tell the truth to the users. This principle is related to the necessity for the data base to reflect reality—but there is an added dimension. It is necessary to design the system, its parameters, and its data base so that unnecessary cushions, personal hedges, and inconsistencies are sorted out. If the formal system is to be used to make day-to-day decisions, the output data must be believable. If it is, the system can substitute information for the physical hedges so often used for buffering in informal systems. A case in point relates to due dates assigned to shop orders launched into the factory. One company had three stamps to be used for their orders: RUSH, CRITICAL, and EMERGENCY! Clearly, here is a case where RUSH stands for *R*outine *U*sual *S*low *H*andling, since it is the lowest order priority. The point to all this is simply that if everything is marked rush, then nothing is rush. It is essential to establish *relative* priorities for shop orders and purchase orders. This is best done by telling the truth about due dates, lead times, and other system parameters. If everyone has to second guess other people's hedges, the resultant mismatch between the system and reality will be great.

The informal system must die. In many companies, there is a formal system for production planning and inventory control (such as RUSH-CRITICAL-EMERGENCY), and an informal system that gets the products shipped *in spite of* the formal system. These informal systems are usually made up of "hot lists" indicating what is *really* needed to meet shipments, physical staging of the materials to make *sure* that they are available, black books for how to *really* make the products, telephone calls, visits over lunch, etc. As long as there is any vestige of an informal system, the incentive to use the formal system is reduced. The only way to kill off the informal system is to design the formal system so well that users always get better information from it than from the informal system. It is also necessary to continually educate the users so that they understand why the formal system produces better results and why all of their efforts are better devoted to solving problems *with* the system, than in inventive ways of going around it.

SYSTEM DYNAMICS

Murphy's law states that if anything can go wrong, it will. The corollary to Murphy's law is that Murphy was an optimist! It is also thought that Murphy formulated his famous law by working in manufacturing. Things are constantly going wrong, and it is essential that the MRP system mirror the actual conditions in the shop. That is, both the physical system and the information system have to cope with scrap, incorrect counts, changes in customer needs, incorrect bills of material, engineering design changes, poor vendor performance, and a myriad of other mishaps.

In this section, we look at the need for quick and accurate transaction processing, and review the replanning activities of the MRP planner in coping with change. We discuss sources of the problems that will occur as a result of data base changes and actions to be taken to ensure that the system is telling the truth, even if the truth hurts.

Transactions during a period

To illustrate transaction processing issues, we use a simple example for one part. Figure 3.1 shows an MRP record for part 1234 that has been produced over the weekend preceding week 1. The planner for part 1234 would receive this MRP record on Monday of week 1.

The planner's first action would be to try to launch the planned order for 50 units in period 1. That is, the MPC system would first check availability of the raw materials for this part, and then issue an order to the shop to make 50 if sufficient raw material is available. Launching would require allocating the necessary raw materials to the shop order, removing the 50 from the planned order release row for part 1234, and creating a scheduled receipt for 50 in week 3, when they are needed. Thereafter, a pick ticket would be sent to the raw material area and work could begin.

Let us assume that during week 1 the following changes occurred, and the transactions were processed :

- The actual disbursements from stock for item 1234 during week 1 were only 20 instead of the planned 30.

FIGURE 3.1 MRP record for part 1234 as of week 1

Lead time = 2
Lot size = 50

		1	2	3	4	5
Gross requirements		30	20	20	0	45
Scheduled receipts		50				
Projected available balance	10	30	10	40	40	45
Planned order releases		50		50		

- The scheduled receipt for 50 due in week 1 was received on Tuesday, but 10 units were rejected, so only 40 were actually received into inventory.
- The inventory was counted on Thursday, and 20 additional pieces were found.
- The requirement date for the 45 pieces in week 5 was changed to week 4.
- Marketing has requested an additional five pieces for samples in week 2.
- The requirement for week 6 has been set at 25.

The resultant MRP record produced over the weekend preceding week 2 is presented as Figure 3.2.

Rescheduling

The MRP record shown in Figure 3.2 illustrates two important activities for MRP planners. These are indicating the sources of problems that will occur as a result of data base changes, and suggesting actions that need to be taken to ensure that the system is telling the truth. Note that the scheduled receipt presently due in week 3 is not needed until week 4. The net result of all the changes to the data base means that it is now scheduled with the wrong due date, and the due date should be changed to week 4. If this change is not made, this job may be worked on ahead of some other job that is really needed earlier, thereby causing problems. The condition shown in Figure 3.2 would be highlighted by an MRP exception message such as "reschedule the receipt currently due in week 3 to week 4."

For the MRP system to not lie to the users, it is imperative to provide accurate relative priority information to fabrication work centers. The first step in doing this is for the planner to reschedule the open order so that the

FIGURE 3.2 MRP record for part 1234 as of week 2

Lead time = 2
Lot size = 50

		2	3	4	5	6
Gross requirements		25	20	45	0	25
Scheduled receipts			50			
Projected available balance	50	25	55	10	10	35
Planned order release				50		

revised priority can be transmitted to the shop floor. Only in this way will the shop know which job to work on next at each work center. The key to doing this job well is for MRP planners to quickly process due date changes as soon as the MRP records reflect the change transactions. Let us now turn to more complex examples of transaction processing, their impact on MRP records, and the resulting needs for rescheduling.

Complex transaction processing

So far, we have illustrated system dynamics by using a single MRP record. However, an action required on the part of an MRP planner may have been caused by a very complex set of data base transactions involving several levels in the bill of materials. As an example, consider the MRP records shown in Figure 3.3, which includes three levels in the product structure. Part C is used as a component in both parts A and B, as well as being sold as a service part. Part C in turn is made from parts X and Y. The arrows in Figure 3.3 depict the pegging data.

The part C MRP record is correctly stated at the beginning of week 1. That is, there would be no exception messages produced at this time. In particular, the two scheduled receipts of 95 and 91, respectively, are scheduled correctly, since delaying either by one week would cause a shortage, and neither has to be expedited to cover any projected shortage.

While the two scheduled receipts for part C are currently scheduled correctly, transactions involving parts A and B can have an impact on the proper

FIGURE 3.3 MRP record relationships for several parts

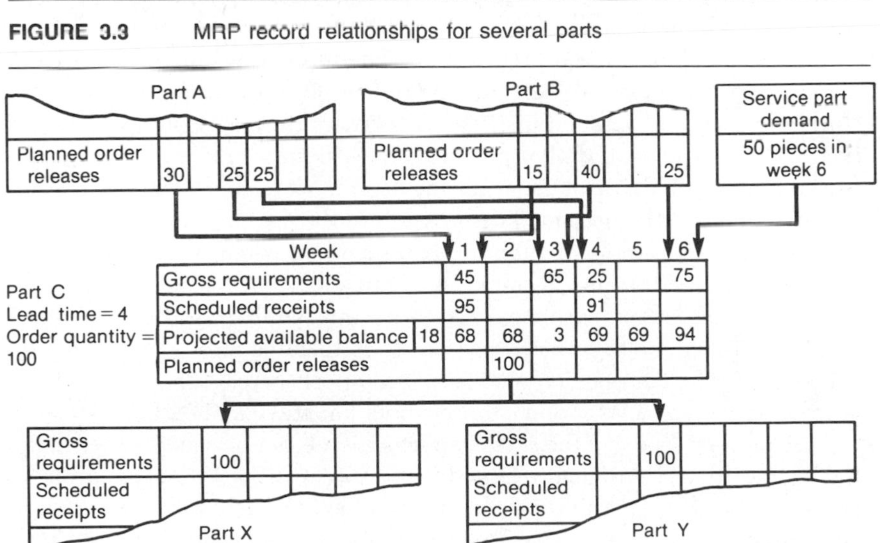

Note: This example is based on one originally developed by Joseph Orlicky, *Material Requirements Planning* (New York: McGraw-Hill, 1975), chap. 3, pp. 44–64.

due dates for these open orders. For example, suppose an inventory count adjustment for part A resulted in a change in the 30 unit planned order release from week 1 to week 3. In this case, the 95 units of part C would not be needed until week 3, necessitating a reschedule. Similarly, any change in timing for the planned order release of 25 units of part A in week 4 would call for a reschedule of the due date for 91 units of part C. Finally, suppose that a transaction requiring 75 additional units of part B in week 5 were processed. This would result in an immediate release of an order for 100 units of part C. This might necessitate rescheduling for parts X and Y. The point here is that actions required on the part of the MRP planner can occur because of a complex set of data base transactions involving many different parts. They may not necessarily directly involve the particular part which is being given attention by the MRP planner.

Procedural inadequacies

MRP replanning and transaction processing activities are two essential aspects of ensuring that the MPC data base remains accurate. However, while these activities are necessary, they are not sufficient to maintain an accurate data base. Some of the procedures used to process transactions simply may be inadequate to the task.

To illustrate inadequate transaction procedures, let us return to the example in Figure 3.3. Note that if 4 or more pieces are scrapped on the shop order for 95, there will be a shortage in week 3, necessitating rescheduling of the order for 91 one week earlier.

What is even more interesting is to see what would happen if 4 pieces were scrapped on the order for 95, and this scrap transaction were not processed. If the scrap is not reported, the MRP records would appear as shown in Figure 3.3, indicating no required rescheduling—when, in fact, that is not true. *If* the shortage were discovered by the person in charge of the stockroom when he or she puts away this order, then only one week would be lost before the next MRP report will show the problem. If, however, the stockroom person does not count, or the person who made the scrap puts the defective parts at the bottom of the box where they go undetected by quality control, then the problem will only be discovered when the assembly lines are trying to build As and Bs in week 3. Such a discovery comes under the category of unpleasant surprises. An interesting sidelight to this problem is that the cure will be to rush down to the shop to get at least 1 piece from the batch of 91. The very person who failed to report the earlier scrap may well now be screaming "Why don't those idiots know what they need!"

Still another aspect of the scrap reporting issue can be seen by noting that the 95 and 91 were originally issued as lot sizes of 100. What this probably means is that five and nine pieces of scrap have occurred already, and the appropriate adjustments have been made in the scheduled receipt data. Note that if these adjustments had *not* been made, the two scheduled receipts would show as 100 each. The resultant 14 (5 + 9) pieces (that do not, in fact, exist) would be reflected in the MRP arithmetic. Thus, the projected available balance at the end of period 5 would be 83 (69 + 14); this is more than enough to cover the gross requirement of 75 in period 6, so the planned order release for 100 in period 2 would not exist and the error would cascade throughout the product structure. Further, even if shop orders are carefully counted as they are put into storage, the five-piece shortage in period 1 is not enough to cause the MRP arithmetic to plan an order. It is only after period 4 (the beginning of period 5) that the additional nine pieces of scrap will be incorporated in the MRP record showing a projected shortage in period 6. This will result in an immediate order, to be completed in one week instead of four! What may be obvious is that if accurate counting is not done, then the shortage is discovered in week 6 when the assembly line goes down. This means that procedures for issuing scrap tickets when scrap occurs and procedures for ensuring that good parts are accurately counted into inventory must be in place. If not, all of the MPC systems will suffer.

The long and the short of all this is that we are back to the principles calling for data integrity. We have to believe the numbers, and an error of as little as *one* piece can cause severe problems. We have to know the truth. We have to tightly control transactions. Moreover, we have to develop iron-clad procedures for processing MPC data base transactions.

PROCEDURAL REFORM

If one were to apply the ABC inventory control principle (where the A items are most important B items less important, and C items least important) to MRP implementation, the C items are the computer and computer programs. The B items are the procedures that must be changed, and the A items are the people issues—education, organizational change, etc. With procedural reform, it is quite possible that every single piece of paper going through the factory will need to be changed. Moreover, new procedures and documents will be required to control things that were previously not controlled. Let us now overview some of the key procedures that support MRP.

Cycle counting

We have seen how an error of as little as one unit in an MRP record can lead to the need for managerial actions. If one thinks of an MRP record of 52 weeks in length, and four rows of information, then there are more than 200 numbers that are displayed. Of all these numbers, the one that can be most accurately validated is the on-hand balance. Furthermore, if it is wrong, the result is a tower of gelatin.

It is critical that the on-hand balances reflected in data records exactly match the physical on-hand balances. The only way to be sure of this match is to compare the two numbers by physical counting. This is the purpose of the annual physical inventory. But the annual inventory count is designed for financial purposes and primarily relates to an *overall* imbalance,—which can include compensating errors. For MRP purposes, this is not good enough. A shortage of one part and an overage of another are two errors—*both* of which may require managerial actions.

An alternative to taking an annual physical inventory is to continuously monitor on-hand balances using cycle counting. One way to do this is to have personnel whose entire job is to cycle count, checking some item on-hand balances every day. Another way is to have stockroom personnel levels set to readily handle peak loads (ins and outs), with slack times used for cycle counting.

Many firms believe that cycle counting is an extra expense, but this is not necessarily true. If it is done right, cycle counting can and should eliminate the need for taking an annual physical inventory. The records held by the MRP data base and verified by cycle counting should be so good that a total physical inventory would induce more mistakes than it would uncover. The costs of stopping all production for several days can very easily justify having a staff of cycle counters.

Cycle counting represents a critical commitment to the achievement of effective MPC system implementation. We know of *no* first-class system that does not use some form of cycle counting. The concept is to have the numbers in the data base regarded in the same way that they are in a bank. It is no less important to know how many part 1234s are in location N-7 than to know how many $20 bills are in a particular drawer in the bank vault. In fact, it may be much more important, since two $10 bills can be substituted for one $20, whereas other items may not be readily substituted for Part 1234.

The commitment to a cycle counting program conveys a degree of seriousness on the part of management to the factory. Someone should be evaluated on the basis of cycle count accuracy. The stockrooms will have to be physically arranged so that inventory accuracy can be achieved. This implies locked areas, limited entry, containers of known weight, accurate measurement devices, specific item areas, shelving, a system that keeps track of items by individual location, and a set of ironclad procedures that capture every possible transaction as goods move in and out of storage. How is it possible to have accurate records if any of the following conditions can occur? (We have seen them all.)

- The engineers get parts for R&D without proper transactions.
- The president (or anyone else) is free to roam the stockroom—can a bank president roam the vault?
- Parts are stored in old cardboard boxes with holes in them.
- Many parts are piled on top of each other.
- Parts are stored in an open yard where they can be lost in the snow.
- The scale for weighing parts belongs in a museum.

- The containers are of uneven, unknown weights, or people are allowed to throw trash in them.

Once someone has their personal performance evaluated in terms of the cycle count accuracy, all of these causes will be isolated, and proper actions will be taken to correct them. The percentage of error encountered by cycle counting is a good barometer or leading indicator for any MPC system. If this error rate is increasing, one can expect more stockouts, frantic expediting, and missed shipments to closely follow. In many firms, the cycle count error rate is periodically reviewed by senior executives of the company.

Cycle Counting Systems. The major message on cycle counting is—do it! However, having said that, let us now turn to the design of a cycle counting system and some techniques that have been successfully used in cycle counting.

One immediate issue in the design of cycle counting systems is how to select the items to be counted. The first need is to determine how many items can be counted in some time period (e.g., a day). With a given work force and some estimates of counts per time period per person, the frequency with which each part is counted can be ascertained. Some companies have found it useful to set the frequency of counting using ABC analysis. A items are counted more frequently than B items, etc. Another selection device is to use the planned order information in the MRP record to advantage. If items are counted just prior to when a new order should be released, any errors can be compensated for by changes in timing and/or amounts. If items are counted just prior to receipt of an order, the on-hand balance should be low. Extending this idea, some firms count when a new batch is put away, since at this time the inventory level should be at a minimum point. Moreover, if the new batch is physically combined with the old, a stockroom person would be handling the parts anyway.

Another selection criterion for cycle counting involves checking any part number that shows a negative on-hand balance, since theoretically this is not possible. Other selection rules include keeping track of the time since the last cycle count, counting items within groups (ABC) in order of last count; keeping track of the item activity (transactions), since those items which have had the most ins and outs may be subject to larger potential error, and applying the opposite logic if transactions are used to verify counts; or allowing users to select parts for counting directly (which can happen for many reasons, including a pending engineering change).

Some companies find it more advantageous to count by location than by part number. That is, the cycle counters are asked to determine the part number and quantity in a specified location. One advantage of this approach is that it is more efficient for cycle counting, since parts in a set of adjacent locations can be counted. It also has the advantage of "finding" parts that are "lost." This scheme is particularly compatible with use of random storage locations (as opposed to specific locations for each part). In addition to better utilization of space, the random location approach has the advantage that *only* the system knows where a part number is located, so the system *must* be used.

The random location system can also provide for rotating stock, since the pick tickets can be devised to pull stock on a first-in, first-out basis. Alternatively, some companies always pull the smallest quantity first, which tends to consolidate inventories into larger batches. Obviously, this kind of system can also issue commands to consolidate if locations become scarce.

Another nice feature of storage by location is the ability to get "free" cycle counting by picking. A pick ticket can indicate that 24 pieces of part 1234 are to be taken from N-7, and that there should thereafter be 3 left. The stock picker is instructed to identify any discrepancies as the stock is picked. Another free cycle counting device is the use of preprinted zero balance cards. Whenever someone takes the last unit from any location, the item and location are written on the card.

In the design of a cycle counting system it is necessary to specify the tolerance for error that will be acceptable. If 10,000 pieces of a very inexpensive item are to be weigh counted, it seems a bit silly to say that an error has occurred if the scale indicates 9,999. A typical set of tolerances is:

Class	*Hand counted*	*Weigh counted*
A	+0% to −0%	+3% to −3%
B	+2% to −2%	+4% to −4%
C	+4% to −4%	+5% to −5%

We have seen some companies approach cycle counting by only verifying the location and eye balling to see whether the count is way off. This is simply not a satisfactory procedure, and its use will lead to poor MPC system performance.

A final technique we have seen used to great advantage is the establishment of a control group of parts, based on a cross section of items, which is counted on a very frequent basis. Initially, this might be only 20 or 30 parts of high activity, which are counted every day. It's purpose is to be able to discover the *causes* of error, because the transactions since the last count are easy to audit. After the cycle counting program is in full operation, the control group might be expanded to about 100 parts, with detailed audit trails of the transactions maintained for each of the parts.

The control group concept leads to a very important point. As important as cycle counting is, in the last analysis its primary purpose is to uncover the causes of errors. The key to achieving cycle count accuracy is to implement ironclad procedures for all transactions so that errors are minimized. Let us now turn to two sets of critical procedures that affect the on-hand balance, the maintenance of shop order data integrity and similar procedural issues in purchase order closeout. Thereafter, we deal with some organizational issues in stockroom operations.

Shop order integrity

Internally fabricated parts are typically controlled by a shop order number, which is the authorization for the job. These numbers are usually assigned sequentially so that all shop orders can be opened, monitored, and closed. The opening of a shop order from an MRP point of view is creating a scheduled receipt, normally as the result of a planned order being launched. This process involves availability checking and allocation.

The shop order typically has a set of shop paper which travels with the material. Included are operation sheets, routings, blueprints, and some means, such as prepunched cards, for reporting work completed.

The open shop order usually produces a pick ticket(s) for the materials to be issued from some storeroom to the shop order. The status of the open order is monitored by the shop-floor control systems. From a data integrity point of view, we have seen that it is also necessary to have procedures for scrap reporting, so that scheduled receipts are shown with accurate counts in the MRP records. Also required are rework procedures to correct materials that can be salvaged.

The closing of a shop order occurs when the order is put into a stockroom. At that time, the data base needs to be updated. For example, the record now must reflect that the stockroom has put away 147 pieces of part 1234, on shop order 456, in location N-7. When accepted, the scheduled receipt is eliminated and the on-hand balance appropriately adjusted. For the transaction to be accepted, system checks are performed to determine the agreement between the part number and the accompanying shop order, the quantity received versus the quantity reported at the last operation in the routing file, whether that last operation has been completed, and whether location N-7 is available.

A key step in this process is the actual counting of the material by stockroom personnel. They should no more accept the count indicated by the last operation than a bank teller would accept your word for the amount of cash in a paper sack you wish to deposit. The operative principle is that the receiver counts. This is the only way that the receiver can be held responsible for the accuracy of the data in his or her area.

Purchase order closeout

Similar procedures are necessary to close out scheduled receipts from vendors. Each "in" transaction is tested against an existing purchase order, the quantity of that order, the previous processing of receiving documentation, etc. We have seen many companies that simply accept the counts on invoices provided by their vendors. The payback from hiring someone to count all receipts (or at least to sample count and keep track of vendor performance) is very short.

The receiving department is typically the place where a batch of purchased material is first recognized as being on the company premises. An arriving shipment has bills of lading which are checked against expected deliveries (scheduled receipts for purchased items). This may be done with a file of outstanding purchase orders, preprinted papers, or an on-line computer system that checks the status of the order. In most companies, a detailed count of the parts is not made at this point. Rather, a check for the number of cartons, the stated volume per carton, the total shipment quantity, and a match against the purchase order are done. The result is a *receiver* transaction which tells the system that the material has arrived, but has not been put into controlled storage on a basis that will allow it to be picked.

Incoming materials are usually routed through receiving inspection before going to the assigned storeroom. At some companies, computerized warehousing (high bay stackers) allows work to be immediately put away, but in a status that is unavailable for picking until inspection has released the batch and inventory control verified the count.

There are, of course, many variations of these procedures, but all accomplish the same basic objectives. For example, we know of one firm that tracks each of the trucks in its large fleet, as well as tracking each unowned truck that enters the area of the factory. This firm has an on-line system to print traveling documentation for each pallet or container as it is unloaded. Again, the objectives are the same: capture the arrival information as soon as possible, track the material flow through the necessary stages prior to storage, count carefully, resolve discrepancies, and perform this quickly. Even if signing bills of lading legally commits the company to some quantity, a speedy verification can usually result in adjustments with vendors.

The stock room

The stockroom is the place where shop orders and purchase orders are finally closed, as well as where materials for shop orders are issued. As such, the stockroom becomes the nerve center for the entire organization. The most immediate impact of this central role played by the stockroom is in personnel requirements. This is not the place to put tired janitors! The need for absolute integrity in stockroom records and the close monitoring of transactions dictate that the person in charge be an agressive professional (preferably mean).

Locking the stockroom in many firms is accomplished by building a wire cage around the stock. Thereafter, the night shift goes over with a ladder, so the top is wired. Then someone gets a cutting torch to cut off the lock. The next logical step is to build an impregnable stockroom. We know of one company that did just that, followed by an interesting result: no shipments. In fact, the impregnable stockroom was the ultimate frustration to the workers who were getting out the products in spite of the MPC system. The problem? Mainly that the actual components used to build end items were different from those specified by the bills of material, so that the assembly department did not have the parts necessary to build end items. Exacerbating this problem was an unrealistic master production schedule. At the end of the month, the company would steal production from next month to make the shipment budget. The parts for these orders were still in the stockroom.

One further dimension of stockroom integrity is worthy of mention. It is not a free good—it will take money to hire a mean professional, and the compensation is fully justified in terms of the responsibility assigned. Moreover, it is also necessary to keep tight control over the stockroom at all hours. How can the mean professional be held responsible if the stockroom is open on the second shift—or even if it is locked but the night foremen are allowed to get things out if they need them. Does anyone on the night shift in a bank have access to the vault?

It is often necessary to extend the definition of stockrooms and to hire more personnel to monitor the larger stockroom areas. For example, many firms do not exercise tight control over raw materials, with machine operators getting more as needed. In the MRP world, a bar of one-inch diameter steel, 16 feet long, is just another part number, and the on-hand balance needs to be correct. All transactions to and from raw materials must be recorded accurately, and both cycle counting and limited access may be required. It may also be necessary to establish procedures for a raw materials salvage operation to cope with problems such as those with parts that are flame cut from large sheets.

The point of all this is simply that tight stockroom control is a necessary but not a sufficient condition for effective MPC implementation. It is necessary to have all data integrity procedures in place and to execute the MPC plans, viz, hit the schedule!

ROUTINE AUDITING

Even the best laid procedural plans will go amuck. Errors will occur, and hopefully the cross checks built into the system will find them. However, when errors do occur, the need still exists to resolve the resulting problems. For example, if an in transaction indicates that 100 pieces of a particular shop order have been put away, and the last fabrication operation before going to stock reported 120 pieces, then there is a discrepancy. Who is right? Where did the other 20 parts go? Is there a need to issue a scrap ticket? Is there an adjustment required in labor reporting? In this section, we review procedures and techniques for routinely auditing data base transactions and for resolving accuracy questions.

Cross checking and "garbage collecting".

An aid to routine auditing of data base transactions is for the systems to provide the maximum amount of cross checking and garbage collecting possible. This includes procedures for using check digits, etc., and more importantly any kind of computerized validation checking possible. For example, supposing that employee 123 wants to report the completion of 100 pieces of part 456, on shop order 789, operation 3. Included in the cross checking would be the following:

- Is employee 123 a legal employee number?
- Is he or she at work today (checked in)?
- Has this employee already checked in on shop order 789?
- Does this employee work in the department associated with operation 3 for part 456?
- Is this employee assigned to the labor grade consistent with this operation?
- Is part 456 a valid part number?
- Is there an open order (scheduled receipt) for part 456 on shop order 789?
- Is this shop order for 100 pieces?
- Has operation 2 been completed?
- Did operation 2 report 100 pieces?

Any of these cross checks could include tolerances for errors. The objective is to use the computer as much as possible to screen out transaction errors and to focus attention on required remedial actions such as new counts, scrap not reported, etc.

Daily reconciliation: an application of principles

The result of any cross check that fails is an exception condition. It will be necessary to have a group of people whose entire job is to audit and reconcile exception conditions. For example, is the in transaction correct or is the purchase order correct? How can we be out of stock in location N-7 when the records indicate that 100 pieces are there? An operator reported work on shop order 1234 which is not valid for the department—was it really shop order 1234? Operation 3 reports 50 pieces and operation 4 reports 48 pieces—is a scrap ticket for 2 pieces needed? Operation 3 reports 50 pieces and operation 4 reports 55 pieces—who is wrong? The assembly department reports none of part 678, yet we show that they have enough to last for three weeks—why?

In an on-line system, many of these discrepancies can be monitored as the transaction is being made. For systems based on batch processing, the minimum goal should be to process all transactions in a 24-hour period or during each night, reconciling all exceptions by about 10 A.M. the following day. It is simply not possible to reconcile errors when the trail gets cold. Going to a machine operator and saying "do you remember that job 1234 that you ran three weeks ago?", will usually yield "no." Moreover, if someone can put in his or her telephone number instead of the part number and get away with it, the system is a joke. Someone will try this, and the objective is to catch the person within 24 hours.

Figure 3.4 is part of an actual daily exception report. This report is the principle auditing tool used by the firm. The document shows 17 parts that generated exception conditions so that they were included on the H/R IN TICKET EXCEPTION REPORT FOR H45. H45 is one of the main stockrooms in this company. The first item, part F16774, shows in the last two columns that 8,375 were reported as finished at the last production operation, but only 7,506 have been located or put into stock.

The 4th through 10th items show invalid part numbers. As indicated by the handwriting, the resolution of this problem is that all seven parts were incorrectly given an F prefix (fabricated part), when, in fact, they should have an A prefix (assembly). Note also, that this exception report shows the location of these seven parts, so that they can be checked, if necessary (Department H45, Bay H41, Row WA, Tier LL).

The Japanese approach

We have now discussed the need for accuracy in the data base, the importance of transactions, the need for auditing, and a new level of discipline in the system. It is important to remember that the need is data base accuracy; transactions, auditing, and discipline are *one* means to that end.

The Japanese have another means that is used in some factories. It is called *just-in-time* manufacture. The relationship to information integrity is most interesting. There is so little inventory in these systems that detailed monitoring of transactions is unnecessary. At the Toyota automobile factory, for example, deliveries of parts from vendors are going out of the door as finished autos within hours. The parts *had* to arrive or the line would stop! Moreover, every worker is also a quality controller, so the parts had to be of the correct quality.

ORGANIZATIONAL CONSIDERATIONS

Proper maintenance of the MRP data base requires three distinct sets of integrated efforts by the organization. First, there is a set of technical efforts that needs to be supported by the computer specialists—to ensure proper

FIGURE 3.4 Daily exception report (H/R in ticket exception report for H45)

C D E	TRANS. DATE	NUMBER	OPTN	SSW	LAM	PL/ PNT	UPHL	ORDER NUMBER	FROM DEPT	QTY PROD	PROD. BY	U/M	QTY LOCTD	DEPT	BAY	RW	TR	SPECIAL INFORMATION	LOCTD BY	TOTAL PROD	TOTAL LOCTD
	04/18	F 16774				PL		JN31318		008375		PCS	0					PARTS PRODUCED ARE NOT LOCATED		008375	007506
	04/19	F 16774				PL		JN35882		006923		PCS	0					PARTS PRODUCED ARE NOT LOCATED		006923	002893
	04/05	F 16775						JN33270		004785		PCS	0					PARTS PRODUCED ARE NOT LOCATED		004785	004122
IT	04/27	F 17127						JN31782	H41	000322	6149	PCS	000322	H45	H41	WA	LL	INVALID PART NUMBER. NOT ON PART MASTER	941	0	0
IT	04/27	F 17127						JN31782	H41	000228	6845	PCS	000228	H45	H41	WA	LL	INVALID PART NUMBER. NOT ON PART MASTER	941	0	0
IT	04/27	F 17127						JN31782	H41	000225	6912	PCS	000225	H45	H41	WA	LL	INVALID PART NUMBER. NOT ON PART MASTER	941	0	0
IT	04/27	F 17127						JN31782	H41	000221	6912	PCS	000221	H45	H41	WA	LL	INVALID PART NUMBER. NOT ON PART MASTER	941	0	0
IT	04/27	F 17127						JN31782	H41	000282		PCS	000282	H45	H41	WA	LL	INVALID PART NUMBER. NOT ON PART MASTER	941	0	0
IT	04/27	F 17127						JN31782	H41	000284	6149	PCS	000284	H45	H41	WA	LL	INVALID PART NUMBER. NOT ON PART MASTER	941	0	0
IT	04/27	F 17132						JN31074	H41	000269	3254	PCS	000269	H45	H41	WA	LL	INVALID PART NUMBER. NOT ON PART MASTER	941	0	0
	04/27	F 17133						JN29631		008066		PCS	0					PARTS PRODUCED ARE NOT LOCATED		008066	006450
	04/11	F 18124						M981		000518		PCS	0					PARTS PRODUCED ARE NOT LOCATED		000518	000000
	03/12	F 18855				PL		JN32242		004581		PCS	0					PARTS PRODUCED ARE NOT LOCATED		004581	000000
	04/06	F 18855				PL		JN35424		005000		PCS	0					PARTS PRODUCED ARE NOT LOCATED		005000	004581
	03/23	F 18871						HR79272		008005		PCS	0					PARTS PRODUCED ARE NOT LOCATED		008065	007855
	04/18	F 19219				PL		JN35873		004000		PCS	0					PARTS PRODUCED ARE NOT LOCATED		004000	003600
	03/29	F 19237						JN30112		002430		PCS	0					PARTS PRODUCED ARE NOT LOCATED		002430	000000

wrong prefix— should be "A"

backup of data files, integration among files, consistent system uses of the files, etc. The second set of efforts is on the part of the system users. In essence, the data base needs to become an integral part of their daily working lives. Finally, some efforts need to be mounted on a companywide basis. These efforts are to encourage a companywide commitment to an integrated data base, and whatever organizational changes are necessary to achieve this goal. This also includes a deliberate effort to base functional planning and decision making on the one integrated data base—for the entire company to sing from the same sheet of music.

The computer side

There is a technical dimension to the design, implementation, and control of an integrated data base, that is largely beyond our present scope. Included are choices of data base languages, computer conversions, architecture of the data base, backup files and backup processing, timing for transaction processing, communication among computer devices, security, and the overall levels of professionalism exhibited by the computer personnel in terms of understanding and ability to deal with integrated data bases. We strongly advise all companies implementing integrated data bases to periodically obtain an independent professional audit of this technical dimension. There is far too much at stake to be subject to unnecessary uncertainties.

At the operational level, it is critical that users and data processing personnel alike understand the nature of linked systems and the transactions in these systems. A revealing analysis in many companies is to ask several different functional areas for some piece of data that should not be subject to uncertainty, such as the shipments two months ago for some particular end item. Many times, the answer to this question is quite different from production to marketing to finance. For instance, at one firm, this question produced three different answers. The differences between production and finance were due to definitions of when the month closed in terms of shipments. Production considered an item shipped when it left the stockroom and entered a truck, whereas finance worked with bills of lading prepared when the trucks left the dock. Thus, reconciliation was possible between production and finance, based on the difference in cutoff dates. However, neither production nor finance could reconcile their version of shipments with that produced by marketing. Marketing used an entirely different system, based on different transactions, linkages, etc. It was not surprising that mistakes were made, since there were different views of what was in inventory and available to ship to customers.

The point of this tale is to show how a single definition of shipments (or any other data element) is required, and how all systems and transactions which use and update this data element need to be integrated and controlled.

The user side

In the last analysis, an MPC system will work only if the required actions, procedures, and transactions are consistent with the ways in which MRP planners and first-line supervisors do their jobs. Detailed execution by departmental foremen and MRP planners must be in synchronization with the system. There is an often told joke about the difference between involvement and commitment being well illustrated by ham and eggs—the pig is committed, whereas the chicken is only involved. It is critical for the users of the system to be *committed* to its continued success.

This commitment does not come by executive fiat. It is necessary to educate the users as to how the actual system works, their part in the overall system, how errors made in transactions affect everyone, how their particular transactions and procedures are to be done, and how informal "fixes" are to be avoided like the plague. Moreover, it is necessary to review the measures of effectiveness employed to evaluate user performance. If users are rewarded for any actions which come at the expense of data integrity, there are serious problems. The job, as well as the job performance, needs to be synchronized with the system. Users are to be rewarded for using the system to solve problems, and for maintaining the accuracy in the data base at high levels.

It is often necessary to change the communication networks for successful MPC system implementation and maintenance. The elimination of buffer inventories increases the need for better coordination between manufacturing, inventory control, purchasing, and all of the other areas that are linked by materials flows. It may be necessary to provide new communication chains for users to solve problems—above and beyond those provided by the MRP system itself. In particular, it is usually necessary to provide fast feedback between users and computer personnel to solve problems of data errors, discrepancies, etc.

Another dimension of user commitment to the system and its maintenance is the need to understand the changes in social networks that are brought about by the implementation of MPC. The technical system is concerned with the processes, tasks, and technology needed to transform inputs to outputs. The social network in which this technical system operates is concerned with the attitudes of people, the relationships among people, reward systems, and authority structures. In the design and implementation of an MPC system, it is very easy to underestimate the changes required in the social network to adapt to the new technical system, and to underestimate the time and cost necessary for these changes to occur.

When users are indeed committed to the system and its continued maintenance, no immediate problem is important enough to warrent solution at the expense of data base integrity. There are too many other people depending *solely* upon the data base for the inputs into their own decision making.

Companywide linkages

A companywide commitment to data base maintenance largely entails an integration of functions and transactions around the one integrated data base. This means, of course, that problems such as how to transact shipments data will be solved. There will be exact divisions of labor and responsibility over specific transactions, and there will be uniform transaction definitions.

More importantly, other company systems can and should be designed to take advantage of the integrated data base. With this redesign, the company also achieves a new level of data maintenance, because a new group of people with new interests is providing one more audit to the data. Of perhaps even more importance, this interfunctional commitment to an integrated data base provides new avenues for cooperation in strategic planning, budgeting, and control.

A fundamental company linkage is with the cost accounting system. One critical portion of MPC systems is accurately reporting every detailed transaction as materials move in and out of stockrooms and through various production conversion steps. This set of transactions provides the basis for a very detailed cost accounting system. Detailed variance analysis can be done for every shop order if desired. Labor reporting and material usage reporting can be done by shop order, with variances for usage, productivity, and other deviations from standards noted. Detailed cost implosions (sometimes called cost roll-ups) for each product can be made as needed, or as variations from cost standards dictate. In short, the MPC data base provides the grounds for a most exact cost accounting system.

The other benefit of using the MPC data base for costing derives from the cost accounting need to identify movement from raw materials into work in process into finished goods. The inventory reporting of these financial movements provides another cross check of data base reliability, and the detailed auditing of the transactions which make up these periodic sums is one more audit trail—now based on the same transaction records. Other examples of cost accounting benefits include the detailed resolution of inventory adjustments, the treatment of obsolete inventories, accounting for scrap, reconciliation of accounts payable to in tickets and purchasing, product costing incorporating engineering and tooling changes, and accounting for new product introductions as well as product phase outs.

With the cost accounting system based on MRP data base transactions, the next logical step is to determine budgets and other financial goals on a consistent basis. In this way, plans are established on the same basis that results are measured. Thus, the establishment of financial budgets and strategic plans becomes integrated with the data base, its operations, its maintenance, and its accounting performance measurement. Still another key linkage for consistency is provided. Moreover, the ability to forecast cash requirements, receivables turnover, and other financial data is substantially increased, because most of these measures are related to material flow decisions.

There can be a negative side to integrating the cost accounting and budgeting procedures as well. If workers are paid based on another system, if cost accounting is only performed in a cursory way, if budgeting is an annual exercise in futility, if forecasting is a game between marketing and production, if a large percentage of the monthly shipments are pushed out in the last few working days with informal methods, or the performance of first-line supervisors is based on measures that can be contrary to execution of routine tasks, then data base integrity is sure to suffer. The point is that job specification, job performance, and job design need to be tailored to management by and of a data base. Organizational changes may be required.

Finally, it is important to indicate the key organizational linkages to marketing. MPC systems are critically linked to order entry and order promising (setting due dates for customer orders). In essence, the master production schedule (MPS) is the interface between marketing and production. It is here that trade-offs are made and the detailed set of marching orders is provided for manufacturing. Achieving that set of orders is manufacturing's job under MPC system constraints. Marketing, in turn, can depend on manufacturing to achieve the planned results. Moreover, marketing's responsibilities are specified in terms of utilizing these outputs to best achieve the goals of the company from a marketing point of view. The result is a new level of communication and cooperation between marketing and manufacturing—and still further pressure to ensure the integrity of the data base that supports this companywide plan of action.

CONCLUDING PRINCIPLES

In the last analysis, the company with a fully operational MPC system is as different from its prior state as an automobile from a horse. The basic day-to-day operations are different, and the entire approach to problem solving becomes integrated around a single companywide data base. The role of general management in planning and controlling the process of organizational change is critical to success. A superb technical design for an MPC system will never be able to compensate for poor procedures and a lack of control over transaction accuracy. To achieve management by a data base and management of a data base, all of the system dynamics must be understood, and ironclad procedures must be designed to keep the information synchronized with the physical flow of material. We offer the following as a set of principles which summarize these concepts:

- MPC systems substitute information for inventory and other forms of organizational slack; the quality of the information directly influences the ability to make this substitution.

- There must be a constant one-for-one match between the physical system and the information in the data base.
- There must be a match between actions and transactions.
- The organization and the reward systems must change to support data base accuracy.
- The costs and training needed to achieve data base accuracy are substantial but yield quick returns.

REFERENCES

Backes, Robert W. "Cycle Counting—A Better Method for Achieving Accurate Inventory Records." *Production and Inventory Management*, 2d Quarter, 1980, pp. 36–44.

Carlson, J. G. H. "Interactive Systems for the Physical Control of Material." *1975 Conference Proceedings*, American Production and Inventory Control Society, pp. 184–89.

Fenton, T. J., and P. J., Rosa, Jr. "How to Live with Your Net Change System." *1975 Conference Proceedings*, American Production and Inventory Control Society, pp. 24–36.

Hall, R. W. "Data Accuracy in Material Flow Control." *1980 Conference Proceedings*, American Production and Inventory Control Society, pp. 128–30.

Herrick, Terry L. "End Item Pegging Made Easier." *Production and Inventory Management*, 3d Quarter 1976.

Hill, Richard E. "Does Top Management Manage Inventory?" *Production and Inventory Management*, 1st Quarter 1974.

Jackson, J. S. "To Peg or Not to Peg." *1973 Conference Proceedings*, American Production and Inventory Control Society, pp. 84–95.

Jordan, H. H. "How to Start a Cycle Counting Program." *1975 Conference Proceedings*, American Production and Inventory Control Society, pp. 190–98.

———. "Cycle Counting for Record Accuracy." *1980 Conference Proceedings*, American Production and Inventory Control Society, pp. 385–86.

Kneppelt, L. R. "Real-Time, On-Line, Distribution in the Manufacturing Environment." *1980 Conference Proceedings*, American Production and Inventory Control Society, pp. 58–60.

Kraemer, R. P. "Record Accuracy Through CRT and Bar Coded Data Collection Systems." *1980 Conference Proceedings*, American Production and Inventory Control Society, pp. 90–93.

Rose, Harvey N. "Auditing of P&IC Systems—The Necessary Ingredient!" *APICS Annual Conference Proceedings*, 1978, pp. 436–54.

Vollmann, T. E., and W. L. Berry. "The Manufacturing Control System Audit: A Key to Productivity and Profit Improvement." University of Iowa, Business School, Discussion Paper Series no. 83–4.

Webber, Michael. "Cycle Counting and Other Physical Controls—What and Why?" *APICS Annual Conference Proceedings*, 1978, pp. 837–45.

4

Capacity planning

In this chapter we discuss the problem of providing sufficient capacity to meet the manufacturing needs of the firm. We focus primarily on techniques for determining the capacity requirements implied in the plans developed by the material planning systems. The managerial objective in planning capacity is to ensure that sufficient capacity is available to accomplish the planned production. The capacity must be available in the right time periods so that the production can be completed at the right time, as well. If sufficient capacity cannot be made available either inside or outside the firm, then the only managerial alternative is to change the material plan to conform to the available capacity.

The chapter is organized around the following five topics:

- The role of the capacity planning system in manufacturing systems: How does it fit? What role does it play?
- Capacity planning and control techniques: How can the capacity implications of a material plan be estimated? How can detailed capacity needs be determined? How can capacity usage be controlled?
- Management and capacity planning: How can managers decide which technique(s) to use? How should they use them?
- Data base requirements: How should the data base be designed for a capacity planning system?

- Example applications: How are capacity planning techniques applied? What outputs are useful for managing capacity?

Some of the techniques in this chapter are closely related to the analogous work in aggregate capacity analysis presented in Chapter 15. The description of finite loading is presented in Chapter 5, rather than here, because of its use as a scheduling model. The production planning discussion in Chapter 9 contains managerial considerations useful for the resource-planning activity.

THE ROLE OF CAPACITY PLANNING IN MPC SYSTEMS

A critical activity that parallels the development of the material plans is the development of capacity plans. Without the provision of adequate capacity or recognition of the existence of excess capacity, the benefits of an otherwise effective MPC system cannot be fully realized. On the one hand, insufficient capacity will quickly lead to deteriorating delivery performance, escalating work-in-process inventories, and frustrated manufacturing personnel who will quickly turn back to the informal system to solve problems. On the other hand, excess capacity is a needless expense that can be reduced. Even firms with advanced material planning capability have found that their inability to provide the appropriate work center capacities is a major stumbling block to achieving maximum benefits. This underscores the importance of developing the capacity planning system in concert with the material planning system, and the need for discussing this topic here.

Hierarchy of capacity planning decisions

The relationship of capacity planning decisions to the other modules of an integrated MPC system is shown in Figure 4.1. Also shown is the scope of capacity planning, starting from an overall plan of resources, proceeding to a rough-cut evaluation of the capacity implications of a particular master production schedule, thereafter moving to the detailed evaluation of capacity requirements based upon detailed MRP records, continuing to finite loading procedures, and ending with input/output techniques to help monitor the plans.

These five levels of capacity planning activities range from large aggregations of capacity for long time periods to very detailed machine scheduling, for an hour or shorter time interval. The primary focus of this chapter will be on rough-cut capacity planning procedures and on the technique called capacity requirements planning. These are central to establishing a correspondence between the capacity plans and the material plans. Since the control of capacity plans is as important as control of material plans, input/output analysis is presented as a method for achieving this control.

Some authorities distinguish between long-, medium-, and short-range capacity planning and control horizons. This chapter is largely devoted to

FIGURE 4.1 Capacity planning in the MPC system

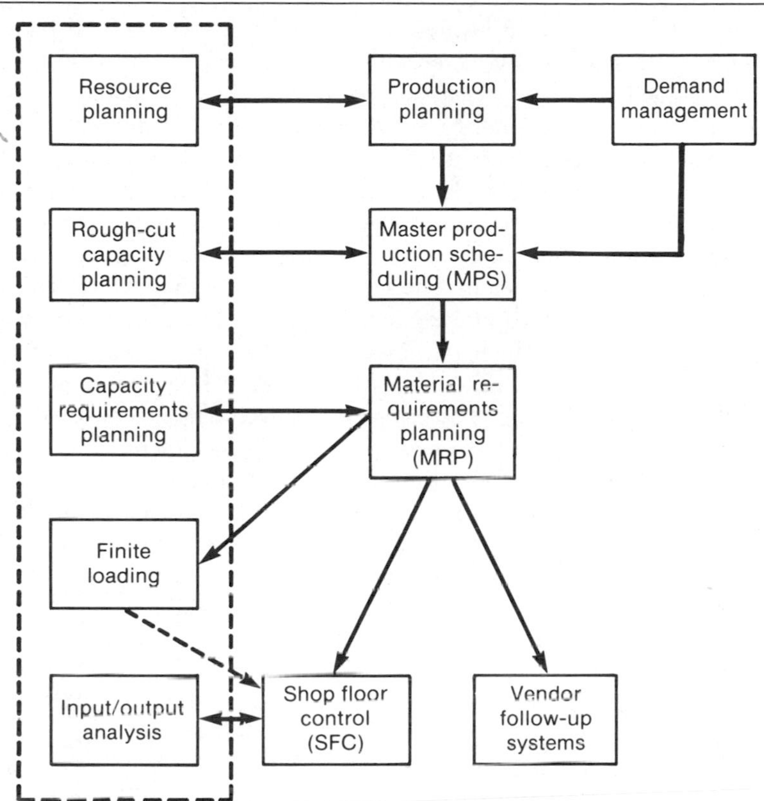

short- to medium-range capacity planning, involving a planning horizon ranging from next week to a year or more in the future. We consider the following questions: what are the techniques, how do they compare, and what benefits are being obtained in actual practice? Short-range capacity requirements can be determined for individual work centers using the capacity requirements planning technique, and for the medium-range using the rough-cut procedures.

Links to other systems modules

The system linkages for the capacity planning modules follow the basic hierarchy just described and illustrated in Figure 4.1. The capacity planning techniques described in this chapter, rough-cut capacity planning and capacity requirements planning, link with the master production schedule and MRP systems, respectively. The linkages are shown as double-headed arrows for a very specific reason. There must be a correspondence between the capacity *required* to execute a given material plan and that made *available* to execute the plan. If this correspondence does not exist, the plan will either be impossible to execute or inefficiently executed. We do not take the position that capacity must always be changed to meet material plans. In fact, whether this is worthwhile or whether the plans should be changed to meet the capacity is a managerial judgment. The capacity planning systems provide the basic information to make that a reasoned judgment.

The resource planning activity is directly linked to the production planning module. It is the most highly aggregated and longest-range capacity planning decision. Resource planning typically involves converting monthly, quarterly, or even annual data from the production plan into aggregate resources such as gross labor-hours, floor space, machine-hours, etc. This level of planning involves new capital expansion (brick and mortar, machine tools, warehouse space, etc.) which requires a time horizon of months or years.

The master production schedule is the primary information source for rough-cut capacity planning. The capacity requirements of a particular master schedule can be estimated by any of the following techniques: capacity planning using overall planning factors (CPOF), capacity bills, or resource profiles. These techniques provide information with which to modify the resource levels or material plan in the medium range to ensure efficient execution of the master production schedule.

Substantially more detailed capacity planning is possible using the capacity requirements planning (CRP) technique. To provide this detail, the material plans produced by the MRP system serve as the basis for calculating time-phased capacity requirements. The data files used by the CRP technique include work in process, routing, scheduled receipts, and planned orders. The information provided by the CRP technique can be used to determine the short-term capacity needs for both key machine centers and labor skills.

The finite loading technique also relates to the MRP detail plans, but can be better viewed as a shop-floor scheduling technique. It, more than any of the other capacity planning techniques, makes clear the relationship between scheduling and capacity availability. Finite loading starts with a specified capacity level for each work center or resource grouping; this capacity is then allocated to work orders. Hence, finite loading is a method for scheduling work orders. The procedures described in this chapter do not deal with scheduling questions. They estimate capacity requirements only, with the schedules of orders considered to be a separate problem. The finite loading process requires linkages to the same files as the CRP technique, as well as to files which specify work center capacities.

Input/output analysis provides a method for monitoring the actual consumption of capacity during the execution of material plans. It is necessarily linked to the execution systems and data base for shop-floor control. Input/output analysis can indicate the need to update capacity plans as actual shop performance deviates from current plans, as well as the need to modify the planning factors used in other capacity-planning techniques.

This overview of the scope of capacity planning sets the stage for the techniques discussed in the chapter. The primary interaction among these techniques is hierarchial; resource planning sets constraints on short- to medium-range capacity planning, which, in turn, constrains detailed scheduling and execution on the shop floor.

CAPACITY PLANNING AND CONTROL TECHNIQUES

In this section we describe four procedures for capacity planning. The first technique is called capacity planning using overall factors (CPOF). This is the simplest of the four techniques and is based only on accounting data. The second, capacity bills, requires more detailed product information. The third, resource profiles, adds a further dimension—the specific timing of capacity requirements. The fourth, capacity requirements planning (CRP), utilizes the entire MRP data base to calculate the capacity required to produce both the detailed open shop orders (scheduled receipts) and the planned orders. We will also discuss the input/output analysis technique for monitoring and controlling the capacity plans.

To describe the four planning techniques, we use a simple example. The example allows us to clearly see the differences in approach, complexity, level of aggregation, data requirements, timing, and accuracy between the techniques. We will then illustrate the input/output analysis procedure, which could be utilized with any of the four planning procedures.

Capacity planning using overall factors (CPOF)

CPOF is a relatively simple approach to rough-cut capacity planning, that is typically done on a manual basis. The data inputs come from the master production schedule (MPS) rather than from MRP detailed time-phased record data. This procedure is usually based upon planning factors derived from standards or historical data for end products. When these planning factors are applied to the MPS data, overall manpower or machine-hour capacity requirements can be estimated. This overall estimate is thereafter allocated to individual work centers on the basis of historical data on shop workloads. CPOF plans are usually stated in terms of weekly or monthly time periods, and are revised as the firm makes changes to the MPS.

The top portion of Figure 4.2 shows the MPS that will serve as the basis for our example. This schedule specifies the quantity of each of two end products to be assembled during each time period. The first step of the CPOF procedure involves calculating the capacity requirements of this schedule for the overall plant. Direct labor standards, indicating the total direct labor-hours required for each end product, are shown in the lower portion of Figure 4.2. Assuming labor productivity of 100 percent of standard, the total direct labor-hour requirement for the first period is 62.80 hours, as shown in Figure 4.3.

FIGURE 4.2 Example problem data

Master production schedule (in units):

	Time period													
End product	*1*	*2*	*3*	*4*	*5*	*6*	*7*	*8*	*9*	*10*	*11*	*12*	*13*	*Total*
A	33	33	33	40	40	40	30	30	30	37	37	37	37	457
B	17	17	17	13	13	13	25	25	25	27	27	27	27	273

Direct labor time per end product unit:

End product	*Total direct labor in standard hours/unit*
A	.95 hours
B	1.85 hours

Source: W. L. Berry, T. G. Schmitt, and T. E. Vollmann, "Capacity Planning Techniques for Manufacturing Control Systems: Information Requirements and Operating Features," Reprinted with permission, November 1982 *Journal of Operations Management,* Journal of the American Production and Inventory Control Society, Inc.

FIGURE 4.3 Estimated capacity requirements using overall factors (CPOF) (in standard direct labor-hours)

Work center	Historical percentage	Period 1	2	3	4	5	6	7	8	9	10	11	12	13	Total hours
100	60.3	37.87	37.87	37.87	37.41	37.41	37.41	45.07	45.07	45.07	51.32	51.32	51.32	51.32	566.33
200	30.4	19.09	19.09	19.09	18.86	18.86	18.86	22.72	22.72	22.72	25.87	25.87	25.87	25.87	285.49
300	9.3	5.84	5.84	5.84	5.78	5.78	5.78	6.96	6.96	6.96	7.91	7.91	7.91	7.91	87.38
Total required capacity		62.80*	62.80	62.80	62.05	62.05	62.05	74.75	74.75	74.75	85.10	85.10	85.10	85.10	939.20

*62.80 = (.95 × 33) + (1.85 × 17) using the standards from Figure 4.2.

Source: W. L. Berry, T. G. Schmitt, and T. E. Vollmann, "Capacity Planning Techniques for Manufacturing Control Systems: Information Requirements and Operating Features," Reprinted with permision, November 1982 *Journal of Operations Management,* Journal of the American Production and Inventory Control Society, Inc.

The second step in this procedure involves using historical ratios to allocate the total capacity required each period to individual work centers. The historical percentage of the total direct labor-hours worked in each of the three work centers during the prior year were used to determine allocation ratios. These data could be derived from the company's accounting records. In the example, 60.3 percent, 30.4 percent, and 9.3 percent of the total direct labor-hours were worked in work centers 100, 200, and 300 respectively. These percentages are used to estimate the anticipated direct labor requirements for each work center. The resulting work center capacity requirements are shown in Figure 4.3, for each period in the MPS.

The CPOF procedure, or variants of it, are found in a number of manufacturing firms. The data requirements are minimal, primarily accounting system data, and the calculations straightforward. As a consequence, the CPOF approximations of the capacity requirements at individual work centers are only valid to the extent that product mixes or historical divisions of work between work centers remain constant. The primary advantages of this procedure are its ease of calculation and minimal data requirements. In many firms, the data are readily available and the computations can be done manually.

Capacity bills

The capacity bill procedure provides a much more direct link between individual end products in the MPS and the capacity required for individual work centers. It takes into account any shifts in product mix. Consequently, it requires more data than the CPOF procedure. Bill of material and routing data are required, and direct labor- or machine-hour data must be available for each operation.

To develop a bill of capacity for the example problem, we use the product structure data for A and B shown in Figure 4.4. Additionally, we need the routing and operation time standard data shown in the top portion of Figure 4.5 for the assembly of products A and B, as well as for the manufacture of component items C, D, E, and F. The bill of capacity indicates the total standard time required to produce one end product in each work center required in its manufacture. The calculations involve multiplying the total time per unit values by the usages indicated in the bill of materials. Summarizing the usage adjusted unit time data by work center produces the bill of capacity for each of the two products shown in the lower portion of Figure 4.5. The bill of capacity can be constructed from engineering data, as we have done here, or similar data might be available in a standard cost system. An alternative approach used by some firms is the bill of capacity only prepared for those work centers regarded as critical.

Once the bill of capacity for each end product has been prepared, the master production schedule can be used to estimate the capacity requirements at individual work centers. The determination of capacity require-

FIGURE 4.4 Product structure data

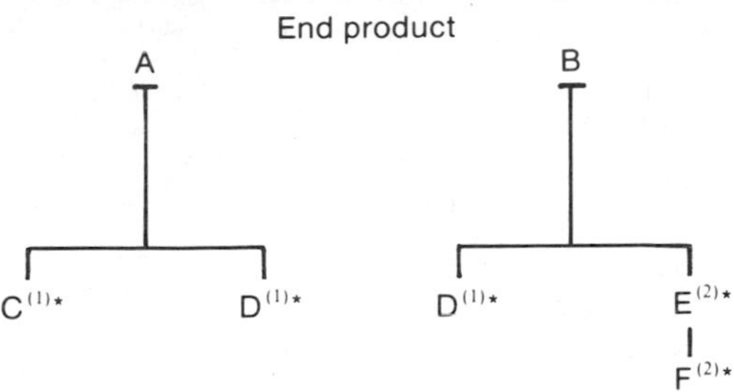

*One unit of component C and one unit of component D are required to produce one unit of end product A. Similarly, one unit of component D and two units of component E are required to produce one unit of end product B. Two units of component F are required to produce one unit of component E.

Source: W. L. Berry, T. G. Schmitt, and T. E. Vollmann, "Capacity Planning Techniques for Manufacturing Control Systems: Information Requirements and Operating Features," Reprinted with permission, November 1982 *Journal of Operations Management*, Journal of the American Production and Inventory Control Society, Inc.

ments for our example is shown in Figure 4.6. The resultant work center estimates differ substantially from the CPOF estimates shown in Figure 4.3. The differences reflect the period-to-period changes in product mix between the projected MPS and historical average figures. The estimates obtained from CPOF are based upon an overall historical ratio of work between machine centers, whereas the capacity bill estimates reflect the actual product mix planned for each period.

It is important to note that the total hours shown for the MPS (939.20) are the same in both Figure 4.3 and Figure 4.6; the differences are in work center estimates for each time period. These differences are far more important in firms which experience significant period-to-period product mix variations than in those that have a relatively constant pattern of work.

Resource profiles

Neither the CPOF nor the capacity bill procedure takes into account the specific timing of the projected workloads at individual work centers. In developing resource profiles, the production lead time data are taken into account to provide time-phased projections of the capacity requirements for individual production facilities.

In the use of any capacity planning technique, the time periods for the capacity plan can be varied (e.g., weeks, months, quarters). Note, however, that when the time periods are long relative to lead times, much of the value of the time-phased information may be lost in the aggregation of the data. In many firms, this means that time periods of greater than one week will mask important changes in capacity requirements.

FIGURE 4.5 Routing and standard time data

End products	*Lot sizes*	*Operation*	*Work center*	*Standard setup hours*	*Standard setup hours per unit*	*Standard run time hours per unit*	*Total hours per unit*
A	40	1 of 1	100	1.0	.250	.025*	.05†
B	20	1 of 1	100	1.0	.050	1.250	1.30
Components							
C	40	1 of 2	200	1.0	.025	.575	.60
		2 of 2	300	1.0	.025	.175	.20
D	60	1 of 1	200	2.0	.033	.067	.10
E	100	1 of 1	200	2.0	.020	.080	.10
F	100	1 of 1	200	2.0	.020	.0425	.0625

Bill of capacity

	End product	
	A	*B*
Work center	*Total time/unit*	*Total time/unit*
100	.05	1.30
200	.70‡	.55§
300	.20	0.00
Total time/unit	.95	1.85

*.025 = setup time ÷ lot size = 1.0/40.

†.05 = standard set up time per unit + standard run time per unit = .025 + 0.25.

‡.70 = .60 + .10 for one C and one D from Figure 4.4.

§.55 = .10 + 2(.10) + 4(.0625) for one D, two Es and four Fs.

Source: W. L. Berry, T. G. Schmitt, and T. E. Vollmann, "Capacity Planning Techniques for Manufacturing Control Systems: Information Requirements and Operating Features," Reprinted with permission, November 1982 *Journal of Operations Management,* Journal of the American Production and Inventory Control Society, Inc.

FIGURE 4.6 Capacity requirements using capacity bills

Work center	Period 1	2	3	4	5	6	7	8	9	10	11	12	13	Total hours	Projected work center percentage
100	23.75*	23.75	23.75	18.90	18.90	18.90	34.00	34.00	34.00	36.95	36.95	36.95	36.95	377.75	40%
200	32.45	32.45	32.45	35.15	35.15	35.15	34.75	34.75	34.75	40.75	40.75	40.75	40.75	470.05	50
300	6.60	6.60	6.60	8.00	8.00	8.00	6.00	6.00	6.00	7.40	7.40	7.40	7.40	91.40	10
Total	62.80	62.80	62.80	62.05	62.05	62.05	74.75	74.75	74.75	85.10	85.10	85.10	85.10	939.20	100%

*23.75 = (33 × .05) + (17 × 1.30) from Figures 4.2 and 4.5.

Source: W. L. Berry, T. G. Schmitt, and T. E. Vollmann, "Capacity Planning Techniques for Manufacturing Control Systems: Information Requirements and Operating Features," Reprinted with permission, November 1982 *Journal of Operations Management,* Journal of the American Production and Inventory Control Society, Inc.

To apply the resource profile procedure to our example, the bills of material, routing, and time standard information in Figures 4.4 and 4.5 are used. We also need to add the production lead time for each end product and component part to our data base. In this simplified example, we use a lead time of one period for the assembly of each end product and one period for each operation required in the production of component parts. Since only one operation is required for producing components D, E, and F, the lead time for producing these components is one time period each. For component C, however, the lead time is two time periods, one for the operation in work center 200 and another for work center 300.

To use the resource profile procedure, a time-phased profile of the capacity requirements for each end item must be prepared. The operation setback charts in Figure 4.7 show this time phasing for end products A and B. The chart for end product A indicates that the final assembly operation is to be completed during period 5. The production of component D must be completed in period 4, prior to the start of final assembly, as must the production of component C. Since component C requires two time periods (one for each operation), it must be started one time period before component D, i.e., at the start of period 3. There are other conventions that are used to define time phasing, but in this example we assume that the master production schedule specifies the number of units of each end product that must be completed by *the end* of the time period indicated. This implies that *all* components must be completed by the end of the preceding period.

For convenience, we have shown the standard hours required for each operation for each product in Figure 4.7. This information is summarized by work center and time period in Figure 4.8, which also shows the capacity requirements generated by the MPS quantities in time period 5 from Figure 4.2 (40 of end product A and 13 of end product B). The capacity requirements shown in Figure 4.8 are only for the MPS quantities in period 5. The MPS quantities for other periods can increase the capacity needed in each period. For example, Figure 4.8 shows that 7.9 hours of capacity are needed in period 4 at work center 200 to support the MPS for period 5. The MPS requirements for period 6 will require another 27.25 hours from work center 200. This results in the total of 35.15 hours shown in Figure 4.9, which provides the overall capacity plan for the current MPS using the resource profile procedure.

A comparison of the capacity plans produced by the capacity bills and the resource profile procedures (Figures 4.6 and 4.9) illustrates the impact of the time-phased capacity information. The total workload created by the master production schedule (939.2 hours) remains the same, as do the work center percentage allocations. The period requirements for work centers 200 and 300 projected by the two techniques vary somewhat, however. A capacity requirement of 8 hours was projected for work center 300 in time period 6 using capacity bills versus 6 hours using resource profiles, a difference of more than 30 percent. This change reflects the difference in the timing of

FIGURE 4.7 Operation set-back charts for end products A and B

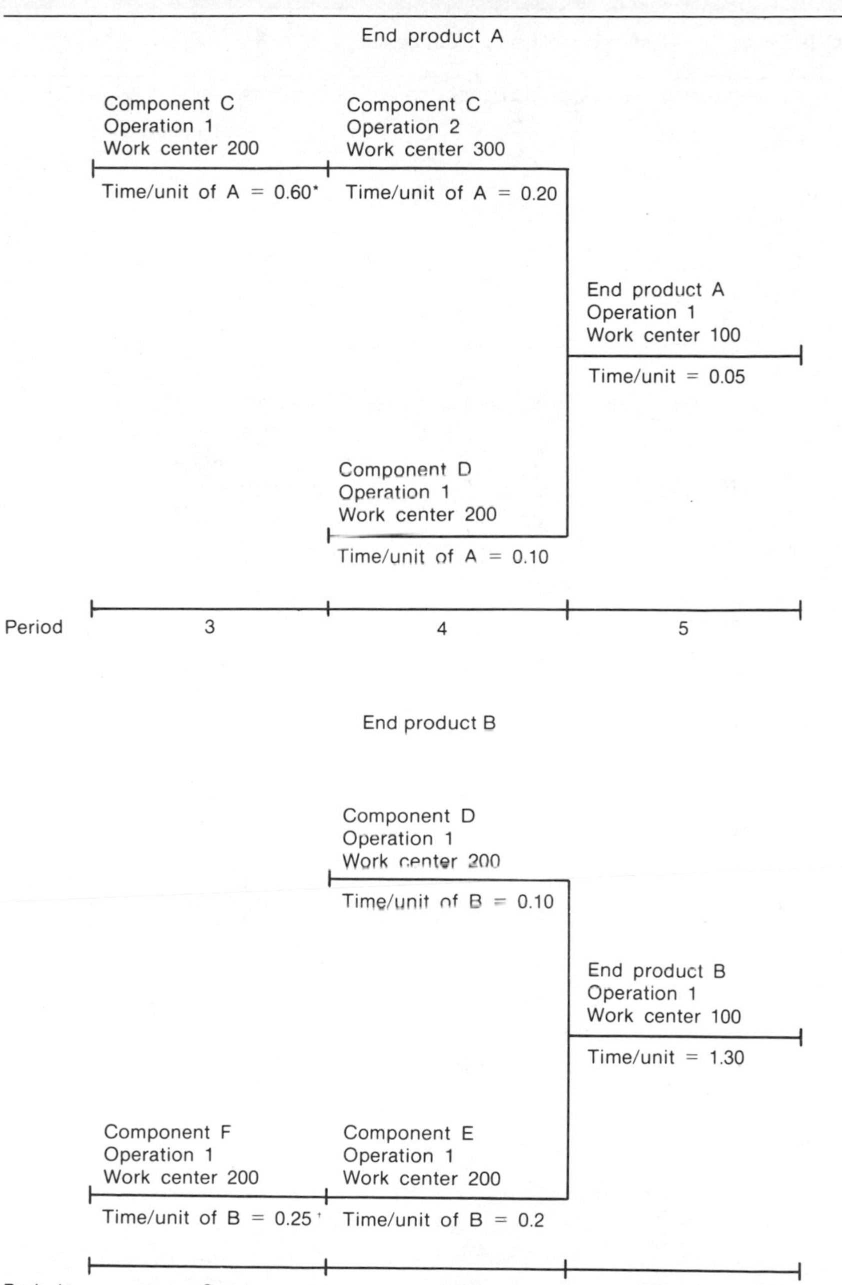

*.60 = Standard time per unit of C × Number of Cs per unit of A = .60 × 1 = .60.

†.25 = Standard time per unit of component F × Number of Fs per unit of B = .0625 × 4 = .25.

Source: W. L. Berry, T. G. Schmitt, and T. E. Vollmann, "Capacity Planning Techniques for Manufacturing Control Systems: Information Requirements and Operating Features," Reprinted with permission, November 1982 *Journal of Operations Management,* Journal of the American Production and Inventory Control Society, Inc.

FIGURE 4.8 Resource profiles by work center

Time required during preceding periods for one end product assembled in period 5:

	Time period		
	3	*4*	*5*
End product A			
Work center 100	0	0	.05
Work center 200	.60	.10	0
Work center 300	0	.20	0
End product B			
Work center 100	0	0	1.30
Work center 200	.25	.30	0

Time-phased capacity requirements generated from MPS for 40 As and 13 Bs in time period 5

	Time period		
	3	*4*	*5*
40 As			
Work center 100	0	0	2
Work center 200	24	4	0
Work center 300	0	8	0
13 Bs			
Work center 100	0	0	16.9
Work center 200	3.25	3.9	0
Work center 300	0	0	0
Total from period 5 MPS			
Work center 100	0	0	18.9
Work center 200	27.25	7.9	0
Work center 300	0	8.0	0

Source: W. L. Berry, T. G. Schmitt, and T. E. Vollmann, "Capacity Planning Techniques for Manufacturing Control Systems: Information Requirements and Operating Features," Reprinted with permission, November 1982 *Journal of Operations Management,* Journal of the American Production and Inventory Control Society, Inc.

resources required to produce the component parts which is taken into account by the resource bill procedure.

Capacity requirements planning (CRP)

Capacity requirements planning (CRP) differs from the resource profile procedure in four respects. First, CRP utilizes the information produced by the MRP explosion process, which includes consideration of all actual lot sizes, as well as the lead times for both open shop orders (scheduled receipts) and orders which are planned for future release (planned orders). Second, the gross to net feature of the MRP system takes into account the production capacity already stored in the form of inventories of both components and assembled products. Third, the shop-floor control system accounts for the

FIGURE 4.9 Capacity requirements using resource profiles

Work center	Past due*	Period 1	2	3	4	5	6	7	8	9	10	11	12	13	Total hours	Work center percentage
100	0.00	23.75	23.75	23.75	18.90	18.90	18.90	34.00	34.00	34.00	36.95	36.95	36.95	36.95	377.75	40%
200	56.50	32.45	35.65	35.15	35.15	32.15	34.75	34.75	39.45	40.75	40.75	40.75	11.80	0	470.05	50
300	6.60	6.60	6.60	8.00	8.00	8.00	6.00	6.00	6.00	7.40	7.40	7.40	7.40	0	91.40	10
Total	63.10	62.80	66.00	66.90	62.05	59.05	59.65	74.75	79.45	82.15	85.10	85.10	56.15	36.95	939.20	100%

*This work should be completed already for products to meet the master production schedule in periods 1 and 2. (If not, it is past due and will add to the capacity required in the upcoming periods.)

Source: W. L. Berry, T. G. Schmitt, and T. E. Vollmann, "Capacity Planning Techniques for Manufacturing Control Systems: Information Requirements and Operating Features," Reprinted with permission, November 1982 *Journal of Operations Management*. Journal of the American Production and Inventory Control Society, Inc.

current status of all work in process in the shop, so that only the capacity needed to *complete the remaining work* on open shop orders is considered in calculating the required work center capacities. Fourth, CRP takes into account the demand for service parts, other demands that may not be accounted for in the MPS, and any additional capacity that might be required by MRP planners reacting to scrap, item record errors, etc. To accomplish this, the CRP procedure requires the same input information as the resource profile procedure (bills of material, routing, time standards, lead times) plus information on MRP planned orders and the current status of open shop orders (MRP scheduled receipts) at individual work centers.

The CRP procedure exploits the MRP information so as to calculate only the capacity required to complete the MPS. By calculating the capacity requirements for actual open shop orders and planned orders in the MRP data base, CRP accounts for the capacity already stored in the form of finished and work-in-process inventories. Since the MRP data include the timing of both these open and planned orders, the potential for improved accuracy in the timing of capacity requirements is realized. This accuracy will be of most importance in the most immediate time periods. Rough-cut techniques can overstate the required capacity by the amount of capacity represented in inventories. In Figure 4.9, for example, the past due or already completed portion of the capacity requirements is 63.1 hours or about a full time period's capacity. This work should already have been completed if we expect to meet the MPS in periods 1 and 2. The potential benefits of CRP are not without cost. A larger data base is required, as well as a much larger computational effort.

The process of preparing a CRP projection is quite similar to that used for resource profiles. The major difference is that the detailed MRP data establish the exact order quantities and timings for use in calculating the capacity required. The resultant capacity needs are summarized by time period and work center in a format similar to that of Figure 4.9. The CRP results would differ from those of the other techniques, primarily in the early periods, but would be a more accurate projection of work center capacity needs. Since the calculations are based on all component parts and end products from the present time period through all periods included in the MRP records (the planning horizon), one can see the enormity of the CRP calculation requirements. This cost is mitigated in some firms by collecting the data as the MRP explosion process is performed.

Figure 4.10 presents one of the MRP records that drive the CRP procedure for our example. To simplify the presentation, we only show the MPS for end product A and the MRP record for one of its components, component C. We have used these data to calculate the capacity requirements for work center 300. These capacity requirements incorporate the influence of lot sizes, inventories, and scheduled receipts for component C. Since item C is processed at work center 300 during the second period of the two-period lead time, the planned order for 40 units due to be released in period 1 requires capacity in period 2 at work center 300. The capacity required is

FIGURE 4.10 CRP example: Detailed calculations

	Period												
	1	*2*	*3*	*4*	*5*	*6*	*7*	*8*	*9*	*10*	*11*	*12*	*13*
Product A *MPS*	33	33	33	40	40	40	30	30	30	37	37	37	37

Component C

Lot size = 40
Lead time = 2

		Period												
		1	*2*	*3*	*4*	*5*	*6*	*7*	*8*	*9*	*10*	*11*	*12*	*13*
Gross requirements		33	33	33	40	40	40	30	30	30	37	37	37	37
Scheduled receipts			40											
Projected available balance	37	4	11	18	18	18	18	28	38	8	11	14	17	20
Planned order releases		40·	40	40	40	40	40		40	40	40	40		

Work Center 300 Capacity Requirements Using CRP

	Period												
	1	*2*	*3*	*4*	*5*	*6*	*7*	*8*	*9*	*10*	*11*	*12*	*13*
Hours of capacity	8	8	8	8	8	8	8	0	8	8	8	8	

Total = 88

Source: W. L. Berry, T. G. Schmitt, and T. E. Vollmann, "Capacity Planning Techniques for Manufacturing Control Systems: Information Requirements and Operating Features," Reprinted with permission, November 1982 *Journal of Operations Management,* Journal of the American Production and Inventory Control Society, Inc.

calculated using the setup and run time data from Figure 4.5 for component C.

For a lot size of 40 units, the labor capacity in work center 300 is 8 hours ($1.0 + 40 \times .175$). Each of the planned orders for component C in Figure 4.10 will require eight hours of capacity at work center 300, one period later. Similarly, the scheduled receipt of 40 units due in period 2 will require eight hours of capacity in week 1. Note that the eight hours of capacity required for the scheduled receipt may not, in fact, be required if this job has already been processed at work center 300 before the beginning of period 1. The actual status of the shop order is required to make the analysis.

In comparing CRP to the other capacity planning procedures, one should not expect that the total capacity requirements for the 13 periods or the period-by-period requirements would be the same. A comparison of the capacity requirements for work center 300 developed by the resource profile procedure (Figure 4.9) and CRP (Figure 4.10) indicates that the total capacity requirements for the 13 periods are less using CRP than resource profiles (88 versus 91.4 hours), and vary considerably on a period-by-period basis. The differences are explained by the initial inventory and the use of lot sizing.

Input/output control

The basic intent in each of the capacity planning techniques is to provide projections of the capacity needs implied by the current material plan, so that timely actions can be taken to balance the capacity needs with capacity available. Once decisions have been made concerning additions to and deletions of capacity, or adjustments to the material plan, a workable capacity plan is the result. The next action is to monitor this plan to determine whether the actions were correct and sufficient. The monitoring also provides the basis for an ongoing correction of capacity planning data.

The basis for monitoring the capacity plan is input/output control. By this we mean that the planned input and planned output of work at a work center will be compared to the actual work input and output. The capacity planning technique used delineates the planned input. The planned output is the result of managerial decision making to specify the capacity level. That is, the planned output is based on manning levels, hours of work, etc. In capacity constrained work centers, the planned output is based on the rate of capacity established by management. In non-capacity constrained work centers, the planned output is equal to the planned input (allowing for some lead time offset).

The actual output at a work center will deviate from the planned output. Often these deviations can be attributed to conditions at the work center itself, such as lower than expected productivity, breakdowns, absences, random variations, or poor product quality. But less than expected output can occur for reasons outside the control of the work center, such as insufficient output from a preceding work center or improper releasing of planned orders. Either of these problems can lead to insufficient input or a "starved" work center. Another reason for a variation between actual input and planned input was shown by our capacity planning model comparisons. That is, some models do not produce very realistic plans!

Input/output analysis also monitors backlog. Backlog represents the cushion between input and output. Arithmetically, it is equal to prior backlog plus or minus the difference between input and output. The planned backlog calculation is based on planned input and planned output. Actual backlog uses actual input and output. The difference between planned backlog and actual backlog represents one measure of the total, or net, input/output deviations. The monitoring of input, output, and backlog typically involves keeping track of the cumulative deviations and comparing them with preset limits.

The input/output report shown in Figure 4.11 is based on work center 200 for our example problem, now shown in weekly time buckets measured in standard labor hours. The report was prepared at the end of period 5, so the actual values are current week-by-week variations in planned input. These could be the result of actual planned orders and scheduled receipts. That is, for example, if the input were planned by CRP, the planned inputs would be based upon the timings for planned orders, the status of scheduled receipts, and routing data. The *actual* input might be the result of any of the causes discussed above.

The planned output for work center 200 has been smoothed. That is, management decided to staff this work center so as to achieve a constant output of 11 hours per week. The result should be to absorb the variations in input with changes in the backlog level. The cumulative planned output for the five weeks (55 hours) is 5 hours more than the cumulative planned input. This reflects a management decision to reduce the backlog from the original level of 20 hours. The process of increasing capacity to reduce backlog recognizes explicitly that the flows must be controlled to change backlog; the backlog cannot be changed in and of itself.

The data in Figure 4.11 summarize the results after five weeks of actual operation. At the end of week 5, the situation requires managerial attention. The cumulative input deviation (+8 hours), the cumulative output deviation (−8 hours), the current backlog (31 hours), or all three could have exceeded the desired limits of control. In this example, the increased backlog is a combination of more than expected input and less than expected output.

FIGURE 4.11 Sample input/output report for work center 200*
(as of the end of period 5)

		Week				
		1	*2*	*3*	*4*	*5*
Planned input		15	15	0	10	10
Actual input		14	13	5	9	17
Cumulative deviation		−1	−3	+2	+1	+8
Planned output		11	11	11	11	11
Actual output		8	10	9	11	9
Cumulative deviation		−3	−4	−6	−6	−8
Actual backlog	20	26	29	25	23	31

Desired backlog: 10 hours

*In standard labor-hours.

One other aspect of monitoring the backlog is important. In general, there is little point in releasing orders to a work center that already has an excessive backlog, except when the order to be released is of higher priority than any in the backlog. In general, the idea is to not release work which cannot be done, but to wait and release that which is really needed. Oliver Wight sums this up as one of the principles of input/output control: "Never put into a manufacturing facility or to a vendor's facility more than you believe that he can produce. Hold backlogs in production and inventory control."

MANAGEMENT AND CAPACITY PLANNING

In the design and use of the capacity planning system, several management considerations must be taken into account. In this section, we will discuss the design of the systems from the perspective of the MPC framework, look at the choices that must be made in tailoring the capacity-planning system to a particular firm, and consider how to use the capacity planning data. The key elements of management's commitment in the design and use of the system are emphasized.

Capacity planning in the MPC system

In Figure 4.1, we show the relationship between the MPC framework and the various capacity planning modules. The five modules range from long-range resource planning to day-to-day control of capacity utilization. In this chapter, we have concentrated on medium- to short-range planning techniques, rough-cut capacity planning and capacity requirements planning, and the input/output control technique for capacity monitoring. Nevertheless there is a vertical relationship among the capacity planning modules as well as the horizontal relationship with the material planning modules of the MPC system. These relationships can affect the managerial choices for the design and use of the capacity planning systems in a specific firm.

An illustration of the importance of the interrelationships in designing and using the capacity planning system comes from considering the impact of production planning and resource planning decisions on shorter-term capacity planning decisions. To the extent that production planning and resource planning are done well, the problems faced in capacity planning can be reduced, since adequate resources have been provided. If, for example, the production plan specifies a very stable rate of output, then changes in the master production schedule (MPS) that require capacity changes are minimal. If the material planning module is functioning effectively, then the MPS will be converted into detailed component production plans with relatively few unexpected capacity requirements.

A good case in point is the use of the *Kanban system* by the Toyota Motor Company and other Japanese firms. For these firms, the production plan calls for a stable rate of output (cars per day). Product mix variations are substantially less than for other automobile companies because Toyota carefully manages the number and timing of option combinations. Order backlogs and finished-goods-inventories also are used to separate the factories from actual customer orders. The result is a shop-floor/vendor control system that is simple, effective, and easy to operate. The careful resource and production planning, and resultant stability means there is little need for these firms to use either rough-cut capacity planning procedures or CRP.

A quite different but equally important linkage that can affect capacity-planning system design is the linkage with the shop-floor control systems at execution time. A key relationship exists in scheduling the effective use of capacity. If sufficient capacity has been provided, and efficient use of that capacity is ensured by good shop floor procedures, then few unpleasant surprises will arise that require capacity analysis and change. Effective shop-floor procedures will utilize the available capacity to process orders according to MRP system priorities, provide insight into potential capacity problems in the short range (a few hours to days), and be responsive to changes in the material plans. Thus, an effective shop-floor control system can reduce the necessary degree of detail and intensity of use of the capacity planning system.

In providing effective control of the capacity plans, the shop-floor control system, again, is key. Good shop-floor control leads to plans that are more likely to be met. The net result is a better match between actual input/output and planned input/output. Again we see attention to the material planning side of the MPC system, in this case the shop-floor control model, having an effect on the capacity planning side.

Choice of a specific technique

The capacity planning techniques discussed in this chapter convert a material plan into capacity requirements. They vary as to accuracy, aggregation level, and ease of preparation. Roughly, as the amount of data and computation time increases, the quality and detail of the capacity requirements improve. The issue is whether the additional costs of supporting more complex procedures are justified by improved decision making and subsequent plant operations. It should also be seen that the quality of the material planning system has an important influence on this trade-off.

Considerations other than that of the quality/cost trade-off can influence the choice of the appropriate capacity planning techniques as well. For example, the length of time it takes to change capacity in particular work centers may necessitate a long-range, aggregate approach. If overtime is not easily used or outside contractors are not readily available, there may be no possible short-term capacity changes. Similarly, if the training period for new employees is quite long or alternate routings are not possible, the effect is the same. In these instances, the need for detailed short-range capacity plans is reduced; the problem often becomes one of utilizing existing capacity more effectively.

If the time frame of the decisions is quarterly or longer, then the accuracy differences between CRP and the rough-cut procedures tend not to be significant. If the inventories are kept low by the MPC systems, the bills of material are shallow (do not have many steps from raw material to finished product), and lead times are short, the differences in the results of the techniques tend to be even less significant.

Another factor that should be taken into account is the need for accuracy in stating the capacity requirements and the magnitude of capacity changes that can be made. If the unit of capacity addition is 1,000 tons per week and requirements vary by only 100 tons, it may be that simpler approximations of the capacity requirements for a particular plan will be sufficient for decision purposes.

One important need in managing the capacity of the company is the ability to perform *what if analysis*. This implies the ability to look at the capacity implications of alternative material plans. This can be done in detail with CRP, but at a substantial computation cost. Alternatively, what if analysis can be accomplished using rough-cut methods directly from the MPS at a lower cost. This means that the MPS can be changed and the capacity implications reviewed for several alternatives with the rough-cut procedures in the time it would take CRP to evaluate a single alternative. Some firms have chosen rough-cut procedures for precisely this reason.

It would be easy to conclude from our presentation of the four capacity planning techniques that CRP, with its ability to account for actual shop conditions and plans, is the preferred technique. It does provide the greatest accuracy, but at a substantial cost. We have argued that specific conditions in a company, such as the rapidity with which capacity can be changed, will influence the choice. We also pointed to use of what if analysis as a factor in the choice. Thus, the choice is not a strict cost/accuracy trade-off. The important point is to determine which technique allows the manager to make the best capacity-related decisions.

Using the capacity plan

All the techniques we have described provide data on which a manager can base a decision. The broad choices are clear—if there is a mismatch between available capacity and required capacity, either the capacity or the material plan should be changed. If capacity is to be changed, the choices include: overtime/undertime authorization, hiring/layoff, increasing/decreasing the number of machine tools or times in use, etc. The capacity requirements can be changed by alternate routings, make or buy decisions, subcontracting, raw material changes, inventory changes, or changing customer promise dates.

In short, the management task is to change the capacity to meet the requirements, the requirements to meet the capacity, or some combination of the two. The factors that enter into this task are costs, market position, flexibility, institutional restrictions, etc. In Europe, Japan, and South America, the task is oriented more toward changing requirements to meet capacity levels than it is in the United States. This is because it is easier to change capacity levels in the United States than in Europe, Japan, or South America.

The choice of capacity planning units can lead to more effective use of the system. Capacity units need not be work centers as defined for manufacturing, engineering, or routing purposes. They can be groupings of the key resources (human or capital) that are important in defining the levels of output of the factory. Many firms plan the capacity solely for key machines (work centers) and gateway operations. These key areas can be managed in detail while other areas fall under resource planning and the shop-floor control system.

Capacity planning choices dictate the diameter of the manufacturing pipeline. Only as much material can be produced as there is capacity for its production, *regardless of the material plan.* Not understanding the critical nature of the management of capacity has led more than one firm into production chaos and serious customer service problems. In the same vein, the relationship between flexibility and capacity must be discussed. One cannot have perfectly balanced material and capacity plans *and* be able to easily produce emergency orders! We know one general manager who depicts his capacity as a pie. He has one slice for recurring business, one for spare parts production, one slice for downtime and maintenance, and a final specific slice for opportunity business. He manages to pay for this excess capacity by winning some very lucrative contracts that require rapid responses. He *does not add* that opportunity business to a capacity plan fully committed to the other aspects of his business.

One final note on capacity planning: Many managers have complained that they cannot manage capacity because they do not know what their capacity is. Therefore, they cannot get started until they have completed some engineering studies, and the engineers are busy right now. In many cases, this is a weak excuse for inaction. Someone has some idea of what capacity is! Use this to get started and then use input/output analysis to improve estimates and knowledge of what can be done. The key is to begin; the major ingredient is courage!

DATA BASE REQUIREMENTS

We have seen that each of the capacity planning techniques requires different systems linkages. These linkages imply different data elements and data base considerations. The managerial use of the different capacity planning techniques and enhancements to improve utility can have data base implications as well.

Data base design consideration

The CPOF, capacity bills, resource profiles, and CRP procedures all use MPS data to develop capacity requirements. The CPOF procedure calculates the overall direct labor requirements for the MPS and allocates this capacity to the work centers on the basis of historically observed workload patterns. By contrast, the capacity bill procedure uses bill of material and routing information to calculate the capacity at work centers and, thus, more accurately reflects the particular mix of end items shown in the MPS. The resource profile procedure time phases the capacity requirements by the lead times for component parts and assemblies used in the manufacture of the end items. The CRP procedure uses additional information from MRP and shop-floor control systems to account for the exact timing and quantities of component parts and end-item production orders.

We see that there is an increasing requirement for data starting with relatively simple accounting system data required by CPOF. The capacity bills, resource profiles, and CRP techniques each require increased amounts of production/inventory control, industrial engineering, and shop-floor control data. These latter procedures incur successively increasing computational cost, as well. The specific data linkages with the material planning modules are shown in Figure 4.1.

Although the size of the data base for capacity bills is much smaller than for CRP, the CRP data base already largely exists if the firm has a working MPR system. For this reason, many firms use CRP systems to answer questions that could be analyzed at far lower computational cost with rough-cut techniques. They do so because there are no additional data base requirements. All that is needed is the additional computer run time, which can be expensive but is usually available.

Several other factors influence the design and maintenance of the data base. The level of detail appropriate for capacity management implies a corresponding level of detail in the data base and in data base maintenance. If the capacity assessments are made in terms of sales dollars or average labor-hours, the data may be extracted from the financial accounting data base. This reduces the complexity of the MPC data base but requires some coordinating data base maintenance.

The use of input/output analysis requires a communication link with the shop-floor control system to gather the data for analysis. A closely related issue that affects data base complexity is labor productivity. Many firms have standard time data which differ widely from actual practice. What is more, this difference can vary between work centers. This fact can greatly complicate the data base design and maintenance problem, since it is critical to keep track of actual production rates to make an accurate conversion of material plans into capacity needs.

Extended capabilities and data base design. We have discussed the desirability of incorporating a what if capability into the capacity planning system. This capability creates demands on the data base design that can be severe. The consideration of computer time has already been raised. The need to evaluate a number of alternative material plans means that the ability to easily change the MPS must be designed in. What is more, the changes must be isolated from the current actual MPS and MRP records, both for the sake of recovery and so as not to create false signals on the shop floor before appropriate analysis and approval have been accomplished.

Along with the capability of *what if* testing runs a parallel set of questions on detailed implementation decisions. The choice of the level of aggregation for capacity planning, the size of the time period for analysis, the number of future periods to be analyzed, and the number and composition of machine centers all influence the size, complexity, and maintenance of the data base. If the basic analysis is taking place with one set of numbers and time periods, then being converted to another for making implementation decisions, mismatches and other problems can occur. On the other hand, designing the system to support any kind of question and any kind of decision may be prohibitively expensive.

We are not arguing here that the manager should be happy with what the computer gives him. Not in the least! The computer can and *should* give the manager what is needed! It is just that the choices of data base design, linkages to other modules, and level of detail required are all closely related. Wise choices in the design stage can lead to more productive systems.

Perhaps the ultimate design objective for the data base and its use is to be able to identify and plan for the key work centers as they change over time. This would require careful attention to the design of the input/output module and the tolerance limits used to trigger attention. It would also require flexibility in the data base to permit analysis of different possible groupings over time and groupings that might not correspond to current work centers or labor categories.

EXAMPLE APPLICATIONS

In this section, we provide examples of the capacity planning techniques in practice. Specifically we look at the use of CRP by the Black & Decker Company and the use of capacity bills by the Twin Disc Company.

Capacity planning at Black & Decker

The Black & Decker Company produces a broad line of consumer workshop, garden, and household products. The production is mostly to stock. Capacity planning at Black & Decker is largely based upon CRP. Figure 4.12 shows the weekly CRP report for one key machine group (KMG073) in department 8–01 of the Hampstead, Maryland plant. It is called the BH "group," but is comprised of a single critical machine. The time periods are weeks (from 741 through 775). For each week, the projection is based on the combined open shop orders (MRP scheduled receipts) and MRP planned orders. The times include setup hours (S/U HRS.) and run-time hours (OP HRS.)

FIGURE 4.12 Black and Decker CRP report

KMG WEEKLY LOADS, HAMPSTEAD

SEQ 1033 KMG 073 DEPT 8-01 CST/CN 063 KMG NAME BH GROUP MACH QTY 1 WEEKLY CAP 106.0

MFG. WEEK	WIP	741	742	743	744	745	746	747	748	749	750	751	752	753	754	755
S/U HRS.	38	5	4	2	5	2	3	6	4	5	2	4	5	3	4	1
OP HRS.	314	104	102	105	95	94	107	111	84	92	41	101	128	100	72	87
TOTAL	352	109	106	107	100	96	110	117	88	97	43	105	133	103	76	88
% OF CAP		103	100	100	94	90	104	110	83	91	40	100	125	97	72	83
MFG. WEEK	756	757	758	759	760	761	762	763	764	765	766	767	768	769	770	771
S/U HRS.	8	1	3	4	3	3	4	5	3	4	9	1	5	5	2	3
OP HRS.	91	92	107	151	65	96	140	86	68	97	117	62	93	98	83	132
TOTAL	99	93	110	155	68	99	144	91	71	101	126	63	98	103	85	135
% OF CAP	93	88	104	146	64	93	136	86	67	96	119	59	92	97	80	125
MFG. WEEK	772	773	774	775												
S/U HRS.	3	6	8	2												
OP HRS.	91	121	134	104												
TOTAL	94	127	142	106												
% OF CAP	89	120	134	100												

AVERAGE FOR
1st 10 Wks 92%
2d 13 Wks 99%
3d 12 Wks 98%
Tot 35 Wks 97%

NUMBER WKS OVER 80%
30

Source: R. W. and T. E. Vollmann, "Black & Decker: Pioneers with MRP," *Case Studies in Materials Requirements Planning,* ed. by E. W. Davis (Falls Church, Va.: American Production and Inventory Control Society, 1978), p. 38.

The weekly capacity of this machine center is 106 hours. Since there is only one machine, 18 hours per day, five days per week, plus 8 hours each on Saturday and Sunday account for all the capacity. The report shows the percent of capacity (% OF CAP) required by the projected arrival of work in each week (planned input). This is shown on Figure 4.12 where 30 out of the 35 weeks shown are loaded to over 80 percent. Black & Decker keeps track of the number of weeks for which the projected needs are in excess of 80 percent of capacity. This is an indicator of potential serious capacity problems. Moreover, the average level for the total 35 week period is shown to be 97 percent.

The capacity problem may be significantly greater than the percent of capacity indicates. The report shows that the current WIP (work in process) or backlog is 352 standard hours. This work is presently at the machine, with 109 standard hours scheduled to arrive in the upcoming week. The work center is already more than three weeks behind schedule. Given the projected load and present capacity, the center will stay behind schedule for the foreseeable future.

To complete the capacity planning picture, Black & Decker uses the MRP data base to analyze capacity loads on a quarterly basis and to prepare a four-week, detailed day-by-day capacity report for each work center. The four-week report is the basis for daily capacity planning decisions. Figure 4.13 shows this daily load report for the next four weeks for the KMG 073 key machine group.

The total values for the weeks show the same capacity problem as does Figure 4.12. Also shown on Figure 4.13 is the actual performance for last week as a part of the input/output control information.

As useful as these capacity planning reports have been to Black & Decker over the years, they do not allow for the level of what if analysis that is desirable. Recently, Black & Decker designed two new systems to support capacity planning. One is a capacity bill approach to rough-cut capacity planning. It produces total dollar output levels by divisions and product groups, work center loadings, and critical machine group capacity requirements directly from the MPS.

The other aid to capacity planning is called *alternations planning*. This approach to what if analysis allows use of the MRP data base to determine the effect of changing the timing or quantities of selected MPS values. These changes can be evaluated in terms of the time-phased capacity requirements on particular machine centers without disturbing the operative data base. The output of the report shows both the current plan and revised plan in a format similar to that of Figure 4.12. This report permits a quick assessment of the effect of MPS changes.

Capacity planning at Twin Disc

The Twin Disc Company manufactures gears, transmissions, and other heavy components for the farm implement and heavy-equipment industries.

FIGURE 4.13 Black and Decker daily machine load report

```
09/15/   Week 741-1                    HAMPSTEAD MACHINE LOAD REPORT                          DEPT. 8-01
COST CTR 002   KMG 073                 BHG ROUTING MACH           1 MACH @ 18 HRS/DAY   18 HRS/DAY AVAIL
```

741										
SCHED OP HRS							TOT SCH	TOT AVAIL	PCT LOAD	CUM AVAIL HRS
-1	-2	-3	-4	-5	-6	-7*				
18	18	19	19	19	8	8	109	106	103	-3

742										
SCHED OP HRS							TOT SCH	TOT AVAIL	PCT LOAD	CUM AVAIL HRS
-1	-2	-3	-4	-5	-6	-7				
18	18	18	18	16	8	10	106	106	100	-3

743										
SCHED OP HRS							TOT SCH	TOT AVAIL	PCT LOAD	CUM AVAIL HRS
-1	-2	-3	-4	-5	-6	-7				
19	19	19	18	17	7	8	107	106	100	-4

744										
SCHED OP HRS							TOT SCH	TOT AVAIL	PCT LOAD	CUM AVAIL HRS
-1	-2	-3	-4	-5	-6	-7				
20	16	18	19	17	7	4	100	106	94	2

HRS PRODUCED LAST WEEK

AHEAD	CURR	BHND	TOTAL	BACKLOG
	15	93	108	352

*Days of the week.

Source: R. W. Hall and T. E. Vollmann, "Black & Decker: Pioneers with MRP," *Case Studies in Materials Requirements Planning,* ed. by E. W. Davis (Falls Church, Va.: American Production and Inventory Control Society, 1978), p. 37.

FIGURE 4.14 Twin Disc capacity bill report

Work center description					Percent utilization of capacity by product line										Remarks
Center	Type	Qty.	No. of shifts	Cap. (hrs/wks)	A	B	C	D	E	F	G	H	I	TOTAL	
03-05 BD	2AC chucker	4	3	1561	22	22	16	3	8	11	11	2		95	
BR	3AC Warner & Swasey	8	3	2966	3	16	46	1	13	2	1	2	—	84	
CA	Reishauer gear grinder	2	3	900			38		22	—	12			72	
CAB	Reishauer gear grinder	2	3	950		10	43		13	2			1	69	
CD	P. & W. gear grinder	1	3	544			59		4					63	
CEA	Maag gear grinder	4	3	3044		10	76		14	5			8	113	Off load to CAB 3:1 ratio
CG	P. & W. gear grinder	4	3	1190			120		8					128	Off load to CA, CD
CI	Pfauter hobber	5	3	2374	6	22	41		9	2	4		2	86	
CJ	Barber colman hobber	1	3	620	27	39	50	1	29	25		8	—	180	Off load to CI, CW
CN	Gear shaver	3	2.5	700	14	37	15		8	9	4			87	
CQ	Gear pointer	1	1	22	13	56	—		12	3				84	
CS	Fellows shaper	1	3	549		37			8	—				45	
CW	Barber colman hobber	3	3	1530	7	12	26	2	8	9	5			70	
CX	Barber colman shaper	1	3	546	—	38	25	7	6	2	24			102	Off load to CS
CY	Fellows shaper	1	3	514	15	77	17		10	12			2	133	Off load to CS
FD	Internal grinder	1	3	285	8	8	10	5	8	4	6			49	Relieve FI and
FI	Internal grinder	1	3	275	25	59	32	11	25	10	9			171	move machine from PLI2
FJ	Surface grinder	1	1	328	6	41	20	1	11	14				93	
FM	Vertical internal grinder	1	2	368		38	57	1	16	1			3	116	Add ½ shift
FY	Gear hone	2	2	528	19	28	11		12	9	5			84	
H	Engine lathe	1	3	427	26	42	29	—	15	8	6		—	126	Off load to HES
HES	W. & S. Lathe—Special	2	2	234	5	43	18		11	12				89	Add 1 shift
JA	Horizontal broach	1	1	90	14	3	53	2	12	3				87	
NH	Gear chamfer	1	3	307	18	42	10		12	11	5			98	
PC	Magnaflux	1	1	240	3	35	48		12	2	2		—	102	Add ½ shift

Source: E. S. Buffa and J. G. Miller, *Production-Inventory Systems: Planning and Control*, 3d ed. (Homewood, Ill.: Richard D. Irwin, 1979), p. 598.

It is primarily a make-to-order firm. One part of the capacity-planning system at Twin Disc involves the use of capacity bills for rough-cut capacity planning. An example ouput from this system is shown in Figure 4.14.

For each machine or work center, the percentage of available capacity required by each of the nine product lines that Twin Disc uses for master production scheduling purposes is shown. For example, the MPS for product line A requires 22 percent of the 1,561 hours of weekly capacity at the 2AC Chucker. The total capacity requirements for all nine product lines indicate a total load of 95 percent of the 2AC Chucker capacity.

Perhaps the most important aspect of this report is the last column. Illustrated here are the managerial actions taken to overcome capacity problems. For example, the Maag gear grinder is loaded to 113 percent of rated capacity by the present MPS. One Reishauer gear grinder, however, is only loaded to 69 percent of its capacity. A decision has been made to use an alternative gear grinder, taking account of the differences in the capacity of the two grinders, roughly a 3 to 1 ratio in the machine-hours required. Other managerial actions shown on the report include moving an additional machine in from another factory and adding more shifts of capacity. The point is that this document is a working document that is used to make effective capacity decisions.

CONCLUDING PRINCIPLES

Several clear principles for the design and use of the capacity planning system emerge from this chapter. Some of the more important are:

- The capacity plans must be developed concurrently with the material plans if the material plans are to be realized.
- The particular capacity planning technique(s) chosen must match the level of detail and actual company circumstances to permit making effective management decisions.
- The better the resource and production planning process, the less difficult the capacity planning process.
- The better the shop-floor control system, the less short-term capacity planning is required.
- The more detail in the capacity planning system, the more data and data base maintenance required.
- It is not always capacity that should change when capacity availability does not equal need.
- Capacity not only must be planned, but the use of that capacity must also be monitored and controlled.
- Capacity-planning techniques can be applied to selected key resources (which need not correspond to production work centers).

REFERENCES

Aherns, Roger. "Basics of Capacity Planning and Control." *APICS 24th Annual Conference Proceedings*, 1981, pp. 232–35.

Anderson, J. C., and R. G. Schroeder. "A Survey of MRP Implementation and Practice." *Proceedings, Material Requirements Planning Implementation Conference*, September 1978.

Belt, Bill. "Integrating Capacity Planning and Capacity Control." *Production and Inventory Management*, 1st Quarter 1976.

Berry, W. L., T. Schmitt, and T. E. Vollmann. "Capacity Planning Techniques for Manufacturing Control Systems: Information Requirements and Operational Features." *Journal of Operations Management* 3, no. 1 (November 1982).

Bolander, Steven F. "Capacity Planning Through Forward Scheduling." APICS, Master Planning Seminar Proceedings, Las Vegas, April 1981, pp. 73–80.

Burlingame, L. J. "Extended Capacity Planning." *APICS Annual Conference Proceedings*, 1974, pp. 83–91.

Capacity Planning and Control Reprints. Falls Church, Va.: American Production and Inventory Control Society, 1975.

Hall, R. W., and T. E. Vollmann. "Black and Decker: Pioneers with MRP." *Case Studies in Materials Requirements Planning.* Falls Church, Va.: American Production and Inventory Control Society, 1978, p. 38.

Lankford, Ray. "Short-Term Planning of Manufacturing Capacity." *APICS 21st Annual Conference Proceedings*, 1978, pp. 37–68.

Reinhart, Leroy D. "Delineation of Capacity Planning Responsibility." *APICS 24th Annual Conference Proceedings*, 1981, pp. 203–6.

Solberg, James J. "Capacity Planning with a Stochastic Flow Model." *AIIE Transactions* 13, no. 2 (June 1981), pp. 116–22.

Van De Mark, Robert L. "Adjust Your Capacity, Do Not Reschedule Your Shop Orders." *APICS 24th Annual Conference Proceedings*, 1981, pp. 148–51.

Wemmerlov, Urban. "A Note on Capacity Planning." *Production and Inventory Management*, 3d Quarter, 1980, pp. 85–89.

Wight, O. W. "Input-Output Control, A Real Handle on Lead Time." *Production and Inventory Management*, 3d Quarter 1970, pp. 9–31.

5

Shop-floor control

This chapter is concerned with the detailed execution of material plans. It treats the detailed scheduling of individual jobs at work centers on the shop floor. An effective shop-floor control system can lead to due date performance that ensures meeting the company's customer service goals. Management of the system can lead to reductions in work-in-process inventories and in production lead times. Development of a suitable system means paying close attention to the match between company needs and system design choices. A key dimension involves feedback from the system on the performance of the shop against plans. This loop-closing aspect provides signals for revising the plans, if necessary.

The chapter is organized around the following five topics:

- A framework for shop-floor control: How does shop-floor control relate to other aspects of material planning and control? What concepts are important for individual firm decisions?
- Shop-floor control techniques: What are the basic concepts and models used for shop-floor control?
- Shop-floor control examples: How have shop-floor control systems been designed and implemented in several different kinds of companies?

- The shop-floor control data base: What are the necessary data elements to support a shop-floor control system, and how are they managed in practice?
- Using the shop-floor control system: What are the critical issues to ensure that shop-floor control plays its proper role in a material planning and control system?

Chapter 5 is linked to Chapter 2 in that MRP provides the material plans that shop-floor control executes. Chapter 3 is also of interest because it is there that we discuss the procedural reforms necessary to ensure accuracy in the shop-floor control data base and priorities. Chapter 13 deals with advanced concepts in scheduling that go beyond the basic scheduling techniques presented in this chapter. Chapter 20 presents a system from Finland and a finite scheduling procedure developed in Israel.

A FRAMEWORK FOR SHOP-FLOOR CONTROL

Shop-floor control is one of the back-end modules in the material planning and control (MPC) system shown in Figure 5.1. It is concerned with managing the detailed flow of material inside the plant. In this section of the chapter, we describe the key MPC system linkages to the shop-floor control (SFC) system and the unique company features which might influence SFC design choices.

MPC system linkages

The primary connection between SFC and the rest of the MPC systems shown in Figure 5.1 comes from the box marked Material and capacity plans. The capacity plan is especially critical to managing the detailed shop-floor flow of material. In essence, the capacity provided represents the resource availabilities for meeting the material plans.

The importance of capacity for SFC is illustrated by considering two extremes. If insufficient capacity is provided, no SFC system will be able to decrease backlogs, improve delivery performance, or improve output. On the other hand, if more than enough capacity exists to produce the peak loads, almost *any* SFC system will achieve material flow objectives. It is in the cases where there are some bottleneck areas and where effective utilization of capacity is important, that we see the utility of good SFC systems.

The material plan provides information to the SFC system and sets performance objectives. The essential objective of SFC is to execute the material plan—to build the right part at the right time. This will result in being able to hit the master production schedule and to satisfy customer service objectives.

A critical information service provided by MRP is to keep the SFC system appraised of all changes in material plans. This means revising due dates and quantities for scheduled receipts as needed, so that correct priorities can be

FIGURE 5.1 Manufacturing planning and control system

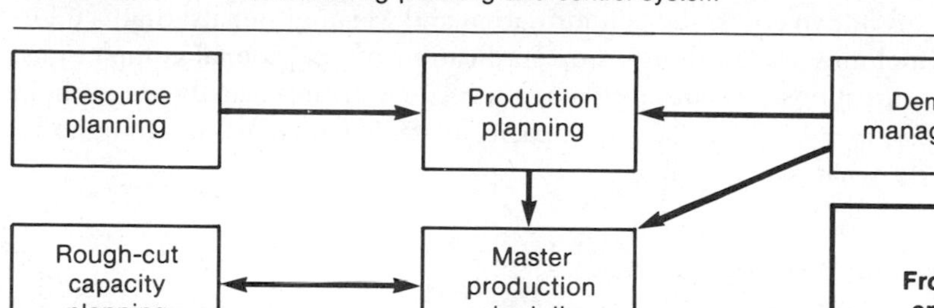

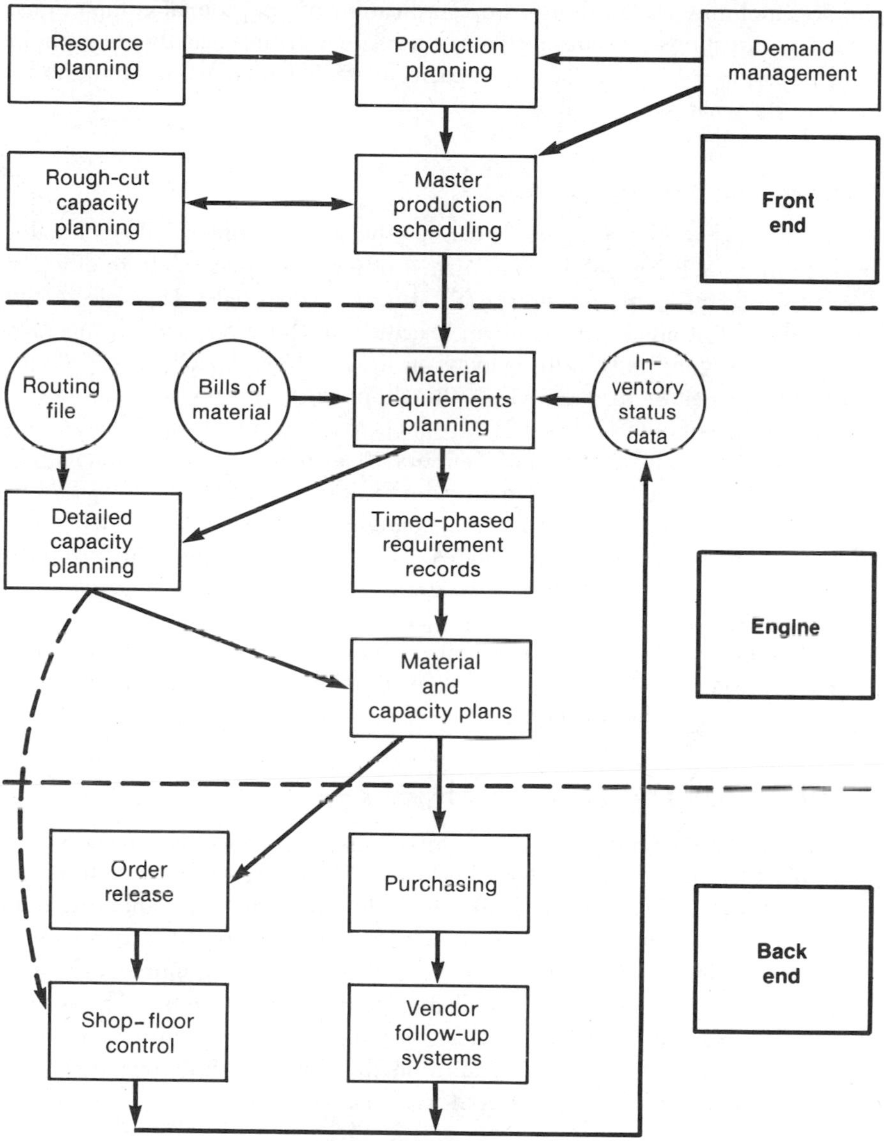

maintained by SFC. The SFC job begins when a component part planner releases an order. The job thereafter might be likened to a duck hunter following a moving target. The SFC system must keep each shop order lined up with its due date—one that is moving—so that the overall MPC is supported.

The linkages to SFC are not all one-way. There is an important feedback from the shop floor to the engine. This is the loop-closing aspect of SFC. The feedback is of two types: status information and warning signals. Status information includes where things are, notification of operational completions, count verifications, accounting data, etc. The warning signals are to help flag inadequacies in material and capacity plans. That is, are we going to be able to do what was planned?

The company environment

We have stated the primary SFC objective as managing the flow of materials to meet MPC plans. In some firms, other objectives relate to efficient use of capacity: labor, machine tools, time, or materials. The role of the particular set of objectives in a firm is critical to the way in which the SFC system is designed. SFC criteria focus on shop orders; capacity criteria focus on the work center through which the shop orders pass.

The choice of objectives for SFC reflects the position of the firm vis-à-vis its competitors, customers, and vendors. It also reflects the fundamental goals of the company and the constraints under which it operates. In Europe, for example, many firms find changing capacity to be much more difficult than it is in the United States. This viewpoint colors the European view of the SFC system. Similarly, some firms have much more complex products and/or process technology than others. The result can be a much more difficult shop-floor management problem and a resultant difference in the appropriate SFC system. The net result is that SFC system design must be tailored somewhat to the needs of the particular firm.

SHOP-FLOOR CONTROL TECHNIQUES

This section begins with a description of basic concepts for shop-floor control. Included are priorities, the loading of a particular job onto a machine center, the elements of lead time, and data inputs. We then examine three approaches to shop-floor control. The first, Gantt charts, provides a graphical understanding of the shop-floor control problem; moreover, Gantt chart models can be used in manual shop-floor control systems. The second approach is based on priority rules for jobs at a work center. The third approach to shop-floor control is finite loading, where an exact schedule of jobs is prepared for each work center.

Basic shop-floor control concepts

Figure 5.2 shows an example product structure for an end item A. This example will serve to demonstrate some of the basic concepts that underlie the shop-floor control techniques. One of the essential inputs to the SFC system is the routing and lead time data for each piece. This is presented in Figure 5.3 for part D and part E of the example. The routing specifies each

FIGURE 5.2 Example product structure diagram

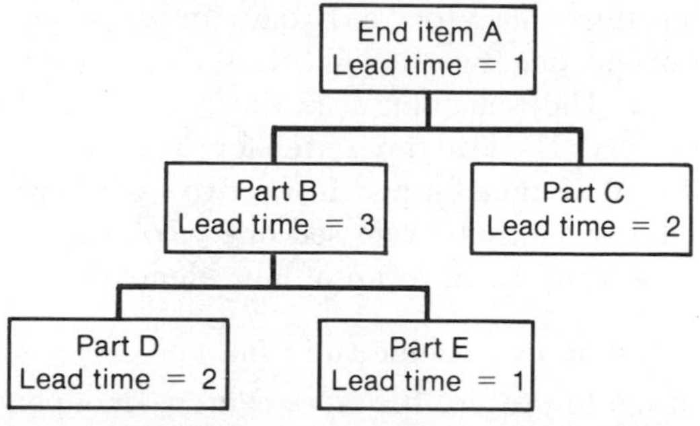

FIGURE 5.3 Routing data and operation set-back chart

Part D routing

Operation	*Work center*	*Run time*	*Setup time*	*Move time*	*Queue time*	*Total time*	*Rounded time*
1	101	1.4	.4	.3	2.0	4.1	4.0
2	109	1.5	.5	.3	2.5	4.8	5.0
3	103	.1	.1	.2	.5	.9	1.0

Total lead time (days) 10.0

Part E routing

Operation	*Work center*	*Run time*	*Setup time*	*Move time*	*Queue time*	*Total time*	*Rounded time*
1	101	.3	.1	.2	.5	1.1	1.0
2	107	.2	.1	.3	.5	1.1	1.0
3	103	.3	.2	.1	1.5	2.1	2.0
4	109	.1	.1	.2	.5	.9	1.0

Total lead time (days) 5.0

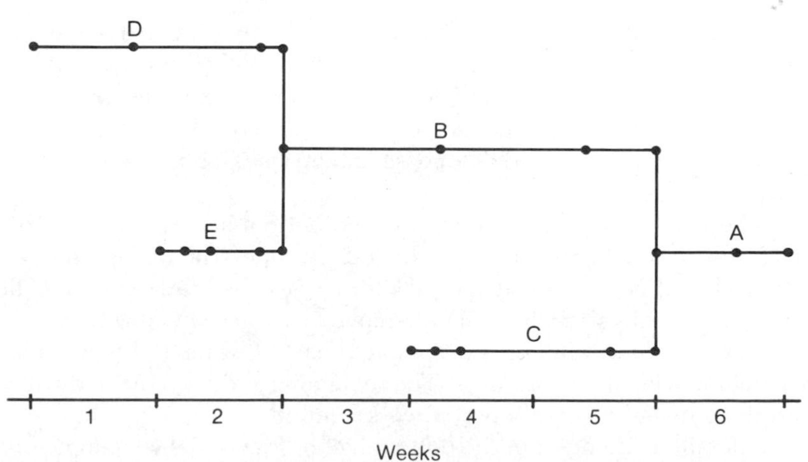

operation to be performed to make the part and which work center will perform the operation.

The production of part D, for example, requires three operations of 4, 5, and 1 days, respectively, for a total of 10 days, or two weeks. Part E requires four operations of one, one, two, and one days, respectively, for a total of five days, or one week. The remaining lead times shown in Figure 5.2 are all derived the same way. The lead times used for MRP must match those in the routing file. If the MRP time for part E was two weeks instead of one week, the orders would constantly be released one week early.

Lead times are typically made up of four elements:

Run time (operation or machine run time per piece × lot size).

Setup time (time to prepare the work center—independent of lot size).

Move time (from one work center to the next).

Queue time (time spent waiting to be processed at a work center which depends upon workload *and* schedule).

Queue time is the critical element. It frequently accounts for 80 percent or more of the total lead time, and it is the most capable of being managed. Reducing queue time means shorter lead time and, therefore, reduced work-in-process inventory. Achieving the reduction requires better scheduling.

The bottom of Figure 5.3 shows an operation set-back chart based on the lead times for each part. The implications of incorrect MRP lead time can be seen clearly here. If the MRP lead time for part E is not the one week calculated from the routing data, the part will either be released early or late to the shop. Neither of these is a desirable outcome. Note that Figure 5.3 shows that both parts D and E go through work center 101 for their first operation. The top half of Figure 5.4 shows the partial schedule for work center 101, with parts D and E scheduled according to the timing given in Figure 5.3.

The bottom half of Figure 5.4 shows two alternative detailed schedules for part D in week 1 at work center 101. The crosshatched portion represents the 1.8 days of lead time required for setup and run time. The first schedule has part D loaded as soon as possible in the four-day schedule shown in the top half of Figure 5.4. The second schedule loads part D into the latest possible time at work center 101.

The key differences between the top and bottom halves of Figure 5.4 are in lead times. The top half includes the queue time. The queue time represents slack that permits the choice of alternative schedules—a form of flexibility. It is also this slack that can be removed by good SFC practice. That is, this schedule allows 4 full days to complete part D, when the actual time on the machine will only be 1.8 days. The remaining 2.2 days, the part will wait in a queue or be moving between work centers.

The detailed schedules in the bottom half of Figure 5.4 contain no queue

FIGURE 5.4 Work center 101 schedules

Parts D and E with MRP lead times

Week 1					Week 2					Week 3				
M	T	W	T	F	M	T	W	T	F	M	T	W	T	F

Part D

E

Alternative detailed schedules for Part D
(Set-up and run time only)

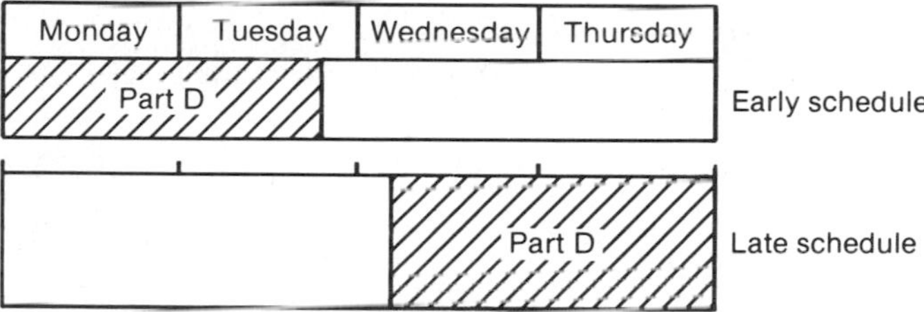

time. These schedules represent the loading of a particular job onto a particular work center for a particular time period. The two alternatives shown in the bottom half of Figure 5.4 are different loadings; one typically chooses between alternative loadings so as to utilize the machine center effectively.

Gantt charts

Gantt or bar charts, such as those presented in Figure 5.4, show a schedule. The operation set-back chart in Figure 5.3 is very similar. It also represents a schedule for when to make each of the five parts based on lead times that include move and queue times.

One form of shop-floor control is to prepare operation set-back charts similar to Figure 5.3 for each job, and use them plus the kind of data presented as Figure 5.3 to prepare Gantt charts such as those in Figure 5.4. That is, the objective is to prepare a schedule for each machine center. This schedule can be based on the assumptions in either the top or bottom half of Figure 5.4, i.e., the schedule may or may not use lead times that include queue and move times.

The more usual practice is to prepare the detailed work center schedule *without* move and queue times. Many firms have systems that do this. The typical approach is a *schedule board* with racks to hold pieces of paper. Each paper is a job and its length represents the time required.

The primary problem with this kind of system is in updating. Actual data must be captured and integrated into an ongoing cycle of replanning. Moreover, a means of communication with the shop floor is usually required since the schedule boards typically reside in planning offices.

Priority sequencing rules

Priority sequencing rules are concerned with which job to run next at a work center. To some extent, these rules can be thought of as producing a loading of jobs onto individual machines, but usually only one job is committed at a time. That is, the job to run *next* is only determined near to the time when the prior job has been completed. The priority sequencing rule is just what the name suggests: a *rule* for what job to process next.

Many different priority sequencing rules have been established. A fairly common one is to base priorities on the type of data contained in Figure 5.3. The lower half of that figure contains scheduled due dates for parts and operations. These due dates can be used as priorities. For example, a priority rule could be: the job to process next is the job with the earliest operation due date. An alternative is to next process the job with the earliest *part* due date. Four other commonly used sequencing rules are:

- Order slack: Sum the setup times and run times for all remaining operations, subtract this from the time remaining (now until the part due date), and call the remainder slack. The rule is to work on that job with the least slack. This rule addresses the problem of work remaining.
- Slack per operation: A variant of order slack is to divide the slack by the number of remaining operations, again taking next the job with the smallest value. The concept of slack per operation is that it will be more difficult to complete jobs with more operations because they will have to be scheduled through more work centers.
- Critical ratio: a rule based on the following ratio:

$$\frac{\text{Time remaining}}{\text{Work remaining}}$$

For calculation, the rule is expressed as:

$$\frac{\text{Due date—Now}}{\text{Lead time remaining (including setup, run, move, and queue)}}$$

If the ratio is 1.0, the job is on time. A ratio less than 1.0 indicates a behind-schedule job, while greater than 1.0 indicates an ahead-of-schedule condition. The rule is to always process that job with the smallest critical ratio next.

- Shortest operation next: This rule ignores all due date information as well as all information about work remaining. It simply says take that job next which can be completed in the shortest time at the work center. This rule maximizes the number of shop orders that go through a work center—and minimizes the number waiting in queue.

In a computerized MRP system, each shop order would be a scheduled receipt for the part. As such, the scheduled receipt has a due date. From this due date, operational due dates could be established by backing off expected operation times if these data are needed to establish priority sequence. The great advantage of this computer based system is that whenever the due date for a scheduled receipt changes, the operation due dates can be changed accordingly. These changes, in turn, lead to priority changes for shop-floor control; the result is an execution system that works on the most needed shop orders first. The objective is for high-priority jobs to move through the shop very quickly, while low-priority jobs are set aside. In this way, the shop-floor control system can indeed execute the dictates of MRP.

In a computer based shop-floor control system, due dates would not be printed on any shop paper that travels with the work-in-process inventory. The shop paper would show the routing or sequence of operations (static data), but not any due dates. The changing (dynamic) due date information would be printed daily in the form of a work center schedule or dispatch list for each work center. It is the dispatch list, not the traveling paper, that shows the priority sequence. The dispatch list can be updated as rapidly as transactions are processed to the MRP data base. The daily dispatch list is, in fact, only one option. It is also possible to keep the data even more current, using cathode-ray tubes for on-line query as to which jobs to run next.

Finite loading

Finite loading systems simulate actual job order starting and stopping to produce a detailed schedule for each shop order and each work center. That is, finite loading does, in fact, *load* all jobs in all necessary work centers for the length of the planning horizon. The result is a set of start and finish dates for each operation at each work center. This schedule is based on the finite capacity limits at each work center. In essence, it is the equivalent of one of the alternative schedules shown in the bottom half of Figure 5.4, but includes *all* of the jobs scheduled for that work center.

Finite loading explicitly establishes a detailed schedule for each job through each work center based on work center capacities and the other jobs that are scheduled. Priority sequencing rules do not consider the work center capacities or the other jobs to be scheduled. For this reason, the priority rules are employed with capacity planning techniques that are based on infinite loading, techniques like resource profiles or capacity requirements planning.

The difference between finite loading and infinite loading is illustrated by Figure 5.5. The top half shows an infinite load for work center 101 as it might be produced by capacity requirements planning (CRP). The lower half of Figure 5.5 shows the capacity profile that would result from finite loading. This result, i.e., the capacity profile, is *not* the objective of finite loading; it is the result of scheduling each job through work centers, but never scheduling more work in a center than the center's capacity.

The finite loading approach will only schedule work in a work center up to its capacity. Thus, the 75 hours of work shown as past due in the top half of Figure 5.5 would be scheduled in week 1 under finite loading techniques. Finite loading does not solve the undercapacity problem illustrated in the top half of Figure 5.5. If the capacity is not increased, only 80 hours of work will come out of this work center each week, regardless of the scheduling

FIGURE 5.5 Infinite versus finite loading (CRP profile for work center 101)

CRP Profile for work center 101

Hours

120

80

40

Capacity

Past due 1 2 3 4 5 6 7 8

Weeks

Finite load capacity profile

Hours

80

40

1 2 3 4 5 6 7 8 9 10

Weeks

Open shop orders

Planned orders

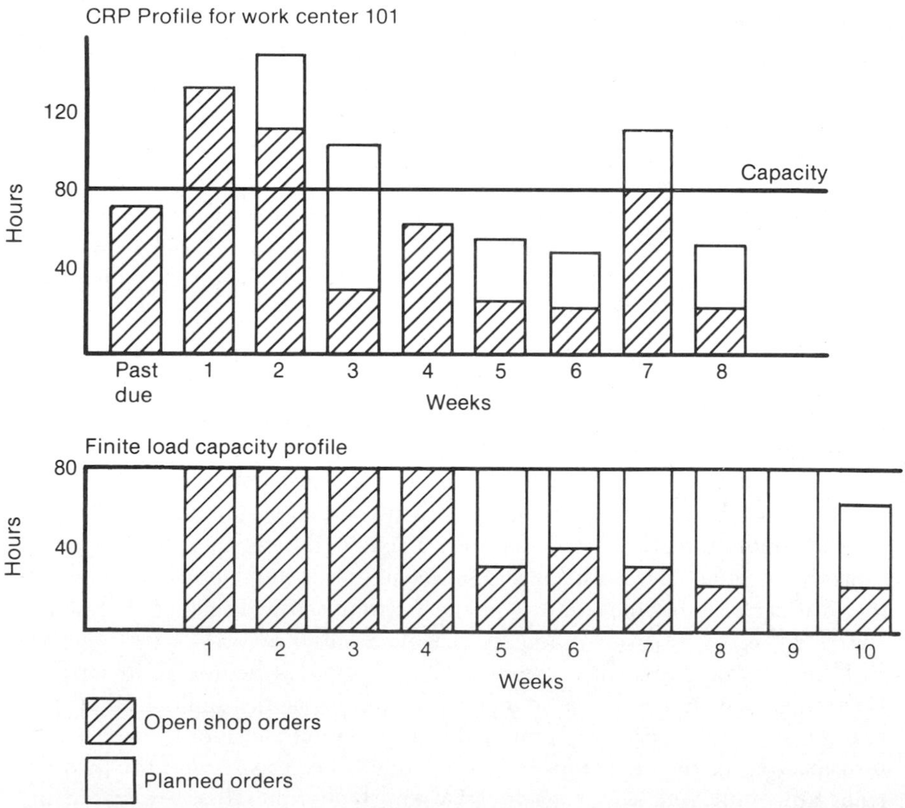

procedure. Finite loading will determine which jobs will come out, based upon priorities.

One output of finite loading is a simulation of how each machine center will operate on a minute-by-minute basis for whatever time horizon is simulated. In one approach to finite loading, the simulated running of work center 101 would proceed as follows, beginning on Monday morning. Assume there is a job already in process, and there are 150 pieces left with a standard time of one minute per piece. Thus, this order would consume the first 150 minutes of capacity; if work started at 8:00 A.M., the machine is loaded until 10:30 A.M. The finite loading system would then select the next order to schedule on the machine, taking account of setup time and run time. This process would be repeated, to simulate the entire working day, then the next day, and so on.

The selection of the next job to schedule is not just based on those jobs that are physically waiting at the work center. Most finite loading systems look at the jobs coming to the work center, when they will be completed at the prior centers, and what priorities these jobs have to decide whether to leave the work center idle and immediately available for the arrival of a particular job. Also, some systems would overlap the operations, so that a job might start at a work center before the completion of all work at the prior center.

The approach of filling a work center job by job is called *vertical loading*. It is consistent with the way most job shop scheduling research is conducted, as well as with the priority scheduling viewpoint. That is, one looks at a work center such as our example center 101, and decides which of a set of jobs (both those at the work center and those scheduled to have had their prior operations processed by the time of the loading) to load next. Another approach is often used for finite loading. It is called *horizontal loading*. In this case, one entire shop order or job (that job with the highest priority) is loaded for all of its operations, then the next highest priority job, and so on. This horizontal approach may well be at odds with a criterion of using a machine center to its maximum capacity. By creating detailed schedules with horizontal loading, the net result can be "holes" in the capacity for a work center. What this implies is that at times a machine is to sit idle, even if a job is available, because a more important job is coming.

Returning to part D in Figure 5.3, we can illustrate the horizontal loading approach. Part D would first be loaded onto work center 101 whenever the previously loaded job is scheduled to be completed. Part D will be scheduled for completion 1.8 days later. At that time, it will be loaded onto work center 109, again as soon as this work center is available. If the prior job at work center 109 has already been completed, this work center will remain idle until part D is completed at work center 101. Finally, part D would be similarly loaded onto work center 103.

Suppose that the next job to be loaded after part D was for part Q, and that the work on part Q commenced in work center 109. Let us also say that in scheduling part D, the result was idle time at work center 109. *If* (and only if) it were possible to schedule part Q into that idle time *without* disturbing the part D schedule, this would be done.

In addition to the horizontal-vertical distinction, there is also the issue of front scheduling versus back scheduling. The back-scheduling approach would take the job backward from its due date. If the resultant schedule indicates that the *start* date has already passed, one has an infeasible schedule for that job. The front-scheduling approach would load the order in as soon as capacity was available in each work center, and thereby determine the expected *completion* date. If the date is beyond the due date, infeasibility is again indicated. The net result is the need for corrective action.

In either horizontal or vertical loading, there is always the choice of which job to schedule next at a work center. The computer uses priority information somewhat like that used in priority scheduling. The same data (due dates, lead times, etc.) are available, but most finite loading systems can also use managerial weighting factors to augment the other data. These factors are typically used to reflect the urgency of particular orders, the importance of the customer, the nature of the work centers through which the job will travel, and so on.

If the finite loading system were run on a Sunday night, the schedules set for a particular work center for Monday should be reasonably accurate. Part of a particular machine center's capacity may already be allocated to a job in process, and perhaps the other jobs to be scheduled are already waiting in queue at the machine center. However, the schedules for Tuesday must deal with Tuesday's expected starting conditions. Moreover, the jobs scheduled for Tuesday are more likely to come from another work center rather than already being at the work center. Differences between the simulated operations and actual operations in those centers will be reflected in the actual job arrivals at the work center. These uncertainties on the shop floor mean that there will be a decay in information validity that grows as the time horizon for the schedule is lengthened.

One way to overcome this decay is to redo the simulation (finite loading) more often. If it is done each night, the next day's plan will be more accurate. The problem with doing finite loading every night is the cost. Finite loading can easily take 10 times as much computer run time as shop-floor control by priority scheduling.

Because finite loading only schedules a work center up to its capacity (and tries to schedule it up to the limit), it will often be true that matching parts have inconsistent due dates. In our example, assembly A is made up of parts B and C. The due dates for both B and C would be identical under MRP. If part B is delayed for two weeks at some work center, there is no reason to rush completion of part C. Finite loading cannot take explicit account of these product structure relationships in the scheduling process. The use of priority information other than MRP due dates can compound this problem.

Proponents of finite loading point to its ability (over CRP) to yield a better forecast of the actual load on each machine center in the near term, say the next few weeks. Although there will be inaccuracies, by simulating the exact flow of orders, the result should be far superior to that based on average queue times. Moreover, the finite loading system will be better than priority scheduling systems for looking out a week or two, because finite systems schedule orders that are one or more work centers away, as well as those at the work center.

The problem of competition between MRP priorities and finite loading, as well as the potential for abusing managerially set priorities, have led many authorities to believe that finite loading is an improper technique that should not be used. The counterargument is that a few companies have, in fact, made it work. It is *not* an easy job. Some critical organizational issues have to be addressed, and the need for accurate standard time estimates, capacities, and other kinds of data integrity is severe.

SHOP-FLOOR CONTROL EXAMPLES

In this section we show how the shop-floor control techniques have been applied in three quite different examples. Ethan Allen has a relatively simple product line, with a small number of levels in the bill of materials, a modest number of component parts, and minimal part commonality. Moreover, one portion of their production process is a line flow. The net result is a fairly straightforward shop-floor control environment. They have implemented a manual system based on Gantt chart methods in most of their factories.

The second example is for the Twin Disc Company. Twin Disc has a large number of component parts, complex product structures, long lead times, complex part commonality, and expensive work centers that they wish to heavily utilize. They have implemented a critical ratio based priority sequencing system.

The final example we consider is Swissair. In the Swissair engine maintenance shop they have a finite loading system for shop-floor control. Each engine to be overhauled is brought in, disassembled, and inspected. It is only at this time that the required work can be determined. They create a unique routing file for each piece part, based on the inspection decisions. The result is a wide variation in the resulting capacity requirements at each work center. The firm employs a large, highly paid work force that is not easily expanded or contracted. Moreover, overtime is more difficult to schedule than is true for most firms in the United States.

The Ethan Allen shop-floor control system

The Ethan Allen Company manufactures and sells home furniture. Production of wood furniture comes from 14 factories which are geographically dispersed. The product line comprises about 1,400 items, which can be further condensed into 980 consolidated item numbers (different finishes for the same item). With 980 end items, each made to stock, the average number of products per factory is only about 70. In fact, some plants make as few as 17 end items while others manufacture as many as 150. The plants with longer product lines tend to have larger numbers of slow-moving items. The result is that for most factories, the number of items in production at any one time is small, say 5 to 30 items. The average number of component parts per end item is only about 40, with a large percentage purchased, so the number of open shop orders for component parts at any one time is in the low hundreds for most factories. Furthermore, the number of operations per order is not large; a standard series of production line steps results in boards of uniform thickness, length, and width. These typically go through only two or three more operations before becoming completed parts. The sum total of all this is a shop scheduling environment that is not overly complex in terms of the number of orders and operations to be scheduled.

Figure 5.6 is a hypothetical item, in this case a shelf, produced at one of the Ethan Allen factories. Figure 5.6 also shows the necessary component parts for this shelf, and Figure 5.7 shows the Gantt-chart-based schedule for the item. Ethan Allen calls this operation set-back chart a "back schedule" because each part is scheduled backwards in time from the desired date for the part to go into the ready-to-assemble inventory (RTA). The RTA stage plays a key role in the Ethan Allen system. This step is designed to achieve proper order closeout for component parts. It also provides a one-week safety lead time.

We now take as an example one part of the shelf, the side (B). Figure 5.8 shows routing information for side B with the lead time for each operation and the total lead time. As seen in Figure 5.8, there are six operations

FIGURE 5.6 Ethan Allen product example: shelves

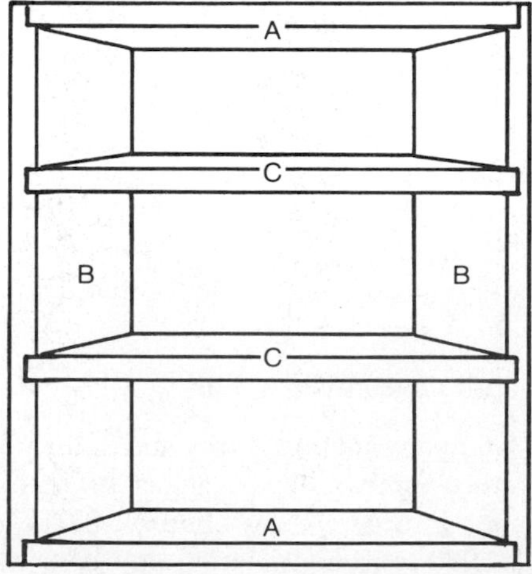

FIGURE 5.7 The Ethan Allen back schedule

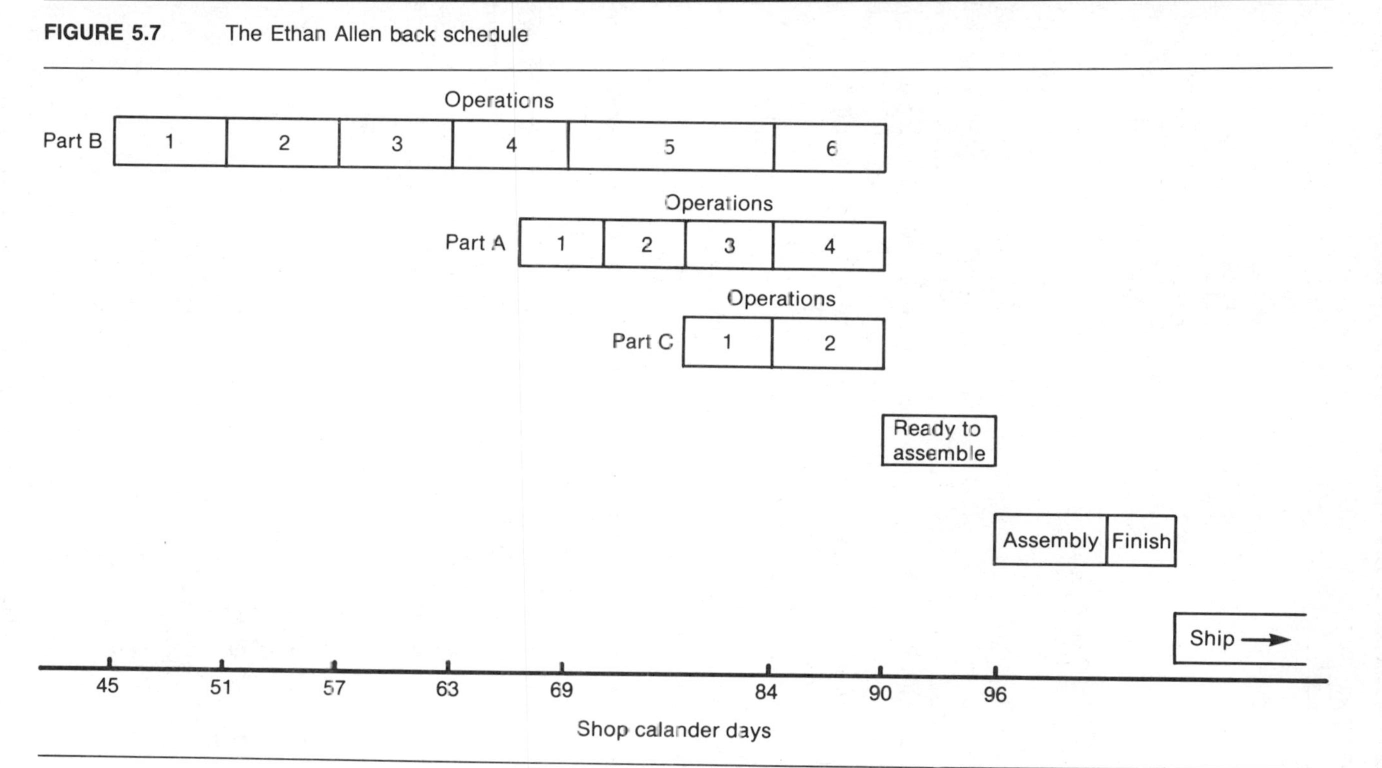

FIGURE 5.8 Routing—side B

Operation	Lead time*
1 Cut to length	1 Week
2 Surface	1 Week
3 Rip	1 Week
4 Surface	1 Week
5 Dado—4 places	2½ Weeks
6 Sand	1 Week

*Consisting of setup time, run time, move time, and queue time.

required to fabricate a side. Figure 5.9 shows the set of shop tickets that correspond to these six operations. In practice, a blank copy of Figure 5.9 is kept in the files, with a copy made for each lot manufactured. Whenever a batch of shelves is to be built, the appropriate due date for each of its component parts, including the side, is taken from the back schedule (Figure 5.7) with the desired assembly date. The due dates for each operation are calculated and handwritten on the shop tickets. There would be one set of shop tickets such as those shown in Figure 5.9, which would travel with each batch of each component part.

To show how the operational due dates are calculated for the shop tickets, let us assume that the factory wished to assemble 100 shelves in shop week

FIGURE 5.9 Shop paper for side B

Side B	Side B
1 Cut to length Quantity ____________ Due date ____________	2 Surface Quantity ____________ Due date ____________
Side B 3 Rip Quantity ____________ Due date ____________	Side B 4 Surface Quantity ____________ Due date ____________
Side B 5 Dado Quantity ____________ Due date ____________	Side B 6 Sand Quantity ____________ Due date ____________

272, that the beginning of that week is shop calendar day 96, and that the shop calendar is based upon six-day working weeks. Use of a shop calendar allows ease of calculation of due dates. Signs in the shop remind all workers of what the current shop day is. The resultant operational due dates for side B would be:

Operation	*Due date*
1	51
2	57
3	63
4	69
5	84
6	90

Sets of shop tickets are created for each batch of component parts, and the resultant orders are issued to the shop according to when they are needed. For example, the side has a due date of 51 for its first operation, cut to length. Since the operation is expected to take six days, this job should ideally be released to the first operation on day 45.

An upside down T-shaped block of wood, called a tilt-up, is placed on top of each batch of component parts. It has clips on both sides of the vertical portion. One clip holds all of the shop tickets in operation sequence. The other is used when an operation has been completed. At that time, the ticket corresponding to the completed operation is removed from the front clip, put on the back clip, and the tilt-up is tipped over. On the bottom it says "move me." A materials handler roams the plant, looking for tilt-ups that indicate movement. When delivered to the department or work center indicated by the next ticket, the back ticket is removed from the load and given to the production control person.

At each work center, the priority sequence rule is to always work on the load with the earliest due date showing on a tilt-up, unless the plant superintendent gives permission to do otherwise. This allows for some deviations to minimize setup or change-over times. These decisions are not left to the workers and first-line supervisors. Their priorities for which job to work on next come from the operational due dates of the back schedule.

In a small office, a copy of each current back schedule is taped to a wall. As each operation is completed, the corresponding portion of the Gantt chart is colored in with a felt-tipped pen. A string is put on the bar chart to indicate the present shop day. Any open space to the left of the string indicates a behind-schedule condition. Any area colored in to the right of the line indicates an ahead-of-schedule condition. By visually reviewing the schedule wall, any scheduling problem can be readily identified.

The exact system described here was implemented in one of Ethan Allen's supplier plants in approximately one month at a critical point in their history. The cash-flow situation was critical, with no ready alternative for additional funding. The system was implemented and the result was a reduction in work-in-process inventory of approximately $300,000. A further reduction was obtained after the system had been in operation for about two years, by decreasing the lead time allowed for each operation. Each job went through production faster, spending less time waiting between operations. The result was reduced work in process, reduced lead time, and better responsiveness to actual customer orders. The system was fully maintained by two people, who prepared all back schedules, routing, and shop tickets. They also monitored shop order progress and updated the schedule wall. This firm had annual sales of approximately $5 million and employed about 200 people.

The key limitation of this shop-floor control system is that the operational due dates are static. That is, all back-schedule due dates are based on the date at which each assembly order is to be started, which is fixed. If, for any reason, one wanted to change this date, all shop papers would have to be physically changed in terms of operational due dates. By freezing the master production schedule for eight weeks out, this problem has been minimized at Ethan Allen.

Critical ratio scheduling at Twin Disc

Twin Disc, Incorporated is a manufacturer of small-lot, heavy-duty transmission equipment. The products are designed to customer specifications, produced in small lots, and range in unit price from several hundred dollars to over $10,000. Annual sales were approximately $200 million at the time of this writing, with more than one half being to four large customers.

The size of the data base for shop-floor scheduling at Twin Disc is considerably larger than that at Ethan Allen. The number of open shop orders is usually about 3,500. Each order typically passes through 10 to 15 operations, and there are more than 300 different machine centers. The average product is made up of approximately 200 parts, and the total part master data base includes about 60,000 separate part numbers.

Twin Disc installed their MRP system in 1964. In 1970, the critical ratio scheduling system was implemented. The MRP system was well understood at that time, and provided the proper basis for updating the priorities for individual shop orders. Let us now see how this shop-floor scheduling system works.

Figure 5.10 is the daily work center schedule. This report is printed during each night, so it is available to the foremen at the beginning of every working day. The sample report shown as Figure 5.10 was printed for February 6, which was Wednesday of manufacturing week 446. (The manufacturing calendar is based on a five-day week.) It is for the BH machine center which is in plant 3, department 5. This machine center works two shifts, and has a weekly rated capacity of 110.9 hours.

FIGURE 5.10 Twin Disc shop-floor control report

DATE 02/06/ DAILY WORK CENTER JOB SCHEDULE WEEK 446 DAY WEDNESDAY

PLANT 03 DEPT 05 MACH. CTR. BH SHIFTS WORKED 2.0 CAPACITY 110.9

PART # ①	PART NAME ②	ORDER # ③	OP # ④	OPER DESC ⑤	-PRIORITY- PO ⑥	PI ⑦	QTY OF OP ⑧	QTY AT OP ⑨	HOURS ⑩	NEXT LOCATION ⑪	WORK REM. ⑫	TIME REM. ⑬
209335H	IMP WHL	@ 438C34	020	FIN	.436		142	142	11.1	0316NB	18.3	8.0
216140A	SPINNER	445C22	010	TURN	1.236		88	88	6.4	0305BQ	18.6	23.0
209308C	IMP WHL	445C67	020	FACE		.430	212	212	16.7	0316NB	18.5	8.0
A 4639A	CARRIER	445B45	010	TURN		2.675	54	54	5.4	**SAME**	8.5	23.0
A 4639A	CARRIER	445B45	020	FACE		2.675	54		5.4	0305YE	6.3	23.0
B 1640A	RETAINER	441B22	010	FACE		4.106	108	108	7.3	0305EG	10.4	43.0
TOTAL HOURS IN THIS MACHINE CENTER									52.3			
PARTS IN PREVIOUS WORK CENTER										PREVIOUS		
208346	IMP WHL	443C31	010	TURN	.437		27	27	4.7	0316NBR	18.2	8.0
203587E	FW PILOT	@ 444C98	010	SEMI-TURN	.462		28	28	4.3	0316NBR	17.3	8.0
208346G	IMP WHL	446A09	010	TURN	.742		250	250	15.4	0316NBR	24.2	18.0
208346A	IMP WHL	446A07	010	TURN	.907		1234	1234	62.2	0316NBR	36.3	33.0
209335H	IMP WHL	@ 446A10	010	TURN	1.388		141	141	11.1	0316NBR	20.1	28.0
B 5164	RETAINER	445C90	020	TURN		2.006	98	98	6.1	0305BQ	11.4	23.0
A 4639B	CARRIER	446B17	010	TURN		2.215	255	255	12.6	0316NBR	10.3	23.0
208457B	IMPELLER	444A44	010	TURN		3.632	10	10	4.1	0316NBR	10.4	38.0
208346C	IMP WHL	446A08	010	TURN		4.105	50	50	5.8	0316NBR	20.2	83.0
TOTAL HOURS FOR THIS MACHINE CENTER IN PREVIOUS CENTERS									126.3			

Source: E. S. Buffa and J. G. Miller, *Production-Inventory Systems: Planning and Control*, 3d ed. (Homewood, Ill.: Richard D. Irwin, 1979), p. 597.

The report is divided into two parts. The top portion shows six orders which are presently at the BH work center, and the lower portion shows those orders which are one work center away from BH. That is, the shop orders at the bottom of the page are not now physically at BH, but their routings indicate that when they are completed at their present work center location, they will be moved to BH for the next operation.

The first two columns on the report are the number and part name. The third column is the shop order number. The fourth and fifth columns are the operation number (i.e., its routing sequence) and a description of the operation. The priority numbers shown in columns 6 and 7 are more easily explained after we discuss the other data. Column 8 shows the quantity that is associated with the shop order, while column 9 shows the quantity that is physically at the work center. This distinction facilitates operation overlapping. Column 10 shows the hours that each of the shop orders is expected to take in the BH center. Notice that this column is totaled for both the jobs in the machine center and for the jobs that are one center away. Column 11 shows where each shop order will go when it leaves BH for those jobs at BH, and where each order is for those jobs coming to BH.

Columns 12 and 13 show the work remaining and time remaining for each shop order. In both cases, the figures are stated in days. The time remaining is calculated by subtracting today's date from the due date shown for each of the shop orders as a scheduled receipt in the appropriate MRP record. For example, if one were to go to the time-phased MRP record for part number 209335H, one would find at least two scheduled receipt quantities; one would be for 142 pieces. Although the record might be printed in weekly time buckets, the convention would be to give it a due date of Friday in week 447. The five days of week 447 plus Wednesday, Thursday and Friday of week 446 yield eight days remaining until this shop order is due to be closed out into inventory. This scheduled receipt for 142 pieces would be pegged to shop order 438C34. A second scheduled receipt for part 209335H would be for 141 pieces, due on Friday of week 451. This order (446A10) is shown as the fifth job in the list of orders one machine center away, with 28 days of time remaining. There could be other open shop orders for part number 209335H as well, but, if so, they are not at BH or at one work center previous to BH.

The work remaining column (12) represents the lead time remaining to complete each order (18.3 days for the first order). This includes setup time, run time, move time, and queue time between operations. We can now define the critical ratio priorities shown as columns 6 and 7:

$$\text{Priority} = \frac{\text{Time remaining}}{\text{Work remaining}}$$

We see there that for the first shop order (8.0/18.3 = .436). This means that this shop order will have to be completed in 43.6 percent of the normal lead time. If this job is not run today, tomorrow's schedule will show a time remaining of 7, and a critical ratio of 7/18.3 = .383. Any order that has a critical ratio priority greater than 1.0 is ahead of schedule, and any priority less than 1.0 indicates a behind-schedule condition (based on total lead time values).

The distinction between columns 6 and 7, PO versus PI, is that in the former case, when the shop order is pegged all the way up through product structures, an actual customer order depends upon this particular shop order. It is a priority for *orders*. PI, on the other hand, is a priority for *inventory*. It means that at the present time no customer order promise depends upon the timely completion of this shop order. The order was issued based upon a forecast of customer orders which has not yet materialized.

The work remaining and associated priorities for the orders that are one work center away are based upon completion of the prior operations. That is, the priorities are those that would exist *if* the job were to arrive at BH today. This allows both sets of jobs to be evaluated on a common base.

The jobs are arranged on the daily work center schedule in priority sequence, PO before PI. This is the sequence that the jobs should be run in, all other things being equal. That is, the company believes in running jobs to support customer orders before those to go into stock to support a forecast, and by running the smallest critical ratio job first, relative priorities are maintained.

In interpreting the shop-floor control report, a foreman knows that a critical ratio of .436 is not a severe problem, providing that *all* of the critical ratios are not less than 1.0. What will happen is that this order will be near the top of the list in each work center schedule as it passes through its routing steps. Since this means that it will be run shortly after arriving at the work center, or perhaps even be started *before* all of the parts are finished at the prior center (i.e., operation overlapping), the queue time will be small and the job should be completed on schedule.

The ability to see jobs that are coming enhances this ability to meet schedules. If the first job in the list of jobs one work center away (part 208346) had a priority of say .1, the BH foreman could go to the foreman in O316NBR (the current location of the job) to see whether the job in BH could be started before all of the parts have been finished in 0316NBR, and perhaps try to overlap the operation following BH, as well.

The report can also be used to sequence jobs to reduce setup times. If the order (446A10) for part number 209335H can be speeded up in 0316NBR, it can be combined on the same setup with order 438C34. Or perhaps running all (or most) of the impeller wheels in sequence makes sense. The report provides relative priority information to the foremen but does not preclude intelligent decision making on his part. The extent to which the foremen can make decisions at variance with the shop-floor control report should be carefully defined. The key is to provide discretion—but not at the expense of missing due dates.

We have already shown how the priority data change on a daily basis, as the time remaining (numerator) grows smaller while the lead time remaining (denominator) stays constant. If a job is not completed, its relative priority will increase as it competes against other jobs for the available work center capacity.

The CAPOSS system at Swissair

Swissair operates approximately 50 aircraft on a worldwide basis. Major maintenance is centralized in Zürich, Switzerland in the Engineering and Maintenance Department (E & M). Approximately 2,600 people are employed in E & M. Swissair also does considerable maintenance work for other airlines.

CAPOSS is an IBM finite scheduling program. The acronym stands for capacity planning and operations sequencing system. The CAPOSS system is used at Swissair for scheduling the engine shop. This shop is responsible for the overhaul of all engines and for the repair of other parts that require operations on engine shop machine tools. The engine shop employs approximately 400 people.

The primary problem in scheduling the engine shop is that more than 60 percent of the repair work on an engine is not definitively known until the engine has been disassembled and inspected. CAPOSS is one of the systems that helps to respond to this inherent level of uncertainty.

Before examining the CAPOSS system itself, it is necessary to briefly overview some other systems and activities which precede it. When an engine is brought in for overhaul, it is disassembled, cleaned, and inspected—all in the minimum time possible. The inspection of a subassembly involves physical measurement and other activities as dictated by detailed maintenance procedures. These procedures originate with the equipment manufacturers. They are translated into German and modified to match Swissair equipment standards. The entire process is done with computerized text editing and is integrated with the overall maintenance control system (MCS) data base.

An inspector uses a video terminal to review the necessary maintenance procedures. Based upon tests and measurements, the inspector determines the necessary repair steps for the subassembly and components. This process is, in essence, the determination of a unique routing file for each part and assembly. These data are essential for CAPOSS. The use of interactive computing allows the routing files to be established quickly. A set of shop papers is immediately printed and attached to the work piece. MCS also keeps track of which parts belongs to which engine.

A production control group working for the engine shop decides whether a particular part is to be reworked to go back into the same engine or a replacement is to be used. This decision is based upon rework requirements, time availability, capacity loads, replacement part availability, and dictates of the manufacturer.

An engine is defined as being made up of 10 modules. Based upon the completion date for the overall engine, due dates are established for when all the parts of any module are required. These are the due dates by which all parts in that module are to be reworked and are one key input to CAPOSS.

Another key input to CAPOSS is the *external priority*. This is a number from 0 to 9, indicating a production control person's priority to be assigned to this order. It represents a subjective input as to how critical this shop order is relative to other orders.

The CAPOSS system first loads each order with infinite capacity loading assumptions, based on operation times plus standard interoperation times (representing move and queue times). If the resultant completion time is greater than the due date for the reworked parts, a delay factor is computed to augment the external priority. Another step is to reduce the move and queue times. This is based on how late the parts are and can result in interoperation times being shortened by as much as 50 percent. After this, the external priorities are combined with move and queue time reductions to produce a new priority number. This priority number is used to pick the job sequence for horizontal finite loading for all the jobs through their required work centers.

The system is run daily on an IBM 370-168 computer. One output is a schedule of all jobs in each worker center. This serves the same function as a daily dispatch report for shop-floor control. Since the outputs are in German, they are not reproduced here. This listing goes to a production control person assigned to each work center grouping. It is this person's job to actually schedule the work. He or she attempts to combine similar jobs (note that a shop order is issued for each part), attempts to assign jobs to workers best able to do the work, etc. The schedule shows what jobs are in the center as well as those not there. The work center production control person also makes sure that all transactions are accurately entered into the data collection system.

The CAPOSS data base is also sorted by engine. An engine shop production control group gets these data. The result is an ability to foresee part shortages. When this occurs, one typical action is to increase the external priority assigned to the particular shop order. This will result in that order being scheduled earlier on each of the next day's work center schedules.

An engine is always scheduled for overhaul in 21 working days. This time is guaranteed to the customer. The CAPOSS schedule is prepared for 15 days into the future, which is more than the time allowed for machine shop operations. For the work center scheduler, only the first few days in the schedule are of importance. For the engine scheduler, all of the time frame is important; relative priority changes are being made constantly.

At the end of the 15-day schedule, any jobs that have not been scheduled are listed in a separate report, along with their capacity requirements. These data indicate potential work center capacity problems. They are studied closely by the production control supervisor. Remedial actions include overtime, alternate routing, and the increased use of replacement parts instead of reworking parts. The production control supervisor discusses these actions with the manager of the engine shop.

THE SHOP-FLOOR CONTROL DATA BASE

Here we consider the detailed data bases and interactions of the shop-floor scheduling system with other data files and systems. We also raise some managerial issues. As we have seen, the data base for shop-floor scheduling typically includes the open shop orders (scheduled receipts from MRP) and their due dates, routing files, engineering standards or other time estimates for operation times, move and queue time data, and the work centers.

The size and complexity of each of these files varies a great deal from company to company. Some firms, such as Ethan Allen factories, deal with an open order file of less than a few hundred shop orders, whereas Twin Disc typically has 3,500 open shop orders. Similarly, the average number of operations per shop order can also vary widely. The same thing is true for the number of work centers to be scheduled. The net result is that the inherent size of the data base and the number of transactions to be processed each day can vary significantly from firm to firm; the resultant systems and supporting data bases have to reflect these complexities.

Still one other aspect of systems and data base design relates to the kind of questions that will be posed to the system. Some firms like to use their shop-floor control system to answer what if questions, such as the implication of acceptance of a particular customer order. Others use their systems to track specific orders and want to determine exact order status on a timely basis. These needs must be considered in the design of the shop-floor control system and its underlying data base. Let us now turn to a concrete example of an operating company, where the focus is on the data base and its interactions, rather than on the shop scheduling techniques.

The Black & Decker Company

Black & Decker manufactures power tools and accessories such as hand drills, circular saws, impact wrenches, and saw blades for both the consumer and industrial markets. The company's main factory is in Hampstead, Maryland. This factory has approximately 1 million square feet of floor space, annual production in excess of $200 million, and employs about 2,500 people.

The Hampstead plant has about 1,200 machines to be scheduled. The typical number of open shop orders exceeds 3,000. The end items are produced for stock, but almost 15 percent of all parts produced are for service part requirements, and the plant also produces parts for other Black & Decker plants.

The Black & Decker MRP (and related) systems were developed and implemented, starting in 1970. Within five years, the valuation of work-in-process inventory had dropped by 21 percent, while production increased at 10 to 20 percent each year. Job completions on schedule improved by 35 percent, and lead times for components dropped by 30 percent. By 1977, the average shop lead times had been reduced from 6 weeks to 2.9 weeks.

SCOPE and PACE. Figure 5.11 shows the primary data base for the Black & Decker manufacturing control systems, and the two main programs which interact with the data base, SCOPE and PACE. SCOPE is an acronym meaning: *S*cheduling and *C*ontrol of *O*rders for *P*roduction *E*conomy. PACE stands for *P*lanned *A*ction and *C*onstant *E*valuation. PACE is the MRP system and SCOPE is the shop-floor system. Parenthetically, Figure 5.11 can be easily compared to Figure 5.1. The finished goods inventory status files are part of the front end, PACE is the engine, and SCOPE is the back end.

SCOPE is the set of computer programs for shop-floor scheduling to execute the plans developed by PACE. SCOPE also has the job of maintaining certain portions of the overall data base. The functions of SCOPE are to:

Schedule orders and plan work center loads.

Coordinate and stage the material for each order.

Release orders to work centers with correct priorities for released orders.

FIGURE 5.11 Black & Decker manufacturing control systems

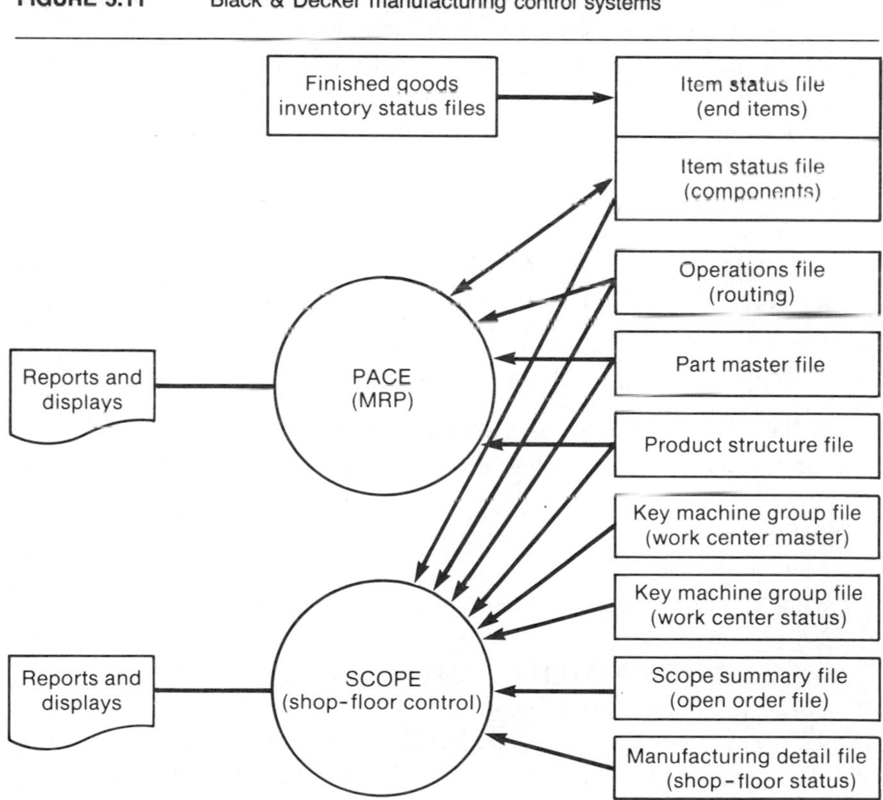

Source: R. W. Hall and T. E. Vollmann, "Black & Decker: Pioneer with MRP," in *Case Studies in Materials Requirements Planning,* ed. E. W. Davis (Falls Church, Va.: American Production and Inventory Control Society, 1978), p. 35.

Monitor and control the flow of orders and maintain order priorities.
Maintain order status data.

The SCOPE system is based on the files shown in Figure 5.11. Those that directly interact with SCOPE are:

ITEM STATUS FILES (COMPONENTS). This file is essentially all of the data necessary to prepare MRP time-phased records.

OPERATIONS FILE (ROUTING). This file keeps all the routing data for each fabricated component part.

PART MASTER FILE. This file keeps all of the data for defining each part number. Included are part number, where used, description, low-level code, unit of measure, engineering change status, order policy, lead time, safety stock, planner code, etc.

PRODUCT STRUCTURE FILE. This file is the bill of materials and related data.

KEY MACHINE GROUP FILE (WORK CENTER MASTER). This file contains all of the work centers, as well as related data such as hours worked per day and hourly capacity per week.

KEY MACHINE GROUP FILE (WORK CENTER STATUS). This file keeps the dynamic data for each work center (called a key machine group) such as which jobs are there, expected jobs, loads, hours ahead, actual results, and backlog.

SCOPE SUMMARY FILE (OPEN ORDER FILE). This file contains all of the scheduled receipts (shop orders) and their present status.

MANUFACTURING DETAIL FILE (SHOP-FLOOR STATUS). This file retains all of the daily transactions for dispatching and labor reporting, e.g., which jobs were worked on, quantities completed, etc.

The SCOPE system in operation consists of the following 10 programs:

INPUT—Checks all incoming data for consistency and validity.

SCHEDULING—Establishes a detailed schedule file for each shop order.

MACHINE LOAD—Generates a projected four-week detailed load for each work center.

CAPACITY PLANNING—Develops a projected 12-month load for each work center.

MATERIAL AVAILABILITY—Checks material availability two weeks ahead before issuance of shop orders.

PRIORITY DISPATCH—Prints a daily work center schedule similar to that used at Twin Disc, but not using critical ratios.

SHOP PAPER—Generates all the necessary paperwork that travels with the shop order.

STATUS UPDATE—Updates all files from daily transactions.

JOB CLOSEOUT—Closes shop orders, prepares summary data; monitors actual counts and actual times.

WORK IN PROCESS—Collects actual costs of closed orders and prepares various data.

Operation/execution of the SCOPE system is similar to that discussed in the Twin Disc example. As at Twin Disc, the priorities are maintained through interaction between the shop-floor scheduling and MRP programs. We have focused on the Black & Decker example as an effective system for maintaining (in great detail) the data on the shop floor. In fact, Black & Decker regard the job of managing the material flows as "management *by* the data base and management *of* the data base."

USING THE SHOP-FLOOR CONTROL SYSTEM

The managerial challenge in shop-floor control is to design, implement, and maintain the right system and data base for the company. The design must take account of the inherent complexity of shop scheduling at that firm, as well as of any indirect barriers to implementation such as an incentive wage system which fosters incorrect reporting. Implementation must also consider the necessary organizational changes, educational requirements, and necessary procedural reforms to achieve data base accuracy.

We have presented several examples that show the necessary match between company conditions and SFC system design. In this section, we consider this issue explicitly. Performance measurement is considered next: Is the SFC system doing what it was designed to do? We then turn to management of lead time—one of the least understood elements of SFC operations. Finally, we discuss some key organizational and management issues facing SFC system users.

Matching the SFC system to the company

We see three critical factors in the design of a specific SFC system. The first relates to the firm's strategic posture in the market. The second factor is the amount and kind of capacity provided for executing the material plans. The third key factor is the nature and complexity of the product, and the process by which the product is produced.

The strategic posture of the company should define the operational objectives of the SFC system. In most of the chapter examples, there is a high implicit customer service objective, which focuses SFC system design on timely production. If a company chooses to compete on the basis of price, however, the primary objective of the SFC system might be to provide high resource utilization. These two objectives, high customer service and high resource utilization, may not be mutually attainable.

There is a close relationship between strategic posture and the amount of capacity provided. In turn, the capacity issue affects the design of the SFC system. One of the costs of providing high levels of customer service may be excess, or highly flexible capacity. An alternative may be a better SFC system. In some market situations, there may be little choice but to provide high service levels. The goal for SFC design in this type of environment is often high flexibility; how to respond to customer needs as quickly as possible. An SFC system that is inherently oriented toward high utilization should not be used. There is no conflict between carrying excess capacity and using it effectively (as opposed to completely).

In some cases, when capacity levels are high relative to demand, the need for a sophisticated SFC system is reduced. When capacity is in short supply, the SFC alternatives have little impact on *average* output rates, but the output of *particular* high-priority jobs can be increased. The key need is to define objectives before finalizing the SFC system design. If capacity is deemed inflexible, the use of finite loading may be indicated, as was the case with Swissair, but finite loading makes less sense if there is surplus capacity.

A concept closely related to the capacity issue is the appropriate unit for shop-floor scheduling. For many firms, it is a group of laborers who get assigned, as needed, to several machines or work centers. In other cases, it may be a unique aggregation of machines that does not match any other work center definition.

The last critical factor in matching the SFC system to the company is the basic product and process design. We saw that Ethan Allen's shallow product structures and short flow times enabled them to use a manual system with static due dates. With more complicated product structures, there is simply too much data for a manual static system to keep synchronized.

The manufacturing process has several attributes that are important in considering SFC alternatives. One is flexibility, a second is speed of manufacture, and still another is the degree to which all products go through the same sequences (flow shop). If the shop is highly flexible, then alternative routing, operation overlapping, and other techniques can be used, but keeping track of things is more difficult. This may call for greater SFC system sophistication. If the products essentially go through a fixed sequence of steps or through the shop quickly, simple systems may work. The Twin Disc system is designed for long processing times through a variety of routings. Murphy's law has much more time to operate, and the system must respond to all its foibles.

If the operations are long, say weeks, then frequent system updating with short horizons may not be necessary. *But*, if scrap is a significant issue, more frequent updating may be important. If, on the other hand, operations are very short, frequent updating may not be either possible or desirable. Some firms go from raw materials to end items in hours.

Performance measurement

Once the SFC system is in place, a key management issue becomes: Is it performing as expected? For systems with a due date orientation, the obvious measure is the extent to which due dates are met. This is *not* an average measure. Both earliness and lateness need to be taken into account. The objective is to have as small a variation around the due date as possible.

Another issue is to *which* due date performance should be pegged. Since we have seen that due dates change, most firms should be concerned with hitting revised due dates. Note, however, that this measure is highly influenced by the degree of stability in other MPC system modules.

It may be desirable to measure due date changes. Three aspects are important: the number of changes, the magnitude of the change, and any inherent bias in the change process. The more due date changes, the more shop-floor execution is complicated. It is much more difficult to change a due date by five weeks than by one. Also, jobs can't *all* be speeded up (expedited). The expedited jobs should be offset by de-expedited jobs (those given *later* due dates).

A related concept is exemplified by the average priority number in priority sequencing rule systems. For example, if *all* numbers in a critical ratio system are less than 1.0, some corrective action needs to be taken.

Resource utilization is the important objective in some SFC systems. Critical resource units need to be defined, their capacities specified, and measures found for monitoring actual results. Two other measures are work-in-process (WIP) inventory and lead time. These can be monitored in absolute magnitude as well as in terms of some other measure, e.g., percent of sales.

Lead time management

Many people think of lead time as a constant such as *pi*. In fact, it is not a value to be measured as much as a parameter to be managed. Of the four elements of lead time (setup, processing, move, and queue), the last two can be compressed with good SFC design and practice.

Lead time and WIP are directly related. Moreover, there are critical feedback linkages which operate. The longer the lead time is perceived to be, the longer the time between order launching date and due date. The longer this time, the more orders in the shop. The more orders in the shop, the longer the queue time (and WIP); we have a self-fulfilling prophecy.

Some WIP will be needed at work centers for which high utilization is important. However, a basic principle of MPC systems is to *substitute information for inventory*. The firm does not need to have jobs physically in front of machines. Orders can be held in a computer and converted to physical units only as needed. Studies reported by Plossl and Welch have shown that for many plants, setup and run time only constitute 10 to 20 percent of the total lead time. The rest is slack that can be substantially cut. George Plossl says also: "Lead times are like mini-skirts—the shorter the better."

One interesting question is how to manage lead time. This means changing data base elements for both SFC and MRP. One alternative is to go through the data base and systematically change all lead times. If they were reduced, the result could be a transient condition of dry gateway work centers. This might be a reasonable price to pay for the resulting WIP reduction.

Changing lead time data elements naturally leads to the question of how they are established in the first place. For most firms, lead time data are usually an input from some functional area such as production control. An alternative is to *calculate* lead time. When one thinks about changing lead times as part of a management process, and when one remembers that SFC lead time must be in tune with MRP lead time offset data, this approach has increasing appeal. One firm calculated lead times in the following way:

The lead time for each operation was set equal to setup plus run time (time per piece × lot size), plus queue time (which includes move time).

The non-queue time was converted to days by dividing the total hours by (7 × number of shifts), assuming 7 productive hours per shift.

The queue time was set equal to two days if the next work center in the routing was in another department, one day if it was in the same department but a different work center, and zero days if it was on the same machine.

The lead time for the total order equals the sum of operation lead times. This time is calculated with an average order quantity, rounded up to a weekly lead time, and used for MRP lead time offsetting.

The selection of the queue time is the critical element in this formula. The values were chosen by taking a sample of 50 parts and using different queue time estimates to yield lead times consistent with production control personnel opinions. The initial estimates were padded, but the company was not very concerned. Once the system was in operation, the estimates for queue times were systematically reduced, a bit at a time. The result was a managed approach to shorter lead times and reduced work in process.

Before leaving this discussion, it is useful to look at the results achieved by one firm. David A. Waliszowski says a $25 million division of Hewlett Packard reduced lead time by 70 percent and increased customer-service levels by 80 percent. This amounted to a $1.7 million reduction in work-in-process inventory and was achieved in three months.

The SFC system users

We turn now to our final issues in using a shop-floor control system. The key questions are: Precisely who is to use the SFC outputs? How are they to be used? What are the relationships between front-line supervisors, MRP planners, and other MPC system personnel?

In the discussion of critical ratio schedules at Twin Disc, we saw how the foremen used the SFC output to make detailed daily decisions which influenced their departments: what to make, when to make it, whom to assign to particular jobs, how to work with other foremen to solve material/capacity problems, etc. At Ethan Allen, the scheduling discretion of the foreman was much more limited. At Swissair, the approach is different. A production control person is assigned to groups of work centers. This person plays the key role in making the detailed daily scheduling decisions.

There is a fundamental difference between these approaches, and the difference is intimately related to the SFC system itself. A priority scheduling rule system is usually easy for first-line supervisors to understand. If they have some flexibility in how to use the system, they can become quite knowledgeable about important trade-offs. A key disadvantage of finite loading system is that they are *not* transparent to the first-line supervisors. It is difficult for them to see why schedules are as they are. Also, there is an implied centralization of authority. The detailed schedules are determined by "the computer"—and the implication is that one is less free to tinker with the results.

Within any SFC system, there are always issues that are not formally included in the analysis. Perhaps a particular job is better given to a particular worker or a particular machine. Perhaps if the sequence of jobs run on a particular machine were changed, a faster changeover could be achieved. Sometimes analysis of the schedule discloses potential late jobs, missed due dates, or poor work center utilization that could be improved. Moreover, there can always be the occasional order that must be added to the schedule.

The approach to solving these problems is twofold. First, many finite loading systems are designed to incorporate such flexibilities as alternate routings, overtime, subcontracting (a form of alternate routing), order splitting, operation splitting, operation overlapping, and preparing combinations of front and back schedules.

The second approach to resolving problems is through manual (i.e., non-programmed) intervention. A person, usually with a cathode ray tube (CRT) display, locates the order for a missing component part, traces its simulated schedule through work centers, and tries to find some way to get the component order completed faster. The way may be to use one of the flexibilities listed above—but one that was not a formal part of the computer logic. What this means is that the use of finite loading clearly recognizes that not all approaches to solving problems can be reasonably put into the computer.

The issues of precisely *who* is going to make the decisions and how much latitude that person will be given are important. A closely related question is who has the better knowledge of how to make this kind of decision? Is it the foremen who know the machines, people, and other constraints, or is it the production control staff person who knows MPC systems? This question naturally leads to several others, including the basic design of the SFC system itself. If foremen are to be the primary users, a transparent system is important. Also important are education and training for these people. In the last analysis, if information is to be traded for inventory and other kinds of slack, first-line supervision increasingly becomes a job of processing information. This may well lead to new job descriptions for first-line supervisors.

The final managerial challenge is to ensure that the formal SFC system is used—and continues to be used. All informal systems must be killed off and not allowed to reappear. No hot lists or other informal scheduling can be allowed, since these come at the cost of degradation in the formal system. In the last analysis, a successful system remains a success only if the users believe in the system and use it for problem solving because it is better than any alternative way to solve problems.

CONCLUDING PRINCIPLES

We see the following principles emerging from this chapter:

- Shop-floor control system design must be in concert with the needs of the firm.
- The shop-floor control system should support users and first-line supervisors, not supplant them.
- Organizational goals and incentives must be congruent with good SFC practice.
- Discretion and decision-making responsibilities in shop-floor control practice need to be carefully defined.
- SFC performance should be defined and monitored.
- Feedback from SFC should provide early warning and status information to other MPC modules.
- Lead times are to be managed.
- The informal system must not be allowed to supplant formal use of SFC.

REFERENCES

APICS, Operations Scheduling Seminar Proceedings, January, 1979.

Baker, Eugene F. "Flow Management: The 'Take Charge' Shop Floor Control System." *APICS 22d Annual Conference Proceedings*, 1979, pp. 169–74.

Belt, Bill. "Input-Output Planning Illustrated." *Production and Inventory Management*, 2d Quarter 1978.

Goddard, W. E. "How to Reduce and Control Lead Times." *1970 APICS Conference Proceedings*, pp. 198–205.

Hall, R. W., and T. E. Vollmann. "Black and Decker: Pioneers with MRP." In *Case Studies in Materials Requirements Planning*, ed. E. W. Davis. Falls Church, Va.: American Production and Inventory Control Society, 1978, pp. 22–47.

Lankford, R. L. "Input/Output Control: Making it Work." *1980 APICS Conference Proceedings*, pp. 419–20.

———. "Scheduling the Job Shop." *1973 APICS Conference Proceedings*, pp. 46–65.

Lockie, Colin S. "Solving Shop Floor Control Problems with Group Technology." *Canadian Association for Product and Inventory Control*, June 1981, pp. 74–80.

May, Neville. "Shop Floor Controls—Principles and Use." *APICS 24th Annual Conference Proceedings*, 1981, pp. 170–74.

Nellemann, D. O. "Shop Floor Control: Closing the Financial Loop." *1980 APICS Conference Proceedings*, pp. 308–12.

Plossl, G. W., and W. E. Welch. *The Role of Top Management in the Control of Inventory*. Reston, Va.: Reston Publishing, 1979, p. 78.

Raffish, Norm. "Let's Help Shop Floor Control." *Production and Inventory Management Review* 1, no. 7 (July 1981), pp. 17–19.

Schonberger, Richard J. "Clearest-Road-Ahead Priorities for Shop Floor Control: Moderating Infinite Capacity Loading Uneveness." *Production and Inventory Management*, 2d Quarter, 1979, pp. 17–27.

Shop Floor Control Reprints, American Production and Inventory Control Society, 1973.

Sulsner, Samuel S. "Basic Shop Floor Control." *Canadian Association for Product and Inventory Control*, June 1981, pp. 81–94.

Waliszowski, David A. "Lead Time Reduction in Multi Flow Job Shops," *1979 APICS Annual Conference Proceedings*.

Wassweiler, W. L. "Fundamentals of Shop Floor Control." *1980 APICS Conference Proceedings*, pp. 352–54.

———. "Material Requirements Planning: The Key to Critical Ratio Effectiveness." *Production and Inventory Management*, 3d Quarter 1972, pp. 89–91.

———. "Material Requirements Planning: The Key to Effective Shop Floor Control." *1973 APICS Conference Proceedings*, pp. 157–65.

———. "Shop-Floor Control." *Annual APICS Conference Proceedings*, 1977, pp. 386–91.

Whitmarsh, J. "MRP is the Only Answer." *Purchasing World*, December 1977, pp. 23–28.

6

Purchasing

It is clearly beyond the scope of this chapter to discuss the entire subject of purchasing. Instead, we concentrate on how manufacturing planning and control (MPC) systems can be integrated into the purchasing activity. The demonstrated results of effecting that integration are impressive. Vendor delivery performance improvements, reduced purchased material inventories, lower prices, sharply decreased vendor lead times, and more satisfactory relationships with vendors have all been attained. Perhaps more importantly, however, is the ability to separate the routine clerical activities from the management aspects of procurement. It is this often touted but little realized objective that allows the human resources to be devoted to the high payoff areas of purchasing.

This chapter is organized around the following five topics:

- Purchasing in MPC: How is the purchasing function integrated into a well-designed manufacturing planning and control system?
- Vendor relationships: What are the relationships that should be established with vendors and how are they monitored?
- Purchasing systems and data base: What are the purchasing systems and the underlying data base to support them?
- Organizational change: What changes are necessary to use these systems effectively?

- Results: What improvements in purchasing performance have been achieved by leading-edge companies?

The ideas in this chapter closely parallel those in Chapter 5, on shop-floor control systems. We view the management of vendor capacity as closely analogous to managing the firm's own capacity resources. Additional technical material on determining purchase order quantities, and some techniques for determining safety stock levels, are found in Chapter 17.

PURCHASING IN MANUFACTURING PLANNING AND CONTROL

Figure 6.1 is again our general model of a manufacturing planning and control (MPC) system. Purchasing is found in the back end. As an execution system, it has the same role as shop-floor control. Within the MPC system, both purchasing and shop-floor control have the objective of executing the detailed planning developed by the material and capacity planning techniques.

In many firms, for each dollar of sales, $.50 or more is spent for purchased items. The potential for improvement is profound. However, many people who work in this functional area of the firm spend the largest portion of their time on low productivity efforts—responding to continuing crises. The integration of MPC systems with purchasing permits a firm to deal more routinely with its vendors. The object is to plan and control vendor capacities through procurement; thereafter, vendor capacities are routinely scheduled in ways analogous to those used in shop-floor control.

Breadth of the purchasing function

The purchasing function encompasses a multitude of activities. Among the most important are:

- Sourcing—finding sources of supply, guaranteeing continuity in supply, ensuring alternative sources of supply, gathering knowledge of procurable resources.
- Value analysis—finding less expensive substitutes, helping to isolate areas where redesign can be particularly appropriate, trying to use more standardized components.
- Contracting—seeking quotations, evaluating quotations, negotiating, establishing relationships with vendors, evaluating vendor performance.
- Budgeting—including price planning, cash-flow forecasting, cost improvement programs, strategic planning.
- Purchasing—committing to specific purchase orders, establishing lot sizes, order releasing.
- Monitoring—controlling the open purchase orders, expediting and de-expediting, order closeout.

FIGURE 6.1 Manufacturing planning and control system

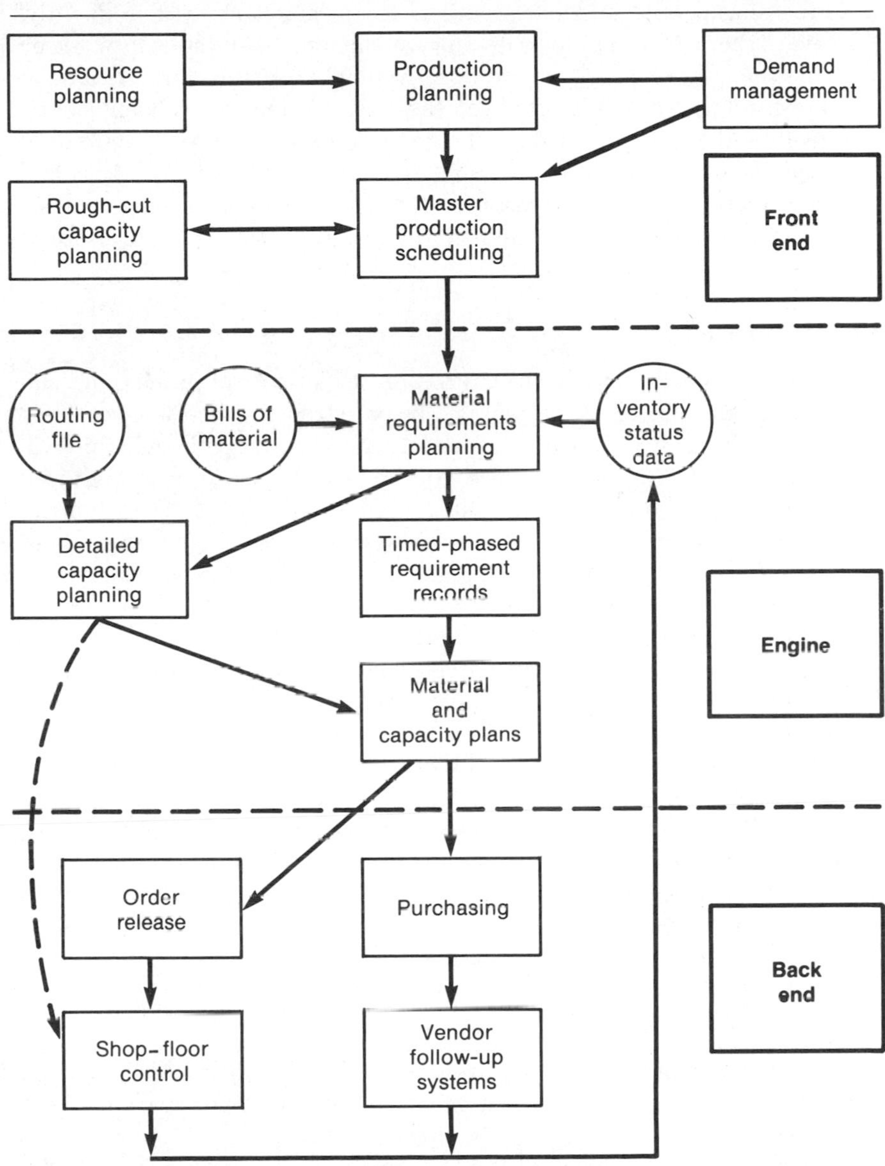

The six categories of purchasing activities listed above are arranged from those of the most long-term importance to the firm to immediate action activities that are of little strategic importance. For most firms, an analysis often indicates that vast portions of everyone's time in the purchasing organization is consumed with purchasing and monitoring. Many firms find more than 50 percent of their purchasing personnel time devoted to clerical work and expediting.

Purchasing people understand this problem and lament it frequently. However, there is an appropriate story about not being able to work on draining the swamp when you are up to your neck in alligators. As long as panic operations are required to keep the assembly line going, panic operations will be the order of the day. The key is to implement MPC systems to routinely keep the assembly line going. Thereafter, the objective is to find the way to rationalize the vast majority of decisions, to separate the vital few from the trivial many, and to eliminate the massive burden of clerical work.

The MPC focus

There have been many books written on the subject of purchasing, and we have but one chapter. Our focus will be on systems; systems for routinely controlling the flows of materials that are purchased. Although this will touch on some of the purchasing activities delineated above, it will not lead in any direct way to all of them. Our emphasis will be on the systems to provide the time and relieve the drudgery and thereafter, on using these systems effectively to implement an organizational climate in which purchasing managers can manage.

At the heart of everything in this chapter is a critical assumption: An MPC system is in place—and it works. There is basic data integrity and a match between planning and execution. The records can be believed and are used for decision making. This assumption is vital, because in many firms, the drudgery in purchasing is directly due to not being able to believe what the formal MPC system says.

To free up procurement personnel for the important tasks, it is necessary to develop routine systems for planning the purchase commitments, executing the plans, monitoring actual conditions, replanning as required, and managing the purchasing detail.

VENDOR RELATIONSHIPS

The primary objective in procurement should be to establish reliable sources of supply that effectively augment the firm's internal capacities. Vendor firms have capacities that can be utilized. Moreover, if the vendor can better utilize his capacities, the resultant savings can be passed along to the final consumer. The major savings in purchasing within an integrated manufacturing planning and control system come from reduction in slack. Slack in purchasing takes the form of larger inventories, extended lead times, extra safety stocks, more obsolete parts, extra capacities, poor vendor performance, expediting, and panic operations. All of these can be reduced if the buyer regards the vendor and his or her capacities with the same reverence extended to internal capacities. From the vendor's perspective, his or her master production schedule is made up of purchase orders and planned orders from customers. One objective of purchasing systems is to help the vendors do a better job of master production scheduling. Doing so will help them produce efficiently and on time.

Quantity planning

With a working MPC system as a given, the quantities to be purchased are clearly depicted by the MRP time-phased records. Scheduled receipts are open purchase orders. Planned orders as they mature (move into the most immediate time bucket), represent the need to issue additional purchase orders. This illustrates the close system linkages between purchasing and other MPC modules.

A key factor in slack reduction has to do with the linkage between production control and purchasing. In many companies, the former group issues orders to buy to purchasing (often called traveling requisitions). These documents are an anachronism from the days when production control was the only group close enough to the real world of the shop to estimate actual needs. This practice retards the development of purchasing as a profession. It builds in extra lead times, provides only a very short horizon, takes little account of vendor capacities or discount schedules, and leads to expediting/panic operations as the way of life.

If one can believe in the MPC system, all of the needs are shown by that system as accurately as they can be known. Murphy's law is still in operation, but the effects of all current conditions (good and bad) are reflected in the data base. Purchasing and production control have the same job: To provide material coverage for those part numbers that have been assigned, in the most effective way possible.

Providing purchasing with access to the entire MPC data base for purchased parts has many important potential advantages. The entire set of planned orders can be used to establish relationships with vendors that go well beyond a particular purchase order. The data can be converted to expected vendor capacity needs. The contractual relationship can be for the total volume, say for a year. Release of actual orders is a separate question, as is the vendor's internal decision for lot sizing.

One job of a purchasing professional is to estimate these capacity needs with the vendor, establish a relationship that, in effect, purchases some specified vendor capacity, determine the terms of the agreement, and monitor the agreement and conditions over time. The release of actual purchase orders is constrained by the agreement, and can become a fairly routine interaction between clerical people at the buying firm and clerical people at the vendor.

We have noted how MPC systems substitute information for inventory and other forms of slack. If one considers the vendor's problem of estimating the demands placed by the buying firm, an excellent example of this substitution can be seen. The vendor's forecasting system will tend to average the demand, which well may be lumpy. Safety stocks and other hedges become necessary. The information contained in the planned order rows of the buying firm's MRP records provide a much better estimate of demand. This will enable the vendor to commit short-term capacity to actual orders and to plan longer-term capacity requirements.

The effort to develop this close relationship does not make sense for all vendors. Some represent only trivial or occasional purchases to the buying firm, and others may regard the buying firm as a trivial customer. But for key purchasing relationships, the buyer should recognize that his purchase orders, as well as his planned purchase orders, should be used as a key component of the vendor's master production schedule.

Another approach to joint buyer-vendor quantity planning can be based on capacity-planning models. Many firms now work with their vendors to plan capacity for several years into the future. Old relationships based on fear of being committed to specific firms, single suppliers, or inflexible quantities are now being replaced with an understanding of the need for mutual, ongoing relationships. The benefits of these relationships can often far outweigh the expected costs of commitment, particularly under present world conditions.

The commitment between the buying firm and the vendor can take many forms, for example, the *blanket order* represents a commitment, by which a buying firm specifies some supplier for some specific items for some time period, often a year. In one form, the blanket order does not commit the firm to any specific quantities, but only provides the vendor with an estimate of needs and the commitment to buy solely from him or her, providing the terms of the contract are maintained. A more definitive buyer-vendor relationship provides a *rolling schedule* of requirements for some time period, with a definite commitment for the buying firm to accept those requirements for a given number of weeks. A variation is to commit to buy some specific product for X weeks plus the vendor's raw materials for an additional Y weeks.

In general, the vendor would prefer the more specific set of commitments. With these, capacity can be specifically committed, and reserve capacity to cover customer whims can be minimized. The key to providing these kinds of commitments is through MPC systems.

An example of this approach, providing information and making commitments to vendors, is that used by the Steelcase Company. Figure 6.2 shows a report for one of their vendors, in this case, Cannon Mills. The items purchased are fabrics for upholstered furniture. Note that all of the orders through the week of 8/26 are asterisked, which means that they are firm commitments on Steelcase's part. Also shown are orders for the next four weeks out. With many of their vendors, Steelcase would commit on these, to the extent of the vendor's investment in raw material.

FIGURE 6.2 Steelcase requirements for Cannon Mills for the week ending 07/22

ALL TAGGED ORDERS (*) ARE FIRM PAGE 1 DATE 07/22

OTHER ORDERS ARE EXPECTED DATES AND QUANTITIES RUN TIME 04-15

PART NUMBER DIV	FINISH CODE	DESCRIPTION NO. DATE BUYER	REC'D LAST WEEK	REQUIREMENTS CURRENT & PAST DUE	7/29	8/05	8/12	8/19	8/26	NEXT 4 WEEKS	FOLLOW-ING 4 WEEKS	ON-HAND	ISSUED LAST WEEK
904550000 4	5350	RED COTTON 9-0553 A 05/08/ 010				400*		400*		400		442	
904550000 4	5351	RED RED ORANGE COTTON 9-0553 A 05/08/ 010		300*	800*	800*	800*	1200*	1200*	1200	1600	359	215
904550000 4	5352	RED ORANGE COTTON 9-0553 A 05/08/ 010	415	765*	800*	800*	400*	800*	800*	400	1200	415	
904550000 4	5353	YELLOW ORANGE COTTON 9-0553 A 05/08/ 010		300* 400*	400*	400*	1200*	800*	400*	800	1200	50	118
904550000 4	5355	YELLOW COTTON 9-0553 A 05/08/ 010	402	331*			400*		400*	400	400	1804	120
904550000 4	5356	YELLOW YELLOW GREEN COTTON 9-3553 A 05/08/ 010		 200*	400*		400*		400*	400		237 237H	
904550000 4	5358	GREEN COTTON 9-0553 A 05/08/ 010				400*	400*		400*	400	400	384	64
904550000 4	5360	BLUE COTTON 9-0553 A 05/08/ 010	416	334*	400*		400*	400*		400	400	416	
904550000 4	5368	TAN VALUE 1 COTTON 9-0553 A 05/08/ 010	1445	1600* 1600*	800*	400*	800*	800*	800*	1600	1600	1502	234
904550000 4	5369	TAN VALUE 2 COTTON 9-0553 A 05/08/ 010	725	 75*				400*	400*	400	400	1305	197

Source: P. L. Carter and R. M. Monczka, "Steelcase, Inc.: MRP in Purchasing," in *Case Studies in Materials Requirements Planning* ed. by E. W. Davis (Falls Church, Va.: American Production and Inventory Control Society, 1978), p. 215.

In this example, the two firms agree on the production of a particular cotton cloth, with a later decision on the specific color it is to be dyed. The job of purchasing is to negotiate the form of the commitment, when and how these "time fences" (cotton versus color) are to be crossed, prices, lot sizes, etc.

The report shown as Figure 6.2 can be sent directly to the vendor. Steelcase has eliminated the use of formal purchase orders for all but occasional purchases. This not only saves on paperwork, but it also cuts response time, another form of slack.

At Steelcase there is an informal agreement that is believed in: Help your vendors when they are acting in your interest. An example was that of an important vendor who was in a cash bind. Steelcase loaned this firm $50,000 interest-free to purchase needed raw materials. The purchasing systems are used extensively, but to *support* professional procurement, not to replace it.

An interesting example of a mutually beneficial commitment is that between the Twin Disc Company and one of its vendors, Neenah Foundry, described by Burlingame and Warren.

For Neenah Foundry, the critical measure of capacity is molds per time period for particular molding centers. The Twin Disc data base has all of its Neenah Foundry castings coded as to which mold center at Neenah is required, and how many castings are made in one mold. The result is an ability to convert all of the Twin Disc requirements into Neenah capacity units of molds per time period.

The two firms have an agreement as to the number of molds per month that are allocated by Neenah to Twin Disc. The length of the agreement is "out as far as Neenah is scheduling into the future." Neenah allowed for changes beyond 90 days and an ability to go 10 percent over or 5 percent under the allotted molds in any one month. The timing for when a commitment to specific end-item castings was required was from 6 to 12 weeks, depending upon the particular casting process.

The benefits from this mold allocation program are significant for both the buyer and the seller. From Twin Disc's point of view, their ability to predict needs is much better in total than for specific items. They are able to wait until only 6 to 12 weeks remain to specify end-item castings, when foundries are quoting 50 week delivery times to others. Twin Disc purchases over 80 percent of its castings and forgings in this way.

From Neenah's point of view, they are able to level out their workload. In one year prior to institution of the mold allocation program, they experienced a swing from a 52-week backlog to not enough work to support the labor force. The program also results in reduced clerical costs because the customers of Neenah on the mold allocation program wait until the last moment to specify end-item castings, avoiding numerous order changes. Neenah has extended the mold allocation program to other customers, and has the goal of devoting at least 50 percent of capacity to this program.

Price planning

Many authorities believe that price determination is secondary to quantity coordination. If the proper planning for vendors is done, lower prices will be achieved. It is less a matter of bargaining than a matter of cooperating. Moreover, most professionals believe that other considerations, such as continuity of supply, quality, and delivery performance, are at least as important as the price.

The establishment of price is, of course, a matter of negotiation in many cases, and this subject is beyond our present scope. With a good plan for quantities and timing for the quantities, as well as an agreement on the terms of commitment, economies can be achieved by the vendor which can be shared.

The primary model for cost estimation is the learning curve. Again, a thorough discussion of this technique is beyond our present scope. The general concept is that for each time the cumulative number of units produced doubles, the average cost per unit should be reduced by some constant percentage. For example, if the average unit cost for the first 100 units were $10, and the firm was on an 80 percent learning curve (20 percent improvement), the expected average unit cost for the first 200 units would be $8, for the first 400 units, $6.40, etc.

The learning model can be built into the price that is negotiated with vendors, either formally or informally. The end result might be a price that is valid for certain quantities with a lower unit price for higher volumes. The quantities expected (and their timing) can be provided by the MPC system.

Another issue in price planning is how the buying firm should respond to a price discount schedule provided by a vendor. The discount may be based on the vendor's perception of learning, or on the allocation of a fixed setup cost over larger volumes. When the demand for an item is lumpy, as it will be with MRP, the determination of the quantity to purchase in each batch is best decided with discrete lot-sizing methods which take into account the price discount schedule.

Vendor scheduling

Vendor scheduling involves release and continuing communication of priorities to released purchase orders. It is the equivalent of shop-floor control, but done for outside work centers. Most of the objectives described for company-owned work centers are applicable to the outside work center, as well. The primary distinction is that to the vendor, each customer is only one of many sources of demand.

Figure 6.3 is a vendor report that is analogous to a shop-floor control report. Again, it is for the Twin Disc Company; the firm calls it the "Open P.O. Buyer Fail-Safe Report." This report lists all of the open purchase orders (scheduled receipts in MRP records), sorted by vendor.

FIGURE 6.3 Twin Disc Company, open p.o. buyer fail-safe report

02/05 OPEN P.O. BUYER FAIL-SAFE REPORT. WEEK-343

BUYER	VENDOR #	PART #	ORDER #	WEEK #	QTY.	FWEEK	FQTY.
D	52487	# 9670A	791930	345	5	345	1
D3	52487	# 9670B	819371	360	50		
D1	52487	# 9682	789410	344	50	338	19
D1	52487	# 9700B	808601	347	35	347	3
D3	52487	# 9753A	819380	352	100		
D3	52487	# 9791A	789561	345	25	348	25
D3	52487	# 9791A	810201	351	65	351	1
D1	52487	# 9813	810211	354	50		
D3	52487	# 9815B	788760	343	15		
D3	52487	# 9824	819390	350	25		
D3	52487	# 9825	793490	346	50	349	15
D1	52487	# 9841	793730	345	50		
D3	52487	# 9870A	758611	347	50		
D1	52487	# 9957	810220	348	25		
D1	52487	#201522	825880	352	1000		
D3	52487	#203717A	822100	354	250		
D1	52487	#205826	819330	349	100	349	38
D3	52487	#205896	826850	358	25		
D3	52487	#205896L	825890	357	50		
D3	52487	#206207	793770	348	200	346	108
D1	52487	#206331	791841	351	50	350	13

Source: E. S. Buffa and J. G. Miller, *Production-Inventory Systems: Planning and Control,* 3d ed. (Homewood, Ill.: Richard D. Irwin, 1979), p. 589.

In Figure 6.3, all of the purchase orders listed are for a single vendor. The first column on the report lists the buyer who placed the purchase order. The second column is vendor number (52487), and the third column is the particular part number on order. The fourth column is the purchase order number for the particular scheduled receipt quantity. Notice, for example, that the sixth and seventh orders are for the same part number, but these are on different purchase orders. The report is printed in part-number sequence within vendor so that *particular* orders can be identified. The fifth column on the report is the due date that was assigned to the purchase order when it was issued. Note that the report was printed at the beginning of week 343. The sixth column is the quantity on the purchase order. Columns seven and eight are of the most interest for vendor scheduling. They are the fail-safe columns. Column seven is the fail week and column eight is the fail quantity. The former is the date at which this order is needed to meet the planned start date of a higher-level assembly. The fail quantity is precisely how many are needed to keep from failing to meet this need.

The first order was issued for five units of part 9670A with a due date of week 345. As of week 343, this due date is still valid. A failure will occur if it is not met. However, it is not essential that all five pieces be delivered. The company can get by if only one of the five is delivered.

"Getting by" has a definite meaning. The fail week and fail quantity are related to actual customer orders. That is, if one were to peg the scheduled receipt for five pieces under purchase order 791930, for part number 9670A, up through product structures, one would find a customer order depending upon one of the five parts being received in week 345. This concept is the direct analog of separating customer orders from inventory orders for jobs in the shop.

What this means is that, for example, the ninth job on the list (part number 9815B) has a due date of the current week. Since there is no information in the FWEEK—FQTY columns, this order, when pegged up, will not be tied to a customer order. It will only go into Twin Disc's inventory.

Many of Twin Disc's vendors have been well enough educated so that this report can be mailed directly to them. It provides a means for them to give priorities to all of the orders from Twin Disc, with continuous updating of their priorities. This information can then be integrated with the competing needs of other firms, in their own MPC systems.

For the example shown in Figure 6.3, this report indicates that the third order in the list (part number 9682) is now critical. It is not due until next week, but based on Twin Disc's present conditions, it was needed five weeks ago. *Why* this is true is not important. If one believes the records, this job is now very urgent. Twin Disc will have to shrink five weeks off the combined lead times for all of assemblies above this part in the product structure to meet the customer promise date. Other purchase orders can be delayed if the vendor wishes to do so. However, Twin Disc is ready to accept their parts on the due dates even though they are not needed until later. This will fulfill their contractual obligations.

Uncertainty protection

Another critical issue in vendor relationship has to do with protection against uncertainty. One approach is the use of safety stocks and safety lead times in MRP systems. A common conclusion is that when one is interested in protection against the due date for an entire order, safety lead time usually is more effective than safety stock. Since in purchasing it is usually the due date for the entire order that is in question, safety lead time is often used.

Neither safety stocks nor safety lead times are cost-free. In both cases, the end result is added inventory investment and lead time extension. Benefits of working more closely with vendors are available here, as well. If a firm has tools that work, an accurate data base, and proper vendor education, the slacks used for uncertainty protection can be sharply reduced.

A different kind of uncertainty protection has to do with more disastrous circumstances such as strikes. A European automobile producer keeps an extra two weeks of inventory on parts made in England to protect against strikes in the English facility and in transport. The Swiss government helps to finance the inventory of many strategic materials in Switzerland to protect the economy against any disruptions in supply.

As for genuine disasters, such as a factory burning down, there is really little that can be done to compensate in the way of inventory. In these cases, the only alternative is response. How to build another plant, shift production to sister plants, etc. In the case of this sort of condition occurring in a supplier plant, one key is to have alternative sourcing plans; another is to help the supplier respond.

Providing protection against these occurrences naturally leads to the concept of multiple sources. Many firms do not want to be totally dependent upon a single source of supply. If they are, it is felt that their bargaining position is weakened. Moreover, some firms want to establish competition among alternative sources for quality, delivery, design improvement, etc.

The other side of this coin is the learning curve. If one supplier can be given all the volume, perhaps the cost per unit can be driven down significantly. In addition, if uncertainties to the vendor are removed, perhaps the firm will become more integrated (and dependent) upon the buying firm. Also, record-keeping and clerical effort increase with multiple sources. More firms are trying to develop a single supplier relationship, working jointly on vendor scheduling and on other critical aspects of professional procurement, such as value analysis. The MPC system provides the foundation for these relationships.

Nonproduction-oriented purchasing

This chapter is largely oriented toward the purchase of items that go directly into the company's products. However, these are not the only items to be purchased. Indirect materials such as cutting oil and tools, supplies such as paper towels and pencils, capital goods such as machine tools, and other items such as company cars and food for the cafeteria, all must also be procured.

To some extent, the establishment of routine system to procure production-oriented materials aids the purchase of nonproduction materials, since time is freed up to more intelligently pursue this other dimension of procurement.

The interesting approach taken by the A.O. Smith Corporation was described by Evans. A. O. Smith designed their purchasing systems to encompass nonproduction materials as well as production materials. To measure price performance on nonproduction materials, they establish *purchasing standards* or reference costs each year for every nonproduction material that is stocked. The accounting variances, which are computed during the year, are grouped by commodity codes. This helps to predict the prices of nonproduction purchases and to better establish purchasing standards. It also fosters standardization of supply needs across organizational units.

The resultant systems and reports are in the same format as those used to control production material purchases. The only difference is the source of the requirements. For production materials, the source is determined from the MPS system by MRP explosion. For nonproduction materials, other means are used to derive requirements. For some items, there is a min-max inventory system. For others, it is a matter of someone initiating a request.

PURCHASING SYSTEMS AND DATA BASE

We turn now to what is perhaps the most important issue in the chapter. Given the set of vendor relationships defined above, what are the specific tools that successful companies are using? Our discussion is again based on the assumption that there is a working MPC system and data integrity.

The procurement functions

Figure 6.4 shows the detailed interaction of purchasing with the front end, engine, and other parts of the manufacturing planning and control system. The set of activities shown as boxes in the middle column depicts the procurement cycle.

The MRP data base provides time-phased record information to both buying and order release. Buying is the activity that encompasses the establishment of the proper vendor relationships discussed previously. This is an ongoing process of estimating quantities, establishing commitment conditions that are mutually beneficial, and working for continuing improvements.

Order release is primarily a clerical job; it is the determination of detailed quantity and timing decisions as constrained by the conditions of buying. Order release also connotes some form of management by exception; when routine actions cannot be executed, buying personnel need to be so advised.

Order follow-up includes vendor scheduling and an ongoing process of assigning priorities. It also includes some exception coding to highlight any conditions that do not agree with plan.

FIGURE 6.4 The purchasing data base and MPC system linkages

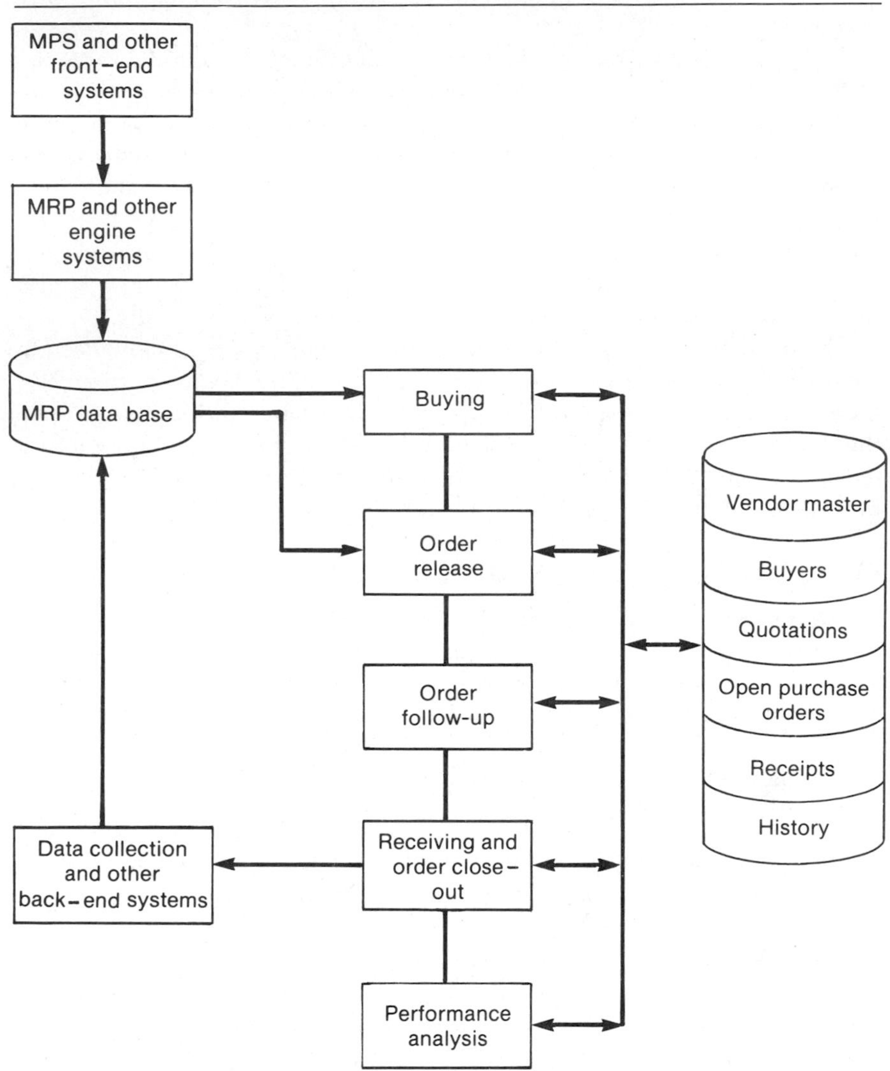

Receiving and order closeout encompass all of the necessary documentation for the receipt of purchase orders, data integrity check procedures, scrap and quality control, and interfaces with accounts payable. It is critical that appropriate data integrity procedures are in place.

Performance analysis is an ongoing evaluation of vendor performance, commodity performance, buyer performance, and overall procurement performance. We will deal with each of these topics after first identifying the key data base elements.

The data base

Figure 6.4 also shows the key files which comprise the purchasing data base. The MRP data base is used as one important source of information. The right-hand portion of Figure 6.4 depicts some of the critical files in the purchasing data base.

The vendor master file includes all of the information which describes each vendor. Included are name, address, telephone number, vendor code, terms of sale, contact(s) in the firm, etc. There would also be direct linkages to the quotations, open purchase orders, receipts, and history files so that vendor-order status performance can be assessed.

The buyers file indicates which buyers are responsible for which part numbers, commodities, and vendors. It would also have linkages to the other files. The quotations file would be all open quotations, requests for quotation, "tickler files" for quotation follow-up actions, and any expiration dates of quotation data.

The open purchase orders file is essentially all of the scheduled receipts from MRP records for purchased parts, plus any purchase orders for non-production materials. In addition to quantity and timing data, all of the data held on a purchase order would be maintained, such as destination, shipping means, terms of sale, etc.

The receipts file maintains all data on receipts, so that order closeout, reconciliation with purchase orders, and accounts payable activities can be supported. The history file contains all of the data on closed purchase orders to support whatever kind of performance analysis is desired by the firm.

Vendor performance

Figure 6.5 is a standard vendor performance report from a software package marketed by Software International Company. This report is for one vendor (ABC Company) for one item (A4792 DPDT SWITCH). This switch is in commodity code DTS, and is bought by ALP.

At the time of the report, there have been two purchase orders closed and one that is still open. The first closed order, issued on 01/15, was due on 02/25, and the last receipt was on 01/25. The order was for 1,000 pieces of which 950 were accepted and 50 were returned. This represents a 5 percent return (RT) rate. The standard cost of those received was $7,125, or $7.125 each. The actual invoice for the 1,000 parts was $7,115.50, or $7.1155 each.

The second closed order shows that the last receipt on 04/05 was later than the due date of 03/30. Also, the returned percentage was 30 percent, and the items were invoiced for $4,000 ($8 each) as against the standard cost

FIGURE 6.5 Software International, purchasing subsystem reports, single item

```
                                                 VENDOR PERFORMANCE

                                               VENDOR PERFORMANCE REPORT
AS OF 12/18                                  *****  DIVISION NAME  *****

VENDOR NO.   VENDOR NAME                                TELEPHONE      CONTACT NAME
103927       ABC CO.                                    301-922-8962   SAM EVANS

ITEM NUMBER          ITEM DESCRIPTION                           COMM.CD            CURRENT BUYER
A4792                DPDT SWITCH                                DTS                ALP

CLOSED       BUY     --------SCHEDULE--------      S   ---------------QUANTITY----------------| SC   RT   RW   Q   ---RECEIPTS----   C

PO NUMBER    ER      ORDERED    DUE      LAST RCPT  F   ORDERED    ACCEPTED   SCRAP   RETURNED   REWORK | %    %    %    F   STANDARD   ACTUAL     F
10923        MNO     01/15/     02/25/   01/25/         1000       950                50                      5             7125.00    7115.50
11014        MNO     02/19/     03/30/   04/05/          500       350               150                     30        *   3562.50    4000.00    *

OPEN         BUY     --------SCHEDULE--------     ---------------QUANTITY---------------     ----BOOKINGS----    --- RECEIPTS ---

PO NUMBER    ER      ORDERED    DUE      LAST RCPT  ORDERED   ACCEPTED   SCRAP   RETURNED   REWORK   STANDARD   ACTUAL      STANDARD  ACTUAL
12176        MNO     09/23/     12/07/   11/21/     2000      800                30                  13830.00   13790.00    5532.00   5516.00 *

ITEM        PERFORMANCE  LATE ORDER  QUALITY COST     ------------ QUANTITY--TOTALS------------    --TOTAL BOOKINGS--   --TOTAL RECEIPTS --
SUMMARY     FLAG   INDEX   PERCENT   RATIO   OVERRUN   ORDERED   ACCEPTED   % SCRAP   % RETURN   % REWORK   STANDARD   ACTUAL     STANDARD   ACTUAL
             *     16.8    56        .87     4.0       3500      2100                 1                     13830.00   13790.00   16219.00   16631.50

TOTALS/VENDOR  PERFORMANCE FLAG=*  INDEX=14  LATE ORD.%=17  QUA RATIO=.39  COST OR.%=1.2      TOTALS   41428.50   41009.00   88378.50   89527.40
```

DESCRIPTION: Provides purchasing with a standard method of comparing the relative performance of vendors. Two reports are provided summarizing vendor performance for the last year or for the current calendar year.

SEQUENCE OF DATA: Sequenced by vendor number. Within vendor, by item number and order status (closed and open), respectively.

OPTIONS: Period (last or current year), the reports to be generated (Part I, II, or both), and variable data.

Source: Software International.

of $3,562.50 ($7.125 each). The return percentage as well as the cost overrun were both judged to be significant enough to generate "flag" conditions. These are shown with an asterisk as a quantity (Q) flag (F) and a cost (C) flag (F).

The one open purchase order has had a partial shipment made against it. The cost data are shown for both the total purchase order (bookings) and the portion that has been received (receipts).

The summary data at the bottom of Figure 6.5 allow all of the performance data for closed and open purchase orders to be grouped into one summary set of performance statistics. The result is an ability to compare the performance of any two vendors for the same purchased component. In the next section, we will see that we can also group these data by commodity group.

Commodity performance

Figure 6.6 is another standard report from Software International. This one again shows the ABC company, but now includes summary performance statistics for all of the parts in commodity code DTS which are supplied by the ABC company (including the part examined in Figure 6.5). The data are presented by part number and then in total for all of these parts. The commodity codes themselves can be defined in whatever way is best for a particular firm.

This performance analysis allows a firm to compare different firms that supply items within the same commodity code. This comparison can lead to choice of vendors, remedial actions, or other buyer-vendor interactions.

It is also possible to group all of the purchases in a particular commodity code with different vendors, so that comparisons can be made across commodity codes. Perhaps all of the purchases in one commodity code are easier to handle than those in another. Perhaps a firm should put its most experienced buyers and clerical personnel in charge of the most troublesome commodity codes. Perhaps it makes sense to chart performance over time for each commodity code to look for performance trends. Perhaps we should use engineering talent to design our way around particular commodity code problems. By collecting the data in commodity groupings, the payoffs from these potential efforts can be better assessed.

Buyer performance

Figure 6.7 is one more performance analysis report from Software International. This time we can see that the same data have been grouped by buyer. This now permits a standardized basis for comparing the performance of buyers. This is an important step in the development of professionalism in the purchasing function.

FIGURE 6.6 Software International, purchasing subsystem reports, summary by vendor

```
                                         VENDOR PERFORMANCE

                                      VENDOR PERFORMANCE REPORT
AS OF 12/18                           *****  DIVISION NAME  *****

COMMODITY CODE      VENDOR NO.      VENDOR NAME                TELEPHONE     CONTACT NAME
DTS                 103927          ABC CO.                    301-922-8962  SAM EVANS

                         PERFM LO QUA CST ---QUANTITY--- U SCRAP RETURN REWORK ---BOOKINGS---       -----RECEIPTS-----
ITEM NUMBER DESCRIPTION  F IND %  R   OV% ORDERED ACCEPTED M %   %      %      STANDARD ACTUAL      STANDARD ACTUAL
A4792       DPDT SWITCH                    3500    2100          3.2           13830.00 13790.00    16219.50 16631.50*
A5317       SPST SWITCH                    7500    7358          1.9           16275.00 15825.00    15966.85 15525.38
B9218       ROTARY SWITCH             1.2  1750    1649          5.8            7472.50  7560.00     7041.23  7123.68
F3092       PUSH-PULL SWITCH               4500    4109          8.7            4185.00  4185.00     3821.37  3821.37

TOTALS/VENDOR  PERFORMANCE FLAG=*INDEX=  LATE ORD.%=  QUA RATIO=  COST OR.%=0.3.  TOTALS  41762.50 41360.00  43048.95 43101.43
```

Source: Software International.

FIGURE 6.7 Software International, purchasing subsystem reports, summary by buyer

BUYER PERFORMANCE

BUYER PERFORMANCE REPORT
***** DIVISION NAME *****

AS OF 10/09

BUYER
MNO

		P PER	LD	QUA	CST	--- QUANTITY ----		U SCR	RET	REW	-----BOOKINGS----		-----RECEIPTS--- C	
ITEM NUMBER	CMC VENDOR NO.	F IND	%	R	OV%	ORDERED	ACCEPTED	M %	%	%	STANDARD	ACTUAL	STANDARD	ACTUAL F
A4792	DTS 103927	17	56	.87	4.C	3500	2100		:1		13830.00	13790.00	16219.50	16631.50*
A4922	DTS 107422	4	7	.2	.5	1700	1678		1		12325.00	11781.00	12165.50	11628.54
A9249	RTS 209731	1	9	.6	.8	800	780		3		5712.00	5656.00	5569.20	5514.60
B9218	RTS 103927	6	4	.4	.3	1350	1318		2		7168.50	7195.50	6998.50	7024.94

BUYER/ITEM PERFORMANCE FLAG=*INDEX= LATE ORD.%= QUA RATIO= COST OR.%= TOTALS

TOTALS/BUYER PERFORMANCE FLAG=*INDEX=4 LATE ORD.%=3.2 QUA RATIO=.3 COST OR.%=3.9 TOTALS 39035.50 38422.50 40752.98 40799.58

****

DESCRIPTION: Provides relative schedule, quality, and cost performance of each buyer.
SEQUENCE OF REPORTS: Sequenced by buyer. Within buyer, by item and vendor.

Source: Software International.

There are many standardized software packages on the market to support purchasing. The three illustrations here from the same firm show how the basic data and definitions of performance can be sorted into several useful forms of analysis. The particular definitions of performance might be different for different applications, but the important concept is the ability to thereafter make comparative analyses.

Overall performance

Before leaving the subject of performance evaluation, let us briefly examine one more report. Figure 6.8 is from the software package marketed by American Software Company. It shows a monthly summary report for the entire purchasing activity. It shows how many purchase orders were opened and closed during the month, and how many are open at the end of the month. These data are presented in terms of line items, purchase orders, and dollar value. The data are also presented on a year-to-date basis. Also shown are all purchase orders issued for more than $10,000.

The lower half of the report breaks down the purchase orders for the month into categories of interest to management. For example, it is easy to see what percentage of the expenditures are to single-source vendors, which are based on competitive quotations, etc. For comparative purposes, the data are presented both for the past month and on a year-to-date basis.

A report similar to Figure 6.8 is a useful summary document for top management. It can also be used to project cash flows necessary to close out the accounts payable. The highlighting of large expenditures can lead to cross-checking with capital appropriation requests, if desired. The potential savings from getting more complete quotations on file or from inadequate lead time purchases might also be estimated.

These performance reports perform an important "loop-closing" function in purchasing in a way analogous to that done based on shop-floor performance.

ORGANIZATIONAL CHANGE

We come now to the fourth critical issue in procurement: What are the organizational changes needed to effectively use MPC systems in procurement?

The Steelcase example

With the necessary vendor relationships, data base, and systems in place, the purchasing job undergoes a fundamental change in character. A professional procurement function can be achieved, with more time spent on how to best utilize vendor strengths to the benefit of the ultimate consumer, and less time spent on day-to-day fire fighting. We have discussed the vendor

FIGURE 6.8 American Gas Corporation, purchase order statistics for September

REGION—CORPORATE SUMMARY	CURRENT MONTH			YEAR TO DATE		
DESCRIPTION	LINE ITEMS	PURCHASE ORDERS	DOLLAR VALUE	LINE ITEMS	PURCHASE ORDERS	DOLLAR VALUE
PURCHASE ORDER ACTIVITY						
PREVIOUS MONTH'S OPEN PURCHASE ORDERS	2,620	501	8,231,674.04	2,620	501	8,231,674.04
NEW P.O.S ISSUED THIS MONTH AND YEAR	1,320	237	1,199,203.78	15,850	3,444	14,390,735.78
OLD P.O.S CLOSED THIS MONTH AND YEAR	1,525	305	1,236,194.67	16,055	3,462	14,427,726.67
CURRENT MONTH'S OPEN PURCHASE ORDERS	2,415	483	8,194,683.15	2,415	483	8,194,683.15
NEW PURCHASE ORDERS OF $10,000 OR MORE	59	15	976,325.19	711	179	12,067,377.23
NEW PURCHASE ORDERS—CODING SUMMARY						
SPECIFIED:						
1A ENGINEERING	34		6,960.23	408		83,522.76
1C OPERATIONS	26		6,339.00	312		76,068.00
1F AVIATION	5		255.15	60		3,061.80
1G GENERAL SERVICES				8		100.00
1K ADMINISTRATIVE	8		2,538.96	96		30,467.52
SINGLE SOURCE:						
2A PARTS FOR EXISTING EQUIPMENT	112		129,445.17	1,344		1,553,342.83
2C ONLY POSITIVE RESPONSE	27		16,315.98	324		195,791.76
2D SPECIALTY ITEMS—ONLY SOURCE	61		90,013.75	732		1,080,165.71
2F MATCHING EXISTING EQUIPMENT	32		7,132.15	384		85,585.57
INADEQUATE LEAD TIME:						
4A PHONE REQUESTS FROM FIELD	176		74,329.87	2,122		891,948.13
4C CONSTRUCTION MATERIALS	28		1,987.65	336		23,844.77
PURCHASING PERFORMED BY OTHERS:						
5A OPERATIONS	4		2,766.01	48		33,312.79
5F GENERAL	9		750.00	108		9,197.63
5J OTHER REGIONS OR CORPORATE	36		315,765.98	432		3,789,180.51
COMPETITIVE PURCHASES:						
6A COMPETITIVE QUOTES IN FILE	211		230,803.07	2,532		2,769,636.36
6B REPETITIVE PURCHASES—SURVEYS	550		313,783.06	6,600		3,765,396.64
6C BLANKET OR CONTRACT						
PURCHASE NOT AT LOWEST COST:						
7 PURCHASE NOT AT LOWEST COST				3		95.25
UNKNOWN OR UNDEFINED PURCHASE CODE:						
X:	1		17.75	1		17.75
TOTAL	1,320		1,199,203.78	15,850		14,390,735.78

Source: Purchasing and Materials Management, Purchasing Systems (Program PPR 210), Atlanta, American Software, 1983.

report for Steelcase, shown in Figure 6.2, and briefly noted the change in attitude toward purchasing in that company. Let us now examine how the organization of the purchasing group was changed. Figure 6.9 is the purchasing organization prior to the implementation of MPC-based systems. The entire operation used to revolve around one person who was in charge of purchased item inventory control and order releases. This individual is shown as the inventory control person in Figure 6.9. This employee negotiated blanket orders with vendors, issued monthly releases against the blanket orders using economic lot sizes, controlled all releases to the vendors, based all decisions on a Kardex file system, and carried 1 to 1½ months of safety stock for individual items. Meanwhile, the buyers functioned as expeditors.

This approach to procurement seemed to work as long as the business did not undergo major changes in volume, mix, or design. In fact, when these changes did occur, orders were issued for the wrong parts and wrong quantities, and the resulting expediting activity was sharply intensified. Unfortunately, at one point, Steelcase approached their increasing problems by computerizing the *existing* system and sending the reports to the vendors. The result was a continuing crisis of operation in purchasing.

Figure 6.10 is the purchasing organization after the MPC-oriented systems were installed. Purchasing people now have the responsibility for planning, scheduling, and inventory control on all purchased items. They are totally responsible for any and all shortages on purchased parts, regardless of the cause.

The primary change is that the persons shown on the left-hand side of

FIGURE 6.9 Steelcase purchasing organization prior to the development of effective MPC systems

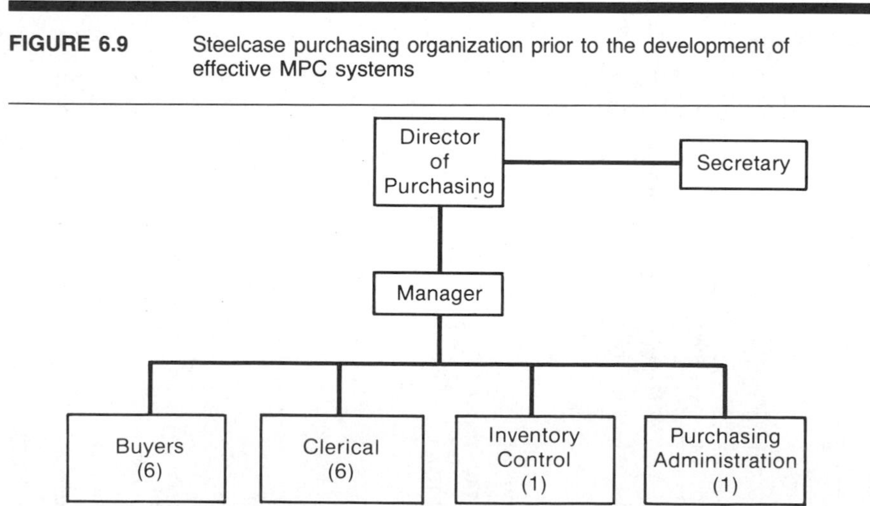

Source: P. L. Carter and R. M. Monczka, "Steelcase, Inc.: MRP in Purchasing," in *Case Studies in Materials Requirements Planning*, ed. by E. W. Davis (Falls Church, Va.: American Production and Inventory Control Society, 1978), p. 123.

FIGURE 6.10 Steelcase purchasing organization after implementation of MPC systems

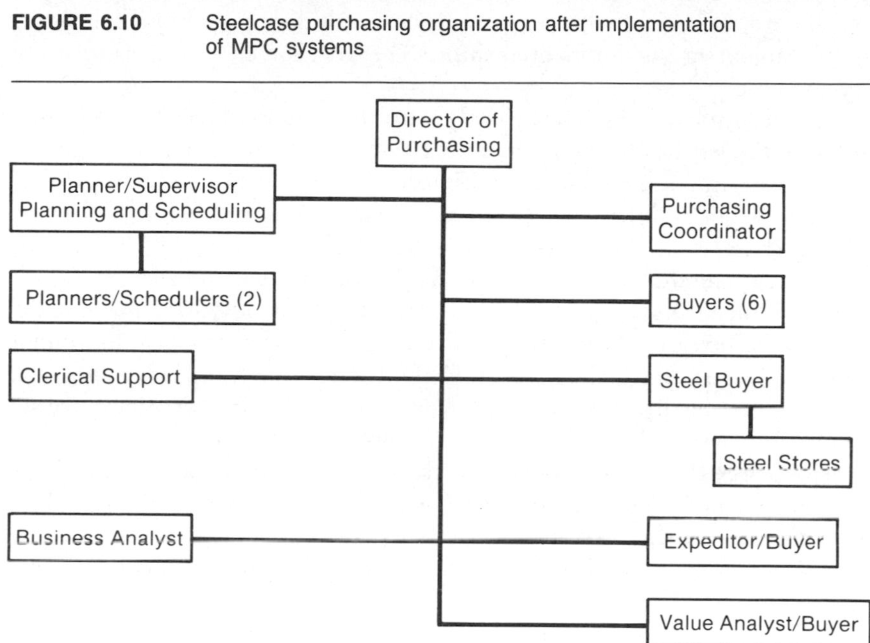

Source: P. L. Carter and R. M. Monczka, "Steelcase, Inc.: MRP in Purchasing," in *Case Studies in Materials Requirements Planning*, ed. by E. W. Davis (Falls Church, Va.: American Production and Inventory Control Society, 1978), p. 123.

Figure 6.10 are now concerned with the detailed releasing and scheduling of and assigning priorities of orders to the vendors. Those on the right-hand side are concerned with buying and vendor relationships. The functions have been separated.

The purchasing coordinator is concerned with all capital equipment purchasing, plus the processing of engineering changes. This latter activity is absolutely vital to determining the best timing and response to design changes. The six buyers are organized around commodity codes, with one responsible for all maintenance, repair, and nonproduction items. The other five buyers purchase production-oriented items. The steel buyer purchases all steel for the company (the largest single expenditure item), manages the steel inventory, and schedules steel slitting.

There is one expeditor/buyer who purchases all fasteners for the company. This person also expedites all rejections of purchased parts, including both rework and returns. The expeditor follows a rule that all dispositions must be made within five days; Steelcase recognizes this as a critical problem area. If they are not handled quickly and properly, the result will be a loss in data integrity. The last person shown in the right-hand side of Figure 6.10 is the value analyst/buyer. This person purchases and coordinates all chrome plating and also works as a specialist in value analysis. In fact, all of the buyers are concerned with value analysis as one key aspect of the ongoing improvement in vendor relationships. The goal for all is "to spend their money wisely."

The group that works most closely with the detailed MRP driven data is show on the left-hand side of Figure 6.10. It is the planner/scheduler group. The two planner/schedulers are in charge of order release, vendor scheduling, and order priority for all purchased parts except fasteners and steel. They manage some 3,800 items, or 1,900 each, on a weekly cycle, since MRP is regenerated over the weekend. On Monday and Tuesday, the planner/schedulers review those 3,800 items, using CRT devices and exception codes. On Tuesday evening, the results are processed to produce the vendor report (Figure 6.2) which is mailed to the vendors on Wednesday morning. As we noted before, this report serves as a purchase order; there are no formal purchase orders used for routine purchasing.

The planner/schedulers represent the day-to-day link between Steelcase and their vendors. These people, in effect, interact with detailed order entry personnel in vendor factories. If problems arise that they cannot solve, the problems escalate to their supervisors and from there to buyers at Steelcase who interact with vendor salespeople.

Use of the vendor report can be illustrated by the intractions with one of Steelcase's plywood, fiberboard, and fiberglass suppliers. Prior to the installation of the new system, Steelcase would typically telephone specific orders against an open blanket order, on a rush or short lead time basis. This meant that the vendor was constantly reacting to problems, and Steelcase was always expediting. With the new report, the activities are very different. The vendor checks the past-due and current columns, and crosses off any orders that have been already shipped but were not reflected on the report because of timing delays. He then puts a high priority on any past-due and current orders not yet shipped, reviews the last two months of demand, and checks the requirements for the next five weeks for any unusual demand to place orders with his vendors. The net result of the new system is that this vendor found his own scheduling much easier because he has better information about future demand.

The benefits that Steelcase achieved from the new system would not have been possible without the organizational changes. The recognition that roles must change and responsibilities shift to use purchasing information as a substitute for inventory, panic operations, and other forms of slack is key. Now, let us generalize from the Steelcase example and take up some related issues.

The procurement job

Figure 6.11 shows the change in a typical buyer's day when MRP-oriented purchasing systems are in use. This figure depicts the changes in pro-

FIGURE 6.11 Typical buyers day

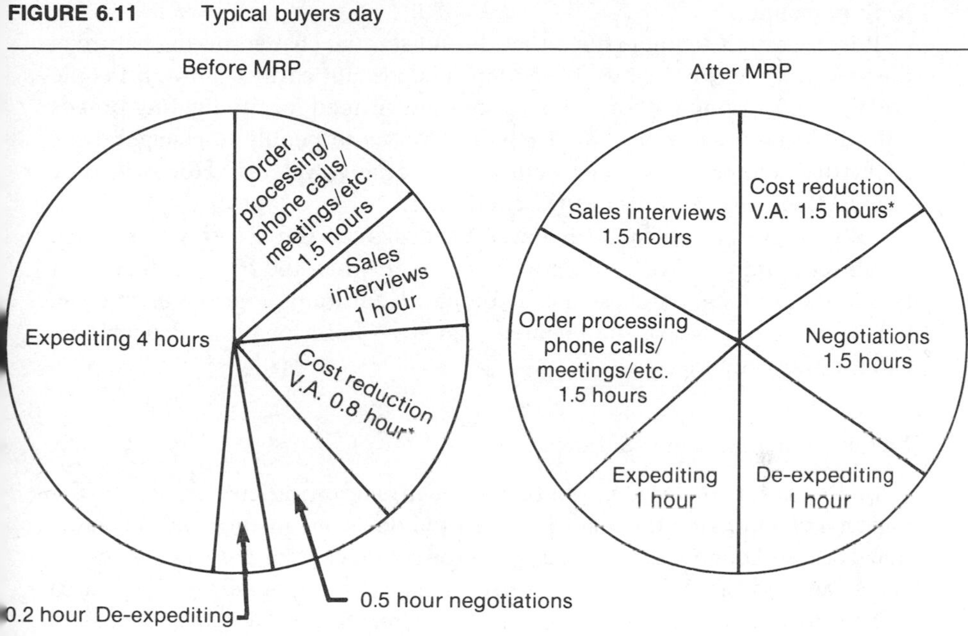

*V.A. = value analysis.
Source: G. Bevis, "Closed-Loop MRP at the Tennant Company," George Bevis Co., P.O. Box 619, Wayzata, Minnesota.

curement that took place at the Tennant Company. As can be seen, prior to the MRP systems, fully one half of the buyer's day was concerned with expediting and very little with de-expediting. After MRP, these two activities are of equal importance, and only take up one fourth of the day. (Note, however, that at Steelcase the *buyer* does virtually none of this activity.) The key difference reflected in Figure 6.11 is that much more time is spent in the series of activities we have called vendor relationships, and much less in clerical detailed fire fighting.

A similar result was reported by Trill for the Reliance Electric Company. Prior to the installation of their MRP systems, negotiation and vendor selection comprised only 8 percent and 7 percent of the buyers' time respectively. Moreover, the clerical people in purchasing were spending 30 percent of their time typing purchase orders, change orders, debit memos, etc., with only 15 percent on expediting. The remaining portion of their time was spent on posting data, filing, and explaining information over the telephone.

With the new system in place, Reliance Electric achieved for buyers a 35 percent savings in time that could now be put to more productive use, a 40 percent savings in overall clerical time, elimination of filing, great reduction of paperwork, savings in equipment and floor space, reductions in lead times, and improved communication between purchasing and other company personnel.

It is important to understand that the substantial changes in the nature of the procurement job that we have identified are not easily achieved. People are used to working with massive paper files. A need for fire fighting breeds a fire fighting organization. Is it possible for these people to change? How about the vendors? Will they believe in the new systems? How will they change their own approaches to scheduling?

All of these are profound issues. The design of the systems to support purchasing from an MPC data base is far easier than the changes that must be made in the way purchasing will operate. Education programs must be an important dimension of the planned changes—both for internal personnel and for the vendors.

Materials management organization

In the last two decades, there has been a growing recognition of the importance of linking the materials-oriented decisions made in various functional areas. At one time, purchasing, production control, forecasting, order entry, and physical distribution were managed independently. Each area had its own goals, specialty, techniques, procedures, systems, data, and organization. Coordination among these different organizational units was achieved through organizational hierarchies, agreed upon high level plans, and, most often, by informal contacts between individuals. The resultant suboptimization was necessary both because there was no overall system design philosophy, and perhaps even more importantly, because there was no integrated data base. The cost of this suboptimization was organizational slack: excess inventories, poor delivery performance, long lead times, overtime costs, the hidden costs of panic operations, and a lack of responsiveness to changes in the business environment.

At this point in time, more and more firms are moving toward a better integration of the various aspects of materials management. To some extent, this integration has been made possible by technological developments in data processing; we now can have an integrated data base. However, there must be an agreed upon integrative philosophy. There must be a consistent set of goals and objectives. Systems must be complementary. Data entry and change must be explicitly defined organizationally to maintain data integrity and ensure a common, complete data base.

In recent times, many firms have approached these issues by the creation of a new managerial position: the materials manager, who is responsible for purchasing, production control, physical storage, transaction processing, traffic, and sometimes distribution. In a survey conducted in 1967, only 3 percent of the firms had a materials manager. Eleven years later, nearly one half of the firms responding to a similar survey had a materials manager.

For procurement, it will be necessary to establish strong links to marketing to know what future sales are anticipated. It is also necessary to have strong ties to engineering to know what new products are coming, what new design changes are anticipated, and where new, less costly or better purchased materials, could help. This purchasing-engineering linkage is more difficult to establish organizationally than some of the others. However, if the routine purchasing decisions are made routinely, there will be more time for key people to work at this critical activity. One way some firms have approached the issue of forming an engineering-materials management linkage is to create a committee for engineering change control. The committee also deals with a somewhat wider scope of interfunctional design issues.

Another linkage of purchasing is to stores. If purchasing is to be held accountable for the investment in purchased items as well as for all stockouts, do they need to have physical control over the purchased items? The answer is no. A stockkeeping group can be developed along with all adequate procedures and safeguards. The stockkeeping responsibility is custodial—purchasing's is financial. However, if both of these groups report to one materials manager, there is even less chance for conflict.

Centralization versus decentralization

The final organizational change issue we consider is whether purchasing should be centralized or decentralized in a multiplant environment, and what role the introduction of MPC systems has in this decision. Some of the classical arguments in favor of centralized procurement are increased clout with the vendors, the ability to obtain larger discounts, the potential for better coordinating orders that go to one vendor, the ability to better divide scarce resources among competing company units, economies of scale in the purchasing activity itself, and the ability to develop a more professional staff.

On the other hand, the arguments in favor of decentralized procurement are the coupling of authority for supply with responsibility for a decentralized facility's output, the potential for diminishing returns if the decentralized facility is large in its own right, unique decentralized requirements, extra time lags (lead times), and the public relations aspects of purchasing locally. This latter factor has increasing importance for multinational organizations. In some companies, the development of fairly autonomous procurement units is important insurance against nationalization.

The decentralization-centralization of procurement issue is rarely clear-cut. For many firms, there is one important commodity such as coffee beans or copper, that is purchased by a central group trying to hedge against price swings. For others, key components may be bought centrally, with local buying of others.

Some people believe that the development of MPC systems forces centralization in purchasing. This is certainly not true. An MPC data base and related systems in procurement make it possible to achieve better integration in the procurement activities of a multiplant company, regardless of the degree of centralization. The question of purchasing centralization or decentralization should be decided on the basis of other arguments. The MPC system provides the basis for the organization to exploit the opportunities for better procurement practice. The use of comparative standard costs, performance by commodity codes, relative vendor performances—all of these are possible in a truly professional multiplant procurement operation supported by modern MPC systems.

RESULTS

The final topic we take up is concerned with the payoffs from integrating effective MPC systems into purchasing. What kind of results have been achieved by the leading-edge companies? The single-word answer is: phenomenal! Many companies have made first-year savings in purchased component costs alone that have more than paid for the entire MPC developmental effort.

Results at Steelcase

We have looked at several examples from the Steelcase Company to illustrate the change in purchasing orientation as well as to describe some other system reports. Let us now see how these systems have paid off.

One of the most striking results of the system institution at Steelcase was great improvement in vendor performance against due dates. When the systems were installed, 35 percent of all outstanding purchase orders were past due and many needed to be rescheduled into the future. After one month, only 20 percent were past due, and after 1½ years only 3.2 percent were past due. These were improvements in the *vendors* performance due to effective use of the new systems.

Productivity in the Steelcase plant was improved, as well. After 1½ years, the number of part numbers short in any single week had dropped from an average of 33 to 4. Better service to the production floor resulted in less rescheduling, fewer split lot sizes, etc.

There was a marked reduction in buyer clerical and follow-up activity. In fact, there was a general reduction in the level of clerical effort throughout purchasing. As noted before, buyers now use their time to spend money wisely rather than to solve immediate crises.

The purchased-material inventory turnover performance was increased substantially. Historically, the inventory had increased by one half of the rate of increase in sales. Over a two-year period after the systems were installed, sales rose 59 percent while purchased item inventories rose only 12 percent. Moreover, there was a far better ability to control inventory levels during a period of sales decline.

Vendor lead times were also reduced. Steelcase's systems provided the vehicle for a redefinition of the concept of lead time to obtain improved delivery performance. With capacity commitments and the MPC system information, lead times were reduced to an absolute minimum. During a period of severe shortage conditions in the United States, Steelcase had no real lead times in excess of five weeks. Later, the Steelcase purchasing manager stated, "Vendor lead times are virtually irrelevant to Steelcase."

Customer service at Steelcase has also improved. When the Sears Tower was built in Chicago, Steelcase contracted to supply office furniture. They shipped five truckloads per day, five days per week, for 20 weeks. Every truck arrived within a few minutes of the scheduled time. In an order for 19,000 chairs for the federal government, an unexpected rush order involved delivery of 2,000 within two weeks. Steelcase procured 3,500 yards of special-color fabric that was delivered in 10 days for the order; this fabric has a normal lead time of 10 weeks.

Finally, the procurement function is regarded as truly professional at Steelcase. Buyers are no longer highly paid expeditors. More and more time is spent on value analysis and other vendor relationship efforts. In a two-year period, the targeted cost reductions through better purchasing was increased 10 fold, from approximately $500,000 per year to $5 million per year. These impressive savings were attainable only after the buyers were freed from routine activities to work on those activities which resulted in the large savings.

Other results

Steelcase is certainly not the only firm which has achieved significant results from improved purchasing based on MPC systems. A similar effort at Signode Corporation, reported by Papesch, resulted in major reductions in shortages, lead time reductions of one fourth to three fourths, faster reaction to increased requirements, and better purging of record error problems.

Although not due to purchasing improvements alone, the Tennant Company has one of the most spectacular MPC success stories. George Bevis, in describing Tennant's results, states that in a 27-month period the purchased material inventory was reduced by 42 percent ($3 million), while the quarterly production rate increased by 66 percent. At the same time, the average daily shortages were reduced from 300 to 5, assembly efficiency increased from 45 to 85 percent, and delivery promises met increased from 50 percent to 90 percent.

Assessing the purchasing function

We are often asked to audit manufacturing planning and control systems. As one portion of this process, it is useful to examine the interactions of MPC systems with purchasing. Here are some of the question we ask:

How is purchasing organized? Is there a materials management approach? What is the relationship between buying (vendor relationship) activities and releasing/vendor scheduling activities? How professional is the group? What is the level of formal education, and training in the use of MPC systems? Are there Kardex, tub, or other large noncomputerized files? What are the computer systems? How good are they? Do people use them? Can a purchasing person (not someone from the computer department) explain their logic to us thoroughly? How are exception conditions handled? With what speed? By whom? Do purchasing people believe in the schedules and MPC systems? Are there any informal systems? How are lead times monitored? Are orders issued as indicated by the MPC systems? What is the frequency of rush orders? How well do the vendors rate this firm as a customer? Is there a formal vendor performance evaluation system? A formal value analysis program? A formal cost improvement program?

Answers to these questions can provide a great deal of insight into the potential improvement in purchasing that can be achieved in a particular firm. Furthermore, it is not a one-time effort. There are *always* improvements to be made through a better integration of a firm's needs with the abilities of its vendors.

CONCLUDING PRINCIPLES

This chapter is devoted to showing how MPC-based systems can provide the basis for a new level of professionalism in procurement. By carefully utilizing the information in an operational MPC system, a firm can help their vendors do business better—better for both the buying firm and the vendor. We see the following basic principles as important:

- Vendor capacities should be planned and controlled with as much diligence as are internal capacities.
- A closer, more intimate working relationship between the buying firm and its vendors should be a primary objective.
- The purchasing data base needs to be integrated with other parts of the MPC system data base.
- Clerical work and managerial work should be separated in the purchasing organization.
- A materials management orientation fosters better interactions between purchasing and other material flow decision-making areas. Companies should seriously consider this option.
- High payoffs have been achieved by firms that have purchasing supported by MPC systems. Achieving the payoffs often requires major reorganization and reorientation of jobs.

REFERENCES

Aiello, Joseph L. "Successful Interaction Between Purchasing and Production and Inventory Control." *APICS 22d Annual Conference Proceedings*, 1979, pp. 234–36.

Alvarez, Ronald. "Purchasing Can Reduce Inventory Investment." *APICS 23d Annual Conference Proceedings*, 1980, pp. 291–93.

Ammer, Dean S. *Material Management and Purchasing.* Homewood, Ill.: Richard D. Irwin, 1980.

Bevis, G. "Closed-Loop MRP at the Tennant Company." Report—The Tennant Company, Minneapolis, Minn.

Burlingame, L. J., and R. A. Warren. "Extended Capacity Planning." *1974 APICS Conference Proceedings*, pp. 83–91.

Carlson, J. G. H. "The Effect of Learning on Production Lots." *1974 APICS Conference Proceedings*, pp. 73–82.

Carter, P. L., and R. M. Monczka. "Steelcase, Inc.: MRP in Purchasing." In *Case Studies in Materials Requirements Planning*, Falls Church, Va.: American Production and Inventory Control Society, 1978, p. 125.

Evans, D. L. "Measuring Purchasing Performance." *1977 APICS Conference Proceedings*, pp. 434–49.

Hoeffer, E. L. "Production Report." *Purchasing* 90, no. 7 (April 16, 1981), pp. 52–66.

Hollingshead, A. W., Jr. "The Linear-Pricing Approach to Purchasing." *Management Review*, September 1971, pp. 14–19.

Kobert, Norman. "Inventory Outlook—Physical Controls Can Save You Time." *Purchasing* 88, no. 6, (March 27, 1980), p. 41.

Monczka, R. M., and P. L. Carter. "Productivity and Performance Measurement in Purchasing." *1976 APICS Conference Proceedings*, pp. 6–9.

"Move to MRP System Helped Steelcase Boom." *Purchasing*, January 25, 1977, pp. 60–63.

Olsen, Robert E. "Bridging the Purchasing—Production Control Credibility Gap." *APICS Annual Conference Proceedings*, 1977, pp. 491–500.

Papesch, Robert M. "Extending Your MRP System into Your Vendor's Shop." *Production and Inventory Management*, 2d Quarter 1978, pp. 47–52.

Piepgras, J. J. "The Inventory Control/Purchasing Relationship: More Than Just Mechanics." *1974 APICS Conference Proceedings*, pp. 36–57.

Ruhl, J., and J. Schorr. "MRP and Purchasing at Steelcase." Report—Steelcase, Inc., Grand Rapids, Mich.

Shaughnessy, Thomas E. "Aggregate Inventory Management: Measurement and Control." *Journal of Purchasing and Materials Management*, Fall 1980, pp. 18–24.

Trill, G. P. "Paypur: A Complete CRT, On-Line, Real Time Procurement System." *1977 APICS Conference Proceedings*, pp. 468–80.

Wallace, Tom. *Purchasing and MRP: More Bang for the Buck.* Atlanta: R. D. Garwood, 1983.

Whitmarsh, J. "MRP is the Only Answer." *Purchasing World*, December 1977, pp. 23–28.

Whybark, D. C. "Evaluating Alternative Quantity Discounts." *Journal of Purchasing and Materials Management*, Summer 1971.

7

Master production scheduling fundamentals

In this chapter, we discuss the basic considerations in constructing and managing a master production schedule. This is a critical module in the manufacturing planning and control system. The effective master production schedule provides the basis for making customer delivery promises, utilizing the capacity of the plant effectively, attaining the strategic objectives of the firm as reflected in the production plan, and resolving trade-offs between manufacturing and marketing. The prerequisites to accomplishing this are to define the master scheduling task in the organization and to provide the master production schedule with the supporting concepts described in this chapter.

The chapter is organized around the following four topics:

- The master production scheduling activity: What is the role of master production scheduling in manufacturing planning and control and its relation to other business activities?
- Master production scheduling techniques: What are the basic MPS tasks and what techniques are available to aid this process?
- The master production scheduler: What does a master production scheduler do and what are the key organizational relationships?
- Examples: How do some actual MPS systems work in practice?

Chapter 7 is closely related to Chapter 8 in which enhancements to the master production scheduling (MPS) process are presented. The production plan, from which the MPS is derived, is discussed in Chapter 9, and Chapter 10 describes the management of the day-to-day demands for plant capacity. MRP concepts, described in Chapters 2 and 3, are applied in this chapter and some advanced MPS concepts are presented in Chapter 14.

THE MASTER PRODUCTION SCHEDULING ACTIVITY

We begin with a brief overview of the master production scheduling (MPS) process. What is the MPS activity and how does it relate to other manufacturing planning and control (MPC) systems, and to other company functions? What is the sequence of tasks performed by the master production scheduler?

At an operational level, the most basic decisions relate to how to construct and update the MPS. This involves the processing of MPS transactions, the maintenance of MPS records and reports, a periodic review and update cycle (we call this "rolling through time"), the processing and response to exception conditions, and the measurement of MPS effectiveness on a routine basis.

On a day-to-day basis, marketing and production are coordinated through the MPS in terms of *order promising*. This is the activity by which customer order requests receive shipment dates. The MPS provides the basis for making these decisions extremely effectively, as long as manufacturing executes the MPS according to plan. When customer orders create a backlog and require promise dates that are unacceptable from a marketing viewpoint, trade-off conditions are established for making changes.

The anticipated build schedule

The master production schedule (MPS) is an anticipated build schedule for manufacturing end products (or product options). As such, it is a statement of production, not a statement of market demand. That is, the MPS is *not* a forecast. The forecast of sales is a critical input into the planning process that is used for the determination of the MPS, but the MPS is not identical to the forecast in most instances. The MPS takes into account capacity limitations as well as desires to utilize capacity fully. This means that some items may be built before they are needed for sale, and other items may not be built even though the marketplace could consume them.

The master production schedule is stated in product specifications. That is, the MPS is stated in part numbers for which bills of material exist. It forms the basic communication link with manufacturing. Since it is a build schedule, it must be stated in terms used to determine component-part needs and other requirements. The MPS cannot, therefore, be stated in overall dollars or some other global unit of measure. The specific products in the MPS can be end-item product designations. Alternatively, the specific products may be groups of items such as models instead of end items. For example, a General Motors assembly plant might state the MPS as so many thousand J-body cars per week, with exact product mix (e.g., Chevrolet, four-door, four-cylinder, etc.) determined with a final assembly schedule (FAS) which is not ascertained until the latest possible moment. If the MPS is to be stated in terms of product groups (e.g., J-body cars) then it will be necessary to create special bills of material (planning bills) for these groups (e.g., an average J-body car planning bill.)

Linkages to other company activities

Figure 7.1 presents our schematic for an overall manufacturing planning and control system. The detailed plan or schedule produced by the MPS drives all of the engine and back-end systems, as well as the rough-cut capacity planning. Not shown in Figure 7.1 explicitly are the feedback linkages. As execution problems are discovered, there are many mechanisms for their resolution, with feedback both to the MPS and to other MPC modules.

The demand management block shown in Figure 7.1 represents the forecasting, order entry, order promising, and physical distribution activities in a company. This includes all of the activities that place demand (requirements) on manufacturing capacities. These demands may take the form of actual and forecast customer orders, branch warehouse requirements, interplant requirements, international requirements, and service part demands. The resultant capacity needs must be coordinated with the MPS on an ongoing basis.

The production plan represents production's role in the strategic business plan for the company. It reflects the desired aggregate output from manufacturing necessary to support the company game plan. In some firms, the production plan is simply stated in terms of the monthly or quarterly sales dollar output for the company as a whole, or for individual plants or businesses. In other firms, the production plan is stated in terms of the number of units to be produced in each major product line monthly for the next year. This aggregate plan constrains the MPS since the sum of the detailed MPS quantities must always equal the whole dictated by the production plan.

Rough-cut capacity planning involves an analysis of the master production schedule to determine the existence of manufacturing facilities which represent potential bottlenecks in the flow of production. That is, the linkage provides a rough evaluation of potential capacity problems from a particular MPS.

The MPS is the basis for key interfunctional trade-offs. The most profound of these is between production and marketing in terms of exact product definition in the MPS. A request to increase production for any item usually results in the need to reduce production on some other item. If production for no item can be reduced, by definition, the production plan and resultant budget for production must be changed.

FIGURE 7.1 Manufacturing planning and control system

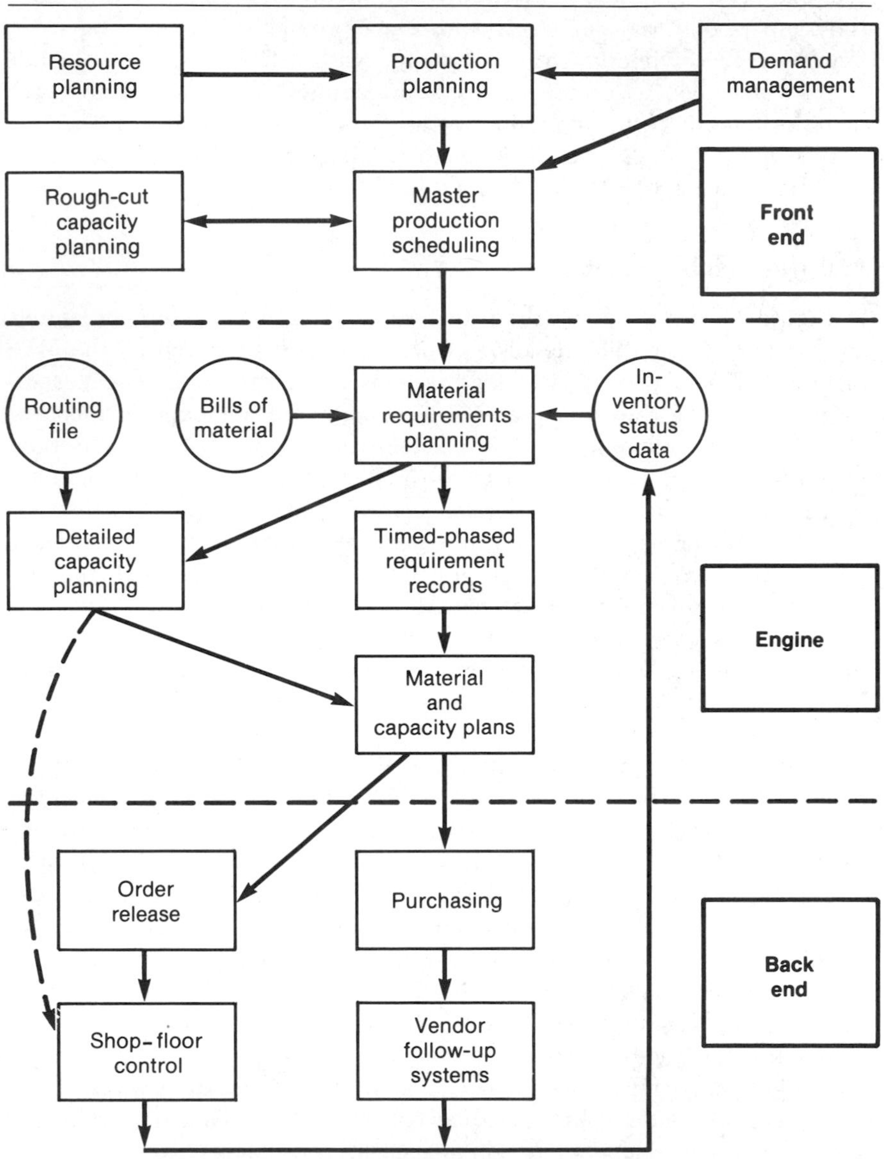

Since the MPS becomes the basis for the manufacturing budget, it follows that financial budgets should be integrated with the production planning/ MPS activities. When the MPS is extended over a time horizon sufficient to make capital equipment purchases, a better basis is provided for capital budgets. On a day-to-day basis, both cash flow and profits can be better forecast by basing these forecasts on the planned production output specified in the MPS.

The MPS environment

The concept of environment, as it relates to master production scheduling, encompasses the production approach used, the variety of products produced, and the markets served by the company. Three classic types of MPS environments have been identified: make to stock, make to order, and assemble to order. The choice between these alternatives is largely one of the unit used for the MPS. That is, is the MPS to be based on end items, specific customer orders, or some group of end items and product options?

The make-to-stock company produces in batches, carrying finished goods inventories for most, if not all of its end items. The MPS is the production statement of how much of and when each of those end items is to be produced. Firms that make to stock are often producing consumer products as opposed to industrial goods, but many industrial goods, such as supply items, are also made to stock.

The choice of MPS unit for the make-to-stock company is fairly straightforward. All use end-item catalogue numbers, but many tend to group these end items into model groupings until the latest possible time in the final assembly schedule. Thus, the Ethan Allen Furniture Company uses a *consolidated item number* for items which are identical except for finish color, running a separate system to allocate a lot size in the MPS to specific finishes at the last possible moment. Similarly, the Black & Decker tool manufacturing firm groups models in a series such as sanders which are similar, except for horsepower, attachments, and private-brand labels. All of the products so grouped are run together in batches to achieve economical runs for component parts and to exploit the learning curve in the final assembly areas.

The make-to-order company, in general, carries no finished-goods inventory and builds each customer order as needed. This form of production is often necessary when there is a very large number of possible product configurations and thus, a small probability of anticipating the exact needs of a customer. In this business environment, customers expect to wait for a large portion of the entire design and manufacturing lead time. Examples include a tugboat manufacturer or a refinery builder.

In the make-to-order company, the MPS unit is typically defined as the particular end item or set of items that comprises a customer order. The definition is difficult since part of the job is to define the product; i.e., *design* takes place as the construction takes place. That is, production often commences before a complete product definition and bill of materials have been determined.

The assemble-to-order firm is typified by an almost limitless number of possible end-item configurations, all of which are made from combinations of basic components and subassemblies. Customer delivery times are often shorter than total lead times, so production must be started in anticipation of customer orders. The large number of end-item possibilities makes forecasting of exact end-item definitions extremely difficult, and stocking of end items very risky. As a result, the assemble-to-order firm attempts to maintain flexibility, starting basic components and subassemblies into production, but in general, not starting final assembly until a customer order is received.

Examples of assemble-to-order firms include General Motors with its endless automobile end-option combinations; the Hyster Company, which makes forklift trucks with options such as engine type, lift height, cab design, speed, type of lift mechanism, and safety equipment; and Tennant Company which makes industrial sweeping machines with many user-designated options.

The assemble-to-order firm typically does not master production schedule end items. The MPS unit is stated in planning bills of material such as an average lift truck of some model series. The MPS unit (planning bill) has as its components a set of common parts and options. The option usages are based on percentage estimates, and their planning in the MPS incorporates buffering or hedging techniques to maximize response flexibility to actual customer orders.

The primary difference between make-to-stock, make-to-order, and assemble-to-order firms is in the definition of the MPS unit. However, many of the techniques for master production scheduling are useful for any kind of MPS unit definition. Moreover, the choice of MPS unit is somewhat open to definition by the firm. Thus, some firms may produce end items that they hold in inventory, yet still use assemble-to-order methodologies and MPS units.

MASTER PRODUCTION SCHEDULING TECHNIQUES

In this section, we present some basic techniques useful for master production scheduling. We start with some graphical models to show the relationships between setting a rate of output, the sales forecast, and the resultant expected inventory balance. We then show how revisions to the plans are made as one rolls through time during a review cycle and takes account of actual conditions. Next, the process of order promising is presented. We show how the entry of actual orders consumes the forecast in this process. Finally, these concepts are incorporated into time-phased record formats.

The basic cumulative charting model

Figure 7.2 shows a highly simplified graphical example of a master production schedule involving an item with a beginning inventory of 20 units, a sales forecast of 10 units per month, and an MPS of 10 units per month as

FIGURE 7.2 Basic cumulative charting example

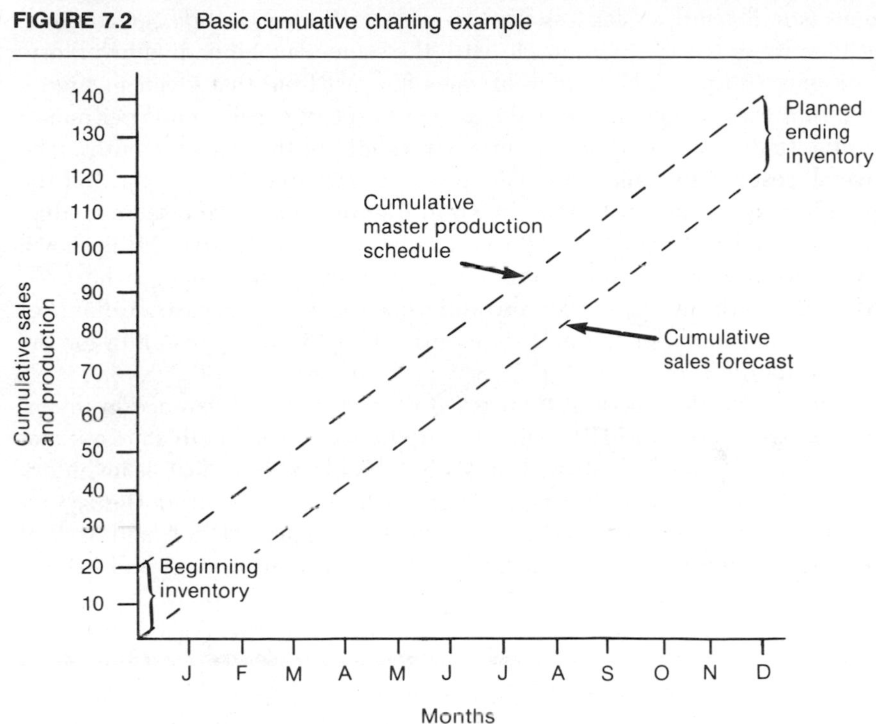

well. These data are shown as a cumulative sales forecast and cumulative MPS; that is, the cumulative sales forecast for the 12 months is 120 units, as is the cumulative master production schedule.

The vertical distance between the cumulative MPS and the cumulative forecast at any point in time represents the expected inventory position at that time, and the horizontal distance represents the amount of inventory expressed in time units. In Figure 7.2, the vertical distance represents a constant expected inventory of 20 units, and the horizontal distance a two-month supply. The cumulative MPS must lie above the cumulative forecast line if the plan is not to incur back orders.

There are several reasons for planning some inventory (the vertical distance) between the cumulative master production schedule and cumulative sales forecast. Forecasts are expected to involve some degree of error, and the MPS is a plan for production which may not be exactly achieved. The distance between the cumulative MPS and the cumulative sales forecast provides a tolerance for errors which buffers production from sales variations. For example, in Figure 7.2, if the actual sales in January were 20 units and the MPS was achieved, there would be no stock-out; if the marketing department still expected that the cumulative sales for the year would be 120 units (some month's sales less than 10 per month), production can continue at the rate of 10 units per month, with the same planned ending inventory.

Figure 7.3 presents a different sales forecast from that given in Figure 7.2. In this case, the marketing department expects to sell 5 units per month for the first six months and 15 units per month for the last six months. The overall result is the same, cumulative sales of 120 units for the year, but the pattern is quite different. Also shown in Figure 7.3 are two master production schedules, A and B. MPS A is the same cumulative MPS shown in Figure 7.2, a constant 10-unit production over the 12-month horizon. MPS B, however, adjusts for the difference in sales forecasts, calling for 5 units per month for the first six months, and 15 units per month for the last six months.

The crosshatched area of Figure 7.3 represents the difference in inventory between the two MPS plans during the year. They both start out and end with the same inventory; but MPS A builds a great deal of inventory during the first six months, which is gradually depleted during the last six months, while MPS B maintains a constant inventory. MPS A and MPS B represent two extreme strategies. MPS A is a *levelling* strategy and MPS B

FIGURE 7.3 Alternative MPS approaches to seasonal sales

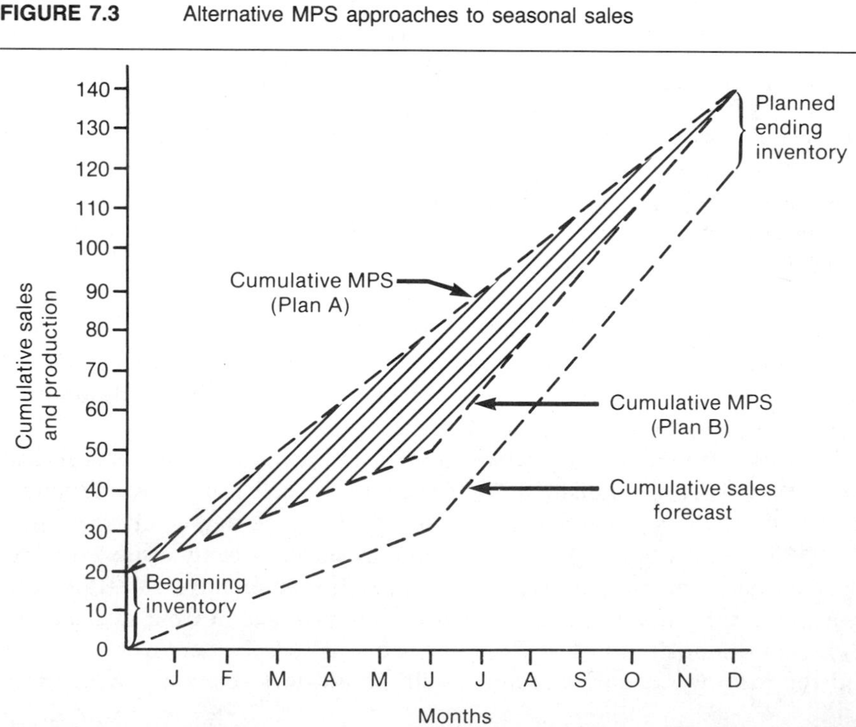

FIGURE 7.4 Lot sizing in the MPS

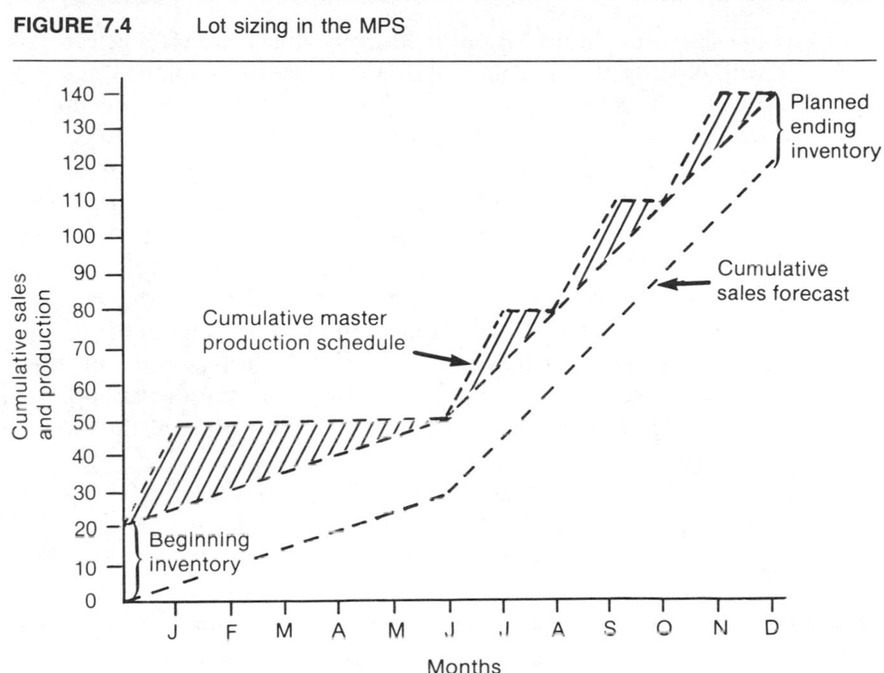

is a *chase* strategy. MPS A calls for no hiring, firing, or capacity adjustments, while MPS B, on the other hand, requires production adjustments to chase the marketplace.

Figure 7.4 presents the same cumulative sales forecast as Figure 7.3, but the MPS incorporates lot sizing. In Figure 7.4 the MPS is established using reorder point logic. An order is placed in the MPS for 30 units (the economic order quantity or EOQ) whenever the inventory (vertical distance) gets to 20 units (the reorder point). Another assumption in Figure 7.4 is that the production takes place continuously for one month. The master production schedule starts out at the beginning inventory position of 20 units (the reorder point), so an order is started for 30 units. It is completed at the end of the first month. This order lasts until the end of June, when the reorder point is again reached. Figure 7.4 shows a total of four batches of 30 units being produced over the 12-month horizon.

Manufacturing in lot sizes of 30 units produces inventories that last between production runs. This is called cycle stock and is illustrated by the crosshatched area of Figure 7.4. The cycle stock could be reduced by reducing the order quantity for the whole schedule or during the first six months only. Similarly, if the company felt that the overall inventory investment was too high for this plan, the order point could be reduced, with less protection against forecast errors.

Rolling through time

Let us now turn to the inclusion of Murphy's law: if anything can go wrong, it will. Rolling through time shows how actual conditions are reflected in the MPS. It is necessary to not only construct the MPS, but also to process actual transactions and make modifications to the MPS.

Figure 7.5 shows the same situation as Figure 7.4, but with the necessary changes to the MPS after one month of actual operations. The lowest line in Figure 7.5 is the original sales forecast, which is the same as that shown in Figure 7.4. Figure 7.5 also shows the original MPS through July. Actual production during January was exactly equal to the MPS. For this reason, the solid line shown in Figure 7.5 as actual production is right on top of the original MPS. The actual sales, however, were 10 units instead of 5 units; the second solid line depicts actual sales. The figure shows the deviation from forecast, the resultant forecast error, and the actual inventory at the end of January (40 instead of 45).

The key question at the end of January is whether the original annual sales forecast is still valid. That is, does the marketing department still believes that the total sales for the year will be 120 units? If so, the revised sales

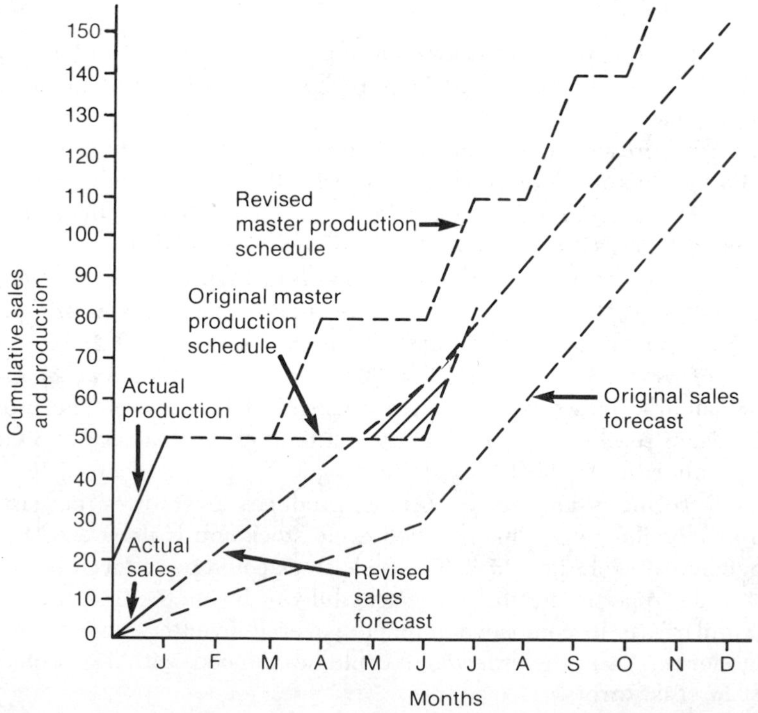

FIGURE 7.5 MPS revision to accommodate revised forecast after one month

forecast is some new dotted line connecting actual sales at the end of January to the 120-unit cumulative sales figure for the year. Let us say that the marketing department has decided that the original forecast was incorrect. A new forecast at the end of January is for 10 units per month for the next five months and 15 units per month for the last six months of the year. This would total 150 units for the year. Since the new forecast incorporates 30 additional units, it is greater than the total planned production for the year. Clearly, some adjustment to the MPS is required if anticipated customer needs are to be met. The first potential problem is seen in the crosshatched area in Figure 7.5. The original master production schedule called for the first batch of 30 units to be started in January and the next batch to be started at the end of June. That is not sufficient to meet the revised forecast at the end of May.

The revised MPS shown as the top line in Figure 7.5 uses the same reorder-point logic used to establish the lot-sized master schedule in Figure 7.4. Figure 7.5 calls for five batches of 30 units to be produced during the year instead of the four batches shown in Figure 7.4. This difference raises the question of whether the company has the capacity to produce five batches in a year. The capacity issue must be resolved before the new MPS is put into effect.

There is one further attribute of the cumulative chart approach that should be explicitly recognized. The process of accumulating is analogous to averaging. The cumulative point on any curve at any time totals all activity from the starting point of the curve. Dividing by the number of months gives the average. Thus, we see that the cumulative notion is similar to one of averaging or smoothing for forecasting. What this means is that minor variations will tend to be absorbed in the cumulative total in the same way that forecasting models tend to damp out random deviations. This is extremely useful; typically, high costs are associated with making production changes, and to the extent that the master production schedule can be prevented from overreacting and actual occurrences can be buffered with inventories, changes will be made only when essential.

Order promising

In many companies, customers do not expect immediate delivery, but place orders for delivery in the future. The delivery date (promise date) is negotiated through a cycle of order promising where the customer either asks when the order can be shipped or else specifies a desired shipment date for the order. If the company has a backlog of orders for future shipments, the order promising task is to determine when the shipment can be made. These activities can be seen in Figure 7.6.

Figure 7.6 builds upon the revised MPS shown in Figure 7.5. The original sales forecast and MPS of Figure 7.5 have been removed, so that only the revised sales forecast and MPS are shown. In addition, we now consider the

FIGURE 7.6 Order promising example

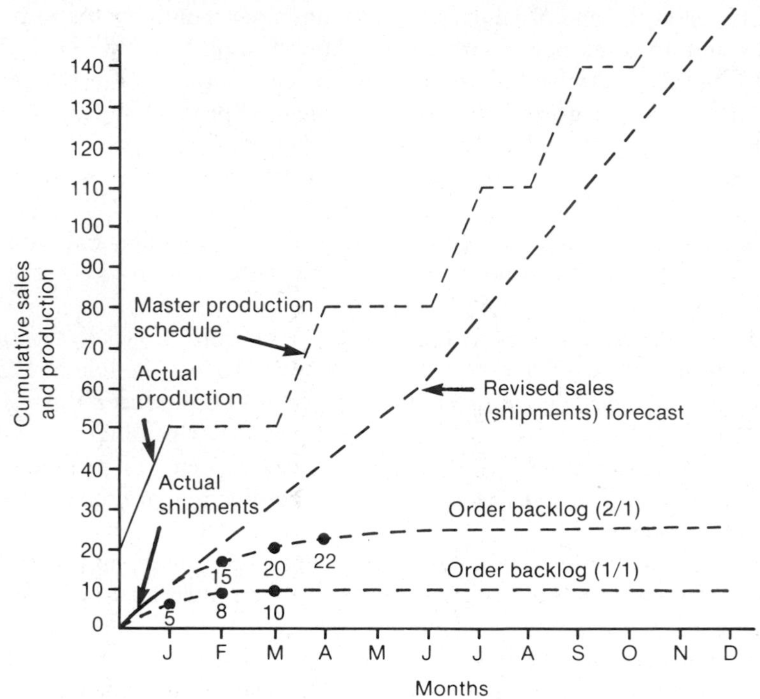

sales forecast line to be for shipments. That is, we are forecasting when items will be shipped, and we are closing out the forecast with shipments, not with sales. The distinction separates various forms of sales (e.g., receipt of order or billing) from our concern here.

The dashed line labeled order backlog (1/1) represents the cumulative backlog of orders that the company had on the first of January. Five units were promised for shipment in January, an additional three units were promised for delivery in February, and an additional two units were promised for delivery in March. No units were promised for delivery after the end of March. Thus, the cumulative order backlog builds to 10 units in March and remains constant thereafter. The actual shipments in January were 10 units. This means that five units shipped in January were not on the books as sold orders going into January. That is, 50 percent of the orders shipped during the month were received during the month. For some companies, this percentage might be significantly higher or lower.

During the month of January, additional orders were received for subsequent period shipping. On January 1, we had three units due to be shipped in February. Two additional units have been booked during the month of

January for February shipment, so the total backlog at the beginning of February for February shipment is five units. An additional three units have been booked for March shipment and an additional two units for April shipment. We see then that the cumulative order backlog as of 2/1 builds to 22 units by the end of April and remains constant from there on.

The difference between the cumulative order backlog as of 2/1 and the cumulative order backlog as of 1/1 (12 units) is the total number of units ordered during the month of January. This may well have been one of the key inputs used by the marketing department in the revision of their sales forecasts.

The cumulative order backlog (including actual shipments) as of 2/1 for the month of February is 15 units. The forecast for the cumulative total shipments as of the end of February is 20 units. We expect to receive orders for five additional units to be shipped during February. Carrying this analysis one month further, we see the cumulative backlog for March at 20 units, and the cumulative forecast as of the end of March at 30 units. This implies that between the first of February and the end of March we expect to receive orders for 10 additional units to be shipped during that period.

A more interesting relationship is seen between the order backlog and the MPS. If we return to the order backlog position for January as of the first of January (5 units), we see that the anticipated production plus beginning inventory is 50 units. This means that we have 45 units "available to promise." That is, it looks as if we could accept orders for shipments during the month of January for up to an additional 45 units.

In actuality, this is not quite true. We could only accept 40 additional units for shipment during January. The reason for this is the next scheduled production for this item does not take place until the beginning of April; therefore, the beginning inventory of 20 units plus the 30 units master scheduled for the month of January have to cover all orders received for January, February, and March. Since we already have orders for 10 units on the books for shipment during that period, we can accept only as many as 40 additional units. Those 40 units could be shipped any time during January, February, or March.

In many firms, accurate order promising allows the company to operate with reduced inventory levels. That is, the order promising activity allows for the sales forecast line to be closer to the MPS. The companies, in effect, buffer uncertainties in demand by their delivery date promises. Rather than carrying safety stocks to absorb uneven customer order patterns, those firms *manage* the delivery dates.

It is extremely difficult to illustrate actual cumulative chart data without using colored lines for the graphs. One firm uses dashed red for MPS, solid red for actual production, dashed blue for forecasting, solid blue for shipments, and green for booked orders. Figures 7.2 through 7.6 have been carefully constructed to avoid intersecting lines. In actual pratice, the colors are essential.

The time-phased record

We turn now to another technique for MPS preparation and maintenance, the time-phased MPS record. The required data are the same as those used in cumulative charting models. The key advantage of time-phased records is that they can be prepared easily by computer; the disadvantage is that the graphical qualities of cumulative charts, which can be very revealing, are lost.

Figure 7.7 presents, in the format of a time-phased MPS record, the same data shown in Figure 7.6. The record shows the condition as of the beginning of January. A comparison of the two figures shows the similarities. The forecast is 10 per month for the first six months and 15 for the last six months. The order backlog on January 1 was five units to be shipped in January, three in February, and two in March. The available row is the expected ending inventory. The convention is to use the greater of forecast or orders to do this, but for this example it is simply: on hand + MPS − forecast. This is equal to the vertical distance between the sales forecast line and MPS line in Figure 7.6. The available-to-promise row basically follows the same logic we used before. The on hand (20) plus the MPS (30) must cover all booked orders (5 + 3 + 2) until the next MPS. The residual (20 + 30 − 5 − 3 − 2 = 40) is the amount not presently committed to customer orders and thus available to promise.

Some companies may choose to show the available-to-promise (ATP) row as cumulative (70 in April), but this is not the approach used in most commercial computer software packages. Keeping the additional increments of ATP separate makes order promising easier and also has the advantage of not

FIGURE 7.7 Basic MPS time-phased record (months)

	J	F	M	A	M	J	J	A	S	O	N	D
Forecast	10	10	10	10	10	10	15	15	15	15	15	15
Orders	5	3	2									
Available	40	30	20	40	30	20	35	20	35	20	35	20
Available to promise	40			30			30		30		30	
MPS	30			30			30		30		30	

On hand = 20

overstating the availability position (i.e., there are not really 70 available to promise in April *and* 40 in January).

Consuming the forecast

One authority on master production scheduling, Richard Ling, originated the idea that actual customer orders *consume* the forecast. That is, we start out with an estimate (the forecast), and actual orders come in to consume (either partially, fully, or over) the estimate. This can be seen in the data of Figure 7.7. Of the 10 units forecast for January, five have been consumed. For February, 3 of 10 have been consumed as have 2 of the 10 for March.

Let us consider Figure 7.7 and see if we can accept the following hypothetical set of customer orders in January, assuming they were received in the sequence listed.

Order number	*Amount*	*Desired month*
1	20	January
2	10	February
3	35	May
4	10	June

The anwer is yes to all but order number 4. Since the total amount requested is 75, and the amount available to promise is only 70 for the first six months, only five units of order number 4 could be shipped. Let us say that the customer would not accept a partial delivery, so we negotiated for delivery in July. The resultant time-phased record at the beginning of February is shown as Figure 7.8, which incorporates the forecast for January of next year.

Obviously, the set of orders received during January represents a major forecast deviation. However, it does allow us to see clearly how we can use the record to make decisions as we roll through time. Let us first review the arithmetic of the process. The on-hand inventory at the beginnning of February is the January beginning inventory (20) + MPS (30) − old orders (5) − January order number 1 (20) = 25.

The available row provides the master production schedulers with a projection of the item availability throughout the planning horizon in a manner analogous to projecting an on-hand inventory balance. The convention of subtracting the *greater* of forecast or orders from the inventory and MPS quantities to calculate the available quantities has an affect here. For February, for example, the available is the 25 units of inventory minus the 13 units on order, for a total of 12. In March, the available quantity is 2, the difference between the February inventory of 12 and the forecast of 10.

FIGURE 7.8 MPS record at beginning of February (months)

	F	M	A	M	J	J	A	S	O	N	D	J
Forecast	10	10	10	10	10	15	15	15	15	15	15	20
Orders	13	2		35		10						
Available	12	2	22	−13	−23	−8	−23	−8	−23	−8	−23	−43
Available to promise	5		0			20		30		30		
MPS			30			30		30		30		

On hand = 25

The available position at the end of some planning horizon is an important piece of information for managing the master production schedule. It is at the end of this planning horizon that the master production schedulers can create additional MPS quantities. If the projected available is positive in that time bucket, then the scheduling of more production of the item may not be necessary. Note, for example, that in January (see Figure 7.7), the December available was 20 and no MPS quantity was entered for December. In the month of February, the available for next January is −43 (see Figure 7.8) due to the forecast of 20 and the consumption of the forecast by the orders booked in January. This indicates that an MPS quantity should be considered for January. The negative available numbers for March through January indicate the desire for more MPS. Whether this can be achieved is a matter of response time and competing needs (other items).

The convention of the greater of forecast or orders means that large orders will be immediately reflected in the availability position. This provides signals to the master production scheduler to consider responding to the order by increasing future item availability, which can be used for booking future orders. The available-to-promise row controls the actual order promising.

To calculate the available-to-promise position, we consider only actual orders and the scheduled production, as indicated by the MPS. We calculate only the incremental available to promise. Note that in Figure 7.8, the 25 units on hand must cover actual orders for February and March since no additional production is scheduled. In April, 30 additional units are scheduled, but none of them is available to promise. The 5 units available to promise in February comes from the 25 on hand minus the 13 units ordered for February and the 2 units ordered for March. Another 5 units of the on hand are needed for the order of 35 in May since the MPS of 30 units in April is not sufficient. This leaves only 5 units available to promise for the months of February through June. Of the 30 units that will be produced in July, 10 will be used for the order in July. This leaves 20 units available to promise in July.

Note that the later customer orders are covered by the later MPS quantities. The 10-unit order for July could have been covered by 5 units in February plus 5 units in July instead of all 10 in July. This would have left no units for promising from February until July, greatly reducing promise flexibility. The convention is to preserve early promise flexibility by reducing the available to promise in as late a period as possible.

The use of both the available row and the available-to-promise (ATP) row is key to effective master production scheduling. Using the ATP to book orders means that no customer promise will be made which cannot be kept. Note that this may mean some orders must be booked at the end of a planning horizon concurrent with the creation of an additional MPS quantity. As actual orders are booked (the order row), or anticipated (forecast row), or shipped (on hand inventory), the available row provides a signal for the creation of an MPS quantity. Once created, the MPS quantity provides the items available to promise for future orders.

The final item of interest in Figure 7.8 is to again focus on the negative available quantities from March through January. These negative quantities indicate potential problems—*if* the forecast is met. However, costly MPS changes should not be made to solve *potential* problems. If a condition arises that creates a negative ATP, that represents a *real* problem.

The time-phased records shown in Figures 7.7 and 7.8 are very similar to MRP records. In fact, the same data can be integrated with standard MRP formats. The primary advantage of doing so is to obtain standard record processing. However, it is necessary to keep track of actual customer orders and the timings of MPS quantities to make ATP calculations, so the MRP data base will need to be expanded.

THE MASTER PRODUCTION SCHEDULER

We turn now to the third of our four topics in master production scheduling fundamentals: Who is the master production scheduler, what does he or she do, and what is the appropriate job description? First, we briefly examine the use of some MRP concepts for the master scheduler.

The MPS as a set of firm planned orders

An interesting advantage of using standard MRP records to manage the master production schedule derives from the firm planned order concept. The firm planned order is similar to any planned order in that it explodes through product structures. However, it is *not* changed in either timing or amount as a result of MRP record processing. It is firm, and can only be changed as the result of action taken by a responsible person.

It is quite useful to think of the MPS as a set of firm planned orders. Thereafter, the job of the master production scheduler is to convert planned orders to firm planned orders, and to *manage* the timing and amounts of the firm-planned orders. The available row in the time-phased record provides the signals for performing this task. Standard MRP exception codes can provide indications of when and to what extent the firm planned orders might not meet the needs.

Managing the timing and amounts of the firm planned orders means that any changes to the MPS have to be carefully evaluated in terms of their resultant impact on material and capacity plans. The key need is to clearly understand the trade-offs between customer needs and other MPC system objectives.

The job

The master production scheduler has the primary responsibility for making any additions or changes to MPS records. He or she also has the primary responsibility for disaggregating the production plan to create the MPS and for ensuring that the sum of the detailed MPS production decisions matches the production plans. This involves analyzing trade-offs, and bringing to the attention of top management any situation in which decisions beyond his or her authority level are required.

As a part of the general feedback process, the master production scheduler should monitor actual performance against the MPS and production plan, and provide a distillation of operating results for higher management. The master production scheduler can also help in the analysis of what if questions by analyzing the impact on the MPS.

The master production scheduler is often responsible for launching the final assembly schedule. This schedule represents the final commitment, taken as late as physically possible, to exact end items. That is, the final assembly schedule has to be based on specific finished-good items. Other master production scheduler activities include an interface with order entry, and an ongoing relationship with production control to evaluate the feasibility of suggested changes.

Much of this activity is in resolving competing demands for limited capacity. Clearly, if several of the records for the master production schedule show a negative available at the end of the planning horizon, some trade-offs must be made. Not everything can be scheduled at once. The management of the firm planned orders must be done within the capacity constraints. An indication of the priority for making those trade-offs is provided by the available position. The lower the number of periods of supply or larger the number of periods of backlog the available position shows, the more urgent the need. If too many are urgent, feedback to marketing may be necessary to change budgets.

Figure 7.9 shows the job description for the master production scheduler at Hyster-Portland. This formal job description makes it clear that the master production scheduler needs to constantly balance conflicting objectives and make trade-offs. The position requires maturity, an understanding of both marketing and finance, and an ability to communicate. Computer software can be a great aid to the master production scheduler, but judgments will always be required.

Managing the MPS data base. For the master production scheduler to operate effectively, it is also critical that there be one single unified data base for the MPS, that it link to the production plan and to MRP, and that clear responsibilities for all transactions be established. This involves not only the usual data integrity issues, but also some organizational issues.

In the case of the MPS, many of the transactions occur in different functional areas. For example, the receipts into finished goods may come from completed assemblies (production), the shipments from order closing (marketing) or bills of lading (finance). It is critical that exact responsibilities be established for transaction processing, and that the data linkages to MPS systems and files be rigorously defined and maintained.

Another critical data base requirement for the MPS is proper control over both engineering and nonengineering changes to the bill of material data base. The MPS is often stated in planning bill units that may not be buildable; e.g., an average J-body car. This requires a more complex bill of material or product structure data base. The result is a greater need to procedurally control all changes to the bill of material and to evaluate the impact of changes both from an engineering point of view and in terms of the effect on nonengineering bills of material.

To support the master production scheduler, the time-phased MPS-record-oriented software system must produce the time-phased records to maintain the data base, provide the linkages to other critical systems, provide MPS monitoring and exception messages, and provide for all MPS transactions. Included are entering of order quantities into the MPS, firm planned order treatment, removing MPS order quantities, changing the latter's timing or amount, converting MPS quantities to final assembly schedule (FAS) quantities, launching final assemblies, monitoring FAS scheduled receipts for timing or quantity changes, closing out FAS receipts into finished-goods inventory, and providing for all customer order entry pegging and promising activities.

EXAMPLES

We turn now to some actual MPS examples. We start with an example from Pfizer, where cumulative charts are used. This technique is not only useful as a means of showing the MPS activities, but can be applied to many MPS problems, as well. We then turn to Ethan Allen and show their approach to master production scheduling. The approach uses a form of time-phased record, and we will see how standard MRP system approaches can be

FIGURE 7.9 Hyster-Portland master production scheduler job description

NAME		JOB TITLE MASTER SCHEDULER
DEPARTMENT NAME CAPACITY AND MATERIAL PLANNING		DATE ASSIGNED TO PRESENT POSITION
LOCATION NAME PORTLAND PLANT	LOC. CODE 02	DATE OF LAST EVALUATION

PREPARED BY: Roger B. Brooks

JOB DESCRIPTION 8-23

RATING

INADEQUATE	MARGINAL	SATISFACTORY	GOOD	SUPERIOR

BASIC FUNCTION:

Responsible for planning, organizing, and controlling the activities of the Master Scheduling Section within the Material and Capacity Planning Department.

REPORTS TO: Capacity and Material Planning Manager

SUPERVISES: Order Entry Administrator, Assembly Schedulers, Master Scheduling Planners

RESPONSIBILITIES:

1. Responsible for creating and maintaining a realistic and valid Master Schedule for all Portland Products. The Master Schedule should reflect requirements for Customer Orders, Stock Orders, the Depot, Product Availability Plan and Option Forecast, Interplant and Export Orders with economic and time consideration for Plant Inventory, Manufacturing Efficiencies, Customer Service and Plant Capacity. Proper Master Scheduling will allow the plant to operate at a steady state during periods of oversold order bookings without a build up of past due job orders and inventories, while simultaneously experiencing no idle capacity on bottleneck work centers.

2. Responsible for accurate, timely and organized order entry of Sales Orders, including IMT's and Export Orders, for all Portland manufactured lift trucks, carriers, winches, sold alones and production parts. Responsible for maintaining communications with the Industrial Truck and Tractor Attachment Sales Order desks to provide accurate and timely customer sales order shipping commitments.

3. Responsible for obtaining shipping instructions for all customers orders via communications with the Industrial Truck and Tractor Attachment Sales Order desks to prevent shipping delays.

4. Responsible for scheduling industrial truck, carrier, sold alone and winch assembly to support customer commitments within the constraints of the Master Schedule, Assembly Department and Parts Bank. Responsible for scheduling major weldments and front ends to support the assembly schedule.

5. Responsible for publishing the Daily Production Report and Final Unit Shipment Report in an accurate and timely manner.

6. Select, develop, and evaluate employees so they, as a group, accomplish the foregoing tasks in a businesslike, efficient, and professional manner.

Source: W. L. Berry, T. E. Vollmann, and D. C. Whybark, *Master Production Scheduling: Principles and Practic* (Falls Church, Va.: American Production and Inventory Control Society, 1979), p. 142.

usefully applied. In presenting these examples, aspects of the job of the master production scheduler are highlighted.

Master production scheduling at Pfizer, Inc.

The minerals, pigments, and metals division of Pfizer, Inc., has several plants using cumulative charting techniques for master production scheduling. An example is the Easton, Pennsylvania, plant, with annual sales of approximately $15 million. This plant produces iron oxides as pigments, ferrites, magnetics, and natural oxides. The products are industrial raw materials used in paints, plastics, food, cosmetics, magnetic inks, recording tapes, etc. The two primary uses are for coloring and for magnetic properties. The products are, in general, made to stock, although we will see that occasionally the demand exceeds capacity with resultant order backlogs.

The Easton plant employs about 250 people, and runs 24 hours per day, seven days per week. Only 50 end items are produced, which are mixed from various combinations of 11 work-in-process (WIP) materials. The 11 WIP materials are all made from scrap iron that has been dissolved in sulfuric acid. After the scrap iron has been dissolved, the neutralized acid is removed, and the residual material is processed in kilns with varying heat, time, and other factors, to create the 11 WIP materials. These, in turn, are washed, dried, and stored. Thereafter, depending upon the desired end product, selected WIP materials are blended, milled, and packaged.

The Easton MPS is stated in end items, in weekly time buckets, covering a quarter (13 weeks) as a general rate or production plan. It is stated in more exact product quantities for a four-week period, and updated every two weeks. The quarterly MPS is done with cumulative charting techniques, essentially the same as those illustrated in Figures 7.2 through 7.6. Before the start of each quarter, the corporate marketing group provides a forecast for each product, expressed as a general rate over the quarter.

As critical orders are received, they can and do vary from the forecast in any one week. Moreover, the marketing forecasts tend to be more accurate for the groupings of products than for the 50 end products individually. The result is necessary adjustments to the MPS, within capacity constraints, to accommodate customer orders as well as possible. These adjustments are made with a document that Easton calls *MRP Explosion* (Figure 7.10).

Figure 7.10 shows the 36 main products (some such as 23 and 34 are combined). The document is prepared every two weeks, covering the next four weeks. The cumulative chart is prepared every four weeks, so it provides the input to the MRP explosion for every other cycle, as well as the estimated demand for every cycle of the MRP explosion. The actual cumulation charts at Easton cannot be meaningfully reproduced without colors, so they are omitted here.

The primary objective in Figure 7.10 is to create the column of Planned

FIGURE 7.10 MRP explosion

Product	Estimated opening inventory	Estimated demand	Planned production	Estimated closing inventory	Production week				Component materials 1716	1721	1722	1728	1731	1732	1743	1750	1780	1789	1799
					1	2	3	4	Q		Q			Q	Q				
1	70	10	0	60															
2	26	408	510	128	170		70	170	510										
3	32	119	289	202		289			115	116	41								
4	9	163	238	84	238						238								
5	201	318	68	−49		68			7	17	27	17							
6	71	143	153	81	153						77			77					
7	60	190	136	6		136					14	68		61					
8	15	14	0	1															
9	65	92	0	−27															
10	36	231	204	9			204								102	102			
11	56	139	0	−83															
12	65	105	0	−40															
13	39	170	0	−131															
14	66	68	0	−2															
RC Total	811	2170	1598	239															
15	12	44	0	−32															
16	60	153	119	26	51			68	119										
17	14	68	51	−3		51			25	26									
18	2	102	0	−100															
19	0	34	34	0	34							17		17					
20	12	9	0	3															
21	15	14	0	1															
RD Total	115	424	204	−105															
22	190	170	136	156		136				136									
23, 34	20, 0	60	0	−40															
24	0	1829	765	−1064		255	255	255											765
25	0	0	0	0															
26, 35	207, 0	102	0	105															
27	129	102	0	27															
28, 36	219, 0	459	136	−104				136									136		
29	85	34	0	51															
30	17	0	0	17															
31	26	136	0	−110															
32	10	85	68	−7			68						34			34			
33	27	68	68	27			68									68			
RE, RP Total	930	3045	1173	−942				Tot	806	295	397	102	34	155	102	204	136		765
Capacity total	1856	5639	2975	−808	646	935	765	629	221	0	315	17	0	94	0	0	0		0
								Wk											
									2177	295	82	85	0	61	0	0	0		
									3170	0	0	0	34	0	102	204	0		255
									4238	0	0	0	0	0	0	0	136		255
							DP/OXD day		17	20.1	18.5	20.1		18.5	18.5	20.1	16.3	16.3	14.8
							OXD days		47.4	14.7	21.5	5.1		8.4	5.5	10.1	8.3		5.7

Quick oxide

$$\frac{82.8 \text{ OXD days}}{28 \text{ days}} = 3.0$$

Regular oxide

$$\frac{89.9 \text{ OXD days}}{28 \text{ days}} = \underline{3.2}$$

Total = 6.2

Note: All data in 1000 pounds.

Source: W. L. Berry, T. E. Vollmann, and D. C. Whybark, *Master Production Scheduling: Principles and Practice* (Falls Church, Va.: American Production and Inventory Control Society, 1979), p. 32.

production numbers. Note that our example shows the column total as 2,975,000 pounds. The plant capacity is 3 million pounds for a four-week period, and the demand of 5,639,000 pounds is in excess of the capacity. This means that pressure is constantly being exerted to get more of each individual product than the total for all products which can be accommodated. Holding to the 3 million-pound constraint will result in unsatisfied demand. This can be seen by the negative values in the column titled Estimated closing inventory which is analogous to the available row in the time-phased record. Trade-offs are required to establish priorities for production.

The set of four columns titled Production week allocates the overall production into weeks. The next 11 columns are the WIP materials necessary to make the products. The totals for these columns represent the exploded demand over the four weeks. This demand is segregated by the week needed in another report. The last two rows, DP/OXD days and OXD days convert the component material needs into equivalent units of capacity. Each WIP material requires a certain amount of time to be processed in the kilns. The DP/OXD day number is the number of pounds (in thousands) of that material that can be processed in a kiln in a 24-hour day. The OXD days is the resultant number of kiln days required to produce the four-week requirement. For example, the column headed 1716 has a total requirement of 806,000 pounds for the four weeks. A kiln can produce 17,000 pounds in 24 hours, so 47.4 kiln days are required to make all the 1716 needed.

A summary of the capacity required is shown in the box at the right of Figure 7.10. Several of the component materials have a Q at the column head. There are, in fact, two types of kilns, "quick oxide" and "regular oxide." The Q is for quick oxide, and the box totals the kiln day requirements for each type of kiln (82.8 and 89.9). When divided by the 28 days in the four-week period, the resultant number of kilns required is determined. Easton, in fact, has three quick-oxide and four regular kilns. These kilns are the limiting capacity or bottleneck operations at Easton. Figure 7.10 ensures that the MPS be constructed to not overplan this capacity while simultaneously loading it to the limit.

The entire MPS effort at Easton is done manually. At the time of this writing, a programmable calculator was being installed to ease the computational burden. It was felt that using the calculator could allow the four-week planning horizon in Figure 7.10 to be extended, the replanning cycle to be done on a weekly basis instead of every two weeks, and the cumulative charts to be updated for every cycle instead of every other cycle.

The Ethan Allen master production schedule

The Ethan Allen Furniture Company produces case goods (wood furniture) in 14 geographically dispersed factories. The total product line in these factories is 980 consolidated item numbers (different finishes for the same item make the number of end items about 50 percent larger). Each consolidated item number is uniquely assigned to a particular assembly line or building station in one of the 14 factories. For each assembly line in each factory there is a capacity established in hours such that if the hours of capacity are fully utilized on all lines, the overall company objectives as stated in their production plan will be met.

A forecast of demand is made for each consolidated item number, using statistical forecasting methods. A lot size for each item is also determined, based upon economic order quantity concepts. For each assembly lot size, the hours required on the assembly line are estimated. For each product, expected weekly priorities are established by dividing the expected beginning inventory by the forecast. In weeks after the first, expected beginning inventory takes account of production and expected sales. The assembly line is loaded to capacity in priority sequence, smallest to largest. Figure 7.11 provides a simplified example for an assembly line with 35 hours of weekly capacity. The simplified example is based on only four products. Actual lines typically manufacture from 15 to 100 different items.

The top section of Figure 7.11 provides the basic data for each of the four products: the beginning inventory, weekly forecast of sales, lot size, and estimated hours to assemble one lot. Note that for product C there is a beginning backlog or oversold condition.

The middle portion of Figure 7.11 is the set of time-phased priority data. For product A in week 1, the beginning inventory of 20 is divided by the weekly forecast of 5, yielding a priority of 4. That is, at the beginning of week 1 there are four weeks of inventory for product A. Similar priority calculations are made for products B, C, and D in week 1.

The rule for assigning products to the assembly line is to take that product with the smallest priority, i.e., the most urgent need. Thus, product C is scheduled for production first. The assignment of product C to the assembly line in week 1 consumes all of the 35 hours of capacity in that week plus 25 hours in week 2. This is so since it takes 60 hours to assembly a batch of 150 of product C.

Moving to week 2, the expected beginning inventory for product A is 15, since the forecast of sales for week 1 is 5. When 15 is divided by the weekly forecast (5) the expected priority for week 2 is 3. Alternatively, if four weeks of sales are in inventory at the beginning of week 1, we would expect to have three weeks of sales at the beginning of week 2, if no production of product A takes place. This means that for each product not produced, its priority number in the succeeding week is reduced by 1. The expected priority for product C at the beginning of week 2 can be computed by finding 35/60 of 150, adding this to the beginning inventory of −30, subtracting 35 units of forecast demand for week one, and dividing the result by the forecast of 35 to give a value of 0.64. The asterisk, indicating that this product is on the assembly line at the beginning of the week, is used here to simplify the calculations. At Ethan Allen, calculations of all priorities are made.

FIGURE 7.11 Simplified Ethan Allen MPS example

Basic Data:

Product	Beginning inventory	Weekly forecast	Lot size	Hours per lot size
A	20	5	50	20
B	50	40	250	80
C	−30	35	150	60
D	25	10	100	30

Priorities:

Product	P_1	P_2	P_3	P_4	P_5	P_6	P_7	P_8
A	4	3			0		−2	*
B	1.25	.25			3.5		1.5	.5
C	−.86	*			−.57		*	.71
D	2.5	1.5			−1.5		6.5	5.5

Schedule:

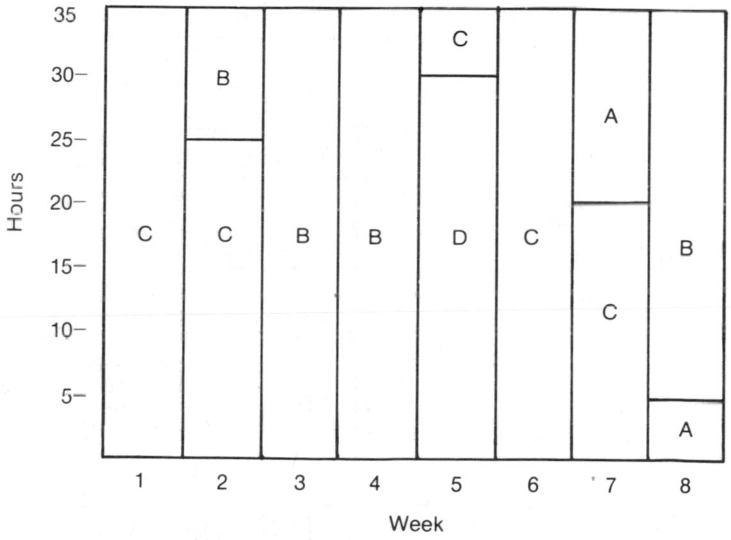

*On the assembly line at the beginning of the week.

The lowest priority product for week 2 is B (.25). Since a lot size of the product takes 80 hours, the capacity is fully utilized until the end of week 4. This is why no priority data are given for weeks 3 and 4. A similar situation is true for week 6 when product C, started in week 5, uses the full week's capacity. By loading each line to its weekly capacity, no more and no less, the match between the production plan dictated for each assembly line and detailed MPS decision making is maintained.

Figure 7.12 shows another way to create the Ethan Allen MPS. Here, the same four products are used. For each, a time-phased order point (TPOP) record is developed. The same schedule shown in the bottom portion of Figure 7.11 is achieved when the line is loaded to capacity in the sequence of when planned orders occur in the TPOP records. That is, product C has the first planned order, then B, then D, etc. Of course, the planned order for D in week 3 is not placed in week 3 because capacity is not available until week

FIGURE 7.12 Ethan Allen MPS example using time-phased order point

		1	2	3	4	5	6	7	8	
Gross requirements		5	5	5	5	5	5	5	5	
Scheduled receipts										A
On hand	20	15	10	5	0	45	40	35	30	
Planned orders						50				

		1	2	3	4	5	6	7	8	
Gross requirements		40	40	40	40	40	40	40	40	
Scheduled receipts										B
On hand	50	10	220	180	140	100	60	20	230	
Planned orders			250						250	

		1	2	3	4	5	6	7	8	
Gross requirements		35	35	35	35	35	35	35	35	
Scheduled receipts										C
On hand	−30	85	50	15	130	95	60	25	140	
Planned orders		150			150				150	

		1	2	3	4	5	6	7	8	
Gross requirements		10	10	10	10	10	10	10	10	
Scheduled receipts										D
On hand	25	15	5	95	85	75	65	55	45	
Planned orders				100						

5. There is also a tie shown in week 8. Both products B and C have planned orders in that week. The tie-breaking decision could produce a resultant schedule that differs slightly from that shown in Figure 7.11.

The great advantage to using TPOP approaches to this problem is that specialized MPS software development is reduced. The TPOP records are produced with MRP logic. The job of the master production scheduler is to convert these planned orders to firm planned orders so that the capacity is properly utilized. At Ethan Allen, the conversion of TPOP planned orders to firm planned orders is largely an automatic activity, so it has been computerized. Note, however, that the objective is to load the assembly stations to their absolute capacity, in priority sequence. Other firms might use other criteria such as favoring those jobs with high profitability, favoring certain customers, or allowing flexibility in the definition of capacity. If so, the detailed decisions made by the master production scheduler would be different.

CONCLUDING PRINCIPLES

The master production schedule (MPS) plays a key role in manufacturing planning and control systems. In this chapter, we have addressed what the MPS is, how it is done, and who does it. We see the following general principles as emerging from this discussion:

- The MPS unit should reflect the company's approach to the business environment in which it operates.
- The MPS is one part of an MPC system—the other parts need to be in place as well.
- Graphical models provide a clear illustration of key MPS trade-offs and decisions.
- Time-phased MPS records should incorporate useful features of standard MRP record processing.
- The order promising activities must be closely coupled to the MPS.
- The master production scheduler must keep the sum of the parts (MPS) equal to the whole (production plan).
- The MPS activity must be clearly defined organizationally.
- The MPS can be usefully considered as a set of firm planned orders.

REFERENCES

Berry, W. L., T. E. Vollman, and D. C. Whybark. *Master Production Scheduling: Principles and Practice.* Falls Church, Va.: American Production and Inventory Control Society, 1979.

Blevins, Preston. "MPS—What It Is and Why You Need It—Without the Jargon and Buzz Words." *APICS Master Planning Seminar Proceedings*, Las Vegas, March 1982, pp. 69–76.

Brenizer, N. W. "The Odyssey of Inventory Management." *Production and Inventory Management* 22, no. 2 (2d Quarter 1981), pp. 22–36.

Brongiel, Bob. "A Manual/Mechanical Approach to Master Scheduling and Operations Planning." *Production and Inventory Management*, 1st Quarter 1979, pp. 66–75.

Camp, Ellis J. "It's the Little Things that Count." *APICS 24th Annual Conference Proceedings*, 1981, pp. 66–69.

Garwood, R. D. "The Making and Remaking of a Master Schedule—Parts 1, 2, and 3." *Hot List*, January/February, and March-June, 1978.

Hoelscher, D. R. "Executing the Manufacturing Plans." *1975 APICS Conference Proceedings*, pp. 447–57.

Kinsey, John W. "Master Production Planning—The Key to Successful Master Scheduling." *APICS 24th Annual Conference Proceedings*, 1981, pp. 81–85.

Ling, R. C., and K. Widmer. "Master Scheduling in a Make-to-Order Plant." *1974 APICS Conference Proceedings*, pp. 304–19.

Proud, John F. "Controlling the Master Schedule." *APICS 23d Annual Conference Proceedings*, 1980, pp. 413–16.

________. "Master Scheduling Requires Time Fences." *APICS 24th Annual Conference Proceedings*, 1981, pp. 61–65.

Raffish, Norm. "Stand Alone MPS: Or Why Wait Two Years?" *APICS 24th Annual Conference Proceedings*, 1981, pp. 54–56.

Smith, Linda M. "MRP—Master Schedule Coordination." *APICS Annual Conference Proceedings*, 1978, pp. 290–98.

Tincher, Michael G. "Master Scheduling—The Bridge Between Marketing and Manufacturing." *APICS Annual Conference Proceedings*, 1981, pp. 57–60.

8

Master production scheduling practice

This chapter is dedicated to the practice of master production scheduling. The techniques described are used to improve the effectiveness of the master production scheduling function and to provide the attendant benefits to the company. The implementation of these techniques leads to a reduced number of items to be master scheduled, closer relationships between production and sales, more stable plans in production, and managed flexibility in the master production schedule. The implementation of these procedures requires detailed design efforts and careful management implementation, but the payoffs are significant.

The chapter is organized around the following six topics:

- Bill of material structuring for the MPS: How can nonengineering uses of the bill of materials improve master production scheduling practice?
- The final assembly schedule: How is the final assembly schedule coordinated with the master production schedule in the assemble-to-order firm?
- Master production scheduling stability: How can a stable master production schedule be developed and maintained?
- Buffering the master production schedule against uncertainty: How can the MPS absorb differences between actual and anticipated customer demands?

- Managing the master production schedule: How can MPS performance be measured, monitored, and controlled on a daily basis?
- Master production scheduling example: How are the concepts for MPS practice implemented in an effective system?

This chapter depends heavily upon fundamental concepts developed in Chapter 7. Specifically, the notions of MPS time-phased records, available-to-promise logic, the environmental differences (make to stock, assemble to order), and rolling through time are all used extensively in the examples in Chapter 8. Chapter 14 presents project scheduling approaches for the make-to-order company, concepts which build upon the ideas developed here.

Chapter 8 is also related to Chapters 9 and 10. The former deals with production planning which provides the appropriate goal that detailed MPS plans must match. The latter deals with demand management; there are critical analogs between MPS activities and the way in which actual demands are managed.

BILL OF MATERIAL STRUCTURING FOR THE MPS

The assemble-to-order firm is typified by an almost limitless number of end-item possibilities made from combinations of basic components and subassemblies. For example, the number of unique General Motors automobiles runs into billions! Moreover, each new product option offered to the consumer tends to double the number of end-item possibilities. What this means is that the MPS unit in the assemble-to-order environment cannot feasibly be based on end items. Defining other units for master production scheduling means creating special bills of material. In this section, we present a few key definitions to clarify what a bill of material is and is not. Thereafter, we discuss modular bills of materials and planning bills of material which facilitate MPS management. With this background it is possible to see how master production scheduling takes place in the assemble-to-order environment.

Key definitions

The *bill of material* is narrowly considered to be an engineering document that specifies the ingredients or subordinate components required to physically make each part number or assembly. A *single-level bill of material* is comprised of only those subordinate components that are immediately required, not the components *of* the components. An *indented bill of material* is a listing of the components, from the end item all the way down to the raw materials; it does show the components of the components.

The *bill of material files* are those computer records designed to provide desired output formats. The term *bill of material structure* relates to the architecture or overall design for the arrangement of bill of material files. The bill of material structure must be such that all desired output formats or reports can be provided. A *bill of material processor* is a computer software package which organizes and maintains linkages in the bill of material files as dictated by the overall architecture (bill of material structure). Most bill of material processors operate using the single-level bill of material and maintaining links or chains between single-level files. It is the bill of material processor that is used in MRP to pass the planned orders for a parent part to gross requirements for its components.

The single-level bill and the indented bill are two alternative output formats of the bill of material. Alternative output formats are useful for different purposes. For example, the single-level bill supports order launching by providing the data for component availability checking, allocation, and picking. The fully indented bill is often used by industrial engineers to determine how the product is to be physically put together and by accounting for cost implosions. A fundamental rule is that a company should have one, and only one, set of bills of material or *product structure* records. This set should be maintained as an entity and be designed so that all legitimate company uses can be satisfied.

The concepts presented in the rest of this section present another way of thinking about the bill of material. The traditional view is from an engineer's point of view, i.e., the way the product is *built*. The key change required to achieve superior master production scheduling is to include some bill of material structures based on the way the product is *sold*. In this way, the bill of material can support some critical planning and management activities.

Constructing a bill of material structure or architecture based on how the product is sold, rather than how it is built, offers some important advantages. Achieving them, however, is not without cost. The primary cost is that the resultant bills of material may no longer relate to the way the product is built. Activities based on *that* structure (e.g., industrial engineering) will have to be based on some new source of data. That is, if the description of how the parts physically go together is not found in the bill of material, an alternative set of records must be maintained. Providing alternative means to satisfy these needs can be costly in terms of both file creation and maintenance.

The modular bill of material

A key use of bill of material files is in translating the MPS into subordinate component requirements. One bill of material structure or architecture calls for the maintenance of all end-item buildable configurations. This bill of material structure is appropriate for the make-to-stock firm where the MPS is stated in end items. For each end item, a single-level bill is maintained which contains those components that physically go into the item. For

General Motors with its billions of possible end items, this bill of material structure is not feasible.

Figure 8.1 shows the dilemma. A solution is to establish the MPS at the option or module level. As indicated, the intent is to state the MPS in units associated with the "waist" of the hourglass. This necessitates that bill of material files be structured accordingly, i.e., the option or module will be defined fully in the bill of material files as a single-level bill of material. Thus, the modular bill of material structure has an architecture that links component parts to options, but does not link either options or components to end-item configurations. If the options are simply buildable subassemblies, then all that is required for the new architecture is to treat the subassemblies as end items; that is, designate them as level zero instead of level one. In most cases, however, the options are not stated as buildable subassemblies, but as options that provide some services to the customer.

Consider, for example, the air-conditioning option for an automobile. The single-level bill of material would show this option or module as consisting of

FIGURE 8.1 The MPS hourglass

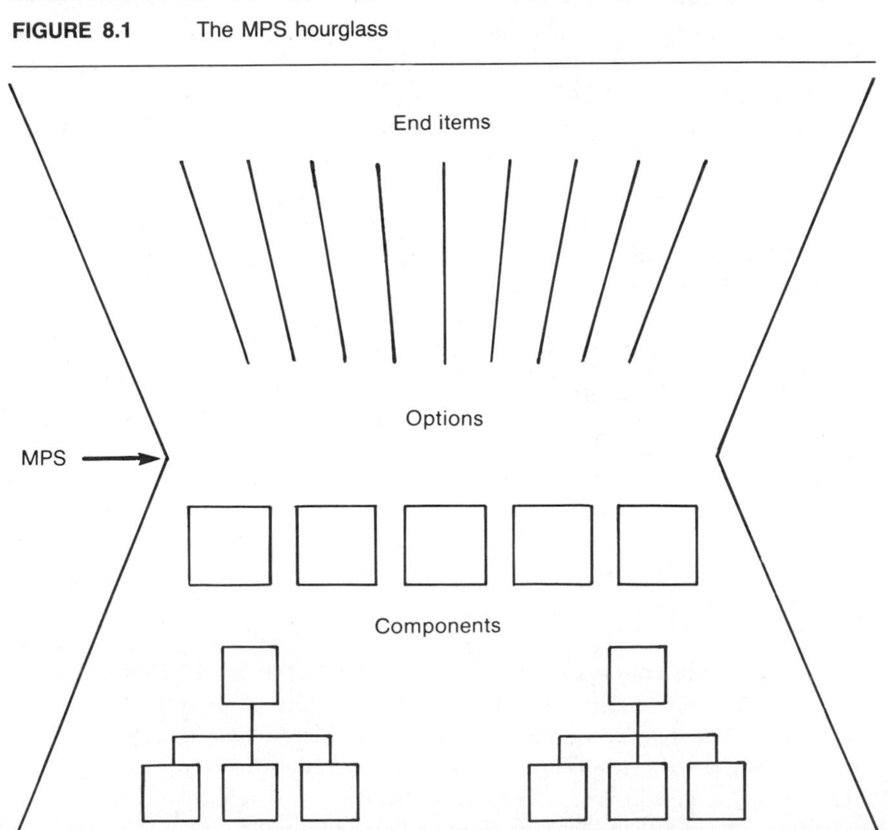

a particular radiator, fan, hoses, compressor, and interior knobs and levers. These items are not, however, assembled together. They are assembled with still other parts as subassemblies which eventually are assembled into the automobile.

The use of the air-conditioning option as a bill of material will pass demand from the customer who wants this option down to the necessary parts It can also be used to forecast demand for air conditioners. However, this bill of material is not useful in the physical building process for air conditioners. For example, the air-conditioning knobs are planned by the bill for the air-conditioning option. They are not planned by the bill of the dashboard assembly where they are installed. Thus, the industrial engineer needs other means to say how the dashboard is to be assembled and from what components.

Using the modular bill of material structure for a firm with a situation similar to that shown in Figure 8.1 permits the MPS to be stated in fewer different units. The MPS is stated in the terms in which it is *sold* rather than in terms in which it is built (i.e., air conditioning, two doors, automatic transmission, fancy trim, etc.). The approach is compatible with marketing perceptions of models, options, and trends in options (e.g., more people buying cars with air conditioning), which tends to improve forecasting. The master scheduling task may be made easier by using modular bills, but order entry tasks are made more complex since each option must be evaluated.

Once the individual customer order (representing a unique collection of options) is entered, it serves the function of a one-time, unique single-level bill of material. That is, it specifies which options or modules are to be included for the particular customer order. It is controlled by a separate final assembly schedule.

The planning bill of material

The restructuring of the bill of material required to better perform MPS activities has led many people to see the techniques and discipline of bill of material approaches as having many applications. An example is the planning bill of material, which is any use of bill of material approaches for planning only, as opposed to use for building the products. The modular bill of material approach just described involves one form of a planning bill since it is used for developing material plans and modules not all of which are buildable.

The most widely used planning bill of material is the *super bill.* The super bill describes the related options or modules that make up the *average* end item. For example, an average General Motors J-body car might have 0.6 Chevrolet unique parts, 2.6 doors, 4.3 cylinders, 0.4 air conditioners, etc. This end item is impossible to build, but using bill of material logic, it is very useful for planning and master production scheduling. Bill of material processing dictates that the super bill be established in the product structure files as a legitimate single-level bill of material. This means that the super bill will show all the possible options as components, with their average decimal usage. The logic of bill of material processing permits decimal multiples for single-level component usages. The super bill combines the modules, or options, with the decimal usage rates to describe the average car. The bill of material logic forces arithmetic consistency in the mutually exclusive options. That is, for example, the sum of two possible engine options needs to equal the total number of automobiles.

The super bill is as much a marketing tool as a manufacturing tool. With it, instead of forecasting and controlling individual modules, the forecast is now stated in terms of the total average units, with attention given to percentage breakdowns (i.e., to the single-level super bill of material), and to *managing* the inventories of modules using the available-to-promise logic on a day-to-day basis as actual customer orders are booked.

Let us consider an artificially small example. The Garden Till Company makes rototillers in the following options:

Horsepower:	3HP, 4HP, 5HP,
Drive Train:	Chain, Gear,
Brand Name:	Taylor, Garden Till, OEM.

The total number of end-item buildable units is 18($3 \times 2 \times 3$). Management at the end-item level would mean each of these would have to be forecast. A super bill for four-horsepower tillers is given in Figure 8.2. Using this artificial end item, an average four-horsepower tiller, only one forecast is needed from marketing. More importantly, the MPS unit can be the super bill. The entry of 1,000 four-horsepower super bill units into the MPS would plan the appropriate quantities of each of the options to build 1,000 four-horsepower units in the average option proportions. Actual orders may not reflect the average in the short run, however.

Figure 8.2 shows the use of safety stocks for the options to absorb variations in the mix. No safety stock is shown for the common parts. What this means is that protection is provided for product mix variances, but not for variances in the overall MPS quantity of four-horsepower tillers. A commitment made to an MPS quantity for the super bill means that exactly that number of common parts will be needed. In the example of Figure 8.2, if 1,000 four-horsepower super bills were entered, the bill of materials would call for 1,000 common parts modules, 600 gear options, 400 chain options, 400 Taylor options, 500 Garden Till options, and 100 OEM options. The safety stocks allow actual customer orders to differ from the usages specified in the bill of material percentage usage.

Although 600 of the 1,000 four-horsepower tillers are expected to be finished in the gear drive option, as many as 750 can be promised because of the safety stock. Similar flexibility exists for all the other options. The safety stocks are maintained with MRP gross to net logic so that appropriate quanti-

FIGURE 8.2 The four-horsepower super bill

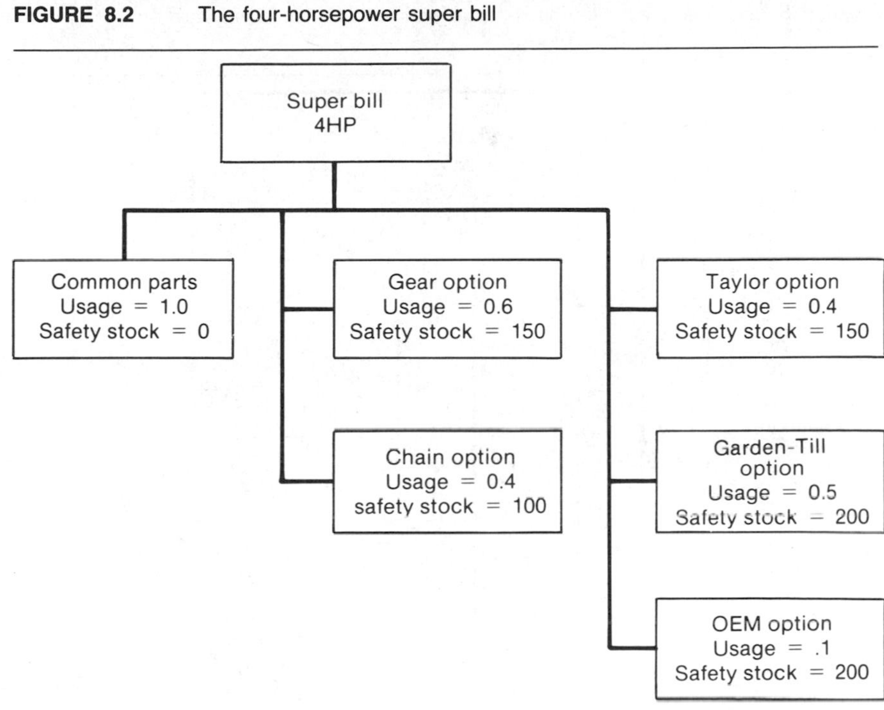

ties are maintained as actual conditions are reflected in replenishment orders. Moreover, the safety stock will exist in matched sets because of the modular bill of material structure. Matched sets occur because when one unit of the module is specified for safety stock, *all* parts required for that unit will be planned. Furthermore, the costs of all safety stocks are readily visible, marketing can and should have the responsibility to optimize the mix.

Order entry using planning bill of material concepts tends to be more complex than when the structure is end-item based. To accept a customer order, the available-to-promise logic must be applied to each option, meaning it is necessary to check each module. Figure 8.3 shows the flow for a particular customer order, in this case for 25 Taylor four horsepower in the Gear Option (T4G). The safety stocks are available for promising and will be maintained by the gross to net logic as additional MPS quantities are planned.

THE FINAL ASSEMBLY SCHEDULE

The final assembly schedule (FAS) is a statement of the exact set of end products to be built over some time period. It is the schedule that serves to plan and control final assembly and test operations; included are the launch-

FIGURE 8.3 Available-to-promise logic with modular bill architecture (order for 25T4G)

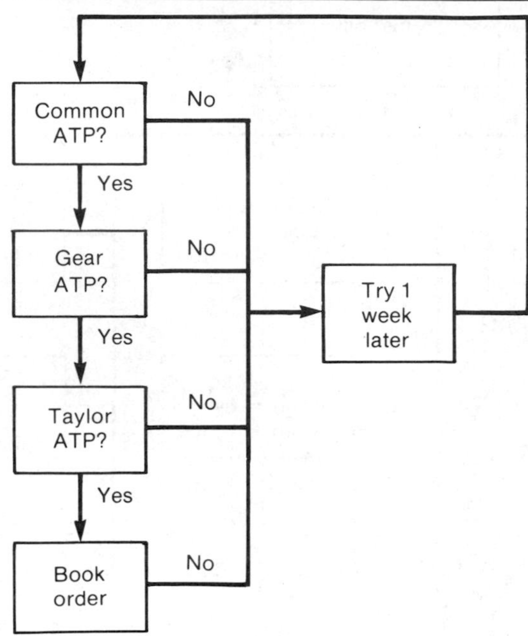

ing of final assembly orders, picking of component parts, subassembly, painting or other finishing, scheduling the fabrication or purchase of any component items not under MPS control but needed for final assembly, and packing. In short, the FAS controls that portion of the business from fabricated components to shipable products. It may be stated in terms of customer orders, end-product items, serial numbers, or special assembly order numbers.

Relation to the MPS

The master production schedule represents an anticipated build schedule. The FAS is the actual build schedule. The MPS disaggregates the production plan into end items, options, or groups of items, whereas the FAS is the last disaggregation—into exact end-item definitions. The distinction is that the MPS generally incorporates forecasts or estimates of actual customer orders in its preparation, with actual orders thereafter imperfectly consuming these forecasts; the FAS represents the last possible adjustment that can be made to the MPS, therefore it is advisable to make that adjustment as late as possible. Any unsold items on the FAS will become part of the firm's finished-goods inventory.

The FAS is distinct and separate from the MPS. The distinction is most clearly seen in the assemble-to-order environment. There, the MPS is typically stated in super bills and options, whereas the FAS must be stated in terms of the exact end-item configurations. However, even in make-to-stock firms such as Ethan Allen or Black & Decker, the MPS is stated in consolidated groups of items, such as all models of a table that differ only in finish, or all models of an electric drill that differ only in speed or gearing. In both cases, flexibility is maintained so that the final commitment to end items can be made as late as possible.

It is important to note that in make-to-stock firms a single-level bill of material is typically maintained for each end item. This means that the conversion from MPS to FAS is simply the substitution of one end-item part number for another. Both are valid, and both explode to components in the same way. For some make-to-stock firms, the MPS is stated in terms of the most common or most complete end item. As actual sales information is received, other end items are substituted. This process continues until a time is reached when all final substitutions are made.

For assemble-to-order and make-to-order firms, end-item bills of material are not maintained. If the FAS is stated in terms of customer orders, it is essential that these orders be translated into the equivalent of a single-level bill of material. That is, these orders must lead to bill of material explosion for order release, picking, etc. This is easily accommodated if the customer order is stated in the same modules as the planning bill. For the tillers, this would mean that the customer order would be stated in brand name, horsepower, and drive train terms.

Avoidance of firming up the FAS until the last possible moment means that the time horizon for the FAS is only as long as dictated by the final assembly lead time (including document preparation and material release). Techniques which help to delay the FAS commitment include bill structuring, close coupling of order entry/promising systems, partial assembly, the stocking of subassemblies, and process/product designs with this objective.

The Hill-Rom FAS

The Hill-Rom Company, a division of Hillenbrand Industries, manufactures hospital furniture and other health-care equipment. One of their products is an over-bed table, which comes in four different models, 10 alternative color high-pressure laminate tops, and four different options of chrome "boots" (to protect the base) and casters. The result is 160 (10 × 4 × 4) end-item possibilities. Let us see how a super bill approach to master production scheduling and final assembly scheduling could work in this environment.

Figure 8.4 shows an example super bill of material for this group of products. The cumulative lead time for over-bed tables is 20 weeks, which means that the MPS must extend at least that far into the future. This means that an

FIGURE 8.4 Over-bed table super bill

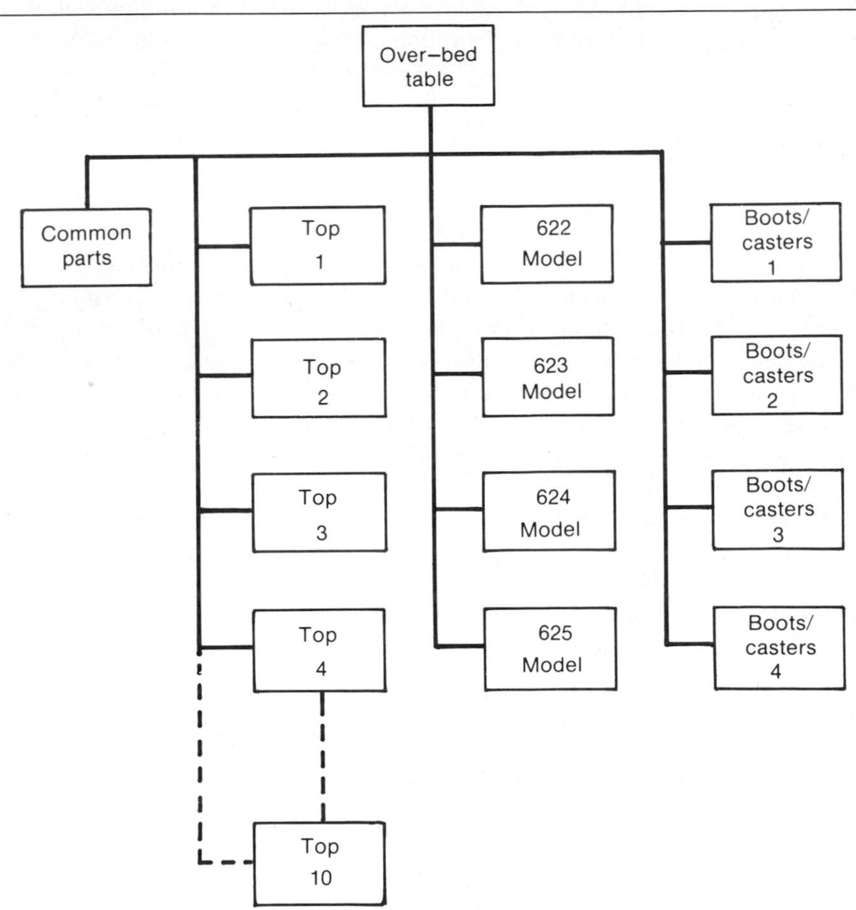

MPS time-phased record must be maintained over at least this time horizon for each of the 19 common part and option bills of material shown in Figure 8.4.

The final assembly lead time for this product is four weeks. Involved is part availability checking, order launching, component part release, welding of subassemblies, snag grinding to smooth welded surfaces, degreasing, painting, subassembly, and final assembly.

Hill-Rom is basically an assemble-to-order company, but some finished-goods inventory is held. This means that for each of the 160 end-item over-bed tables, an on-hand balance record must be maintained. This is incorporated in a time-phased FAS record. The overall need is for 19 time-phased

MPS records for each option and the common parts, maintained for week 5 through at least week 20, plus 160 time-phased FAS records, maintained for each end item for weeks 1 through 4.

The FAS job is to convert MPS records into FAS records as we roll through time. This job is done by the master production scheduler interacting with marketing, since the FAS represents the final culmination of the MPS process.

A related task is order promising, since customer orders may be promised out of the FAS system (on hand or in final assembly) or out of the MPS system (option by option, as done in Figure 8.3). Figures 8.5, 8.6, and 8.7 show this process. In Figure 8.5, we show an FAS record. This record is for one of the 160 end items and is maintained only for the length of the FAS lead time, four weeks. The record is for the 622 model, with "gunstock" colored top, and 01B boots/caster combination; the finished-good item number which identifies this configuration is 17123–01B GUN.

FIGURE 8.5 FAS record for 17123-01B GUN table

Part no.	*Item*	*FAS lead time*	*On hand*
7123-01B GUN	*Over-bed Table*	*4*	*120*

Week	1	2	3	4	
Orders	10			30	Before booking order F 5264
Available	160	160	210	230	
Available to promise	160		50	20	
FAS	50		50	50	

Week	1	2	3	4	
Orders	10		200	30	After booking order F 5264
Available	160	160	10	30	
Available to promise	10			20	
FAS	50		50	50	

MPS pegging detail				*Actual order pegging detail*			
Week	*Shop Order*	*Quantities*	*Action*	*Week*	*Quantity*	*Customer Order*	*Code*
1	011	50		1	10	F 5117	F
3	027	50		3	200	F 5264	F
4	039	50		4	30	F 5193	F

Note that there are *only* orders in the record (no forecasts), and they are used to compute the available row. This convention recognizes that the FAS is finishing out products in a specific configuration. The 50 units that will be completed this week are not subject to uncertainty. If no customer order is received for these, they will go into stock; essentially, a "sales order" has been written by the company.

Figure 8.5 also shows an order for 200 units being booked. The customer has requested shipment of the complete order as soon as possible. The available-to-promise (ATP) logic leads to putting the order into week 3 since only 160 units can be promised prior to week 3. This is shown in the "before" and "after" sections of Figure 8.5. The bottom section of the figure shows the supporting pegging data for the orders. The customer orders are pegged with an F code (satisfied from the FAS system).

Next we assume that another customer order is received, requesting shipment in week 6. Since this is outside the FAS it can be satisfied from the MPS. Figure 8.6 shows the MPS record for the common-parts option. Note that the MPS quantities are for common and option part numbers. Moreover, inventories for these options can exist, even though the physical inventory would be only a collection of parts. (On-hand balance for common parts is 10.) The MPS option quantities can also be committed to final assembly

FIGURE 8.6 MPS record for common parts

Part no.	*Item*	*MPS lead time*
1234	*Common parts*	*20*

Week	5	6	7	8	20	21	
Forecast	75	75	75	75	75	75	
Orders	10						Before
Available	−15	210	235	160	125	50	booking
Available to promise	50	300	100				order
MPS	50	300	100	0			
On hand = 10							

Week	5	6	7	8	20	21	
Forecast	75	75	75	75	75	75	
Orders	10	200					After
Available	−15	85	110	35	0	−75	booking
Available to promise	50	100	100				order
MPS	50	300	100				
On hand = 10							

FIGURE 8.7 Available-to-promise logic

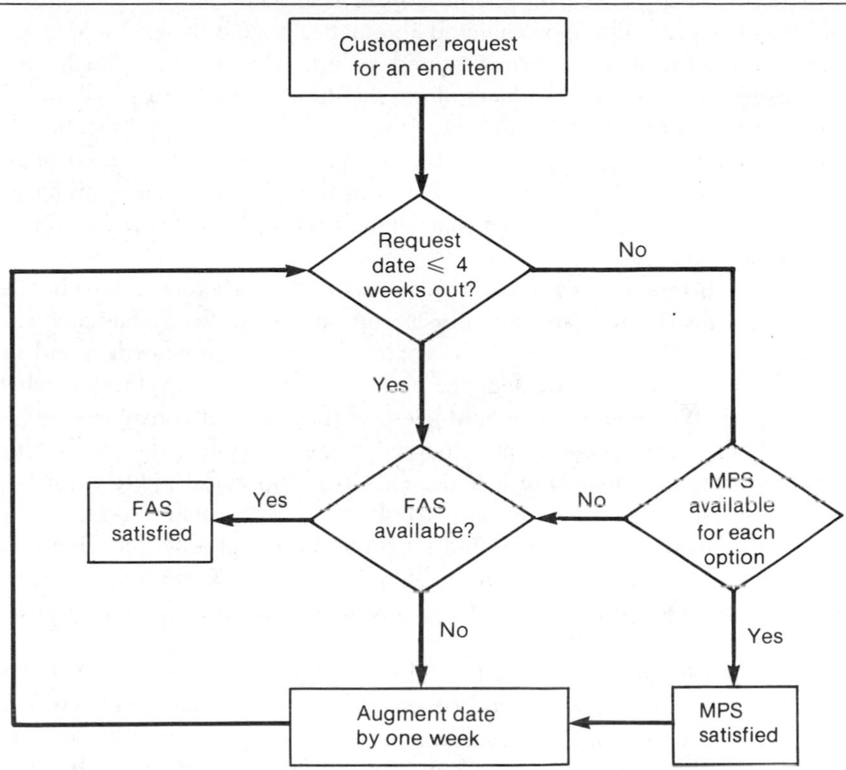

specific end items. When final assembly starts, it takes four weeks to finish out the end item. Figure 8.7 shows the ATP logic required to book any customer order in the Hill-Rom system.

MPS STABILITY

A stable master production schedule translates into stable component schedules, which mean improved performance in plant operations. Too many changes in the MPS are costly in terms of reduced productivity. However, two few changes can lead to poor customer service levels and increased inventory. The objective is to strike a balance where stability is monitored and managed. The techniques most used to achieve MPS stability are firm planned order treatment for the MPS quantities, frozen time periods for the MPS, and time fencing to establish clear guidelines for the kinds of changes that can be made in various periods.

Firm planned order treatment

Black & Decker. A firm planned order is a planned order with timing and quantity that will not be changed automatically, and the entire MPS can be considered as a set of firm planned orders. That is, once the MPS is established, processing any change in it should be the sole responsibility of the master production scheduler after careful analysis of the implications of the change. The stability provided by firm planned order treatment of the MPS is particularly important to the rest of the fabrication and purchasing activities in the firm. It ensures that all supporting activities are aiming at the same target.

The firm planned order is particularly useful to ensure that all the changes in physical distribution are not transferred directly back to manufacturing through the MPS. Black & Decker creates the firm planned orders and the MPS in a way that isolate the logistics activities from the shop. First, marketing owns the finished-goods inventories, so they are not considered in the MPS time-phased records by manufacturing. Second, the marketing/logistics group does use the finished-goods inventories and TPOP records to determine when they next need to request an MPS quantity. Third, the times and quantities are negotiated with the master production scheduler. In this way, physical distribution problems are *first* reviewed by marketing/logistics before negotiating for MPS quantities or changes that require expediting in manufacturing.

The Black & Decker approach is illustrated in Figures 8.8 and 8.9. The first shows the MPS time-phased record for a model series of belt sanders. Note that it is exactly in MRP format and, in fact, is maintained as any other MRP record. Figure 8.8 does, however, show the creation of the firm-planned orders. The gross requirements come down directly as planned orders. This is done by specifying zero lead time, lot-for-lot order sizing, and no on-hand inventories. Any lot can be assembled in the same week it is launched, and the lot sizes put into the gross requirements are those negotiated with logistics. The result is de facto firm planned order status for these planned orders which are the MPS quantities. Just like firm planned orders, the only way they can change is by a manual shift in the gross requirements.

Figure 8.8 is for the model series 80070681–00. Each item is a belt sander but with different accessories, and one is sold under a private brand name. In the pegging data (STATUS) portion of Figure 8.8, the end-item model numbers can be seen as the last two digits of the reference number. This overall model series is comprised of four individual end-item models, 01, 00, 09, and 10. This section is read left to right, requirements first, then open orders, then planned orders. Thus the past-due requirement of 6,500 (also shown as current) is made up of 5,500 model 09 and 1,000 model 10, both due last week, week number 139.

Figure 8.9 shows the same item from the marketing/logistics viewpoint. Marketing/logistics monitor the finished-goods inventory for these make-

FIGURE 8.8
Black & Decker time-phased MPS record

WEEK 140 **INVENTORY STATUS** CODE- A FOR 80070581-00 (PART NUMBER OR RAW MATERIAL CODE) CLASS OF FAMILY — I N D I V I D U A L - P A R T (TITLE OF INQUIRY) — REQUESTED BY VANCE (NAME) 843 01 (DEPT. NO.)

CATEGORY	PART NUMBER OR RAW MATERIAL CODE	DESCRIPTION	UNIT OF MEASURE	ABC CODE	FAMILY CODE	CLASS CODE	BUYER CODE	STANDARDIZATION CODE	LAST EFFECTIVE ECN NUMBER	PACKAGE ASSEMBLY	UNIT FAMILY MASTER	UNIT ASSEMBLY	LINE CODE	PHANTOM	SERVICE ONLY	SPECIAL CUTTER	DATE OF LAST C/C	DATE LAST TRANS.	ECN PEND	LOC
1	80070681-00	PA BELT SANDERS	50			207			46812	X			2				000	138	P	8

ORDER CODE	LEAD TIME S/A	LEAD TIME COMP	PRODUCTION LOT SIZE	SCRAP FACTOR	SAFETY STOCK	MINIMUM PURCHASE QUANTITY	PURCHASE CONVERSION QUANTITY	NUMBER ORDERS LAST YEAR	NUMBER ORDERS YEAR TO DATE	USAGE LAST YEAR	EST.	USAGE YEAR TO DATE	TOTAL STANDARD COST	SET-UP COST PER LOT	RUN COST (COST EACH LESS SET-UP)	QUANTITY BALANCES ON HAND	RECEIVED	STAGED	LOCATION PLANT	AREA
F				00				0	0	38002		45291	NOT AVAIL						8	

	PAST DUE	CURRENT WEEK	WEEK - 141	WEEK - 142	WEEK - 143	WEEK - 144	WEEK - 145	WEEK - 146	WEEK - 147	WEEK - 148	WEEK - 149	WEEK - 150	WEEK - 151	WEEK - 152
REQUIREMENT	6500	6500			9000				9000				6500	
ALLOCATIONS														
ON ORDER	6500	6500												
AVAILABILITY					9000-	9000-	9000-	9000-	18000-	18000-	18000-	18000-	24500-	24500-
PLANNED ORDERS					9000				9000				6500	

	WEEK - 153	WEEK - 154	WEEK - 155	WEEK - 156	WEEK - 157	WEEK - 158	WEEK - 159	WEEK - 160	WEEK - 161	WEEK - 162	WEEK - 163	WEEK - 164	WEEK - 165	WEEK - 166
REQUIREMENT			8500				8000					9000		
ALLOCATIONS														
ON ORDER														
AVAILABILITY	24500-	24500-	33000-	33000-	33000-	33000-	41000-	41000-	41000-	41000-	41000-	50000-	50000-	50000-
PLANNED ORDERS			8500				8000					9000		

	WEEK - 167	WEEK - 168	WEEK - 169	WEEK - 170	WEEK - 171	WEEK - 172	WEEK - 173	WEEK - 174	WEEK - 175	WEEK - 176	WEEK - 177	WEEK - 178	WEEK - 179	WEEK - 180
REQUIREMENT		9000			9000				9000				9000	
ALLOCATIONS														
ON ORDER														
AVAILABILITY	50000-	59000-	59000-	59000-	68000-	68000-	68000-	68000-	77000-	77000-	77000-	77000-	86000-	86000-
PLANNED ORDERS		9000			9000				9000				9000	

	WEEK - 181	WEEK - 182	WEEK - 183	WEEK - 184	WEEK - 185	WEEK - 186	WEEK - 187	WEEK - 188	WEEK - 189	WEEK - 190	WEEK - 191			TOTALS
REQUIREMENT			9000											101500
ALLOCATIONS														
ON ORDER														6500
AVAILABILITY	86000-	86000-	95000-	95000-	95000-	95000-	95000-	95000-	95000-	95000-	95000-			95000
PLANNED ORDERS			9000											95000

ORDERS OUT OF PHASE

* A - ALLOCATION; B - SERVICE/SUBSIDIARY ALLOCATION; H - PURCHASE ORDER ON HOLD; I - TRANSFER ALLOCATION; J - MFG. ORDER - FIRST OPERATION COMPLETE; M - MANUFACTURING ORDER; P - PURCHASE ORDER; R - REQUIREMENT; S - MFG. ORDER - SHOP PAPER ISSUED; T - TRANSFER ORDER; U - PLANNED ORDER

† AUTH. P - PART, U - UNIT; CO-ORD. S - SCHEDULE SHEET, C - COORDINATED; CONTROL ECN A - DROP IN ON USE-UP, B - PKG. ASSEM. CONTROLS ECN, C - A + B ABOVE

STATUS

* CODE	WEEK	REFERENCE NUMBER (LOC. / MFG. NO. BUYER, PURCHASE ORDER / LOT / MOD.)	QUANTITY	† AUTH.	CO-ORD	CONTROL ECN
		REQUIREMENTS				
R	147	000706818409	9000	U		B
R	155	000706818809	7000	U		B
R	164	000706819209	7500	U		
R	168	000706819410	1000			
R	175	000705810209	3000			
R	183	000705810609	7000			
		OPEN-ORDERS				
		PLND-ORDERS				
U	151	000706813610	1000	U		
U	159	000706819009	8000	U		
U	168	000706819401	500			
U	171	000706819609	6000			
U	179	000706810409	9000			
		NO WHERE USED				

* CODE	WEEK	REFERENCE NUMBER	QUANTITY	† AUTH.	CO-ORD	CONTROL ECN
R	139	000706818209	5500	U		
R	151	000706818609	5500	U		
R	155	000706818810	1000	U		B
R	164	000706819210	1000	U		
R	171	000706819601	1000			
R	175	000706810210	1000			
R	183	000706810610	1500			
S	139	000706818209	5500	U	C	
U	143	000706818309	9000	U		
U	155	000706818801	500	U		
U	164	000706819201	500	U		
U	168	000706819409	7500			
U	171	000706819610	2000			
U	183	000706810601	500			
		HAS COMPONENTS				

* CODE	WEEK	REFERENCE NUMBER	QUANTITY	† AUTH.	CO-ORD	CONTROL ECN
R	139	000706818210	1000	U		
R	151	000706818610	1000	U		
R	159	000706819009	8000	U		B
R	168	000706819401	500			
R	171	000706819609	6000			
R	179	000706810409	9000			
S	139	000706818210	1000	U	C	
U	147	000706818409	9000	U		
U	155	000706818809	7000	U		
U	164	000706819209	7500	U		
U	168	000706819410	1000			
U	175	000706810209	8000			
U	183	000706810609	7000			
		HAS OP FILE				

* CODE	WEEK	REFERENCE NUMBER	QUANTITY	† AUTH.	CO-ORD	CONTROL ECN
R	143	000706818309	9000	U		
R	155	000706818801	500	U		B
R	164	000706819201	500	U		
R	168	000706819409	7500			
R	171	000706819610	2000			
R	183	000706810601	500			
U	151	000706818609	5500	U		
U	155	000706818810	1000	U		
U	164	000706819210	1000	U		
U	171	000706819601	1000			
U	175	000706810210	1000			
U	183	000706810610	1500			

BLACK & DECKER MFG. CO. FORM NO. 30020

Source: W. L. Berry, T. E. Vollmann, and D. C. Whybark, *Master Production Scheduling: Principles and Practice* (Falls Church, Va.: American Production and Inventory Control Society, 1979), p. 67.

FIGURE 8.9 Black & Decker marketing/logistics MPS record

07/01/ MONTHLY TOOL INVENTORY PLANNING REPORT—PLANNING DIVISION 02 PAGE 0167

FAMILY IDENT	PROD CODE	CATALOG NUMBER	DESCRIPTION	MFG-MOD NUMBERS	E C	P-L-A-N-T CUR	LT	FUT	PROD P/GRP	UNIT GSV	UNIT A STD C	LOT SIZE	SAFETY STOCK		END-OF-MONTH BOH	B/O
020560	444	7450-01	BELT SANDER 220V	070681-01		60	00	00	040020	58.20	29.86	25		M	1176	6
	450	7450-06	BELT SNDR 240V	000000-00		60	00	00	020560	59.75	27.14	500		M		
	451	7451	BEST BELT SANDER W/	070681-09		60	00	00	020560	50.15	31.01	5000		M	907	6844
	461	7461	2SPD DUST COLL SNDR	070681-10		60	00	00	020560	61.06	38.23	1000		M	898	

PROD CODE	NET BOH	PAST DUE	JUL 140 ORDERS	SALES	EOM-INV	AUG 143 ORDERS	SALES	EOM-INV	SEP 148 ORDERS	SALES	EOM-INV	OCT 152 ORDERS	SALES	EOM-INV
444	1170	14		95	1089		620	469		25	444		305	139
450														
451	5937-	16	5500	4333	4754-		8278	13032-	19000	5759	901-	5500	5038	329-
461	898	640	1000	443	2095		715	1380		872	508	1000	605	903
TOTALS	3869-	670	6500	4871	1570-		9613	11183-	18000	6656	161	6500	5948	713

Source: W. L. Berry, T. E. Vollmann, and D. C. Whybark, *Master Production Scheduling: Principles and Practice* (Falls Church, Va.: American Production and Inventory Control Society, 1979), p. 68.

to-stock-items, and they use data like those in Figure 8.9 in the process. Figure 8.9 is a portion of the TPOP record, which is printed in monthly time buckets. The exact dates, kept inside the computer, are the same as in the manufacturing system except for a lead time offset.

In Figure 8.9 the ORDERS columns show the model 09 order of 5,500 and the model 10 order of 1,000 sanders. The equivalent marketing record uses the product codes of 451 and 461 for 09 and 10 respectively. Each of the remaining orders in Figure 8.9 can be matched with planned orders in Figure 8.8, except that the printout grouping into monthly time buckets combines two manufacturing planned orders for 9,000 each into one marketing order of 18,000 in the month of September.

Note in Figure 8.9 that the inventories (NET BOH) include a −5,937 for model 451, along with positive inventories for two of the other models, and no activity at this time for the 450 model. The negative inventory is for the private-brand product. This product is essentially made to order, not made to stock, and the negative balance is an unfilled order. The key point is that the level and composition of finished-goods inventory is a marketing decision. At Black & Decker, that is where these decisions are made, and the result is a stabilized set of firm planned orders in manufacturing.

Ethan Allen. Construction of the Ethan Allen MPS is based upon TPOP records, with assembly lines loaded up to exact capacities, and the sequence of MPS items determined by the date sequence of planned orders. This process might seem to lead to a great deal of repositioning of MPS quantities. That is, as actual sales occur, forecast errors will tend to reorder the MPS. In fact, this does not occur, because the planned orders from TPOP records are "frozen," or firm planned, under certain conditions.

Ethan Allen uses three types of firm planned orders for the MPS. These are illustrated in Figure 8.10. In essence, any firm planned order is frozen in that it will not be automatically repositioned by any computer logic. All MPS quantities for the next eight weeks are considered to be frozen or firm planned at Ethan Allen. In addition, any MPS quantity that has been used to make a customer promise (i.e., a customer order is pegged to that MPS batch) is also a firm planned order. The third type of firm planned order used in the Ethan Allen MPS is for what they call the *manual forecast*. Included are contract sales (e.g., items to a motel chain), market specials (i.e., items to go on special promotion), and new items (MPS is when the product is to be introduced). All of the blank space in Figure 8.10 is filled with a TPOP-based scheduling technique. Computerized MPS logic will fill in the holes up to the capacity limit without disturbing any firm planned order.

Freezing and time fencing

Figure 8.10 shows the first eight weeks in the Ethan Allen MPS as being frozen. This means that *no* changes inside of eight weeks are possible. In reality, no may be a bit extreme. If the president dictates a change, it will probably happen, but such occurrences are very rare at Ethan Allen.

FIGURE 8.10 Ethan Allen firm planned order approach

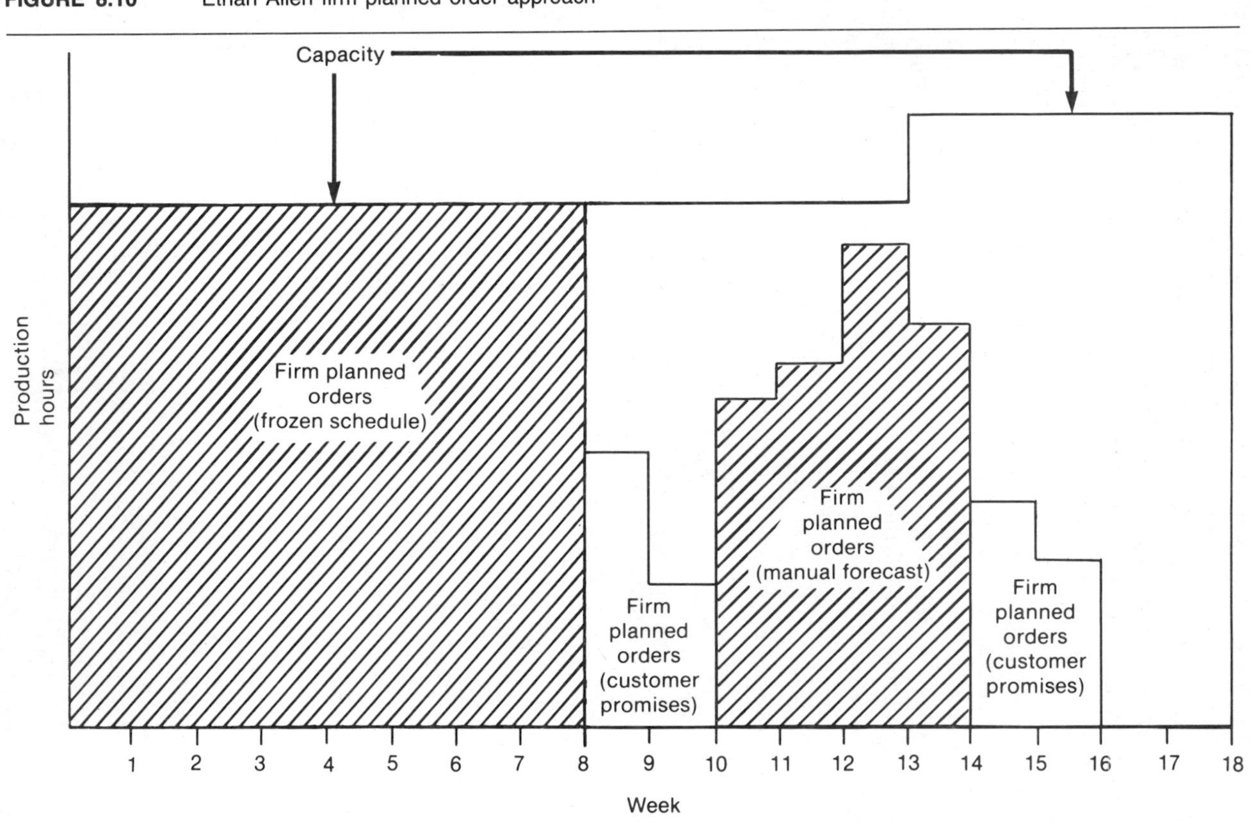

Source: W. L. Berry, T. E. Vollmann, and D. C. Whybark, *Master Production Scheduling: Principles and Practice* (Falls Church, Va.: American Production and Inventory Control Society, 1979), p. 51.

Many firms do not like to use the term frozen, saying that anything is negotiable—but the negotiations get tougher as we approach the present time. However, the use of a frozen period provides a very stable target for manufacturing to hit. It also removes most alibis for missing the schedule!

Time fencing is an extension of the freeze concept. Many firms set time fences that specify periods in which various types of change can be handled. For example, Black & Decker has three time fences, 26, 13, and 8 weeks. The implication is that beyond 26 weeks the marketing/logistics people can make any change as long as the sum of all MPS records is synchronized with the production plan. From weeks 13 to 25, substitutions of one end item for another are permitted, providing the required component parts will be available and the production plan is not violated. From weeks 8 to 13, the MPS is quite rigid, but minor changes within a model series can be made, if component parts are available. The eight-week time fence at Black & Decker is basically a freeze period similar to that at Ethan Allen, but occasional changes are made within this timing. In fact, assembly lines have been shut down to make changes—but the occurrence is so rare that everyone in the factory remembers when this happens! To achieve the level of productivity necessary to remain competitive, stability in short-range manufacturing plans is essential.

The establishment of time fences is critically related to lead times. When planning bills of materials are used, the two critical lead times are the cumulative lead time for all components and assemblies, and the final assembly lead time. These two lead times result in the *planning* time fence and the *demand* time fence, respectively. These are minimum time periods for which material commitment decisions have to be in place. The major part of the MPS job is to manage the process of crossing the time fences as we roll through time. This is illustrated with the Hill-Rom records in Figures 8.5, 8.6, and 8.11.

In Figure 8.5 we show the FAS for an over-bed table, end-item number 17123–01B GUN. This four-week record is inside the demand fence for Hill-Rom. Once this fence is crossed, i.e., decisions are made to roll common parts and options into final assemblies, the items will either go to customer orders or to stock. We are only concerned about demand in this period, not forecast, since the commitment has been made. That is, the demand time fence is the period of last commitment to an end item.

The planning time fence is 20 weeks out for the Hill-Rom MPS record. This is the lead time for which major commitments to purchased material and expensive component fabrication must be made. Crossing the planning fence means that consumption of manufacturing capacity is begun. It is within the planning fence that the master production scheduler uses firm planned orders, since changes in the timing of planned orders outside the planning fence do not affect the material plans in any major way.

The records in Figure 8.11 show the position during the processing cycle. No more orders were booked after the records depicted in Figures 8.5 and 8.6. Consider the FAS record in Figure 8.11. The inventory of end items is

FIGURE 8.11 Hill-Rom records after rolling through time

Part no.	Item	FAS lead time		On hand		
17123-01B GUN	*Over-bed table*	*4*		*160*		
Week		2	3	4	5	FAS record
Orders			200	30	2	
Available		160	10	30	28	
Available to promise		10		18		
FAS			50	50		

Part no.	Item	MPS lead time						
1234	*Common parts*	*20*						
Week		6	7	8	9	21	22	MPS record
Forecast		75	75	75	75	75	75	
Orders		200						
Available		150	175	100	125	−10	−85	
Available to promise		150	100		100			
MPS		300	100		100			
On hand = 50								

now 160 (120 units last week + 50 units assembled − 10 units booked for last week). There is an order for 2 units in week 5, which is part of the 10-unit order shown in week 5 on the MPS record of Figure 8.6. That is, the orders for 10 units shown in week 5 on the MPS record in Figure 8.6 have 2 of the 10 committed to the 17123–01B GUN item.

Note that the two units now shown in the FAS orders row in week 5 of Figure 8.11 for the end item have consumed ATP from week 4. That is, so far in the processing cycle, *no* common parts (and other options) have been committed from the MPS records to 17123–01B GUN. That decision is, in fact, a key part of the processing cycle. Figure 8.6 shows 10 units of common parts on hand plus an MPS of 50 in week 5. Any or all of these 60 common units can be committed to specific end items. The situation depicted on the top of Figure 8.11 shows that the 60 common parts units can be committed to end items *other* than the 17123–01B GUN. The MPS decision is to *which* of the 160 end items to commit, or whether to hold more common parts as inventories, thereby postponing the time of commitment to specific end items.

The master production scheduler must worry about the planning fence 20 weeks out. In Figure 8.6, we show how the booking of the customer order for 200 in week 6, drives the availability in week 21 to negative. This is the signal to consider scheduling an MPS quantity for week 21. If the logic used after the planning fence is MRP planned-order logic, a planned order would already appear for that week.

When the record is processed for the next week, the result would be as shown as the bottom portion of Figure 8.11. Since no more orders were booked than the 200 in week 6 plus the previously booked 10 in week 5, the availability position is changed (i.e., we didn't sell the 75 forecast for week 5). The available position in week 21 is still negative and *might* require an MPS quantity. To make this decision, the master production scheduler will need to evaluate the priorities for other MPS units and the capacity available. The task then is to allocate the available capacity to the competing needs so as to maximize the available-to-promise positions and remain synchronized with the production plan.

Some firms work very creatively to keep the planning and demand time fence periods to minimum levels. For example, some people ignore low-cost items in establishing the planning fence. These are kept in excess supply. The planning fence becomes that point in time, that, when crossed, will mean commitments to expensive components.

An interesting definition of the make-to-order company can be seen from the process of rolling across time fences. If the demand time fence is reached and no consumer order has been received, the choice is whether to build to stock or not to assemble. The latter choice will underutilize capacity and the firm is, in fact, a make-to-order company.

BUFFERING THE MPS AGAINST UNCERTAINTY

MPS stability is achieved through firm planned order treatment and time fencing. Stability precedes buffering because by stabilizing the MPS, a great deal of uncertainty is removed. If sufficient stocks of component parts are to be carried to permit constant MPS changes, manufacturing becomes chaotic! Further, the ability to adequately judge manufacturing performance is severely limited. Conceptually, the approach is to first stabilize, then to incrementally add safety stocks or other buffering mechanisms to increase flexibility, assessing the additional costs versus the attendant benefits.

MPS buffering should be for the sole purpose of hedging against forecast errors. A separate issue is the feedback loop to control errors in achieving the stated MPS. The two issues should be treated separately in the approach to the MPS so that the costs of safety stock and other buffers can be clearly matched to marketplace reponse objectives. That is, it is manufacturing's job to hit the schedule—as exactly as possible. It should not be necessary to carry safety stocks or provide other hedges against poor manufacturing performance. All buffering objectives should be concentrated on responding to actual customer demand. This is achieved by maximizing available-to-promise flexibility.

Safety stock

For the make-to-stock company, safety stocks are generally maintained at the finished-goods level. Physical placement of the safety stocks and their replenishment are issues that can be treated with the technique called *distribution requirements planning*. The amount of finished-goods safety stock to hold is based on the trade-off of inventory and holding costs, with safety levels related to the magnitude of forecast errors.

The amount of safety stock that has to be held is also related to the time interval over which safety is provided. That is, if an item is assembled every week, as opposed to once per year, the smaller-lot-size inventory provides less protection against a stock-out; but if the final assembly timing can be changed with short lead time, protection is provided by adaptations in the MPS.

This may sound like a blow struck against MPS stability, but it is not. The time fences need to be set, and when it is time to freeze, it must be done. But at the same time, if lead times can be reduced, freezing can be done on a close-in basis rather than out several periods in the future.

Ethan Allen has made a conscious effort to reduce the lot sizes for the final assembly lines (but not the component-part lot sizes). The result is that each item tends to be produced more often, and finished goods inventories are more rapidly adjusted across all items. That item most in need of being manufactured will be placed into the first nonfrozen time period.

Some firms maintain safety stocks in raw materials. In essence, this provides a reduction in lead times. Raw material safety stocks also serve the function of withholding commitment. Rather than cutting a raw material into a specific component, flexibility to cut it into many alternative components is maintained. This holding back of the commitment can also be extended to holding sets of parts that might be assembled into different end-item configurations, unpainted units that can be any color, etc.

In many make-to-order firms, competitive pressures dictate customer delivery date promises that have timings shorter than the cumulative lead times. This necessitates some procurement and manufacturing in anticipation of customer orders. Raw-material safety stocks are one approach. Another is to keep long-lead-time items, such as castings, in stock and force engineering to make those items very common (i.e., force engineering to use common castings). Another is to start fabrication of specific piece parts and perhaps even assemblies. The more delivery lead times are reduced, the more committed to end-item configurations the company becomes—which also means the less unique the end-item design can be.

Option overplanning

In the assemble-to-order firm, the entire product design concept is to provide maximum response to customer needs, with standardized subassemblies and construction methods.

Safety stocks in product options, often called overplanning, maximize flexibility to respond to customer requirements using available-to-promise logic. The use of a planning bill facilitates this process. The MPS commitment is stated in total super bill units, and so common parts are not overplanned. Options are overplanned by incorporating safety stocks.

As actual orders are received, gross to netting takes place, and replenishment orders are planned to bring safety stocks to their desired levels. Engineering design is concentrated on trying to get as many expensive components as possible into the common-parts module so they don't need to be carried as safety stock. Option overplanning can be more extensive if safety stocks are made up of relatively inexpensive components.

One key issue in option overplanning needs to be understood. From an MPS point of view, a common part is only common *if* it remains uncommitted to a particular end item or assembly until the final assembly schedule (FAS) time fence. That is, for example, in the Hill-Rom over-bed table, the table top core to which the high-pressure laminate is attached is *not* a common part in the super bill. The same chip-board core is indeed used in every over-bed table, but it must be committed to a particular color before final assemblies. That is, the manufacture of the tops themselves is not a part of the FAS. They are built before, and held in inventory as subassemblies. It is necessary to overplan top cores because a top core in white cannot be put into a green over-bed table.

Safety stock timing

Safety stocks, particularly those used for option overplanning, need to be viewed with a time-phased orientation. As actual orders come in, uncertainties are resolved. As this occurs, the need for safety stocks is reduced in those periods where the uncertainty in option mix has been reduced. Suppose, for example, that an MPS commitment were made to 10 units (super bill) at some planning fence. At some time later, let us say seven of those units were sold and that the product is sold in both right-hand and left-hand models. The maximum number of either right-hand or left-hand ATP that should be carried at this time is three, since no more than three of either can be promised. Any more should be deexpedited or reflected in the quantity needed at the next replanning cycle. All safety stocks should ideally only exist at that point in time when uncertainty is possible, and also be consistent in amount with the remaining degree of uncertainty.

Hedging

The safety stock timing issue leads to another key buffering issue in master production scheduling. Up to now, we have talked about buffering against product-mix variation, but we have yet to discuss product-volume variations. The latter relate to changes in the overall demand level of a model series or super bill. Although the production plan may have been set for a model series, there may well be times when the company would like to respond to particular marketing opportunities, perhaps trading off increases of this series with reduction for some other model series.

The Tennant Company does volume hedging very well. (They also use planning bill techniques for product-mix buffering.) The volume hedge for Tennant is always kept just beyond the planning time fence. That is, for each model series a hedge, established by the master production scheduler, is set. This hedge or buffer is put in the period just beyond the time period for which they will have to commit to large-scale component part purchases. The issue at a periodic review meeting is whether or not to let the hedge quantity come over the planning time fence and thereby set in motion the chain of material decisions which changes the overall volume level for a model series.

MANAGING THE MPS

We turn now to the fifth of our six issues in MPS practice: How does one measure, monitor, and control detailed day-to-day performance against the MPS? The first prerequisite for control is to have a realistic MPS. Most basic management textbooks describe how it is critical to only hold people accountable for performance levels that are attainable. This means that the MPS cannot be a wish list, and it should not have any significant portion that is past due. In fact, we claim that significant past due is a major indication of a "sick manufacturing planning and control system."

Stability and proper buffering are also important because the objective is to remove all alibis and excuses for not attaining the performance for which the proper budget has been provided. Successful companies hit the production plan every month, and they do the best job possible to disaggregate the plan to reflect actual product mix in the MPS.

The overstated MPS

Most authorities have warned that the MPS must not be overstated. To do so destroys the relative priorities developed by MRP and shop-floor control; more importantly, the overstated MPS erodes belief in the formal system, thereby reinstituting the informal system of hot lists and black books. Walter Goddard, a well-known MPS expert, no longer tells companies not to overstate the MPS, because at some point the temptation is overwhelming; he now tells them to learn from the experience so they will not do it again!

A key to not overstating the MPS is to always force the sum of the MPS to equal the production plan. Then, when someone wants to add something, the question is, "Of what do you want less?" The company must give up what is referred to as *the standard manufacturing answer*. The standard manufacturing answer to whether more output of some product is possible is: "We do not know, but we will try like hell!"

The company *must* know. There should be an overall output budget for manufacturing. Capacity should be in place, which matches (is not more or less than) the budget. Manufacturing and marketing should work diligently to respond to product-mix changes, but within the overall budgetary constraint. The correct response to whether more output of some product is possible is, "What else can be reduced?" If nothing, then the answer is either "No," or "The output budget and concomitant resources to increase capacities will have to be changed."

MPS measures

There is an old Vermont story about the fellow who was asked: "How is your wife?" His answer: "Compared to what?" The measurement of the MPS has to be established in concrete terms which reflect the fundamental goals of the firm. This is not as easy as it might seem. At one time, Ethan Allen evaluated each factory on the basis of dollar output per week. At one plant, an assembly line produced both plastic-topped tables and all-wood tables. The plastic-topped tables sold for more and could be assembled in roughly half the time since the top was purchased as a completed subassembly. Obviously, the factory favored plastic-topped tables, even when the inventories were high on those items and low on wood tables.

It was necessary for Ethan Allen to change the measure for evaluating plant performance. Each line in each plant is now scheduled by the techniques we have described, and performance is based upon hitting the schedule.

Another important measure of MPS and other MPC systems is customer service. In virtually every company, customer service is an area of concern. However, in many firms, a tight definition of precisely how the measure is to be made is lacking. Measurement is a critical step in control, and each firm will need to express the way in which this important aspect of their operation is to be measured.

It is to be expected that whatever measure for customer service is chosen, the firm may have problems similar to those of Ethan Allen when evaluating plants with dollar output. However, the way to find the problems and thereafter eliminate them is, in fact, to start with *some* measure, no matter how crude, and evolve.

Appropriate measures will vary a great deal from firm to firm, reflecting the type of market response typical in the industry and the particular company. Ethan Allen measures customer service in terms of hitting the order acknowlegement or promise dates. Pfizer measures the frequency and causes of late shipments at their Easton, Pennsylvania, plant. Black & Decker measures their customer service in distribution, in terms of a 95 percent ability to deliver any customer order from inventory. Some assemble-to-order firms evaluate production against the production plan, which is to deliver a specific number of each model to marketing in the agreed upon time frame. They also evaluate customer service in terms of how long customers have to wait until they can get a specific end item. This is an indication of how well the production plan is being disaggregated.

Monitoring the MPS at Ethan Allen

The Ethan Allen firm planned order approach to its MPS is depicted in Figure 8.10. We also know that each plant is evaluated on hitting the MPS, so it should be useful to see how the detailed monitoring takes place and how the overall company operations have been affected.

Every Tuesday morning, the Ethan Allen vice president of manufacturing receives a report detailing the performance of each factory in the prior week. Figure 8.12 is an example of this overall performance report, and Figure 8.13 is the detail for one factory, located at Beecher Falls, Vermont.

Figure 8.12 is a short summary of overall performance, showing one plant, Boonville, as having had poor performance. The last two comments about packed production and outside suppliers show the total production achieved in these two categories.

The STATIONS in Figure 8.13 are the assembly lines, and their capacities are stated in hours. The PRIORITY data reflect the expected operating conditions 18 weeks in the future. If each of those priority numbers were 18, the expectation is that the plant will be exactly meeting customer needs 18 weeks in the future. This particular factory will be seriously behind in terms of meeting anticipated customer demands. This is a question of capacity that is reflected in the comments about each station. For example, for the 06 station, the detail indicates that 10 extra weeks of capacity are required to catch up. Note, however, that the lack of capacity does not mean that the plant is not meeting its schedule. All eight lines are reported as "no misses." This means that in the week covered by this report, the plant met its schedule exactly. The jobs in the schedule are being run. The schedule is loaded up to capacity—not in excess of capacity. The lack of adequate capacity will mean longer delivery times to customers, but not missed schedules.

By evaluating the reports illustrated by Figures 8.12 and 8.13, which plants are performing according to expectations is very clear. Life in the factories is much more calm with performance more clearly defined. No longer do salespeople, customers, marketing people, and other executives call the factories. The interface between the functions is reflected in the master production schedule, and the job of each factory is to hit its MPS. In a sense, what the entire master scheduling effort has done for Ethan Allen is to achieve centralized management of decentralized operations. The operations of the factory are geographically dispersed over wide areas, but the

FIGURE 8.12 Ethan Allen summary MPS performance

April 5,

To: Bill Morrissey

From: Marty Stern

Production schedule review
4/1

Summary:

Nine of the 14 factories operating hit their schedules 100 percent.

Performance against schedule was poor this week at one of the factories: Boonville - 75 percent

Packed production was 196 million over total scheduled. 11 of the factories reporting met or exceeded their schedule.

The outside suppliers produced 171 million under their schedule bringing total production to 25 million over scheduled goal.

cc: Marshall Ames
Barney Kvingedal
Ray Dinkel
Walter Blisky
Andy Boscoe
Steve Kammerer
Tom Ericson
Bob Schneble
Hank Walker

Source: W. L. Berry, T. E. Vollmann, and D. C. Whybark, *Master Production Scheduling: Principles and Practice* (Falls Church, Va.: American Production and Inventory Control Society, 1979), p. 54.

evaluation of those operations is very carefully performed in the corporate offices. The execution responsibility and criteria are unambiguously defined for each plant.

One of the most important benefits of the master production scheduling system for Ethan Allen lies in the fact that the system is upward compatible. That is, the system is transparent, and will work with 5 factories or 25 factories, with new ones easily added. Centralized coordination is maintained, and performance is very clear, with the result being an important tool to support

FIGURE 8.13 Ethan Allen detailed MPS performance (for one factory)

SUMMARY OF SCHEDULE REVIEW

PLANT: BEECHER FALLS

FROM: MARTY STERN

SCHEDULE DATE 3/27/78
THRU WEEK OF 8/28/78

STATION		CAPACITY*	PRIORITY		PROD.SCHED. DOLLARS	PRODUCTION GOAL
06-Cases		175.0	1	$	240.1	232.0
07-C/Hutch	*	10.0	11		10.0	9.0
08-Hutch	*	15.0	14		17.9	19.0
20-Beds	*	60.0	1		85.7	84.0
21-Misc.		3.0	11		3.7	4.0
22-Bookstack		70.0	3		33.0	31.0
24-Desks	*	10.0	8		8.8	10.0
26-Mirrors		25.0	12		23.0	19.0
PLANT TOTAL				$	422.2	408.0

Station 06 -- Cases: Other than misses caused by reporting date change (Canbury closed Good Friday) no misses. Items such as 10-4017, 4066, 4512P, 4522P, 11-5215, 5223 delayed 1 to 4 weeks. Nine items service position improved. Some jobs outside frozen schedule should have been made "A" jobs and shifting would not have occurred. Priority down to 1 from 2. To schedule through priority 18 requires 10 weeks capacity, slightly higher than last months 9 3/4 weeks.

Station 07 -- C/Hutch: No misses. Delayed 3 of 5 items on this line. Priority down to 11 from 14. 7 weeks capacity will schedule thru priority 18, up from 5 weeks.

Station 08 -- Hutch: No misses, Delayed 2 items, pulled 3 ahead. (Plant comments base the shift on purchase parts). Priority up to 14 from 3. To schedule thru priority 18 requires 3 weeks capacity, down from 6 weeks.

Station 20 -- No misses. Delayed the 11-5632-5. Pulled a number of beds ahead. Priority unchanged at 1. 8 weeks capacity, down from 10 3/4 weeks will schedule thru priority 18.

Station 21 -- Misc.: No misses. Some shifting but orders are O.K. Priority up from 10 to 11. 3 weeks capacity, same as last month, will schedule thru priority 18.

Station 22 -- Bookstack: No misses. Built 1 assembly ahead. Priority up to 3 from 2. To schedule thru priority 18 requires 4 1/2 weeks capacity down from 6 weeks.

Station 24 -- Desks: No misses. Built 1 assembly ahead. Some shifting, no delays. Priority up to 8 from 4. 3 1/2 weeks capacity, down from 5 1/2 weeks, will schedule thru priority 18.

Station 26 -- No misses. Some shifting but ahead only. Priority up to 12 from 1. 2 3/4 weeks capacity, down from 8 weeks will schedule thru priority 18.

Source: W. L. Berry, T. E. Vollmann, and D. C. Whybark, *Master Production Scheduling: Principles and Practice* (Falls Church, Va.: American Production and Inventory Control Society, 1979), p. 55.

orderly growth for the company. The company has roughly tripled in size since the start of the master production scheduling effort.

MPS EXAMPLE: HYSTER, PORTLAND

We finish this chapter on MPS concepts with one complete example, which illustrates the MPS items developed in the chapter.

The Portland, Oregon plant of Hyster, Inc., produces forklift trucks, straddle carriers, and towing winches (for mounting on the rear of crawler tractors). The straddle carriers are made to order, but both towing winches and lift trucks are assemble-to-order products, with virtually unlimited end-item possibilities. The lift trucks are divided into three model series, with a super bill of materials for each; there are six super bills to cover the towing-winch models. Each of these super bills is made up of various options with percentage usage factors.

MPS overview

Figure 8.14 gives an indication of the end-item definition complexity. This figure represents the option choices for one model series of forklift truck. The option groups used in the super bill are closely related to their sales options, but they are not identical, since some options preclude others and dictate still other options. For example, the gasoline engine option dictates a particular frame and air cleaner. The powershift transmission *with* a gasoline engine dictates still another set of options such as radiator, flywheel, and hydraulic hoses.

A 12-month production plan is established at corporate headquarters stated in super bill terms. Each month, this plan is revised (new month added). It is stated in the number of units of each model series to have available to ship in each month. If no customer order exists at the time when commitment must be made to an exact end item (demand time fence), marketing issues a stock order for the model unit, which will become part of marketing's finished-goods inventory.

Order promising is based on available-to-promise logic. The first ATP checked is for the model common parts, then for each optional feature desired. The process is straightforward, but each order is so complex in terms of optional choices that even with a cathode ray tube (CRT) unit, it takes an average of one hour to promise an order and peg each option to the customer order.

The MPS system at Hyster Portland was installed along with MRP. The software is a commercial package, sold by Software International, using net change. The MRP and MPS are run daily, and the MPS produces time-phased records for each of approximately 1,400 MPS super bills and options. The Portland factory had to make major changes in its approach to production planning/inventory control to adapt to the system, but the results have been dramatic. Performance against factory schedules has improved, delivery performance is much better, inventory levels are reduced, and marketing is kept fully informed as each order progresses through the various stages of manufacturing. Marketing is also extremely happy with the reduction, of the time at which they have to issue a firm end-item stock order to the plant from 45 days to 14 days.

FIGURE 8.14 Product option matrix—model A lift truck order entry

ORDER ENTRY

LIFT TRK 'A'			GAS O/C	GAS P/S	LPG O/C	LPG P/S	PERKINS O/C	PERKINS P/S	DETROIT O/C	DETROIT P/S
COMMON PARTS			001, 022, 100, 125, 133, 144, 001F, 144F, 125F, 133F, 103F	001, 023, 100, 125, 133, 144, 001F, 144F, 125F, 133F, 108F	001, 024, 100, 125, 133, 144, 001F, 144F, 125F, 133F, 108F	001, 025, 100, 125, 133, 144, 001F, 144F, 125F, 133F, 108F	001, 026, 100, 125, 133, 144, 001F, 144F, 125F, 133F, 108F	001, 027, 100, 125, 133, 144, 001F, 144F, 125F, 133F, 108F	001, 028, 100, 125, 133, 144, 001F, 144F, 125F, 133F, 108F	001, 029, 100, 125, 133, 144, 001F, 144F 125F, 133F 108F
ENGINE	GAS		002, 005, 006, 019, 030, 032, 035	002, 005, 006, 020, 031, 033, 036						
	LPG				003, 005, 019, 030, 032	003, 005, 020, 031, 033				
	PERKINS						008, 004, 006, 019, 032, 035	008, 004, 006, 020, 033, 036		
	DETROIT								007, 004, 006, 019, 035	007, 004, 006, 020, 036
AXLE	HYPOID	SOLID	012, 056, 134, 130	021, 037, 056, 134, 130	012, 056, 134, 130	021, 037, 056, 130, 130	012, 056, 134, 130	021, 037, 056, 134, 130	012, 056, 134, 130	021, 038, 056, 134, 130
		PNEUMATIC	012, 056, 134, 060, 130	021, 037, 056, 134, 060, 130	012, 056, 134, 060, 130	021, 037, 056, 134, 060, 130	012, 056, 134, 060, 130	021, 037, 056, 134, 060, 130	012, 056, 134, 060, 130	021, 038, 056, 134, 060, 130
	PLANETARY	SOLID	014, 057, 106, 116, 120	013, 057, 106, 116, 121	014, 057, 106, 116, 120	013, 057, 106, 116, 121	014, 057, 106, 116, 120	013, 057, 106, 116, 121	014, 057, 106, 116, 120	013, 057, 106, 116, 114
		PNEUMATIC	014, 057, 106, 116, 120, 061	013, 057, 106, 116, 121, 061	014, 057, 106, 116, 120, 061	013, 057, 106, 116, 121, 061	014, 057, 106, 116, 120, 061	013, 057, 106, 116, 121, 061	014, 057, 106, 116, 120, 061	013, 057, 106, 116, 114, 061
CAB			181, 619, 620, 626	181, 619, 621, 626	009, 181, 619, 620, 626	009, 181, 619, 621, 626	181, 619, 620, 626	181, 619, 621, 626	181, 619, 620, 626	181, 619, 621, 626
W/O CAB			182	182	010, 182	010, 182	182	182	182	182
HEATER & DEFROSTER			661	661	661	661	662	663	664	665
STANDARD VALVE			017, 080	018, 080	017, 080	018, 080	017, 080	018, 080	017, 080	018, 080
3-WAY VALVE	DIRECT		081, 015, 079, 086, 087	081, 016, 079, 086, 087	081, 015, 079, 086, 087	081, 016, 079, 086, 087	081, 015, 079, 086, 087	081, 016, 079, 086, 087	081, 015, 079, 086, 087	081, 016, 079, 086, 087
	PUSH		082, 015, 079, 086, 087	082, 016, 079, 086, 087	082, 015, 079, 086, 087	082, 016, 079, 086, 087	082, 015, 079, 086, 087	082, 016, 079, 086, 087	082, 015, 079, 086, 087	082, 016, 079, 086, 087
4-WAY VALVE			015, 079, 083, 085, 087	016, 079, 083, 085, 087	015, 079, 083, 085, 087	016, 079, 083, 085, 087	015, 079, 083, 085, 087	016, 079, 083, 085, 087	015, 079, 083, 085, 087	016, 079, 083, 085, 087
5-WAY VALVE			015, 079, 084, 085, 087	016, 079, 084, 085, 087	015, 079, 084, 085, 087	016, 079, 084, 085, 087	015, 079, 084, 085, 087	016, 079, 084, 085, 087	015, 079, 084, 085, 087	016, 079, 084, 085, 087
ATT. PARTS – 3 4 5			680 681 682	680 681 682	680 681 682	680 681 682	680 681 682	680 681 682	680 681 682	680 681 682
STD. A/C			044, 047, 050	044, 047, 050	044	044	044, 050	044, 050		
H.D. A/C			054	054			054	054	STD.	STD.

Note: Each box represents MPS option groups specified by salable option features for this model.

Source: W. L. Berry, T. E. Vollmann, and D. C. Whybark, *Master Production Scheduling: Principles and Practice* (Falls Church, Va.: American Production and Inventory Control Society, 1979), p. 140.

The MPS records

We turn now to the detailed MPS records at Hyster. This discussion will illustrate the consumption of the forecast by actual customers, time fencing, planning bills, and buffering.

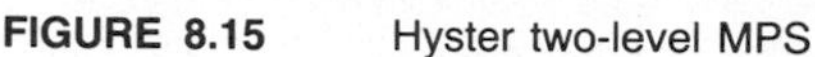

FIGURE 8.15 Hyster two-level MPS

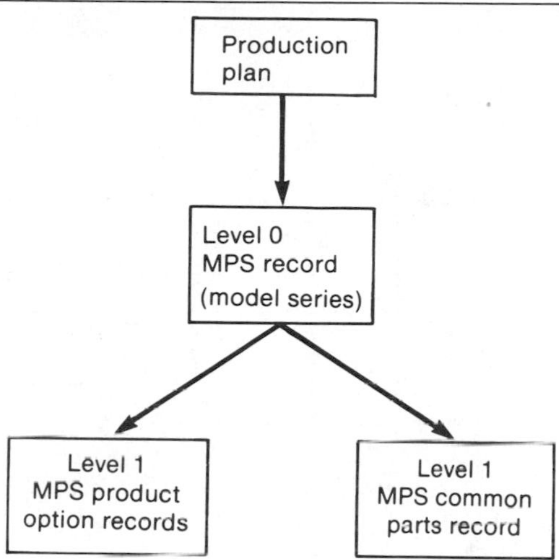

Figure 8.15 provides an overview of the Hyster approach. The detailed MPS decision making takes place at two levels: the level 0 records which manage the model series, and the level one MPS records for the common parts and each of the options. The level 0 model series is essentially the super bill. The overall direction for the MPS is provided from the production plan. The sum of the parts (in this case the level 0 model series record) is kept in concert with the overall dictates of the production plan.

Figure 8.16 gives the MPS for one level (0) series ("A"). The MPS quantities come from the production plan for this model series and are treated as firm planned orders. These are shown in the row labeled MPS START. The time buckets are printed in weekly increments for the weeks 8/21 to 1/15. Thereafter they are printed in four-week buckets. In the four-week buckets, the quantities shown are supported by the detail provided (in weekly buckets) in the lower right-hand portion of Figure 8.16. For example, the monthly bucket quantity for 1/15–273 is 49. This is the sum of the quantities shown in the weeks of 273 (13), 278 (12), 283 (12), and 288 (12).

Figure 8.17 is the level 1 MPS record for the common parts. The row titled PROD FORECAST is the same as the MPS START row from Figure 8.16. That is, for each model series A, one set of common parts is required. The production forecast row shows this explosion.

The common parts record shown in Figure 8.17 contains some other useful information. For example, the customer orders which have been booked for the model series A trucks are displayed in the SOLD row, and are listed along with the sales order number in the pegging data section shown in the

FIGURE 8.16 Model series A—level 0 MPS record

```
                                   SUMMARY MATERIAL PLAN INQUIRY                          PAGE 0001
        - 178    BATCH  080                                                    RUN DATE 08/21/   - 178

*  *    *   *    *   *    *     CONTROL # MRPS2402    USER   ABC  ITEM INV  MAKE UNI COM BUY PHS MAS
ITEM NUMBER      DESCRIPTION                          CODE1  COD  TYPE STAT BUY MEA COD PLN OUT SCH  UNIT-COST  LOW-LVL
A                MODEL SERIES  A                                   00   10   1   0      MS   0   1        .00      000

ALLOCATED  REQ+ALLO ORDER O-QTY OR TLEAD SAFETY  ON ORDER   I S S U E S      R E C E I P T S    L A S T   Y E A R    ENGINEERING
 QUANTITY  QUANTITY CODE   POQ-WKS TIME  STOCK   QUANTITY   QUANTITY TIMES   QUANTITY TIMES     ISSUES    RECEIPTS  NUMB RD  DATE
        0         0 A           0     0      0          0          0     0          0     0          0          0          000000

USER  SHRK SET-UP   CARRY   L E A D   T I M E S           M O D I F I E R S          PRIMARY AREAS  ON-HAND  EXP-DED UNT ALT UM/AUM
CODE2 FACT  COST    RATE   RUN SET QUEM PURCH ACCUM   MINIMUM  MAXIMUM MULTIPLE      ASSY   FABR    PROB-DAT COM PAR MEA UM  FACTOR
        0%   .00    .000     0   0    0     0    0.         0        0        0                        0      1   2   0   0   1.006

                                         D I S T R I B U T I O N   O F   O N - H A N D
    TOTAL   LOCATION        PRIMEA     FLRSTK
        0   ON HAND              0          0
            TO BE RECVD          0
 HOLD QTY   STOCK DATE    00/00/00
        0   TRANS DATE    08/17/78
```

	OVERDUE	08/21-178	08/28-183	09/05-188	09/11-192	09/18-197	09/25-202	10/02-207	10/09-212	10/16-217	10/23-222
PROD FORECAST	0	0	0	0	0	0	0	0	0	0	0
SOLD	0	0	0	0	0	0	0	0	0	0	0
SCH. RECPTS	0	0	0	0	0	0	0	0	0	0	0
PROJ OH	0	0	0	2	8	20	33	48	63	78	93
MPS START	0	0	0	2	6	12	13	15	15	15	15

	10/30-227	11/06-232	11/13-237	11/20-242	11/27-245	12/04-250	12/11-255	12/18-260	01/03-265	01/08-268
PROD FORECAST	0	0	0	0	0	0	0	0	0	0
SOLD	0	0	0	0	0	0	0	0	0	0
SCH. RECPTS	0	0	0	0	0	0	0	0	0	0
PROJ OH	108	123	137	148	163	178	193	206	215	228
MPS START	15	15	14	11	15	15	15	13	9	13

	01/15-273	02/12-293	03/12-313	04/09-333	05/07-353	06/04-372	07/02-392	07/30-411	FUTURE 08/27-431	TOTAL
PROD FORECAST	0	0	0	0	0	0	0	0	0	0
SOLD	0	0	0	0	0	0	0	0	0	0
SCH. RECPTS	0	0	0	0	0	0	0	0	0	0
PROJ OH	277	311	346	382	412	451	489	522	522	
MPS START	49	34	35	36	30	39	38	33	0	522

FIRST PLANNED ORDER NEED DATE IS 188 MAGIC NO.# GA23A
QUANTITY IS 2

............P L A N   M A S T E R   S C H E D U L E S..................

QUANTITY	DUE DATE	RESCHEDULE TO DATE	RESCHEDULE TO QUANTITY	QUANTITY	DUE DATE	RESCHEDULE TO DATE	RESCHEDULE TO QUANTITY
2	188			6	192		
12	197			13	202		
15	207			15	212		
15	217			15	222		
15	227			15	232		
14	237			11	242		
15	245			15	250		
15	255			13	260		
9	265			13	268		
13	273			12	278		
12	283			12	288		
11	293			6	298		
10	303			7	308		
10	313			7	318		
10	323			8	328		
10	333			10	338		
6	343			10	348		
7	353			9	358		
6	363			8	368		
10	372			10	377		

MPS AS FPO's:
Production Plan in
Weekly Time Buckets.

```
06-50                              SUMMARY MATERIAL PLAN INQUIRY                          PAGE 0002
AS OF 08/21/   - 178   BATCH  080                                              RUN DATE 08/21/   - 178
```

............P L A N   M A S T E R   S C H E D U L E S..................

QUANTITY	DUE DATE	RESCHEDULE TO DATE	RESCHEDULE TO QUANTITY	QUANTITY	DUE DATE	RESCHEDULE TO DATE	RESCHEDULE TO QUANTITY
10	382			9	387		
8	392			11	396		
10	401			9	406		
11	411			11	416		
11	421						

Source: W. L. Berry, T. E. Vollmann, and D. C. Whybark, *Master Production Scheduling: Principles and Practice* (Falls Church,

Model series A—common parts level 1 MPS record

06-50
AS OF 08/21/ - 178 BATCH 080

SUMMARY MATERIAL PLAN INQUIRY

PAGE 0005
RUN DATE 08/21/ - 178

ITEM NUMBER	DESCRIPTION	CONTROL #	USER CODE1	ABC COD	ITEM TYPE	INV STAT	MAKE BUY	UNT MEA	COM COD	BUY PLN	PHS OUT	MAS SCH	UNIT-COST	LOW-LVL
005	MOD A - O/C XMSN	MRPS2402	62%		00	10	1	0		MS	0	1	.00	002

ALLOCATED QUANTITY	REQ+ALLO QUANTITY	ORDER CODE	O-QTY OR POQ-WKS	TLEAD TIME	SAFETY STOCK	ON ORDER QUANTITY	ISSUES QUANTITY	ISSUES TIMES	RECEIPTS QUANTITY	RECEIPTS TIMES	LAST ISSUES	YEAR RECEIPTS	ENGINEERING NUMB	RD	DATE
22	347	A	0	8	0	0	0	0	0	0	0	0			000000

USER CODE2	SHRK FACT	SET-UP COST	CARRY RATE	LEAD TIMES RUN	SET	QUEM	PURCH	ACCUM	MODIFIERS MINIMUM	MAXIMUM	MULTIPLE	PRIMARY AREAS ASSY	FABR	ON-HAND PROB-DAT	EXP-DED COM	PAR	UNT MEA	ALT UM	UM/AUM FACTOR
24 W	0%	.00	.000	8	0	0	0	0	0	0	0			183	1	2	0	0	1.006

DISTRIBUTION OF ON-HAND

TOTAL	LOCATION	PRIMEA	FL=STK
0	ON HAND	0	0
	TO BE RECVD	0	
HOLD QTY	STOCK DATE	00/00/00	
0	TRANS DATE	08/17/	

	OVERDUE	08/21-178	08/28-183	09/05-188	09/11-192	09/18-197	09/25-202	10/02-207	10/09-212	10/16-217	10/23-222
PROD FORECAST	0	0	3	2	3	8	8	9	10	9	9
SOLD	0	0	3	6	5	2	1	0	0	0	0
SCH. RECPTS	0	0	0	0	0	0	0	0	0	0	0
PROJ OH	0	0	[illegible]	0	1	1-	0	0	1-	0	0
MPS START	9 *	7	9	8	10	9	9	10	9	9	10

	10/30-227	11/06-232	11/13-237	11/20-242	11/27-245	12/04-250	12/11-255	12/18-260	01/03-265	01/08-268
PROD FORECAST	10	[illegible]	9	6	10	9	9	8	6	8
SOLD	0	[illegible]	0	0	0	0	0	0	0	0
SCH. RECPTS	0	[illegible]	0	0	0	0	0	0	0	0
PROJ OH	1-	[illegible]	1-	0	1-	0	0	0	0	0
MPS START	8	[illegible]	9	10	9	8	6	8	8	7

	01/15-273	02/12-293	03/12-313	04/09-333	05/07-353	06/04-372	07/02-392	07/30-411	FUTURE 08/27-431	TOTAL
PROD FORECAST	31	21	21	23	18	25	23	21	0	325
SOLD	0	0	0	0	0	0	0	0	0	22
SCH. RECPTS	0	0	0	0	0	0	0	0	0	0
PROJ OH	1-	1-	0	0	0	1-	0	1-	1-	
MPS START	26	21	24	19	22	23	26	6	0	346

ALLOCATIONS (Sales Orders)

DATE	QUANTITY	PARENT ITEM NUMBER	ORDER NUMBER	
183	1		S01	NYS
183	1		S02	NYS
183	1		S03	NYS
183	1		S04	NYS
183	1		S05	NYS
183	1		S06	NYS
183	1		S07	NYS
183	1		S08	NYS
188	1		S14	NYS
188	1		S15	NYS
188	1		S16	NYS
188	1		S17	NYS
188	1		S18	NYS
188	1		S19	NYS
192	1		S24	NYS
192	1		S25	NYS
192	1		S26	NYS
192	1		S27	NYS
192	1		S28	NYS
197	1		S32	NYS
197	1		S33	NYS

PLAN MASTER SCHEDULES (MPS Firm Planned Orders)

QUANTITY	DUE DATE	RESCHEDULE TO DATE	RESCHEDULE TO QUANTITY	QUANTITY	DUE DATE	RESCHEDULE TO DATE	RESCHEDULE TO QUANTITY
9	183			7	188		
9	192			8	197		
10	202			9	207		
9	212			10	217		
9	222			9	227		
10	232			8	237		
7	242			9	245		
10	250			9	255		
8	260			6	265		
8	268			8	273		
7	278			8	283		
7	288			7	293		
4	298			6	303		
4	308			7	313		
4	318			6	323		
5	328			6	333		
7	338			3	343		
7	348			4	353		
5	358			4	363		
5	368			6	372		

06-50
AS OF 08/21/ - 178 BATCH 080

SUMMARY MATERIAL PLAN INQUIRY

PAGE 0006
RUN DATE 08/21/ - 178

ALLOCATIONS

DATE	QUANTITY	PARENT ITEM NUMBER	ORDER NUMBER	
202	1		S34	NYS

FIRST PLANNED ORDER NEED DATE IS 183 MAGIC NO.# RK237
QUANTITY IS 9

PLAN MASTER SCHEDULES

QUANTITY	DUE DATE	RESCHEDULE TO DATE	RESCHEDULE TO QUANTITY	QUANTITY	DUE DATE	RESCHEDULE TO DATE	RESCHEDULE TO QUANTITY
7	377			6	382		
5	387			5	392		
7	396			6	401		
6	406			7	411		
7	416			6	421		

Note: Due to confidentiality, the above data is sample information only. Under normal operating circumstances, the MPS START would never be allowed to fall OVERDUE.

Source: W. L. Berry, T. E. Vollmann, and D. C. Whybark, *Master Production Scheduling: Principles and Practice* (Falls Church, Va.: American Production and Inventory Control Society, 1979), p. 151.

lower left-hand corner. As an example, 13 model series A units have been booked for the week 8/28. Each of the individual orders which support these sales are shown in the sales order pegging data (183). When customer orders are booked by Hyster both the PROD FORECAST in the common parts MPS record (Figure 8.17) and the MPS START in the model series A MPS record (Figure 8.16) are decreased by the amount of the sales order. The resultant data are used to make available-to-promise calculations.

The firm planned orders for the common parts grouping are shown in the MPS START row and are also listed (pegged) in the lower right-hand corner of Figure 8.17. The firm planned orders are offset by a planned lead time of two weeks. As an example, 12 units are scheduled to be started in the week beginning 8/21, and these units are due in week 9/5. The pegging data in the lower right-hand corner of Figure 8.17 show the due date for the firm planned orders instead of the order release date, e.g., 12 units are due in the week beginning with day 188. This 12-unit firm planned order covers the requirements for 2 units of PROD FORECAST in week 9/5 (exploded from the MPS record in Figure 8.16) and 10 units of sold orders in the same week.

Figure 8.18 is the level 1 MPS record for one of the model series A options, an oil clutch. For this record, the row labeled PROD FORECAST is not the same as the MPS START row from Figure 8.16. In the header information of Figure 8.18 under USER CODE 1 it says 62 percent. This indicates that Hyster expects 62 percent of the model series A lift trucks to have an oil clutch specification. Thus, the MPS START data in Figure 8.16 are multiplied by .62 to obtain the PROD FORECAST data in Figure 8.18.

An exact multiplication of the MPS START data in Figure 8.16 by .62 will not yield the data in the PROD FORECAST row of Figure 8.18. The system will always round off, but it keeps track of the cumulative round-off amount so that this is always less than one unit. For example, the MPS START (Figure 8.16) for 9/5 is 2. When multiplied by .62, the result is 1.24. The PROD FORECAST (Figure 8.18) is rounded up to 2. In the following week the MPS START is 6; multiplied by .62, this equals 3.72. But since the earlier rounding was .76 (2 − 1.24), the PROD FORECAST for week 9/11 is 3. There remains a cumulative rounding of .04 (.76 − .72).

Buffering

The safety stock aspects of the common parts MPS record shown as Figure 8.17 are contained in the projected on-hand balance row. The PROJ OH row equals the MPS firm planned order receipts minus the PROD FORECAST minus the SOLD orders. This projected on-hand row can be used to determine whether the MPS record contains any safety stock, i.e., when the supply of units is not matched with the actual plus forecast demand for the item. Since the PROJ OH row for the common parts in Figure 8.17 contains all zeros, there is no safety stock for the common parts.

There is no overplanning or safety stock for the common parts, since they

FIGURE 6.18

Model series A—level 1 oil clutch MPS record

```
AS OF 08/21/   - 178   BATCH 080          SUMMARY MATERIAL PLAN INQUIRY                                        PAGE 0005
                                                                                                  RUN DATE 08/21/  - 178
ITEM NUMBER        DESCRIPTION            CONTROL # MRPS2402   USER   ABC  ITEM INV  MAKE UNT COM BUY PHS MAS
005                MOD A - O/C XMSN                            CODE1  COD  TYPE STAT BUY  MFA COD PLN OUT SCH  UNIT-COST  LOW-LVL
                                                               62%         00   10   1    0       MS  0   1    .00        002

ALLOCATED  REQ+ALLO ORDER O-QTY OR TLEAD SAFETY  ON ORDER   I S S U E S     R E C E I P T S   L A S T  Y E A R   ENGINEERING
QUANTITY   QUANTITY CODE  POQ-WKS  TIME  STOCK   QUANTITY   QUANTITY TIMES  QUANTITY TIMES    ISSUES   RECEIPTS  NUMB RD DATE
22         347      A     0        6     0       0          0        0      0        0        0        0                 000000

USER   SHRK SET-UP  CARRY  L E A D  T I M E S            M O D I F I E R S          PRIMARY AREAS  ON-HAND  EXP-DFD UNT ALT UM/AUM
CODE2  FACT COST    RATE   RUN SFT QUEM PURCH ACCUM  MINIMUM MAXIMUM MULTIPLE       ASSY  FABR     PROB-DAT COM PAR MEA UM  FACTOR
24 W   0%   .00     .000   8   0   0    0     0      0       0       0                             183      1   2   0   0   1.006

TOTAL      LOCATION       PRIMEA        D I S T R I B U T I O N   O F   O N - H A N D
  0        ON HAND          0           FLPSTK
           TO BE RECVD      0             0
HOLD QTY   STOCK DATE     00/00/00
  0        TRANS DATE     03/17/
```

	OVERDUE	08/21-178	08/28-183	09/05-188	09/11-192	09/18-197	09/25-202	10/02-207	10/09-212	10/16-217	10/23-222
PROD FORECAST	0	0	0	2	3	8	8	9	10	9	9
SOLD	0	0	8	6	5	2	1	0	0	0	0
SCH. RECPTS	0	0	0	0	0	0	0	0	0	0	0
PROJ OH	0	0	1	0	1	1-	0	0	1-	0	0
MPS START	9 *	7	9	8	10	9	9	10	9	9	10

	10/30-227	11/06-232	11/13-237	11/20-242	11/27-245	12/04-250	12/11-255	12/18-260	01/03-265	01/08-268
PROD FORECAST	10	9	9	6	10	9	9	8	6	8
SOLD	0	0	0	0	0	0	0	0	0	0
SCH. RECPTS	0	0	0	0	0	0	0	0	0	0
PROJ OH	1-	0	1-	0	1-	0	0	0	0	0
MPS START	8	7	9	10	9	8	6	8	8	7

	01/15-273	02/12-293	03/12-313	04/09-333	05/07-353	06/04-372	07/02-392	07/30-411	FUTURE 08/27-431	TOTAL
PROD FORECAST	31	21	21	23	18	25	23	21	0	325
SOLD	0	0	0	0	0	0	0	0	0	22
SCH. RECPTS	0	0	0	0	0	0	0	0	0	0
PROJ OH	1-	1-	0	0	0	1-	0	1-	1-	
MPS START	26	21	24	19	22	23	26	6	0	346

............A L L O C A T I O N S....................

DATE	QUANTITY	PARENT ITEM NUMBER	ORDER NUMBER	
183	1		S01	NYS
183	1		S02	NYS
183	1		S03	NYS
183	1		S04	NYS
183	1		S05	NYS
183	1		S06	NYS
183	1		S07	NYS
183	1		S08	NYS
188	1		S14	NYS
188	1		S15	NYS
188	1		S16	NYS
188	1		S17	NYS
188	1		S18	NYS
188	1		S19	NYS
192	1		S24	NYS
192	1		S25	NYS
192	1		S26	NYS
192	1		S27	NYS
192	1		S28	NYS
197	1		S32	NYS
197	1		S33	NYS

............P L A N   M A S T E R   S C H E D U L E S............

QUANTITY	DUE DATE	RESCHEDULE TO DATE	QUANTITY	QUANTITY	DUE DATE	RESCHEDULE TO DATE	QUANTITY
9	183			7	188		
9	192			8	197		
10	202			9	207		
9	212			10	217		
9	222			9	227		
10	232			8	237		
7	242			9	245		
10	250			9	255		
8	260			6	265		
8	268			8	273		
7	278			8	283		
7	288			7	293		
4	298			6	303		
4	308			7	313		
4	318			6	323		
5	328			6	333		
7	338			3	343		
7	348			4	353		
5	358			4	363		
5	368			6	372		

```
06-50
AS OF 08/21/   - 178   BATCH 080          SUMMARY MATERIAL PLAN INQUIRY                                        PAGE 0006
                                                                                                  RUN DATE 08/21/  - 178
```

............A L L O C A T I O N S....................

DATE	QUANTITY	PARENT ITEM NUMBER	ORDER NUMBER	
202	1		S34	NYS

FIRST PLANNED ORDER NEED DATE IS 183 MAGIC NO. RK237
QUANTITY IS 9

............P L A N   M A S T E R   S C H E D U L E S............

QUANTITY	DUE DATE	RESCHEDULE TO DATE	QUANTITY	QUANTITY	DUE DATE	RESCHEDULE TO DATE	QUANTITY
7	377			6	382		
5	387			5	392		
7	396			6	401		
6	406			7	411		
7	416			6	421		

Note: Due to confidentiality, the above data is sample information only. Under normal operating circumstances, the MPS START would never be allowed to fall OVERDUE.

Source: W. L. Berry, T. E. Vollmann, and D. C. Whybark, *Master Production Scheduling: Principles and Practice* (Falls Church, Va.: American Production and Inventory Control Society, 1979), p. 152.

are used one-for-one on each model series A truck. However, since some safety stock is often planned for product options, the MPS records for these items often deliberately include a projected on-hand balance. Exception messages are generated to indicate those situations. That is, a positive projected on-hand row balance indicates that the current material plan (supply) exceeds the projected usage (booked orders plus production forecast), reflecting the existence of time-phased safety stock. Such an example can be seen for the oil clutch product option in Figure 8.18. Similarly, when the PROJ OH row contains negative figures, the current material plan is inadequate to meet the projected usage for the item and the exception message signals the need for the master scheduler to review such an item. The negative balance probably does not indicate an inability to meet final assembly needs. It likely indicates a more limited ability to respond to customer orders than is indicated by the percentage usage of that option.

For example, in Figure 8.18, the PROJ OH is −1 in the week of 9/18. This comes about because eight units are in the MPS START for 9/5; two units are SOLD for 9/18 and eight units are forecast to be sold that week. There is a PROJ OH of one from the prior week (9/11). This one unit plus the eight-unit MPS is short of the expected total requirements (8 + 2) by one unit. But, what this really means is that if the PROD FORECAST is perfect up to the week of 9/18, only seven more units can be provided for delivery in that week. In the following week, the expected deficiency is recovered.

The Hyster example also illustrates the timing of the safety stock as well as its quantity. For example, Figure 8.18 shows the projected on hand to be zero for the week of 8/21 and to be +1 in the week of 8/28. That is, there is no safety stock in 8/21 and one unit in 8/28. But for the week of 8/28 there is also no uncertainty! That is, the PROD FORECAST is zero. The only requirement is eight actual customer orders. Thus, any safety stock would be redundant.

As actual customer orders come in, they will specify the oil clutch option or they will not. The forecast for the oil clutch option will be consumed—albeit somewhat erratically. The 1 unit of projected on hand in week 9/11 means that although 62 percent of the 6 units of model A left to be sold in week 9/11 are anticipated to be with an oil clutch (.62 × 6 = 3 with cumulative rounding), in fact, actual consumer orders with an oil clutch can be promised for 3 + 1 = 4 units. The master production scheduler will take this into account when launching the next order for oil clutch options and in any necessary replanning of open shop orders.

What this means is that safety stocks are only used to buffer uncertainty in actual customer orders. As order entry takes place, the uncertainties are resolved. As soon as actual orders are known, there is no need to forecast them. Therefore all safety stocks can be de-expedited in timing until a period where there is forecast demand. At this point uncertainty exists as to the option mix of customer orders.

CONCLUDING PRINCIPLES

A working MPS system can provide extensive benefits to the firm—so extensive that a superior MPS is a powerful competitive weapon. The following general principles summarize the key points made in this chapter:

- Minimize the number of items in the MPS.
- Design planning bills to match the way the products are sold.
- Available-to-promise logic should be used for customer order promising, in support of planning bills of materials.
- Avoid firming up the FAS until the latest possible time.
- Stability must be designed into the MPS and be managed.
- Safety stocks should be highly visible and managed both in amount and timing.
- The MPS should be evaluated with a formal performance measurement system.

REFERENCES

Berry, W. L., T. E. Vollmann, and D. C. Whybark. *Master Production Scheduling: Principles and Practice*. Falls Church, Va.: American Production and Inventory Control Society, 1979.

Bobeck, C. J., and R. W. Hall. "The Master Schedule—A New Financial Planning Tool." *1976 APICS Conference Proceedings*, pp. 111–19.

DeWelt, R. L. "Integrating Cost Accounting with Inventory Control and MRP." *1975 APICS Conference Proceedings*, pp. 277–86.

Dippold, V. F. "Master Production Schedule, Black and Decker Study." *1975 Conference APICS Proceedings*, pp. 358–66.

Gallagher, G. R. "How to Develop a Realistic Master Schedule." *Management Review*, April 1980, pp. 19–25.

Mather, H. "Which Comes First, the Bill of Material or the Master Production Schedule?" *1980 APICS Conference Proceedings*, pp. 404–7.

Master Production Scheduling Reprints. Falls Church, Va.: American Production and Inventory Control Society, 1977.

Miller, J. G. "Hedging the Master Schedule." In *Disaggregation Problems in Manufacturing and Service Organizations*, ed. L. P. Ritzman. Martinus Nijhoff, Social Sciences Division, 1979.

Orlicky, J. A., G. W. Plossl, and O. W. Wight. "Structuring the Bill of Material for MRP." *Production and Inventory Management*, 13, no. 4 (4th Quarter 1972), pp. 18–42.

Proud, John F. "Controlling the Master Schedule." *Production and Inventory Management* 22, no. 2 (2d Quarter 1981), pp. 78–90.

9

Production planning

Production planning is probably the least understood aspect of manufacturing planning and control. However, the payoffs from a well-designed and executed production-planning system are very large. In this chapter, we discuss the process by which the aggregate levels of production are determined. The managerial objective is to develop an integrated game plan for which the manufacturing portion *is* the production plan. The production plan, therefore, links strategic goals to production and is coordinated with sales objectives, resource availabilities, and financial budgets. If the production plan is not integrated, production managers cannot be held responsible for meeting the plan, and informal approaches will develop to overcome inconsistencies.

Our discussion of production planning is organized around the following four topics:

- Production planning in the firm: What is production planning? How does it link with strategic management and other MPC system modules?
- The production-planning process: What are the fundamental activities in production planning and what techniques can be used?
- The new management obligations: What are the key responsibilities for ensuring an effective production-planning system?

- Operating production-planning systems: What is the state of the art in practice?

This chapter is focused on managerial concepts for integrated planning. Mathematical and other technical aspects of aggregate production planning are emphasized in Chapter 15. Useful background for the concepts in this chapter can be found in Chapter 8 on planning bills of material and in Chapter 10 on demand management.

THE PRODUCTION PLANNING IN THE FIRM

The production plan provides key communication links from top management to manufacturing. It determines the basis for focusing the detailed production resources to achieve the strategic objectives of the firm. By providing the framework within which the master production schedule is developed, the subsequent MPC systems, material resources, and capacities of the plant are planned and controlled on a basis consistent with these objectives. We now describe the production plan in terms of the role it plays in top management, some of the necessary conditions for effective production planning, the linkages to other MPC system modules, and some of the payoffs from effective production planning.

Production planning and management

The production plan provides a direct and consistent dialogue between manufacturing and top management, as well as between manufacturing and the other functions. As shown in Figure 9.1, many of the key linkages of production planning are *outside* of the manufacturing planning and control (MPC) system. As such, the plan necessarily must be stated in terms that are meaningful to the nonmanufacturing executives of the company. Only in this way, can the top-management game plan, shown in Figure 9.1, become consistent for each of the basic functional areas. Moreover, the production plan also has to be stated in terms that can be used by MPC system modules, so that detailed manufacturing decisions are kept in concert with the overall strategic objectives reflected in the game plan.

The basis for consistency of the functional plans is the resolution of broad trade-offs at the top management level. Suppose, for example, there is an opportunity to expand into a new market, and marketing requests additional production to do so. With a specified production plan, this could only be accomplished by decreasing production for some other product group. If this is seen as undesirable, i.e., the new market is to be direct add-on, by definition, a new game plan is required—with an updated and consistent set of plans in marketing, finance, and production. The feasibility of the added production must be resolved and agreed upon before detailed execution steps are taken.

FIGURE 9.1 Key linkages of production planning

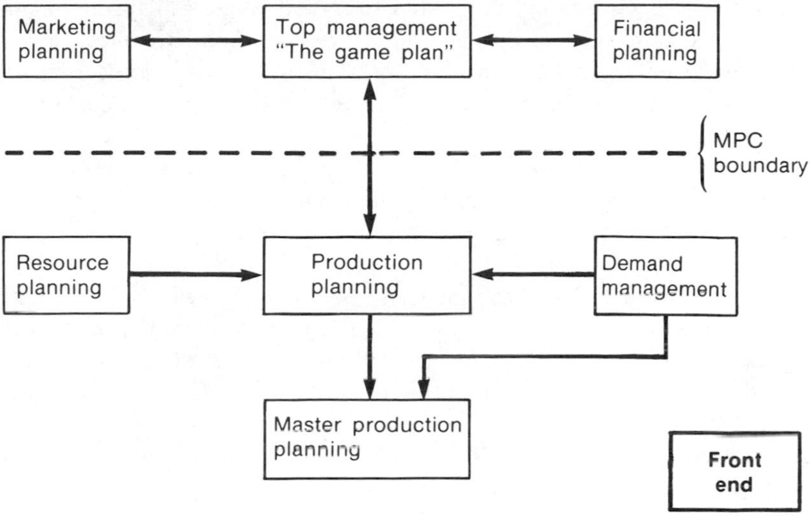

The production plan states the mission that manufacturing must accomplish if the overall objectives of the firm are to be met. How the production plan is to be accomplished in terms of detailed manufacturing and procurement decisions is a problem for manufacturing management. With an agreed upon game plan, the job in manufacturing is to "hit the production plan." Similar job definitions exist in marketing and finance.

An interesting chicken-and-egg question sometimes arises about the production plan and the detailed plans that result from the MPC system. Conceptually, production planning should precede and direct MPC decision making. Production planning provides the basis for making the more detailed set of MPC decisions. In some firms, however, it is only after the MPC systems are in place that the resultant production-planning decisions are clearly defined. In these cases, the first production plans are no more than a summation of the individual decisions. They are the *result* of other detailed decisions rather than an input to those decisions. Even so, they provide the basis for management review.

The planning performed in other MPC systems is necessarily detailed and the language is quite different from that required for production planning. The production plan might be in dollars or aggregate units of output per month, while the MPS could be in end products per week. The MPS might be stated in special bills of materials to manage complicated options and not correspond to the units used to communicate with top management.

To perform the necessary communication role, the production plan must be stated in commonly understood, aggregated terms. In some companies, the production plan is stated as the dollar value of total monthly or quarterly output. Other firms break this total output down by individual factories or by major product lines. Still other firms state the production plan in terms of total units for each product line. Measures that relate to capacity, such as direct labor-hours, tons of product, etc., are also used by some firms. The key requirement is that the production plan be stated in some commonly understood homogenous unit, that thereafter can be kept in concert with other plans.

The overall context within which the trade-offs are made and the production plan developed is increasingly called *game planning*. The game plan reflects the strategy (e.g., increased market share) and tactics (e.g., increased inventory for improved service) that are *doable* by the firm. It is not a set of uncoordinated wishes that some people would like to see realized. The manufacturing part of the game plan is the production plan.

The production plan is *not* a forecast of demand! It is the planned production, stated on an aggregate basis, for which manufacturing management is to be held responsible. The production plan is not necessarily equal to a forecast of aggregate demand. For example, it may not be profitable to satisfy all demands, in which case the production would be less than the forecast. Conversely, a strategic objective of improved customer service could result in aggregate production in excess of aggregate demand. These are important management trade-offs.

An important reason for making a clean separation of the production plan and the forecast is a behavioral one. A forecast is always wrong! Therefore, we cannot honestly hold someone responsible for making a forecast come true. On the other hand, once there is agreement to the plan, responsibilities can be assigned.

Trade-offs also exist with finance. For example, limitations on available capital may limit inventory levels or capacity expansions. The costs of leveling production rates in the face of seasonal demand need to be carefully weighed. Still another example might be a special promotion. Perhaps the extra volume should be built ahead during slack capacity times. Overtime is an alternative—and so is limiting the size of the promotion!

Production planning and MPC systems

Up to this point, we have emphasized the linkages of production planning to activities outside of the MPC system boundaries. These linkages are often referred to as top management's handle on the business. To provide execution support for the production plan, it is necessary to have linkages to the MPC systems. The most fundamental linkage is the master production schedule (MPS) which is a disaggregation of the production plan. The result drives the detailed scheduling through MRP and other MPC systems.

The MPS must be kept in concert with the production plan. As the individual daily scheduling decisions to produce specific mixes of actual end items and/ or options are made, the parity between the sum of the MPS quantities and the production plan must be maintained. If the relationship is maintained, then "hitting the schedule" (MPS) means the agreed upon production plan will be met, as well.

Another critical linkage, shown in Figure 9.1, is the link with demand management. Demand management encompasses order entry, order promising, and physical distribution coordination, as well as forecasting. This module must capture every source of demand against manufacturing capacity, such as interplant transfers, international requirements, and service parts. In some firms, one or more of these sources of demand may be of more consequence than others. For the firm with distribution warehouses, for example, the replenishment of those warehouses may create quite a different set of demands on manufacturing than is true for other firms. The contribution of demand management, insofar as production planning is concerned, is to ensure that the influence of all aspects of demand is included and properly coordinated.

As a tangential activity, the match between actual and forecast demand is monitored in the demand management module. As actual demand conditions depart from forecast, the necessity for revising the production plan increases. Thus, the assessment of the impact of the changes on the production plan and the desirability of making a change is dependent on this linkage. It is critical for top management to change the plans rather than to let the forecast errors per se change the aggregate production output level.

The other direct MPC linkage to production planning, shown in Figure 9.1, is with resource planning. This activity encompasses the long-range planning of facilities. Involved is the translation of extended production plans into capacity requirements, usually on a gross or aggregate basis. In some firms, the unit of measure might be constant dollar output rates, in others, it might be man-hours, head counts, machine-hours, key-facility-hours, tons of output, or some other output measure. The need is to plan capacity, at least in aggregate terms, for a horizon at least as long as it takes to make major changes.

Resource planning is directly related to production planning, since in the short term, the resources available provide a set of constraints to production planning. In the longer run, to the extent that production plans call for more resources than available, financial appropriations are indicated. A key goal of the linkage between production planning and resource planning is to answer what if questions. The maintenance of current resource-planning factors, related to the product groupings used for planning, is the basis for performing this analysis.

Much of the very near-term production plan is constrained by available material supplies. The levels of currently available raw material, parts, and subassemblies limit what can be produced in the short run, even if other resources are available. This is often hard to assess unless the information links from the MRP and shop status data bases are effective.

Links through the MPS system to MRP and other MPC systems provide the basic data to perform the what if simulations of alternative plans. Having the ability to quickly evaluate alternatives can greatly facilitate the game-planning process by providing good information for evaluating trade-offs. This is *not* an argument to always change the production plan. On the contrary, having the ability to demonstrate the impact of proposed changes may reduce the number of instances in which production "loses" in these negotiations.

The value of the production-planning activity is certainly questionable if there is no monitoring of performance. This requires linkages to the data on shipments/sales, aggregated into the production-planning groupings. The measurement of performance is an important input to the planning process itself. Insofar as deviations in output are occurring, they must be taken into account. If the plan cannot be realized, the entire value of the production-planning process is called into question.

One final performance aspect where effort must be expended is in the reconciliation of the MPS with the production plan. As day-to-day MPS decisions are made, it is possible to move away from the production plan unless constant vigilance is applied. Like other performance monitoring, it requires a frequent evaluation of status and comparison to plan.

Payoffs

Game planning is top management's handle on the business. It provides important visibility of the critical interactions between marketing, production, and finance. If marketing wants higher inventories, but the top-management decision is that there is not sufficient capital to support the inventories, the production plan will be so designed. Once such critical trade-off decisions are made, the production plan provides the basis for monitoring and controlling manufacturing performance in a way that provides a much more clear division of responsibilities than is true under conventional budgetary controls.

Under such planning, it is manufacturing's job to hit the schedule. This can eliminate the battle over "ownership" of finished-goods inventory. If actual inventory levels do not agree with planned inventory levels, that is basically not a manufacturing problem, *if* they hit the schedule. It is either a marketing problem (they did not sell according to plan) or a problem of product-mix management in the demand management activity (the wrong individual items were made).

The production plan provides the basis for day-to-day, tough-minded trade-off decisions, as well. If marketing wants more of some items, they must be asked "Of what do you want less?" There is no other response, because the production of the same amount of everything else and more of something would violate the agreed upon production plan. In the absence of a new, expanded production plan, production and marketing must work to allocate the scarce capacity to the competing needs (via the master production schedule).

The reverse situation is also true. If the production plan calls for more than marketing currently needs, detailed decisions should be reached as to which items will go into inventory. Manufacturing commits people, capacities, and materials to reach company objectives. The issue is only how best to convert these resources into particular end products.

Better integration between functional areas is one of the major payoffs from production planning. Once a consistent game plan between top levels of the functional areas is developed, it can be translated into detailed plans that are in concert with the top-level agreements. This results in a set of common goals, improved communication, and transparent systems.

Without a production plan, the expectation is that somehow the job will get done—and in fact, it does get done, but at a price. That price is organizational slack: extra inventories, poor customer service, excess capacity, long lead time, panic operations, and poor response to new opportunities. Informal systems will, of necessity, come into being. Detailed decisions will be made by clerical-level personnel with no guiding policy except "get it out the door as best we can." The annual budget cycle will not be tied in with detailed plans and will probably be inconsistent and out of date before it is one month old. Marketing requests for products will not be made so as to keep the sum of the detailed end products in line with the budget. In many cases, the detailed requests for the first month are double the expected 1/12 of the year's forecast volume. Only at the end of the year does the reconciliation between requests and budget take place, but in the meantime it has been up to manufacturing to decide what they really need.

We have seen many companies with these symptoms. Where are these costs reflected? There is no special place in the chart of accounts for them, but they will be paid in the bottom-line profit results.

THE PRODUCTION-PLANNING PROCESS

Our interest in this section is on aids to the management of the production-planning process. Specifically, we will be concerned with routinizing the process, the game-planning output, cumulative charting, the tabular plan display, and what if analyses.

Routinizing production and game planning

The game- and production-planning process typically begins with an updated sales forecast covering the next year or more. Any desired increases or decreases to inventory or backlog levels are added or subtracted, and the result is the production plan. The most immediate portion of this plan will not be capable of being changed, since commitments to manpower, equipment, and materials already will have been made. An effective production-planning process will typically have explicit time fences for when the aggregate plan can be increased or decreased; there also well may be tight constraints on the amounts of increase or decrease. An example might be no changes during the most immediate month, up to +10 percent or −20 percent in next month, etc. Effective production planning also implies periodicity. That is, it is useful to perform the production- and game-planning process on a regular, routine cycle.

Performing the game-planning function on a regular basis has several benefits. It tends to institutionalize the process which forces a consideration that might otherwise be postponed, of changed conditions and trade-offs. The routine also keeps the information channels open for forecast changes, different conditions, and new opportunities. Performing the task routinely also helps ensure a separation between the forecasts and the plan.

The frequency of the cycle varies from firm to firm, depending upon the stability of the business, the cost of planning, and the ability to monitor performance. The trade-off is a difficult one. There is a high cost to planning involving data gathering, meetings, what if analysis, and other staff report activities. On the other hand, delaying the planning process increases the chance of significant departures of reality from plan, creating the opportunity for informal systems to take over. Ironically, the more successful firms can use a less frequent cycle because of the ability of their formal systems to keep the firm on plan and warn of impending problems. A common schedule among successful firms is to review the plans monthly and revise the plans quarterly or when necessary. An example of the monthly cycle at Ethan Allen is shown in Figure 9.2.

Ethan Allen is a make-to-stock furniture manufacturer; so much of their demand forecasting is based on routine extrapolation of historical data. The first event shown in Figure 9.2, "determine (manual forecast)," is to forecast the nonroutine items. These include large contract sales (such as to a motel chain), new items for which there are no historical data, and market specials.

The second event shown in Figure 9.2 is the end of the month. Following immediately is a six-month economic review. This is a report which attempts to summarize the future economic conditions in the furniture industry. At the same time, the sales screening report is prepared. It is a review of the actual sales in light of the forecast, to make any necessary changes before the preparation of the new routine statistical forecast.

The sixth event shown in Figure 9.2 ("set output level for next six months"), is the production plan. A group of executives reviews the economic outlook, present inventory levels, statistical forecasts, and other factors. The net result is a rate of output in total dollars for Ethan Allen production. The subsequent events are devoted to preparing reports based on this production plan, allocating the total to individual factories, and preparing the detailed MPS which supports the production plan.

FIGURE 9.2 Example monthly cycle for production planning

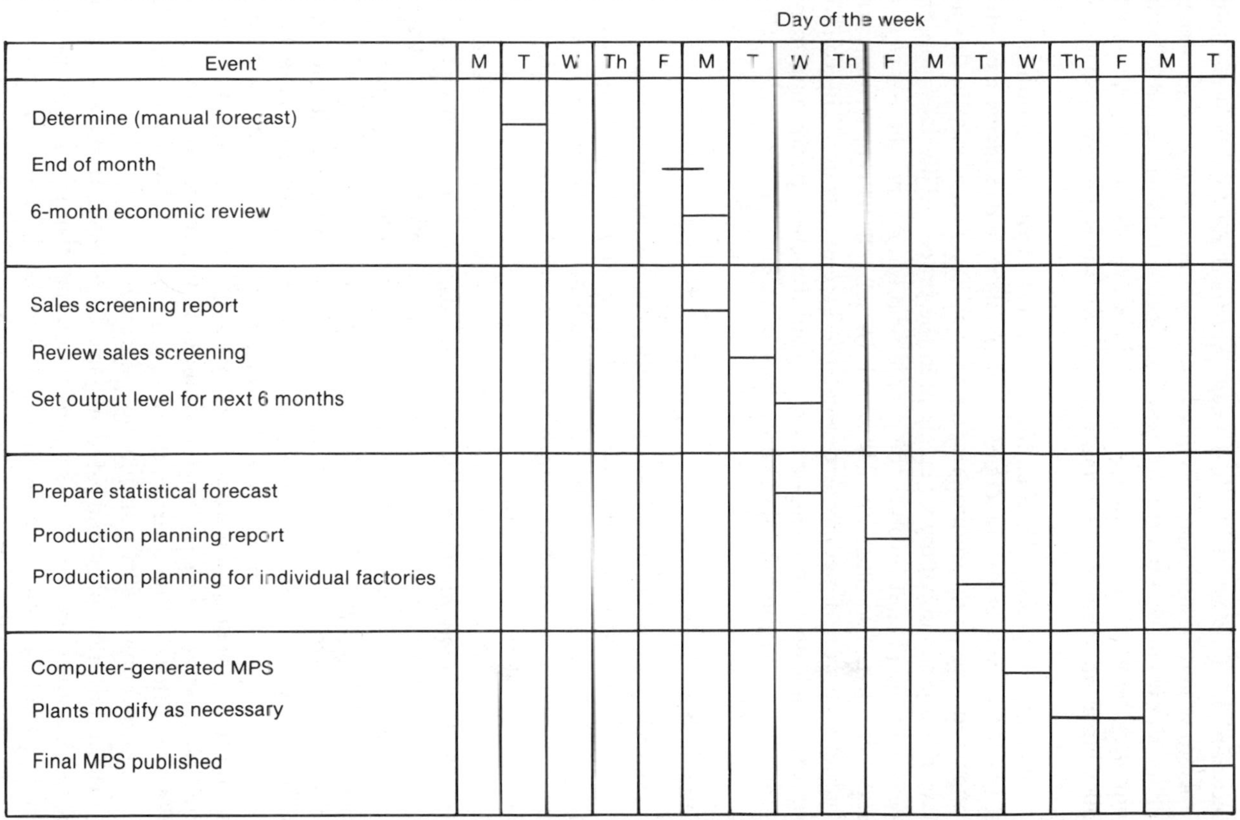

Event	M	T	W	Th	F	M	T	W	Th	F	M	T	W	Th	F	M	T
	Day of the week																
Determine (manual forecast)																	
End of month																	
6-month economic review																	
Sales screening report																	
Review sales screening																	
Set output level for next 6 months																	
Prepare statistical forecast																	
Production planning report																	
Production planning for individual factories																	
Computer-generated MPS																	
Plants modify as necessary																	
Final MPS published																	

Source: W. L. Berry, T. E. Vollmann, and D. C. Whybark, *Master Production Scheduling: Principles and Practice* (Falls Church, Va.: American Production and Inventory Control Society, 1979), p. 45.

The other discipline required in routinizing the production and game-planning process is to replan when conditions indicate it is necessary. If information from the demand management module indicates differences between the forecast and actual have exceeded reasonable error limits, replanning may be necessary. Similarly, if conditions change in manufacturing, or a new market opportunity arises, or the capital market shifts, replanning may be needed. So, though regularizing has its advantages, slavishly following a timetable and ignoring actual conditions is not wise management practice.

Since the purpose of the planning process is to arrive at a coordinated set of plans for each of the functions (a game plan), mechanisms for getting support for the plans are important. Clearly, a minimum step in this is to have the top functional officer involved in the process. This does more than legitimize the plan; it involves the people who can resolve the issues in the trade-off stage. A second step that is used by some firms is to virtually write contracts between functions as to what the agreements are. The contracts serve to underscore the importance of each function performing to plan rather than returning to informal practice.

Cumulative charts

The use of cumulative charts has utility in displaying the relationship between the production plan (or alternative plans) and the forecast of expected shipments. A cumulative chart clearly shows the buildup or drawdown of inventory, and can show where additional resources are necessary. An example is shown in Figure 9.3.

The information used to construct the cumulative chart must contain shipments to meet *all* demands: forecast needs, new items, special promotions, customer demands at the plants, intercompany shipments, etc. This serves as a basic input to the planning process, although no guarantee is made that all possible demand will be satisfied.

Once the forecast of cumulative shipments is prepared, any inventory adjustments need to be taken into account. In the example in Figure 9.3, we start with 10 tons in inventory and management decides that a 5-ton minimum (plan A) reflects this directly. Only enough production is planned for the first quarter to provide for the shipments and reduce the inventory to five tons. After the first quarter, the production is varied to just maintain the five-ton inventory. This plan "chases" shipments.

The production plan, indicated in plan B, is *level.* It starts out at the beginning inventory and shows a production rate that is constant, provides the five-ton minimum inventory at the end of the third quarter, and always has enough cumulative inventory and production to meet the shipments required. This plan is clearly different from the shipment pattern, which could also be different from the forecast of demand. Production plan B builds

FIGURE 9.3 Example cumulative chart

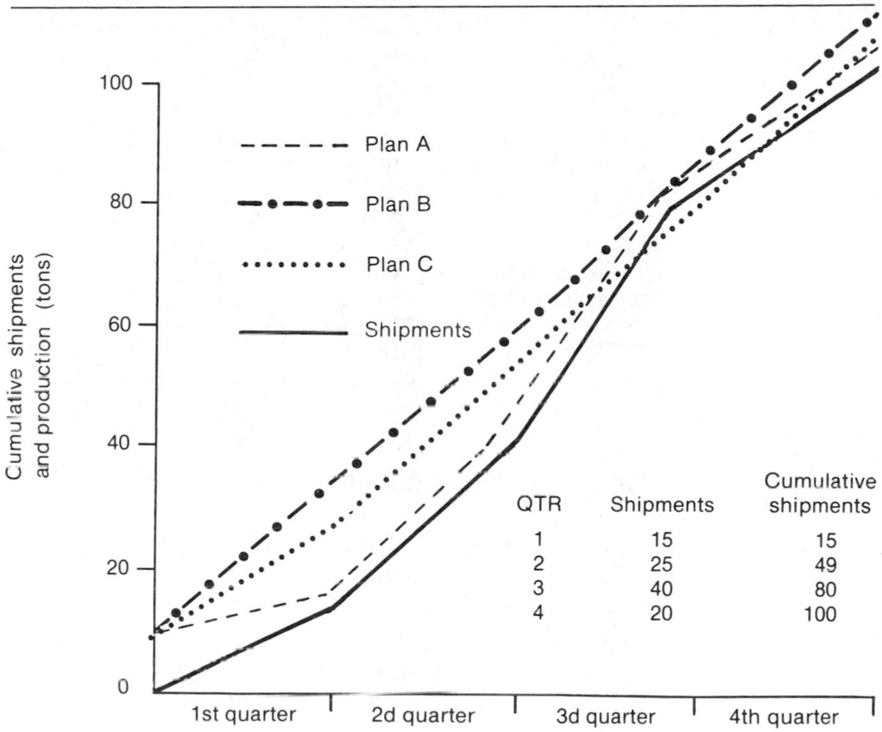

QTR	Shipments	Cumulative shipments
1	15	15
2	25	49
3	40	80
4	20	100

up an inventory to meet the peak shipments, while production plan A varies the rate of production.

We have also shown an infeasible plan for production, indicated as plan C in Figure 9.3. Plan C provides enough production plus beginning inventory to meet all the shipments for the year and provides a five-ton year-end inventory. Toward the end of the third quarter, however, the company would be building a backlog and would not be holding an inventory. If this is not acceptable, either more resources must be made available for manufacturing or the shipment schedule must be changed.

Tabular plans

It is much more common to see tabular than graphical representations of the production plans. A tabular representation of the data in Figure 9.3 is given in Figure 9.4. The implications of the strategy of varying production (plan A) are quite clear from this display. A 40-ton capacity is needed in the third quarter. If this is not available in-house, outside contracting would be

FIGURE 9.4 Tabular production plans for A and B from Figure 9.3

	Quarter			
	1	*2*	*3*	*4*
Plan A:				
Opening inventory	10	5	5	5
Planned production	10	25	40	20
Available for shipping	20	30	45	25
Shipments	15	25	40	20
Plan B:				
Opening inventory	10	20	20	5
Planned production	25	25	25	25
Available for shipping	35	45	45	30
Shipments	15	25	40	20

needed. The production planned for the first quarter is 10 tons, which is only one fourth of the maximum planned. This variation in production means using part-time people, hiring and laying off, or some other method of ajdusting the human resources. In many countries, this is virtually impossible.

On the other hand, plan B does not show such fluctuations in production. The rate is a constant 25 tons per quarter. Consequently, all the advantages of a stable work force can be realized by this plan. To do this, however, requires a buildup of 20 tons of inventory. This could be extremely expensive at the current costs of capital. In addition, space may be limited, causing further increases in costs.

As long as the plans are feasible, that is, the shipment schedule can be met and sufficient capital can be found to store any inventory, the specific choice between production alternatives A and B (or combinations in between) might rest with manufacturing. If problems of insufficient capacity, labor force changes, warehouses, or capital availability exist, then the plan necessarily will have inputs from other organizational areas.

What if analysis

The quality of analysis that precedes the finalization of the production plan can be greatly enhanced by being able to easily answer what if questions. The types of questions that are raised in this analysis relate to levels of manpower, machine-hours, inventory, subcontracting, etc., required under alternative plans. Quick answers to these questions will permit the evaluation of more alternatives than otherwise would be considered.

We can illustrate the ideas of what if analysis with the data in Figure 9.4. The simplicity of the data for plans A and B is for illustrative purposes and is

FIGURE 9.5 What if analysis of the two plans in Figure 9.4

	Quarter			
	1	*2*	*3*	*4*
Plan A:				
Inventory ($1,000)	20	10	10	10
Employees	5	12.5	20	10
Percent of capacity	33	83	133	66
Plan B:				
Inventory ($1,000)	20	40	40	10
Employees	12.5	12.5	12.5	12.5
Percent of capacity	83	83	83	83

not a limitation of the technique. The two plans already incorporate elements of what if analysis. The inventory levels that would result from each alternative have been calculated. Extending these levels by the dollar value of the inventory would provide the investment levels required by each plan.

To evaluate the labor implications of the alternatives requires extending the production by a labor factor. This may involve an explicit treatment of the product mix if the different lines use different levels of labor. The same may be necessary to determine the effect on machine-hours, floor space, or other key resources. The analysis of plans A and B shown in Figure 9.5 was made using a value of $2,000 per ton of inventory, 2 tons per employee per quarter, and a machine capacity of 30 tons per quarter.

The example in Figure 9.5 is a simple one and does not take into account many important considerations that apply in real situations (weekly time periods, work-in-process inventory, different product mixes, etc.). Even in the most complicated of circumstances, however, the process is straightforward and is mostly a matter of doing the arithmetic. There is merit in tying the what if analysis capability into the MPC system at the production planning level, but the calculations and data required are rarely in excess of the capacity of a personal computer using available software.

THE NEW MANAGEMENT OBLIGATIONS

A great deal must change in many companies to move to a true planning-based style of management. It is clear from our discussion so far that the top-management role in this is critical and must not be one of lip service only. In this section, we look at some dimensions of the top-management and departmental roles, as well as the integration with strategic planning. We also consider the stability and management control of the plan.

Top-management role

The first obligation of top management is to commit to the game-planning process. This means a major change in many firms. The change involves the routine aspects of establishing the framework for game planning: getting the forecasts, setting the meetings, preparing the plans, etc. The change may also imply modifications of performance measurement and reward structures to align them with the plan. It should be expected at the outset that there will be many existing goals and performance measures that are in conflict with the integration provided by a working game-planning system. These should be rooted out and explicitly changed. Enforcing the changes implies a need to abide by and provide an example of the discipline required to manage with the planning system. This implies that even top management must act within the planned flexibility range for individual actions and must evaluate possible changes that lie outside the limits.

As a part of the commitment to the planning process, top management *must force* the resolution of trade-offs between functions prior to approving plans. The production plan provides a transparent basis for resolving these conflicts. It should provide the basic implications of the choices, even if it does not make the decisions any easier. If the trade-offs are not made at this level, they will be forced into the mix of day-to-day activities of operating people who will have to resolve them—perhaps unfavorably. If, for example, manufacturing continues long runs of products in the face of declining demand, the mismatch between production and the market will be in increased inventories.

The game-planning activities must encompass *all* formal plans in an integrated fashion. If budgeting is a separate activity, it will not relate to the game plan and the operating managers will need to make a choice. Similarly, if the profit forecast is based solely on the sales forecast (revenue) and accounting data (standard costs) and does not take into account the implications for production, its value is doubtful. The intention of the game-planning process is to produce plans, budgets, objectives, and goals that are complete and integrated; and are used by managers to make decisions and provide the basis for evaluating performance. If other planning activities or evaluation documents are in place, the end result will be poor execution. An unfortunate but frequent approach is to invest management time in the production planning activity, but thereafter allow the company to be run by a separate performance measurement system or budget.

Departmental roles

The primary obligation under game planning is to "hit the plan." This is true for all departments involved: manufacturing, sales, engineering, finance, etc. A secondary obligation in the environment is this need to communicate when something will prevent a department from hitting the plan.

If there is a problem, the sooner it can be evaluated in terms of other departmental plans, the better. The obligation to communication provides the basis for keeping the plans of *all* departments consistent when changes are necessary.

The process of budgeting usually needs to change and to be integrated with game planning and subsequent departmental plans. In many firms, budgeting is done on an annual basis, using data that are not a part of the material planning and control system. The manufacturing budgets are often based upon historical cost relationships and a separation of fixed and variable expenses. These data are not as precise as those that can be obtained by utilizing the material-control-system data base. By using the data base, a tentative master schedule can be simulated to examine the exact component part needs and expected costs. The resultant budget can be analyzed for the effect of product-mix change as well as for performance against standards.

Another important aspect of relating budgeting to the game-planning activity and underlying MPC systems and data base is that the cycle can be done more frequently. The data should not have to be collected—they always exist in up-to-date form. Moreover, inconsistencies are substantially reduced. The budget should always be in agreement with the production plan which, in turn, is in concert with the disaggregated end items and components that support the plan. The result should be far fewer occasions when an operating manager has to choose between his budget and satisfying the production plan.

With budgeting and production planning done on the same basis with the same underlying dynamic data base, it is natural to incorporate cost accounting. The result is an ability to perform detailed variance accounting, as well as an important cross check on transaction accuracy.

The most obvious need for integrated planning and control is between marketing and production. Yet it is often the most difficult to accomplish. There are needs to ensure product availability for special promotions, to match customer orders with specific production lots, to coordinate distribution activities with production, and a host of other cross-functional problems.

The job of marketing under integrated game planning is to sell what is in the sales plan. It is necessary to instill the feeling that overselling is just as bad as underselling. In either case, there will be a mismatch with manufacturing output, financial requirements, and inventory/backlog levels. If the opportunity arises to sell more than the plan, it needs to be formally evaluated by means of a change in the game plan. By going through this process, the timing for when this increase can be properly supported by both manufacturing and finance will be ascertained. And once the formal plan has been changed, it is again the job of each function to achieve its specified objectives—no more and no less.

Similarly, it is manufacturing's job to achieve the plan—exactly. Overproduction may well mean that more capacity and resources are being utilized than are required. Underproduction possibly means the reverse (not enough resources) or it means poor performance. In either case, performance against the plan is poor. This can either be the fault of the standard setting process or inadequate performance. Both problems require corrective action.

When manufacturing is hitting the schedule, it is a straightforward job for marketing to be able to provide good customer order promises and other forms of customer service. It is also a straightforward job for finance to plan cash flows and to anticipate financial performance.

If the production-planning results cannot be achieved, it must be the clear responsibility of whoever cannot meet plan to report this condition promptly. If, for example, a major supplier cannot meet his or her commitments, the impact on the detailed marketing and production plans must be quickly ascertained.

Integrating strategic planning

Strategic planning is an important direction-setting activity that is done in different ways. Some companies approach this problem primarily as an extension of budgeting. Typically, these firms use a bottom-up process, which is largely an extrapolation of the departmental budgets based upon growth assumptions and cost-volume analysis. One key aspect of the strategic plan in these firms is to integrate these bottom-up extrapolations into a coherent whole. Another is to critically evaluate the overall outcome from a corporate point of view.

A more recent approach to strategic planning is to have the plan based more on products and less on organizational units. The company's products are typically grouped into strategic business units (SBUs), with each SBU evaluated in terms of its strengths and weaknesses vis-à-vis similar business units made and marketed by competitors. The budgetary process in this case is done on an SBU basis, rather than on an organizational unit basis. The business units are evaluated in terms of their competitive strength, their relative advantage (usually based on learning curve models), life cycles, and cash flow patterns (e.g., when does an SBU need cash and when is it a cash provider?) From a strategic point of view, the objective is to carefully manage a portfolio of SBUs to the overall advantage of the firm.

The role of game planning and the departmental plans to support these strategic planning efforts can be profound. In the case of the production plan, the overall data base and systems ensure that game plans will be in concert with disaggregated decision making. In other words, MRP and related systems ensure that the strategic planning decisions are executed!

All the advantages of integrating production planning with budgeting also apply if strategic planning is basically an extrapolation of budgeting. When the SBU focus is taken, it makes sense to state the production plan in the same SBU units; that is, rather than using dollar outputs per time unit, state the production plan in SBU terminology.

Controlling the production plan

A special responsibility involves control of performance against the plan. As a prerequisite to control, the game-planning process should be widely understood in the firm. The seriousness with which it is regarded should also be communicated, as well as the exact numerical volumes that pertain to each of the organization's functional units. In other words, it is necessary that the planning process be transparent, with clear communication of expectations, to control actual results. For the production plan, this means wide dissemination of the plan and its implications for managers.

Another dimension of control is periodic reporting. Performance against the production plan should be widely disseminated. When actual results differ from plans, analyses of where these deviations came from should be made and communicated.

An example of this communication is seen at the Tennant Company. Some of their more important measures of performance and reporting frequency are:

Measure	*Reporting*
Conformity of the master production schedule to the production plan	Weekly
Capacity utilization	Weekly
Delivery performance	Daily
Actual production to master production schedule performance	Weekly
Inventory/backlog performance	Weekly

At a recent point in their history, Tennant had not missed a quarterly production plan for the previous 2½ years. Moreover, the monthly production plan had been met in 10 out of 12 months for each of the previous years. All of these results are well known inside the company, and they are widely disseminated outside, too. The importance of the production plan is well understood at all levels of the firm.

Key issues in production planning are when to make changes to the plan, how often to replan, and how stable to keep the plan from period to period. There is no doubt that a stable production plan results in far fewer execution problems by the detailed master production scheduling, MRP, and other execution systems. Stability also fosters the achievement of some steady state operations where capacity can be more effectively utilized.

At Tennant, changes to the production plan are batched until the next review, unless they are required to prevent major problems. In other companies, stability in the plan is maintained by providing time fences for changes and permissible ranges of deviation from plan. Flexibility within the plan can be provided by planning adequate inventories or other forms of capacity to absorb deviations within an agreed upon range.

Several Japanese companies such as Toyota use a material planning and control system called Kanban. There are many aspects of the system that are based on manual controls. Both the system and the results at companies using it (e.g., a turnover ratio of working assets that is 10 times that of Western automobile producers) seem unbelievable to most Americans and Europeans. One key to making this system work is a very stable production plan. The output rate is held constant for long periods of time, and only modified after extensive analysis. This means that the rate of production at each step of the manufacturing process can be held to very constant levels, providing the benefits of stability and predictability.

The other side of this coin is seen by considering the approach of Chrysler in 1974–75. In the face of diminishing sales, they continued to produce in excess of sales. The result was a buildup of finished-goods inventory that exceeded 100 days of sales. The results on their financial statements were very significant. The lesson is that stability is very desirable, but one must also be responsive to any significant shifts in either manfacturing or the marketplace. Finished-goods inventories and other backlogs can decouple the marketplace from day-to-day shocks, but long-run changes have to be reflected in the basic production plan itself.

OPERATING PRODUCTION-PLANNING SYSTEMS

In this section, we show examples of production-planning practice. In particular, we present some of the organizational aspects of production planning at the Bendix Corporation, the entire process for the Mohawk Electric Company, and the way the Hill-Rom Company uses SBU-related bills of material for tying the production plan to their strategic business units.

Production planning at Bendix

The production-planning function at Bendix is called master production planning (MPP). In describing it, Kenneth A. Wantuck, Corporate Director—Materials Management, says, MPP is management's game plan for the conduct of business. It is a specific, validated, management-level statement of the production levels at which a company is to operate, considering customer requirements, sales goals, inventory investment and profit objectives. This description is consistent with the description provided here. The company has organized and formalized the process to make it happen as described.

As a part of the organizational dimension, Bendix formed an MPP committee with top-management membership. This committee oversees the integration of all business plans in the organization and meets at least monthly to update the plan. The top-management commitment is ratified by signatures to the plan including that of the general manager. The plan is stated in product families and sets the parameters for the master schedule. The committee requires performance measurement and rescheduling. For example, no past-due production is allowed to accumulate. Past-due production is rescheduled into the future, subject to the resource constraints of the plan. This prevents a "bow wave" of work from appearing in the first month of the plan.

Figure 9.6 provides a summary of the elements of the MPP process at Bendix. By following this checklist, the plan is integrated with the budgeting process of the company and the other functional plans. Performance reporting is required to ensure that the plan is a working document. Since implementation of the process, Wantuck reports:

- A European subsidiary improved productivity by 9 percent and increased inventory turnover by 30 percent over a three-year period.
- A domestic automotive component division was able to maintain favorable investment ratios despite reductions of more than 30 percent in customer orders.
- A Canadian subsidiary reduced its inventories by $4 million while improving customer service within the first year of MPP implementation.

Mohawk's integrated planning process

The Mohawk Electric Company (a disguised name for an actual Midwestern firm) manufactures electrical switches, controls, and measurement instruments for industrial applications. Three main product lines—energy management devices, tachographs, and data systems represent annual sales of $25 to $30 million, with a price range of $15 to $50,000 per unit. About 10,000 units are sold each year, involving some 5,000 unique final-product catalogue numbers. Approximately 70 percent of the sales volume is shipped directly from the finished-goods inventory of the firm.

The production plan and master production schedule are established quarterly as a part of the regular budgetary planning activities of the firm. For most of Mohawk's business, the master production schedule is stated in terms of the number of units to be produced for each end product (catalogue number) during the next four quarters.

The overall production lead time (covering the purchasing, fabrication, and assembly operations) generally exceeds the delivery time quoted to the firm's customers. Thus, the production plan and master production schedule are primarily based on sales forecasts and financial plans—instead of on actual customer orders. The budgetary planning process is outlined in Figure 9.7. Once every quarter, the company's sales, finance, and manufacturing executives prepare an overall business game plan covering the next four quarters that includes: (a) a sales forecast for each of the firm's three product lines (energy management devices, tachographs, and data systems); and (b) a

FIGURE 9.6 Production planning guidelines at the Bendix Corporation

BENDIX

MASTER PRODUCTION PLANNING

CHECKLIST

MANAGEMENT ELEMENTS

- ☐ FORMAL MPP COMMITTEE, WHICH INCLUDES THE GENERAL MANAGER, CONTROLLER, AND FUNCTIONAL DIRECTORS (I.E., MARKETING, MANUFACTURING, MATERIAL, ETC.)
- ☐ MONTHLY REVIEW MEETINGS TO REVISE AND UPDATE THE MPP
- ☐ COMMITMENT FROM DIRECTORS THAT THE MPP WILL BE FOLLOWED
- ☐ SIGNATURE APPROVAL BY THE GENERAL MANAGER
- ☐ USED AS THE BASIS FOR BUDGETING AND FINANCIAL FORECASTING
- ☐ USED AS THE BASIS FOR DOWNSTREAM MASTER SCHEDULES AND CUSTOMER COMMITMENTS
- ☐ REQUIRES MPP COMMITTEE APPROVAL FOR CHANGES IN SCOPE

MPP DOCUMENT ELEMENTS

- ☐ CONTAINS THE MINIMUM NUMBER OF PRODUCT FAMILIES THAT FULLY DESCRIBE THE BUSINESS (INCLUDING SPARES AND REPAIRS)
- ☐ COVERS A TIME PERIOD (PLANNING HORIZON) EQUAL TO OR GREATER THAN THE LONGEST PRODUCT FAMILY LEAD TIME (PROCUREMENT TIME + MANUFACTURING TIME)
- ☐ IS SUBDIVIDED INTO MONTHLY PERIODS, AS A MINIMUM
- ☐ RECONCILES SALES FORECASTS AND CUSTOMER ORDERS TO REALISTIC SHIPPING PLANS, SHOWING RESULTING SHORTAGES/SURPLUS
- ☐ DESCRIBES THE ACTUAL PRODUCTION PLAN, WHICH USUALLY DIFFERS FROM THE SHIPPING PLANS
- ☐ HAS BEEN VALIDATED WITH RESPECT TO REALISTIC:
  - MACHINE CAPACITY
  - LABOR SHIFT/OVERTIME PLAN
  - VENDOR CAPACITY AND LEAD TIME
  - MATERIAL AVAILABILITY

ADMINISTRATIVE ELEMENTS

- ☐ CONVERTED TO A MASTER SCHEDULE, BY PART NUMBER, IN WEEKLY TIME PERIODS, WHICH CONFORMS TO THE MPP
- ☐ ADMINISTERED BY A MASTER SCHEDULER, WHO MAY ONLY MAKE MIX CHANGES WITHIN THE SCOPE OF THE MPP
- ☐ PERFORMANCE MEASURED AT LEAST WEEKLY AND REPORTED TO THE GENERAL MANAGER
- ☐ UNCOMPLETED WORK RESCHEDULED INTO FUTURE TIME PERIODS, SUBJECT TO MPP SCOPE RESTRAINTS

Source: K. A. Wantuck, "Master Production Planning at Bendix," *Inventories and Production Magazine,* July–August 1983, p. 14.

FIGURE 9.7 Mohawk Company, quarterly budgeting cycle activities

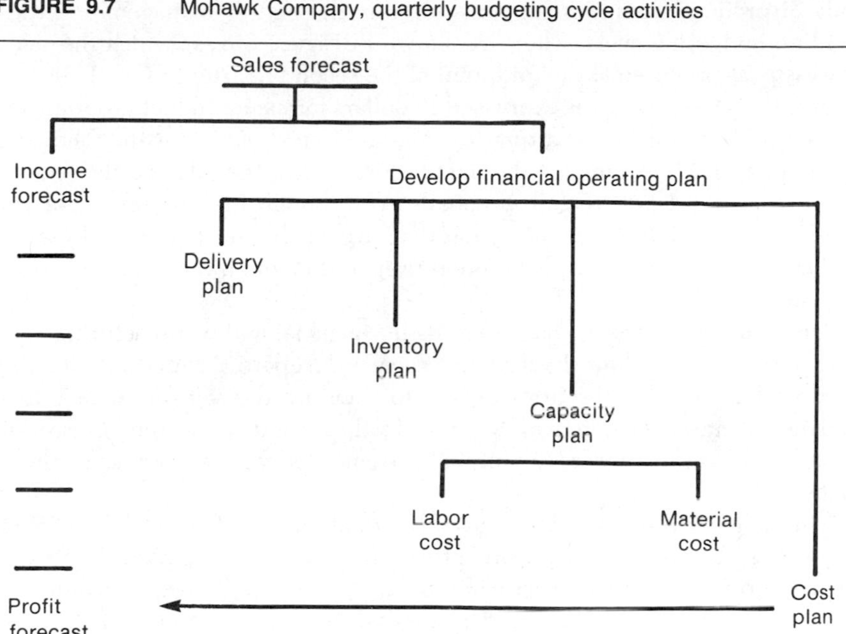

detailed financial operating plan that specifies a forecast of plant shipments (Mohawk calls this the "delivery plan"; in fact, it is the production plan), inventory level targets (the inventory plan), and a capacity plan (covering both a manpower and a materials budget). Once these plans have been prepared to produce an overall profit forecast for the firm, work can begin on preparing (revising) the master production schedule that also covers the next four quarters.

The budgeting cycle, performed at the midpoint of each quarter, begins with the preparation of a sales forecast for each of the firm's three product lines. Sales forecasting is the responsibility of a general manager who has the profit responsibility for a particular product line. In preparing the sales forecast, the general manager, the financial staff, and the marketing organization work closely with a separate field sales organization. The initial sales forecast is for one year in the future. This forecast is stated both in terms of dollar sales and unit sales, and corresponds to the product groupings used by the financial staff to value inventory and measure gross profit levels.

As an example, the energy management product line represents annual sales of $15 to $18 million in total. This product line includes some 75 individual product categories, each representing annual sales of $25,000 to $2.5 million. While a separate forecast is prepared for all of the 75 different product categories, some of these sales forecasts are combined to reduce the number of product categories considered in the budgeting cycle. In fact, only 21 product groupings are considered in the energy management product line budgeting cycle. They are shown in Figure 9.8 for which the sales forecast was prepared at the midpoint of the second quarter in year 1. In this figure, the sales forecast is expressed in dollars for each product grouping on a monthly basis for the next quarter, and a quarterly basis for the following three quarters. In producing the data in Figure 9.8, the sales for the second quarter of year 1 are treated as actual, even though the quarter is not yet finished. As a result, the monthly forecasts are for the third quarter of year 1, and the quarterly forecasts have been prepared through the second quarter of year 2.

Once the sales forecast has been made, financial and manufacturing representatives become involved in the cycle to prepare a game plan for the product line. One of the first steps is to translate the sales forecast into a delivery plan (production plan) for manufacturing and an income forecast for finance. The company uses the tabular presentation form for preparing these plans.

The delivery plan is a statement of the total planned factory deliveries to customers, to finished-goods inventory, and to other company locations. Representatives from manufacturing, finance, and sales develop the delivery plan. The sales forecast, desired changes to inventory, potential capacity constraints, vendor deliveries, cash requirements, personnel available, etc., are considered, and adjustments to the sales forecasts (plan), and/or inventory plan are negotiated, if necessary. If, for example, manufacturing cannot produce the volume necessary to satisfy both the sales plan and an increase in inventory, the cycle stops and a new sales and/or inventory plan is agreed upon. This production plan, therefore, is a very important and integral part of the entire process; subsequent planning does *not* proceed until there is complete agreement between the sales, finance, and manufacturing representatives.

The next step in the cycle is the conversion of the delivery plan into a capacity plan for each product line and for the plant in total. Figure 9.9 illustrates the development of the capacity plan for the energy management product line considering the labor content of the sales forecast, the forecast labor content of the two identified inventories (finished goods and work in process), and the labor content of the forecast interplant transfers both to and from this plant. The bottom line in the energy management section of Figure 9.9 (TOTAL LABOR INPUT) indicates the plant capacity requirements for this product line for the periods indicated where capacity is stated in terms of direct labor dollars. For example, $199,000 of direct labor input is planned for January, year 1. This represents about two thirds of the total direct labor input (capacity) for the Mohawk plant in January ($290,000)—which is shown on the next line of Figure 9.9. Since there are 21 working days in January, this means an average of $13,800 of direct labor input per

FIGURE 9.8 Mohawk Company, summary sales forecast, energy management products ($000)*

Product Grouping	History				Year 1					Year 2 1 Qtr.	Year 2 2d Qtr.
	Year 2	Year 1	Year 0	1st Qtr.	2d Qtr.	July	Aug.	Sept.	4th Qtr.		
Singlephase	886	700	265	51	23	13	14	14	41	41	39
Polyphase	4059	1699	349	46	32	20	20	20	60	60	50
Con-Ed	402	108	—								
Lincoln Billing	1609	1354	1412	451	351	102	161	146	409	527	435
Meter Timeswitch	331	224	188	63	76	20	30	27	77	78	69
Sockets	41	57	84	13	14	2	2	2	6	6	10
	7328	4142	2298	624	496	157	227	209	593	712	603
Lincoln Nonbilling	2301	2721	1837	725	560	149	176	204	529	528	586
Line Controls	615	698	358	97	120	15	21	22	58	83	90
Timeswitch	882	1107	708	186	185	43	55	76	174	262	202
	3798	4526	2903	1008	865	207	252	302	761	873	878
Transformers 600V	2767	3139	2248	666	559	193	254	281	728	756	677
Transformers 15KV	383	528	410	232	110	45	50	60	155	201	175
D.C. Meters	143	200	102	70	59	7	18	18	43	53	56
	3293	3867	2760	968	728	245	322	359	926	1010	908
Survey Recorders	695	826	901	321	355	99	162	132	373	398	367
S.R. Systems				8	95	—	178	45	223	237	141
Digital Pulse Rec.	460	436	225	119	174	43	48	50	141	126	140
C.M.E.	663	443	407	153	168	6	31	57	94	145	145
	1818	1710	1533	601	792	148	419	284	851	906	788
Parts—Winchester & Memphis	1348	1466	1027	405	413	75	135	135	345	395	390
Misc.	407	307	276	224	82	24	32	33	89	120	129
Repairs (Replacement Parts)	37	46	53	16	10	3	3	4	10	10	12
	444	353	329	240	92	27	35	37	99	130	141
Resale:											
Demand Control	—	2	151	64	56	42	52	53	147	172	110
Sigma-form	482	443	—								
	482	445	151	64	56	42	52	53	147	172	110
Total	18511	16509	11001	3910	3442	901	1442	1379	3722	4198	3818

*Prepared at the midpoint of the second quarter of year 1.

Source: W. L. Berry, R. A. Mohrman, and T. R. Callarman, "Master Scheduling and Capacity Planning: A Case Study" (Bloomington: Indiana University Graduate School of Business, Discussion Paper No. 73, 1977).

FIGURE 9.9 Mohawk Company, aggregate production and inventory plan ($000)*

Labor forecast	*Year 0*		*Year 1*						*Year 2*	*Year 3*
	8/31 Actual	*12/31 4th Qtr.*	*1/31 Jan.*	*2/29 Feb.*	*3/31 Mar.*	*6/30 2d Qtr.*	*9/31 3d Qtr.*	*12/31 4th Qtr.*	*12/31 1977*	*12/31 1978*
Energy management:										
Finished Goods inventory	$ 244	$ 240	$ 250	$ 270	$ 275	$ 310	$ 300	$ 300	$ 300	$ 300
Work-in-Process inventory	862	825	825	805	800	800	800	800	800	800
Subtotal	$1,106	$1,065	$1,075	$1,075	$1,075	$1,110	$1,100	$1,100	$1,100	$1,100
Net change		⟨41⟩	10	—	—	35	⟨10⟩	—	—	—
Labor in sales forecast		599	176	168	210	540	531	542	2,196	2,146
Transfer from Memphis		⟨54⟩	⟨12⟩	⟨12⟩	⟨12⟩	⟨36⟩	⟨36⟩	⟨36⟩	⟨144⟩	⟨144⟩
Transfer to Memphis		72	25	25	15	13	13	13	52	52
Total labor input		$ 576	$ 199	$ 181	$ 213	$ 552	$ 498	$ 519	$2,104	$2,054
Plant total:										
Labor input	$ 210	$ 829	$ 290	$ 273	$ 342	$ 847	$ 745	$ 830	$3,243	$3,706
Days per period	20	61	21	20	25	62	52	57	236	236
Average labor per day	$ 10.5	$ 13.6	$ 13.8	$ 13.6	$ 13.7	$ 13.7	$ 14.3	$ 14.6	$ 13.7	$ 15.7

*Measured in direct labor dollars.

Source: W. L. Berry, R. A. Mohrman, and T. R. Callarman, "Master Scheduling and Capacity Planning: A Case Study" (Bloomington: Indiana University Graduate School of Business, Discussion Paper No. 73, 1977).

day. This translates into a total manpower level for the plant, using planning factors for the number of dollars of direct labor per man/day.

Three factors are considered in arriving at the capacity plan. First, the direct labor content of the sales forecast is determined, using standard cost system data. The direct labor content of the sales forecast for the energy management product line is shown in Figure 9.9 (labeled Labor in Sales Forecast). Note that $176,000 of direct labor is required to support the sales forecast for January of year 1. Next, the labor dollars in the sales forecasts are modified to account for any buildup or depletion of inventories that is planned for the coming year. Figure 9.9 indicates the desired levels over the next year, including both finished-goods and work-in-process inventories. The levels (also measured in terms of direct labor dollars) indicate the cash requirements that are needed to finance the inventory during the next year, as well. Note that a reduction in inventory of $41,000 is planned for the fourth quarter of year 0, while an increase of $10,000 is planned for January, year 1. These changes need to be considered in planning the direct labor input for the energy management product line. Thus, the increase of $10,000 in January means that $186,000 of direct labor is needed in this month instead of $176,000. The third factor needed in determining the plant capacity is interplant sales of equipment. Figure 9.9 shows that $12,000 of labor will be expended by the Memphis plant for products sold by this plant. An additional $25,000 in labor will be expended here for products sold by Memphis. Thus, there is a net addition of $13,000 in direct labor required above and beyond the sales by this plant. When added to the $10,000 inventory increase and the $176,000 of labor in the sales forecast, the total labor input for January, year 1, is $199,000.

After all the negotiations are complete, the budgeting cycle has produced an overall game plan for the business which includes an approved sales plan, a delivery plan, an inventory plan, and a capacity plan. Several additional steps are performed in the budgeting cycle, which involve preparing a direct material budget indicating the purchasing dollars required to support the delivery plan, and a cost plan which specifies a budget of indirect manufacturing and administrative expenses. Other operating plans in addition to the basic production plan, involving engineering and marketing plans, are also included in the budgeting cycle. These plans are then combined by the finance staff to produce a profit forecast for each product line (profit center).

Hill-Rom's use of planning bills of material

The use of planning bill of material concepts can be very useful in the production planning process. For an example, we look at the application being developed at Hill-Rom, a manufacturer of hospital beds, related equipment, and accessories for hospitals and nursing homes.

Hill-Rom has expanded the planning bill concept to what they call the "super-duper" bill. An abbreviated example is shown in Figure 9.10. Using

FIGURE 9.10 Hill-Rom "super-duper" bill

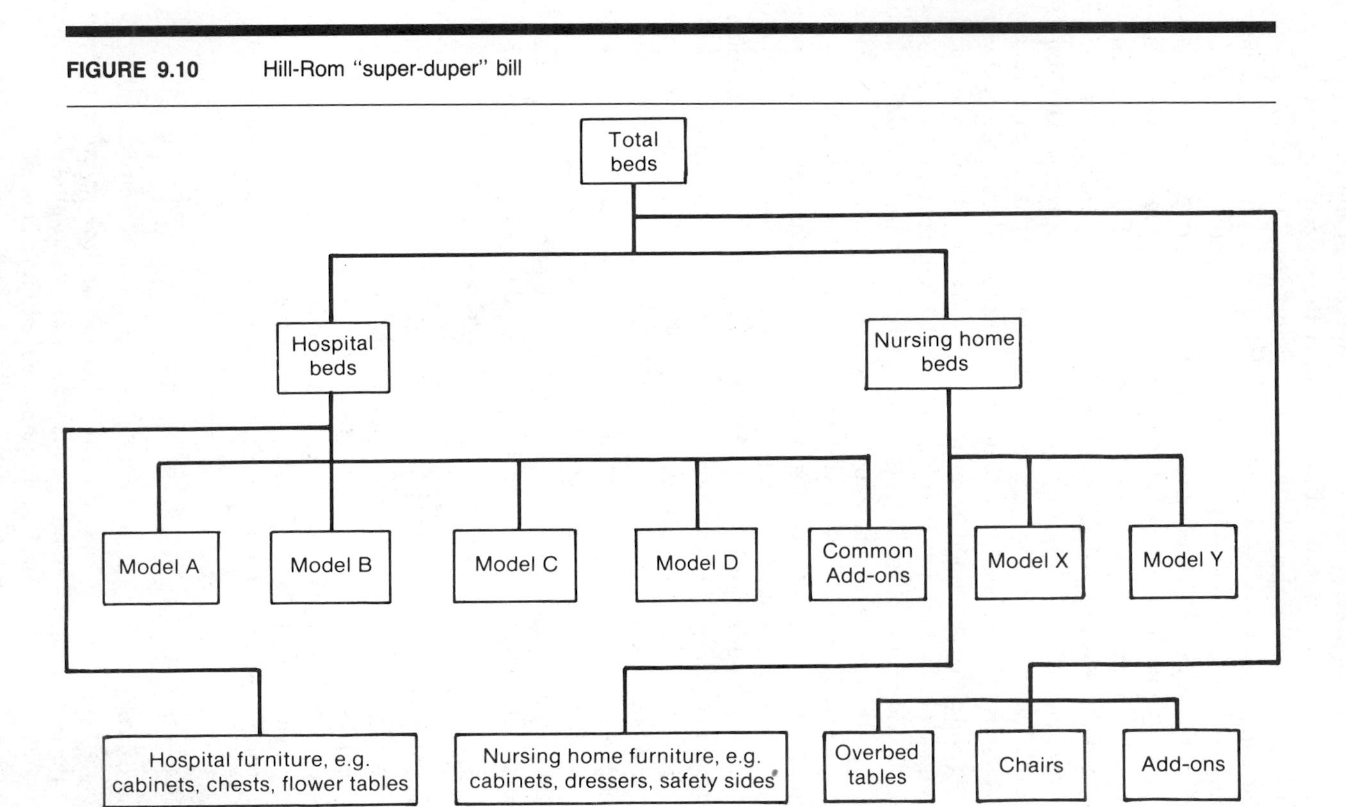

this approach, only one unit is forecast, total bed sales. All other forecasts are treated as bill of material relationships. For example, the forecast for the super bill group, over-bed tables, is a percentage of overall bed sales.

One of the marketing people at Hill-Rom found the super-duper bill concept ideal for implementing an idea he had been thinking about for some time. He believed that the company makes trigger products and trailer products. Beds are trigger products, whereas over-bed tables, chairs, and add-ons such as trapezes or intravenous fluid rods are trailer products. The purchase of trailer products is dependent upon the purchase of trigger products in somewhat the same relationship as components to end items. This relationship means that, rather than forecasting the demand for over-bed tables, Hill-Rom tracks and maintains the percentage relationship between the sales of beds and over-bed tables.

This bill of material relationship will probably be a better estimate than a direct forecast of over-bed tables. If one expects bed sales to go up or down, by treating over-bed tables as a trailer product with a bill of material linkage, there is an automatic adjustment made in over-bed table forecasts, as in all the trailer products.

The use of bill of material approaches to forecasting also forces a logical consistency. There was a time when the forecast for 84-inch mattresses at Hill-Rom exceeded the combined forecasts for beds that use 84-inch mattresses. By treating these relationships with bill of material approaches, these inconsistencies, which will always result from independent estimating, are reduced.

The production planning unit for these products at Hill-Rom is total beds. Furthermore, the percentage split into hospital beds and nursing home beds is not only estimated, it is managed. Sales personnel are held to specified tolerance limits on this split because the capacity and net profit implications of the percentage split are important.

Below each of these two super-duper bills are super bills for the various model series. Finally, there is another trigger-trailer relationship between the total hospital bed sales and hospital furniture such as cabinets, flower tables, etc. The same kind of bill of material relationship is used to forecast nursing home furniture sales. These various bill of material relationships pass the planning information down through the MPC system in a logically consistent way.

At the time of this writing, the approach described here was not yet fully implemented. The firm is still working on the bill of material design, engineering change integration, and other aspects of the relationship to the MPC. The directions are clear, however.

Finally, this entire approach is consistent with the way the firm does its strategic planning, which is in terms of strategic business units (SBUs). The SBUs are to be established as super bills. The result will be a very close integration of MPC and strategic planning.

CONCLUDING PRINCIPLES

Production and game planning are key inputs to MPC systems. They represent management's handle on the business. This chapter emphasizes the key relationships of top management and functional management in the development and maintenance of an effective production plan. We summarize our discussion with the following important principles:

- The production plan is not a forecast; it must be a managerial statement of desired production output.
- The production plan should be a part of the game-planning process so that it will be in complete agreement with the other functional plans (sales plan, budget, etc.) that make up the game plan.
- The trade-offs required to frame the production plan must be made *prior* to final approval of the plan.
- There must be top-management involvement in the game-planning process, which should be directly related to strategic planning.
- The MPC system should be used to perform the routine activities and provide the routine data so that management time can be devoted to the important tasks. The MPC system also should be used to facilitate what if analyses at the production-planing level.
- Review of performance against plan and forecast performance are both needed to prompt replanning when necessary.
- The production plan should provide the MPS parameters, and flexibility should be specifically defined. The sum of the detailed MPS must always equal the production plan.
- The production plan should tie the strategic activities of the company directly through the MPS to the execution modules of the MPC.

REFERENCES

Berry, W. L., R. A. Mohrman, and T. Callarman. "Master Scheduling and Capacity Planning: A Case Study." *The Manufacturing Productivity Education Committee*, Purdue University, 1977.

Bitran, Gabriel R., Elizabeth A. Haas, and Arnoldo C. Hax. "Hierarchical Production Planning: A Single Stage System." *Operations Research* 29, no. 4 (July-August 1981), pp. 717–43.

Goldratt, Eliyanu. "The Unbalanced Plant." *APICS 24th Annual Conference Proceedings*, 1981, pp. 195–99.

Hall, Robert. "Driving the Productivity Machine: Production Planning and Control in Japan." (Falls Church, Va.: APICS, 1981).

Holt, C. C., F. Modigliani, J. F. Muth, and H. A. Simon. *Planning Production, Inventories, and Workforce*, New York: Prentice-Hall, 1960.

Motwane, Aman A. "How to Organize a Production Planning Department." *APICS 24th Annual Conference Proceedings*, 1981, pp. 347–50.

Pendleton, W. E. "MRP II Begins with the Strategic Plan." *1980 APICS Conference Proceedings*, pp. 252–55.

Peterson, Rein, and Edward A. Silver. *Decision Systems for Inventory Management and Production Planning*. New York: John Wiley & Sons, 1979.

Skinner, C. W. *Manufacturing in the Corporate Strategy*. New York: John Wiley & Sons, 1978.

Visagie, Martin S. "Production Planning—It Touches Us All." *APICS 24th Annual Conference Proceedings*, 1981, pp. 142–44.

Wantuck, K. A. "Master Production Planning at Bendix." *Inventories and Production Magazine*, July-August 1981, pp. 12–16.

10

Demand management

This chapter covers the highly integrative activity we call demand management. It is through demand management that all potential demands on manufacturing capacity are collected and coordinated. This activity manages the day-to-day interactions between the customers and the company. A well-developed demand management module within the manufacturing planning and control (MPC) system results in several significant benefits. The proper planning of all externally and internally generated demands means that capacity can be better planned and controlled. Timely and *honest* customer order promises can be made. Physical distribution activities can be improved significantly. This chapter shows how these benefits can be achieved; the focus is less on techniques than on the management underpinnings and concepts necessary to perform this integrative activity.

The chapter is organized around the following four topics:

- Demand management in MPC systems: What role does demand management play in the MPC system?
- Demand management techniques: What techniques have proven useful for demand management practice?
- Managing demand: How to live with demand management on a day-to-day basis.
- Company examples: Effective demand management in practice.

There are several chapters in this book that are closely related to demand management. Chapters 7 and 8 deal with master production scheduling, which is intimately tied to demand management. The detailed logistics activities required to move products to the customers are treated in Chapter 19. Technical material related to forecasting is found in Chapter 16 and to inventory management in Chapters 17 and 18.

DEMAND MANAGEMENT IN MANUFACTURING PLANNING AND CONTROL SYSTEMS

Demand management encompasses forecasting, order entry, order-delivery-date promising, physical distribution, and other customer-contact-related activities. Demand management is also concerned with other sources of demand for manufacturing capacity. Included are service-part demands, intracompany requirements, and pipeline inventory stocking. All quantities and timing for demands must be planned and controlled.

For many firms, the planning and control of demand quantities and timings are a day-to-day interactive dialogue with customers. For other firms, particularly in the process industries, the critical coordination is in scheduling large inter- and intracompany requirements. For still others, physical distribution is critical, since the factory must support a warehouse replenishment program which can differ significantly from the pattern of final customer demand.

Demand management is a gateway module in manufacturing planning and control providing the link to the marketplace. The activities performed here provide the coordination between manufacturing and the marketplace, sister plants, and warehouses. It is through demand management that a channel of communication is maintained between the MPC systems and their "customers." Specific demands initiate actions throughout MPC, which ultimately result in the delivery of products and the consumption of materials and capacities.

The external aspects of the demand management module are depicted in Figure 10.1 as the double-ended arrow connected to the marketplace outside the MPC system.

The importance of identifying all sources of demand is obvious, but sometimes overlooked. If the material and capacity resources are to be planned effectively, *all* sources of demand must be identified: spare parts, distribution, inventory changes, new items, promotions, etc. It is only when all demand sources are accounted for that realistic MPC plans can be developed.

Demand management and production planning

The exact linkage of demand management and production planning depends to some extent on the way in which production planning is done in the

FIGURE 10.1 Demand management in the MPC system

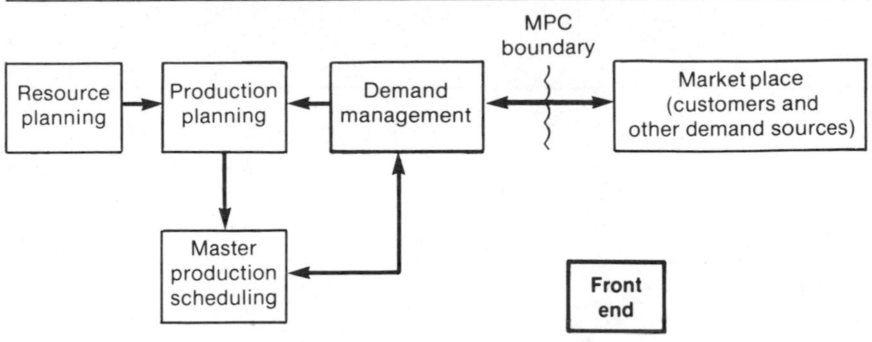

firm. If the production plan is a quarterly statement of output in dollars or some other financial measure, then the key requirement for demand planning is for synchronization with this target. If the delivery timings for significant customer orders will affect the production plan, this information needs to be understood by production planning. Similarly, a major change in distribution inventory policy might influence the production plan.

The overall level of service-part demand also has to be included in the production plan. For many firms, the individual service-part items are forecast; the extension by selling prices and summation for the production-planning period is one way to incorporate this source of demand into production planning.

A major change in intercompany demand can also play an important role in production planning. This means that all transfers of products into and out of a plant must be explicitly incorporated into the required budgets.

Demand management and master production scheduling

The interactions of demand management and master production scheduling (MPS) are frequent and detailed. Figure 10.2 shows how two time fences might be used in an MPS. The net result is three areas, which are sometimes called "frozen," "slushy," and "liquid." The way in which the MPS is stated in these three areas is often different. The key point here is that the MPS capacity is filled with customer orders in the short run and forecasts in the long run. This leads to an understanding of order entry as a process of consuming the forecast—sometimes in small bites and sometimes in large bites.

The *available-to-promise* concept is a key to managing the consumption of the forecast by actual customer orders. As an important part of our present discussion, it is critical to point out that for some firms the customer orders can be partially made of interplant requirements and/or distribution requirements.

FIGURE 10.2 MPS time fences—forecasts consumed by orders

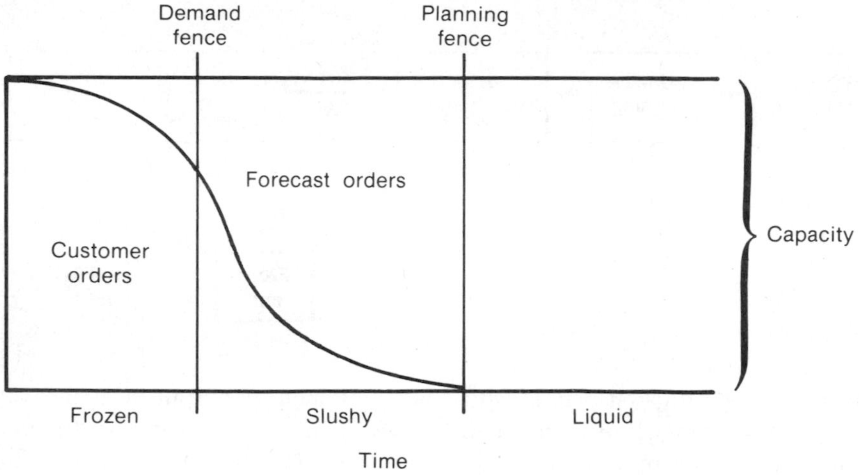

The spare-part issue is a bit more complex in most firms. The demand for spare parts is typically forecast on an item-by-item basis and added to the gross requirement data in the corresponding MRP records. The actual spare-part demand will, of course, vary around the forecast. The variability can be buffered with safety stocks. The point is, there is *not* an explicit treatment of each spare part by a master production schedule. This would take too long; moreover, the simplified approach will work reasonably well.

A key problem might be raised if spare-part demand is not incorporated at the MPS level; the resulting capacity requirements will not be reflected in rough-cut capacity planning models. The requirements would, however, be seen by the detailed capacity requirements planning models that are driven from MRP records.

To adequately perform rough-cut capacity planning, the service-part demand will have to be included. This could be done on a rough basis by estimating the service-part demand in monetary units and using some base to convert it to machine center hours. Alternatively, one could prepare a bill of capacity for each service-part and multiply by the forecast service-part demand levels. The principle is clear: the capacity must be provided for *all* sources of demand.

Outbound product flow

Distribution activities are planned on the basis of the information developed in the demand management function. Customer delivery promise dates, inventory resupply shipments, interplant shipments, and so on, are all used to develop short-term transportation schedules. The information used for master production schedules can be integrated with distribution planning, as well. The information can be used to plan and control warehouse resupply. Moreover, transportation capacity, warehouse capacity, and the other resources within which the day-to-day distribution function will operate can also be better planned and controlled with this information.

Integration of distribution with master production scheduling can have very high payoffs for some firms. In essence, the resupply shipping decisions are demand inputs which must be satisfied by the MPS. Conversely, the MPS provides a set of product availabilities that can be put into the distribution planning system.

Distribution requirements planning (DRP) is a methodology for properly coordinating the replenishment of distribution inventories. The key concept is to use the MRP time-phased logic to lay out a set of planned replenishment shipments to each warehouse or distribution center. As was shown in Figure 10.2, the first or most immediate portion of the plan is frozen, then there is a slushy part, and then there is a liquid portion. By summing all the warehouse replenishment shipment plans into an MRP record, one is able to obtain the demands on the central stock inventory. That is, the planned orders (shipments) in each warehouse record are passed as gross requirements to the central stock inventory. Replenishments for the central inventory are, in fact, the MPS.

It is through the conversion of the day-to-day customer orders into product shipments that the service levels for the company are realized. Careful management of the actual demands can provide the stability needed for efficient production, and that stability provides the basis for realistic customer promises and services. The booking of actual orders also serves to monitor activity against forecasts. As changes occur in the market plan, demand management can and should routinely pick them up, indicating when managerial attention is required.

Data capture

The data capture and monitoring activities of demand management fall into two broad categories, the basic market and the product mix. The activity most appropriate for production-planning monitoring is basic market trends and patterns. The data monitored should correspond to the units used in production planning. The intent is to determine, on an ongoing basis, the general levels of actual business to compare with the production plan.

The second activity is concerned with managing the product mix for purposes of master production scheduling and customer order promising. Since final demand will be in catalog numbers or stockkeeping units, the day-to-day conversion of specific demands to MPC actions requires managing the mix of individual products.

For both basic market and product-mix activities, it is important that *demand* data be captured where possible. Many companies use sales instead of demand for purposes of making "demand" projections. Unless all demands have been satisfied, sales can understate the actual demand. In other instances, we know of firms that use shipments as the basis for making demand projections. In one such instance, the company concluded that their demand was increasing since their shipments were increasing. It was not until they had committed to increased raw-material purchases that they realized the increased shipments were replacement orders for overseas customers. It seems that two successive overseas shipments were lost at sea.

Dealing with day-to-day customer orders

A primary function of the demand management module is converting specific day-to-day customer orders into detailed MPC actions. It is through the demand management function that the actual demands consume the planned materials and capacities. The conversion of actual customer demands into production actions must be performed regardless of whether the firm manufactures make-to-stock, make-to-order, or assemble-to-order products. The details may be somewhat different, depending on the nature of the manufacturing/marketing environment of the company.

In make-to-order environments, the primary activity is the specification of customer delivery dates. This must be related to the master production schedule to determine when the material will be available to meet a specific customer request. While this function is often performed the same way for assemble-to-order products, a communication with the final assembly schedule may also be needed to set promise dates. In both of these environments, there is a communication from the customer (a request) and to the customer (a delivery date) through the demand management module. These aspects of demand management are known by such names as order entry, order booking, and customer order service.

In a make-to-stock environment, demand management does not ordinarily make customer promise dates. Since the material is in stock, the customer is most often served from the inventory. In the event that there is insufficient inventory for a specific request, the customer needs to be told when the material will be available, or, if there is under allocation, told what portion of the request can be satisfied. The conversion of customer orders to MPC actions in the make-to-stock environment occurs to resupply the inventory from which sales are made. This conversion is largely through forecasting, since the resupply decision is well beyond any backlog of customer orders.

In all of the environments, extraordinary demands often must be accommodated. Examples include advance orders in the make-to-stock environment, unexpected interplant needs, large spare-part orders, provision of demonstration units, and increased channel inventories. These all represent "real" demands on the material system.

The capture of actual demand and its comparison to forecasts can provide important early warning information to management. By bringing managerial attention to demand information that is outside of some expected range of forecast errors, executives can evaluate the market to see whether changes have, in fact, been taking place. This could lead to a revision of the production plan and subsequent material availability.

The demand data captured on specific products can be used to monitor the actual product mix, and also to change material plans. Even though the overall level of demand remains fixed, the specific allocation of those demands among products may change. Capturing this information and monitoring changes in the mix is necessary to keep the production of individual products in line with the marketplace. As products are made and delivered to customers, the service levels of the organization are realized. An important activity within demand management is capturing the data on the actual customer-service performance of the company. The requirement is to capture data on unsatisfied demand in make-to-stock environments and actual versus promised delivery performance in make- or assemble-to-order environments.

DEMAND MANAGEMENT TECHNIQUES

The techniques dealt with in this section have the primary objective of increasing the managerial focus of demand management.

Facilitating the forecasting task

There are several reasons for aggregating industrial product items in both time and level of detail for forecasting purposes. This must be done with caution, however. The aggregation of individual products into families, geographical areas, or product types, for example, must be done in ways that are compatible with the planning systems. The product groupings must also be developed so that the forecast unit is sensible for the forecasters. Provided these guidelines are followed, product groupings can be used to facilitate the forecasting task.

It is a well-known phenomenon that *long-term or product-line forecasts are better than detail forecasts*. This is just a verbalization of a statistical verity. Consider the example shown in Figure 10.3. The monthly sales average 20 units per day, but vary randomly with a standard deviation of 2 units. This means that 95 percent of the monthly demands would lie between 16 and 24 units (assuming a normal distribution). This corresponds to a forecast error of plus or minus 20 percent around the forecast of 20 units per day.

Now suppose that instead of forecasting the demand on a monthly basis, an annual forecast of demand is prepared. In this case, a forecast of 240 units is made for the year. The resulting standard deviation would be 6.9 units (assuming the monthly sales were independent). This corresponds to a 95 percent range of 226 to 254 units or a plus or minus 5.8 percent deviation. The reduction from plus or minus 20 percent to plus or minus 5.8 percent is

FIGURE 10.3 Effect of aggregating on forecast accuracy

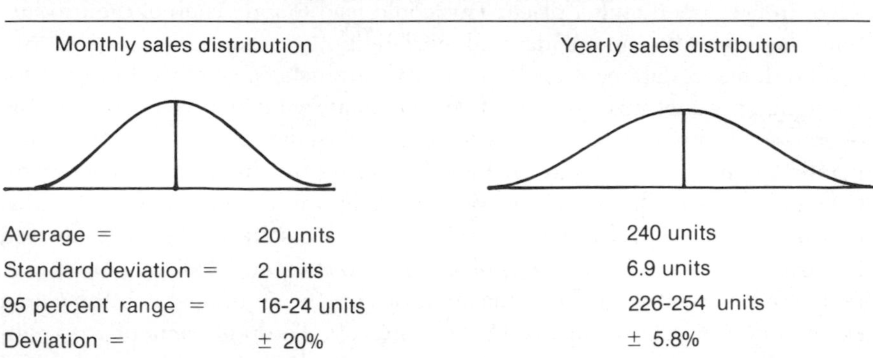

	Monthly	Yearly
Average =	20 units	240 units
Standard deviation =	2 units	6.9 units
95 percent range =	16-24 units	226-254 units
Deviation =	± 20%	± 5.8%

due to using a much longer time period. The same effect can be seen in forecasting the demand for product families instead of for individual items.

The use of aggregate product forecast data can be illustrated with a survey concerning forecast accuracy taken by Polysar International of plant, distribution, scheduling, sales, and transportation managers. The results of the survey are shown in Figure 10.4. Even though the persons surveyed used detailed information to make labor, inventory, scheduling, traffic, and warehousing decisions, they recognized the magnitude of the forecast error in the detailed product-item forecasts. Their conclusion was to prepare short-term, detailed forecasts routinely and develop methods to live with the forecast errors.

One means of dealing with the inherent difficulty of forecasting individual items is to forecast ratios or percentages of aggregated forecasts rather than stockkeeping units (SKU) directly. Figure 10.5 shows the reduction in detail possible by the technique. For Jag's Coffee Company there are four grinds,

FIGURE 10.4 Realistic levels of deviation of actual versus forecast (percent)

Time →

Item detail ↓	1 month	1 quarter	1 year
Total volume	± 12	8	8
Family	15	10	8
Type in family	15		12
Grade in type	30		
SKU †	50		

*Average of a Polysar International Survey.
†Stockkeeping unit.

four package sizes, and three brands. This is a maximum total of 4 × 4 × 3 = 48 possible combinations, of which only 20 had sales in the period covered by the example. If the percentages of the total coffee sales by each of the brands, sizes, and grinds are computed, there are only 12 separate items (11 mix ratios and total coffee sales) to be concerned with. That is, one could forecast total coffee sales and break them down into brands, sizes, or grinds on a percentage basis.

For many firms, product-mix ratios remain fairly constant over time. In such cases, managerial attention can be directly on forecasting overall sales. Percentage forecasting can be used to routinize the individual item forecasting problem. Moreover, if the master scheduler keeps MPS records for each of the product options, it may not be necessary to forecast individual items. The important job is not *forecasting* individual end items, it is *building* them and keeping due-date promises. Demand management is designed to facilitate the process.

The example of Figure 10.5 also shows the need for applying judgment in forecasting. If the promotion package size was for a single promotion, it should be dropped from the forecast. It also helps if the manufacturing step subject to the greatest forecast error can be postponed as long as possible. For example, if the labeling of the package or the filling of the package can be postponed, a reduction in forecast error might be realized because specific customer orders will be on hand before the commitment to any particular item is made.

FIGURE 10.5 Sales in tons by brand, size, and grind of Jag's Coffee Company

Brand and size	*Grind**				*Total*		*Total*	*Percent*
	I	*R*	*D*	*S*				
Jingle						Coffee	440	100
Packet	10				10	Brand		
Regular	20	40	30		90	Jingle	130	30
Giant		20	10		30	Jangle	80	18
						Jungle	230	52
Jangle						Size		
Packet	10				10	Packet	20	4
Regular	15	10	20		45	Regular	225	52
Promotion	5	5			10	Promotion	10	2
Giant		5	10		15	Giant	185	42
Jungle						Grind		
Regular		40	40	10	90	Grind I	60	14
Giant		50	50	40	140	Grind R	170	39
						Grind D	160	36
						Grind S	50	11
Total	60	170	160	50	440			

*I = instant, R = regular, D = drip, S = special.

There is one final point about forecast errors: Many efforts to reduce them are wasted—since they will not go away. A better alternative to improved forecasting found by many firms is improved systems for *responding* to forecast errors. The gross to net logic of MRP prevents forecast errors from compounding, since the net requirements are simply changed from period to period as the actual inventory deviates from the projected inventory.

Distribution requirements planning (DRP)

The basic MRP record and logic can be applied to distribution material flows using distribution requirements planning. When several distribution centers or warehouses are in operation, DRP is an excellent way to coordinate the input of demand information to the master production schedule. The DRP records for one item stored in two warehouses and the central (factory) warehouse are shown in Figure 10.6.

In creating the DRP records, the warehouses are typically coded as the zero level on the bill of material (BOM). Level one is the central warehouse or distribution center. The MRP explosion logic combines the firm planned orders and planned orders (sometimes called planned shipments, as in our example), at the warehouse. This is shown in Figure 10.6. The warehouses have forecasts as their gross requirements, since the demand on the warehouses is independent demand. (In some advanced firms, the level zero of the BOM is extended beyond the warehouses to their key customers. The benefits of this close integration can be substantial.)

DRP brings the full range of MRP techniques to distribution. The exception messages, pegging, and firm planned order concepts are all applied to managing the replenishment of the warehouses. Moreover, the MPS can be viewed as a set of firm planned orders determined in timing and amount in such a way as to economically group the central warehouse gross requirements.

The process of combining a forecast with the MRP records is called *time-phased order point (TPOP)* logic. That is, if the forecasts were uniform and perfect, the records would simulate the results of using order-point logic at the warehouse. The application of this logic to warehouse A from Figure 10.6 is shown in Figure 10.7. In Figure 10.7, four successive periods of replanning are shown.

In this example, actual sales vary from 16 to 24 around the forecast of 20 units. The actual sales of 18 in period 1 have no impact on the planned shipments, while the actual sales of 24 units in period 2 changes the plan. The additional sales in period 2 have the effect of increasing the net requirements, which leads to planning a shipment in period 3 rather than period 4. The sales in period 3 were less than expected, so the net requirements are less and the planned shipment in period 5 is changed to period 6. Thus, the gross to net logic results in modifications of the shipping plans to keep them matched to the current market situation.

FIGURE 10.6 DRP records for two warehouses and the factory

Warehouse A
(Lead time = 1 period, shipping quantity = 40, safety stock = 6)

		Period 1	2	3	4	5
Forecast requirements		20	20	20	20	20
Scheduled receipts		40				
Projected available balance	6	26	6	26	6	26
Planned shipments			40		40	

Warehouse B
(Lead time = 2 periods, shipping quantity = 100, safety stock = 20)

		Period 1	2	3	4	5
Forecast requirements		60	60	60	60	60
Scheduled receipts		100				
Projected available balance	63	103	43	83	23	63
Planned shipments		100		100		

Central (factory) warehouse
(Lead time = 1 period, production quantity = 200, safety stock = 50)

		Period 1	2	3	4	5
Gross requirements		100	40	100	40	0
Scheduled receipts						
Projected available balance	217	117	77	177	137	137
Planned order releases			200			

Filtering the demand input to the MPS

There is one negative aspect of the TPOP logic in the example of Figure 10.7. The deviations of the actual sales around the forecast were reflected in changed shipping plans. These changes could have a destabilizing impact on the master schedule and shop. Two techniques for stabilizing the informa-

FIGURE 10.7 Records for a single SKU at one warehouse with time-phased order point logic

(Lead time = 1 period, shipping quantity = 40, safety stock = 6)

Period		1	2	3	4	5
Forecast requirements		20	20	20	20	20
Scheduled receipts		40				
Projected available balance	6	26	6	26	6	26
Planned shipments			40		40	

Actual demand for period 1 = 18

Period		2	3	4	5	6
Forecast requirements		20	20	20	20	20
Scheduled receipts						
Projected available balance	28	8	28	8	28	8
Planned shipments		40		40		

Actual demand for period 2 = 24

Period		3	4	5	6	7
Forecast requirements		20	20	20	20	20
Scheduled receipts		40				
Projected available balance	4	24	44	24	44	24
Planned shipments		40		40		

Actual demand for period 3 = 16

Period		4	5	6	7	8
Forecast requirements		20	20	20	20	20
Scheduled receipts		40				
Projected available balance	28	48	28	8	28	8
Planned shipments				40		

tion flow, firm planned orders and error addback, are described in this section.

Firm planned order. An example of the application of the firm planned order (shipment) concept to the warehouse example is shown in Figure 10.8. Firm planned shipments are designated by the planners and are not under system control. That is, they are not automatically replanned as conditions change, but are maintained in the period designated by the planner. By using firm planned shipments, the record shows the what if results of maintaining the present order pattern. By using MRP records to display this pattern, standard exception messages will be generated. That is, for example, if a present plan violates a stated safety stock objective, this would be highlighted by MRP exception coding.

In the example record for period 3, the firm planned shipment of 40 in period 4 is not rescheduled to period 3, even though the projected available inventory balance for period 4 is less than the safety stock. Thus, the master scheduler can review the implications of *not* changing before deciding whether the changes should be made. In this case, the decision might be to opt for consistency in the information, knowing that there still is some projected safety stock and the next order is due to arrive in period 5.

Error addback. Another method for stabilizing the MPS is the error addback method. This method assumes that the forecasts are unbiased, or accurate on the average. This means that any unsold forecast in one period will be made up for in the subsequent period, or any sales exceeding forecast now will reduce sales in the next periods. Using this method, errors are added (or subtracted) from future requirements to reflect the expected impact of actual sales on projected sales. An example is shown in Figure 10.9, which applies this concept to the warehouse example. Note that the planned shipments are under system control, i.e., the firm planned orders are not used.

The records in this example show the planned orders in exactly the same periods as in the firm planned shipment case. The adjustments to the forecast requirements ensure stability in the information. It is apparent that the effectiveness of this technique diminishes if the forecast is not unbiased. For example, if the reduced demand that occurred in periods 3 and 4 is part of a continuing trend, the procedure will break down. In this case, it will continue to build inventory as though the reduced demand will be made up in the future. This means that the forecasts must be carefully monitored and changed when necessary so that the procedure can be started again. One convenient measure for evaluating forecast accuracy is the cumulative forecast error. If this exceeds a specified quantity, the item forecast should be reviewed. For example, in period 4, the cumulative error has reached +7 (a value exceeding the safety stock); this might be used to indicate the need to review the forecast for this item.

In all cases, stability in the MPS is enhanced by using freezing techniques to hold schedules firm, and time fences to specify the management level

FIGURE 10.8 Record for a single SKU at one warehouse with firm planned order (shipments) logic

(Lead time = 1 period, shipping quantity = 40, safety stock = 6)

Period		1	2	3	4	5
Forecast requirements		20	20	20	20	20
Scheduled receipts		40				
Projected available balance	6	26	6	26	6	26
Firm planned shipments			40		40	

Actual demand for period 1 = 18

Period		2	3	4	5	6
Forecast requirements		20	20	20	20	20
Scheduled receipts						
Projected available balance	28	8	28	8	28	8
Firm planned shipments		40		40		40

Actual demand for period 2 = 24

Period		3	4	5	6	7
Forecast requirements		20	20	20	20	20
Scheduled receipts		40				
Projected available balance	4	24	4	24	4	24
Firm planned shipments			40		40	

Actual demand for period 3 = 16

Period		4	5	6	7	8
Forecast requirements		20	20	20	20	20
Scheduled receipts						
Projected available balance	28	8	28	8	28	8
Firm planned shipments		40		40		40

FIGURE 10.9 Record for a single SKU at one warehouse with error addback

(Lead time = 1, shipping quantity = 40, safety stock = 6)

Period		1	2	3	4	5
Forecast requirements		20	20	20	20	20
Scheduled receipts		40				
Projected available balance	6	26	6	26	6	26
Planned shipments			40		40	

Period 1 demand = 18, cumulative error = +2

Period		2	3	4	5	6
Forecast requirements		22	20	20	20	20
Scheduled receipts						
Projected available balance	28	6	26	6	26	6
Planned shipments		40		40		

Period 2 demand = 24, cumulative error = −2

Period		3	4	5	6	7
Forecast requirements		18	20	20	20	20
Scheduled receipts		40				
Projected available balance	4	26	6	26	6	26
Planned shipments			40		40	

Period 3 demand = 16, cumulative error = +2

Period		4	5	6	7	8
Forecast requirements		22	20	20	20	20
Scheduled receipts						
Projected available balance	28	6	26	6	26	6
Planned shipments		40		40		

Period 4 demand = 15, cumulative error = +7

required to formally approve a change request. For make-to-order or assemble-to-order products, stability is also related to the discipline applied in booking customer orders. Key in accomplishing this is the use of the available-to-promise concept. Figure 10.10 provides an example from the Jag's Coffee Company problem, using the 60 tons per period of instant coffee from Figure 10.5 as the basis.

The example shows that all of the instant coffee available in the first two periods is committed to customer orders already booked. No additional promises for delivery in the first two periods are possible without changing the commitment on one of the orders already booked. There are 120 tons of production planned for period 3, of which 70 tons are already promised. The remaining 50 tons are available for promise as early as period 3. If a customer wanted more than 50 tons to be delivered in one shipment, that customer would have to wait until at least period 5, unless one of the orders presently promised for delivery in periods 1, 2, or 3 could be rescheduled to period 5 or later, or unless the MPS itself was changed. The production of 120 units of instant coffee currently scheduled in period 1 must be nearly completed.

Flexibility planning

The focus on stability in the information system and MPS should not be taken as an argument for inflexibility. Indeed, we argued earlier that mechanisms for dealing with the forecast errors were often more important than attempts to reduce forecast errors. This means a form of flexibility is needed, particularly to accommodate short-term variations in the mix of SKUs being sold.

FIGURE 10.10 Application of available-to-promise logic to Jag's instant coffee production

	Period 1	2	3	4	5
Forecast	60	60	60	60	60
Booked orders	90	80	50	20	0
Available	80	0	60	0	60
Available to promise	0		50		120
Master schedule production	120		120		120

On hand = 50

In the make-to-stock examples of Figures 10.6 to 10.9, we saw the use of safety stock in the distribution warehouse as a form of buffer against larger than forecast demands. The use of safety stock in inventories is quite common. Less common is the use of safety lead time. In instances where the finished product is transported to a distant inventory location, such as a warehouse or distribution center, there is often a range of time during which the delivery can take place. The forecast error in this case is in terms of the time of arrival, not the quantity that will arrive. In these circumstances, dispatching shipments earlier than would be necessary on the average provides a safety lead time buffer against late-arriving shipments. In this case, both the shipment date and the scheduled delivery date are advanced by the amount of the safety lead time so that the system is driven by the correct data.

For make-to-order products, the use of hedging provides an effective, easily managed buffering technique. An example is given in Figure 10.11 for Jag's regular grind coffee. The figure shows the records for three steps of the production process. Green coffee beans are removed from storage and prepared for roasting. This takes one period. Next, the roasting of the prepared beans is done over three periods. Finally, the roasted beans are ground. The lead time for the final step is one period.

The records trace the planned orders through the process from the master schedule for regular grind coffee to green bean preparation. Since the demand for regular grind coffee is calculated as a percent of the total coffee forecast, and variations can occur in the mix between instant, regular, drip, and special grinds, the company wants the flexibility to respond to product-mix changes. However, they don't want to hold excess regular grind coffee in inventory.

The approach is to establish a hedge of 20 tons five periods from now. This is done by creating a hedge time fence at period five and introducing a 20-ton master schedule entry. We presume in this example that this has been done and the system has been operating for some time. Currently we are at the beginning of period 121 and the hedge of 20 units has just come over the time fence into period 125. Note that previously placed orders (scheduled receipts) and planned orders balance out the requirements and no inventory is shown except for prepared green coffee beans.

If there is no indication that the mix has changed, the hedge quantity is not required, and the 20 hedge units are pushed back over the fence to period 126 (top arrow in Figure 10.11). This will reduce the gross requirement for regular grind coffee from 360 to 340 tons in period 125 and will change the planned order in period 124. The effect is passed through the roasted bean record to the prepared green beans. At this point, the scheduled receipt of 340 and the inventory of 20 would have been enough to satisfy the gross requirement for 360, but it is not necessary, so the 20 tons will be held in prepared green bean inventory. Pushing out the hedge unit

FIGURE 10.11 An example of hedging for regular grind Jag's coffee

(Hedge time fence = 5 periods)
(Regular grind coffee: lead time = 1 period)

Period		121	122	123	124	125	126
Master schedule		340	0	340	0	340	0
Hedge quantity						20 →	20
Gross Requirements		340		340		340 →	20
Scheduled receipts		340					
Projected available balance	0	0	0	0	0	0	0
Planned order releases			340		340 →	20	

(Roasted beans: lead time = 3 periods)

Period		121	122	123	124	125	126
Gross requirements		0	340	0	340 →	20	0
Scheduled receipts			340				
Projected available balance	0	0	0	0	0	0	0
Planned order releases		340 →	20				

(Prepared green beans: lead time = 1 period)

Period		121	122	123	124	125	126
Gross requirements		340 →	20	0	0	0	0
Scheduled receipts		340	0				
Projected available balance	20	20	0	0	0	0	0
Planned order releases							

in subsequent periods will leave the 20 tons of prepared green beans in inventory.

If the hedge quantity had been allowed to remain within the time fence, a planned order for 360 tons of roasted coffee beans would have been issued and the 20 tons of prepared green beans would have started on the way to becoming roasted coffee beans. Should the hedge quantity have been required, it would be ground during period 124 and would be available in period 125. The placement of the hedge fence indicates how quickly a response can be made to product volume changes.

Setting the time fence and managing the hedge units must take into account both economic trade-offs and current conditions. Setting the time fence too early means that the inventory will be carried at higher levels in the product structure, which often decreases alternative uses of basic materials. Also, too short a time fence may not provide enough time to evaluate whether the mix ratio is changing. Similarly, it makes no sense to provide flexibility where it is not needed. Over the period when all the planned available coffee is committed to specific customer orders, there is no need for flexibility since the exact product mix is known (e.g., in the frozen part of Figure 10.2). In this circumstance, the hedge should be pushed out until there is still some forecast usage that has not been consumed by actual orders.

MANAGING DEMAND

In this section we are concerned with managerial issues related to the performance of day-to-day demand management tasks.

Organizing for demand management

Many, if not all, of the activities that we have associated with demand management are already performed in most companies. In many instances, the organizational responsibility for performing these activities is widely scattered throughout the firm. The finance or credit department performs credit-checking and order-screening activities associated with customer orders. The order-entry or booking activities are performed in the sales or customer service departments. The outbound product activities are associated with the distribution, traffic, or logistics departments of firms.

In some companies, a materials management function has been established which is responsible for coordinating most of the demand management activities. The organizational responsibility for demand management tends to be very much a function of the history and nature of the organization. It is much less important, however, that there be a unified organizational home for all the activities, than that they be appropriately defined and coordinated.

In marketing-oriented firms where close contact with the demand trends and good customer relations are required for success, the demand management function might well be performed by the marketing or sales organization. In those firms for which the development of the product requires close interaction between engineering and customers, the activities might be performed in a technical services department. The materials management organization has grown up in firms that feel it important to manage the flow of materials from purchasing raw materials through the production process to the customer. In such firms, which span both industrial and consumer products, the demand management function can be a part of the materials management activity. In all instances, it is necessary to clearly assign responsibilities to make sure that nothing is left to chance.

If flexibility is a key objective, then the rules for interacting with the system and customers must be carefully designed and enforced by management so the system can provide this flexibility. By this we mean that customer order processing must be established and enforced through the master production scheduling system. It means carefully establishing the rules under which particular special customers will be served. For example, if an extraordinarily large order is received at a field warehouse, procedures need to be established for determining whether that order will be allowed to consume a large portion of the local inventory or be passed back to the factory. Limits within which changes can be made must be defined and enforced. If any of these procedures are violated by a manager who says, "I don't care how you do it but customer X must get his order by time Y," the demand management activity is seriously undercut.

A very useful technique for assisting in defining and managing these areas of responsibility is to tie them to time fences. Abbott Laboratories, Ltd. of Canada has developed a highly formalized set of time fences. Figure 10.12 shows the four levels of change responsibility within the company. As a change request affects the MPS nearer to the current date, the responsibility for authorizing the change moves up in the organization. This procedure does not preclude a change but does force a higher-level of review for schedule changes to be made in the near term.

The underlying concept for approval procedures is to take the informal bargaining out of the system. By establishing and enforcing such procedures for order entry, customer delivery date promising, changes to the material system, and responses to mix changes in the product line, everyone plays by the same rules. In the Abbott example, flexibility is part of the change procedure, but the difficulty of making a change increases as the cost of making that change increases. It is clear that this is more a matter of management discipline than technique. The ability to respond: "What don't you want?" to the, "I have to have it right away" for a particular customer request will help immensely in establishing this discipline.

Managing service levels

One way of helping the organization live with a formal system for placing demands on the manufacturing organization is to explicitly set levels of service and publicize them throughout the organization. Substantial theoretical work has been performed concerning the setting of service levels for finished-goods inventory. This work indicates that inventory investment increases exponentially as service-level objectives are increased. More impor-

FIGURE 10.12 Approval fences for master scheduling change at Abbott Laboratories, Ltd.

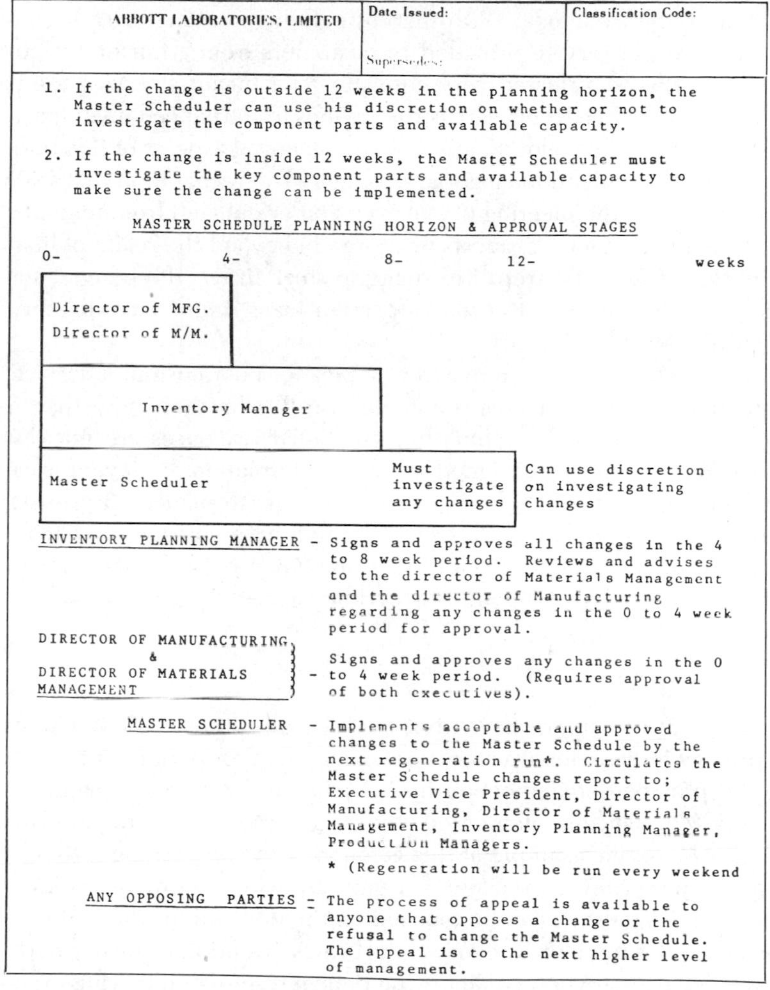

ABBOTT LABORATORIES, LIMITED | Date Issued: | Supersedes: | Classification Code:

1. If the change is outside 12 weeks in the planning horizon, the Master Scheduler can use his discretion on whether or not to investigate the component parts and available capacity.

2. If the change is inside 12 weeks, the Master Scheduler must investigate the key component parts and available capacity to make sure the change can be implemented.

MASTER SCHEDULE PLANNING HORIZON & APPROVAL STAGES

0- 4- 8- 12- weeks

Director of MFG.
Director of M/M.

Inventory Manager

Master Scheduler | Must investigate any changes | Can use discretion on investigating changes

INVENTORY PLANNING MANAGER - Signs and approves all changes in the 4 to 8 week period. Reviews and advises to the director of Materials Management and the director of Manufacturing regarding any changes in the 0 to 4 week period for approval.

DIRECTOR OF MANUFACTURING & DIRECTOR OF MATERIALS MANAGEMENT - Signs and approves any changes in the 0 to 4 week period. (Requires approval of both executives).

MASTER SCHEDULER - Implements acceptable and approved changes to the Master Schedule by the next regeneration run*. Circulates the Master Schedule changes report to; Executive Vice President, Director of Manufacturing, Director of Materials Management, Inventory Planning Manager, Production Managers.

* (Regeneration will be run every weekend

ANY OPPOSING PARTIES - The process of appeal is available to anyone that opposes a change or the refusal to change the Master Schedule. The appeal is to the next higher level of management.

Source: W. L. Berry, T. E. Vollmann, and D. C. Whybark, *Master Production Scheduling: Principles and Practice* (Falls Church, Va.: American Production and Inventory Control Society, 1979), p. 83.

tantly, there is a need for discipline in the management of service levels. Simply stated, this means understanding that something less than a 100 percent service-level target implies that occasionally there *will* be a stock-out. Truly understanding and living with that can be difficult. It is often the case that a stock-out or late delivery focuses so much attention on a given transaction that the people respond to prevent its recurrence. This is frequently the origin of the impossible order given to many inventory clerks: "Keep the inventory low but don't stock-out."

The determination of appropriate service levels requires very careful consideration of the trade-offs. With increasingly high costs of carrying inventory, the levels of service provided to customers from a finished-goods inventory must be reevaluated very honestly. This means assessing the value of maintaining service levels versus the savings from reduced inventory. The statistical materials developed to solve the technical aspects of this trade-off do not solve the difficult managerial problem. The recognition that 100 percent service, i.e., the meeting of every customer demand from inventory or at the time the customer requests it, is simply beyond the realm of financial possibility, is a key first step. For make-to-stock firms, 100 percent service implies huge inventories. For make-to-order firms, immediate delivery implies substantial idle capacity.

Lest one interpret these remarks as a plea for poor customer service, let us state emphatically that such is not the case. We firmly believe that major improvements are possible, but that emotional responses are not the answer. MPC systems are designed to trade information for inventories and other kinds of slack—including poor delivery performances. By using the systems well, one can be close order coupled with customers; that is, demand management can often lead to substantial improvements in customer service *without* massive inventories or idle capacity.

Using the system

An effective demand management module will gather marketing information, provide forecast information, screen and monitor performance information, and provide detailed action instructions to the material planning and control system. Once implemented, the system can be used to perform routine tasks. A specific example of this is found in the forecasting activity. The system can perform the breakout of item sales within a product family, and management's attention can be focused on the demand for the family itself. Focusing on the broader category both brings attention to bear where it is most needed and prevents squandering human resources on trying to reduce forecast error, which is unlikely. It is only through the support of the system that this redirection of human resources can be accomplished.

The management control function also runs through the formal MPC activities. Gathering intelligence on actual conditions in the marketplace provides the basis for deciding whether or not to change the game plan (production plan, sales plan, budget, etc.) of the organization and for determining the appropriate level of flexibility. Again, the approach is to use the system to gather this information and then apply management talent where it is needed.

Perhaps the most important change that improved management in this area can effect is the ability to be honest with customers. In our experience, customers prefer honest, even if they are unpleasant, answers to inaccurate information. An effective manufacturing planning and control system with discipline in order promising and service-level maintenance provides the basis for honest communication with customers. They can be told when to expect delivery or when inventory will be replenished, and can count on it. Providing the basis for honest communication with the customers can pay handsome dividends in terms of customer loyalty.

COMPANY EXAMPLES

In this section, we present several illustrations of actual demand management practice, as well as records that demonstrate the key concepts we have discussed in this chapter. Material gathered from Abbott Laboratories, the Tennant Company, and Dow Corning is used in these illustrations.

Abbott Laboratories, Inc.: Forecasting

Abbott Laboratories Incorporated, located in North Chicago, Illinois, is a multinational health-care firm. The company's product line includes pharmaceutical products for professional and personal use, medical electronics, cosmetics, and related chemical/pharmaceutical products. The products in this example are produced on a make-to-stock basis; the company has a reputation for maintaining a high level of customer service. Figure 10.13 is an example of the forecasting process used for these products.

The forecasting procedure at Abbott Laboratories uses many of the techniques that were suggested earlier in this chapter. In this example, the first step in the process is to develop the monthly forecasts by product. The initial input is a computer-developed forecast which uses data on customer demand and provides a basis for marketing review and approval. Figure 10.13 shows that marketing left the forecast the same for the months of April and May but changed it for June. Management judgment is used in reviewing the forecast for these monthly totals. Next, the forecast is broken down by distribution center by a computer program using the demand history data base.

The process of dividing up the forecast by distribution center begins with determining the historical percentage of each product sold by each distribution center. This is illustrated in Step III in Figure 10.13. These percentage breakdowns are then applied by the computer to the approved total forecast to develop the monthly forecast by distribution center.

At Step IV in Figure 10.13, the forecast is broken down further by week within the month. Again, this is done by the computer using procedures to take into account split weeks, vacations, etc. The result is a weekly forecast for each product at each distribution warehouse.

FIGURE 10.13 Developing detailed SKU forecasts at Abbott Laboratories

Illustration of Weekly Forecast
Development for a Product
(by distribution center)

	April	May	June
Week*	1–4	5–8	9–12
Step I: Computer developed forecast by product (preliminary forecast)	520	648	712
Step II: Marketing revision and/or approval (final forecast)	520 (OK)	648 (OK)	620 (Revised by Mkt.)

Step III: Computer proration of monthly forecast by distribution center (DC)

DC	*Forecast*†	*Percent of total FC*
#218	155	‡31%
#233	310	62%
#244	35	7%
Total	500	100%

April	*May*	*June*
§160	200	192
320	400	394
40	48	44
520	648	620

Step IV: Development of weekly forecast

DC	Week: 1	2	3	4	5	6	7	8	9
#218	‖40	40	40	40	50	50	50	50	48
#233	80	80	80	80	100	100	100	100	96
#244	10	10	10	10	12	12	12	12	11

*Four weeks per month used to simplify example.

†Each DC Forecast is done independently through the use of an exponential smoothing technique based on past DC sales history.

Sample of calculations (within computer):

‡155 ÷ 500 = 31%

§31% × 520 = 160 (Rounded)

‖160 ÷ 20 days/mo. × 5 days/wk. = 40/wk.

Source: D. C. Whybark, "Abbott Laboratories, Inc.," in *Studies in Material Requirement Planning,* ed. E. W. Davis (Falls Church, Va.: America Production and Inventory Control Society, 1977), p. 17.

These forecasts are then utilized as gross requirements data for the time-phased order point records for each of the warehouses. The result of thereafter applying MRP logic is the planned shipments for replenishing inventory from the factory. Data on actual demand are captured at the warehouses. The gross to net logic and safety stock are used to absorb the fluctuations between sales and forecasts.

An interesting reaction occurred when the weekly projections of product sales at each warehouse were provided to the warehouse supervisors. By having the planned information, in many instances they were able to use their knowledge of the local purchasing patterns to adjust the distribution of the forecast within each month to better plan inventory resupply. Even though the information was quite detailed, they were able to review the weekly patterns and adjust them within the monthly totals provided by the computer breakdown of the marketing approved forecast.

Tennant Company: Order promising and flexibility management

The Tennant Company manufactures industrial floor-maintenance equipment and associated cleaning products. The equipment varies from small walk-behind cleaners to larger operator-driven units. The machines are used for both indoor and outdoor applications. They are divided into families for planning and scheduling purposes. Within each family there are a large number of customer specified options and accessories for each machine.

Customer order promising is done explicitly from the machine availability plan prepared by the material planning and control system. Specifically, this is performed by the order entry function using a report of machine status, an example of which is provided in Figure 10.14. The first line of the document shows the status of machines in the E2 family. This report includes machines that have already been assembled and machines in various stages of preparation for customer delivery, as well as machines scheduled for future production. This example shows that all but one of the machines scheduled for production in the next seven weeks are promised to customers. The earliest possible customer delivery date promise is for a machine in week 7 (manufacturing day 211, June 5th). Although this report has a different format than the available-to-promise logic illustrated earlier, it contains the same basic information and is used in the same way.

The next two lines indicate two of the options available for the E2 family. They are the gas and LP motor options. This provides a second level of order entry testing. The only machine that will be available in the week of June 5th is an LP machine. This is seen by the fact that there is no commitment to the LP motor available in the week of June 5th. This logic of testing product availability illustrates the process of order entry that matches customer requests to the availability of scheduled machines and options at Tennant.

Figure 10.15 illustrates the production version of the same document in somewhat greater detail. This MPS control report has basic parts, unique gas parts, and unique LP parts, as did the order entry document. It is first important to notice that exactly the same information is available through this to manufacturing as was available to order entry. Additional information in this report is of interest in illustrating the management of flexibility. First of all, there are specifically identified time fences for the basic parts at manufacturing day 276 and 436 (note the vertical lines of slashes), and different

FIGURE 10.14 Tennant's report of machine status—the customer promising document

```
                                            D A I L Y   M A C H I N E   R E S E R V A T I O N   R E P O R T        MFG DATE 182

                                                     1    2    3    4    5    6    7    8    9   10   11   12   13   14   15
16100 PARTS BASIC E2                         FINAL 182  186  191  196  201  206  211  216  221  226  231  236  241  246  251  LATER
    PARTS-BASIC             E2LINE #16100     LOGS AP26 MY01 MY08 MY15 MY22 MY29 JN05 JN12 JN19 JN26 JL03 JL10 JL17 JL24 JL31 CMTMNT
     CRTD UNCR TEST RWRK ASSY PULD SCHEDULED         1    1    1    2    2    1    2    1    1    1    1    1    1    1    1
        3    4                     STOCK CMT                                                                                  1
             1    1         1    1 CUST CMT   1 OF   1    1    1    2    2    1    1
                                - - - - - - - - - - - - - - - - - - - - - - - - - - - - - - - - - - - - - - - - - - - - - - - - -
17005 FINAL ASSY E2
    PARTS-UNIQUE-GAS        E2LINE #16102
     CRTD UNCR TEST RWRK ASSY PULD SCHEDULED         1    1         2    2    1    1    1    1    1    1    1    1    1
        1    2                     STOCK CMT                                                                                  1
                  1         1    1 CUST CMT   1 OF   1    1         2    2    1    1
                                - - - - - - - - - - - - - - - - - - - - - - - - - - - - - - - - - - - - - - - - - - - - - - - - -
                                                     1    2    3    4    5    6    7    8    9   10   11   12   13   14   15
17006  FINAL ASSY E2 LP                      FINAL 182  186  191  196  201  206  211  216  221  226  231  236  241  246  251  LATER
    PARTS-UNIQUE- LP        E2LINE #16103     LOGS AP26 MY01 MY08 MY15 MY22 MY29 JN05 JN12 JN19 JN26 JL03 JL10 JL17 JL24 JL31 CMTMNT
     CRTD UNCR TEST RWRK ASSY PULD SCHEDULED                   1                   1    1    1    1    1         1    1    1
        2    2                     STOCK CMT
             1                     CUST CMT                    1
```

Source: W. L. Berry, T. E. Vollmann, and D. C. Whybark, *Master Production Scheduling: Principles and Practice* (Falls Church, Va.: American Production and Inventory Control Society, 1979), p. 163.

fences identified on the records for the gas and LP parts. These time fences are defined to indicate the time frames in which management wants flexibility. For the basic parts, the fence set at manufacturing day 276 is a *volume hedge* fence. Its purpose is to provide flexibility to accommodate an increase in overall demand for the E2 family. The fence for the gas and LP engines provides the flexibility for adapting to mix changes which occur between these two options.

The hedge concept is applied as was illustrated in Figure 10.11. For example, in the basic parts, the hedge unit indicated in period 276 has just crossed the time fence and the master scheduler will move it out unless a management decision is made to increase the volume for the E2 family to include the hedge quantity. The fences for the options indicate the flexibility range for product mix changes. The number of gas and LP options within the time fences exceeds the basic parts that are scheduled. This provides flexibility to adjust to day-to-day swings in the demand for product options without having too large amounts of inventory.

The hedge units are managed explicitly, which means that the amount of flexibility is highly visible and reviewed continually. A great deal of computer information on time fences, hedge percentages, and current status is available to the master production scheduler to assist in the management of the hedges. An important concept is to provide the flexibility in volume and product mix only where necessary. This is noted by the fact that no hedge units are provided prior to manufacturing day 211. There is no need to provide flexibility before that time, since all available machines and options are covered by customer orders.

With all the formality of this system and the support that it provides the planners, there is still a major element of management discipline that makes this system work. On asking Doug Hoelscher, Director of Manufacturing at the time these reports were gathered, what would happen if a salesperson tried to promise delivery of an E2 prior to week 211, his response was, "We'd fire the person."

The discipline at Tennant runs through to manufacturing, as well. Under the new responsibilities created by formal systems, the manufacturing mandate is to produce the scheduled products. In the event that no customer order is available for an item that is approaching final assembly, management will release a stock commitment for that item. If no customer order is received by the time the item goes to final assembly, it is produced in an easily retrofitted model and goes into inventory. This inventory is owned by *the top-management committee* of Tennant. Top management feels that the commitment to meeting the plans, be they in manufacturing or marketing, is important enough that *they* will own any finished goods that are unsold. They recognize that, if marketing is to make the sales plan, any currently unsold machines will be sold in the future. This is an example of the error addback stability technique illustrated in Figure 10.9.

FIGURE 10.15 Tennant flexibility management document

M A S T E R   S C H E D U L E   C O N T R O L   R E P O R T
MFG DATE 182

E2 FAMILY

16100 PARTS-BASIC E2LINE — D.RATIO 100% — SHORT RANGE HEDGE 10% 15% 20% — TIME FENCES 00 20 52 00 — BACKLOG 2 — LONG RANGE HEDGE % % % — LAST REVIEW 417

SEQ 0560

	ADJ.																									
	APR			MAY					JUN				JUL					AUG				SEP				OCT
	181	186	191	196	201	206	211	216	221	226	231	236	241	246	251	256	261	266	271	276	281	286	291	296	301	306
PLANNED		1	1	1	2	2	1	(2)	1	1	1	1	1	1	1	1	2	1	1	1/	1	1	1	1	1	1
HEDGE M/S		1	1	1	2	2	1	2	1	1	1	1	1	1	1	1	2	1	1	1/ 2/	1	1	1	1 2	1	1
COMMITTED		1	1	1	2	2	1	1												/						

				NOV					DEC				JAN					FEB				MAR				APR
	311	316	321	326	331	336	341	346	351	356	361	366	371	376	381	386	391	396	401	406	411	416	421	426	431	436
PLANNED	1	1	1	1	1	1	1	1	2	1	1	1	2	1	2	1	1	2	1	1	1	1	1	2	1	1/
HEDGE M/S	1	1	1 2	1	1	1	1 2	1	2	1	1 2	1	2	1	1 3	1	1	2	1 2	1	1	1	1	2	1	/ 1/
COMMITTED																										1/

				MAY					JUN				JUL					AUG				SEP				OCT
	441	446	451	456	461	466	471	476	481	486	491	496	501	506	511	516	521	526	531	536	541	546	551	556	561	566
PLANNED	1	1	1	2	1	2	1	2	1	2	1	2	1	2	1	2	1	2	2	1	2	1	2	1	2	1
HEDGE M/S	1	1	1	2	1	2	1	2	1	2	1	2	1	2	1	2	1	2	2	1	2	1	2	1	2	1

				NOV					DEC					JAN				FEB				MAR				
	571	576	581	586	591	596	601	606	611	616	621	626	631	636	641	646	651	656	661	666	671	676	681	686	691	696
PLANNED	2	1	2	1	2	1	2	1	2	1	2	1	2	1	2	1	2	1	2	1	2	1	2	1	2	1
HEDGE M/S	2	1	2	1	2	1	2	1	2	1	2	1	2	1	2	1	2	1	2	1	2	1	2	1	2	1

16102 PARTS-UNIQUE-GAS E2LINE — D.RATIO 65% — SHORT RANGE HEDGE 45% 50% 55% — TIME FENCES 00 03 16 00 — BACKLOG 2 — LONG RANGE HEDGE % % % — LAST REVIEW 417

SEQ 0570

	ADJ.																									
	APR			MAY					JUN				JUL					AUG				SEP				OCT
	181	186	191	196	201	206	211	216	221	226	231	236	241	246	251	256	261	266	271	276	281	286	291	296	301	306
PLANNED		1	1	/	2	2	1	1	1			1	1	1			1/	2	1			1	1	1		1	1
HEDGE M/S		1	1	/ /	2	2	1	1	1	1 1	1 1	1	1	1	1 1		/ 1/	2	1		1 1	1	1	1	1 1	1	1
COMMITTED		1	1	/	2	2	1	1									/										

				NOV					DEC				JAN					FEB				MAR				APR
	311	316	321	326	331	336	341	346	351	356	361	366	371	376	381	386	391	396	401	406	411	416	421	426	431	436
PLANNED	1			1	1		1	1	1	1		1	1	1	1		1	1	1	1		1		1	1	
HEDGE M/S	1		1 1	1	1		1	1	1	1	1 1	1	1	1	1 2		1	1	1 2	1		1		1	1	
COMMITTED																										1

				MAY					JUN				JUL					AUG				SEP				OCT
	441	446	451	456	461	466	471	476	481	486	491	496	501	506	511	516	521	526	531	536	541	546	551	556	561	566
PLANNED		1	1	1	1	1	1	1		1	1	1		1	1	1	1	1	1	1	1		1	1	1	1
HEDGE M/S		1	1	1	1	1	1	1		1	1	1		1	1	1	1	1	1	1	1		1	1	1	1

				NOV					DEC					JAN				FEB				MAR				
	571	576	581	586	591	596	601	606	611	616	621	626	631	636	641	646	651	656	661	666	671	676	681	686	691	696
PLANNED	1		1	1	1	1	1	1	1	1	1	1	1		1	1	1	1	1	1	1	1	1	1	1	1
HEDGE																				1	1	1	1	1	1	1

FIGURE 10.15 *(concluded)*

```
                               M A S T E R   S C H E D U L E   C O N T R O L   R E P O R T                        TIME 02.45
                                                                    MFG DATE 182                                  PAGE  21
16103     PARTS-UNIQUE- LP        E2LINE  D.RATIO   SHORT RANGE HEDGE   TIME FENCES     BACKLOG   LONG RANGE HEDGE   LAST REVIEW
                                            35%      45%   50%   55%    00 03 16 00        2          %     %     %        417

SEQ 0580       -APR/--------MAY--------/--------JUN----/--------JUL--------/--------AUG----/--------SEP----/--------OCT
ADJ.            181  186  191  196  201  206  211  216  221  226  231  236  241  246  251  256  261  266  271  276  281  286  291  296  301  306
PLANNED                    1/                   1         1    1                   1    1    /              1    1                   1

HEDGE                       /                        1              1         1              /
M/S                        1/                   1    1    1    1    1         1    1    1    /              1    1                   1
COMMITTED                  1/                                                                /

               --------/--------NOV----/--------DEC----/--------JAN--------/--------FEB----/--------MAR----/--------APR
                311  316  321  326  331  336  341  346  351  356  361  366  371  376  381  386  391  396  401  406  411  416  421  426  431  436
PLANNED               1    1              1              1         1         1         1    1         1              1         1    1         1

HEDGE                                          1
M/S                   1    1              1    1         1         1         1         1    1         1              1         1    1         1
COMMITTED

               --------/--------MAY----/--------JUN----/--------JUL--------/--------AUG----/--------SEP----/--------OCT
                441  446  451  456  461  466  471  476  481  486  491  496  501  506  511  516  521  526  531  536  541  546  551  556  561  566
PLANNED           1              1         1         1    1    1         1    1    1         1         1    1         1    1    1         1

HEDGE
M/S               1              1         1         1    1    1         1    1    1         1         1    1         1    1    1         1

               --------/--------NOV----/--------DEC--------/--------JAN----/--------FEB----/--------MAR--------/-------
                571  576  581  586  591  596  601  606  611  616  621  626  631  636  641  646  651  656  661  666  671  676  681  686  691  696
PLANNED           1    1    1         1         1         1         1         1    1    1         1         1         1         1         1

HEDGE
M/S               1    1    1         1         1         1         1         1    1    1         1         1         1         1         1
```

Source: W. L. Berry, T. E. Vollmann, and D. C. Whybark, *Master Production Scheduling. Principles and Practice* (Falls Church, Va.: American Production and Inventory Control Society, 1979), p. 166–67.

Dow Corning: Integration of all demand sources

Figure 10.16 shows a set of distribution requirements planning (DRP) records for the Dow Corning Corporation. The first four DRP records are for four regional warehouses. The last record combines the data for the first four. The record rows allow the company to keep track of the critical data elements. The first row, CUST ORD, is actual sold customer orders. PROJ SAL is forecast sales, and the integration of forecast with actual, permits Dow Corning to make available-to-promise calculations. STK TRNS is stock in transit or scheduled receipts. FP/R RST is firm planned receipts of restocks (receipts of firm planned orders). PROJ INV is the projected available balance, and PLND RST is planned restock or planned orders.

From a managerial viewpoint, it is important to see that the DRP approach results in the correct demand management data base. It is critical to differentiate between actual sales and forecast sales, to keep track of scheduled receipts, planned orders, and firm planned orders, and to do *all* of this by particular location. DRP provides both the data base and the methodology for integration at Dow Corning.

It is critical that *all* demand sources be included in the company's plans. There is one remaining source of demand management data that often must be included in the demand management data base. This is the set of time-phased demands represented by interplant transfers. Dow Corning has this problem in addition to the DRP considerations. Figure 10.17 shows this final consolidation of demand for Dow Corning. It is this consolidation which is used to establish and monitor the MPS. The top half of Figure 10.17 shows the overall consolidated MRP record. The bottom half presents the pegging detail. Note that the number 10,560 is circled on this report. In Figure 10.16 we circled the number 24 in the total distribution requirements row for the same time period. Figure 10.17 also shows the item as a 440-pound (20-kilo) package. The requirement of 24 times 440 equals 10,560. That is, the 10,560 in Figure 10.17 is the requirement, in pounds, for restocking the field warehouses.

Figure 10.17 has other important sources of demand. They include international transfers, interplant transfers, and firm planned orders from different organizational units. Again, the resulting data base is correct. One must keep track of each of these sources of demand, with proper timing and amounts. The summation of these data is a critical input to the MPS activity.

CONCLUDING PRINCIPLES

This chapter has focused on the integrative nature of demand planning. It is necessary to capture all sources of demand, to maintain a proper demand management data base, and to carefully integrate demand management both with production planning and with the detailed MPS decision making. We

FIGURE 10.16 Dow Corning DRP records

FIELD WAREHOUSE RESTOCK REFERENCE REPORT

MM NO.	PROD#	CC	PRODUCT NAME	SIZE	BUS/BPU		PROJECTION
1112490	26050	31		440 LB	20	21	3

RP	PT	SP	LT	OFST	CONF	MIN	MULT	MAX	SAFSTK	ONHAND	INTRAN	OP
B1	01	A1	14	THUR	75.0	4	4	0	4	27	0	G

	PERIOD	1	2	3	4	5	6	7	8	9	10	11	12	13	14	15	16
	PSTDUE	09/04	09/11	09/18	09/25	10/02	10/09	10/16	10/23	10/30	11/06	11/13	11/20	11/27	12/04	12/11	12/18
CUST ORD	0	0	0	0	1	2	0	0	0	0	0	0	0	0	0	0	0
PROJ SAL	0	1	0	1	1	2	0	0	0	1	0	1	0	1	0	1	0
STK TRNS	0	0	0	0	0	0	0	0	0	0	0	0	0	0	0	0	0
FP/R RST	0	0	0	0	0	0	0	0	0	0	0	0	0	0	0	0	0
PROJ INV	23	22	22	21	20	18	18	18	18	17	17	16	16	15	15	14	14
PLND RST	0	0	0	0	0	0	0	0	0	0	0	0	0	0	0	0	0

0185=E/E PROD/DOM MUST BE ON PKG SLIP

MM NO.	PROD#	CC	PRODUCT NAME	SIZE	BUS/BFU		PROJECTION
1112490	26050	31		440 LB	20	21	42

RP	PT	SP	LT	OFST	CONF	MIN	MULT	MAX	SAFSTK	ONHAND	INTRAN	OP
C1	01	A1	15	FRI	75.0	4	4	0	16	7	0	G

	PERIOD	1	2	3	4	5	6	7	8	9	10	11	12	13	14	15	16
	PSTDUE	09/04	09/11	09/18	09/25	10/02	10/09	10/16	10/23	10/30	11/06	11/13	11/20	11/27	12/04	12/11	12/18
CUST ORD	0	7	0	0	0	0	0	0	0	0	0	0	0	0	0	0	0
PROJ SAL	0	9	11	11	11	10	10	10	10	10	11	11	6	11	10	11	8
STK TRNS	0	0	0	0	0	0	0	0	0	0	0	0	0	0	0	0	0
FP/R RST	0	0	40	0	0	0	0	60	0	0	0	0	0	0	0	0	0
PROJ INV	-9	-18	11	0	-11	-21	-31	19	9	-1	-12	-23	-29	-40	-50	-61	-69
PLND RST	0	0	0	0	0	0	0	52	0	0	0	0	0	52	0	0	0

MM NO.	PROD#	CC	PRODUCT NAME	SIZE	BUS/BPU		PROJECTION
1112490	26050	31		440 LB	20	21	26

RP	PT	SP	LT	OFST	CONF	MIN	MULT	MAX	SAFSTK	ONHAND	INTRAN	OP
F1	01	A1	14	TUE	75.0	4	4	0	19	1	0	G

	PERIOD	1	2	3	4	5	6	7	8	9	10	11	12	13	14	15	16
	PSTDUE	09/04	09/11	09/18	09/25	10/02	10/09	10/16	10/23	10/30	11/06	11/13	11/20	11/27	12/04	12/11	12/18
CUST ORD	0	0	0	0	0	0	0	0	0	0	0	0	0	0	0	0	0
PROJ SAL	0	5	7	7	7	7	5	7	7	7	6	7	5	7	7	8	7
STK TRNS	0	0	0	0	0	0	0	0	0	0	0	0	0	0	0	0	0
FP/R RST	0	0	0	0	0	0	0	24	0	0	0	0	0	0	0	0	0
PROJ INV	-18	-23	-30	-37	-44	-51	-56	-39	-46	-53	-59	-65	-71	-78	-85	-93	-100
PLND RST	40	0	0	0	0	0	40	0	0	0	0	0	40	0	0	0	0

FIGURE 10.16 *(concluded)*

FIELD WAREHOUSE RESTOCK REFERENCE REPORT

```
MM NO.    PROD# CC   PRODUCT NAME                     SIZE    BUS/BPU  PROJECTION
1112490   26050 31                                   440 LB   20  21         18

        RP  PT  SP  LT  OFST    CONF      MIN     MULT     MAX  SAFSTK  ONHAND  INTRAN  OP
        G2  01  A1  14  MON     85.0        4        4       0      14       4       0   G
```

	PERIOD	1	2	3	4	5	6	7	8	9	10	11	12	13	14	15	16
	PSTDUE	09/04	09/11	09/18	09/25	10/02	10/09	10/16	10/23	10/30	11/06	11/13	11/20	11/27	12/04	12/11	12/18
CUST ORD	0	0	0	0	0	0	0	0	0	0	0	0	0	0	0	0	0
PROJ SAL	0	4	5	4	5	4	4	5	4	4	5	5	4	4	5	4	4
STK TRNS	0	0	0	0	0	0	0	0	0	0	0	0	0	0	0	0	0
FP/R RST	0	0	0	16	0	0	0	0	20	0	0	0	0	0	0	0	0
PROJ INV	-10	-14	-19	-7	-12	-16	-20	-25	-9	-13	-18	-23	-27	-31	-36	-40	-44
PLND RST	0	0	0	0	24	0	0	0	0	0	24	0	0	0	0	0	28

```
*** TOTAL ***   SAFSTK    ONHAND    INTRAN
                    53        39         0
```

	PERIOD	1	2	3	4	5	6	7	8	9	10	11	12	13	14	15	16
	PSTDUE	09/04	09/11	09/18	09/25	10/02	10/09	10/16	10/23	10/30	11/06	11/13	11/20	11/27	12/04	12/11	12/18
CUST ORD	0	7	0	0	1	2	0	0	0	0	0	0	0	0	0	0	0
PROJ SAL	0	19	23	23	24	23	19	22	21	22	22	24	15	23	22	24	19
STK TRNS	0	0	0	0	0	0	0	0	0	0	0	0	0	0	0	0	0
FP/R RST	0	0	40	16	0	0	0	84	20	0	0	0	0	0	0	0	0
PROJ INV	-14	-33	-16	-23	-47	-70	-89	-27	-28	-50	-72	-96	-111	-134	-156	-180	-199
PLND RST	40	0	0	0	24	0	40	52	0	0	24	0	40	52	0	0	28

Source: W. L. Berry, T. E. Vollmann, and D. C. Whybark, *Master Production Scheduling: Principles and Practice* (Falls Church, Va.: American Production and Inventory Control Society, 1979), p. 103–4.

FIGURE 10.17 Dow Corning consolidated demand

DESCRIPTION	UNITS	AV	OP	FIX QTY	MIN QTY	MAX QTY	MULT QTY	MAX Q/D	CUTOFF	WW	LT	SU	RN	QA	PUR
	LB	1	A	0	440	0	440	0			5	M			

CI	SAF-STK	6MO TOTAL	ACCOUNT	INVENTORY STATUS APPVD	IN-TEST	INTRANS	REJECTED
	0	384221	TOTAL ***	59400	0	0	0

WEEK OF	PST DUE	09/02	09/09	09/16	09/23	09/30	10/07	10/14	10/21	10/28	11/04	11/11	11/18	11/25	12/02	12/09	12/16
TOTAL REQRMT	25122	24850	10823	20504	10322	187	63547	23067	1947	147	12441	1882	19458	28429	7310	5551	17526
ON ORDER	0	0	0	0	0	0	0	0	0	0	0	0	0	0	0	0	0
PROJ ON HAND	34278	9428	-1395	-21899	-32721	-32908	-96455	-119522	-121469	-121616	-134057	-135939	-155397	-183826	-191136	-196687	-214213
PLND ORDER	0	0	1760	20240	11000	0	63300	22880	2200	0	12320	1760	19800	28160	7480	5720	17160

WEEK OF	12/23	12/30	01/06	01/13	01/20	01/27	02/03	02/10	02/17	02/24	TOTAL
TOTAL REQRMT	6553	24171	33733	6013	6991	10853	5574	9093	3813	3814	384221
ON ORDER	0	0	0	0	0	0	0	0	0	0	0
PROJ ON HAND	-220766	-244937	-278670	-284683	-291674	-302527	-308101	-317194	-321007	-324821	0
PLND ORDER	6600	24200	33880	6160	6600	11000	5720	8800	3960	3960	325160

PEGGED REQUIREMENTS - PRODUCING PLANT

MATRL.IRC	ORIGIN OF REQUIREMNTS	DESCRIPTION	PST DUE	09/02	09/09	09/16	09/23	09/30	10/07	10/14	10/21	10/28	11/04	11/11
FIRM:														
INTERNATIONAL TRANS ORDERS					7040	13200								
INTERPLANT TRANSFER ORDERS														
C1	01			24640					45760					
U3	**													1
MANUFACTURING FP/R ORDERS-DIFFERENT UNIT														
A0	07		7522											
		** FIRM TOTAL **	7522	24640	7040	13200			45760					1
PLANNED:														
REMAINING FORECAST PLANT SALES				210	263	264	262	187	187	187	187	147	121	121
FLD WAREHOUSE PLANNED RESTOCK			17600				10560		17600	22880			12320	1760
MANUFACTURING PLANNED ORDERS-SAME UNIT														
A0	01 2GA 200 FL 100 CS EL,LB,440#				3520	7040					1760			
		** TOTAL **			3520	7040					1760			
		** PLANNED TOTAL **	17600	210	3783	7304	10822	187	17787	23067	1947	147	12441	1881
		MASTER MATERIAL TOTAL **	25122	24850	10823	20504	10822	187	63547	23067	1947	147	12441	1882

Source: W. L. Berry, T. E. Vollmann, and D. C. Whybark, *Master Production Scheduling: Principles and Practice* (Falls Church, Va.: American Production and Inventory Control Society, 1979), p. 101.

see the following key principles as important to accomplishing these objectives:

- MPC systems must take into account *all* sources of demand, properly identified as to time, quantity, location, and source.
- Order promising must be done using available-to-promise concepts.
- Specific customer-service standards must be developed and maintained.
- The management of outbound product flows must be coordinated through the master production schedules.
- Attaining more accurate forecasts may be an impossible dream. Management attention should be focused on the system to provide appropriate responses to actual conditions and forecast errors.
- Flexibility must be explicitly planned into the system.
- To provide helpful stability in the factory, demand management and MPS activities need to be closely coordinated.
- Intelligent customer promises should be the rule of the day, rather than wishful thinking.
- Clear definitions of authority and responsibility for demand management activities must be made to obtain the attendant benefits.

REFERENCES

American Production and Inventory Control Society. *Interfaces Seminar Proceedings*, March 1980.

Berry, W. L., T. E. Vollmann, and D. C. Whybark. *Master Production Scheduling—Principles and Practice*. Falls Church, Va.: *American Production and Inventory Control Society*, 1979.

Borgendale, Mac. "Spare Parts: Deciding What to Stock at Each Location." *APICS Service Parts Seminar Proceedings*, Las Vegas, April 1981, pp. 1–4.

Brown, R. G. *Materials Management Systems*. New York: Wiley Interscience, 1977.

Haskins, Robert E. "Demand Management by Exception (Not by Exception Report)." *Inventories and Production Magazine*, July-August 1981.

Herron, David P. "Profit Oriented Techniques for Managing Independent Demand Inventories." *Production and Inventory Management*, 3d Quarter 1974.

Martin, Andre. "DRP: Another Resource Planning System." *Production and Inventory Management Review*, December 1982.

Moore, A. J. "Forecasting the Unforecastable: The Customer's Mind." *Production and Inventory Management*, 1st Quarter 1974.

Perry, W. "The Principles of Distribution Resource Planning (DRP)." *Production and Inventory Management*, December 1982.

Ray, W. D. "Computation of Reorder Levels when the Demands are Correlated and the Lead Time Random." *Journal of the Operational Research Society* 32, no. 1 (January 1981), pp. 27–34.

Shycon, H. N., and C. R. Sprague. "Put a Price Tag on Your Customer Service." *Harvard Business Review*, July-August 1975.

11

Implementation

This chapter is devoted exclusively to the issue of implementing an effective manufacturing planning and control system. The focus is almost exclusively managerial, since that is where the ultimate responsibility lies. This chapter raises some fundamental issues involving organization, management, procedures, and resources. Addressing these issues is critical to implementing a truly effective MPC system, and doing so on a timely basis with realized results at each step in the process.

The chapter is organized around the following six topics:

- Assessing the situation: How does a firm rigorously determine the magnitude and appropriate direction for the implementation effort?
- Management of and by the data base: Why is management of an integrated data base a critical prerequisite to success?
- Organizational implications: What are the organizational changes needed for implementing a truly effective system?
- Plan of attack: How should the detailed implementation plan be established and managed?
- Education: How should the required educational effort be defined and executed?
- Auditing: Why is periodic auditing of the system essential at any stage of development? Why is it a general management responsibility?

Elements of implementation issues are raised in virtually every preceding chapter, as the various manufacturing planning and control system modules are discussed. In particular, Chapter 3 discusses in considerable detail issues of data integrity which are important to successful implementation. Formal project planning and control techniques which could be used for an MPC implementation project are covered in Chapter 14.

ASSESSING THE SITUATION

In this section, we are interested in providing a yardstick by which the current effectiveness of the MPC system can be measured. This is a first step in defining what needs to be done. The second involves developing a sense of the needs of the organization by evaluating the environment in which the system must function and the first areas for improvement. Before turning to some examples, we also want to raise a third issue. This is an evolutionary point of view toward the MPC implementation process.

Establishing the yardstick of performance

Clearly, the model to which we feel a company should be moving is our general MPC schematic, now presented as Figure 11.1. A first step in establishing the current position of the company is to determine how well each of these modules is performed. The first test is one of completeness. Are there any gaps in the current MPC system or is performance so poor in any activity that it might just as well not exist?

A way of assessing the performance of the system has been suggested by Oliver Wight, a well-known manufacturing consultant. He addresses the implementation issue by defining MRP based companies as falling into one of the following four categories:

A *Class A* MRP user is one that uses MRP in a closed loop mode. They have material requirements planning, capacity planning and control, shop-floor dispatching, and vendor scheduling systems in place and being used; and management uses the system to run the business. They participate in production planning. They sign off on the production plans. They constantly monitor performance on inventory record accuracy, bill of material accuracy, routing accuracy, attainment of the master schedule, attainment of the capacity plans, etc.

In a Class A company, the MRP system provides the game plan that sales, finance, manufacturing, purchasing, and engineering people all work to. They *use* the formal system. The foremen and the purchasing people work to the schedules. There is no shortage list to override the schedules and answer the question, What material is really needed when?—that answer comes from the formal MRP system.

Companies using MRP II have gone even a step beyond Class A. They have tied in the financial system and developed simulation capabilities so that the "what if" questions can be answered using the system. In this type

FIGURE 11.1 Manufacturing planning and control system

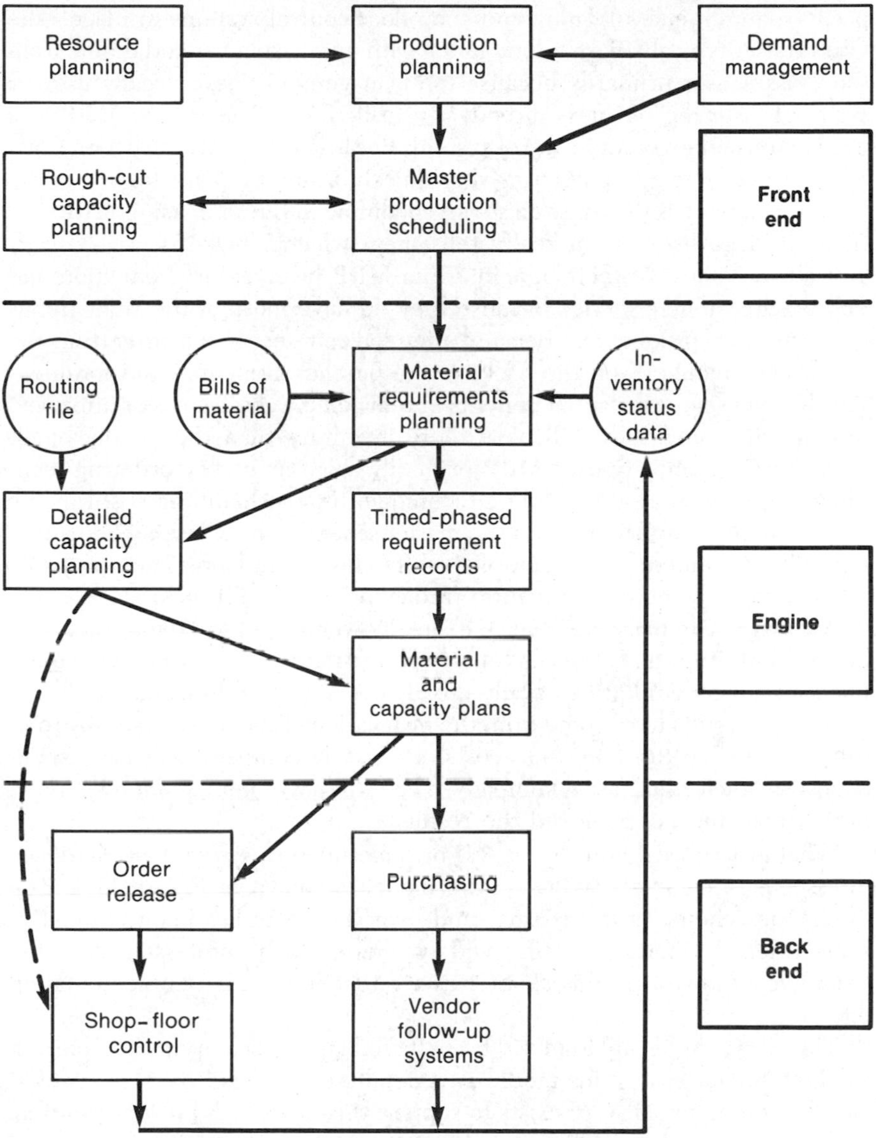

of company, management can work with one set of numbers to run the business because the operating system and the financial system use the same numbers.

Technically, then, an MRP II system has the financial and operating systems married together and has a simulation capability. But, the important point is that the system is used as a company game plan. This is what really makes a company Class A.

A *Class B* company has material requirements planning and usually capacity requirements planning and shop-floor control systems in place. The Class B user typically hasn't done much with purchasing yet and differs from the Class A user primarily because top management doesn't really use the system to run the business directly. Instead, Class B users see MRP as a production and inventory control system. Because of this, it's easy for a Class B user to become a Class C user very quickly. Another characteristic of the Class B company is that they do *some* scheduling in the shop using MRP, but their shortage list is what really tells them what to make. Class B users typically see most of their benefits from MRP in inventory reduction and improved customer service because they do have more of the right things going through production. Because they haven't succeeded in getting the expediting "monkey" off the backs of the purchasing people and foremen, they haven't seen substantial benefits in reduced purchase costs or improved productivity—and they still have more inventory than they really need.

A *Class C* company uses MRP primarily as an inventory ordering technique rather than as a scheduling technique. Shop scheduling is still being done from the shortage list, and the master schedule in a Class C company is typically overstated. They have not really closed the loop. They probably will get some benefits in inventory reduction as a result of MRP.

A *Class D* company only has MRP really working in the data processing department. Typically, their inventory records are poor. If they have a defined master schedule, it's usually grossly overstated and mismanaged, and little or no results have come from the installation of the MRP system. Ironically, except for the education costs, a Class D company will have spent almost as much as a Class A company. They will have spent about 80 percent of the total, but not achieved the results.

What is described here as MRP II or sometimes as "closed loop MRP" is, in essence, a complete MPC system model as shown in Figure 11.1. The evaluation scheme is interesting, and over the years has been applied to some research efforts. It is also widely referenced by professionals in the field. We will use it in this chapter as a yardstick to judge implementation efforts.

The MPC model in Figure 11.1 is based upon a computer-supported, integrated data base. This model is generally understood by MPC professionals, computer software exists to support this model, and it represents an overall system objective. Furthermore, the MPC model presents a useful way to divide the overall system objective into subsystem projects. The critical implementation question is which projects to take on, and in what order.

The company environment

To some extent, all companies tend to consider themselves as unique—often to the detriment of system implementation. However, there are indeed aspects of each company's situation that make some system modules more appropriate than others for implementation emphasis.

The firm that manufactures many components through complex fabrication steps will want to put in place a shop-floor control system to carefully monitor and manage the progress of their orders. On the other hand, the firm that purchases a large percentage of its components for assembly will be more interested in systems to support purchasing.

A company that has very expensive machine tools in a job-shop environment may be more concerned with capacity planning and control than is the firm which utilizes simple bench-assembly methods. Similarly, a company that has a complex flow of final assembly may be very anxious to establish a level flow of work through these operations.

Many times, the make-to-stock firm will concentrate its original systems effort on distribution and inventories of finished goods. The make-to-order firm which produces complex items in unique designs may require a sophisticated system for the management of customer orders—from quotation through design, to manufacture and shipping. The assemble-to-order firm typically requires a significant effort to create planning bills of material, as well as order-promising logic.

A different sort of environmental consideration is the organizational climate and receptiveness to the implementation of various systems. We have seen firms where the achievement of accurate shop-floor reporting is not difficult, and others where conditions such as incentive wage systems virtually preclude the accurate reporting of actual production or shop-floor conditions on a timely basis.

At a more fundamental level, but still a key environmental issue, is the extent of managerial identification with improved systems for materials flow. We list management commitment as a key implementation success variable. Has management recognized the need? Do they have the appropriate *total* level of commitment?

Each of these issues, from the manufacturing process to the management attitudes, are basic elements of the assessment process. They must be honestly addressed if appropriate implementation priorities and resources are to be developed.

An evolutionary point of view

In many instances, the assessment of the environment will lead to pessimistic conclusions. What can be done without appropriate environmental factors? Is the only resort to roll over and play dead? This issue always comes up at the educational seminars we hold. One participant summed up his feelings as: "This is all well and good, and I really see how these systems could do marvelous things for my company. But next week I will return to my job and within hours I will have out my gun and knife, shooting and stabbing as usual."

Our response is that the only way to eat an elephant is one bite at a time, and it doesn't make a great deal of difference if one starts at the tail or the trunk. The key is to critically assess where your company is, and where it would like to be. (Class A in the long run!) Who are you, and what authority and resources do you control? What confederations can you make that will yield results? Where can you take a bite of the elephant that will yield clearcut results that can be used to widen the commitment? What parts of the elephant should be avoided now because success will be too long in coming?

What all of this means is that although our general model for MPC systems applies to every firm, and the ultimate goal is Class A status, the emphasis given at any point in time must be assessed on an individual company basis. George Bevis is often quoted for his remark that "MRP is a journey not a destination." There are many ways to drive from New York to California, but the key is always to safely reach some intermediate destination. Let us briefly illustrate these points with two examples.

The Ethan Allen implementation

At a very early stage, the newly appointed assistant vice president of manufacturing at the Ethan Allen Furniture Company saw the clear need to better plan and control production in a widely decentralized set of manufacturing plants. The assessment of where they were at the time versus where they wanted to be revealed a vast need for change. An example of the gap is provided by the product structure data base. Not only did the company not have a computerized bill of materials, they did not even have part drawings! Products were made by launching an end item in terms of rough sizes for wooden pieces, finding a sample piece hanging on a nail somewhere, and making more like it. Tolerances were expressed as: "Machine to fit."

There was no uniformity of building techniques among the factories, and each plant had completely different names for parts as well as ways to make them. It was clear that the company needed to construct a product structure data base, but when it was considered at the time, management was convinced that this effort could not succeed. The effort was too massive for the very limited resources available, it would be far too long before results would be seen on the bottom line, and the effort would be the first to be set aside for fire fighting or for any cost reduction that was mandated.

The area selected for implementation first was master production scheduling (MPS), and the original effort was confined to only one factory. When this factory could be scheduled in a way that was clearly superior to past practices, word spread throughout the other factories and the plant managers were clamoring to use the new system. Once the MPS system was in use, the need for shop-floor control systems to move parts in sequence with assembly dictates was clear—these systems were put in with minimal effort. Thereafter, the need for data accuracy was keenly felt, so locked storeroom concepts began to be applied. And so it went. Interestingly, this natural evolution eventually came to the product structure data base, the need for standardization of methods and parts, and a consistent cost-accounting system. The journey has taken 15 years and is still not over.

The Black & Decker journey

The Black & Decker systems for controlling material flows have been widely publicized throughout the world. Their MRP system is always included on the list of Class A companies. However, to assume that they have arrived, or that no significant improvement potential exists, or that they cannot make mistakes, is just not correct. In fact, several years ago the company took the actions necessary to free up some of the key people originally responsible for MRP, with the open-ended assignment to look for new improvement potential. They selected engineering as the area, focusing on how to design and group parts for manufacture so as to substantially reduce setup times. They are also working on alterations planning, a technique to assess the capacity impact of proposed changes. Moreover, in a seminar at Indiana University on state-of-the-art MPS systems, it seemed clear that Black & Decker could profit by applying the distribution requirements planning concepts developed by Abbott Laboratories.

As far as mistakes are concerned, in 1974 the demand for their products was outstripping capacity, and they committed the sin that seems irresistible at some point in time. They overloaded the master schedule, which transmitted impossible loads throughout the company. It turned out to be a costly education program.

The key point in the Black & Decker story is that there is no ultimate weapon. There is always room for improvement, no matter how good the system is. The system is never a substitute for management direction, and improvements can be best achieved by conscious effort—committing the time of key players, backed up with adequate resources.

MANAGEMENT OF AND BY THE DATA BASE

The achievement of data integrity, the procedural reforms necessary to obtain transaction accuracy, and the necessary changes in job descriptions are critical to success. Virtually every expert states that this aspect of implementation is typically underestimated both in its importance and in the efforts required to attain the required integrity. With poor data integrity, Class D operation is the inevitable best result. In a survey of 326 MRP companies by John Anderson and Roger Schroeder, a strong correlation was found between the degree of record accuracy and the Wight classification scheme. Class A companies have better record accuracy than Class B, which, in turn, have better accuracy performance than Class C, etc. In this section, we present a checklist of critical data integrity issues.

Data elements

All of the following data elements must be accurate to high levels—more than 90 percent and preferably more than 95 percent—before implementation can be considered successful. Moreover, in the rush to obtain implementation, a firm may decide to switch over to the new system without these levels of accuracy in the mistaken view that things will get straightened out. In fact, the result may be just the opposite; the system may become a bad joke, with users scrambling to get information from other sources, a death knell to the implementation project. The accuracy measure here is not an average measure. Pluses and minuses *do not* cancel out. Being five parts over on A does not make up for the shortage of five parts on B. The result is two errors.

- Item Master: Has this critical file been well defined, and have all of the necessary data elements been entered?
- Bill of Materials: Have the product structure records been properly defined for MPC purposes, and have they been checked for accuracy?
- Inventory Records: Does the company have secure storerooms, a cycle counting program, and results that are measured to accuracy levels in excess of 90 percent?
- Routing: Is the set of manufacturing operations for each fabricated part accurate? Has a detailed review been made prior to implementation?
- Open Orders: Does the company have an accurate list of open shop orders, with no tag ends that do not actually exist? Can the quantities be verified by physical count? Can these records be loaded as scheduled receipts on the MRP data base?
- Purchase Orders: Can the tests for open orders be applied to open purchase orders? Is purchase order creation based upon MRP-driven needs? Are purchasing lead times reasonably accurate? Have they been reviewed for MRP lead time offsetting?
- Master Production Schedule: Does the master schedule reflect what is actually being built—on a weekly (or smaller time increment) basis? Are there any ways that changes to final build schedules can be achieved outside of the formal MPS or FAS (final assembly schedule)?

The above list is not intended to be exhaustive. Clearly, other files such as locations, rejected materials, vendor master, machine centers, etc. are also required.

Transaction procedures

Hand in hand with accurate initial data is the need to keep the data accurate, i.e., data maintenance. It is not enough to get accurate data into the computer once. Tight control over the data elements is required on an ongoing basis. For each data element, some organizational unit or person needs to be assigned the sole responsibility for maintaining the data and making any required changes.

The key to data maintenance is ironclad procedures to control every transaction to the data base. It is imperative that each of the files listed above be maintained so that there is no discrepancy between what the file depicts and the actual situation. That is, the system must not lie to the users. To achieve this truth, new procedures are typically required. Some of the most important transaction procedures include:

- Item master maintenance.
- Engineering change (and effectivity dates).
- Cycle counting.
- Inventory adjustments.
- Routing changes (and effectivity dates).
- Order launching—including availability checking and allocation.
- Material and part picking.
- Scrap reporting.
- Rework.
- Receipt tickets and order closeout.
- Receiving, purchase order closeout, returns to vendors, reconciliation, and links to accounts payable.
- Changes, additions, and deletions to the MPS.
- Rejected materials.
- Nonproduction uses of materials.
- Nonbill of material needs for production.
- Order entry, customer due date promising, and changes to open customer orders.

This is a formidable list, and again, for any particular company there will be other procedures required. The degree of change implied is all too easily underestimated.

Using the system

The final key element in management by a data base and management of a data base is to reemphasize the "by" portion of this dictate. It is absolutely essential that informal systems be supplanted—and kept from reappearing. No handwritten hot lists should be allowed to override the formal system, expediting as a formal job should disappear, and any problem solution which comes at the expense of accurate data is to be avoided at all cost. In short, the system should become the sole basis for decision making, with no other record-keeping systems used. The following dictates are representative of the commitment required:

- Get rid of all Kardex or other paper files.
- Don't allow any other set of duplicate records.
- Be sure that only one bill of materials exists.
- Be on constant alert to see whether foremen need black books to run their parts.
- Implement an ongoing audit function.
- Maintain a high level of professional management information system support for the MPC system.
- Don't expect "the system" not to require change and upgrading.
- Insist on an adequate level of system documentation.
- Understand that user education is not a one-time process.

ORGANIZATIONAL IMPLICATIONS

Implementing a Class A system may well be the largest single change in operations that a company can undertake. The achievement of Class A status requires new levels of discipline, attention to detail, and use of formal systems. With a Class A system, a new level of integration is achieved, so that front-end plans and budgets are synchronized with day-to-day detailed decision making. The organizational objective is to make plans that are valid and attainable, and thereafter hold people strictly accountable for achieving these plans.

In company after company we have seen, the first task of the production planning manager is to second guess the sales forecast. Sales personnel resources were consumed in the preparation of the forecast, but no one used it. The budget was produced independently, and production decisions were based on guesses of "real" sales needs. This still remains a common form of management.

In many companies, no one can be held accountable for execution because the formal plans are simply not used, attainable, or valid. People at the middle-management level ignore the formal plans and execute informal plans, acting in what they think are the best interests of the company. The formal plans call for production of unneeded items, no production of needed items, and sometimes more total production per time period than is possible. In a Class A system, everyone's job is to hit the formally stated schedule. No one is allowed to second guess, and the formal system is always the management plan. No production manager is permitted to say that he or she did not make some item because sales did not need it. The manager's job is always to hit the schedule. This shifts responsibility for preparing a valid schedule squarely to where it belongs.

These suggestions hit people in some organizations very hard. It is assigning new responsibilities and holding people to meet them that raises the greatest number of "we can't do that" responses. The key implementation question is "what is the alternative?" When we ask why a company that is promising all deliveries within two weeks has actual deliveries that vary from four to eight weeks, the answer is often, "We have to promise two weeks because of competition." When confronted with the possibility of *honest* but later than two-week delivery promises, the answer is "We can't do that." The alternative is clear—continued lies to customers.

In one European firm, the organizational cost to implement the MPC system was very high but the alternative was worse. Facing a deteriorating competitive position and profitability, the top management of the firm realized the need for an effective MPC system. The constraints of only making promises to customers from the MPS and not being able to go to the shop floor to get orders for particular customers, led the sales manager to resign. Moreover, the manufacturing manager didn't like the discipline required by the formal system and left, along with the inventory planner.

We are not advocating radical surgery with this example, but organizational change might be costly and requires management commitment. The results for this European firm were tripled gross margins, a fivefold increase in their inventory turns, and a virtual elimination of late delivery penalties. That was certainly preferable to the alternative, and it was worth the high cost in organizational change.

Slack reduction

The firm with poor systems has extra inventories, extra lead times, extra capacity, extra personnel, excessive overtime, long delivery times, and other kinds of slack built into its operations. These elements of slack allow various organizational units to be operated quite independently of each other. Under good MPC operations, the objective is, in fact, to reduce these slack conditions. The result is a need for better scheduling and other kinds of improved communication among organizational subunits to compensate for the reduced slack.

The company will have a need for new kinds of dialogue either supported by formal organization changes or by other mechanisms, such as regularly scheduled committee meetings. These committee meetings have to be taken quite seriously since they usually are a part of a processing cycle that requires a timely decision. If one member doesn't turn up, there will have to be some "default" rule applied, and the no-show will be just as responsible!

One new level of communication that becomes quite important is between first-line management and the computer department. Murphy's law is always at work, and the foremen will occasionally get reports with "mysterious" data. The resolution of these problems on a timely basis is very important for the health of the system.

Job design

Achievement of Class A implementation status means a significant change in the way people do their jobs. It follows then that the means of evaluating job effectiveness must change. Jobs must be designed and evaluated on a basis that is consistent with system transactions and system performance measures. Accountability needs to be established on a basis that is congruent with the new job designs. Foremen should be held accountable for meeting the schedules. Stockroom personnel should be evaluated in terms of stockroom accuracy measures. Planners should be evaluated for inventory levels and for shortages of manufactured or purchased materials. Purchasing buyers should be evaluated in terms of material cost reductions, service improvements, and vendor performance.

An interesting implication of these changes was observed at a large heavy-equipment manufacturer. The continuing addition of systems to be executed on the shop floor resulted in a fundamental change in the job of the foreman. Instead of someone who moved iron and yelled a lot, the foreman became more of an information processor. One result was rethinking the career path which leads to a foreman's job. The MPC-system driven company is fundamentally different from its predecessor.

The organization will have to adapt to the system. Many successful implementors now see that the key is to change the organization to match the system, rather than vice versa. That is not to say that the system is not tailored to meet the needs of a particular environment, but only to say that activities at the operational level after Class A implementation are different. They are as different as the job of a barnstormer is from that of a professional pilot.

The Class A MPC system can be achieved under any form of organization. Many people have asked whether it is necessary to install a materials management organization before implementing MPC systems. The materials management type of formal organization is no guarantee of success and it is not a prerequisite to success. However, because of the interactions among organizational subunits and the reduction of slack which formerly allowed them to operate more independently, many companies have adopted a materials management form of organization to support their systems to control materials flow.

A materials management organization typically integrates production planning, purchasing, traffic, distribution, and all physical inventory control activities within one organizational unit. Also included are formal feedbacks associated with transaction error resolution, shop-floor control, and vendor follow-up systems.

The exact form of a materials management organization can vary from firm to firm over time. However, there is a general evolution toward more complete organizational integration. The reduction of slack requires more close working relationships. The integrated materials management form of organization has been helpful in achieving these relationships in many firms.

An interesting example of introducing the materials management form of organization can be seen in the experience of the Xerox Corporation. The information systems group, the division producing copiers and duplicators, went through a number of changes in their materials management organization as the products went through their life cycle. When the products were new, the designs were in a great state of flux and all emphasis was on design improvements and maximum output. At a later stage, competition was more intense, the designs were stable, and emphasis shifted to productivity and cost reduction.

Top management commitment

The final organizational implication for Class A implementation is the requirement of a deep and lasting commitment from the top management of the company. We have already noted the survey of MRP companies that found a strong correlation between data accuracy and good measures of effectiveness by the Wight classification scheme. An even stronger correlation existed between the level of top-management support and the A, B, C, and D measurement of success. All authorities state that this commitment is critical to success, and empirical evidence backs up this claim.

Another interesting result of this survey was that the authors found a strong correlation between success and the level of support provided by the marketing group. Those companies that have active participation from the marketing department during MPC system design and implementation seem to be more likely to achieve Class A status than those where marketing personnel play a weak or nonexistent role.

Top-management commitment means a great deal more than a chief executive giving his or her blessing to the MPC systems. The key to commitment is not even in providing the necessary funding for the effort. It is first and foremost to recognize that the MPC effort will require the sole use of some of the best people in the organization for a significant period of time. These people have to be identified, they have to be freed from present responsibilities (hire replacements if necessary), they have to be molded into an effective team, and they have to have the authority and responsibility to do the job.

Top-management commitment also relates to understanding how achievement of Class A MRP status will affect the entire company. The top management should provide leadership for the change, rather than playing a passive role. This kind of leadership means that one companywide system is the goal; that this system will be used for budgeting and for strategic planning; that marketing decisions such as customer order promising will be made within the system; that key trade-offs are made in the MPS; that the accounting and finance systems will at some point be integrated with the companywide data base; that engineering will support the effort to whatever degree necessary; that manufacturing's job will be to hit the schedule, and that an ongoing companywide education program, beginning with top management, will be put in place. George Bevis has said that the key to success at the Tennant Company (another Class A system user) was when he clearly understood that he personally had to make an active commitment to the MPC systems. At the time, he was executive vice president for the company. He had to change the way he thought about manufacturing and carry this change through the organization.

In some firms, effective systems have been installed despite lack of top-management support. In one instance we know of, the resources were provided at the vice presidential level and the president never did understand some of the fundamental changes that were taking place in the company. This strategy is risky and is to be avoided if possible. In some firms, however, there is no other way.

PLAN OF ATTACK

We have already discussed how a plan of attack has to be tailored to the company environment and perceptions at a point in time. To some extent, material control systems have been oversold and oversimplified. The result is that many people seriously underestimate the magnitude of the implementation task and have unrealistic expectations of what can be done, how much is reasonable, what subsystems should be started first, and when they should quit.

Defining the scope

The question of what model to start on is a bit more complex than the analogy of eating an elephant one bite at a time. Some idea of the task and priorities for improvement help define the starting point. For example, many companies only turn to the MPS after the MRP explosion, data integrity, shop-floor control, and purchasing follow-up systems are in place. Without the MPS, the result can often be sophisticated systems to execute insanity. Moreover, with some degree of stability at the front end of the system, the resulting problems in execution are significantly lessened. The other side of the coin is that a sophisticated MPS that cannot be executed will not be widely acclaimed by the organization. But any improvement in the MPS should make management, even with crude execution systems, easier. The resolution of this dilemma hinges on a careful assessment of organizational readiness for change and where change is needed.

One key aspect of defining the project scope is to have in mind a specific group of users for each system that is designed. The system should be designed to support some day-to-day decision problem faced by either an existing group of users or some group of users that is to be put together by a specific organizational change. If the system is designed for some nonexistent group of users or, worse yet, is designed to make decisions automatically, the chances of success are reduced substantially.

Since the first impact of a materials control system will be felt in the factory, it follows that the first group of users should probably be somewhere in the manufacturing organization (including materials management). At least one of the key users should be a member of the design team. In that way, he or she will be continually assessing the system design in terms of what is possible and what key problems are to be solved.

The question of when to quit is partly related to the notion of a journey rather than a trip. Note that the journey has to be periodically redefined and refunded. A further dimension of this continuing effort is that most companies expect to implement the system and that thereafter it will remain relatively static. Experience runs counter to this belief. In most firms, there is an ongoing need for system improvements, reformatting of data, inclusion of different facts on output reports, evolution from paper outputs to cathode ray tubes, new cross checks for data integrity, etc. These efforts are important and need to be encouraged to some degree, because by so doing the users develop a genuine identity with the systems and they feel that their needs are being met. On the other hand, too much attention to this kind of effort can come at the expense of development in other subsystems. Moreover, sometimes a problem symptom will later be eliminated after other system efforts. The need is for a degree of balance, and an eye to the long term, while not ignoring legitimate short-term user needs. The long-term commitment of the users, obtained by solving their short-term needs, is an important element of this balance.

Project management

Perhaps the most critical dimension to the plan of attack is the proper use of project teams. An MPC system has to be designed and implemented in subsystem units. It is critical to properly define the scope of each subsystem and to manage its design and implementation.

We see the need for three kinds or layers of project management teams, but there are overlaps between them during the evolution of the MPC system. The most important level of project management is what we call the primary project team. This is a group of about five to eight people coming from different functional areas. Their task is to define the detailed set of subsystem projects, order the priorities, make sure that each subsystem project remains congruent with the overall MPC system efforts, and act as a conduit to and from their respective functional areas and user groups.

The primary project team needs to report to a special top-management steering committee. This second group serves as a decision-making group when MPC efforts require coordination that exceeds the authority of the primary project team. An example might be the need to coordinate some aspects of marketing and design engineering. The steering committee is also the source of resources for the project teams. It will be necessary to earmark critical resource persons and allocate funding to the MPC system efforts. The steering committee will be needed to reconcile these needs with competing needs in the company.

The third level of project management is the team assigned to a detailed MPC subsystem, such as stockroom data integrity, bill of material structuring, engineering change control, or master production scheduling. In the early stage of the MPC system effort, it is often true that members of the primary project team serve as members of detailed project teams. This is very useful to broaden their understanding of the MPC system and to develop realistic expectations of how long the subprojects should take, what organizational changes are required, how to define educational needs, etc.

The primary project team

The group of five to eight persons on the primary project team should definitely include a representative from marketing, one from engineering, one from line manufacturing, and one from the computer department. Beyond this organizational representation, the only need is for bright, hard workers, preferably with some history of getting projects accomplished. Many teams also include a member from finance. This is particularly important when the short-term scope of the project is to incorporate cost-accounting systems or critical interfaces with systems such as labor cost reporting.

The project team should be a core of people who are largely freed from other responsibilities during the course of the project. They should be physically located in some separate area with minimal contact with their previous jobs and associates. The team should be comprised of people from within the company. There is a tendency to believe that this kind of talent can better be hired. This is not usually the case for two critical reasons. First, the supply of qualified professionals in this field is severely limited; most of the best ones are happily employed. Second, even if the talent were available, the organization must make the necessary adaptations to use the new systems on its own. It is critical to know what the changes will be, what the major roadblocks are, who will be supportive, and who will need to receive special handling. It is only insiders who have this kind of knowledge.

A further dimension of using insider project teams is the opportunity for individual growth that participation in this kind of project offers. The primary project team is going to evolve into a highly professional group, and the materials management based on MPC systems will similarly be more professional than formerly. The result is that there should be some very nice jobs available for productive members of the project teams. There are not many chances for rapid advancement in status and compensation in industrial organizations that outstrip the demonstrated results on a MPC project team.

The use of insider project teams does not mean that the team should not receive outside counsel. On the contrary, use of a qualified professional consultant can be extremely valuable. This person can help in defining the project scope, in providing education for the project teams, in defining the education program for the company, and in auditing results. Another role that can be well performed by an outsider is that of conscience. It is very useful to have an outsider come around and ask whether the project is on target, whether anyone has been removed from the team or has been diverted, and whether directions are being maintained.

One person on the primary project team has to serve as the project leader. It is tempting to believe that this person needs to be able to perform miracles while serving coffee to the team. People with those qualifications are hard to find. The key attribute of the project leader is that he or she should have a demonstrated track record for management in the company. The person needs to be decisive, to know how to assign task authority and responsibility, and to provide leadership to the team. It is also important to know how to deal with top management.

The primary project team leader must be a user, definitely not someone from the computer department. Ideally, the project leadership will be viewed as a temporary assignment, with the intent to return to a position where he or she uses the system.

A source of leadership in the primary project team is from one key member of the top-management steering committee. This member serves as top management's representative, and should be more knowledgeable about the MPC project than the other members of the steering committee. A good choice might be the vice president of manufacturing. In some firms, this person goes so far as to assume personal reponsibility for the success or failure of the MPC project. This level of commitment places MPC system implementation in the same category as any major corporate goal. Building a new factory based on new technology is a useful analog.

The Swissair project team. A good example of how detailed MPC subsystem projects can be defined and managed is provided by Swissair's engineering and maintenance department. Maintenance on Swissair aircraft is performed in Zurich. This facility also provides maintenance service for other airlines. Total employment in the maintenance group is approximately 2,600.

The development of the Swissair integrated maintenance and control system (MCS) was started in 1971. The overall system is shown as Figure 11.2. It is divided into about 50 subsystems or segments; Figure 11.2 also shows the necessary sequential nature of introducing these segments. Figure 11.3 provides English-language descriptions for those segments which have been implemented, the year each segment was implemented, and the developmental effort in man-years in the segment. The overall developmental effort for the 15 implemented segments is 260 man-years and approximately 25 million SF ($12.5 million U.S.). Annual running costs are approximately 7 million SF ($3.5 million U.S).

These costs are more than offset by direct savings, primarily in labor

FIGURE 11.2 Swissair maintentance and control system

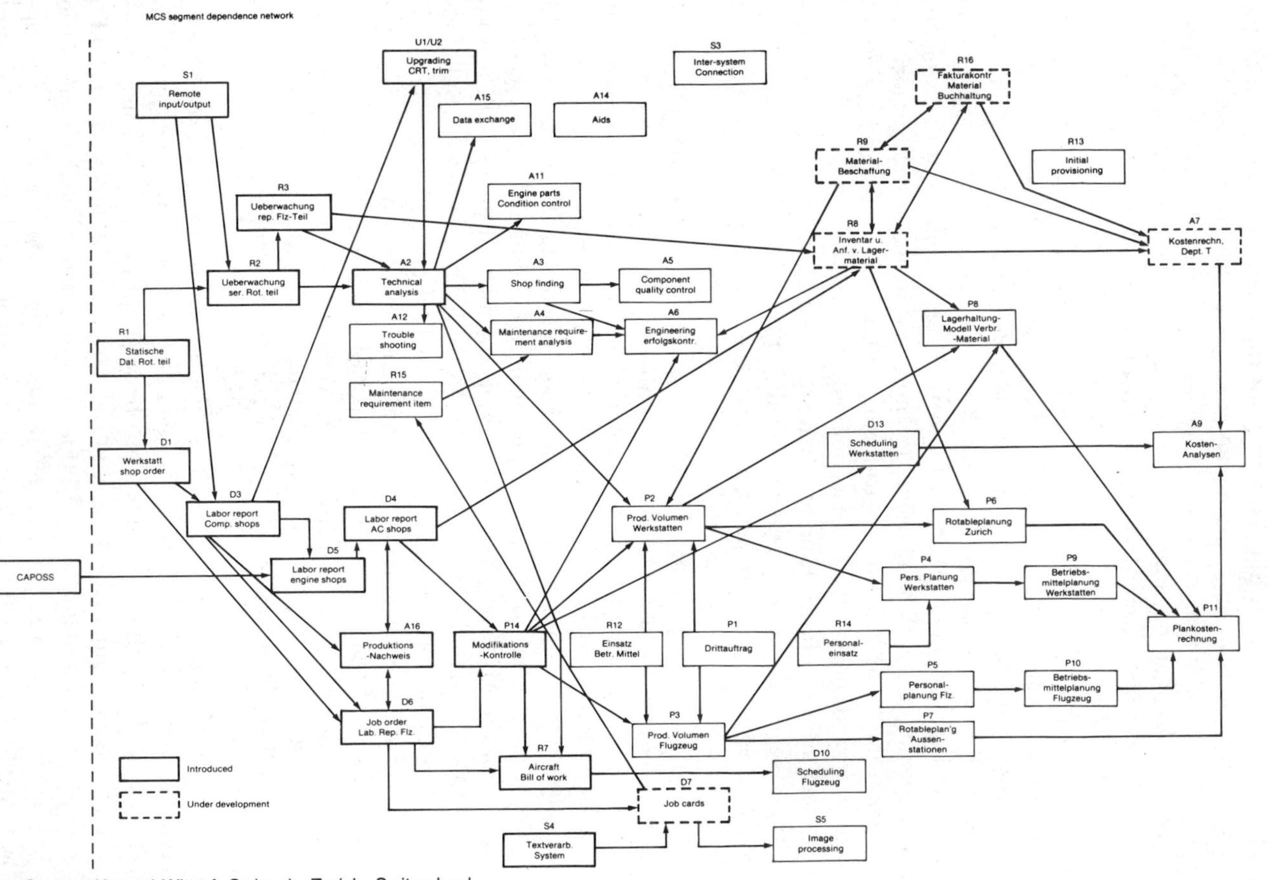

Source: Konrad Wittorf, Swissair, Zurich, Switzerland.

FIGURE 11.3 Swissair implemented system segments

Area	*Segment*	*Function*	*Year of implementation*	*Development effort (man-years)*
Rotable control	R1	Establish a master rotable record including all static data necessary for rotables control and labor reporting in the rotables workshops	1975	21.4
	R2	Register location and running times of rotables and control their time limits	1975	19.7
	R3	Control all rotable and repairable parts during rework time, set workshop priorities and monitor alert values	1978	15.3
Task management	D1	Establish a master labor record including all static data necessary for job planning and control in workshops	1975	14.4
	D3	Print work papers on request, record and compare man hours with standards registered in the system for component shops	1975	24.4
	D4	Same functions as D3 but for aircraft supporting shops	1976	6.5
	D5	Same function as D3 but for engine work shop. Integration of the CAPOSS package into the MCS	1976	10.3
	D6	Establish a master labor record and a system for automated printing of work papers and for recording man hours spent in aircraft maintenance and overhaul	1977	21.4
	R7	Support the selection of jobs for the next aircraft visit (bill of work)	1981	15.5
Production control	A16	Replace the previous reports about man hours	1976–77	14.1
Technical analysis	A2	Provide statistical data concerning technical occurrences such as pilot complaints, maintenance complaints, and component changes	1978	21.8
Modification control	P14	Control origin, implementation, and status of modifications	1980	15.0
Support segments	S1	Specify and supervise the installation of remote input/output facilities	1974	7.5
	U1/U2	Establish functions for direct access to the central EDP system and introduce CRT terminals. Upgrade some S1 functions to this access mode	1977–79	10.0
	S4	Provide a text management system which can be integrated with data processing. First used for overhaul manuals	1979	3.5

Source: Konrad Wittorf, Swissair, Zurich, Switzerland.

costs, through increased productivity. From a strategic point of view, the Swissair MCS system represents a long-term competitive weapon. Use of these systems should permit Swissair to obtain an increasing volume of third-party maintenance work. Even though Swiss labor costs are very high, the downtime of aircraft for maintenance can be reduced substantially, resulting in a greater ability to schedule flight hours for each aircraft so maintained.

One key to the Swissair MCS system is the development of each of the segments as a separate project, with its own project team. The segments are constrained to be not longer than approximately 20 man-years of effort and 2 to 3 years in elapsed time. The overall organization and management of the MCS project is shown in Figure 11.4. One key aspect of this organization is the general manager—planning and control. This person chairs the project management committee, as well as serving as a member of the steering committee as a project management representative. In essence, he or she is the top management representative for the detailed MCS project planning and control. This manager spends at least one day per week reviewing the exact status of each segment project.

The management organization for an individual segment project is illustrated in Figure 11.5. Each project encompasses the same set of six phases,

FIGURE 11.4 Swissair project organization

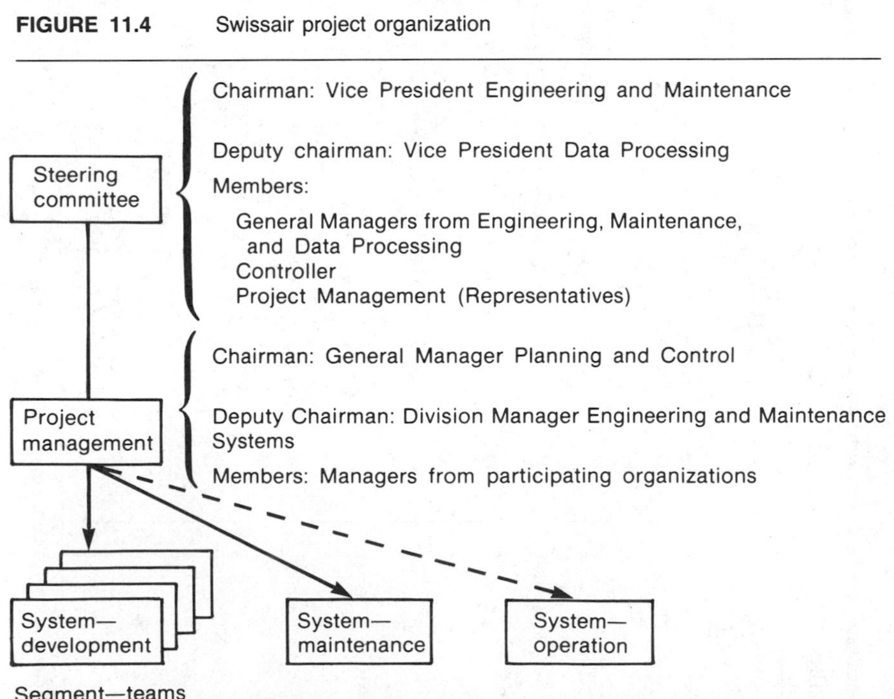

Source: Konrad Wittorf, Swissair, Zurich, Switzerland.

FIGURE 11.5 Swissair segment teams: Participation in development phases

Skill / Phase	User	System-specialist: System planner (user)	System-specialist: System analyst (EDP)	Programmer
Outline	+	⊕	+	
Functional specialist	+	⊕	+	
Program development			⊕	+
User-procedures	+	⊕		
User-tests	+	⊕	+	
Introduction	⊕	+	+	

\+ Participation

◯ Responsible

Source: Konrad Wittorf, Swissair, Zurich, Switzerland.

which are clearly defined as the rows in the matrix of Figure 11.5. The columns of this matrix show four key project team members. These entries in the matrix show which of these members participate in each phase, and who is responsible for project leadership during that phase.

The first important observation is that it is a user who will have ultimate responsibility for implementing the system. Since he or she knows this at the outset, there is careful attention given to all of the other phases so that a usable system will result. The second observation is that the EDP (electronic data processing) person is responsible only for computer program development, and it is the only activity that involves the programmers. According to the definition of the project phases, functional specification is not complete until an unambiguous programming job is defined.

The key responsibilities shown in Figure 11.5 are those of the system planner. This is a person who is basically a user, not a computer expert. It is a career assignment for fast-track career persons. They have the major job of defining the exact scope of a segment, including the expected costs, timings, and benefits. They also have the major responsibility of designing the new procedures, testing the system, and making it ready for introduction.

These people have a long-run career interest in becoming managers in a user department. They do not look to careers in data processing. Neither do they have a long-run interest in being project leaders. As one developmental step in their career, they take on one or two of these projects. If the results are favorable, they are eligible for a significant line-management job.

The final aspect of Figure 11.5 of interest is that, in reality, the system planner and the EDP system analyst act as a duo. This is to ensure that if either of them leaves the company during the duration of the effort, Swissair does not suffer irreparable damage to the project.

Project definition

The precise project definition will be company specific, depending upon their circumstances. However, each plan should have clear timings and milestones, and should perform the tasks in the correct sequences. Some form of project scheduling such as PERT or CPM is appropriate, but a bar chart approach can be used. Figure 11.6 is a partial example, which incorporates most of the key elements necessary for a firm starting from informal systems to achieve the basic engine portion of the MPC system in Figure 11.1.

One critical aspect of project definition is to subdivide the overall task into subprojects that each have well-defined milestones. If the project takes too long before concrete benefits are achieved, users will lose interest and chances for success are reduced. We personally feel that a reasonable approach for firms entering into these systems for the first time is to restrict each project to no more than one year in length. If timing slips, and 15 months elapse, the chances for success are probably still fairly good; but if two years elapse before some operating unit sees demonstrable results, the project can be in trouble.

A final comment on project definition is that once a detailed project plan has been agreed to, try very hard to adhere to the plan, resisting the temptation to go off in other directions. Unless the steering committee has been notified and is in agreement with a revision of the plan, don't permit deviations. Implementation may be a journey instead of a destination, but the journey must not become random.

EDUCATION

It is almost impossible to overemphasize the role of education in achieving a Class A system implementation. One of the questions asked in the Anderson and Schroeder survey was: "What is the major problem that your firm has faced in implementing MRP?" At the top of the list of replies is: Education of personnel.

Education levels and requirements

We see four distinct focuses or levels of education needed for implementation. Figure 11.7 shows these four levels as a pyramid. At the top is the top-management group; this group may be identical to the steering committee. They need to attend a short course on MPC systems, go to follow-up

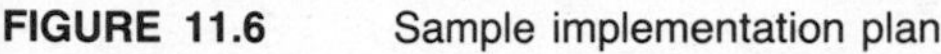

FIGURE 11.6 Sample implementation plan

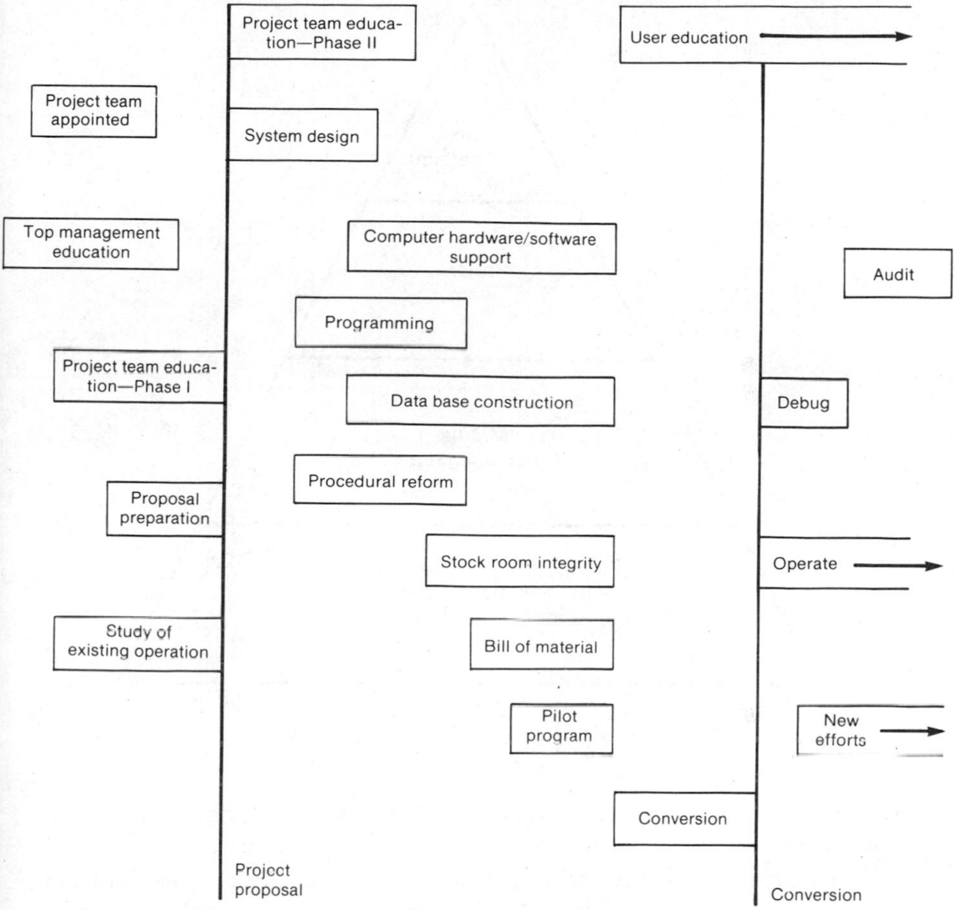

seminars on a regular basis, read top-management materials dealing with MPC systems, and stay abreast of current company efforts.

The next level of education is for the primary project team and the detailed project teams. The primary project team and the leaders of detailed projects should become true professionals, knowledgeable about the state of the art in this field. This is not an easy job, and it is ongoing. But the size of the MPC investment mandates having this level of knowledge resident within the firm.

This knowledge can be partially purchased through consultants and obtained from hardware/software vendors, but a firm should be especially wary

FIGURE 11.7 Education requirements

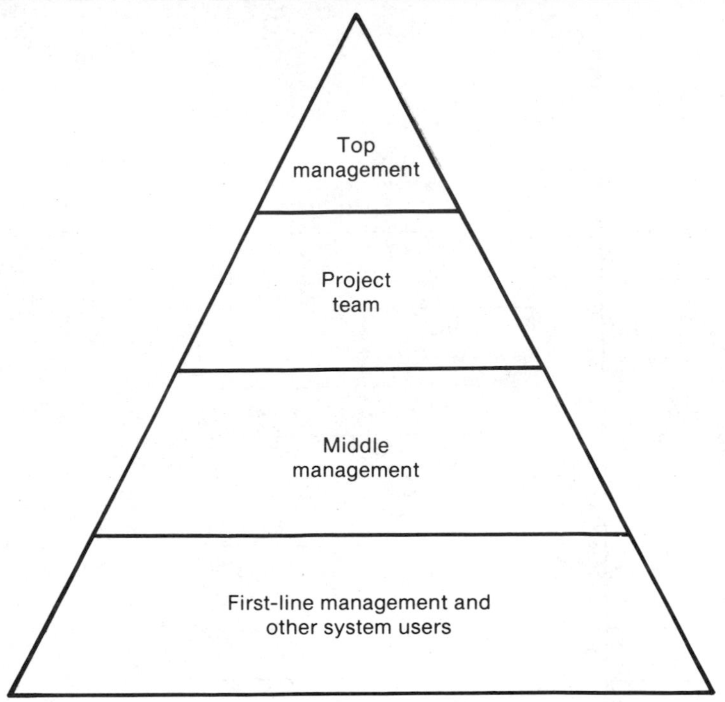

of letting its knowledge base depend too heavily on outsiders, particularly when those outsiders are trying to sell expensive products.

The primary project team needs to attend seminars on a regular basis, be active in professional societies, attend conferences and meetings of the societies, read journals in the field, and interact with other professionals in this area of interest. The leaders of detailed projects need to attend educational seminars especially devoted to their particular projects. The American Production and Inventory Control Society (APICS) has a professional certification program based on a series of examinations; achievement of this certification status is a reasonable goal for persons who intend to manage through MPC systems.

The third layer of education shown in Figure 11.7 is for the middle managers of the company. It will be necessary for all of these to receive education. This could take the form of attending two or three seminars of three to four days duration. This group needs to get outside of the company, learn the general approach of these systems and then see how they have been applied in several other firms. By seeing the before/after conditions through case studies and other means, the general direction of the efforts as well as the degree of change necessary to make them effective can be seen. One simply needs to take off the blinders imposed by existing company practices to see what these systems have to offer.

The outside education is followed up by inside education in the systems being designed for the firm. With an outside perspective, the middle managers can now more actively participate in the design of the systems that are going to affect their working lives. This participation goes a long way toward ensuring that the system is *our* system, instead of *the* system.

The final layer of education shown in Figure 11.7 is for first-line supervisors and other system users. In the last analysis, implementation will succeed or fail on the factory floor. It is essential that foremen and others execute the system, process transactions accurately, be rewarded for working within the system, and keep the informal system dead and buried.

There has been a tendency in some companies to consider the education for foremen, stockroom personnel, production planners, buyers, and other users as a narrow job of training. This focus is only on the use of the system as it affects the person's individual area. A much better point of view includes broad-based education about why the system has been adopted, what it does for the firm, and most important, how decisions made in each area (by specific people) are linked together. When the foreman sees exactly how unreported scrap causes an incorrect scheduled receipt that can result in a rush order back to his or her own department, he or she will be much more interested in data accuracy than if someone simply says—"We want you to always report scrap." The objective is not only to train people in procedures, but to provide them with a new framework and understanding. They need to be able to see why certain procedures are necessary and how they should treat some action that has not been previously explained.

Some sort of in-house program for this group is usually most appropriate. Some firms have had success with videotapes, but the best programs we have seen are a mixture of overview concepts and specific company examples. This can often best be achieved by the project team designing an education program, perhaps aided by a consultant. The program can also usefully employ middle managers, who will learn greatly from the process as the teachers.

An education program

The successful firm may find it wise to design the entire education program as part of the project. This can be the best way to address the entire span of educational needs depicted in Figure 11.7. Moreover, it is necessary to include redundancy. We have personal experience with the same users asking questions in a seminar that were clearly covered in an earlier seminar they attended. One simply must take a fairly pessimistic view of how much can be absorbed in one session, and realize that people forget quickly. It will be necessary to give the message several times, hopefully in somewhat different ways.

In addition to the need for redundancy, there is a natural turnover in personnel. People leave or take other assignments, and new personnel must be trained and educated. Since many aspects of executing a Class A system run counter to the work experiences of people, it is important not to expect very much from prior on-the-job training. The new foreman might know how to put some number into a computer terminal because a prior boss showed him or her how, but the chances are slim that there was a clear explanation of *why*. Often the worst possible training comes from expecting a new person to learn the ropes by watching someone else. The why rarely gets conveyed this way, and professionalism suffers. One further goal of a broad-based education program should be to locate personnel who can get enthusiastic about material control systems and can grow into more responsible positions. There is always a need for these people, particularly those who have firsthand experience.

The final dimension of an educational program we want to mention is the degree of organizational change required to implement Class A systems. This process can be the largest single change in people's working lives. Education can represent a much less direct threat to people than other change approaches. If educational programs and exercises can be set up that clearly show how one way of doing something is better than another, acceptance can be a much easier task and the changes much more easily made.

AUDITING

The process of implementing an MPC system deserves some sort of periodic audit. Furthermore, we have closely examined fully implemented systems in many companies, including some of the best in the world. There is not one that could not be improved. Top management should make sure that the best improvement plans are being formulated and that the existing systems are continuing to do the job for which they were designed. In this brief overview of auditing, we present three main ideas. The first is a checklist of system features that should be included in a Class A system. Next, we present a brief view of how we conduct an audit and how one can diagnose poor system health. Finally, we present a section on cost/benefit analysis in the attempt to provide better expectation guidelines for MPC system implementation.

Class A queries

In addition to the brief description of a Class A company presented earlier, the following checklist of system questions should be considered in evaluating any MPC control system.

- Are the time buckets used for planning no longer than one week?
- Is the planning (regeneration) at least weekly?
- Is performance against schedule evaluated on a weekly or more frequent basis using concrete measurements?
- Is there a defined measure of customer service?
- Is production held responsible for hitting the schedule and not for finished-good inventory levels?
- Is any past-due portion of the master production schedule held to less than one week's capacity?
- Are the capacity implications of the production plan and MPS evaluated on a long-term resource need and rough-cut basis?
- Are the detailed aspects of capacity planning using capacity requirements planning a key part of manufacturing planning?
- Is there an input-output or other system in place to compare machine center outputs with expectations?
- Does the shop-floor control system provide daily dispatch lists for departmental foremen?
- Are the daily dispatch lists the sole source of priority information for the foremen?
- Is an inventory cycle counting procedure in place with periodic measurement and evaluation?
- Are all records in the computer (no handwritten documents)?
- Are accuracy levels maintained for bills of material?
- Is there a well-functioning approach to the control of engineering changes?
- Are shop orders closed out religiously (no tag ends, counts reconciled, etc.)?
- Are other critical procedures to control transactions adequate, such as rejected materials, rework, etc.?
- Does the system incorporate pegging?
- Does the system have firm planned order capabilities?
- Do planners use bottom-up replanning to solve material availability problems?
- Are state-of-the-art purchasing systems in use, and are vendor capacities planned with the same vigor as internal capacities?
- Is vendor performance routinely measured?
- Is the system integrated with finished-goods planning and control?

This is a formidable list of questions, and it is not all-inclusive. Moreover, some negative responses may be more tolerable than others for a given company. Let us now turn to the approach we have found useful in auditing a company's MPC systems.

The routine audit

As one part of a routine audit, we feel that the company's approaches should be evaluated against state-of-the-art system features. The firm that evaluates its approach to material control systems against the set of questions posed above can accomplish this. A somewhat different perspective is to examine the general level of effectiveness of each of the firm's particular systems. That is, whatever the stated system design, do the systems in fact work? Are they in use? What else is needed for users to do their jobs?

Our approach to this issue is a routine audit involving several steps. First, it is necessary to take whatever amount of time is necessary to understand the systems that are in place, how the documents are created, what data files are used to process the records, etc. This is not to say, however, that one is auditing the computer program or the computerized data base. Effective use of the computer is a separate technical issue. The intent of the MPC audit is to clearly understand the set of output documents, how they are linked, who uses them, and what to do with them.

It is very important to adopt a viewpoint of substantial ignorance at the outset. We ask to be shown exact current output data and examine these documents in considerable detail. We take the position that one needs to understand what all of the data items are on each report, where they come from, and what arithmetical operations are performed to get them. We examine several actual records to see whether we can understand the numbers, and whether the stated logic can be applied to produce the sample results.

One often finds logical inconsistencies in this process, such as negative inventory values, records with all zeros in some field, etc. These are sure clues that all is not well. It is also of interest to reconcile documents that presumably should have been produced from a common set of data. An example is shipments for some common time period from records in marketing, finance, and manufacturing.

As a side issue of this analysis, one sometimes finds that the in-house experts cannot explain how the documents are created, what they truly contain, who will use them, and how they are used. Inconsistencies in their beliefs must similarly be explained in sufficient detail.

After gaining an understanding of the system, the audit should turn to those who use the output documents. If a foreman who is asked for the daily dispatch list replies: "My daily what?" one begins to wonder whether systems are really being used. On the other hand, if it is in his or her pocket, with pencil lines and fingerprints, one begins to feel that the system outputs are used and the system matches reality. Similar checks should be made in other areas. Is it possible for one of us as an outsider to look important and gain entry into the stockroom? Is the door locked? Who has the keys? What is done on the night shift? Ask a stockroom person to produce the current inventory listing and pick parts at random. Can each of these parts be found in the exact amounts in the exact location? How do the stockroom people feel about data accuracy? Ask them how many times the parts are not there. Ask whether the engineers come in to get parts for R&D without proper paperwork. Check out the receiving area. Are there boxes of goods there? Ask how long they have been there. Find out how the system is notified of arrivals. How are counts verified? Look at the documents that accompany work in process. Do they make sense? Are all fields properly filled out?

Visit the assembly department. Ask whether they are now working on the jobs that the system has indicated they should be working on. Ask whether there is an end-of-the-month bulge in shipments. Ask how many times they run out of parts.

Talk to the master scheduler. Ask him or her to show you how the MPS is prepared. Ask about the support obtained from marketing. Ask if they get silly forecast data that they have to override.

Audit the level of education being used in the company. Who does it? Who gets it? How often? What is the program? Is an overall level of understanding considered important? Does the foreman know how a shop order is created? Is top management knowledgeable about the MPS system or do they believe that education is important—for my subordinates! Are the members of the design team active professionally? Do they attend seminars, workshops, and conferences?

In sum, the routine audit starts with the posture that one believes nothing unless proven. The objective is to find out what is supposed to be the case and whether actuality matches the system. In the last analysis, a system is only effective when used.

The MPC system audit is not a witch-hunt. Whatever systems are presently in use is simply a matter of fact. It is not the fault of the users that it is not any better. Making it better requires action plans, project teams, and resources. The MPC audit attempts to help the company assess where it truly is, where it might be, and how to get there.

Cost/benefit analysis

We firmly believe that one important aspect of any MPC system implementation should be a well-defined cost/benefit study. There are far too many large system projects that proceed without sufficient analysis of costs and benefits, or that have had the benefits computed on an after-the-fact basis. An MPC system effort represents a substantial investment for the firm; the fact that the data are hard to estimate with precision should not preclude rigorous analysis.

For every project, the costs and benefits will be a bit unique, depending upon the scope of the project and the conditions prevailing at the time. However, to the extent that critical costs and benefits of the effort can be included as a set of time-phased expectations, the steering committee can review the project performance more effectively. Moreover, to the extent that major expenditures are specified up front, there will be fewer unpleasant surprises. It may well be easier to sell an entire package with a large price at one time than to be continually "returning to the well."

The kinds of cost that are usually important to plan and budget for are:

- Personnel costs for people assigned to the project on a full-time basis. (Try to identify specific people so that their bosses will be committed to their absence.)
- Personnel costs for people assigned on a part-time basis. (Again, try to obtain a commitment for who and when.)
- Computer hardware costs—any necessary enhancements in hardware should be specified.
- Computer software costs—purchased software and outside personnel to install software.
- Personnel expenses for company systems people who will work on the project (when, who, duration).
- Outside professional services, such as consultants, education, contract programming, etc.

The indirect costs of managerial time and opportunity costs of placing this system implementation at the highest priority level for the company should perhaps be acknowledged, but not explicitly accounted for.

The benefits can be assessed in a multitude of ways. We feel that the commitment to some concrete statement of benefit measured on an agreed upon basis, rather than precisely how the benefits are measured, is the key. Some possibilities include: Pro forma accounting statements—these can be generally based on certain operating ratios and improvements in those ratios, and thereafter matched with actual results. The problem with the pro forma approach, however, is that bottom-line results are a function of many causes. It may be hard to isolate the exact contribution of the MPC system.

It may be necessary to assess the benefits through improvements in other surrogate measures. Possibilities include:

- Shipping budget performance.
- Labor utilization rates.
- Productivity measures.
- Expediting budget.
- Obsolete inventory write-off.
- Cycle count accuracy.
- Overtime hours.
- Purchased component costs.
- Vendor delivery performance.
- Premium shipment costs.
- Customer delivery promise performance.

- Spare-part service levels.
- Obsolete inventory reduction.
- Raw-material inventory as a percentage of sales.
- Work-in-process inventory as a percentage of sales.
- Finished-goods inventory as a percentage of sales.
- Safety-stock inventory as a percentage of sales.
- Inventory turnover.
- Annual accounting inventory adjustment.

Any of these measures may be appropriate, but the need is to clearly specify how the exact measurement is to be made and when various improvements are to be obtained. Almost every company will choose a different set, and perhaps a different way to measure; but this should be part of the up-front effort so that actual progress can be compared to expectations, and so that the project teams will know when they are meeting the agreed upon expectations.

Many subjective benefits can also be stated, but the problems of concrete measurement are more complex. Among the subjective benefits that firms may wish to achieve are the following:

- Customer relations.
- Competitive position.
- Professionalism.
- Morale and *esprit de corps*.
- Coordination between finance, marketing, and production.
- Accounting control.
- Product quality.

Both the subjective and objective measures should be specified and made a part of each working contract between a particular project team and the steering committee. The original, perhaps tentative, set of objectives should be specified as well as possible and made a part of the formal proposal by the team to the steering committee.

As actual work progresses, any evolution in the anticipated costs and benefits should be directly discussed in progress meetings. A finalized time-phased set of expected costs and benefits should be put forth at the time of major conversion, and continuing audits should be carried out thereafter to measure actual results versus plans.

One final word of caution: These assessments of cost/benefit often look too good! It is probably sensible to focus on a few key measures, ones that have a close relationship to the bottom line, and to be somewhat conservative. A major management responsibility is to truly control the costs. To put a team together with a year to complete the first requirement and then let them drift along will ensure cost overruns. It also will allow enthusiasm to wane, which reduces the possibilities of achieving the long-run benefits. The greatest early leverage is to hold persons responsible to hit the design schedule, and in that way control timings and costs.

The timing issue may be even more critical than the cost issue. The benefits from MPC systems are usually so substantial that cost overruns are easily covered. *But*, if timings are allowed to slip, the result is people resources being used longer than originally planned. This leads to the need for reassigning priorities to project work in the firm. Usually, systems personnel (and others) are being requested to work on many projects. When the actual time durations on these projects slip, one result can be political infighting over resources.

CONCLUDING PRINCIPLES

In this chapter we have tried to focus attention on the major problem in MPC systems—how to get implemented results. The following principles summarize the major points:

- MPC system efforts should start with an assessment of where the firm is and what can be done.
- The total MPC system implementation effort should be divided into manageable subtasks so that each yields concrete benefits.
- One should start with a subsystem that can be implemented quickly and that will be of recognized use to some readily identified user group.
- An early goal should be data integrity because of its fundamental importance.
- Management should be prepared to install new organizational forms to facilitate MPC implementation and operation.
- Key users must be on project teams.
- Performance on project teams should be congruent with career planning.
- Education programs should be designed for all levels of the organization.
- The design scope for each particular project should be carefully defined and maintained unless broad agreement on redefinition is reached.
- Project definition and project management techniques should be used to manage the implementation.
- Management should audit, audit, and audit.
- An objective assessment of costs and benefits should be part of any MPC-system implementation program.

REFERENCES

Belt, Bill. "Men, Spindles and Materials Requirements Planning: Enhancing Implementation." *Production and Inventory Management*, lst Quarter 1979, pp. 54–65.

Benson, P. B., A. V. Hill, and T. R. Hoffman. "Manufacturing Systems of the Future—A Delphi Study." *Production and Inventory Management Journal*, 3d Quarter 1982, pp. 97–98.

Bevis, G. E. "Closed Loop MRP at the Tennant Company." Report—The Tennant Company, Minneapolis, Minn.

Brenezir, Ned W. "The Bottom Line Begins at the Top." *Production and Inventory Management*, 3d Quarter 1977.

Davis, E. W. "Material Requirements Planning in a Fabrication and Assembly Environment: Ingersoll Rand Case Study." Pennsauken, N.J.: Auerback Publishers, 1982.

Fisher, Kenneth. "How to Implement MRP Successfully." *Production and Inventory Management* 22, no. 4 (4th Quarter 1981), pp. 36–54.

Flosi, Thomas L. "How to Manage an MRP Implementation." *APICS Management Seminar Proceedings*, Las Vegas, March 1982, pp. 79–88.

Glaza, Thomas L. "Gaining and Retaining Management Commitment." *APICS 23d Annual Conference Proceedings*, 1980, pp. 222–25.

Gunder, William M. "Manufacturing Control Systems Implementation—A Practical Approach," BCT Associates, 1979.

Hall, R. W., and T. E. Vollmann. "Planning Your Material Requirements." *Harvard Business Review*, September/October 1978.

Jordan, H. H. "Developing an Integrated Production and Inventory Control System." *1972 APICS Conference Proceedings*, pp. 28–34.

MRP Re-Implementation: You Too Can Be Successful." *APICS National Conference Proceedings*, Boston, October 1981, pp. 119–20.

Maertz, William E. "MRP's Fourth Requirement." *Production and Inventory Management*, 3d Quarter 1979, pp. 81–84.

Nicholas, John M. "Developing Effective Teams for Systems Design and Implementation." *Production and Inventory Management*, 3d Quarter 1980, pp. 37–47.

Prather, Kirk L. "From Warfare to Cooperation: PIC Team Building." *APICS Management Seminar Proceedings*, Las Vegas, March 1982, pp. 88–94.

"Productivity: Out of MRP—A New Game Plan." *Modern Materials Handling*. January 1981, pp. 63–82.

Schroder, R. G. *Material Requirements Planning: A Study of Implementation and Practice*. Falls Church, Va.: American Production and Inventory Control Society, 1981.

Schroder, R. G., J. C. Anderson, S. E. Tupy, and E. M. White. "A Study of MRP Benefits and Costs." *Journal of Operations Management* 2, no. 1 (October 1981).

Spampani, P. B. "Manufacturing and Material Control Systems Development Program." *1973 APICS Conference Proceedings*, pp. 171–85.

Tersine, Richard J. "Production and Operations: A Systems Construct." *Production and Inventory Management*, 4th Quarter 1977.

"The Trick of Materials Requirements Planning." *Business Week*, June 4, 1979, pp. 72D–72J.

Van Dierdonck, R. J. M., and J. G. Miller. "Designing Production Planning and Control Systems." *Journal of Operations Management* 1, no. 1 (1980), pp. 37–46.

White, E. M., J. C. Anderson, R. G. Schroeder, and S. E. Tupy. "A Study of the MRP Implementation Process." *Journal of Operations Management* 2, no. 3 (May 1982).

Wight, Oliver W. "MRP II—Manufacturing Resource Planning." *Modern Materials Handling*, September 1979, pp. 78–94.

________. *MRP II: Unlocking America's Productivity Potential.* Williston, Vt.: Oliver Wight, Ltd. Publications, 1981.

12

Advanced concepts in material requirements planning

This chapter is concerned with some advanced issues in material requirements planning (MRP). Some of the concepts and conventions discussed can lead to improvement in well-functioning basic systems. Most of the concepts presented are of a "fine tuning" nature and can provide additional benefits to the company.

We take the point of view that the first, most important phase in MRP is to get the system installed, to make it a part of an ongoing managerial process, to get users trained in the use of MRP, to understand the critical linkages with other areas, to achieve high levels of data integrity, and to link MRP with the other modules of the front end, engine, and back end of manufacturing planning and control (MPC) systems. Having achieved this first phase, many firms then turn to the advanced issues discussed in this chapter.

Chapter 12 is organized around the following five topics:

- Determination of manufacturing order quantities: What are the basic trade-offs in lot sizing in the MRP environment, and what techniques are useful?
- Determination of purchase order quantities: How should lot sizes be chosen when purchasing discounts are in effect?

- Buffering concepts: What are the types of uncertainties in MRP, and how can one buffer against these uncertainties?
- Nervousness: Why are MRP systems subject to nervousness and how do firms deal with system nervousness?
- Other advanced MRP concepts: What conventions have been successfully applied? How are they useful?

Chapter 12 is linked with Chapters 2 and 3 in that this chapter presupposes understanding of MRP systems, record processing, systems dynamics, etc. Chapter 12 is also linked to Chapters 17 and 18 where several inventory concepts (lot sizing, buffering, and service levels) are treated. The focus here is on the dependent demand (MRP) environment whereas Chapters 17 and 18 largely deal with systems for independent demand. Additional buffering concepts are dealt with in Chapters 7 and 8 (master production scheduling) and in Chapter 10 (demand management).

DETERMINATION OF MANUFACTURING ORDER QUANTITIES

The MRP system converts the master production schedule into a time-phased schedule for all intermediate assemblies and component parts. The detailed schedules are comprised of two parts, scheduled receipts (open orders) and planned orders. The scheduled receipts each have had the quantity and timing (due date) determined for release to the shop. The quantities and timings for planned orders are determined by the MRP logic using the inventory position, the gross requirements data, and a specific procedure for determining the quantities—the lot-sizing procedure.

A number of procedures have been developed for MRP systems, ranging from ordering as required (lot-for-lot), to simple decision rules, and finally to extensive optimizing procedures. In this section, we describe five such lot-sizing procedures.

The primary consideration in the development of lot-sizing procedures for MRP is the nature of the requirements data. The demand dependency relationship from the product structures and the time-phased gross requirements mean that the requirements for an item might appear as illustrated in Figure 12.1. First, it is important to notice that the requirements do *not*

FIGURE 12.1 Example problem: Weekly requirements schedule

Week number	1	2	3	4	5	6	7	8	9	10	11	12
Requirements	10	10	15	20	70	180	250	270	230	40	0	10

Ordering cost = S = $300 per order
Inventory carrying cost = C_H = $2 per unit per week

Source: W. L. Berry, "Lot Sizing Procedures for Requirements Planning Systems: A Framework for Analyses," Second quarter 1972, *Production and Inventory Management,* Journal of the American Production and Inventory Control Society, Inc.

reflect the key independent demand assumption of a constant uniform demand. Second, the requirements are *discrete* since they are stated on a period-by-period basis (time phased) rather than as a rate (for example, an average of so much per month or year). Finally, the requirements can be *lumpy*. That is, they can vary substantially from period to period and even have several periods for which there are no requirements.

MRP lot-sizing procedures are designed specifically for the discrete demand case. One problem in selecting a procedure is that reductions in inventory-related costs can generally be achieved only by using increasingly complex procedures. Such procedures require more computations in making lot-sizing determinations. A second problem has to do with local optimization. The lot-sizing procedure used for one part in a MRP system has a direct impact on the gross requirements data passed to its component parts. The use of procedures other than lot-for-lot tends to make the lumpiness of the requirements data grow larger farther down in the product structure.

The manufacturing lot size problem is basically one of converting the requirements into a series of replenishment orders. If we consider this problem on a local level, that is, only in terms of the one part and not its components, the problem involves determining how to group the time-phased requirements data into a schedule of replenishment orders that minimizes the combined costs of placing manufacturing orders and carrying inventory.

Since MRP systems are normally operated on a daily or weekly basis, i.e., batch processed, the timing affects the assumptions commonly made in using MRP lot-sizing procedures. These assumptions are as follows. First, since the component requirements are aggregated by time period for planning purposes, we assume that all of the requirements for each period must be available at the beginning of the period. Second, we assume that all of the requirements for a given period must be met and cannot be back ordered. Third, since the system is operated on a periodic basis, the ordering decisions are assumed to occur at regular time intervals, for example, daily or weekly. Fourth, the requirements are assumed to be properly offset for manufacturing lead time. Finally, we assume that the component requirements are satisfied at a uniform rate during each period. Therefore, the average inventory level will be used in computing the inventory carrying costs.

In the following sections, we shall illustrate the results obtained by applying five different ordering procedures to the example data given in Figure 12.1. Furthermore, this example will be used to illustrate the manner in which these procedures vary in their assumptions and the extent to which they utilize all of the available data in making lot-sizing decisions.

Economic order quantities (EOQ)

Because of its simplicity, the economic order quantity (EOQ) formula is often used as a decision rule for placing orders in a requirements-planning system. As we shall illustrate in the following example, however, the EOQ model frequently must be modified in requirements planning system applications. Since the EOQ is based upon the assumption of constant uniform demand, the resulting total cost expression will not necessarily be valid for requirements planning applications.

The results obtained by ordering material in economic lot sizes for the example data are presented in Figure 12.2. In this example, the average weekly demand of 92.1 units for the entire requirements schedule was used in the EOQ formula to compute the economic lot size. Note, too, that the order quantities are shown when received, and that the average inventory for each period was used in computing the inventory carrying cost.

This example illustrates several problems with using economic lot sizes. When the requirements are not equal from period to period, as is often the case in MRP, fixed EOQ lot sizes result in a mismatch between the order quantities and the requirements values. This can mean excess inventory must be carried forward from week to week. As an example, 41 units are carried over into week 6 when a new order is received.

In addition, the order quantity must be increased in those periods where the requirements exceed the economic lot size plus the amount of inventory carried over into the period. An example of this occurs in week 7. This modification is clearly preferable to the alternative of placing orders earlier to meet the demand in such periods, since this would only increase the inventory carrying costs. Likewise, the alternative of placing multiple orders in a given period would needlessly increase the ordering cost.

Finally, the use of the average weekly requirements figure in computing the economic lot size ignores a considerable amount of other information contained in the requirements schedule. This information has to do with the magnitude of demand. For instance, there appear to be two levels of component demand in this example. The first covers weeks 1 to 4 and 10 to 12; the second covers weeks 5 to 9. By computing an economic lot size for each of these time intervals and placing orders accordingly, the total cost can be reduced by more than $1,000. Yet this proposal would be much more diffi-

FIGURE 12.2 Economic order quantity example

Week number	1	2	3	4	5	6	7	8	9	10	11	12
Requirements	10	10	15	20	70	180	250	270	230	40	0	10
Order quantity	166					166	223	270	230	166		
Beginning inventory	166	156	146	131	111	207	250	270	230	166	126	126
Ending inventory	156	146	131	111	41	27	0	0	0	126	126	116

Ordering cost	$1,800
Inventory carrying cost	3,065
Total cost	$4,865
(Economic lot size = 166)	

Source: W. L. Berry, "Lot Sizing Procedures for Requirements Planning Systems: A Framework for Analysis," Second quarter, 1972, *Production and Inventory Management,* page 22. Journal of the American Production and Inventory Control Society, Inc.

cult to implement because the determination of different demand levels would require a very complex decision rule.

Periodic order quantities (POQ)

One way of reducing the high inventory carrying cost associated with fixed lot sizes is to use the EOQ formula to compute an economic time interval between replenishment orders. This is done by dividing the EOQ by the mean demand rate. In the example above, the economic time interval would be approximately two weeks (166/92.1 = 1.8). The procedure then calls for ordering *exactly* the requirements for this interval. Applying this procedure to the data in our example (Figure 12.1) produces Figure 12.3. One result is the same number of orders as the EOQ procedure, but with lot sizes ranging from 20 to 520 units. Consequently, the inventory carrying cost has been reduced by 30 percent, thereby improving the total cost of the 12-week requirements schedule by 19 percent in comparison with the EOQ result above.

Although the periodic order quantity (POQ) procedure improves the inventory cost performance by allowing the lot sizes to vary, like the EOQ procedure it, too, ignores much of the information contained in the requirements schedule. That is, the replenishment orders are constrained to occur at fixed time intervals, thereby ruling out the possibility of combining orders during periods of light product demand, e.g., during weeks 1 through 4 in the example. If, for example, the orders placed in weeks 1 and 3 were combined and a single order were placed in week 1 for 55 units, the combined costs can be further reduced by $160 or 4 percent.

Part period balancing (PPB)

The part period balancing procedure uses all of the information provided by the requirements schedule. In determining the lot size for an order, this procedure tries to equate the total costs of placing orders and carrying inven-

FIGURE 12.3 Periodic order quantity example

Week number	1	2	3	4	5	6	7	8	9	10	11	12
Requirements	10	10	15	20	70	180	250	270	230	40	0	10
Order quantity	20		35		250		520		270			10
Beginning inventory	20	10	35	20	250	180	520	270	270	40	0	10
Ending inventory	10	0	20	0	180	0	270	0	40	0	0	0

Ordering cost	$1,800
Inventory carrying cost	2,145
Total cost	$3,945

Source: W. L. Berry, "Lot Sizing Procedures for Requirements Planning Systems: A Framework for Analysis," Second quarter, 1972, *Production and Inventory Management*, page 23. Journal of the American Production and Inventory Control Society, Inc.

tory. This point can be illustrated by considering the alternative lot-size choices available at the beginning of week 1. These include placing an order covering the requirements for:

1. Week 1 only.
2. Weeks 1 and 2
3. Weeks 1, 2, and 3.
4. Weeks 1, 2, 3, and 4.
5. Weeks 1, 2, 3, 4, 5, etc.

The inventory carrying costs for these five alternatives are shown below. These calculations are based on the average inventory per period.

1. $(\$2) \cdot [(1/2) \cdot (10)] = \$10.$
2. $(\$2) \cdot [(1/2) \cdot (10) + (3/2) \cdot (10)] = \$40.$
3. $(\$2) \cdot [(1/2) \cdot (10) + (3/2) \cdot (10) + (5/2)\,(15)] = \$115.$
4. $(\$2) \cdot [(1/2) \cdot (10) + (3/2) \cdot 10 + (5/2) \cdot (15) + (7/2) \cdot (20)] = \$255.$
5. $(\$2) \cdot [(1/2) \cdot (10) + (3/2) \cdot (10) + (5/2) \cdot (15) + (7/2) \cdot (20) + (9/2) \cdot (70)] = \$885.$

In this case, the inventory carrying cost for alternative 4, ordering 55 units to cover the demand for the first four weeks, most nearly approximates the ordering cost of \$300. That is, alternative 4 "balances" the cost of carrying inventory with ordering. Therefore, an order should be placed at the beginning of the first week and the next ordering decision need not be made until the beginning of week 5.

When this procedure is applied to the example data, the result is Figure 12.4. As seen, the total inventory cost is reduced by almost \$500, or is 13 percent lower than the cost obtained with the periodic order quantity procedure. Notice that this procedure permits both the lot size and the time between orders to vary. Thus, for example, in periods of low requirements, this procedure results in smaller lot sizes and longer time intervals between

FIGURE 12.4 Part period balancing example

Week number	1	2	3	4	5	6	7	8	9	10	11	12
Requirements	10	10	15	20	70	180	250	270	230	40	0	10
Order quantity	55				70	180	250	270	270			10
Beginning inventory	55	45	35	20	70	180	250	270	270	40	0	10
Ending inventory	45	35	20	0	0	0	0	0	40	0	0	0

Ordering cost	\$2,100
Inventory carrying cost	1,385
Total cost	\$3,485

Source: W. L. Berry, "Lot Sizing Procedures for Requirements Planning Systems: A Framework for Analysis," Second quarter, 1972, *Production and Inventory Management,* page 25. Journal of the American Production and Inventory Control Society, Inc.

orders than occur for periods of high demand. This results in lower inventory-related costs.

Despite the fact that this procedure utilizes all of the information available, it will not always yield the minimum-cost ordering plan. Although this procedure can produce low-cost ordering plans, it may miss the minimum cost plan since it does not evaluate all of the possibilities for ordering material to satisfy the demand in each week of the requirements schedule.

McLaren's order moment (MOM)

This procedure is quite similar to the part period balancing procedure. It evaluates the cost of placing orders for an integral number of future periods, e.g., for period 1 only; periods 1 and 2; periods 1, 2, and 3, etc. However, instead of equating the total costs of placing orders and carrying inventory directly in determining order quantities, as in the case of the part period balancing procedure, the order moment procedure uses a part period accumulation principle.

A part period is one unit of inventory carried for one period. The total number of part periods accumulated across the planning horizon is proportional to the total inventory carrying cost. The McLaren order moment procedure determines the lot size for individual orders by matching the number of accumulated part periods to the number that would be incurred if an order for an EOQ were placed under the conditions of constant demand. This is accomplished by first calculating a target number of part periods, and then accumulating the actual period-by-period part periods until the target is reached. The target value is calculated as follows:

$$OMT = \bar{D}\left[\sum_{t=1}^{T^*-1} t + (TBO - T^*)T^*\right] \tag{12.1}$$

where:

OMT = Order moment target.
$\bar{D}$ = Average requirements per week.
TBO = EOQ/$\bar{D}$.
T^* = The largest integer less than (or equal to) the TBO.

The order moment procedure accumulates requirements from consecutive periods into a tentative order until the accumulated part periods reach or exceed OMT in period k, using the following equation:

$$\sum_{t=1}^{k} (k - 1)D_k \geqslant OMT \tag{12.2}$$

In the period when the accumulated part periods first reach or exceed the OMT value, a second test is made before the lot size for the current order quantity is determined.

The second test is made to see whether it is worthwhile to include one more period's requirement in the order. The test involves comparing the carrying cost incurred by including the requirement for period k in the current order with the cost of placing a new order for that period's requirements in period k. This comparison is made using the following equation:

$$C_H(k - 1)\, D_k \leqslant C_P \tag{12.3}$$

where:

C_H = The inventory carrying cost per period.
k = The period currently under consideration.
D_k = The requirements for period k.
C_P = The ordering cost.

When the accumulated part periods exceed OMT and $C_H(k - 1)\, D_k \leqslant C_P$, the order quantity covers the requirements for periods 1 through k. However, when the accumulated part periods exceed OMT and when $C_H(k - 1)\, D_k > C_P$, the order quantity covers the requirements for periods 1 through $k - 1$.

The example shown in Figure 12.5 applies the MOM procedure to our example data. Note that the accumulated part periods first exceed the OMT target in week 4 when $(1 \cdot 10 + 2 \cdot 15 + 3 \cdot 20) > 73.7$. Since the cost of carrying the 20 units required in week 4 is less than the cost of placing an order in week 4 ($120 < 300$) in this case, the first order is placed in week 1

FIGURE 12.5 McLaren's order moment example

Week number	1	2	3	4	5	6	7	8	9	10	11	12
Requirements	10	10	15	20	70	180	250	270	230	40	0	10
Order quantity	55				70	180	250	270	280			
Beginning inventory	55	45	35	20	70	180	250	270	280	50	10	10
Ending inventory	45	35	20	0	0	0	0	0	50	50	10	0
Part periods	0	10	40	100	180†	250†	270†	230†	0	40	40	70
Exceed target?	No	No	No	Yes	Yes	Yes	Yes	Yes	–	–	–	No, but end of record
$C_H(k-1)D_k$	–	–	–	120	360	500	540	460				60

$\overline{D} = 92.1$
EOQ = 166.2
TBO = 166.2/92.1 = 1.8
$T^* = 1.0$
OMT = 92.1[1.8 − 1)(1)] = 73.7

Ordering cost = $1,800
Inventory carrying cost = 1,445
Total cost = $3,245

† Measured in the following week.

Source: B. J. McLaren, "A Study of Multiple Level Lot-Sizing Techniques for Material Requirements Planning Systems." (Ph.D. dissertation, Purdue University, 1977).

for 55 units. Then, since the accumulated part periods exceed OMT in weeks 5 through 8, and the cost of carrying the next week's requirement exceeds the ordering cost, weekly orders are placed during that time interval.

The total cost of using the order moment procedure in this example is $3,245, which is 7 percent less than the total cost for the part period balancing procedure. In fact, the MOM procedure found the optimal solution in this particular example.

Wagner-Whitin algorithm

One optimizing procedure for determining the minimun-cost ordering plan for a time-phased requirements schedule is the Wagner-Whitin algorithm. Basically, this procedure evaluates all of the possible ways of ordering material to meet the demand in each week of the requirements schedule, using dynamic programming. We will not attempt to describe the computational aspects of the Wagner-Whitin algorithm, in the space available to us here. Rather, we shall note the difference in performance between this procedure and the part period balancing procedure.

When the Wagner-Whitin algorithm is applied to the example, the results are shown as Figure 12.6. (Note that the order quantities are identical to those in Figure 12.5.) The total inventory cost is reduced by $240, or 7 percent, in comparison with the ordering plan produced by the part period balancing procedure in Figure 12.4. The difference between these two plans occurs in the lot size ordered in week 9. The part period balancing procedure did not consider the combined cost of placing orders in both weeks 9 and 12. By spending an additional $60 to carry 10 units of inventory forward from week 9 to 12, the $300 ordering cost in week 12 is avoided. In this case, a saving of $240 in total cost can be achieved. The increase in the number of ordering alternatives considered, however, clearly increases the computations needed in making ordering decisions.

FIGURE 12.6 Wagner-Whitin example

Week number	1	2	3	4	5	6	7	8	9	10	11	12
Requirements	10	10	15	20	70	180	250	270	230	40	0	10
Order quantity	55				70	180	250	270	280			
Beginning inventory	55	45	35	20	70	180	250	270	280	50	10	10
Ending inventory	45	35	20	0	0	0	0	0	50	10	10	0

Ordering cost	$1,800
Inventory carrying cost	1,445
Total cost	$3,245

Source: W. L. Berry, "Lot Sizing Procedures for Requirements Planning Systems: A Framework for Analysis," Second quarter, 1972, *Production and Inventory Management,* page 26. Journal of the American Production and Inventory Control Society, Inc.

Simulation experiments

The example problem we have used to illustrate the procedures is for only one product item, without regard for *its* components, with no rolling through time, and with only a fixed number of weeks of requirements. To better understand the performance of lot-sizing procedures, they should be compared in circumstances more closely related to the dynamics of an industrial situation. Many simulation experiments have been performed to do exactly that.

Figure 12.7 presents summary experimental results. The first experiment shown in this figure is for a single level (i.e., one MRP record) with no uncertainty. MOM, PPB, and POQ are compared to Wagner-Whitin. MOM produces results about 3 percent more costly, PPB about 6 percent, and POQ about 11 percent. The order of magnitude of these differences is more important than the absolute magnitude. Savings of 3 percent in total costs may not be trivial.

Moving down to the third experiment, we see the results for a multilevel situation, again with no uncertainty. In this case, the comparison is not against Wagner-Whitin, but against a dynamic programming procedure that produces close to optimal results in a multilevel environment. The key finding in this experiment is that the results are roughly the same as in the first comparisons, although POQ does do about 50 percent worse than before.

Perhaps the most interesting result in Figure 12.7 is to compare the first and third experiments to the *second* experiment. The second experiment is for a single-level procedure, but *with* uncertainty expressed in the gross

FIGURE 12.7 Summary experimental results

	Procedure			
	Wagner-Whitin	*MOM*	*PPB*	*POQ*
Experiment 1: Percent over Wagner-Whitin cost; Single level, no uncertainty*	0	3.06	5.74	10.72
Experiment 2: Percent over Wagner-Whitin cost; Single level, uncertainty*	0	2.71	−.67	2.58
Experiment 3: Percent over nearly optimal procedure; Multilevel, no uncertainty†	.77	3.07	6.92	16.91
Computing time†	.30	.11	.10	.08

* These results are from U. Wemmerlöv and D. C. Whybark, "Lot-Sizing under Uncertainty in a Rolling Horizon Environment." Proceedings, Midwest AIDS Conference, Milwaukee, April 1982.

† These results are from B. J. McLaren "A Study of Multiple Level Lot-Sizing Techniques for Material Requirements Planning Systems" (Ph.D. dissertation, Purdue University, 1977). The multilevel procedure was designed specifically to take into account the relationships of a single part to its components and parents. The computing time is the average CPU time for one sample problem.

requirements data. The results here are quite mixed. Note that PPB does *better* than Wagner-Whitin, and both MOM and POQ are within 3 percent of Wagner-Whitin.

The conditions modeled in the second experiment replicate conditions likely to be found in actual industrial situations. Moreover, other studies show that as uncertainty grows increasingly larger, it becomes very hard to distinguish between the lot-sizing procedures' performance.

The message is clear. Lot-sizing enhancements to an MRP system should only be done *after* major uncertainties have been removed from the system. That is, *after* data integrity is in place, other MPC system modules are working, stability is present at the MPS level, etc. If the MPC is not performing effectively, that is the place to start, *not* with lot-sizing procedures.

DETERMINATION OF PURCHASE ORDER QUANTITIES

So far, we have discussed procedures for determining lot sizes for manufactured items in an MRP environment. In many firms, a high percentage of component items are purchased from external sources. The purchase quantity decision can be very complex when price discounts are available for placing orders in large quantities and/or when transportation savings are available for shipping full carload quantities instead of less than carload lots. We start this section with a brief description of the purchasing discount problem, and then turn to three procedures which take into account such discounts: least unit cost, least period cost, and McLaren order moment.

The purchasing discount problem

To illustrate each of these procedures, an example problem will be used based on the first four periods' requirements shown in Figure 12.8. Note that in addition to the ordering and the inventory carrying costs used in the previous examples, base and discount prices and the discount quantity have been added for this item.

A convention has developed in the purchasing research literature that affects the procedures we will describe. The purchasing procedures use *pe-*

FIGURE 12.8 Example purchase discount problem

Period	1	2	3	4	5	6	7	8	9	10	11	12
Requirements	80	100	124	100	50	50	100	125	125	100	50	100

Ordering cost = \$100
Inventory carrying cost = \$2/period/unit
Base price = \$500/unit
Discount price = \$450/unit
Discount quantity = 350 units

riod-end inventory balances to calculate the inventory carrying cost. This is not the same convention as that used previously for the manufacturing lot-size calculations. To be consistent with the previous purchasing lot-sizing research, we will use the period-end inventory convention.

The increase of the quantity discount information adds complexity to the solution of this ordering problem. Moreover, the specification of an "all units" discount, i.e., a $500/unit price for units 1 through 349 and a $450 price for a *total* order quantity exceeding 349 units, presents further computational difficulties. Alternatively, an "additional units" discount is sometimes specified, i.e., a $500/unit price for units 1 through 349 and a $450/unit price for any *additional* units ordered in excess of 349. Unlike the additional units discount schedule, the all units discount applies to all units purchased when at least the discount quantity is purchased. The all units discount is considerably more common in industry than the additional units discount, and creates a considerably more difficult decision problem.

The ordering procedures we now consider assume the use of an all units discount, as well as the earlier assumptions listed for the manufacturing order quantities under MRP (except average inventory). In addition, several conventions are followed for all of the procedures. One is to consider orders sequentially, which would cover an increasing number of periods. For the example shown in Figure 12.8, this would be orders of 80 (1 period), 180 (2 periods), etc. In addition, an order for the exact discount quantity (350 units) is considered. Another convention is that calculations are made for at least the number of periods needed to reach the discount quantity (period 4 in the example). An explanation of the details of each procedure is provided in the following paragraphs.

Least unit cost. The least unit cost (LUC) procedure evaluates different order quantities by accumulating requirements, at least through the period in which the discount can be obtained until the cost/unit starts to increase. The order is placed for the quantity that provides the least unit cost. There are three steps in using this procedure. First, requirements are accumulated through an integral number of periods until the quantity to be ordered is sufficient to qualify for the discount price. The next step is to determine whether the discount should be accepted on the basis of the least unit cost criterion. The final step is to evaluate ordering a quantity exactly equal to the discount quantity. If the least unit cost criterion indicates that neither the integral number of periods nor exactly the discount quantity is the most economical order, the order will be placed for a quantity without the discount.

These steps are illustrated using Figure 12.9 and the example problem shown in Figure 12.8. The setup cost of $100 is incurred once it has been determined that an order will be placed. The inventory carrying cost is accumulated at $2 per unit times the number of periods it will be carried until the period in which it is used. The base price per unit is $500 per unit until a point during period 4, hereafter called "period 3*," the time at

FIGURE 12.9 Least unit cost example

Period	Require-ments	Cumulative require-ments	Setup cost	Inventory carrying cost	Unit purchase price	Cumulative total cost	Cost/unit
1	80	80	$100	$ 0	$500	$ 40,100	$501.25
2	100	180	100	200	500	90,300†	501.67
3	124	304	100	696	500	152,796	502.62
3*	64	350	100	972	450	158,572	453.06
4	100	404	100	1,296	450	183,196	453.46

†(180 × 500) + $100 + $200 = $90,300.

which the cumulative requirements exactly equal the discount quantity and where the unit price drops to $450. The additional inventory carrying cost will be (350 − 304) × $2 × 3 periods ($276) as the remaining 46 units would not be used until period 4. The total inventory carrying cost for period 3* is $276 + $696 = $972. Cost per unit is the total cost divided by the cumulative requirements. When the cost per unit increases (as in period 4) and the discount quantity has been surpassed, the LUC heuristic chooses as the lot size the quantity which provides minimum cost per unit (i.e., $453.06, lot size = 350).

Least period cost. The least period cost (LPC) works in the same manner as the least unit cost procedure, except that the criterion for lot sizing is changed. The calculation of costs in LPC is the same as in the LUC procedure (Figure 12.9). The difference between LPC and LUC is that LPC uses the lowest cost per *period* to determine the lot size instead of the lowest cost per *unit*. The number of periods of demand considered is the divisor for the cost/period calculation. At period 3* where the exact discount quantity is considered, the period is determined by adding the fraction of the period proportional to the quantity required to qualify for the discount [3 + (350 − 304)/100] = 3.46, where 100 is the requirement in the split period (4). The LPC procedure uses the cost per period as the criterion for lot sizing, and for this example, the lot size would be 80, as is indicated in Figure 12.10.

McLaren's order moment. The McLaren's order moment (MOM) procedure works somewhat differently. First, the attractiveness of the discount is measured by calculating the number of part periods of inventory that would have to be carried to offset the potential savings from the discount. Part periods are accumulated by summing the number of units to be carried times the number of periods they are carried. Next, the actual number of part periods necessary to qualify for the discount is determined from the requirements and the decision whether to order exactly the discount quantity is made, even if it means splitting requirements to qualify exactly for the discount. If the discount is favorable, the order placed will be for the dis-

FIGURE 12.10 Least period cost example

Period	Cumulative requirements	Cumulative total cost	Cost/period
1	80	$ 40,100	$40,100
2	180	90,930	45,150
3	304	152,796	50,932
3*	350	158,572	45,930
4	404	193,196	45,799

count quantity. If it is unfavorable, McLaren's procedure for determining a lot size without discounts is used.

Figure 12.11 presents an application of the McLaren procedure to the example purchase discount problem. The first step is to calculate the number of part periods that would exactly offset the savings available from the discount. This is termed the *target level* and is the dollar savings gained by taking the discount divided by the incremental cost of carrying an additional unit for one period. Equation (12.4) expresses the calculation of the target level. To perform the lot sizing , the actual cumulative part periods until the discount quantity is exceeded are computed and tested against the target level, as shown in Figure 12.11.

$$\text{Target level} = \frac{(\text{Base price} - \text{Discount price}) \times \text{Discount quantity}}{\text{Inventory carrying cost per period}}$$
$$= [(\$500 - \$450) \times 350]/2 = \$8{,}750 \qquad (12.4)$$

At period 4, the cumulative requirements exceed the discount quantity, and the cumulative part-periods are less than the target level. This indicates that the discount will more than offset the extra carrying costs associated with the larger quantity. The lot size is set to 350. The requirements in period 4 are then reset to 404 − 350 = 54. Note that if the number of part periods exceeds the target at four periods, the comparison is made for exactly 350 units to determine whether splitting the period's requirements is worthwhile.

FIGURE 12.11 McLaren's order moment example

Period	Requirements	Cumulative requirements	Part periods	Cumulative part periods
1	80	80	80 × 0 = 0	0
2	100	180	100 × 1 = 100	100
3	124	304	124 × 2 = 248	348
4	100	404	100 × 3 = 300	648

The essence of the MOM procedure is to first answer the question, is it worthwhile to carry the extra inventory required to qualify for the quantity discount? The target level states how much extra inventory *can* be carried (in part period terms) and still make the discount worthwhile. If the amount that *must* be carried, given the actual requirements, is less, the decision is to order the discount quantity. To decide whether to purchase even more than the discount quantity, the look-ahead feature is employed. It is described next.

Look-ahead feature

Each of the three purchase discount procedures can be used with a *look-ahead* enhancement. After the procedure has determined the initial lot size, the look-ahead feature performs a check to see whether the cost of carrying an additional period's requirements (or the remainder of a period which has had its requirements split), is less than the cost of the setup required to supply that period's requirements in a separate order. If the cost of carrying the additional inventory is less, the requirements are added to the original lot and the look-ahead procedure is repeated on the following period's requirements, and again for the next period until it no longer pays to carry the additional inventory.

An illustration of the look-ahead feature will be developed for the example purchase discount problem. For the least unit cost example in Figure 12.9, a lot size of 350 units has been determined. The remaining requirements in period 4 are 54. Using the look-ahead test, calculate the carrying cost of 54 units to period 4 and campare it to the setup cost:

$$54 \text{ units} \times 3 \text{ periods} \times \$2/\text{unit} = \$324$$
$$\text{Setup cost} = \$100$$

The look-ahead test fails if carrying costs exceed the setup cost; the lot size remains at 350. If the carrying cost had been less than the setup cost, the additional units would be included in the lot size and the look-ahead feature would be applied to the requirements in period 5.

Performance comparison

Simulation experiments have been conducted to evaluate the performance of these three lot-sizing procedures. One set of experimental results is shown in Figure 12.12. Here the least period cost (LPC) and the least unit cost (LUC) procedures have been evaluated against a mixed integer programming (MIP) procedure. The results indicate that the LUC procedure is superior to LPC.

A second set of simulation experiments provides a performance comparison of the least unit cost (LUC) and the McLaren order moment (MOM)

FIGURE 12.12 Summary experimental results: LPC versus LUC

Procedure	*Average percentage above optimal cost*	*Maximum percentage above optimal cost*	*Percentage of solutions that were optimal*	*Average CPU time (seconds)*
MIP	0	0	100	97.46
LPC	2.376	11.12	34	.0029
LUC	.021	.22	68	.0030

Source: T. E. Callarman and D. C. Whybark, *Purchase Quantity Discounts in an MRP Environment,* Discussion Paper no. 72 (Indiana University, 1977).

procedures. In these experiments, the look-ahead feature was a part of the comparison. The results in Figure 12.13 indicate that the LUC heuristic results in average costs that are slightly better than those with MOM. In addition, a cost improvement is indicated for the look-ahead feature for both the MOM and LUC procedures. The computer time, though small in absolute terms, is substantially less for MOM than the LUC procedure and is even more favorable with look ahead.

From a practical standpoint, there is little cost difference between the LUC and MOM procedures with the look-ahead feature. They both are superior to the LPC procedure. Also, the cost differences may appear small in an absolute sense. Three points must be made about this. First, the comparisons are among reasonable procedures and may understate the saving over practice. Secondly, even a small unit saving for a company whose purchases represent a large proportion of the cost of goods sold can be a large total which passes right through to the bottom line. Finally, the savings shown are based on *total* cost. If just the controllable costs (setup, inventory, and potential discount) are used, the percentage differences are highly magnified.

FIGURE 12.13 Summary experimental results: LUC versus MOM

Procedure	*Mean cost/unit*	*Mean percent above LUC cost*	*Average CPU time (seconds)*
LUC (with look ahead)	$477.99	0.000	.0384
MOM (with look ahead)	478.00	0.002	.0137
LUC (without look ahead)	478.53	0.114	.0438
MOM (without look ahead)	479.04	0.215	.0217

Source: A. D. Hemphill and D. C. Whybark, *A Simulation Comparison of MRP Purchase Discount Procedures,* Discussion Paper no. 96 (Indiana University, 1978).

BUFFERING CONCEPTS

In this section we deal with another advanced concept in MRP, the use of buffering mechanisms to protect against uncertainties. We do, however, want to make the same proviso that was made for lot sizing: Buffering is not the way to make up for a poorly operating MRP system. First things must come first.

Categories of uncertainty

There are two basic sources of uncertainty that affect an MRP system: demand and supply uncertainty. These are further separated into two types: quantity uncertainty and timing uncertainty. The combination of sources and types provides the four categories of uncertainty that are summarized in Figure 12.14 and illustrated in Figure 12.15.

Demand timing uncertainty is illustrated in Figure 12.15 by timing changes in the requirements from period to period. For example, the projected requirements for 372 units in period 7 have actually occurred in period 4. This shift might have resulted from a change in the promise date to a customer or from a change in a planned order for a higher-level item on which this item is used.

Supply timing uncertainty can arise from variations in vendor lead times or shop flow times. Thus, once an order is released, the exact timing of its arrival is uncertain. In Figure 12.15, for example, a receipt scheduled for period 3 actually arrived in period 1. Note that in this case the uncertainty is not over the amount of the order, but over its timing. The entire order may be late or early.

Demand quantity uncertainty is manifest when the amount of a requirement varies, perhaps randomly, about some mean value. This might occur when the master production schedule is increased or decreased to reflect changes in customer orders or the demand forecast. It can also occur when there are changes on higher level items on which this item is used, or when

FIGURE 12.14 Categories of uncertainty in MRP systems

	Sources	
Types	*Demand*	*Supply*
Timing	Requirements shift from one period to another	Orders not received when due
Quantity	Requirements for more or less than planned	Orders received for more or less than planned

Source: D. C. Whybark and J. G. Williams, "Material Requirements Planning under Uncertainty," *Decision Sciences*, October 1976, p. 598.

FIGURE 12.15 Examples of the four catagories of uncertainty

	Periods									
	1	*2*	*3*	*4*	*5*	*6*	*7*	*8*	*9*	*10*
Demand timing:										
Projected requirements	0	0	0	0	0	0	372	130	0	255
Actual requirements	0	0	0	372	130	0	146	255	143	0
Supply timing:										
Planned receipts	0	0	502	0	0	403	0	0	144	0
Actual receipts	502	0	0	0	0	403	0	0	144	0
Demand quantity:										
Projected requirements	85	122	42	190	83	48	41	46	108	207
Actual requirements	103	77	0	101	124	15	0	100	80	226
Supply quantity:										
Planned receipts	0	161	0	271	51	0	81	109	0	327
Actual receipts	0	158	0	277	50	0	77	113	0	321

Source: D. C. Whybark and J. G. Williams, "Material Requirements Planning under Uncertainty," *Decision Sciences,* October 1976, p. 599.

there are variations in inventory levels. In the example of Figure 12.15, the period 1 projected requirements of 85 actually involved a usage of 103 units.

Supply quantity uncertainty typically arises when there are shortages of lower level material, when production lots incur scrap losses, or when production overruns occur. Figure 12.15 illustrates this category of uncertainty, where the actual quantity received varied around the planned receipts.

Safety stock and safety lead time

There are two basic ways to buffer uncertainty in an MRP system. One of these is to specify a quantity of safety stock in much the same manner as is done with statistical inventory control techniques. The second method, safety lead time, plans order releases earlier than indicated by the requirements plan and schedules their receipt earlier than the required due date. Both approaches produce an increase in inventory levels to provide a buffer against uncertainty, but the techniques operate quite differently. The differences are illustrated in Figure 12.16.

In the first case shown in Figure 12.16, no buffering is used. A net requirement occurs in period 5, and a planned order is created in period 3 to cover it. In the second case, a safety stock of 20 units is specified. This means that the safety stock level will be broken in period 3 unless an order is received. The MRP logic thus creates a planned order in period 1 to prevent this condition. The final case in Figure 12.16 illustrates use of safety lead time. In this example, a safety lead time of one period is included. The net result is the planned order being created in period 2 with a due date of period 4.

FIGURE 12.16 Safety stock and safety lead time buffering

Order quantity = 50 units
Lead time = 2 periods

Period

No buffering used		*1*	*2*	*3*	*4*	*5*
Gross requirements		20	40	20	0	30
Scheduled receipts			50			
Projected available balance	40	20	30	10	10	30
Planned order releases				50		

Safety stock = 20 units		*1*	*2*	*3*	*4*	*5*
Gross requirements		20	40	20	0	30
Scheduled receipts			50			
Projected available balance	40	20	30	60	60	30
Planned order releases		50				

Safety lead time = 1 period		*1*	*2*	*3*	*4*	*5*
Gross requirements		20	40	20	0	30
Scheduled receipts			50			
Projected available balance	40	20	30	10	60	30
Planned order releases			50			

Source: D. C. Whybark and J. G. Williams, "Material Requirements Planning under Uncertainty," *Decision Sciences*, October 1976, p. 601.

Most MRP software packages can easily accommodate safety stock, since the planned orders can be determined simply by subtracting the safety stock from the initial inventory balance when determining the projected available balance. Safety lead time is a bit more difficult. This cannot be achieved by simply inflating the lead time by the amount of the safety lead time. In our example, this approach would not produce the result shown as the last case in Figure 12.16. The due date for the order would be period 5 instead of period 4. Thus, the planned due date, as well as the planned release date, must be changed.

Both safety stock and safety lead time illustrate the fundamental problem with all MRP buffering techniques: They lie to the system. The *real* need date for the planned order shown in Figure 12.16 is week 5. If the *real* lead time is two periods, the *real* launch date should be period 3. Putting in buffers can lead to behavioral problems in the shop, since the resulting schedules do not tell the truth. An informal system may be created to tell people what is really needed. This, in turn, might lead to larger buffers. There is a critical need to communicate the reasoning behind the use of safety stock and safety lead times, and to create a working MPC system that minimizes the need for buffers.

Safety stock and safety lead performance comparisons

Simulation experiments have been reported which indicate that there is a preference for using either safety stock or safety lead time, depending upon the category of uncertainty to be buffered. These results show a distinct preference for using safety lead time in all cases where demand or supply *timing* uncertainty exists. Likewise, the experiments show a strong preference for using safety stock in all cases where there is uncertainty in either the demand or supply *quantity*.

Typical results from these experiments are shown in Figures 12.17 and 12.18. Figure 12.17 compares safety stock and safety lead time for simulated

FIGURE 12.17 Experimental results: Average inventory versus service level with timing uncertainty

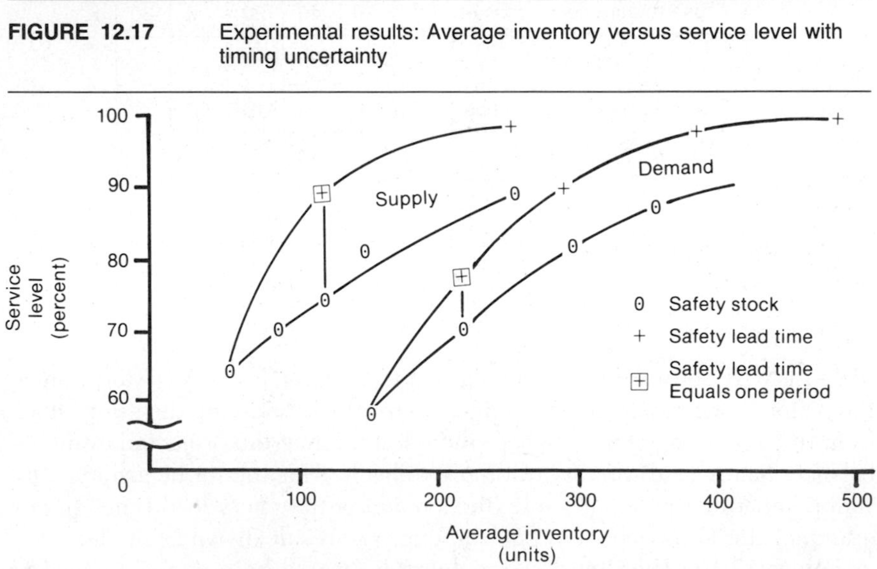

Source: D. C. Whybark and J. G. Williams, "Material Requirements Planning under Uncertainty," *Decision Sciences,* October 1976, p. 602.

FIGURE 12.18 Experimental results: Average inventory versus service level with quantity uncertainty

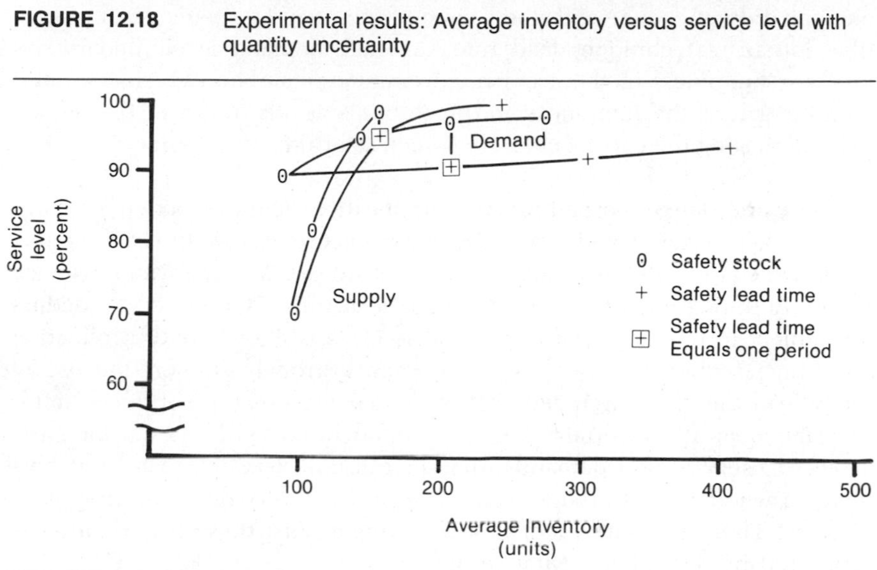

Source: D. C. Whybark and J. G. Williams, "Material Requirements Planning under Uncertainty," *Decision Sciences,* October 1976, p. 603.

situations similar to the top two examples shown in Figure 12.15. The horizontal axis shows the average inventory held, and the vertical axis depicts the service level in percentage terms, that is, the horizontal axis is based on the period-by-period actual inventory values in the simulation; the vertical axis is based upon the frequency with which the actual requirements were met from inventory.

For both the supply and the demand timing uncertainty cases, Figure 12.17 shows a strong preference for safety lead time buffering. For any given level of inventory, a higher service level can be achieved with safety lead time than with safety stock. For any given level of service, safety lead time can provide the level with a smaller inventory investment.

Figure 12.18 shows the comparison for uncertainty in quantities. This simulated situation is similar to the bottom two examples shown in Figure 12.15. The results are a bit more difficult to see since the graphs for supply and demand uncertainty overlap. Nevertheless, the results are again clear. For any given level of inventory investment, higher service levels are achieved by the use of safety stocks than by the use of safety lead times. This result is true for situations involving quantity uncertainty in both demand and supply.

The results of the experiments provide general guidelines for choosing between the two buffering techniques. Under conditions of uncertainty in timing, safety lead time is the preferred technique, while safety stock is preferred under conditions of quantity uncertainty. The experimental conclusions did not change with the source of the uncertainty (demand or supply), lot-sizing technique, lead time, average demand level, uncertainty level, or lumpiness in the gross requirements data. The experiments also indicate that as the lumpiness and uncertainty levels increase, the importance of making the correct choice between safety stock and safety lead time increases.

There are some important practical implications of these guidelines. Supply timing uncertainty and demand quantity uncertainty are the two categories for which the differences in service levels are largest. An obvious instance of supply timing uncertainty is in vendor lead times. Orders from vendors are subject to timing uncertainty because of variability in both production and transportation times. These experiments strongly support the use of safety lead time for purchased parts experiencing this type of uncertainty. Demand quantity uncertainty often is found in an MRP system for parts subject to service part demand. Another cause of demand quantity uncertainty is when an end product can be made from very different options or features. The use of safety stock for buffering against these uncertainties is supported by the experimental results.

Other buffering mechanisms

Before leaving the discussion of uncertainty, it is useful to consider some additional alternatives for dealing with uncertainty. One useful way to cope with uncertainty is to reduce it. That is, rather than living with uncertainty, an alternative is to reduce it to an absolute minimum. In fact, that is one of the major objectives of MPC systems.

For example, increasing the accuracy of demand forecasts and the development of effective procedures for translating the demand for products into master schedules reduces the amount of uncertainty that is transmitted to the MRP system. Along these same lines, freezing the master schedule for some period of time achieves the same result. Developing an effective priority system for moving parts and components through the shop reduces the uncertainty in lead times. Responsive shop-floor control systems can achieve better due date performance, thereby reducing uncertainty. Procedures that improve the accuracy of the data in the MRP system reduce uncertainty regarding on-hand inventory levels. Increased inspection and more stringent quality control procedures reduce the number of defective units in a production lot. Other activities could be mentioned, but all focus on the reduction of the amount of uncertainty that needs to be accommodated in an MRP system.

Another way to deal with uncertainty in an MRP system is to provide for slack in the production system in one way or another. Production slack is caused by having additional time, manpower, machine capacity, etc., over that which is specifically needed to produce the planned amount of product. This extra production capacity could be used to produce an oversized lot to allow for shrinkage in that lot through the process. It could be used to allow for the production of lots on overtime or for additional machinery to speed their progress through the shop. Thus, providing additional capacity in the shop allows for accommodating greater quantities than are planned in a given time period, or for expediting jobs through the shop. It must be understood however, that slack costs money. In fact, the objective of a good MPC system should be to *reduce* the slack.

NERVOUSNESS

Several enhancements to MRP systems have been described in this chapter. However, it should be recognized that some of the lot-sizing procedures can contribute to the problem of "nervousness," i.e., instability, in the MRP plans. In this section, we discuss the problem of nervousness in MRP systems and guidelines for reducing the magnitude of this problem.

Sources of MRP system nervousness

MRP system nervousness is commonly defined as changes in MRP plans, which are produced even though there are not significant changes in the master production schedule. The changes can involve the quantity or timing of planned orders or scheduled receipts. The example shown as Figure 12.19 illustrates just such a case. Here, a reduction of one unit in the master schedule in week 2 produced a significant change in the planned orders for item A. This change had an even more profound impact on component part B. It is hard to imagine that a *reduction* at the MPS level could create a past-due condition, but that is precisely what is illustrated in Figure 12.19. The example illustrates how the change caused by a relatively minor shift in the master schedule is amplified by the use of the periodic order quantity (POQ) lot-sizing procedure.

There are a number of ways that relatively minor changes in the MRP system can create nervousness and instability in the MRP plans. These include planned orders which are released in an unplanned quantity or which are prematurely released, unplanned demand (as for spare parts or engineering requirements), and shifts in MRP parameter values such as safety stock, safety lead time, or planned lead-time values. The nervousness created by such changes is most damaging in MRP systems with many levels in the product structure. Furthermore, the use of some lot-sizing techniques, such as POQ, can amplify the system nervousness at lower levels in the product structure, as indicated by the example in Figure 12.19.

Reducing MRP system nervousness

There are several ways of reducing the nervousness in MRP systems. First, it is important to reduce the causes of changes to the MRP plan. It is important to introduce stability into the master schedule through such de-

FIGURE 12.19 MRP system nervousness example

Before reducing second-week requirements by one unit:
Item A
POQ = 5 weeks
Lead time = 2 weeks

Week		1	2	3	4	5	6	7	8
Gross requirements		2	24	3	5	1	3	4	50
Scheduled receipts									
Projected available balance	28	26	2	13	8	7	4	0	0
Planned order releases		14					50		

Component B
POQ = 5 weeks
Lead time = 4 weeks

Week		1	2	3	4	5	6	7	8
Gross requirements		14					50		
Scheduled receipts		14							
Projected available balance	2	2	2	2	2	2	0	0	0
Planned order releases			48						

After second-week requirement change:
Item A
POQ = 5 weeks
Lead time = 2 weeks

Week		1	2	3	4	5	6	7	8
Gross requirements		2	(23)	3	5	1	3	4	50
Scheduled receipts					58	57	54	50	0
Projected available balance	28	26	3	0	**58**	**57**	**54**	**50**	**0**
Planned order releases			63						

Component B
POQ = 5 weeks
Lead time = 4 weeks

Week		1	2	3	4	5	6	7	8
Gross requirements			63						
Scheduled receipts		14							
Projected available balance	2	16	−47						
Planned order releases	(47)								

Past due →

vices as freezing and time fences. Similarly, it is important to reduce the incidence of unplanned demands by incorporating spare parts forecasts into MRP record gross requirements. Furthermore, it is necessary to follow the MRP plan with regard to the timing and the quantity of planned order releases. Finally, it is important to control the introduction of parameter changes such as changes in safety stock levels or planned lead times. All of these actions will help dampen the small adjustments that can trigger MRP system nervousness.

A second guideline for reducing MRP system nervousness involves the selective use of lot-sizing procedures. That is, if nervousness still exists after reducing the causes above, different lot-sizing procedures might be used at different product structure levels. One approach is to use fixed order quantities at the top level, using either fixed order quantities or lot-for-lot at intermediate levels, and using period order quantities at the bottom level. Since the fixed order quantity procedure passes along only order timing changes (and not changes in order quantity), this procedure tends to dampen lot-size-induced nervousness. Clearly the fixed order quantity values need to be monitored, since changes in the level of requirements may tend to make such quantities uneconomical over time.

A third guideline for reducing nervousness involves the use of the firm planned order in MRP (or MPS) records. The use of firm planned orders tends to stabilize the requirements for lower-level items. The offsetting cost, however, is the necessary maintenance of firm planned orders by MRP planners.

These guidelines provide methods for reducing nervousness in MRP plans. There is a distinction, however, between nervousness in the MRP *plans* and nervousness in the *execution* of MRP system plans. Nervousness in the execution of the plans can also influence behavior. If the system users see the plans changing, they may make arbitrary or defensive decisions. This can further aggravate changes in plans.

One way to deal with the execution issue is simply to reduce the frequency with which the updated information is passed to system users. This suggestion would argue against the use of net change MRP systems, or at least against publishing every change. An alternative is simply to have more intelligent users. A well-trained user responding to the problem indicated in Figure 12.19 might, through bottom-up replanning, change the lot sizes to eliminate the problem. However, Figure 12.19 does indicate that this is not an easy problem to detect. Many aspects are counter-intuitive. The fact still is that more intelligent users will make more intelligent execution decisions. User education may be the best initial investment!

OTHER ADVANCED MRP CONCEPTS

There are several additional MRP concepts or conventions that are used in practice to facilitate use of the system. The applicability of some of these ideas depends upon the company environment. In this section, we briefly deal with timing conventions, bucketless MRP systems, phantom assemblies, scrap allowances, and automatic updating of MRP data base elements.

Timing conventions

The timing convention we have used in the MRP records throughout this book has been that a gross requirement was due at the *beginning* of the period. Other conventions are sometimes used, and to some extent, any convention will work if it is consistently applied and universally understood.

If shop paper for an order specifies a due date in a particular week, this is interpreted as meaning the *end* of that week. That is, if an order is due in week 3 and is done by Friday of week 3, it is on time. This obviously cannot work if the order is to satisfy a gross requirement for which it was assumed that completion would be at the beginning of week 3.

The problem is only partially solved by making the due date Monday. It still takes time to close out the shop order, recognize the new on-hand balance, create shop orders for the parent item, pick the parts, move them, and begin work. For this reason, some firms make the due dates for a shop order the week prior to the one in which the parent item is to start. This timing convention has the same result as using one week of safety lead time. In fact, behaviorally, the shop may use all of the week except the weekend by not completing the order until Friday.

Bucketless systems

To some extent, the problems of timing conventions are tied to the use of time buckets. When the buckets are small enough, the problems are reduced significantly. However, smaller buckets mean more buckets, which increases the review, storage, and computation costs. A bucketless MRP system specifies the exact release and due dates for each requirement, scheduled receipt, and planned order. The managerial reports are printed out on whatever basis is required, including by exact dates.

Bucketless MRP systems are a better way to use the computer. Above and beyond that, the approach can allow for better maintenance of lead time offsets and provide more precise time-phased information. The approach is consistent with state-of-the-art software, and many firms are now successfully using bucketless systems.

Phantom assemblies

Another issue related to timing has to do with *phantom assemblies*. In essence, a phantom assembly is any assembly that does not go into and out of inventory. That is, it is an assembly that exists physically but is normally not stored, so inventory transactions are not posted against it. An example would be the assembly of a drawer in a chest that is made as the chest is being assembled. Still another example is the chest itself which is assembled but thereafter finished (stain, etc.). We see then that many times there can be phantoms within phantoms.

The need for phantom assemblies can potentially be eliminated by redesigning the bill of materials and engineering drawings. Note that in the drawer/chest example, this would mean having the drawer parts listed on the single-level bill of materials for the chest, and the drawer itself no longer existing. This will not always work. There are times when the phantom does exist; i.e., the drawer does not get assembled into the chest and must be inventoried. This can occur when more subassemblies (drawers) than needed are produced or when the subassemblies are sold as service parts.

If subassemblies are not treated as phantoms, the bill of material processing logic will necessarily create orders for *both* chests *and* drawers. One reason, therefore, that firms use phantom assemblies is to avoid the work and time associated with closing out shop orders and opening new shop orders. That is, the objective of the phantom assembly treatment of the drawers is to pull drawer parts automatically by only launching orders for chest assemblies and not drawer assemblies.

The phantom condition can also exist in areas that are not truly assemblies. For example, many firms do not typically inventory parts coming off a paint line (even though painted parts have different part numbers than unpainted ones); they simply flow into final assembly and not through inventory, *unless* they are to be used for service parts or extras are produced.

Phantom bill treatment in MRP requires special processing. The net requirements for the phantom bills must be determined (in case there are any inventories) so they can be passed down to the component, but without creating explicit records. The trick to gross to netting the phantom requirements is to explicitly code a phantom bill (to avoid producing the record) and use a zero lead time offset. Whenever a specific need for phantom items occurs, say for service parts, the phantom itself can be treated as any other MRP record item, with usual order-launching treatment.

Scrap allowances

A concept closely tied to buffering is the use of scrap allowances in calculating the lot size to start into production to reach some desired lot size going into the stockroom. It is a fairly straightforward procedure to use any lot-sizing procedure to determine the lot size and then adjust the result to take account of the scrap allowance. One issue that arises is whether the quantity shown on the shop paper (and as a scheduled receipt), should be the *starting* quantity or the *expected finished* quantity. Practice suggests the use of the former. This requires, however, that each actual occurrence of scrap be transacted and reflected in updated plans.

The overall issue of the scrap allowance is similar to the use of safety stocks for quantity uncertainty buffering. In fact, the two issues are clearly related. One or both of these buffers could be used in a particular situation. The point is that if scrap losses occur, they must be planned for and buffered. It also means that this may be an area where tight control can lead to performance improvements.

Automatic updating

The final enhancement issue we consider is the use of the computer to automatically perform a transaction normally done by MRP planners. A good case in point is the updating of scheduled receipt due dates as indicated by exception coding. That is, the computer software tells an MRP planner that the due date for a scheduled receipt needs to be moved from week 7 to week 6. Why not let the computer do it automatically?

We raise this issue here, under advanced concepts, because the operational issue is similar to that of more sophisticated lot sizing: It is OK—*after* one has the basic house in order. When an MRP system is in place, data integrity is good, the other MPC systems are in place, and users are well trained, *then* automatic updating might make sense.

There are two good reasons for doing the updating of scheduled receipt data automatically. First, the new data will be passed more quickly to shop-floor control; the result will be a more responsive shop-floor control system. The second reason is to save time and effort for the MRP planners. Typically, a large percentage of the exception messages involve minor repositioning of scheduled receipt data. If this is done by the computer, time can be freed up for more useful pursuits.

The key question of whether to do automatic updating or not is behavioral and partly related to system nervousness. Are the users ready for it? Do *they* want it? Will *they* still be accountable for the results? Will *they* have a hand in specifying the logic used to automatically update? Once again, we see this enhancement intimately tied to the development of intelligent system users.

CONCLUDING PRINCIPLES

Chapter 12 describes several advanced concepts and conventions in MRP systems. Many of the ideas are of research interest, but all of them have practical implications, as well. There are, in fact, certain kinds of enhancements that can be made in a well-operating MRP system, if made by knowledgeable professionals, and if implemented with knowledgeable users. We see the following principles as critical:

- MRP enhancement should be done *after* a basic MPC system is in place.
- Discrete lot-sizing procedures for manufacturing can reduce inventory-associated costs. Some procedures work better than others.
- Selecting the appropriate lot-sizing procedure for purchasing can also lead to cost savings.

- Safety stocks are a preferred buffer when the uncertainty is of the quantity category.
- Safety lead times are preferred when uncertainty is of the timing category.
- MRP system nervousness can result from lot-sizing rules, parameter changes, and other causes. The MPC professional must understand this issue and take appropriate precautions.
- In the last analysis, MRP system enhancements depend upon the growth of ever more intelligent users.

REFERENCES

Berry, W. L. "Lot Sizing Procedures for Requirements Planning Systems: A Framework for Analysis." *Production and Inventory Management* 13, no. 2 (2d Quarter 1972), pp. 19–33.

Callarman, T. E., and D. C. Whybark. "Purchase Quantity Discounts in an MRP Environment." Discussion Paper No. 72, Indiana University, 1977.

Dixon, P. S., and E. A. Silver. "A Heuristic Solution Procedure for the Multi-Item, Single Level, Limited Capacity, Lot-Sizing Problem." *Journal of Operations Management* 2, no. 1 (1981).

Elk, Roger D., and James C. Hershauer. "Extended MRP Systems for Evaluating Master Schedules and Materials Requirements Plans." *Production and Inventory Management*, 2d Quarter 1980, pp. 53–66.

Hemphill, A. D., and D. C. Whybark. "A Simulation Comparison of MRP Purchase Discount Procedures." Discussion Paper No. 96, Indiana University, 1978.

Karni, R., and Y. Roll. "A Heuristic Algorithm for the Multi-Item, Lot-Sizing Problem with Capacity Constraints." *AIIE Transactions* 14, no. 4 (December 1982).

McLaren, B. J. "A Study of Multiple Level Lot Sizing Techniques for Material Requirements Planning Systems." Unpublished Ph.D. dissertation, Purdue University, 1977.

Newson, E. F. P. "Multi-Item Lot Size Scheduling by Heuristic, Part I: With Fixed Resources." *Management Science* 21, no. 10 (1975).

Silver, E. A., and H. C. Meal. "A Simple Modification of the EOQ for the Case of a Varying Demand Rate." *Production and Inventory Management*, 4th Quarter 1969.

Steele, D. C. "The Nervous MRP System: How to do Battle." *Production and Inventory Management* 16, no. 4 (April 1973).

Steinberg, E., and A. Napier. "Optimal Multi-level Lot Sizing for Requirements Planning Systems." *Management Science* 26, no. 12 (December 1980), pp. 1258–72.

Wagner, H. M., and T. M. Whitin. "Dynamic Version of the Economic Lot Size Model." *Management Science*, October 1958, pp. 89–96.

Wemmerlöv, U., and D. C. Whybark. "Lot Sizing Under Uncertainty in a Rolling Horizon Environment." Working paper, Indiana University, 1981.

Whybark, D. C., and J. G. Williams. "Material Requirements Planning Under Uncertainty." *Decision Sciences* 7, no. 4 (October 1976).

13

Advanced concepts in scheduling

This chapter addresses advanced issues in scheduling, with primary emphasis on the detailed scheduling of individual jobs through work centers in a shop. The intent is to provide direction for the firm that has a working MPC system in place and wishes to enhance the shop floor control module. The approaches in this chapter presume that effective front-end, engine, and back-end systems are in place. Chapter 13 provides an application perspective to some of the research that has been done in scheduling. It is completely beyond our scope to even summarize the vast amount of research done on this topic. Rather, our interest here is to focus on some basic concepts and results, and show how these results might be applied in certain operating situations.

Chapter 13 is organized around the following four topical areas:

- A scheduling framework: What are the key definitions, performance criteria, and kinds of scheduling problems studied?
- Research approaches: What are the basic scheduling problem structures, and what approaches have been formulated for their solution?
- Basic research findings: What are the scheduling results that have been consistently verified in the research, and what are their practical implications?

- Advanced research findings: What findings from advanced research seem to be particularly helpful in assigning jobs or labor to machines?

Chapter 13 is most closely linked to Chapter 5, which describes basic shop-floor control systems and their place within an overall MPC system. There are also indirect links to Chapter 6 concerning the scheduling of vendors, to Chapters 7 and 8 for master production scheduling, to Chapter 14 which deals with project scheduling for engineered products, and to Chapter 19 which includes a treatment of vehicle scheduling.

A SCHEDULING FRAMEWORK

There are many ways to think about scheduling as well as different kinds of scheduling problems and decisions. Before delving into scheduling research, we think it is useful to first develop a brief framework for scheduling. Included are some key definitions, the criteria for judging scheduling performance, and some important dimensions of scheduling problems.

Definitions

The *Random House Dictionary* has several definitions of the word *schedule*. The three most useful for our purposes are:

A plan or procedure, usually written, for a proposed objective, especially with reference to the sequence of and time allocated for each item or operation necessary to its completion.

A series of items to be handled or of events to occur at or during a particular time or period.

(Verb, transitive) To make a schedule or plan for a certain date.

The first definition allows us to think of a schedule that has a series of sequential steps, or a routing. The entire sequence of operations, the necessary sequential constraints, the time estimates for each activity, and the required resource capacities for each activity are inputs to the development of the detailed plan or schedule.

The first definition also allows us to think of component part scheduling based upon product structures, with scheduling of components for subassemblies and, in turn, subassemblies to support end-item assembly. Material requirements planning (MRP) is the system which establishes the necessary disaggregation of end-item scheduling to subassembly and component scheduling. The associated resource capacity requirements are also established by the material plans.

The second definition of a schedule, as a series of events to occur during some time period, is particularly useful when considering the scheduling of capacities. Rather than looking at the schedule of a part or an end item, we can look at the resultant load or set of capacity requirements for each machine center, labor center, or other defined unit of capacity. The objective becomes one of satisfying, as well as possible, the due date constraints imposed by the end-item schedule, while at the same time scheduling the series of activities or jobs to be accomplished during each time period so as to utilize capacity resources effectively.

The last definition of schedule is as a transitive verb. That is, someone prepares a schedule either for when an end item will be completed or for what series of activities or jobs are to be completed during a specified time by the work center of interest. Implied in this definition is repetition of the scheduling task. The schedule is prepared, actual performance is observed, and rescheduling takes place as uncertain events become resolved; e.g., forecasts of customer orders become actual customer orders, planned results become actual results.

Performance criteria

There are three primary objectives or goals that typically apply to scheduling problems. The first goal concerns *due dates*: one typically wants to avoid late job completion. The second goal concerns *flow times*: this objective is to minimize the time that a job spends in the system, from creation or opening of a shop order until it is closed. The final goal concerns *work center utilization:* one wants to fully utilize the capacity of expensive equipment and personnel.

These three objectives are often conflicting. One can do a better job of meeting due dates if more capacity is provided and the work center capacity is less intensively utilized. Similarly, more capacity will typically reduce flow time, but at reduced capacity utilization. If extra jobs are released to the shop they will tend to have longer flow times, but capacity can be better utilized and *perhaps* due date performance can be improved.

For each of the three primary scheduling objectives, it is necessary to establish exact performance measures. Moreover, for each objective there are competing measures. Meeting due dates might be simply specified on a yes/no basis. More typically, however, due date performance is based on "lateness." The *average lateness* for jobs is one measure, but this raises the issue of "earliness." Are early jobs allowed to offset late jobs in order to calculate the average? Is earliness also undesirable? Is maximum lateness an issue? We follow the convention that lateness measures both positive and negative deviations from the due date.

Another alternative is to measure the variability of actual completion dates against due dates with an objective of minimizing the variance of lateness. But this measure raises the question of which due date should be used to measure performance in an MRP environment when due dates are routinely revised by the MRP system.

Similar problems arise with flow times. Is the measure the average flow time, the variance in flow time, or the maximum flow time? Should flow time be weighted by some monetary value to favor shorter flow times for expensive work?

Work-center utilization measures have equal problems. Is one interested in the utilization of all work centers or in selected centers? How does one select? How is utilization to be measured?

The measurement issues are important to the MPC professional, both for understanding what particular research results mean and for establishing the appropriate performance criteria in applying the concepts. That is, an operating scheduling system must have unambiguous definitions of performance, and these measures must be congruent with the basic objectives of the firm. It is imperative to understand the performance criteria utilized in particular research studies and to carefully assess the match between those criteria and what is truly important in an actual company.

Shop structure

Another facet of a scheduling framework relates to the shop structure that is being studied. One important structure is that of the flow-shop variety. That is, all the jobs tend to go through a fixed sequence of the same routing steps. Other structures are more of a job shop nature involving custom-made products. Each particular job tends to have a unique routing, jobs go from one work center to another in a somewhat random pattern, and the time required at a particular work center is also highly variable. The scheduling complexity and constraints in a flow shop can be quite different from those in a job shop. The appropriateness of particular performance criteria and scheduling systems should reflect those differences.

One dimension of shop structure has been clarified in scheduling research. It is tempting to think that what works well in a shop with 10 work centers will not work well in a shop with 100 work centers. This, in fact, is not so. If they both have other attributes that are the same (e.g., shop structure or percentage capacity utilization), the conclusions drawn from a relatively small shop will be very similar to those appropriate for a large shop.

Product structure

Product structure is another facet of the scheduling environment that needs to be defined for a particular situation. One question is the existence of either single part or assembly routings. The issue is whether the scheduling problem is dealing only with individual jobs or if one necessarily must worry about matched sets of parts (jobs). That is, does one have to schedule each of the components of an assembly to ensure that all are done at the same time? Some companies have a large percentage of their jobs that are essentially one piece part per customer order. Others necessarily must produce parts and assemblies.

Assembly scheduling is partially addressed by MRP in that the due dates for components are coordinated by the MRP planning process. It is in this context that MRP is best seen as a scheduling technique. The detailed execution/scheduling of MRP plans is sometimes a separate issue. To the extent that the scheduling procedure attempts to deal with maintaining matched set due dates, the scheduling task becomes very complex. Note that in finite loading approaches due dates are typically adjusted to reflect finite capacity constraints (which implies the performance criterion is work center utilization).

The type of processing time distribution is another product structure issue. Most of the analytical research studies have been based upon processing times which are represented by the negative exponential distribution. Some simulation studies have used empirical distributions. The practical issue is again the extent to which the research results are robust enough to apply to the wide variety of applied scheduling situations.

Another issue in both research and practice is the use of alternative routings. The design and maintenance of alternative routing files can be an enormous job. Moreover, the decision rules for when to use alternative routings can be quite complex. On the other hand, alternative routings can improve operating performance. If one work center is overloaded and another work center is underloaded, improvements in due date performance, flow times, and work center utilization can be achieved by the use of alternative routings.

A related issue is the use of operation overlapping. If a job can be started at a work center *before* it is completely finished on the previous work center, improvements in scheduling performance can be achieved. Overlapping is a form of scheduling that increases flexibility, but it does not come without cost. It is necessary to have good information on time requirements and to start successive operations only when they will not run out of work (i.e., when operation two requires less time per unit than operation one, it can only be started when a sufficient queue at the second operation exists).

Still another issue concerning product structure is the extent to which setup times remain the same, regardless of the sequence in which jobs are processed. Thus in some firms there is a potential setup time saving to be made by better sequencing of jobs through a work center. However, it is only after an investment is made in developing a data base and an appropriate scheduling system that these savings can be realized.

Work center capacities

A final facet of a framework for scheduling relates to work center capacities. One issue is the extent to which the capacities are fixed or variable. This is analogous to the alternate routing issue. The extent to which the capacity for a particular work center can be increased or decreased and the time delay to achieve the change in capacity both affect scheduling performance.

A related issue is the degree to which the capacity of a particular work center is limited by the capacity of machines or the capacity of labor. The benefit of a labor-limited system versus a machine-limited system is the possibility of increased flexibility, since the same labor capacity can be assigned to several different machines. The extent to which a workforce has multiple skills and the degree of flexibility specified by union contracts on these matters clearly influence this issue.

RESEARCH APPROACHES

There have been two basic kinds of scheduling problems studied in the research—static scheduling problems and dynamic scheduling problems. Some, but not all, of the results that apply to one of these situations also apply to the other. The static problem consists of a fixed set of jobs to be scheduled until they are all completed. The machine centers can begin either empty (i.e., no jobs on them) or with some existing load. At the end of the study, the machine centers are empty.

The dynamic scheduling problem deals with an ongoing situation. New jobs are continually being added to the system, and the emphasis is on the long-term performance of scheduling approaches. The dynamic case matches most shop-floor control problems but not all of them. For example, the scheduling of a unique make-to-order product might be better seen as a static scheduling problem. For such situations, the objective is to minimize the total time to run *only* this product. Similarly, there are some situations when "customers" can only arrive after some opening time, and all of them are processed.

Static scheduling approaches

The static scheduling problem consists of a fixed set of jobs to be run. The typical assumptions are that the entire set of jobs arrive simultaneously and that all work centers are available at that time. Most of the static scheduling research has been conducted using a criterion called minimum "make-span"; i.e., the minimum total time to process all of the jobs. This is a flow time criterion, not a due date or work center utilization criterion. Furthermore, the minimum make-span criterion is not the same as the average flow time criterion.

Static scheduling research has been performed using deterministic processing times (known and nonvarying) and stochastic processing times (subject to random variations). Methods for dealing with deterministic times can be divided into those that produce optimum results and those utilizing heuristic scheduling procedures. In general, optimization methods are only applicable to relatively small problems. The computational difficulty tends to increase exponentially with problem size.

Large-scale problems are usually treated with heuristic procedures called dispatching or sequencing, rules. These are logical rules for choosing which available job to select for processing at a particular machine center. In using dispatching rules, the scheduling decisions are made sequentially, rather than all at once. This is especially beneficial when processing times are uncertain, since the rule can decide which job to process next based on those jobs that are *actually* available to process, rather than those that are *supposed* to be available.

Dynamic scheduling approaches

Dynamic scheduling problems are those in which new jobs are continually being added over time. The processing times for these jobs can be either deterministic or stochastic, but most research has focused on the latter case. Analytic approaches have been based on queuing models which provide expected steady state conditions for certain kinds of situations and time distributions. The criteria applied in the queueing studies typically involve the average flow time, the average work-in-process or number of jobs in the system, and the machine center utilization.

One approach in the dynamic scheduling studies is to use different scheduling (dispatching) rules at the work centers. The use of some rules gives better results for certain criteria. The original work in queuing studies was devoted to single-machine systems, later work extended the results to multiple machines. However, as the size of the system increases, simulation is the most frequently used research methodology. Moreover, simulation allows one to forgo the time limiting assumptions that are inherent in most analytical queuing approaches.

Simulation studies of large-scale scheduling problems are again mainly based on dispatching rules. There are a substantial number of these studies, and an understanding of certain basic conclusions is essential for the MPC professional. Some of the results are quite counterintuitive. Furthermore, an understanding of some basic simulation issues, such as sample size requirements and run lengths as a function of problem complexity, are useful for the person contemplating a simulation study for a particular firm.

BASIC RESEARCH FINDINGS

In this section we overview some of the basic research work that has been done in scheduling. We start with an analysis of a simple system and then turn to more complex systems. Finally, we summarize the results into a set of lessons for scheduling practice. An important element in this section is the interaction between the scheduling procedure used and the performance objective. In order to choose a procedure it is first necessary to choose a performance criterion. However, some criteria lead to procedures that seem to work well under a wide variety of conditions.

The one-machine case

Research on single-machine scheduling has been largely based on the static problem of how to best schedule a fixed set of jobs through a single machine, when all jobs are available at the start of the scheduling period. It is further assumed that setup times are independent of the sequence.

If the objective is to *minimize the total time* to run the entire set of jobs (i.e., the minimum make span), it does not make any difference in which order the jobs are run. In this case the make span will equal the sum of all setup and run times under any sequence of jobs. However, if the objective is to *minimize the average time* that each job spends at the machine (setup plus run plus waiting times), then it can be shown that this will be accomplished by sequencing the jobs in ascending order according to their total processing time (setup plus run time). As an example, if three jobs with individual processing times of one, five, and eight hours, respectively, are scheduled, the *total time* required to run the *entire* batch under any sequence is 14 hours. If the jobs are processed in ascending order, the average time that each job spends in the system is (1 + 6 + 14)/3 = 7 hours. However, if the jobs are processed in the reverse order, the average time in the system is (8 + 13 + 14)/3 = 11.67 hours.

This result has an important consequence. The average time in the system will always be minimized by selecting the next job for processing that has the shortest processing time at the current operation. This rule for sequencing jobs at a work center (called shortest processing time or SPT) provides excellent results when using the average time in system criterion.

SPT also performs well on the criterion of *minimizing the average number of jobs in the system.* We have noted previously that work-in-process inventory levels and average flow time are directly related measures. If one is increased or reduced, the other will change in the same direction. It can be shown analytically that the SPT rule will again provide superior performance when the work-in-process criterion is applied in the single-machine case.

When the criterion is to *minimize the average job lateness*, it can again be demonstrated that SPT is the best rule for sequencing jobs for the single machine case. To introduce the criterion of lateness, it is first necessary to establish due dates for the jobs. However, an interesting aspect of the research is that no matter what procedure is used to establish the due dates, the minimization of the *average job lateness* will be achieved by SPT.

Another criterion is to *minimize the maximum job lateness.* In this case, the best sequencing rule is to run the jobs in due date order, from earliest due date to latest due date. This result can also be proven analytically. Still another measure of scheduling performance that is often of interest is that of *minimizing the order lateness variance.* This criterion is also best served by running the jobs in due date sequence, earliest to latest, since doing so minimizes the deviations from due dates of the individual jobs.

Since there are relatively few applied examples of the one-machine scheduling problem, this research tends to be more useful for gaining insights into the behavior of scheduling rules under particular criteria than for direct scheduling applications. The issue from both a pragmatic and research point of view is the extent to which the conclusions from this work are applicable to more complex problem environments.

The most important conclusion to be drawn from the single-machine research is that the SPT rule represents the best way to pick the next job to run if the objective is to minimize the average time per job, minimize the average number of jobs in the system, or to minimize the average job lateness. However, if the objective is to minimize either the maximum lateness of any job or the lateness variance, then the jobs should run in due date sequence.

The two-machine case

The development of scheduling procedures for the two-machine case is somewhat more complex than for single-machine systems. In the two-machine case, both machines have to be scheduled to best satisfy whatever criterion is selected. Moreover, job routings need to be considered. In general, any job could be routed to either of the machines for the first operation. In a "flow shop" model (as opposed to a job shop) the assumption is that each of the jobs always goes first to one machine and then to the second. For analytically based research, additional assumptions, such as those for the one-machine case, are made. For example, all jobs are available at the start of the schedule, and setup times are independent.

A set of rules has been developed to minimize the make span in the two-machine case. Note that while the minimum make span does not depend on the sequencing of jobs in the one-machine case, this is not true in the two-machine case. Additionally, if the total time to run the entire batch of jobs is to be minimized, this does not ensure that either the average time each job spends in the system or the average number of jobs in the system will also be minimized.

The following scheduling rules to minimize make span in a flow shop were developed by Johnson:

Select the job with the minimum processing time on either machine 1 or machine 2. If this time is associated with machine 1, schedule this job first. If it is for machine 2, schedule this job last in the series of jobs to be run. Remove this job from further consideration.

Select the job with the next smallest processing time and proceed as above (if machine 1, schedule it second; if machine 2, next to last). Any ties can be broken randomly.

Continue this process until all of the jobs have been scheduled.

The intuitive logic behind this rule is that the minimum time to complete the set of jobs has to be the larger of the sum of all the run times at the first machine plus the smallest run time at the second machine, or the sum of all the run times at the second machine plus the smallest run time at the first machine.

These rules can also be applied to the three-machine case if some limiting assumptions are made. Additional research has shown that these limiting assumptions can be relaxed using branch and bound algorithms and integer-programming methods. Problems of greater complexity have also been formulated as integer-programming models, but solutions are generally feasible only for very small problems.

There are several important observations to be made from these research efforts. First, the size of problems that can be treated with analytical methods is small and of limited applicability for the "real world." Second, the computer time required to solve scheduling problems with analytical methods grows exponentially with the number of jobs and/or machines to be scheduled. Third, the performance measure, minimizing the make span, is not the same as minimizing the average time in the system or average number of jobs in the system. Moreover, any of these criteria are not necessarily related to the job lateness criterion. Fourth, the static scheduling assumptions (beginning with all machines idle, all jobs available, and ending with all jobs processed and all machines idle) clearly influence the results. Fifth, there is no randomness reflected in any of the machine processing times, which could reduce the applicability of the techniques. Finally, on the positive side, it is important to note that the two-machine scheduling rules utilize the shortest processing time logic. The application of the SPT in the two-machine case is not exactly the same as it was in the single-machine case, but it is clearly an essential element in producing the desired scheduling performance in both problem situations.

Queuing model approaches

The application of queuing models to scheduling problems allows for a relaxation of some of the limiting constraints mentioned above. In particular, the queuing approaches deal with the dynamic problem rather than the static problem. Randomness in the interarrival and service times are considered, and steady state results are provided for average flow time, average work-in-process, expected work center utilization, and average waiting time.

The queuing research first examined the single-machine case and then was expanded to the multiple-machine case. The single-machine research has shown that again the SPT rule for sequencing jobs yields the best performance for the average completion time, average work-in-process level, and average waiting time criteria. Applying queuing theory to the multiple-machine case requires the use of such limiting assumptions that the results are only interesting from a research point of view. To examine realistic, multiple-machine, dynamic scheduling situations, simulation models are most often used. With simulation, one can examine the performance of various rules against several criteria. The size of the problems studied (work centers and jobs) can be expanded, the effects of startup and ending conditions can be considered, and any kind of product structure, interarrival time patterns, or shop capacity, can be accommodated. The primary research questions addressed in simulation studies include the following. Which dispatching rules for sequencing jobs at work centers perform best? For which criteria? Are some "classes" of rules better than others for some classes of criteria or "classes" of problems?

Sequencing rules

Figure 13.1 illustrates a typical scheduling environment for a complex job shop. At any time, if a set of n jobs is to be scheduled on m machines, there are $(n!)^m$ possible ways to schedule the jobs, and the schedule could change with the addition of new jobs. For any problem that involves more than a few machines or a few jobs, the computational complexity of finding the best schedule is beyond the capacity of modern computers.

Complex routings are shown in Figure 13.1. For example, after processing at machine center A, jobs may be sent for further processing to machine centers B, D, or F. Similarly, some jobs are completed after being processed at machine center A and go directly to finished component inventories. Also note that a job might flow from machine center A to machine center D, then back to A.

A sequencing or dispatch rule is depicted in Figure 13.1 between each queue and its associated work center. This indicates that a dispatching rule exists for choosing the next job in the queue for processing. The question of interest is which sequencing rule will achieve good performance against some scheduling criterion.

There are a large number of sequencing rules that have appeared in research and in practice. Each could be used in scheduling jobs. The following are some well-known rules with their desirable properties:

R (random). Pick any job in the queue with equal probability. This rule is often used as a benchmark for other rules.

FCFS (first come/first serve). This rule is sometimes deemed to be "fair," in that jobs are processed in the order in which they arrived at the work center.

SPT (shortest processing time). As noted, this rule tends to reduce both work-in-process inventory, the average job completion (flow) time, and average job lateness.

EDD (earliest due date). This rule seems to work well for criteria associated with job lateness.

CR (critical ratio). This rule is widely used in practice. The priority index is calculated using (due date—now)/(lead time remaining).

LWR (least work remaining). This rule is an extension of SPT in that it considers *all* of the processing time remaining until the job is completed.

FOR (fewest operations remaining). Another SPT variant that considers the number of successive operations.

ST (slack time). A variant of EDD which subtracts the sum of setup and

FIGURE 13.1 The scheduling environment

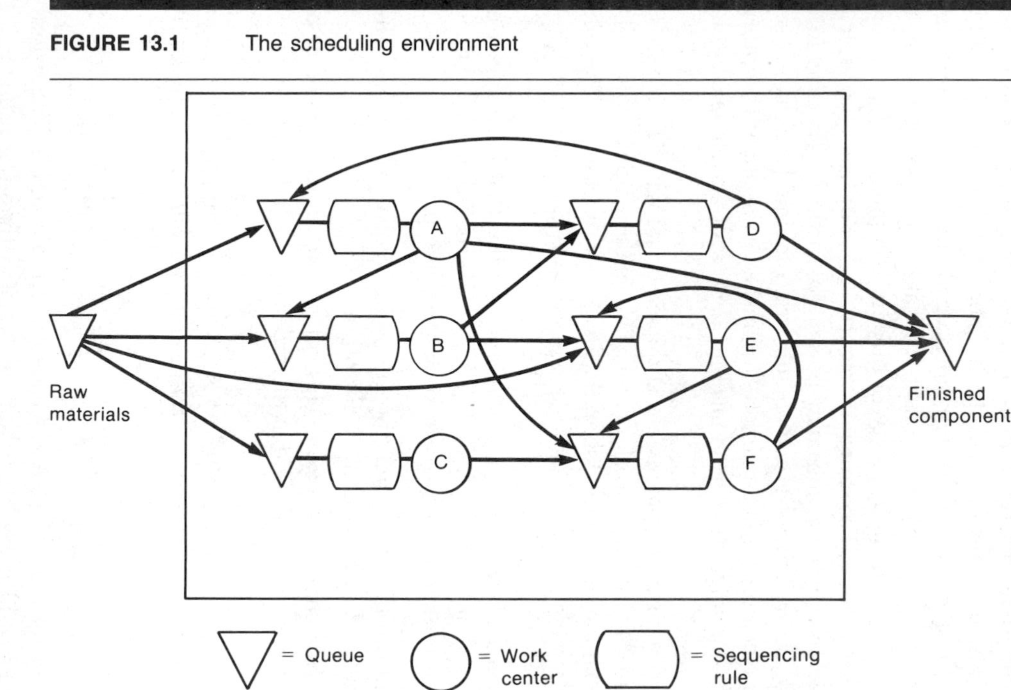

processing times from the time remaining until the due date. The resulting value is called "slack." Jobs are run in order of the smallest amount of slack.

ST/O (slack time per operation). A variant of ST which divides the slack time by the number of remaining operations, again sequencing jobs in order of the smallest value first.

NQ (next queue). A different kind of rule which is based on machine utilization. The idea is to consider the queues at each of the succeeding work centers to which the jobs will go and select the job for processing that is going to the smallest queue (measured either in hours or perhaps in jobs).

LSU (least setup). Still another rule is to pick that job which minimizes the changeover time on the machine. In this way capacity utilization is maximized. Note this rule explicitly recognizes dependencies between setup times and job sequence.

This list is not meant to be exhaustive. There are many other rules, variants of these rules, and combinations of these rules that have been studied. In some cases, the use of one rule under certain conditions and the use of another under other conditions has been studied.

One issue highlighted in Figure 13.1 is whether the same rule should be used at each work center. One might, for example, build a case for using SPT at the "gateway" work centers and using some due date oriented rules for downstream centers. Or perhaps the selection of a rule should depend on the size of the queue or the amount of work that is ahead of or behind schedule.

Another issue in selecting sequencing rules is their cost of usage. Some of the rules, such as random, first come/first serve, shortest processing time, earliest due date, and fewest operations remaining, are easily implemented since they do not require information other than that related to the job itself. Other rules, such as the critical ratio, least work remaining, slack time, and slack time per operation rules, require more complex information as well as time-dependent calculations. The next queue and least setup rules require even more information, involving the congestion existing at other work centers, or a dynamic changeover cost matrix.

Sequencing research results

There has been extensive research on the performance of different sequencing rules. We will highlight some of these efforts and draw conclusions for practice. One of the early comprehensive simulation studies on sequencing rules was performed by Conway. He examined 39 different sequencing rules, each tested using the same set of 10,000 jobs. Results from the first 400 and last 900 were not included in the results in order to eliminate startup and ending conditions. Figure 13.2 reports some results from this study. They are reported for two criteria: the average time in system and the variance of the time in the system. As we have noted, the average time in the

FIGURE 13.2 Simulation results for various sequencing rules

Sequencing rule	*Average time in system*	*Variance of time in system*
SPT	34.0	2,318
EDD	63.7	6,780
ST/O	66.1	5,460
FCFS	74.4	5,739
R	74.7	10,822

Source: R. W. Conway, W. L. Maxwell, and L. W. Miller, *Theory of Scheduling* ©1967, Addison-Wesley Publishing Co. Inc., Reading, Ma. Page 287, Table C–3. Reprinted with permission.

system measure is directly related to work-in-process inventory and the average number of jobs in the system. This measure is also directly related to the average job lateness. The results reported in Figure 13.2 clearly show that the SPT rule performs quite well for this set of criteria.

There is, however, a concern in using SPT. In many studies, SPT has been found to have a higher variance of time in system than other rules. In addition, it can allow some jobs with long processing times to wait in queue for a substantial period of time, thereby causing severe due-date problems for a few jobs. However, since the SPT rule can complete the average job in a relatively short period of time compared with other rules, it produces a much smaller average job lateness. Therefore, the overall lateness performance might be much less severe than one might think. Figure 13.3 shows simulation results using various lateness criteria.

Figure 13.3 shows that the slack time per operation (ST/O) rule is best in terms of the percentage of jobs late. However, the SPT rule is a close second, and SPT is considerably better than the earliest due date (EDD) rule. The earliest due date rule has a much lower variance of job lateness than SPT, but the *average* lateness measure of SPT might be better enough to compensate for the high job lateness variance associated with SPT.

FIGURE 13.3 Simulation results for other criteria

Sequence rule	*Average job lateness**	*Variance of job lateness*	*Percentage of jobs late*
ST/O	−12.8	226	3.7
SPT	−44.9	2,878	5.0
EDD	−15.5	432	17.8
FCFS	−4.5	1,686	44.8

*Minus sign means that jobs are early on average.

Source: R. W. Conway, W. L. Maxwell, and L. W. Miller, *Theory of Scheduling* ©1967, Addison-Wesley Publishing Co. Inc., Reading, Ma. Page 287, Table C–3. Reprinted with permission.

Additional studies have been done where job due dates were established using a variety of procedures. The performance of SPT has been shown to be better than other rules even under those conditions where due dates are assigned a bit less "rationally"; i.e., where the due dates are set without regard to the work content involved in processing the job. In studies where the shop utilization was varied, SPT has been found to be less sensitive to changes in the capacity utilization of the work centers than other sequencing rules.

Several rules were tested in a simulation study by Nanot using very large sample sizes (number of orders scheduled) and several combinations of shop load and routing (job shop versus flow shop) conditions. The general results support SPT as a superior rule in terms of average time in system and the related measures. Again, Nanot found the time in system variance is higher than for some of the other rules. Nanot also concluded that the results did not seem to be sensitive to changes in the shop load and routing conditions.

Other research efforts have attempted to combine SPT with other scheduling rules in order to obtain most of the benefits of SPT without the large time in system variance. One approach has been to alternate SPT with FCFS (first-come, first-serve) to "clean out the work centers" at periodic intervals. Other combinations of SPT with ST/O or with critical ratio produce similar results.

One of the most consistent results of the simulation experiments has been to demonstrate that SPT is a very good dispatching rule for many criteria. This conclusion is robust and is supported by a variety of simulation studies. This result runs counter to what many practioners believe: To ignore due dates for sequencing jobs seems irresponsible. But since the use of SPT results in reduced lead times and work-in-process inventories, the benefits might argue for its implementation. Conway sums it up well in one of his conclusions:

> The priority rule under which the job with the shortest processing time is selected (SPT) clearly dominates all the other rules tested. Its performance under every measure was very good, it was an important factor in each of the rules that exhibit a "best" performance under some measure, and is simpler and easier to implement than the rules that surpass it in performance. It surely should be considered the "standard" in scheduling research, against which candidate procedures must demonstrate their virtue.

Implications for practice

A key limitation of all of the research discussed so far is that the assignment of due dates is done once and they are not revised over time. This differs from shop floor control systems operating as part of an effective MPC system; due dates are continually revised as one portion of the MRP planner's job. Many operating shop floor control systems use critical ratio as a dispatching rule. It is based on the following formula:

$$\frac{\text{Due date} - \text{Now}}{\text{Lead time remaining}}$$

The due date is the date of a scheduled receipt in an MRP record. It is to be expected that these due dates will change over time since Murphy's law is always at work. The unanswered question is what is the influence of changes in order due dates on the research conclusions formulated above (especially on the benefits of using SPT)? It seems that there are at least three possibilities:

1. SPT is dead: long live critical ratio.
2. SPT still works—our intuition is wrong.
3. Design a critical ratio/SPT hybrid or a hybrid based on some other due date-oriented rule with SPT. For example, at Twin Disc where critical ratio is used, jobs are segregated into PO jobs (pegged to actual customer orders) and PI (pegged to forecast usage). A hybrid rule is to first run all PO jobs with a critical ratio less than 1.0, in critical ratio sequence, then sequence all other jobs by SPT.

Black & Decker uses a similar hybrid approach. Most jobs are processed on the basis of SPT. But the importance of lateness grows exponentially until lateness becomes important enough to override SPT. Thus, no job can "get lost" because of a long processing time at some operation. This and other practical experiments lead us to believe that hybrid rules will be developed and implemented in many other firms as the management of due dates (lead times) becomes more effective.

One important practical result of the research on job shop scheduling has been to clearly understand the combinational nature of the problem. The computational costs rise rapidly as a function of problem complexity even when optimal solutions are not being sought. As the number of jobs to be scheduled and the number of work centers increase, the time to prepare a schedule increases much more rapidly. Thus the size of many actual manufacturing shops means that many of the techniques used for research are not computationally economical for solving day-to-day scheduling problems. For this reason, simulation-based finite loading systems used in practice, such as the CAPOSS system, typically use simplifying assumptions such as horizontal loading and groupings of machines to create fewer machine centers.

The computational costs of completely simulating all job arrivals and all possible schedules for each machine and worker can be prohibitively high for many actual applications. The use of the simplifying assumptions in these situations leads to an interesting research question: To what extent could improvements be made in the various criteria if more exact scheduling techniques were used?

A related practical question is the application of scheduling research to a specific company situation. There is a temptation for the serious practioner to become interested in certain research questions. For example, the plant with a well-functioning MPC system contemplating a hybrid SPT/critical ratio rule might be interested in trying it out in a simulated environment before implementing it in the shop. A knowledge of scheduling research (considerably beyond that covered in this chapter) should be a prerequisite. The impact of shop capacity loads, starting conditions, number of jobs processed, which jobs to measure, performance criteria, number of machine centers to study, and other factors are all important to understand *before* doing extensive simulation studies. Without first attending to these questions, it is quite easy to consume large quantities of computer time with dubious results.

ADVANCED RESEARCH FINDINGS

In this final section, we discuss several additional research studies that we see as being of particular relevance to MPC practice. These studies focus on the determination of lead times (management of due dates) for manufactured items and the determination of labor assignments in manufacturing operations. In most cases, this research has not yet provided definitive conclusions for the practicing professional. However, in each case we think that important practical issues are raised and that the practicing professional can make use of the available, though perhaps tentative, conclusions.

Due date setting procedures

The scheduling procedures presented so far in this chapter have assumed that the due dates for individual jobs are *givens*. Yet in many firms, the setting of due dates is often assigned to manufacturing and is frequently the subject of intense negotiations between manufacturing and marketing personnel. Many times due dates must be set at the time of order receipt or when bidding for an order. An effective MPC system can help by providing appropriate information regarding the availability of material and capacity, as well as information concerning the resource requirements for individual jobs. As an example, the assignment of due dates for make-to-order products is normally made on the basis of raw material and equipment capacity availabilities. Likewise, due dates for manufactured components in MRP systems are set by determining the length of the planned lead time for such items. Therefore, the establishment of lead time offsets and due dates is a vital and ongoing function in a manufacturing system. The achievement of these due dates is fostered by a well-functioning shop floor control system based on good dispatching rules.

Although very little research has been reported on the management of lead times (due dates), some useful insights have been provided by Baker and Bertrand. They analyzed the effectiveness of three different procedures for estimating lead times and setting due dates for a job shop. Specifically, they set due dates for orders by adding an estimate of the manufacturing time to the date the order is received. The three methods used for establishing the value of manufacturing time are:

CON: A *constant* time allowance for manufacturing *all* jobs; i.e., the same lead time is added to all jobs at receipt date to calculate the due date.

SLK: A time allowance that provides an equal (constant) waiting time or slack for *all* jobs; i.e., the due date is set equal to the receipt date plus the sum of all processing times, plus a fixed additional time for waiting.

TWK: A time allowance that is proportional to the total processing time for a job; i.e., the lead time to be added to the receipt date is a multiple of the sum of all processing times.

Each of the procedures has a single parameter (the constant time, the waiting time, or the multiple) to be determined. Other informational needs are similar to those of usual shop floor control problems. The first procedure is easily implemented in many firms since the shop floor control system data base requirements are minimal. The other two procedures, however, require an estimate of the processing time for a job in order to set the due date. The experiment was concerned with the degree of improvement in manufacturing performance to be obtained by implementing the more complex due date procedures, SLK and TWK.

The evaluative criterion was "due date tightness." It is presumed that tight due dates (or short lead times) are strategically more desirable than loose due dates. Tight due dates provide a competitive advantage by permitting the firm to offer an improved level of customer service as well as achieve lower costs through reductions in work-in-process inventory. The approach of the experiments was to set each of the three parameters such that *no* late deliveries occurred. That is, the parameters are chosen so that the longest lead time is just sufficient. Thereafter, the actual lead times are observed in the simulation. The preferred procedure is the one that achieves the smallest mean lead time.

The experiments involved a single-machine system using the shortest processing time (SPT) dispatching rule for all three due date setting rules. However, they were conducted under a wide variety of operating conditions: 80 percent to 99 percent machine utilization, a variety of jobs, 20 replications, and use of both exponentially and normally distributed processing times. The exponentially distributed processing times gave a much greater degree of variability in achieved lead times (coefficient of variation, $c_v = 1.0$) than the normally distributed processing time ($c_v = .25$). Two releasing rules were used as well. The random release rule meant that orders were issued to the shop as soon as received. The "controlled" release rule meant that jobs were released when work-in-process inventory levels fell below a "trigger point". The trigger point was chosen so as to provide a specified average number of jobs in the shop.

The results indicate that the SLK and TWK procedures set tighter due dates than the CON procedure. As shown in Figure 13.4, these two procedures provided as much as a 50 percent reduction in the lead time required for manufacturing (in comparison with the CON procedure) under exponentially distributed processing times. Much smaller differences were noted when normally distributed processing times were used. Furthermore, there was a clear preference for the TWK procedure (as opposed to the SLK procedure) when random work releasing was used. In using controlled work releasing, preference shifts to the TWK procedure at higher levels of machine utilization.

While considerably more research is required (especially for multiple machines) and significant modifications of the procedures may be discovered, we believe there are some important messages that this research suggests. In particular, the results indicate the important potential for reductions in lead time and work-in-process inventory when due dates are set in relation to job processing times. An important step in implementing these procedures is that of determining how much variability exists in the processing times in a shop. An indication of high variability (e.g., coefficient of variation of 1.0 or more) would suggest the potential for major improvements in manufacturing performance.

We see these results as particularly important as firms systematically reduce work-in-process inventories. As long as lead times are 90 percent waiting, the influence of processing times and processing time variability is masked. When lead times are reduced, processing time will become a larger element of the total lead time and thus more important to take into account.

Dynamic due dates

The determination of due dates for orders in a job shop is one aspect of the management of due dates in scheduling. A second aspect has to do with maintaining *valid* due dates as orders progress through the manufacturing process. The need for due date maintenance arises from the dynamic nature of the manufacturing environment. Management actions, such as master production schedule changes, planned lead time adjustments, bill of material modifications, etc., can create the need to reschedule manufacturing orders and to revise the priorities given to the shop. Likewise, variations in shop conditions, such as unexpected scrap, unplanned transactions, etc., can also create the need to revise job due dates.

Many firms have systems and procedures which result in changes in open order due dates. This practice is referred to as *dynamic due date maintenance*. The primary argument for this practice is that the shop should be using accurate and timely information in dispatching jobs to machines in order to provide a high level of customer service. In spite of its widespread

FIGURE 13.4 Simulation results for manufacturing lead time estimating procedures

Treatment	Mean number of jobs	Utilization	Mean manufacturing lead time			Frequency best		
			TWK	*SLK*	*CON*	*TWK*	*SLK*	*CON*
Exponential times, random release	4.00	0.80	4.43	9.04	10.14	20	0	0
	5.67	0.85	5.63	10.37	11.39	20	0	0
	9.00	0.90	6.20	11.79	12.76	20	0	0
Exponential times, controlled release,	4.00		5.26	4.53	8.79	3	17	0
	5.67		6.51	6.23	10.09	7	13	0
	9.00		8.28	9.51	13.49	17	3	0
Normal times, random release	4.28	0.90	7.20	7.70	7.72	16	2	2
	9.59	0.95	10.06	10.70	10.75	16	2	2
	52.09	0.99	10.44	10.99	11.07	20	0	0
Normal times, controlled release	4.28		6.65	5.31	5.90	0	20	0
	9.59		12.35	10.61	11.18	0	20	0
	52.09		48.53	53.10	53.64	20	0	0

*Number of times in the 20 replications that each procedure performed the best (i.e., produced the lowest mean manufacturing lead time).

Source: K. R. Baker and J. W. M. Bertrand, "A Comparison of Due Date Selection Rules," Reprinted with permission from *AIIE Transactions,* vol. 13, no. 2, June 1981, pp. 128–129. Copyright © Institute of Industrial Engineers, Inc., 25 Technology Park/Atlanta, Norcross, GA 30092.

use, there is some controversy over the advisability of implementing dynamic due date maintenance systems. Some suggest that the use of dynamic due dates can have an adverse impact on scheduling performance because of system "nervousness." Steele, for example, argues that a job shop can function effectively only if open order priorities are stable enough to generate some coherent action on the shop floor. He defines a scheduling system with *unstable* open order priorities as a nervous scheduling system which can lead to shop floor distrust and overriding of formal priorities. A second behavioral argument against dynamic due date maintenance is that the volume of rescheduling messages might innundate the production planner so that he or she is unable to process the necessary changes in a timely fashion.

In such cases the production planner may simply stop trying to perform an impossible task; the shop could lose faith in the priority system and revert to using an "informal" system; or ill-chosen or misleading rescheduling messages may be communicated to the shop. Any or all of these responses may cause the shop and inventory system performance to deteriorate.

While much of the scheduling research has been directed at determining the "best" heuristics for scheduling a shop in order to meet fixed or open order due dates, very little experimental research has addressed the problem of whether and how to respond to these issues when the actual need date for an open order changes while the order is being processed by the shop.

In one study conducted to determine the impact of using *dynamically* updated due dates on manufacturing performance, Berry and Rao evaluated the use of dynamic due dates with the critical ratio scheduling rule in a make-to-stock environment. They studied the scheduling of products produced by a job shop for a finished goods inventory which was controlled using an economic lot size/reorder point system. The *dynamic* due dates used in critical ratio scheduling were produced using the following formula:

$$\text{Due date} = \text{Current date} + \frac{\text{On-hand inventory balance} - \text{Buffer stock}}{\text{Average daily usage}}$$

The result is that larger than expected demand for a product will move the due date for an open order for that item closer to the current date, thereby increasing the critical ratio scheduling priority.

The results of this study were counterintuitive. They showed that the use of dynamic due dates produced a significant increase in the combined costs of setup, carrying work-in-process and finished product inventory, and inventory shortages. Nervousness in the dispatching rule priorities caused both the mean and variance of the job flow times to increase, thereby increasing the work-in-process inventory level and reducing the customer service level.

In a related study by Hausman and Scudder the use of dynamic inventory information in priority scheduling rules was evaluated for a jet engine repair facility. This facility performed the disassembly, manufacture of component parts, and re-assembly of jet engines. Quick turnaround times were of importance to the customer, so the study used the time-weighted final product (engine) back orders as the measure of performance. The inventory management policy was a continuous review, one-for-one (S-1, S) inventory policy, and the product had a multilevel product structure.

The repair facility had 10 machines. The study compared the back order performance of a wide range of priority sequencing rules. These included: static rules (earliest due date, FCFS, etc.), dynamic rules (minimum slack time per operation, critical ratio, etc.), and rules that consider additional information. Two of the latter rules and their variations proved to be the most effective priority scheduling rules tested. These two rules were:

Inventory based: Select the job with the smallest value of net inventory. (Net inventory equals current on-hand inventory minus back orders for the component type.)

Multiple use: Select the job which is required by the largest number of modules (subassemblies) awaiting parts for assembly.

Both of these rules incorporate dynamic information regarding the expected component work-in-process inventory. In effect, the development of the priority index information used in these rules is similar to the gross-to-netting procedures used in an MRP system.

The use of dynamic work-in-process, finished component, and subassembly requirement information provided significant improvements in operating performance. For example, the inventory based rule resulted in 3.67 mean delay days as opposed to 6.03 for critical ratio and 7.28 for the shortest processing time rule. For the repair facility, a two-day improvement in the mean delay time represents a savings of one engine from the spares inventory, $2 million.

The seemingly contradictory results observed in the previous studies are partially explained in work by Penlesky. He evaluates the use of several dynamic due date procedures. He also examines the use of simple procedures for selectively implementing a few of the many due date changes that would normally be implemented (filtering procedures). In particular, the study is concerned with determining what types of job-related information are important to consider in formulating open order rescheduling procedures and evaluating the impact of the rescheduling on manufacturing performance in MRP systems.

Three different filters for making rescheduling decisions are considered: the ability, the magnitude, and the horizon filters. The purpose of the ability filter is to assure that only attainable due date adjustments are passed along to the shop. In using this procedure:

1. All *rescheduling out* actions (when the new due date is later than the previous due date) are implemented.

2. The implementation of *reschedule-in* actions depends upon one of three conditions:
   a. If the machine setup and processing time remaining is less than the time until the new due date, the new due date is implemented.
   b. If the machine setup and processing time remaining is less than the time until the old due date but greater than the time until the new date, the due date is set to the present time plus the machine setup and processing time to complete the order.
   c. If the machine setup and processing time remaining exceeds the time allowed until the old due date, no change is made to the old due date.

Different information is considered by the magnitude and the horizon filters. These procedures are designed to filter out trivial due date adjustments by means of a *threshold* value. In the magnitude procedure, if the absolute value of the difference between the new and the old due dates exceeds a threshold value (T_m), the change in the due date is implemented. Similarly, the horizon procedure is designed to filter out those due date changes which are too far out in the planning horizon to be of any immediate concern to the production planner. Only if the old due date falls within the period of interest (T_H) is the new due date implemented. By setting parameter values for T_m and T_H, the number of rescheduling changes to be filtered out can be adjusted. The procedures will implement all changes when $T_m = 0$ and $T_H = \infty$, providing full dynamic procedures. Static dates are obtained when $T_m = \infty$ and $T_H = 0$.

Simulation experiments were used to investigate the effect of incorporating dynamic due date information in the sequencing rules and the use of the filtering procedures. These experiments were conducted using a make-to-stock job shop simulator, with both component manufacturing and assembly operations, controlled by an MRP system. The procedures were tested under differing values of machine utilization, uncertainty in the master production schedule, length of the planned lead times, and size of production order quantities. The three measures of effectiveness used were the end product customer service level, the combined work-in-process and finished item inventory level, and the number of rescheduling changes implemented.

The results shown in Figure 13.5 indicate that the gains in performance to be obtained by using dynamic due dates depend on the shop operating conditions. These results indicate that under certain operating conditions, dynamic due date information can provide improvements in customer service and total inventory level. The results help explain the apparently contradictory results reported by Berry/Rao and Hausman/Scudder. While both studies were conducted under high machine utilization conditions, small lot sizes (a single unit) were used in the Hausman and Scudder experiments (these correspond to experiments 6 and 8 in Figure 13.5, where performance

FIGURE 13.5 Percentage improvements in service and inventory levels using dynamic due dates*

			Low master schedule uncertainty		*High master schedule uncertainty*	
Periodic order quantity	*Planned lead time*	*Performance measure*	*Low machine utilization*	*High machine utilization*	*Low machine utilization*	*High machine utilization*
Small	Low	Experiment number	1	2	3	4
		Customer service level	3.4	—	15.2	—
		Total inventory level	—	—	10.5	—
	High	Experiment number	5	6	7	8
		Customer service level	.5	9.3	4.8	31.8
		Total inventory level	—	5.1	—	8.3
Large	Low	Experiment number	9	10	11	12
		Customer service level	4.3	—	14.3	—
		Total inventory level	—	—	8.0	—
	High	Experiment number	13	14	15	16
		Customer service level	2.5	—	6.2	—
		Total inventory level	—	—	—	—

*(Static − Dynamic) ÷ Static) × 100; calculated only in those cases where there was a statistically significant difference in the performance measure between the two procedures.

Source: R. J. Penlesky, "Open Order Rescheduling Heuristics For MRP Systems in Manufacturing Firms," unpublished doctoral dissertation, Indiana University, 1982.

gains were obtained), and much larger order quantities (economic order quantities involving several periods of demand) were used in the study reported by Berry and Rao (these correspond to experiments 14 and 16 in Figure 13.5, where no improvements in performance were observed).

Another important conclusion can be drawn from the results in Figure 13.5. The dynamic due dates can provide a reduction in the total inventory level while *simultaneously* providing an improvement in customer service; e.g., in experiments 3, 6, 8, and 11. Even though the magnitude varies, the attainment of simultaneous improvements in customer service and inventory levels is possible using dynamic due dates.

The performance comparison of the filtering procedures is shown in Figure 13.6 for experiment number 8 of Figure 13.5. Two observations can be made regarding these results. First, there is no significant difference in performance between the filtering procedures and the dynamic due date procedure without filtering. All rescheduling procedures produced a significant improvement in performance over the static procedures. Second, the magnitude and horizon filters provide comparable performance to the dynamic rescheduling procedure—but with far fewer rescheduling actions implemented. Therefore, it would seem that the benefits of dynamic rescheduling can be achieved by *selectively* implementing the rescheduling actions. By filtering the rescheduling messages, the information processing costs and the adverse behavioral effects of system nervousness can be reduced without an adverse effect on operating performance.

Labor limited systems

The scheduling research results presented so far are useful when dispatching (sequencing) rules represent the principal means of controlling the flow of work in a plant. In many firms, in addition to assigning jobs to work

FIGURE 13.6 Results of applying the filtering procedures

		Customer service level		*Total inventory level*	
Procedure	*Filter level**	*Mean*	*Standard deviation*	*Mean*	*Standard deviation*
Static due dates	0	.651	.084	14,357	895
Ability filter	100	.871	.048	12,990	412
Magnitude filter	53	.873	.041	12,873	919
Horizon filter	45	.831	.055	13,190	958
Dynamic due dates without filtering	100	.858	.049	13,161	999

Note: Data from experiment 8 of Figure 13.5.
*Percent of indicated reschedules that were implemented.
Source: R. J. Penlesky, "Open Order Rescheduling Heuristics for MRP Systems in Manufacturing Firms," unpublished doctoral dissertation, Indiana University, 1982, p. 148.

centers, there is a need to make labor assignment decisions as well. Labor assignment decisions are an important factor in controlling work flow when labor capacity is a critical resource in completing work. This can occur even when only one particular labor skill is the bottleneck resource. In such instances, the system is said to be labor limited.

Labor limitations provide an additional dimension to shop floor scheduling that is particularly important in the present economic climate. In many firms excess capacity exists in many machine centers. The controllable cost is labor, and the primary scheduling job is how to assign labor to machine centers. Good labor scheduling practice provides the possibility of varying the labor capacity at work centers to better match the day-to-day fluctuations in work loads. To the extent that flexibility in assigning people to work centers exists, improvements in manufacturing performance can be gained; e.g., reduced flow times, better customer service, and decreased work-in-process inventory. However, the degree to which flexibility in making labor assignments exists depends on factors such as the amount of cross-training in the work force, the existence of favorable employee work rules, the costs of shifting people between work centers, etc.

A comprehensive framework for the control of work flow in labor-limited systems has been provided by Nelson. The framework lists three major elements for controlling of work flow in scheduling:

1. Determining which job to do next at a work center (dispatching).
2. Determining when a person is available for transfer to another work center (degree of central control).
3. Determining the work center to which an available person is to be assigned (work center selection).

Various decision rules, using information similar to that used in making dispatching decisions, have been suggested for making the latter two decisions. The decision rules suggested by Nelson for determining the availability of a person for transfer utilize a central control parameter, d, that varies between 0 and 1. When $d = 1$, the person is always available for reassignment to another machine. When $d = 0$, the person cannot be reassigned as long as there are jobs waiting in the queue at the person's current work center assignment. The proportion of scheduling decisions in which a person is available for transfer can be controlled by adjusting the value of d between 0 and 1.

Two different approaches to transfer availability are suggested by Fryer. One considers time, and the other considers the queue. The approach suggests that the person must be idle for t or more minutes before a transfer can be made. The queue-oriented approach suggests making a transfer only when the person's work center queue has less than q jobs waiting for processing. Labor flexibility is increased by decreasing the value of t or increasing the value of q.

The third decision in the framework, deciding to which work center a person should be assigned, can be made using decision rules that are quite similar to dispatching rules. Priorities for assigning labor to unattended work centers can be determined on the basis of which work center has as its next job to process:

1. The shortest job (SPT).
2. The job that has been in the shop the longest (FISFS).
3. The job that has been waiting at the current work center the longest (FCFS).
4. The most jobs in the queue.
5. Random assignment (as a base line for comparison)

These decision rules are combined with the decision rules for making dispatching and labor availability decisions to control the work flow.

Simulation experiments have been conducted to evaluate the performance of the different work flow control rules suggested for labor-limited systems. These studies generally measure the improvement in the job flow time performance. An interesting general finding is that while changes in dispatching rules involve a tradeoff between the mean and variance in job flow times, changes in labor assignment rules often can reduce both measures simultaneously. These results can be seen in Figure 13.7.

The importance of labor flexibility in a shop is also demonstrated by experiments involving the labor flexibility factor, d. A change between no labor flexibility ($d - 1$) and complete labor flexibility ($d = 0$) resulted in a 12 percent and 39 percent reduction in the mean and variance of job flow times, respectively.

The research on labor assignment rules demonstrates the importance of cross-training and labor assignment flexibility. Moreover, it provides a view that both labor and job dispatching can have a major impact in controlling work flow through a shop. With an operating shop floor control system in place, it well might be that further performance improvements will come from better design of labor assignments and from operational changes that permit greater flexibility in labor assignments.

Lessons for practice

In this section we have overviewed several advanced studies on scheduling. The three major research streams selected are due date setting, dynamic due dates, and labor limited scheduling systems. Each of these advanced research areas offers some important insights to the professional who has an operating MPC system and is interested in further enhancements.

The research on due date setting suggests that important reductions in manufacturing flow times and work-in-process inventory can be achieved by adopting lead time setting procedures that are based on job processing

FIGURE 13.7 Time and number of jobs in system

Size of labor force	Statistic: / Queue discipline	Mean time and mean number in system*			Variance of time in system			Variance of number in system		
		FCFS	FISFS	SPT	FCFS	FISFS	SPT	FCFS	FISFS	SPT
4		17.7	17.7	9.4	488	295	612	201	205	24
3	Labor assignment rule 0	11.0	11.0	7.0	200	125	295	76	80	17
	Labor assignment rule 1	10.2			173			54		
	Labor assignment rule 2		10.5			102			63	
	Labor assignment rule 3			6.6			343			15
	Labor assignment rule 4	10.1	10.1	6.4	169	97	281	50	53	11
2	Labor assignment rule 0	8.7	8.7	6.2	158	147	186	65	67	23
	Labor assignment rule 1	8.7			153			49		
	Labor assignment rule 2		8.7			147			67	
	Labor assignment rule 3			5.0			285			10
	Labor assignment rule 4	8.7	8.8	5.1	154	89	293	46	48	9
1	Labor assignment rule 0	8.3	8.3	5.5	157	174	176	74	69	24
	Labor assignment rule 1	8.3			149			48		
	Labor assignment rule 2		8.3			174			69	
	Labor assignment rule 3			4.2			296			9
	Labor assignment rule 4	8.3	8.3	4.4	150	174	298	45	69	8

Note: Labor assignment rules:
0 = Random labor assignment to a work center
1 = FCFS labor assignment to a work center
2 = FISFS labor assignment to a work center
3 = SPT labor assignment to a work center
4 = Most jobs in queue labor assignment to a work center
*Parameters chosen so that the mean time and the mean number in the system were equal.
Source: R. T. Nelson, "Labor and Machine Limited Production Systems," *Management Science* 13, no. 9 (May 1967), p. 660.

times. Using this information to set the lead time offset data for MRP and shop floor control will be particularly important as lead times (and work-in-process inventory levels) are systematically reduced.

The research on managing open order due dates suggests that performance benefits can be gained by implementing dynamic due date procedures under certain operating conditions. The improvements, however, are influenced by shop structure considerations such as order quantity sizes and lead times. The research on filtering procedures suggests that gains in manufacturing performance can be achieved by implementing a relatively small proportion of the suggested due date changes.

The research on labor-limited scheduling shows the potential that an increase in labor flexibility can have on manufacturing performance. In many firms today the combined capacity of its work centers far exceeds its labor capacity. In such cases there is an important potential for reassigning the work force to better match the day-to-day variations in work. This is particularly so if the benefits of job sequencing have already been achieved with a functioning shop floor control system. Broadening the scheduling approach to include the assignment of people to work centers as well as the sequencing of jobs can provide major reductions in manufacturing flow times and work-in-process inventory. Critical elements in achieving these benefits concern the cross-training of employees on different machines, and the negotiation of favorable employee work rules. A firm which is able to implement these procedures can achieve an important competitive edge.

CONCLUDING PRINCIPLES

The advanced scheduling concepts described in this chapter lead to the following concluding principles:

- The objective(s) to be achieved in scheduling must be determined before a sequencing rule can be selected since different rules provide different results.
- The shortest processing time rule, contrary to one's intuition, can produce important results and should be considered as a standard in designing shop floor control systems.
- Important improvements in manufacturing performance can be gained by introducing flexibility in scheduling; e.g., through the use of alternate routings, adjustments in labor assignments, overlap scheduling, etc.
- Manufacturing lead time setting is an important consideration in scheduling. Processing times should be a basic data input.
- Proper maintenance of due dates can provide major improvements in manufacturing performance.
- Shop floor nervousness can be diminished by using due date filtering procedures.
- Labor assignment procedures can have an important impact in improving the mean and variance of job flow times simultaneously.

REFERENCES

Baker, K. R. *Introduction to Sequencing and Scheduling.* New York: John Wiley and Sons, 1974.

Baker, K. R., and J. W. M. Bertrand. "A Comparison of Due-Date Selection Rules." *AIIE Transactions,* June 1981.

Berry, W. L. "Priority Scheduling and Inventory Control in Job Lot Manufacturing Systems." *AIIE Transactions* 4, no. 4 (December 1972).

Berry, W. L., and V. Rao. "Critical Ratio Scheduling: An Experimental Analysis." *Management Science* 22, no. 2 (October 1975).

Cantellow, D. G., S. L. Burton, and R. M. Laing. "An Automatic Model for Purchase Decisions." *Operations Research Quarterly,* Special Conference Issue, 1969.

Carroll, D. C. "Heuristic Sequencing of Single and Multiple Component Jobs." Ph.D. dissertation, Alfred P. Sloan School of Management, Massachusetts Institute of Technology, 1965.

Conway, R. W., W. L. Maxwell, and L. W. Miller. *Theory of Scheduling*. Reading, Mass.: Addison-Wesley, 1967.

Day, J. E., and M. P. Hottenstein. "Review of Sequencing Research." *Naval Research Logistics Quarterly* 17 (March 1970).

Eilon, S., and I. G. Chowdbury. "Due Dates in Job Shop Scheduling." *International Journal of Production Research* 14, no. 2 (1976).

Elvers, D. A. "Job Shop Dispatching Using Various Due-Date Setting Criteria." *Production and Inventory Management* 14, no. 4 (December 1973).

Erhorn, Craig R. "Handling Less Than Lead Time Schedule Changes." *Production and Inventory Management* 22, no. 3 (3d Quarter 1981), pp. 27–32.

Fryer, J. S. "Labor Flexibility in Multiechelon Dual-Constraint Job Shops." *Management Science* 20, no. 7 (March 1974).

———. "Operating Policies in Multiechelon Dual Constraint Job Shops." *Management Science* 19, no. 9 (May 1973).

Graves, S. "A Review of Production Scheduling." *Operations Research* 29, no. 4 (July/August 1981).

Hausman, W. H., and G. D. Scudder. "Priority Scheduling Rules for Repairable Inventory Systems." *Management Science* 28, no. 11 (November 1982).

Holstein, W. K., and W. L. Berry. "The Labor Assignment Decision: An Application of Work Flow Structure Information." *Management Science* 18, no. 7 (March 1972).

Jackson, J. S. "Can You Trust the Computer to Reschedule?" *1974 APICS Conference Proceedings*, pp. 216–24.

Johnson, S. M. "Optimal Two and Three-Stage Production Schedules with Setup Time Included." *Naval Research Logistics Quarterly* 1 (1954), pp. 61–68.

Kanet, J. J. "On the Advisability of Operation Due Dates." *1980 APICS Conference Proceedings*, pp. 355–57.

Nanot, Y. R. "An Experimental Investigation and Comparative Evaluation of Priority Discipline in Job Shop Queueing Networks." Management Sciences Research Project, Research Report no. 87, University of California, Los Angeles, December 1963.

Nelson, R. T. "Labor and Machine Limited Production Systems." *Management Science* 13, no. 9 (May 1967).

———. "A Simulation of Labor Efficiency and Centralized Assignment in a Production Model." *Management Science* 17, no. 2 (October 1970).

———. "Dual-Resource Constrained Series Service Systems." *Operations Research* 16, no. 2 (March/April 1968).

Orlicky, J. A. "Rescheduling with Tomorrow's MRP Systems." *Production and Inventory Management*, June 1976.

Panwalker, S. S., and W. Iskander. "A Survey of Scheduling Rules." *Operations Research* 25 (January 1977).

Penlesky, R. J. "Open Order Rescheduling Heuristics for MRP Systems in Manufacturing Firms." Unpublished Ph.D. dissertation, Indiana University, 1982.

Putnam, A. O., R. Everdell, G. H. Dorman, R. R. Cronan, and L. H. Lundgren. "Updating Critical Ratio and Slack Time Priority Scheduling Rules." *Production and Inventory Management* 12, no. 4 (1971).

Steele, D. C. "The Nervous MRP System: How to Do Battle." *Production and Inventory Management* 16 (December, 1975).

Weeks, J. K. "A Simulation Study of Predictable Due-Dates." *Management Science* 25, no. 4 (April 1973).

Wemmerlov, U. "Design Factors in MRP Systems: A Limited Survey." *Production and Inventory Management* 20 (December 1979).

Whitaker, John H. "Managing—To Get Better Results in Less Time." *Production and Inventory Management*, 4th Quarter 1975.

Woolsey, R. E. D. "A Survey of Quick and Dirty Methods for Production Scheduling." *1972 APICS Conference Proceedings*, pp. 309–30.

14

MPC systems for engineered products

This chapter is concerned with the planning and scheduling of complex make-to-order products produced on a project basis. Examples include the manufacture of custom-engineered products such as those produced by the ship-building, electrical apparatus, and the construction industries. In these situations the planning and scheduling effort necessarily includes the preproduction project activities, such as product development, engineering design, and drafting, as well as purchasing and manufacturing. The planning and control of such products can clearly be accomplished using conventional project planning and control methods such as PERT (project evaluation and review technique) and CPM (critical path method), and we describe the use of these techniques in this chapter. However, some firms have taken a very different approach to the planning and scheduling of make-to-order products, as in the Elliott Corporation example described in this chapter. That is, the MPC system is extended and bill of material techniques have been applied to plan and schedule preproduction activities such as engineering and drafting. There are important advantages in extending standard MPC procedures to cover preproduction activities for a firm that already has an MPC system in place for manufacturing and purchasing. A single system for scheduling both preproduction and manufacturing activities enables a consistent control method to be applied to all project activities. Moreover, since, in many firms, other products, e.g. make-to-stock or assemble-to-order products, are produced in addition to make-to-order products, it is important to have consistent systems for material planning, capacity planning, and shop-floor control.

Again, Chapter 14 focuses on enhancements to a working MPC system. When this is the case, and if the firm is increasingly concerned with the scheduling of highly engineered custom made products, the ideas in this chapter can pay important dividends. The chapter is organized around the following five topics:

- Basic project-planning techniques: What are the fundamental data for project scheduling, and how are individual activities scheduled?
- Enhancing the project plan: How can uncertainties in activity times and resource limitations be incorporated into the plan?
- Project planning with MPC systems: How can MRP and other MPC techniques be applied to project scheduling?
- Project control: How can project planning be routinely updated, and what techniques highlight problem areas?
- Examples: How have project scheduling techniques and MPC techniques been creatively applied to solve actual problems?

This chapter has close parallels with the material in Chapters 5 and 13 which describe scheduling and routine updates to scheduling. There is also a linkage to Chapters 7 and 8, dealing with master production scheduling, since Chapter 14 develops concepts useful for master production scheduling for make-to-order companies. We rely on the concepts of MRP and the bill of material ideas presented in Chapters 2 and 8 to show how project management can be accomplished with MPC system modules.

BASIC PROJECT-PLANNING TECHNIQUES

Project-planning techniques have been utilized for more than 25 years in the management of complex, one-of-a-kind projects. The project evaluation and review technique (PERT) and critical path method (CPM) are well-known project-planning techniques. Both techniques involve breaking down a total project into individual activities or tasks, and recognizing the sequential constraints among the tasks. Thereafter, a schedule for the timing of each task is developed, indicating the start and finish times, plus any flexibilities in the timing for the tasks. In order to understand how project planning with MPC approaches can lead to important benefits, we will first review the methodology and terminology of the basic project-planning techniques.

Basic data

The first steps in planning a project are to break the overall project down into individual activities or tasks to be accomplished, and to estimate the time required to complete each activity. This will form a key part of the

FIGURE 14.1 Norwalk project data base

Activity	*Description*	*Time*	*Preceding activities*
A	Engineering design	3 weeks	—
B	Drafting	2 weeks	A
C	Customer approval	1 week	A
D	Purchase material	4 weeks	B, C
E	Fabricate tank	3 weeks	D
F	Fabricate top	2 weeks	D
G	Fabricate base	1 week	D
H	Assemble top to tank	4 weeks	E, F
I	Assemble tank to base and test	2 weeks	G, H

project data base. As an example, the sales department at a pressure vessel manufacturing firm has recently been successful in bidding on a pressure vessel project. This particular pressure vessel is to be custom designed for installation at the Norwalk Chemical Plant. As soon as the project bid was accepted by the customer, the sales, engineering, and manufacturing departments met to prepare a schedule for the design, purchasing, and production work on the project. This committee determined that nine activities need to be performed in this project. These activities and the estimated time to complete each of them are listed in Figure 14.1.

One of the problems in defining the project tasks is to determine the scope of each activity. For example, in the Norwalk project, the first activity is to complete the engineering design work for the pressure vessel. This involves preparing the engineering specifications for the three major components of the vessel: the tank top, the tank, and the base. Alternatively, this activity might be divided into three separate activities: design the tank top, design the tank, and design the base unit. Decisions regarding the scope of the individual activities depend on the level of detail required to plan and control the project, and the resources to be utilized in executing an activity.

In this example, the same engineering group is responsible for designing the tank top, tank, and base unit. Combining these three tasks into a single activity simplifies the definition of this activity. However, if the customer delivery lead time were short and the overall project length needed to be reduced, there might be an advantage in specifying separate activities for each of these tasks. That is, scheduling the base-unit design work first might permit an earlier start on the succeeding activities, e.g., drafting, purchasing, and manufacturing.

Determining the precedence relationships

Once the individual project activities have been specified and time estimates have been prepared, the next step is to ascertain the sequence in which these activities must be completed, i.e., their precedence relationships. These are also a part of the project data base. Several precedence relationships are evident in the Norwalk project activities listed in Figure 14.1. For example, the tank cannot be fabricated (Activity E) until the steel and fittings have been purchased (Activity D). Similarly, the top cannot be assembled to the tank (Activity H) until after the tank and top have been fabricated (Activities E and F). The precedence relationships follow directly from the nature of the activities themselves. Some of the project activities need to be performed in a given sequence, such as purchasing material, fabricating the tank, and assembling the tank top to the tank in the Norwalk project. Other project activities can be performed concurrently. For example, the tank, the tank top, and the base unit can be manufactured in any order or simultaneously once the necessary material has been purchased.

The extent to which the project activities can be performed concurrently, instead of sequentially, will have an important impact on determining the overall length of the project. An examination of the activities shown in Figure 14.1 indicates why this is true. If all the activities *must* be performed in sequence, starting with Activity A and ending with Activity I, 22 weeks would be required to complete the project. However, if there were *no* precedence relationships among these activities, the project would be completed in 4 weeks—the length of time required to complete the longest activity. We see then that this project will take somewhere between 4 and 22 weeks to complete. The key to determining where in this 18-week time span the completion of the Norwalk project will take place can be provided by the application of network models.

Developing a network diagram

Two alternatives have been developed which utilize a network-based approach to project scheduling: PERT and CPM. Both approaches are, however, quite similar in application. They both involve the use of a network diagram to structure the precedence relationships of the activities, to prepare the project schedule, and to allocate resources to project activities. There are, however, some unique features of these two techniques, which will be briefly noted.

The first step in using CPM or PERT in scheduling project activities involves the construction of a network diagram. A network diagram identifies the sequence in which the project activities are to be accomplished. Under CPM, the network diagram is referred to as an *activities on node diagram.* Under PERT, the network diagram is referred to as an *activities on arrow diagram.* Since both network scheduling approaches are quite similar, this chapter will focus on the use of CPM. Using the activities on node approach, individual activities are displayed as circles (nodes), and arrows connect these nodes to indicate the precedence relationships among the activities which are to be performed in completing the project. The network diagram begins with the activity which starts the project and ends with the

FIGURE 14.2 Example CPM network diagram—Norwalk project

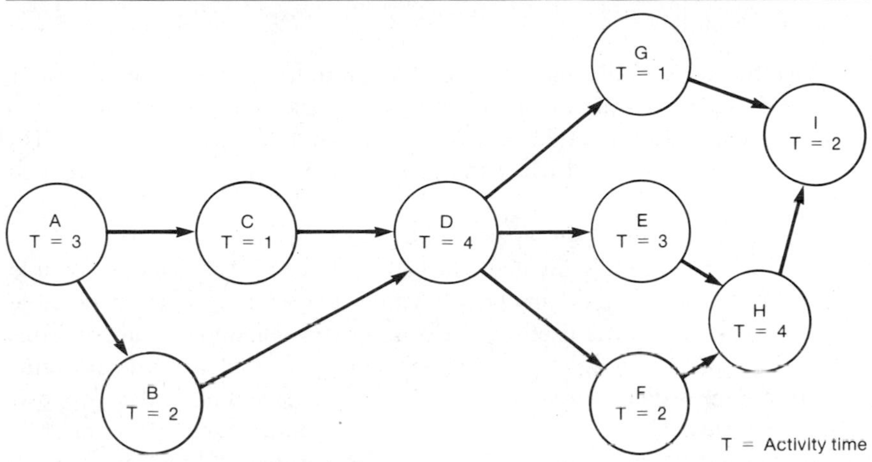

activity which completes the project. Often there are two additional activities used to specifically designate the start of the project and the completion of the project. If used, they must be incorporated into the project data base. When the network diagram has been completed, it forms the basis from which the project schedule is constructed. An example CPM network diagram for the Norwalk project is shown as Figure 14.2.

The CPM network diagram for the Norwalk project begins with the engineering design activity (A) and ends with the assembly of the tank to base and testing activity (I). Once activity A has been completed, the diagram indicates that activities B and C can be started and performed concurrently. Similarly, the diagram indicates that both activities B and C must be completed before activity D (purchasing) can be started. Next, the diagram indicates that the fabrication activities E, F, and G cannot begin until the purchasing activity D is completed. Finally, the project cannot be finished (activity I) until both activities G and H have been completed.

The network diagram provides a picture of the sequence of activities required to complete the project. In the Norwalk project, six different paths (sequences of activities) can be observed (Figure 14.2). One of these paths, for example, is A–C–D–F–H–I. Within a given sequence, e.g., A–C–D–F–H–I, each activity must be completed in turn before the following activity can be started. Note that each of these six activity sequences (paths) can be performed concurrently. The minimum project duration will, therefore, equal the *longest* of the times required to complete the activity sequences. The six sequences and their associated times are:

A–C–D–F–H–I (16 weeks), A–C–D–G–I (11 weeks),
A–C–D–E–H–I (17 weeks), A–B–D–G–I (12 weeks),
A–B–D–E–H–I (18 weeks), and A–B–D–F–H–I (17 weeks)

Since the activities on path A–B–D–E–H–I require the longest overall time of 18 weeks, this establishes the minimum project length.

Project scheduling

Once the network diagram has been completed, a project schedule can be prepared. This schedule involves determining the starting and completion times for each project activity, to meet the minimum project length. This schedule can be prepared using the routine logic of project-planning techniques.

The network diagram serves as the basis to develop not one but two CPM schedules. One schedule involves starting each activity as early as possible, while the second schedule involves starting each activity as late as possible. The network diagram is used in performing the scheduling computations, and both project schedules are typically noted on the network diagram.

Early-start project schedule. The early-start schedule is developed by making a *forward pass* through the network diagram, taking into account the required time for each project activity. The early-start time (S_E) and the early finish time (F_E) are determined for each activity and noted on the network diagram, using the conventions shown in Figure 14.3.

There are four rules for calculating the early start and finish times for each activity:

1. The early-start time for the initial activity in the network is set equal to zero, i.e., $S_E = 0$ for the START activity.
2. An activity can begin as soon as its preceding activity has been completed, i.e., $S_E =$ the F_E for the preceding activity.
3. The activity early-finish time equals the early-start time plus the activity time, i.e., $F_E = S_E + T$.

FIGURE 14.3 Activity scheduling information

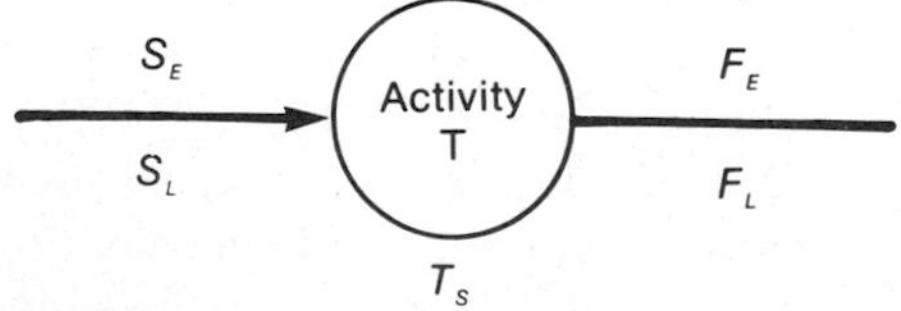

where:

S_E = Activity early-start time.
F_E = Activity early-finish time.
S_L = Activity late-start time.
F_L = Activity late-finish time.
T = Activity time.
T_S = Activity total slack time.

4. When an activity or circle on the network diagram has more than one predecessor activity, i.e., more than one arrow entering the node, the activity early-start time equals the largest early-finish time of the preceding activities, i.e., S_E = largest of (F_{E1}, F_{E2} ··· F_{En}) for an activity having n predecessors.

The determination of the early-start and early-finish times for a project, using these four rules, is illustrated with the numbers *on top of the nodes* in Figure 14.4 for the Norwalk project. Since the initial activity (A) is the starting activity for the project, its early-start time (S_E) is set equal to zero. This activity requires three weeks to complete, so its early-finish time (F_E) equals three. Therefore, the early-start time for activity B equals three, and since activity B requires two weeks to complete, its early-finish time (F_E) equals the end of week five. Setting the early-start and finish times for these two activities provides an illustration of rules 1 through 3. The early-start and early-finish times for each of the remaining activities in the Norwalk project are shown in Figure 14.4.

The application of rules 1 through 4 to the activities in Figure 14.4 provides the early-start (S_E) and early-finish times (F_E) for this project. When both the activity times and the precedence relationships between the project activities have been considered, it appears that this project cannot be completed earlier than the end of week 18. An alternative schedule can be constructed for the project in which the activities are scheduled as late as possible to meet this earliest project completion date. This schedule, called the late-start and finish schedule, helps to define managerial flexibility in scheduling individual project activities.

Late-start schedule The late-start schedule is prepared by making a *backward pass* through the network diagram, beginning with a stated project completion date for the last project activity, and working backward toward the first activity in the project. This scheduling procedure produces a late start (S_L) and a late-finish time (F_L) for each activity. These times are usually noted under the nodes on the network diagram using the conventions shown previously in Figure 14.3. There are four more rules for calculating the late-start and late-finish times for each activity:

5. The late-finish time for the final activity in the network is set equal to the earliest project completion date, i.e., F_L = The F_E for the final activity.
6. The late-finish time for an activity equals the late-start time for the activity immediately succeeding it, i.e., F_L = The S_L for the succeeding activity.
7. The activity late-start time equals the late-finish time minus the activity time, i.e., $S_L = F_L - T$.
8. When an activity has more than one successor activity, i.e., more than one arrow leaving the node, the late-finish time for that activity is the

FIGURE 14.4 Norwalk project network schedule

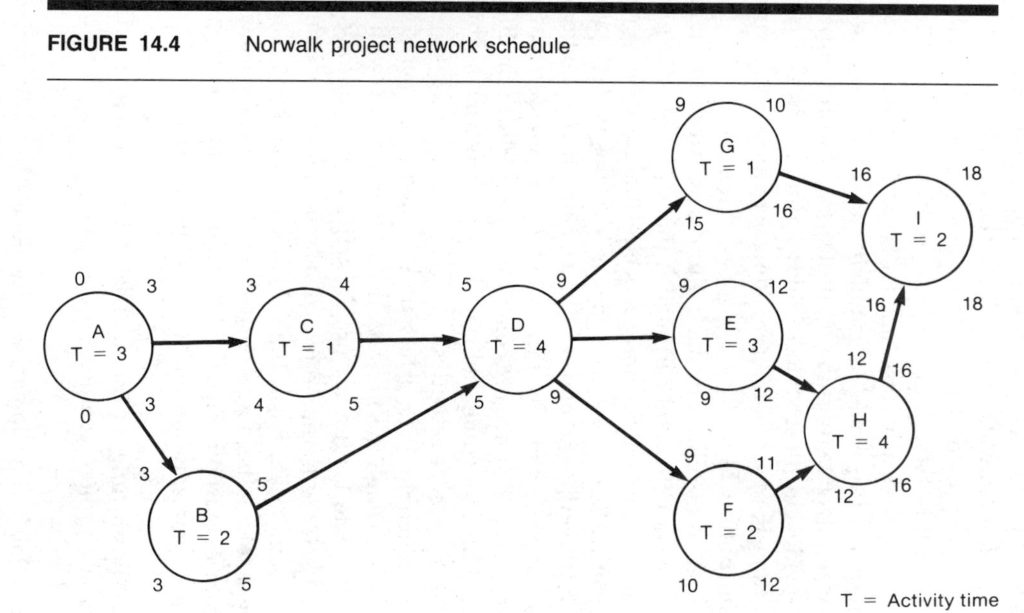

smallest of the late-start times for those activities immediately succeeding that activity, i.e., F_L = smallest of $(S_{L1}, S_{L2}, \ldots S_{Ln})$ for an activity having n successors.

The application of these rules to determine the late-start (S_L) and late-finish (F_L) time for each activity in the Norwalk project is illustrated by the data shown *below the nodes* in Figure 14.4.

Slack

Once the early- and late-start times have been determined for all of the activities in a project network, the total slack time for each activity in the project can be determined. The total slack time for an activity (T_S) is defined as the difference between its late-and early-start times ($T_S = S_L - S_E$). Alternatively, the total slack (T_S) for an activity can be calculated as the difference between the early-and late-finish times, i.e., $T_S = F_L - F_E$). The total slack time for each activity in the Norwalk project is shown in Figure 14.5, and the detailed calculations are given in Figure 14.6. For example, note that activity G can be started as early as the end of week 9 at the early-start time (S_E) and as late as the end of week 15 (S_L) without affecting the project completion date of the end of week 18. Therefore, the total slack time (T_S) for activity G is 15 − 9, or 6 weeks. The total slack time measure indicates the degree of flexibility that management has in scheduling the start time of a particular activity to best utilize the available resources or to respond to local conditions.

FIGURE 14.5 Norwalk project network schedule

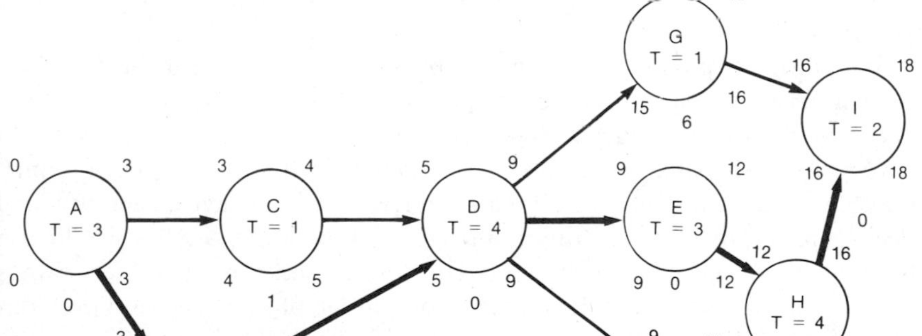

FIGURE 14.6 Norwalk project schedule

Activity	S_E	S_L	T_S
A	0	0	0
B	3	3	0
C	3	4	1
D	5	5	0
E	9	9	0
F	9	10	1
G	9	15	6
H	12	12	0
I	16	16	0

The critical path. Several of the activities shown in Figure 14.6 have a total slack time of zero, indicating that management has no flexibility in scheduling these activities. For example, since the early-start time for activity B equals its late-start time, this activity must be started at the end of week 3 or the completion of the entire project will be delayed beyond the end of week 18. Similarly, activities A, D, E, H, and I all have a total slack time of zero.

The fact that activities A, B, D, E, H, and I have a zero total slack time (T_S), and must be performed in the sequence shown in Figure 14.5, means that they form a *critical path* in completing the Norwalk project. A delay in starting any of the activities on the critical path in the project network means that the project cannot be completed at the end of week 18. The determination of the critical path in a project network enables management to focus attention on those activities which are most crucial in completing the project on time. Other activities which do not lie on the critical path, do not warrant the same degree of managerial attention since there is some flexibility (as indicated by the total slack times) in both starting and completing these activities.

It is entirely possible for there to be more than one critical path in a project network. As an example, suppose that activity C required two weeks to complete instead of one. In this case, the Norwalk project network would have two critical paths, A–C–D–E–H–I and A–B–D–E–H–I, both requiring 18 weeks to complete. In this case, activity C would have an activity total slack time (T_S) of zero, and the timely completion of this activity would also be of major concern to management. The determination of the critical path is a key element in ensuring the on-time completion of a project, and provides management with an important tool for identifying those project activities that deserve special attention in managing the project.

ENHANCING THE PROJECT PLAN

There are several implied assumptions in the basic project-planning techniques as explained above. Activity times are uncertain estimates of the actual times required. Resources are not unlimited, and the company may have several projects in process. This section briefly describes how some of these real-world considerations can be added to the basic project-planning model.

Probabilistic project networks

The network diagram analysis and the project schedules presented up to this point have assumed that the activity times are deterministic. That is, each activity will take exactly the time allotted, and will not vary. Yet, in reality, the time for very few project activities is known with complete certainty before a project is undertaken, and it is often desirable to introduce information into the network analysis which reflects the uncertainty inherent in activity times.

The PERT formulation of the project scheduling problem allows for this uncertainty by establishing three time estimates: optimistic, most likely, and pessimistic, for each activity. The result is an expected time value for each activity, and for the project in total. This additional information provides for probabilistic assessments of activity and completion times, and provides the basis for using simulation to analyze complex projects.

Resource allocation

A major issue in project scheduling is how a particular project can be scheduled so as to best integrate with available resources. That is, it is important to satisfy the time constraints imposed by a project, while at the same time scheduling the series of activities so as to utilize resources effectively. These are important issues involving both the management of the demands placed on an operating facility and the setting of realistic project completion dates.

It is important to have a method for checking the resource requirements indicated by a project schedule before a commitment is made to either a project completion date or, in the case of one-of-a-kind manufacturing, the delivery of product to a customer. It may be that a given project requires more resources, e.g., more welders in the fabrication shop, than are available in a particular time period. Another project schedule might call for a very erratic use of some resource. To the extent that slack exists, flexibility in scheduling project activities also exists. Slack might make it possible to adjust the project schedule to better utilize resources. There are several techniques available for adjusting project schedules to level the resource requirements. These include the use of *time charts* and some computerized procedures that have been developed for use with network scheduling techniques, such as the SPAR-1 technique described by Weist and Levy.

Time charts The time chart offers a simple visual check on the project resource requirements and can be used effectively for projects that have a relatively small number of activities. The time chart indicates the timing of individual project activities relative to one another. The time chart can be used to display a project network on a time scale, showing the activity early- and late-start and finish times, thereby indicating management flexibility in project scheduling.

A time chart for Norwalk is shown as Figure 14.7. Each activity is designated by an arrow, with the arrowhead indicating the completion time of an activity and the tail of the arrow marking the start time for the activity. For example, activity B in Figure 14.7 starts at the end of week 3 and is completed at the end of week 5. The critical path activities (A–B–D–E–H–I) are shown together at the top of Figure 14.7, and the remaining activities are shown scheduled at their late start and finish times. The dashed line preceding each of the noncritical activities indicates the slack time for the activity. For example, activity G is scheduled during week 16 and has six weeks of slack time. Also shown in Figure 14.7 are the personnel requirements and a convention for their inclusion on the time chart.

To evaluate the resource requirements for the project, the project data base must be expanded to include the resources required to complete each

FIGURE 14.7 Norwalk project time chart

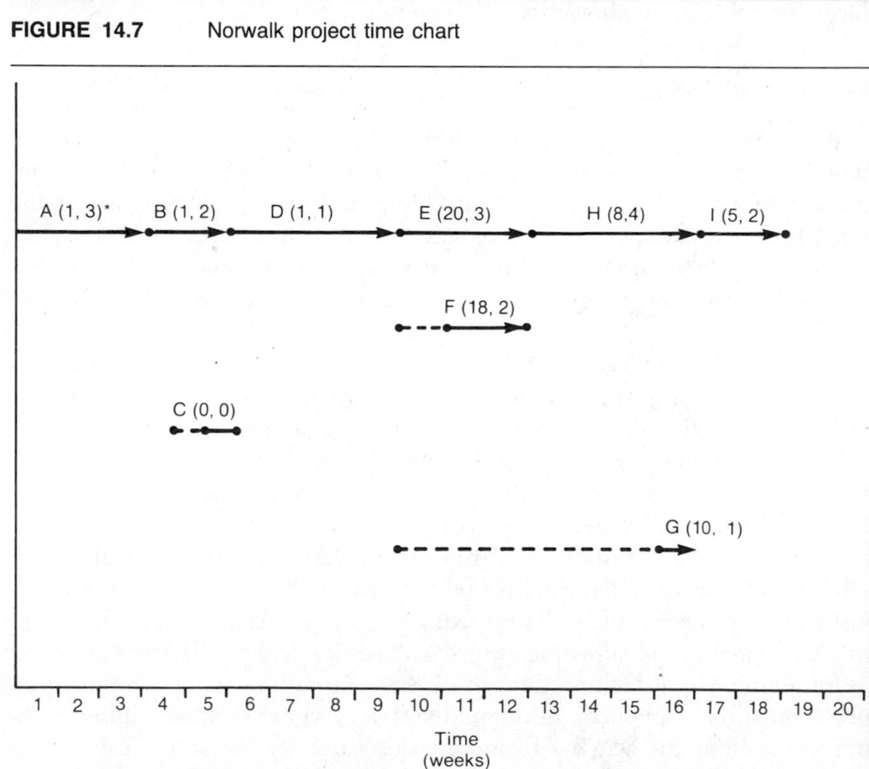

*A(1,3) means activity A requires one person for three weeks. In general (X,Y) means X persons for Y weeks. Any additional activity time requires other resources, e.g. in activities C and D.

FIGURE 14.8 Norwalk project resource requirements

Activity	Resource requirements
A	1 engineer for 3 weeks
B	1 draftsman for 2 weeks
C	—
D	1 buyer for 1 week plus 3 weeks of supplier lead time
E	20 fabrication shop employees for 3 weeks
F	18 fabrication shop employees for 2 weeks
G	10 fabrication shop employees for 1 week
H	8 assembly shop employees for 4 weeks
I	5 assembly shop employees for 2 weeks

activity. The resource requirements for each activity in the Norwalk project are listed in Figure 14.8. These are added to the time chart to determine the resource requirements for each activity in every time period during the project.

The resource requirements noted on the time chart can be summarized for every time period in the project to indicate the total requirements for each type of resource. This has been done in Figure 14.9 for the fabrication

FIGURE 14.9 Fabrication shop personnel requirements for the Norwalk project

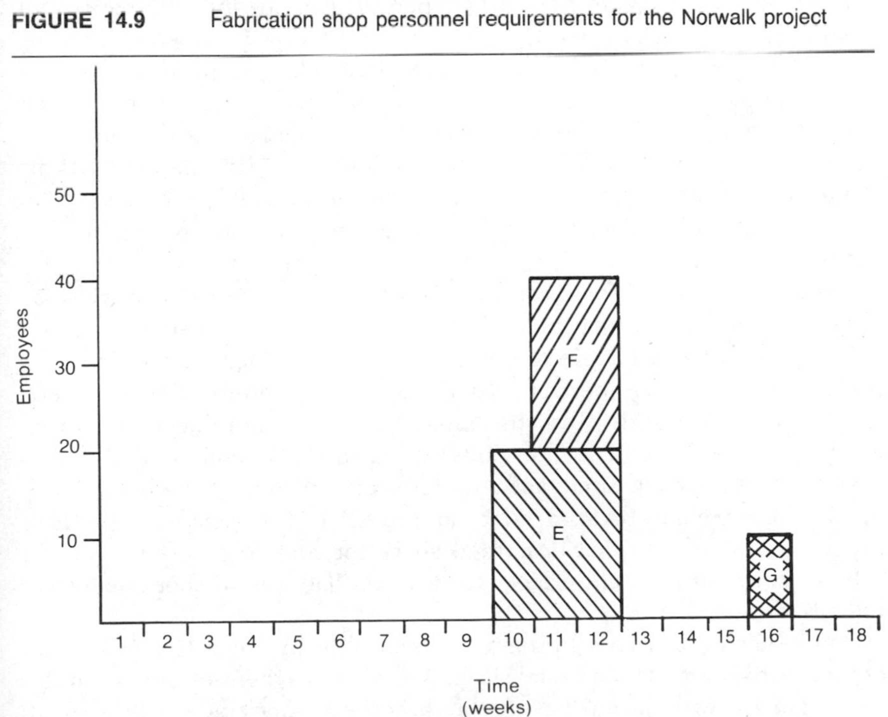

shop employees for each week in the 18-week schedule for the Norwalk project. These requirements can be evaluated in light of the workload that has been already placed on the fabrication shop by other projects in process. The fabrication shop load table in Figure 14.10 provides a time-phased forecast of the current workload (i.e., without the Norwalk project) in the fabrication shop.

When the 18-week schedule for the Norwalk project is analyzed using the resource requirements and shop load information in Figures 14.9 and 14.10, it is apparent that the total requirements would now exceed the available fabrication shop manpower in weeks 12 and 16. The fact is that 38 more fabrication shop workers would be required in weeks 12 and 16 if the Norwalk project were undertaken. The 38 fabrication shop employees that would be needed in week 12 would exceed the availability of 20 out of the 100 limit shown on the shop load table in Figure 14.10. Similarly, the Norwalk project requirements for week 16 would also exceed the total manpower available, since there is none available and the Norwalk project requires 10 people.

Often, the project schedule can be adjusted to meet the resource limitations by shifting those activities which have slack times to an earlier start time. For example, activity F has one week of slack, and could be started as early as the end of week 9. Starting activity F one week earlier will alleviate the resource problem in week 12. Similarly, the slack time of six weeks indicated for activity G in Figure 14.7 permits two possible alternatives for solving the problem in week 16. Activity G can either be scheduled during week 14, or perhaps during weeks 14 and 15 using five people each week. In some cases, the use of available slack time in scheduling project activities will not permit the project to be scheduled within the available resources. In these cases, the project beginning and completion dates may need to be changed or additional resources obtained to accommodate the order. This may require some negotiation between manufacturing, marketing, and the customer.

Computer methods for resource allocation The time chart provides an important managerial tool for both presenting a project schedule and for adjusting a project schedule to meet resource limitations. However, when projects with large numbers of activities are encountered, or when several projects are scheduled to use the same facilities (multiproject situations), computer-based scheduling methods are needed. Several computer programs for resource allocation and multiproject scheduling have been developed. These include RAMPS, MS^2, and SPAR-1. The logic used by these programs is similar to that described above for adjusting the schedule for activity F in the Norwalk project to meet the fabrication shop manpower limitation.

For example, the SPAR-1 program lists all of the project activities in order of their early-start date and total slack. Activities are then selected from this list, beginning with the one having the earliest early-start date and the small-

FIGURE 14.10 Fabrication shop load table

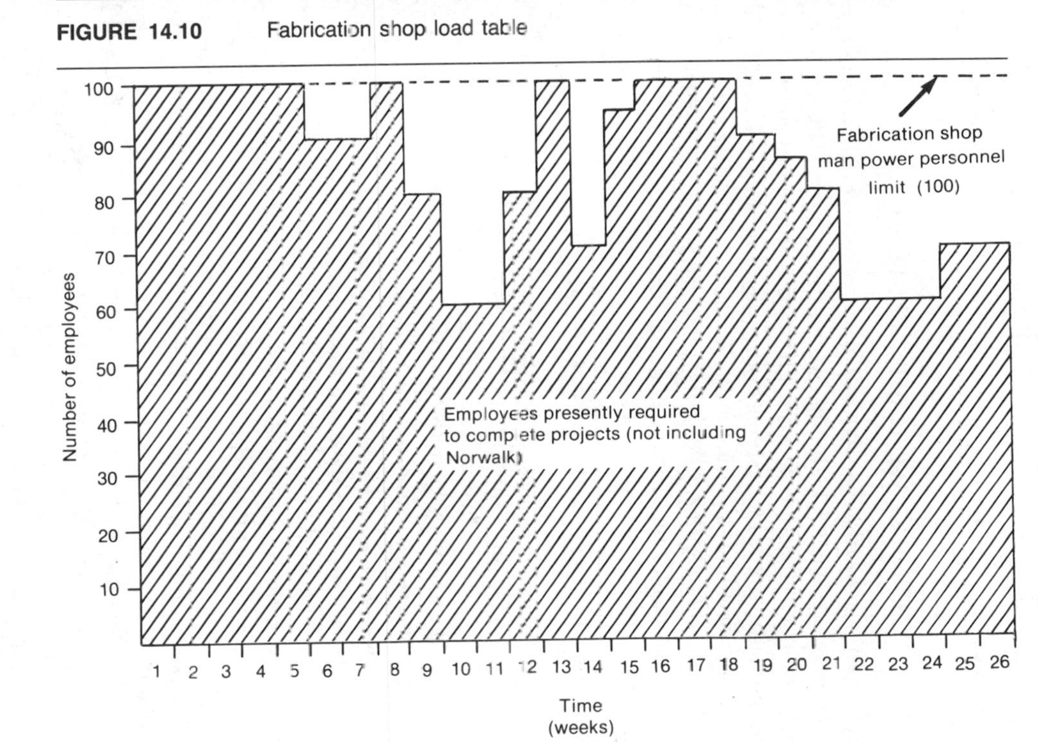

est slack time, and are scheduled period by period, using the available resources, until the entire project has been scheduled. In this way, the activities on the critical path have a high probability of being scheduled at their early-start date, since they have no slack. The SPAR-1 program has additional scheduling procedures for increasing the utilization of project resources or for decreasing the length of the project schedule. These procedures can have an important impact on the use of project resources to meet resource limitations, and are often the only feasible means of performing such analysis on large-scale projects or in multiproject situations.

PROJECT PLANNING WITH MPC SYSTEMS

Now that we have reviewed the basic objectives, methodologies, and terminology of project scheduling, we will show how MPC systems can be used to achieve the same objectives, but with significant improvements. In particular, applying MPC systems to the planning and control of highly engineered products allows an integrated approach to all phases of creation of the product, from conception to design, contracting through prototyping, and into production—all in sharply reduced lead times.

Developing a project bill of material

An alternative to the basic project management approaches is to apply the bill of material concepts used by an MRP system. This involves preparing a project bill of material that reflects the activities and their precedence relationships, and modeling the activity times as lead times. The project BOM can then be processed using routine MRP logic to construct a project schedule. Both MRP and PERT/CPM approaches provide the necessary project schedule. However, the MRP approach allows a direct integration with other MPC modules. It also facilitates the integration of this project with the planning and control of projects currently in progress.

The first step in using MRP logic to schedule project activities is to develop the project bill of material. The individual project activities are displayed as part numbers, and the BOM level structure is used to indicate the sequence in which the project activities will be performed. The project bill begins with the final project activity. Each project activity is listed below, down to and including the activity that starts the project.

Figure 14.11 is a project bill of material for the Norwalk project. In this figure, the final project activity (*I*) is identified as level zero in the BOM. Activities that must be completed before the final activity can begin are coded as level-one activities (in this case activities G and H). This process of identifying the low-level code numbers for the project activities continues until all project activities are included on the bill of material. In the example, activity A has a low-level code of 5. This is the lowest level and corresponds to the initial activity of the project.

FIGURE 14.11 Norwalk project bill of materials

	Low-level code	*Activity*	*Activity time (weeks)*
Assemble tank to base and test	0	I	2
Assemble top to tank	1	H	4
Fabricate top	2	F	2
Fabricate tank	2	E	3
Purchase material	3	D	4
Customer approval	4	C	1
Drafting	4	B	2
Engineering	5	A	3
Fabricate base	1	G	1

The bill of material structure shown in Figure 14.11 uses indenting to show the sequential constraints for the Norwalk project. The indention and low-level coding lead to creation of single-level bills of material. That is, the data associated with activity I would list parts H and G as components in a single-level BOM. Similarly, H would list E and F, E would list D, D would list C and B, and B would list A.

A comparison of Figure 14.11 with Figure 14.5 shows one of the anomalies of using MPC approaches for project scheduling. In PERT/CPM scheduling, an activity is often a predecessor to more than one other activity. For example, activity D is shown in Figure 14.5 as a predecessor to activities G, E, and F. In Figure 14.11, however, D is shown only as a component of E. If it were also shown as a component of F and G, the implication would be that three Ds are needed. The trick is how to choose the correct activity to which each activity should be a predecessor; that is, to design the indented project bill. This is accomplished by using the same logic as is used in making the backward pass for developing the latest start schedule. Using this approach an activity such as D is attached to the predecessor that has the earliest late start time (activity E in this example).

Constructing the project bill is simplified in many firms by utilizing information from previous projects of a similar nature. For example, while the pressure vessel in the example is custom-designed for Norwalk, it is quite possible that a similar vessel may have been built previously for a different customer. This means that the project bill for the previous vessel could be modified to specify the details of the Norwalk project bill. The use of previous project bills reduces the time and effort involved in developing the data base required for project planning and control. In fact, the project-planning data base in a firm may consist of project bill modules for various activities, for example, for various tank types, tops, or base-unit types, that tend to repeat from one project to another.

FIGURE 14.12 Norwalk project bill of materials—revised

	Low-level code	Activity*	Activity time (weeks)
Assemble tank to base and test	0	I	2
Assemble top to tank	1	H	4
Fabricate tank	2	E	3
Purchase material	3	D^2	1
Customer approval	4	C^2	1
Drafting	5	B^2	.5
Engineering	6	A^2	1
Fabricate top	2	F	2
Purchase material	3	D^3	1
Customer approval	4	C^3	1
Drafting	5	B^3	.5
Engineering	6	A^3	1
Fabricate base	1	G	1
Purchase material	2	D^1	2
Customer approval	3	C^1	1
Drafting	4	B^1	1
Engineering	5	A^1	1

*The superscripts (D^2) are on an activity from Figure 14.11 that has been broken into separate components. The value of the superscript shows which separate component group it belongs to.

The construction of the project bill is what makes the MPC approach to project planning so desirable. An entire project often includes such activities as contract negotiation, design engineering, drafting, customer approval, testing, etc. All of these activities can be included in the project schedule under the MPC approach along with the manufacturing steps. By using a project bill from a previous customer order, one can convert each of the activities to the exact one needed for the new project. In using project planning methods based on MPC models, the priorities are established for when each of the activities must be completed. In fact, a schedule can be developed based on these priorities. The MPC approach to project scheduling also enables us to obtain information analogous to that supplied by the shop-floor control, capacity planning, and other MPC systems. Moreover, the periodic regeneration of this information that is an integral part of an MRP system results in a continual replanning of each project, recognizing actual events.

Creativity in designing the project bill of material can help in meeting the schedule objectives. For example, in Figure 14.12 the engineering, drafting, customer approval, and purchasing activities have been broken down into separate activities for each of the product components—the tank, the tank top, and the base. By redefining the project activities, time requirements, and precedence relationships, the planned project length can be reduced from 18 to 12.5 weeks, or by 30 percent, even though the total time for all activities has increased. Clearly, these modifications have complicated the

FIGURE 14.13 Norwalk MRP schedule (due date = week 20)

	Low-level code	*Activity*	*Activity time*	*Late-start time*	*Late-finish time*
Assemble tank to base and test	0	I	2	18	20
Assemble top to tank	1	H	4	14	18
Fabricate top	2	F	2	12	14
Fabricate tank	2	E	3	11	14
Purchase material	3	D	4	7	11
Customer approval	4	C	1	6	7
Drafting	4	B	2	5	7
Engineering	5	A	3	2	5
Fabricate base	1	G	1	17	18

project bill and have added some complexity in the coordination of activities such as the customer approval step, but there might be important gains in reducing the time to complete the project.

MRP scheduling

Once the project bill has been prepared, a project schedule can be developed using MRP logic. This schedule is identical to the late-start schedule developed using CPM. That is, MRP makes a backward pass through the project, beginning with a stated project completion date for the last project activity and working toward the first activity in the project.

This backward pass is a direct result of applying MRP logic. The due date for the level-zero activity, offset by the level-zero lead time, results in the due date for each of its component activities, and so on. Figure 14.13 applies this MRP logic to the basic Norwalk project bill of materials (Figure 14.11), with a project due date arbitrarily set at the end of week 20.

The critical path

The information in the MRP schedule indicates the critical path in the project schedule. It is found by determining the earliest of the late-start dates in the project and then tracing the path connecting that activity to the final activity in the project. In MRP terms, this can be accomplished with pegging, i.e., moving from a low-level item through the successive bill of material levels to the end-product item, using selective where-used pointers. In the Norwalk project, activity A has the earliest of the late-start dates, i.e., week 2, and the critical path is A–B–D–E–H–I.

The managerial concern for the critical path activities is identical to that described earlier in using network scheduling methods. That is, the critical path represents the minimum project length, and managerial attention should be directed at shortening the activities on the critical path if the overall project length currently exceeds the customer delivery requirement.

Slack

Management information regarding the amount of slack time for individual project activities could also be developed from the MRP schedule. All of the activities that do not lie on the critical path have some degree of slack time; thereby providing the flexibility for scheduling project activities. The methods for determining the slack time for individual project activities are, however, much more complex using MRP logic than with CPM. This occurs because all activities are scheduled at their latest start and completion times under MRP scheduling, and the two-pass (forward and backward) scheduling procedure is not employed as it was in the network scheduling procedures. That is, the MRP scheduling procedure removes all slack as a basic part of the logic. MRP schedules *all* activities to be on the critical path.

Uncertainty in activity times

As in network scheduling, the MRP project scheduling method has assumed that the activity times are fixed and will not vary. This is analogous to the use of a fixed lead time for MRP scheduling. When uncertainty in lead times is recognized in scheduling manufacturing operations under MRP, safety lead time can be introduced. The safety lead time is often used to allow for the possibility that the activity/operation may take longer than anticipated.

The primary way that MPC systems deal with activity time uncertainty is through the replanning process (regeneration) and with priority setting in shop-floor control. That is, the total MPC approach to project planning and control recognizes lead time uncertainty as something to control and manage. The periodic regeneration of MRP is particularly useful for this aspect of project planning and control.

PROJECT CONTROL

We have differentiated between the front-end and engine systems used to prepare manufacturing plans and the back-end systems that ensure the proper control/execution of those plans. The methods presented so far in this chapter have been primarily concerned with the preparation of a schedule (plan) at the start of a project. We turn now to ongoing project control and replanning activities.

The issues in developing workable execution systems for project management are the same as in routine manufacturing. There is first a need to communicate the project to those responsible for individual project activities, and to indicate scheduling priorities. Next, there is a need to track actual performance and detect differences between actual progress and the plan. These two issues are similar to those concerning the design and use of shop-floor control and purchasing systems, and the importance of exception message processing. One result of using MPC approaches for project scheduling is that shop-floor control reports can be generated for many functions or areas, such as design engineering. More fundamentally, as each functional area uses the same tools for planning and control, it finds a new basis for communications and improvement in operating results.

Executing the project plan

The process of opening and closing shop orders has an exact counterpart in the development of execution systems for project activities. Here, a project activity can be considered as a shop order. That is, at some point an order for a project activity should be released to the appropriate processing unit, e.g., engineering, drafting, purchasing, manufacturing, etc. At some later date, this order needs to be closed out. The opening and closing of an order for executing a project activity signals the entry and the departure of that activity from an active project execution system data base. There are direct counterparts to the control of manufacturing orders. There is no point in releasing orders (activities) to a work center (project processing unit) that is already overloaded, unless the new activities are of higher priority. This implies that a priority system is in place—and working properly.

The Norwalk project provides a good illustration of the project execution system data base. Activities E, F, and G are all fabrication shop activities. Because of resource limitations, these activities have been scheduled to start and complete as follows:

Activity E: start Monday, week 10 and complete Friday, week 12.
Activity F: start Monday, week 10 and complete Friday, week 11.
Activity G: start Monday, week 14 and complete Friday, week 14.

Several procedures could be used for releasing orders for these activities to the fabrication shop. Under MRP scheduling, the orders might be released to the shop, say, one week prior to the scheduled start date, e.g., Monday of week 13 in the case of activity G. Under network scheduling, the orders could be released on the early-start date, e.g., Monday of week 9 in the case of activity G. In either case, a system for indicating relative priorities, and keeping these priorities current, must be employed.

Figure 14.14 presents a hypothetical shop-floor control report that could have been made for one of the fabrication shop departments, the welding department. It shows all three activities for the Norwalk project, and priority data as they would be generated with critical ratio scheduling.

This report indicates the priority for processing each of the project activities (shop orders). The priority index equals the time remaining until the

FIGURE 14.14 Fabrication—shop-floor control report

#10 welding station—Monday, week 11:

Shop order	*Item*	*Priority*	*Activity scheduled start date*	*Activity scheduled completion date*	*Previous operation*	*Next operation*	*Shop time remaining**
Norwalk	Activity F	.625†	Monday, week 10	Friday, week 11	Burnout	Weld	8
Norwalk	Activity E	2.5‡	Monday, week 10	Friday, week 12	Weld	Inspection	4
Norwalk	Activity G	4.0§	Monday, week 14	Friday, week 14	—	Weld	5

*In days.
†5/8.
‡10/4.
§20/5.

scheduled completion for the activity divided by the shop time remaining to complete the activity. For example, activity F has five days remaining between today's date and the scheduled completion date, and eight days of shop time remaining to be completed. The critical ratio in this case is .625. A critical ratio of less than 1.0 indicates that an item is behind schedule and the project *may* be delayed. Therefore, the shop-floor control report can be used for order-tracking purposes to detect significant deviations in the project schedule. It can also be used for priority purposes in controlling the project activities, and for better planning the utilization of capacity at a work center or project-processing unit.

Similar shop-floor control reports can be developed for non-shop oriented activities such as engineering, drafting, customer approval, purchasing, etc. Here, the intent of the report is the same: i.e., to assign priorities, track project progress, and plan capacity utilization. The use of such information in preproduction activities is clearly important in focusing engineering effort on those activities that need early design. It is important that materials be purchased and shop activities begun as needed. Without the proper kind of document, shown in Figure 14.14, the engineering group could easily start their design efforts on items that are not of the highest priority. This could make it impossible to complete the project on schedule.

Engineering and other preproduction work centers can also benefit from standard exception messages in MRP systems. For example, a typical exception message will list all part numbers that are invalid. By putting in all parts yet to be engineered for a specific project with the same illegal part number prefix, the exception code will automatically list them if they are still to be engineered. As engineering is completed, illegal numbers are replaced with valid part numbers.

Shop-floor control reports for engineering, drafting, and purchasing units can also provide critical capacity information in areas where standard time estimates are often not available. For example, engineering man-hours may be estimated from the listing of engineering activities on the shop-floor control report. Authorizations for overtime or additional personnel can be based on this information. Similarly, the application of capacity requirements planning procedures could lead to more fundamental knowledge of manpower requirements. Rough-cut capacity planning techniques could examine the potential impact of proposed projects by using similar BOMs and determining the implied capacity needs. Changes to projects can be evaluated with alterations planning approaches.

Still another approach to scheduling detailed project activities is finite loading. The approach used in SPAR-1 and other resource loading models is quite similar to that used in finite loading. When one understands the need for finite loading to be seen as a shop-floor control technique that is to be used for replanning on a continuous basis, one can see how project control is critical.

Rolling the project schedule

Once the project is under way, deviations from the schedule will always occur, and it is important to evaluate the project performance periodically to make any necessary adjustments. Two items are typically of interest in monitoring the project performance: the performance against the schedule and the performance against the budget.

The techniques presented in this chapter provide a means of evaluating the project performance against the schedule. For example, the shop-floor control reports will reflect those activities (orders) which are behind schedule. Using the reports, the project planner can spot significant deviations that require direct line-management action to minimize the impact of deviations on the overall project schedule. In execution systems for project management, the design and use of exception messages facilitate this process greatly.

When significant deviations occur in project performance, the network schedule or the MRP schedule should be updated to reflect current status. For example, suppose a customer delay of two weeks occurred in the customer approval activity in the Norwalk project. This means that instead of completing activity C by the end of week 5, it will not be completed until the end of week 7. The project planner must determine whether any of the remaining activities on the critical path (D–E–H–I) can be compressed into a shorter time or whether the completion of the project must now be delayed. In either case, it is critical that the new scheduling decisions be incorporated into the overall schedule. This is directly analogous to the MRP dictate of "not lying to the system."

Rescheduling actions can have a significant impact on the priorities for other activities in the Norwalk project, and in the scheduling of project resources. A customer delay of two weeks can mean that the project will be delayed even further because of resource limitations. Regular updating of the project schedule is crucial if a realistic project plan is to exist for the organization. The regular replanning cycle (regeneration) of MRP facilitates the updating process. Moreover, the use of MRP bottom-up replanning is useful to solve project scheduling problems.

Replanning or updating the project plan involves several tasks. As actual activity times are known, they must be incorporated into the network diagram or into the MRP planning cycle. Moreover, the remaining times required for activities which are still in progress are often determined by estimating percentage completions. For example, if an activity estimated to take eight days has been in progress for three days and is estimated to be 25 percent complete, six more days of work would be required, making the overall activity time nine days instead of eight. Any revisions in time estimates for activities which have not been started should also be made, and the network diagram (or MRP schedule) revised. The revised project schedule forms the basis for evaluating the time performance of the project and for making any changes in the project schedule or capacity levels.

Activity time estimation and control

One key element in project management is development of the activity time estimates. Where do these numbers come from? How are they derived? We see some important benefits coming from paying close attention to the methods used in developing lead time data for MPC systems.

Lead times for MPC are defined as machine time plus setup time plus move time plus queue time. Using these as analogs to project scheduling, one might ask: Does a particular time estimate include setup time, and if so, how? Is this time at a work center (machine) or are we talking about a labor-constrained resource? Does the estimate allow for waiting or not? What percentage is waiting? How do we track actual time and update estimates? Can we use input/output analysis to monitor actual progress against estimates?

A related issue concerns assumptions about the use of resources in project scheduling. Can a 20-man-day activity be done equally well by one person for 20 days, 20 people for one day, or 5 people for four days? Can resources be substituted freely? Are there learning curve effects? How important are they?

Monitoring project costs

So far we have focused on the problem of monitoring project performance in terms of time. It is also usually important to monitor the actual cost against the budget, and to prepare updated estimates of the cost to complete the project. To do this, it is necessary to break the project budget down by activity or groups of activities, and to routinely collect actual project costs on a consistent basis.

The project budget by activity is readily integrated with MRP scheduling. Routine cost implosions can be made to summarize all, or portions, of the project budget. The shop-floor control feedback system can be used to accumulate actual cost information by project activity, as well as reporting the actual time requirements of the project. The net result is that routine MPC execution systems can be used to monitor both time and cost performance of a project.

EXAMPLES

The project-scheduling techniques described in this chapter have been applied in a wide variety of industries. We describe three quite different applications. The first illustrates project scheduling on a manual basis to plan and control a large plant expansion program. The key point in this example is the need to define the project creatively so as to include "soft" activities (those that require significant managerial time, but which are often ignored). The second application illustrates the use of computerized software for the installation of management information systems. The final example is the use of MRP scheduling for the routine planning and control of large make-to-order products.

Plant expansion at Ethan Allen

At one point, the Ethan Allen Furniture Company needed to undertake a major expansion program in seven furniture factories. The typical expansion project consisted of an increase of 100 percent or more in a factory's production volume. The scope of the project included the design and construction of large buildings, the layout and purchase of new equipment, the rearrangement of existing facilities, and the hiring and training of new employees. Large capital expenditures were committed to these projects, and there were substantial pressures to get the additional production volume on line as soon as possible. The vice president of manufacturing was responsible for the time and cost performance of the expansion projects. Previous plant expansion projects had typically been finished behind schedule and over the budgeted costs.

Each of the major plant expansion projects was planned as an individual CPM network. The number of activities in the individual projects ranged from 30 to 50. A partial listing of the activities for one of the projects is shown in Figure 14.15 along with the initial time estimates. A CPM network diagram showing the precedence relationships and the early start/finish schedule for this project is shown in Figure 14.16. The activities noted in the middle and lower portion of the network diagram are largely concerned with the installation of control systems to support the manufacturing operations.

During the expansion projects, the network diagrams were updated on a weekly basis to reflect actual progress. This approach not only provided more detailed project plans and improved control over project performance at Ethan Allen, but produced an interesting side benefit, as well. Previously, management attention was largely focused on the "hard" aspects of expansion projects, i.e., the construction of buildings, the location of equipment, etc. Very little attention was directed toward the "soft" aspects of the project, i.e., the design of the production and quality control systems, the training of new employees, etc.

By scheduling, both types of activities, as shown in Figure 14.16, attention was directed to the soft activities. The resources required for these activities were almost always managerial, and the analysis of the resource requirements for these key people in the Ethan Allen projects revealed a major reason for past poor performance. Poor time and cost performance in previous expansion projects occurred when the managerial resource was

FIGURE 14.15 Ethan Allen plant expansion project—partial activity listing

Number	*Activity*	*Time (weeks)*
1	Detailed layout	4
2	Build buildings	16
3	Utilities layout	3
4	Install machine-room utilities	12
5	Purchase machinery	16
6	Move machine room	2
7	Demolish old machine room	2
8	Install rough mill utilities	10
9	Move rough mill	2
10	Purchase finishing equipment	16
11	Install finishing utilities	10
12	Move finishing room	4
13	Start-up and build up production	18
14	Build sticker shed	26
15	Build dry kilns	11
16	Demolish old shed and kilns	2
17	Build dry shed	24
18	Schedule project	1
19	Quality control system	3
20	Plant maintenance and protection	2
21	Shop-floor scheduling system	10

Source: Company records

overloaded. The use of CPM methods in the expansion projects at Ethan Allen helped to use this resource more effectively and to monitor project performance.

Management information systems projects at Cummins Engine Company

Cummins Engine Company is a large U.S. Manufacturer of diesel engines. They use a computer-based project scheduling system to plan and schedule management information system (MIS) projects. The computer application involves both the initial planning and the ongoing control of the projects. Cummins employs approximately 80 people in the MIS Department with several of the major systems projects planned and controlled using PERT project management techniques.

One of the firm's recent projects involved the installation of a computerized accounts receivable management system. The project was subdivided into several development phases, with each phase controlled through PERT analysis. The computer program development phase of the project included 31 project activities and required more than 34 weeks to complete. A description of the first 11 activities, their precedence relationships, and the normal times are shown in Figure 14.17. The PERT network diagram con-

FIGURE 14.16 Ethan Allen plant expansion project—CPM network diagram

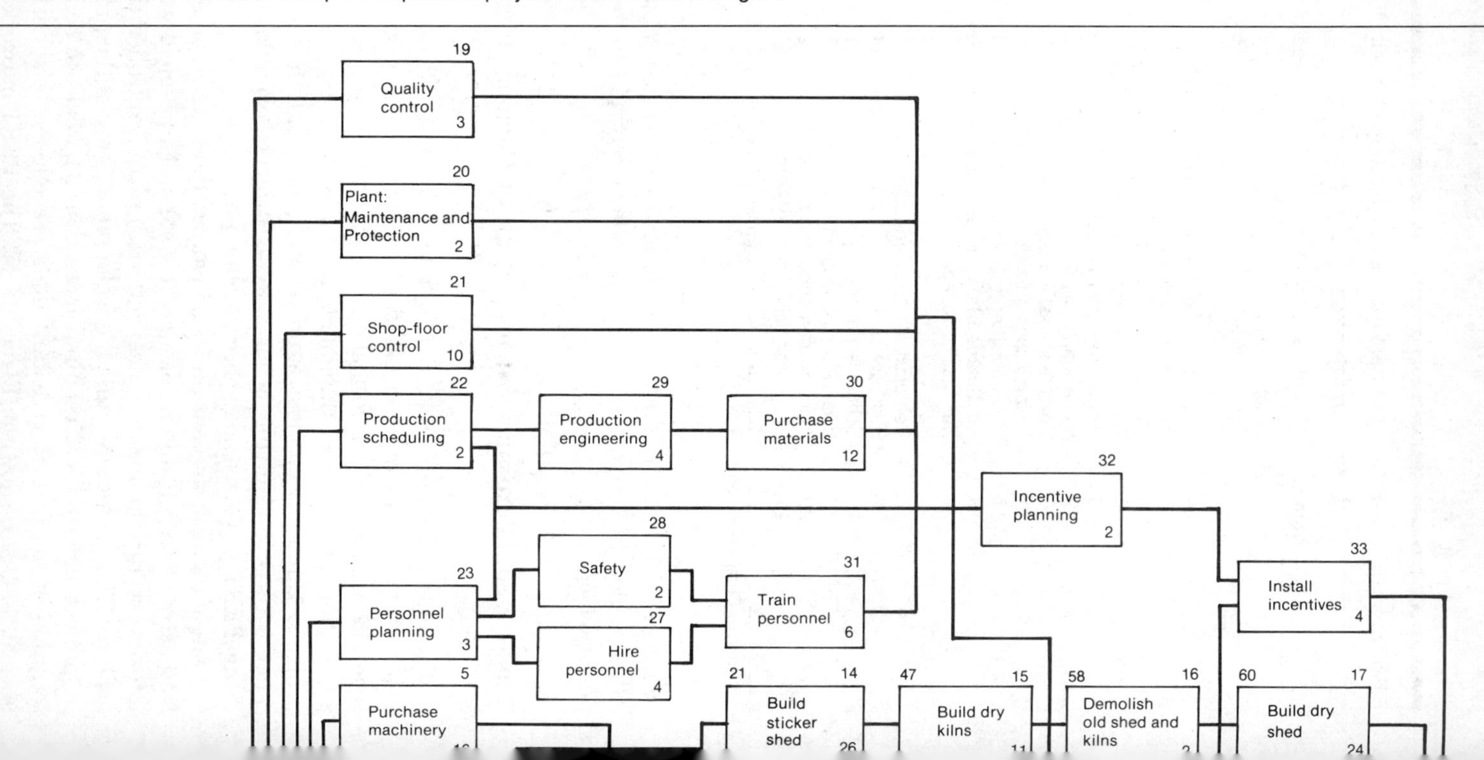

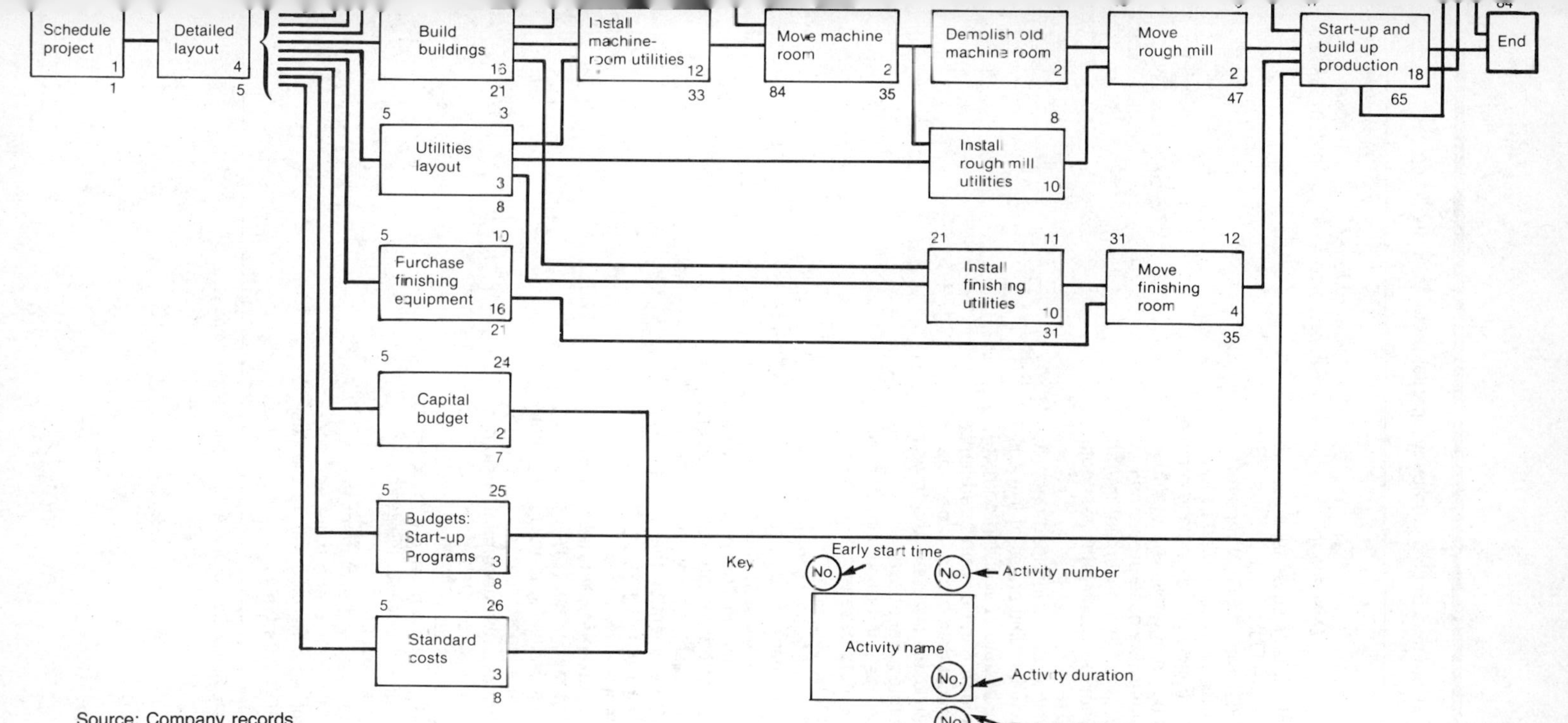

Source: Company records

FIGURE 14.17 Cummins Engine Company—partial project activity listing

Activity	*Description*	*Prerequisite/ corequisite task*	*Estimated elapsed time (weeks)*
1.	Obtain data base general requirements—Obtain the various PSB, DBD, and SYSGEN requirements for the data base load programs, the transaction data base maintenance programs, and the customer data base programs	—	2
2.	Code, test, and document the programs for loading the test data bases	1	5
3.	Develop conversion load data. Accumulate test cases of live customer data in verifying correct program and system operation	—	5
4.	Load test data bases—Load the applicable test data and transaction test data base	1, 2, 3	1
5.	Code, test, and document transaction data base maintenance programs	1	7
6.	Implement transaction data base maintenance and support programs (milestone date—01JUL)	4, 5	1
7.	Develop data dictionary element descriptors for the new customer data base. Identify and define each element on the data base exclusive of the open item segments	—	6
8.	Load customer data base MFS and load the screen (CRT) descriptions pertaining to customer data base support	7	1
9.	Code, test, and document customer data base programs	4, 8, 5	12
10.	Load terms table. Define and develop each term and its ramifications and develop the terms table/data base	—	5
11.	Code, test, and document the edit 1, edit 2, and proof and control reporting modules for the customer data base	—	4.5

Source: D. F. Aldrich, Senior Consultant, Arthur Young and Company.

taining all 31 activities is presented as Figure 14.18. Note that in the PERT network diagram, the activities are represented by arrows, and the completion of distinct project events is depicted by the nodes.

A major feature of this MIS project-scheduling system is the regular reporting of the status of each project activity. The project schedule report shown in Figure 14.19 provides an example of the routine project status information available. This report lists all of the project activities that remain to be completed and their early-late start/finish times. It also lists these activities in order by their total slack time. Note that some of the activities have a negative total slack time, which means that the project is behind schedule as of the current reporting date.

The same information is also listed in the time chart report shown in Figure 14.20. This report provides a time-phased display of the activities yet to be completed. The activity time is marked by an XXXX, while negative total slack time is indicated by − −, and positive total slack time by ++++. These reports provide management with the information necessary to assess the current status of a project, and to indicate where resource levels might be adjusted to improve project performance.

Make-to-order products at Elliott Company, Division of Carrier Corporation

The Jeanette, Pennsylvania, plant of the Elliott Company, manufactures large air and gas compressors, and steam turbine devices. The products are highly engineered, using state-of-the-art manufacturing techniques and materials. The engineered apparatus products are designed and built to customer specifications, to accomplish a specific function. The products typically weigh 50 tons and take a year or more to produce. More than half of this lead time is made up of order processing, design engineering, and purchasing.

The scheduling of each customer order is based upon the assignment of an imaginary (planning) bill of materials to each major piece of equipment. This bill is established by using elements of previously built products that are similar to the product on the customer order. This imaginary bill of materials is then processed by standard MRP logic. The lead times to produce the components on the imaginary bill of materials include estimated times to perform the engineering design and do the necessary drafting, in addition to the manufacturing lead times. The result is a proper ordering of when each component should be designed, the priorities for all customer orders relative to the due dates, and a capacity requirement profile for each work center. The capacity profiles are produced for engineering and drafting work centers on a routine basis. Figure 14.21 is one of the imaginary bills of material.

Figure 14.22 is part of an exception report showing behind-schedule project activities. For example, the first item on the list is nine weeks behind schedule, has project engineer A in charge, and is presently in engineering

FIGURE 14.18 Cummins Engine Company—accounts receivable management system PERT network diagram*

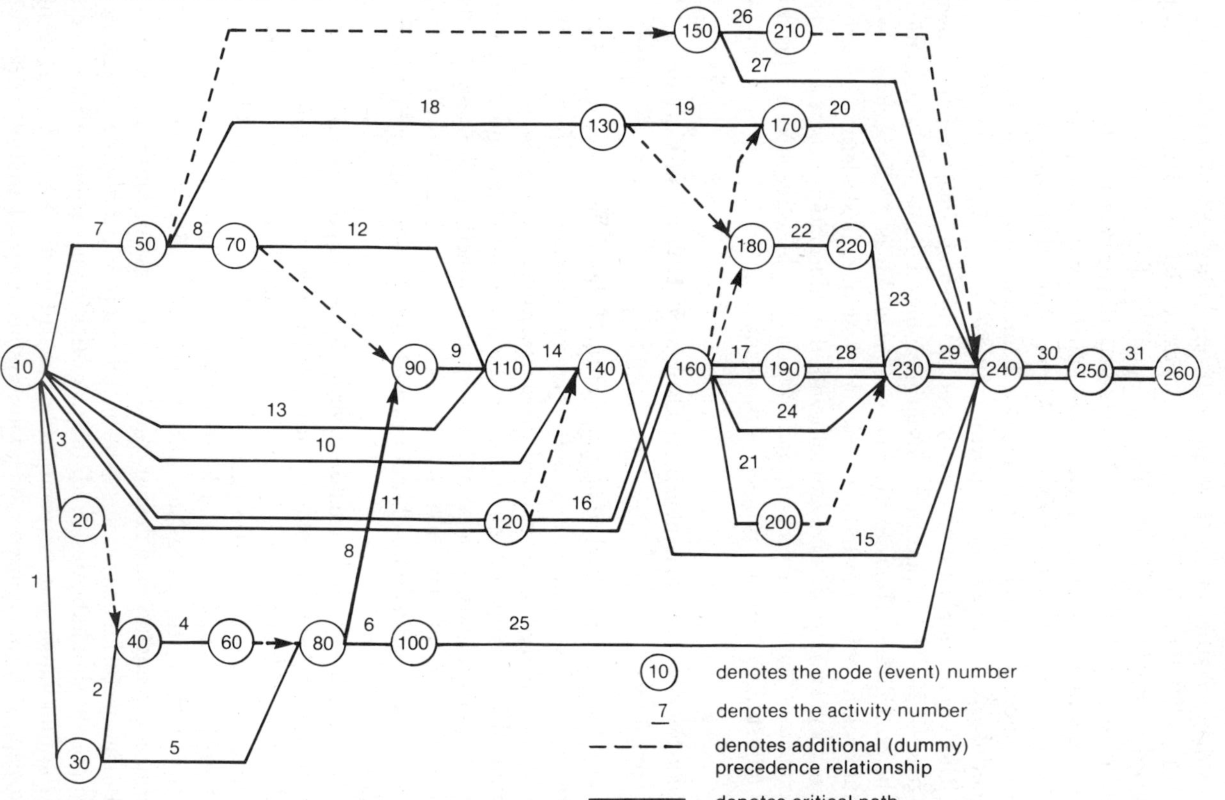

*PERT/CPM analysis—34 weeks elapsed time.

Source: D. F. Aldrich, Senior Consultant, Arthur Young and Company.

FIGURE 14.19 Cummins Engine Company—accounts receivable management system project schedule report

Accounts receivable management system— *Critical path PERT listing*

Run date 8/15 *Scheduled finish 2/15*

Node	Nos.	Activity description		Activity	Duration	Slack	Earliest Start	Earliest Finish	Latest Start	Latest Finish
50	70	Cust DB MFS Screens	Load	8	1.0	−11.6	8/15	8/22	5/26	6/2
90	110	Cust DBM Maint Programs	Develop	9	12.0	−11.6	8/22	11/14	6/2	8/25
110	140	USER Cust DB Maint—CRT	Train	14	2.0	−11.6	11/14	11/28	8/25	9/8
140	240	Customer Data Base	Implement	15	1.0	−11.6	11/28	12/5	9/8	9/15
70	90	Dummy		0	.0	−11.6	8/22	8/22	6/2	6/2
60	80	Dummy		0	.0	−10.6	8/15	8/15	6/2	6/2
80	90	Cust Data Base	Load	8	.0	−10.6	8/15	8/15	6/2	6/2
10	110	USER Org Structure	Establish	13	8.0	− 6.6	8/15	10/10	7/1	8/25
70	110	Cust DP User Manual	Develop	12	6.0	− 5.6	8/22	10/3	7/14	8/25
10	120	Edit-1, Edit-2, PAC-Cust	Develop	11	4.5	− 5.1	8/15	9/16	7/11	8/11
120	160	MPS RFD Batch & Online	Obtain	16	1.0	− 5.1	9/16	9/23	8/11	8/18
160	190	BMP Update Programs	Develop	17	11.0	− 5.1	9/23	12/9	8/18	11/3
190	230	Acceptance Test Criteria	Develop	28	6.0	− 5.1	12/9	1/20	11/3	12/15
240	250	DP OPS Review-Document	Review	30	3.0	− 4.3	2/10	3/3	1/11	2/1
230	240	Conduct Structured Test	Test	29	3.0	− 3.7	1/20	2/10	12/25	1/15
250	260	Mngt Review-TFST Results	Review	31	1.0	− 3.3	3/3	3/10	2/8	2/15
10	140	Terms Table	Load	10	5.0	− 1.6	8/15	9/19	8/4	9/8
120	140	Dummy		0	.0	− 1.1	9/16	9/16	9/8	9/8
80	100	Trans DB Maint & Sup PBM	Implement	6	1.0	4.2	8/15	8/22	9/14	9/21
100	240	All Interface Sys To MFS	Develop	25	16.0	4.2	8/22	12/12	9/21	1/11
160	200	Cash Related Programs	Develop	21	8.0	5.3	9/23	11/18	10/30	12/25
180	220	Cash & Adj MFS Screens	Load	22	1.0	5.3	9/23	10/1	10/30	11/6
220	230	Cash & Adj On-Line PGMS	Develop	23	7.0	5.3	10/1	11/18	11/6	12/25
160	180	Dummy		0	.0	5.3	9/23	9/23	10/30	10/30
200	230	Dummy		0	.0	5.3	11/18	11/18	12/25	12/25
170	240	Inv & Inq Programs	Develop	20	10.0	5.7	9/23	11/2	11/2	1/11
160	170	Dummy		0	.0	5.7	9/23	9/23	11/2	11/2
50	130	DD Element Disc-DPN ITM	Develop	18	4.0	6.2	8/15	9/12	9/28	10/26
130	170	Inv & Inq MFS Screens	Load	19	1.0	6.2	9/12	9/19	10/26	11/2
160	230	RPT RBMS & Monthend PGM	Develop	24	7.0	6.3	9/23	11/11	11/6	12/26
130	180	Dummy		0	.0	6.8	9/12	9/12	10/30	10/30
150	210	User Manuals and Proc	Develop	26	8.0	13.2	8/15	10/10	11/16	1/11
50	150	Dummy		0	.0	13.2	8/15	8/15	11/16	11/16
210	240	Dummy		0	.0	13.2	10/10	10/10	1/11	1/11
150	240	Training Requirements	Develop	27	6.0	15.2	8/15	9/26	12/1	1/11
20	40	Dummy		0	.0	26.2	8/15	8/15	2/16	2/15

Source: D. F. Aldrich, Senior Consultant, Arthur Young and Company.

FIGURE 14.20 Cummins Engine Company $\underline{m}$ on accounts receivable management system time chart report

```
ACCOUNTS RECEIVABLE MANAGEMENT SYSTEM - PGMDEV

RUN DATE 8/15                                                                      SCHEDULED FINISH 2/15
                                                                         ----------------------------------------------
NODE  NOS.         DESCRIPTION                         DURA SLK   ACTIVITY   JUL            OCT            DEC            APR
                                                                             1              1              30             1
 80   100   TRANS DB MAINT & SUP PGM     IMPLMENT     1.0  4.2      6              ++++0x
 50    70   CUST DB MFS SCREENS            LOAD       1.0-11.6      8        ------0x
 90   110   CUST DBM MAINT PROGRAMS       DEVELOP    12.0-11.6      9        -------0xxxxxxxxxxxx
 10   140   TERMS TABLE                    LOAD       5.0- 1.6     10            --0xxxxx
 10   120   EDIT-1, EDIT-2, PAC-CUST      DEVELOP     4.5- 5.1     11        -----0xxxxx
 70   110   CUST DP USER MANUAL           DEVELOP     5.0- 5.6     12         ------0xxxxxx
 10   110   USER ORG. STRUCTURE          ESTABLISH    8.0- 6.6     13        ------0xxxxxxxx
110   140   USER CUST DB MAINT-CRT         TRAIN      7.0-11.6     14               ------------0xx
140   240   CUSTOMER DATA BASE           IMPLMENT     1.0-11.6     15                 ------------0x
120   160   MPS RFD BATCH & ONLINE        OBTAIN      1.0- 5.1     16             -----0x
160   190   BMP UPDATE PROGRAMS           DEVELOP    11.0- 5.1     17              -----0xxxxxxxxxx
 50   130   DDT ELEMENT DISC.-DPN ITM     DEVELOP     4.0  6.2     18              ++++++0xxxx
130   170   INV & INQ MFS SCREENS          LOAD       1.0  6.2     19                  ++++++0x
170   240   INV & INQ PROGRAMS            DEVELOP    10.0  5.7     20                   ++++++0xxxxxxxxxx
160   200   CASH RELATED PROGRAMS         DEVELOP     8.0  5.3     21                   +++++0xxxxxxxx
180   220   CASH & ADJ MFS SCREENS         LOAD       1.0  5.3     22                   +++++0x
220   230   CASH & ADJ ONLINE PGMS        DEVELOP     7.0  5.3     23                    +++++0xxxxxxx
160   230   RPT RBMS & MONTHEND PGM       DEVELOP     7.0  6.3     24                   ++++++0xxxxxxx
100   240   ALL INTERFACE SYS TO MFS      DEVELOP    16.0  4.2     25               ++++0xxxxxxxxxxxxxxx
150   210   USER MANUALS AND PROC         DEVELOP     8.0 13.2     26              ++++++++++++0xxxxxxxx
150   240   TRAINING REQUIREMENTS         DEVELOP     6.0 15.2     27              ++++++++++++++0xxxxxx
190   230   ACCEPTANCE TEST CRITERIA      DEVELOP     6.0- 5.1     28                         -----0xxxxxx
230   240   CONDUCT STRUCTURED TEST        TEST       3.0- 3.7     29                                ----0xxx
240   250   DP OPS REVIEW-DOCUMENT        REVIEW      3.0- 4.3     30                                   ----0xxx
250   260   MNGT REVIEW-TFST RESULTS      REVIEW      1.0- 3.3     31                                       ---0x
 20    40   DUMMY                                      .0 26.2      0              +++++++++++++++++++++++++0
 50   150   DUMMY                                      .0 13.2      0              +++++++++++++0
 70    90   DUMMY                                      .0-11.6      0        -------0
 60    80   DUMMY                                      .0-10.6      0        ------0
 80    90   CUST DATA BASE                 LOAD        .0-10.6      8        ------0
120   140   DUMMY                                      .0- 1.1      0                 -0
130   180   DUMMY                                      .0  6.8      0                  +++++++0
160   170   DUMMY                                      .0  5.7      0                   ++++++0
160   180   DUMMY                                      .0  5.3      0                   +++++0
200   230   DUMMY                                      .0  5.3      0                           +++++0
210   240   DUMMY                                      .0 13.2      0                      +++++++++++++0
```

Note: xxx denotes activity duration, +++ denotes positive slack, --- denotes negative slack
Source: D. F. Aldrich, Senior Consultant, Arthur Young and Company.

FIGURE 14.21 Imaginary bill of materials for Elliott Company

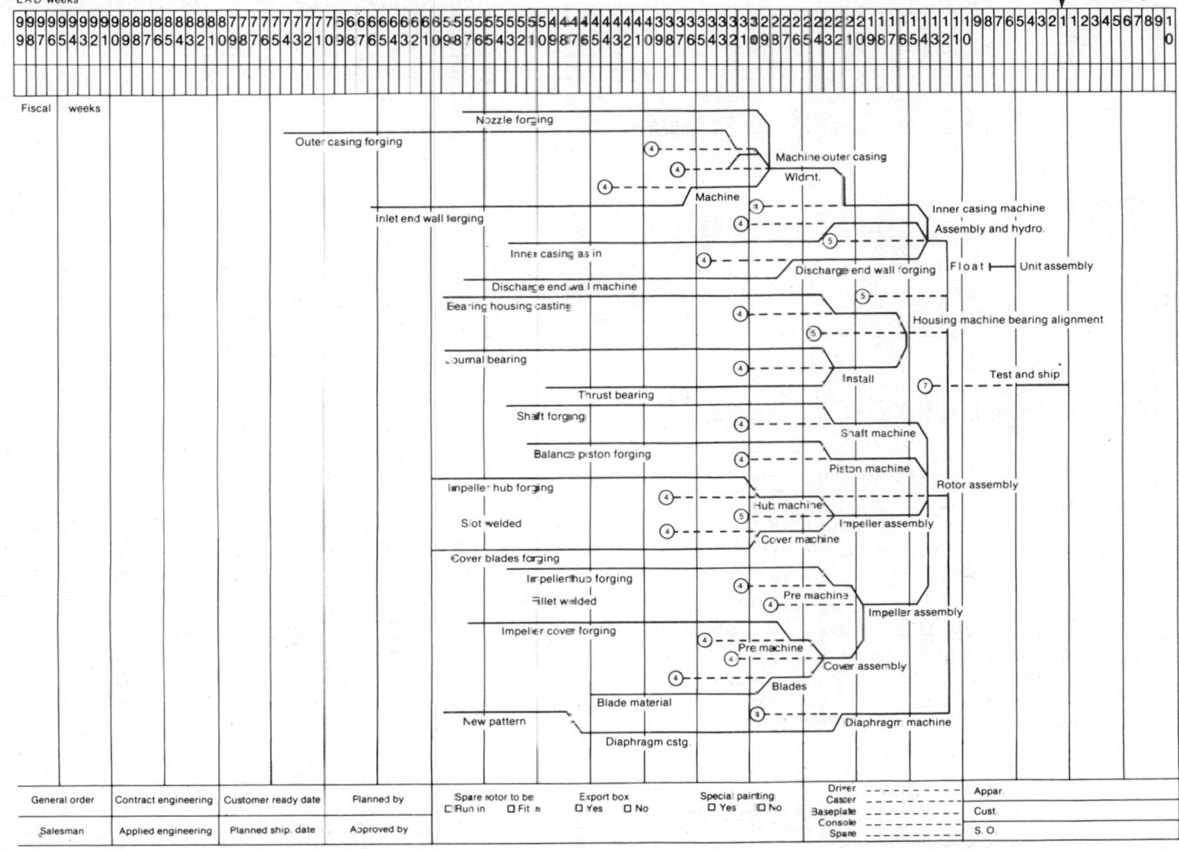

Source: W. L. Berry, T. E. Vollmann, and D. C. Whybark, *Master Production Scheduling: Principles and Practice* (Falls Church, Va.: American Production and Inventory Control Society, 1979), p. 124.

FIGURE 14.22 Late project status report for Elliott Company

Report no. ELCH08391 — *Engineered apparatus project engineering records scheduled for action*

Shop order	*Description*	*Quantity*	*Rel. no.*	*Project engineer*	*EAC Project engineering schedule*	*Project engineer prom.*	*Status (weeks)*
A528156000	Piping Agreement	1.0	H3P	A	356	446	−9
A528157000	Piping Agreement	1.0	H3P	A	376	446	−7
A628502000	Purchase Response	1.0	P3		326	386	−6
A628503000	Purchase Response		P3		326	386	−6
A628505000	Coupling	1.0	S5	V	326	386	−6
A528196000	Major Components	1.0	S5	A	466	516	−5
A628505000	Release of S2	1.0	S3	V	336	386	−5
A528164000	Coupling	1.0	S2T		356	386	−3
	Coupling	1.0	S2T		356	386	−3
A528187000	Oil Schematic	1.0	M1P	A	356	386	−3
	Piping Agreement	1.0	H3P	A	416	446	−3
V025094000	Pipe Agreement	1.0	M3P	O	376	406	−3
A528175000	Piping Agreement	1.0	H3P	A	366	386	−2
A528027000	Place Pr	1.0	S2		376	385	−1
A528043000	Purch Response	1.0	P2P		376	386	−1
	Major Components	1.0	S5	N	376	386	−1
A528131000	Lube Information	1.0	SAP		376	386	−1
	Firm Incomplete	1.0	S1A		376	386	−1
A528142000	Purchase Response	1.0	P3		376	386	−1

Source: W. L. Berry, T. E. Vollmann, and D. C. Whybark, *Master Production Scheduling: Principles and Practice* (Falls Church, Va.: American Production and Inventory Control Society, 1979), p. 125.

department H3P. The report is printed in order of those jobs in the worst status. Elliott uses shop-floor control and other MPC system modules to plan and control each customer order during the several months each is in progress. In two years of using these systems, performance against customer promise dates improved by 50 percent; inventory levels were reduced by 23 percent; and meanwhile, there was a 32 percent increase in sales volume. The advantages were achieved by better planning and control of *all* aspects of the business, from order entry through engineering, to the shop floor. Both hard and soft activities are planned/controlled, with the MPC-based systems for project management.

CONCLUDING PRINCIPLES

In this chapter we have shown that projects can be planned either with CPM/PERT methodologies or with MRP approaches. When it comes to the control dimension of projects, MPC/MRP has several key advantages. We see the following general principles for project planning:

- Projects and make-to-order products should be managed with systems with both planning and control features.

- The analogs between project scheduling and manufacturing planning and control should be well understood—and exploited. The differences must be understood, as well.
- MPC system modules should be applied to project-planning and control problems—especially if their approaches are also used for the regular manufacturing operations.
- Feedback information on project performance should be incorporated into revised plans in a periodic replanning cycle.
- Project cost performance should be based on the MPC transaction data base.
- Historical data on similar projects should be used to more quickly establish a new project as part of the overall planning/control effort. The use of planning bills of material facilitates this process.

REFERENCES

Berry, W. L., T. E. Vollmann, and D. C. Whybark. *Master Production Scheduling: Principles and Practice.* Falls Church, Va.: American Production and Inventory Control Society, 1979, p. 124.

Budnick, F. S., R. Mojena, and T. E. Vollmann. *Principles of Operations Research for Management.* Homewood, Ill.: Richard D. Irwin, 1977, Chap. 14.

Davis, E. W. *Project Management: Techniques, Applications and Management Issues.* Publication No. 3 in Institute of Industrial Engineers Monograph Series, 1976.

Donelson, W. S. "Project Planning and Control." *Datamation*, June 1976, pp. 73–75.

Hoffman, G. "Project Cost Control: Dynamic Risk Analysis of Randomly Ordered Sequential Decisions under Uncertainty," *Interfaces*, vol. 12, no. 3, 1982.

Moder, J., E. W. Davis, and C. Phillips. *Project Management with CPM and PERT.* New York: Van Nostrand-Reinhold, 1983.

Peterson, Eric. "Project Management Building Block." *Production and Inventory Management* 1, no. 12 (December 1981), p. 25.

________. "Project Management: We Cannot Afford to Fail." *Product and Inventory Management* 1, no. 9 (September 1981), pp. 56–58.

Stelter, Keith. "So You're Going to Install MRP." *APICS 24th Annual Conference Proceedings*, 1981, pp. 99–101.

Trill, Gilbert P. "You Can Do It, Charlie Brown." *APICS 24th Annual Conference Proceedings*, 1981, pp. 433–36.

Wiest, Jerome D. "Precedence Diagramming Method: Some Unusual Characteristics and Their Implications for Project Managers." *Journal of Operations Management* 1, no. 3 (February 1981) pp. 121–30.

Wiest, J. D., and F. K. Levy. *A Management Guide to PERT/CPM*, 2nd ed. Englewood Cliffs, N.J.: Prentice-Hall, 1977, pp. 120–23.

15

Aggregate capacity analysis

This chapter deals with modeling procedures for the establishment of an overall or aggregate plan, and the disaggregation of the plan. The basic issue is, given a set of product demands, stated in some common denominator, what levels of resources should be provided in each period? There has been a long history of academic research on aggregate capacity planning models. Theory has outstripped application by a wide margin. However, as firms implement MPC systems, there is a natural evolution toward questions of overall planning which provide direction to the other MPC system modules. We are cautiously optimistic that theory and practice are converging. This chapter provides a basic understanding of how that convergence might occur. It is organized around the following four topics:

- The aggregate capacity planning problem: What are the basic trade-offs and approaches for dealing with this question?
- Basic modeling approaches: What are the fundamental models that have been proposed in this area?
- Disaggregation: How can aggregate plans be disaggregated, and how does one deal with multiple plants?
- State of the art: What are the roadblocks to implementation, and the current application status?

Chapter 15 has a close linkage with Chapter 9 on production planning. There are also linkages to Chapters 7 and 8 on master production scheduling, and Chapter 4 on capacity planning. The Ethan Allen approach to aggregate capacity is discussed in Chapter 15. Other MPC system modules at Ethan Allen are discussed in other chapters, which provide a background to their aggregate planning. In particular, Chapter 7 shows how Ethan Allen develops and maintains its master production schedule.

THE AGGREGATE CAPACITY PLANNING PROBLEM

To illustrate the nature of the aggregate capacity planning problem, we will use an example based on an actual firm which has a seasonal sales pattern. We raise the issues in the context of a single facility, following the traditional research formulation of the aggregate production-planning problem. In this context, the problem is to find a low-cost combination of inventories, overtime, changes in work force levels and other capacity variations that meet the production requirements of the company. We first present a cumulative charting approach, and then examine tabular representation of the alternative strategies.

The basic trade-offs

Figure 15.1 presents the forecast of aggregate sales for our example, the XYZ Company, for the year. The total is aggregated in dollar terms for *all* of the plant's output for the year and is about $130 million. The monthly totals vary from a high of $15.8 million to a low of $7 million. Figure 15.2 shows these monthly sales data in the form of a cumulative chart (solid line). In addition, the dashed straight line in Figure 15.2 represents the cumulative production, at a constant rate of production. The aggregate capacity planning problem is to choose a low-cost cumulative production plan with a line on the cumulative chart that is always on or above the cumulative forecast line.

The cumulative chart shows clearly the implications of alternative plans. For example, the vertical distance between the dashed line and the solid line in our example represents the expected inventory at each point in time. If no inventory is to be held, the cumulative production line would be equal to the cumulative sales line. This policy is called the *chase strategy* production chases sales. The opposite extreme is called a *level policy*, where production is at a constant uniform rate of output, with inventory buildups and depletions. Effecting changes in production output requires changes in the work force level, hours worked, and subcontracting.

To convert aggregate output into capacity for planning purposes, a planning factor is used. In our example, the XYZ Company keeps a planning statistic which they use to convert gross sales dollars into aggregate labor capacity requirements. This statistic, obtained from accounting records, indicates that on the average each direct labor-hour produces $30 in sales. This

FIGURE 15.1 XYZ Company monthly sales forecast ($000,000)

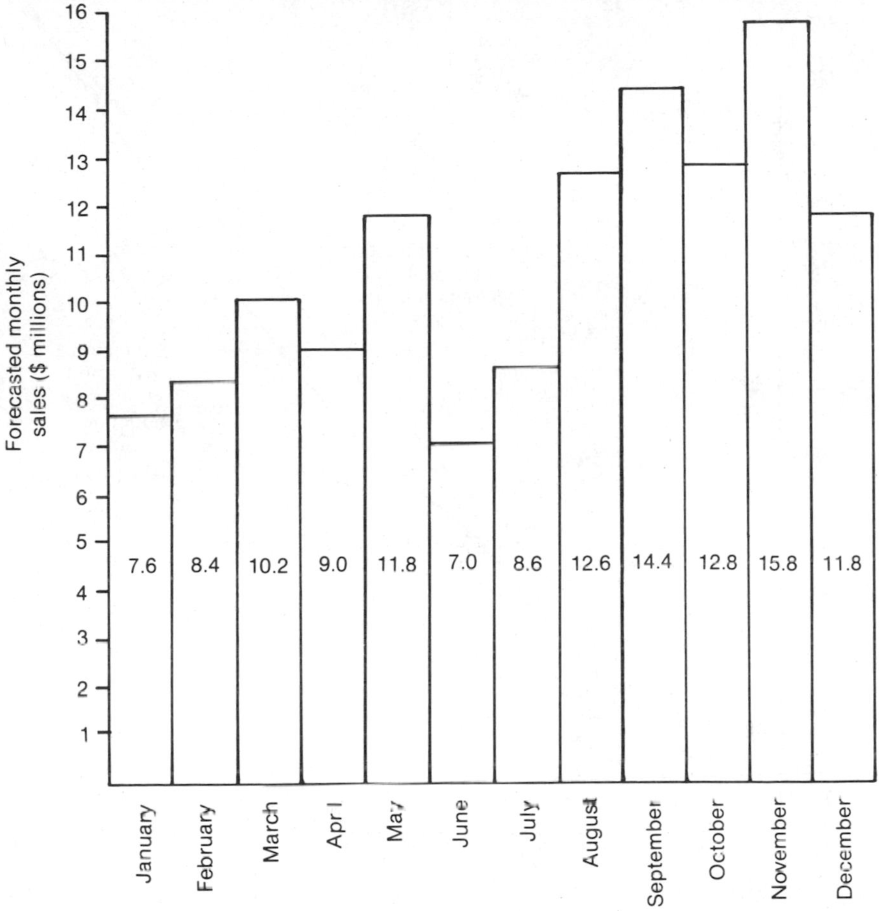
Forecasted monthly sales ($ millions)
16
15
14
13
12
11
10
9
8
7
6
5
4
3
2
1
7.6
8.4
10.2
9.0
11.8
7.0
8.6
12.6
14.4
12.8
15.8
11.8
January
February
March
April
May
June
July
August
September
October
November
December

Total sales for the year = $130 million.

factor is used to convert the sales forecast data in Figure 15.1 into a labor-hour forecast. The first column in Figure 15.3 shows the conversion.

The second column of Figure 15.3 presents the working days in each month for the year. This is an important addition, since the number varies sharply from month to month. The lowest number occurs in July, which only has 10 working days. This is due to the annual two-week shutdown during July.

If the total labor-hour requirements for the year's sales (4,333,333 hours) is divided by the number of working days (243), the result (17,832) is the number of labor-hours necessary to work each day if level production is to be

FIGURE 15.2 XYZ Company cumulative chart

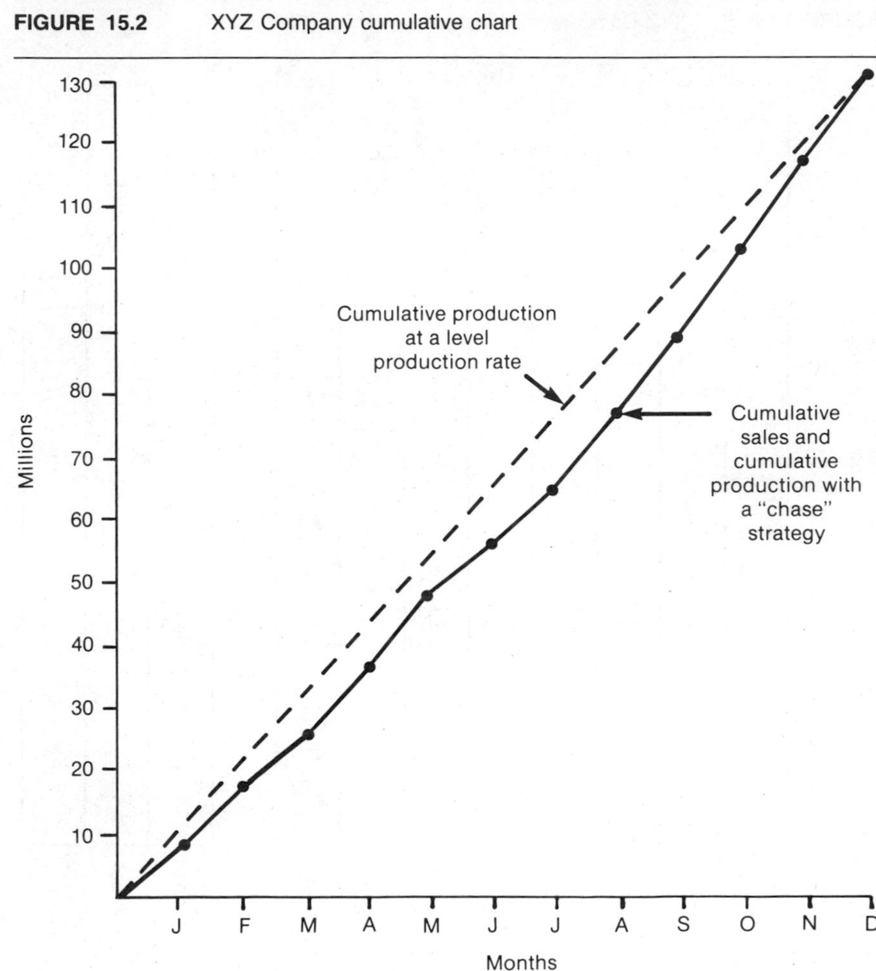

employed. Dividing the result by eight working hours per day gives an implied constant labor force of 2,229 workers required to produce the year's forecast.

The third column of Figure 15.3 represents one approach to a pure chase strategy. For this example, the working week is held at 40 hours, and the size of the labor force is varied as needed to only produce the forecast sales. For example, the January forecast sales are $7.6 million. When divided by $30, the resultant labor-hour capacity requirement is 253,333. When this result is divided by 20 working days, we obtain a need for 12,667 labor-hours each day. If each worker puts in an eight-hour day, the implied work force for January is 1,583 workers.

FIGURE 15.3 XYZ Company labor capacity requirements

	Chase strategy (Inventory = 0)				*Level production*
Months	*Sales in labor-hours (000s)*	*Working days*	*Variable work force**	*Variable workweek†*	*Variable inventory* ($000)*
January	253	20	1,583	28.4	3,099
February	280	21	1,667	29.6	5,933
March	340	23	1,848	33.1	8,037
April	300	20	1,875	33.7	9,737
May	393	22	2,235	40.2	9,706
June	233	22	1,326	23.9	14,475
July	287	10	3,583	64.4	11,224
August	420	23	2,283	41.0	10,929
September	480	20	3,000	53.8	7,228
October	427	22	2,424	43.5	6,197
November	527	20	3,292	59.1	1,096
December	393	20	2,458	44.2	0‡
Total	4,333	243	2,229	40.0	0

* Work force = 2,229.
† Workweek = 40 hours.
‡ The month-by-month detailed calculations will result in a December ending inventory of approximately −$5,000. This is because a work force of 2,229 workers is slightly less than necessary to create $130 million of sales in 243 working days.

The month-to-month differences between the implied work force levels represent hiring/firing decisions. For example, the decision for February would be to hire an additional 84 workers over the January total (1,667 − 1,583). The impact of the hire/fire decisions is especially severe during the summer months. It would be necessary to fire 909 workers in June, but to hire 2,257 in July.

In most circumstances, it would only be a firm like a summer resort or a farm that harvests an agricultural commodity that could consider such a high level of hiring and firing. In many Western countries, it is very difficult to hire and fire workers. In Western Europe and parts of South America, it is virtually impossible to fire workers—the cost is very high.

The next to last column in Figure 15.3 is another approach to a chase strategy. In this case, the labor force is kept at a constant level of 2,229 workers, but the length of the working week is varied as necessary to provide the labor-hours dictated by the first column. Again, the same kinds of variations are seen, but in the hours worked this time. Clearly, the plant shutdown in July causes severe overtime problems, if this strategy is followed. This could be mitigated against by continuing to work at a more normal level of output in June.

The last column in Figure 15.3 shows a "pure" level strategy. This is essentially the dashed line in Figure 15.2, with allowances for the exact numbers of working days in each month. In this example, 2,229 workers would need to be employed for eight hours on each of the 243 working days in the year to meet the forecast sales levels.

In January, the 2,229 workers, working for 20 days of eight hours each, will create $10,699,200 of goods, using the planning factor of $30 of end product per labor-hour. Since the sales forecast for January is $7 million, the expected inventory at the end of January is $3,099,000. The value shown in Figure 15.3 for February, $5,933,000, includes the January ending inventory plus the net addition to inventory created during February. Planned inventory will increase during each month that the implied workweek (next to last column) is less than 40 hours, and decrease if the implied workweek is greater than 40 hours.

The basic trade-offs of aggregate capacity analysis are clearly seen in this example. They involve inventory accumulations, hiring and firing, undertime and overtime, and alternative capacity forms such as outside contracting. The evaluation of these trade-offs is very much firm specific.

Evaluating alternatives

The cumulative chart in Figure 15.2 and the tabular presentation in Figure 15.3 show the implications of the pure chase and level production strategies. So far in the example, nothing has been said about evaluating the trade-offs involved. The management issue is how to choose between them or how to construct an alternative that is superior to either of the pure strategies. To do this rigorously, it is necessary to establish cost data that relate to the alternative aggregate capacity planning methods. But in many firms, relevant cost data are not readily available. In such cases, the analysis could be conducted, using executive opinion.

Suppose, for example, that no explicit cost data exist for aggregate capacity planning at the XYZ company. In that case, the executives at XYZ could evaluate data such as those in Figure 15.3 to point out situations they do not like. The implications of revised plans could be quickly calculated, using a programmable calculator or a micro-computer, for subsequent evaluation by the executives. For example, the work force could be allowed to build up as indicated from January through May for the chase strategy and be held at 2,235 for June instead of dropping to 1,326. The resulting inventory would be included in the analysis performed for July and beyond. If this process of revising and evaluating were continued until the managerial group was satisfied, it could be possible to imply, from the choices made, the relative importance or costs assigned to various conditions.

For illustrating the analysis when cost data are available, we will assume that the cost data in Figure 15.4 were provided for the XYZ company. The cost to hire an employee is estimated to be $200, whereas the cost to fire is $500. The average labor cost at XYZ is $5 per hour, and any overtime work has a 50 percent premium. That is, for overtime work, the average person

FIGURE 15.4 XYZ Company aggregate capacity planning data

Hiring cost	$200 per employee
Firing cost	$500 per employee
Regular labor cost	$5 per hour
Overtime premium cost	$2.50 per hour
Undertime premium cost	$3.00 per hour
Inventory carring cost	2 percent per month (applied to the monthly ending inventory)
Beginning inventory	0 units
Beginning labor force	1,583 persons

earns $7.50 for each hour. The cost of "undertime" is more difficult to assess, but clearly there is a heavy morale cost associated with working less than a normal workweek (40 hours). In some firms, the cost may be as much as the regular wage rate, meaning that people are kept on the payroll with no work to do. At the XYZ Company, the people are sent home but the company estimates the cost is still about $3 per hour, even though no direct payment is made to the work force. The final cost element is the inventory carrying cost. This is estimated to be 2 percent per month, based upon the monthly ending inventory value.

One question that needs to be addressed before performing the aggregate capacity analysis is the starting conditions. That is, are there any inventories and what is the beginning work force level? From Figure 15.4, we see there is zero beginning inventory and a work force of 1,583 (the desired level for January) at the beginning of the year.

In Figure 15.5 the Hire/Fire column for the first alternative specifically states the necessary additions and deletions to the work force to comply with the levels indicated in Figure 15.3. The Cost column is simply the hire and fire cost for these actions. No regular labor costs are shown in Figure 15.5, since they will be the same for each of the alternative plans considered. That is, the same number of working hours will be used for every plan, although some will be paid an overtime premium. This results in an incremental cost of a pure hire-fire policy with the given cost values of $2,708,300.

The second alternative in Figure 15.5 is to also maintain a zero inventory level, but to do this with a constant work force of 2,229 persons. The length of the workweek will be adjusted according to the dictates of the next to last column of Figure 15.3, the column that shows the length of the workweek required to produce the sales with 2,229 people. As noted, we again begin with a work force of 1,583, so the first and only hire-fire action is to add 646 workers.

The cost for January ($439,477) is based on the cost of hiring 646 workers (646 × 200 = $129,200) plus the cost of having each worker idle for 11.6 hours (40 − 28.4) per week at $3 per hour. This means that each worker will

FIGURE 15.5 Costs of alternative aggregate plans

	Zero inventory hire-fire as required		*Zero inventory/ overtime-undertime/ constant work force = 2,229*		*Level production/ constant work force = 2,229*		*Mixed strategy**				
Month	*Hire-fire*	*Cost*	*Hire-fire*	*Cost*	*Hire-fire*	*Cost*	*Hire-fire*	*Work force*	*Workweek*	*Inventory ($000)*	*Cost*
January	—	—	+646	$ 439,477	+646	$ 191,180	—	1,583	40.0	$ 0	—
February	+84	$ 16,800	—	292,088	—	118,660	+84	1,667	40.0	0	$ 16,800
March	+181	36,200	—	212,245	—	160,740	+181	1,848	40.0	0	36,200
April	+27	5,400	—	168,512	—	194,740	+27	1,875	40.0	0	5,400
May	+360	72,000	—	4,904	—	194,120	+360	2,235	40.0	0	72,000
June	−909	454,500	—	473,707	—	289,500	—	2,235	40.0	4,081	96,020
July	+2257	451,400	—	271,938	—	224,480	—	2,235	40.0	1,565	31,300
August	−1300	650,000	—	25,633	—	218,580	—	2,235	40.0	1,302	26,040
September	+717	143,400	—	307,602	—	144,560	+494	2,729	40.0	1	98,820
October	−576	288,000	—	85,817	—	123,940	—	2,729	40.0	1,610	33,200
November	+868	173,600	—	425,739	—	21,920	—	2,729	43.3	0	90,875
December	−834	417,000	—	93,618	—	0	−271	2,458	40.0	0	135,000
Total		$2,708,300		$2,801,280		$1,882,420					$641,155

* Hire until May. Constant work force until September (build inventory). Build inventory in October. Overtime in November. Fire in December.

average undertime work in the amount of 2.32 hours per day (11.6/5). At $3 per hour, 20 working days per month, and 2,229 workers, the undertime premium cost for January is $310,277. When added to the hiring cost of $129,200, the total cost for January is calculated as $439,477.

An illustration of overtime cost can be seen for July. The required work-week is 64.4 hours, or 4.88 hours of overtime per worker each day on the average. Since there are 10 working days in the month, each overtime hour has a premium cost of $2.50, and there are 2,229 workers, the total overtime premium for the month is $271,938. The total expected cost for the year, with an overtime/undertime strategy, is $2,801,280.

The third alternative shown in Figure 15.5 is the level strategy. In this case, enough people are added to the work force in January to raise it from 1,583 to 2,229 workers. Each worker puts in a constant 40-hour week, and inventories are varied, as indicated in the last column of Figure 15.3. When each of these planned inventory values is multiplied by 2 percent, the costs indicated in Figure 15.5 are obtained (for example, February = $5,933,000 × .02 = $118,660).

The last alternative evaluated in Figure 15.5 is a mixed strategy. The plan calls for adding employees as necessary from January through May, but thereafter keeps the resultant work force constant (2,235) until September. This means that some inventories are held during June, July, and August. In September, the work force is again expanded, this time by 494 workers, to provide the necessary output levels. This is determined by subtracting the August ending inventory of $1,302,000 from the September forecast of $14.4 million to get a net requirement of $13,098,000. At eight hours per day for 20 days and $30 per hour, it takes 2,729 workers to produce this amount.

The plan calls for this work force level to be maintained during October, which results in an addition to inventory of $1,610,000 which is needed in November. To meet the sales forecast of $15 million in November, however, it is necessary to work overtime for 3.3 hours each week. The lower level of forecast in December results in a layoff of 271 workers.

This plan may not be the best plan possible. For example, it is less costly to carry the extra inventory produced by 271 workers in December ($26,016), than to lay off all 271 workers ($135,500). The analysis thus far has not considered the desirable ending conditions in terms of work force levels. The valuation of any particular ending work force level must be made in light of the following year's sales forecast. The determination of mixed strategies that improve costs over those obtained by employing pure strategies can be guided by mathematical models. We consider some of these in the following section.

BASIC MODELING APPROACHES

In this section, we present an overview of the analytical models which have been suggested for the aggregate capacity planning problem. The academic literature has long been concerned with what has been called the aggregate production planning problem. We start by formulating this problem as a linear programming model. This approach is relatively straightforward, but is necessarily limited to cases where there are linear relationships in the input data. We then overview an approach which allows for quadratic cost data assumptions, the linear decision rule. Thereafter, we discuss an approach based on modeling managers' behavior and, finally, we present search procedures which are capable of solving problems with cost data that are not easily defined mathematically.

Linear programming

There have been many linear programming formulations for the aggregate capacity planning problem. The objective is typically to find the lowest-cost plan, considering when to hire and fire, how much inventory to hold, when to use overtime and undertime, etc., while always meeting the sales forecast. One formulation, based on measuring aggregate sales and inventories in terms of direct labor hours, follows. Minimize:

$$z = \sum_{t=1}^{m} (C_H H_t + C_F F_t + C_R X_t + C_o Y_t + C_I I_t + C_u U_t)$$

Subject to:

1. Inventory constraint:

$$I_{t-1} + X_t + Y_t - \mathrm{I}_t = D_t$$
$$I_t \geq B_t$$

2. Regular time production constraint:

$$X_t - A_1 W_t + U_t = 0$$

3. Overtime production constraint:

$$Y_t - A_2 W_t + S_t = 0$$

4. Work force level change constraint:

$$W_t - W_{t-1} - H_t + F_t = 0$$

5. Initializing constraints:

$$W_0 = A_3$$
$$I_0 = A_4$$
$$W_m = A_5$$

where:

C_H = The cost of hiring an employee.
C_F = The cost of firing an employee.

C_R = The cost per labor-hour of regular time production.
C_o = The cost per labor-hour of overtime production.
C_I = The cost of carrying one labor-hour of work per time period t.
C_u = The cost per labor-hour of idle time on regular time production.
H_t = The number of employees hired in period t.
F_t = The number of employees fired in period t.
X_t = The regular time production hours scheduled in period t.
Y_t = The overtime production hours scheduled in period t.
I_t = The hours stored in inventory at the end of period t.
U_t = The number of idle time regular production hours in period t.
D_t = The hours of production to be sold in period t.
B_t = The minimum number of hours to be stored in inventory in period t.
A_1 = The maximum number of regular time hours to be worked per employee per period.
W_t = The number of people employed in period t.
A_2 = The maximum number of overtime hours to be worked per employee per period.
S_t = The number of unused overtime hours per period per employee.
A_3 = The initial employment level.
A_4 = The initial inventory level.
A_5 = The desired number of employees in period m (the last period in the planning horizon).

Similar models have been successfully formulated for several variations of the aggregate planning problems. In general, however, few real-world aggregate planning problems appear to be compatible with the linear assumptions. For some plans, discrete steps, such as adding a second shift, are required. For many companies, the unit cost of hiring or firing large numbers of employees is much larger than that associated with small labor force changes. Moreover, economies of scale are not taken into account by linear programming formulations. Let us now turn to another approach which partially overcomes linear assumption limitations.

The linear decision rule

The linear decision rule (LDR) for aggregate capacity planning was developed by Holt, Modigliani, Muth, and Simon in the 1950s. The primary application was in a paint producing company. The following statement describes the problem as perceived by those authors:

> Background: The effort to carry sufficient inventory of each product at warehouses and retail stores had built up total inventories that seemed excessively large. Nevertheless, demand runs on individual products resulted in stockouts, lost sales, and extreme demands on factory production during the peak sales season. One technique for coping with this situation was use of several types of priority orders on the factory in addition to normal replenish-

ment orders. There was some interest in the company in the possibility of ameliorating the situation by centralizing information on stocks and sales at all levels, with the probable exception of information from independent retailers. That such a policy might pay off was indicated by the fact that an informal and partial system of this sort was said to have worked quite well.

The company was also interested in stabilizing production throughout the year. It was felt that employees tended to reduce their efforts in the off-season in an attempt to spread out the work. A policy of smooth production would possibly remove fear of seasonal layoffs and improve efficiency. It might also reduce the premium costs associated with overtime payments during the peak season. However, stabilized production would lead to higher inventory costs because of wide seasonal fluctuations in sales.

The factory management wanted to schedule economical production runs of each product without excessively large inventories at the factory warehouse. The factory problem was further complicated by emergency orders from the warehouses, which required prompt filling to keep customers satisfied and to minimize lost sales.

Although the LDR does not attempt to solve all these detailed problems, it concentrates on the overall planning and control of operations. It does so in the framework of the aggregate capacity planning problem, and control is established by resolving the problem periodically. The major difference between the LDR model and linear programming models is the approach taken to cost input data. The four cost elements considered in LDR are regular payroll cost, hire/fire cost, overtime/undertime cost, and inventory/backlog cost.

The regular payroll cost is simply a linear function of the number of workers employed. For the other three cost elements, however, a quadratic cost function is used. For example, the hire/fire cost is defined as:

$$64.3(W_t - W_{t-1})^2$$

where:

W_t = The work force to be established for the tth month.
W_{t-1} = The prior month's work force.
64.3 = Analytically derived coefficient for best fitting the squared differences in work force levels to actual operating cost results.

Figure 15.6 is an example quadratic hire/fire cost function, along with the presumed actual cost data. The presumed actual cost data only approximate the quadratic function. However, in some ways, the implication that each hire or fire decision results in ever-increasing unit costs is consistent with many managerial opinions.

The total cost function for the paint company was made up of the four cost elements. Because there are back-order costs in the LDR formulation, the problem is to minimize the total cost function. Since the cost data are linear and quadratic, the solution to the problem can be derived by calculus. The

FIGURE 15.6 LDR quadratic cost function for work force changes

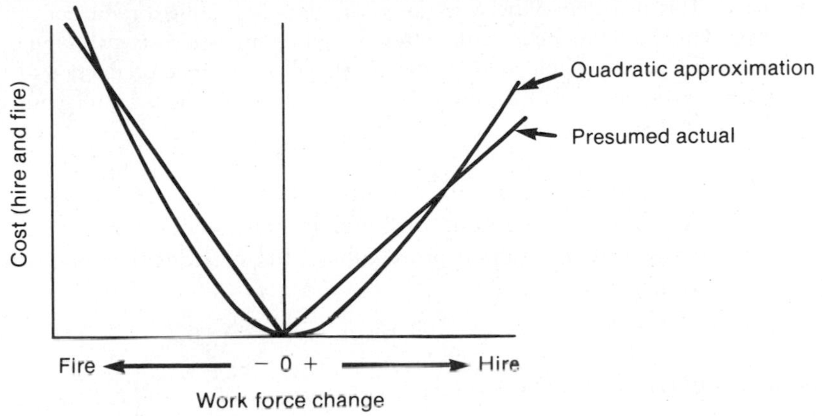

result is a set of two decision rules specifying the production output rate and the work force level in each month.

The LDR was implemented at the paint company. However, several years later, John Gordon visited the company to assess current results. He describes some of the findings:

> After considerable study and investigation it became apparent that although top management thought the rules were being used to determine aggregate production and work force, a more intuitive and long-standing system was in fact being used. The production control clerk whose responsibility it was to calculate the production and work force sizes, as well as convert these into item orders, was doing just that and posting the results in the form of job tickets on the production control board. When the foremen came into the production control office for a job ticket, they surveyed the available tickets for one that agreed with their intuitive feeling or judgment. If they found one they took it but if they did not they simply wrote out a ticket which corresponded with their feeling. Over the history of the use of the rules it turned out that about 50 percent of the tickets were used and the others ignored. Management, however, had the feeling that the rules were being used except in the odd case when judgment indicated that they should be overruled. At a later date the calculations associated with the rules were centralized with the installation of a data-processing center. The personnel in the center became concerned when their reports indicated that many of the production orders that they had issued were ignored. Consequently, and with the compliance of higher management, they instituted a reporting system which fed back to the plant management, and the foremen, a cumulative listing of outstanding production orders. After a short delay the length of this cumulative list began to diminish until it all but vanished. But in the meantime the inventory of finished goods associated with this plant rose steadily to alarming proportions,

especially in some obsolete items. Further investigation revealed that although the rules were indicating the size of the work force, no action was ever taken to reduce the work force because it was against the policy of the company. This meant that the work force rule was indicating a reduction in the work force; the production rule, attempting to minimize costs given the present work force level but anticipating layoff, called for some production for the excess work force. The rules are interactive, but in this case the interaction had been eliminated.

The moral to the story seems clear: One must never assume that the real world matches the model without auditing. In fact, any system that is not readily understood by the users is more subject to overrides than one where the logic is transparent.

The management coefficients model

A rather unique approach to aggregate capacity planning has been formulated by Bowman. He suggests that the production rate for any period would be set by the following, very general decision rule:

$$P_t = aW_{t-1} - bI_{t-1} + cF_{t+1} + K$$

where:

P_t = The production rate set for period t.
W_{t-1} = The work force in the previous period.
I_{t-1} = The ending inventory for the previous period.
F_{t+1} = The forecast of demand for the next period.
a, b, c, and K = Constants.

Bowman's approach is to first gather historical data for P, W, I, and F. Thereafter, through regression analysis, the values of a, b, c, and K are estimated. The result is a decision rule based upon past managerial behavior without any explicit cost functions. The assumption is that managers know what is important, even if they cannot readily state explicit costs. However, managers may either overreact to specific circumstances or delay in making adjustments. In both cases, a bias comes into their decision making. The regression analysis of the management coefficients model will average out this bias for future decisions.

Bowman compared the performance of the management coefficient model with LDR and actual company practice in four firms. In three out of four cases, the management coefficient model produced results superior to those made by the company, and in two cases the results were also superior to LDR. Later research has tended to confirm the efficiency of Bowman's approach, lending credence to approaches that supplement the application of experienced judgment.

Search decision rules

We have noted that linear programming models are limited by the linear cost assumptions. The ability to use quadratric costs in LDR is somewhat mitigating, but one is still constrained to cost functions that have convenient analytical features. The search decision rule (SDR) methodology helps overcome this restriction. SDR approaches allow one to state the cost data inputs in very general terms. The only requirement is that a computer program be constructed which will unambiguously evaluate the cost of any production plan. The procedure then searches among alternative plans (in a guided fashion) for the plan of minimum cost. Unlike linear programming and LDR, there is no guarantee of mathematical optimality with SDR. However, the increased realism in input data provides the potential for solving a problem more in line with managerial perceptions.

Several researchers have worked with search procedures for the aggregate capacity planning problem. Taubert compared the SDR with LDR for the paint company problem. He found that the SDR results were very close to those obtained by LDR. The technique has been applied in a number of applications. The versatility of the underlying approach provided makes it especially attractive for real-world applications.

DISAGGREGATION

Thus far, we have considered only the establishment of a global plan of production. This plan will necessarily have to be broken down or disaggregated into specific products and detailed production actions. Moreover, the aggregate capacity problem, as formulated up to now, has been based on a single facility (although it is conceivable that a facility subscript could be used in the linear programming model). For many firms, the problem of determining which facility will produce which products, in which quantities, is an important prerequisite to planning at each facility. In this section, we consider an approach that takes this into account. First, however, we discuss disaggregation of single-facility aggregate plans.

The disaggregation problem

One of the issues that is receiving increased attention is the conversion of overall aggregate plans into detailed product plans. That is, managers must make day-to-day decisions on a product and unit basis, rather than at the overall output level. The concept of disaggregation facilitates this process and ameliorates mismatches between plan and execution. In essence, disaggregation is concerned with overall capacity planning as well as with consistent lower-level capacity decisions. It recognizes that aggregate decisions constrain the disaggregated actions. It is therefore concerned with the issue of how to break the total or aggregate plan into plans for subunits of capacity.

Disaggregation is an important field of study. There is very little theory to guide practice, and the number of applications to date are limited. The disaggregation frame of reference is that of trying to facilitate the process of maintaining a match between the production plan and the master production schedule. The aggregate production plan must be the sum of the production called for by the detailed master production schedule (MPS). Very little help for providing this match is available. The planning issue is how to keep the two in concert. Some firms are coping with this problem in creative ways, but they are acting independently. Some of the new research efforts offer potential help, but there is much to be done.

Hierarchical production planning

One approach to aggregate capacity analysis that is based upon disaggregation concepts and can accommodate multiple facilities is hierachical production planning. The approach incorporates a philosophy of matching product aggregations to decision-making levels in the organization. Thus, the approach is not a single mathematical model, but utilizes a series of models, where they can be formulated. Since the disaggregation follows organization lines, managerial input is possible at each stage. A single schema of the approach is shown in Figure 15.7.

The development of hierarchical production planning (HPP) has been the effort of a group of researchers (Britan, Haas, Hax, Meal, and others) over several years. Some of the work has involved mathematical contributions, while others increase the depth or breadth of application (incorporating distribution centers or levels of detail in a factory). All, however, are based on some fundamental principles.

One principle has been mentioned already: the disaggregation should follow organizational lines. Another principle is that it is only necessary to provide information at the aggregation level appropriate to the decision. Thus, it is not necessary to use detailed part information for the plant assignment decisions. Finally, it is necessary to schedule only for the lead time needed to change decisions. That means that detailed plans can be made for periods as short as the manufacturing lead times.

The process of planning follows the schema of Figure 15.7. It first involves the specification of which products to produce in which factories. The products are combined in logical family groupings to facilitate the aggregation, assignment to factories, and modeling processes. The assignment to factories is based on the minimization of capital investment cost, manufacturing cost, and transportation cost.

Once the assignment to factories has been done and managerial inputs incorporated, an aggregate production plan is made for each plant. The procedure for the determination of the aggregate production plan could be any of those discussed previously. The aggregate plan specifies production levels, inventory levels, overtime, etc., for the plant. This plan is constrained by the specific products and volumes assigned to the plant.

FIGURE 15.7 Hierarchical planning schema

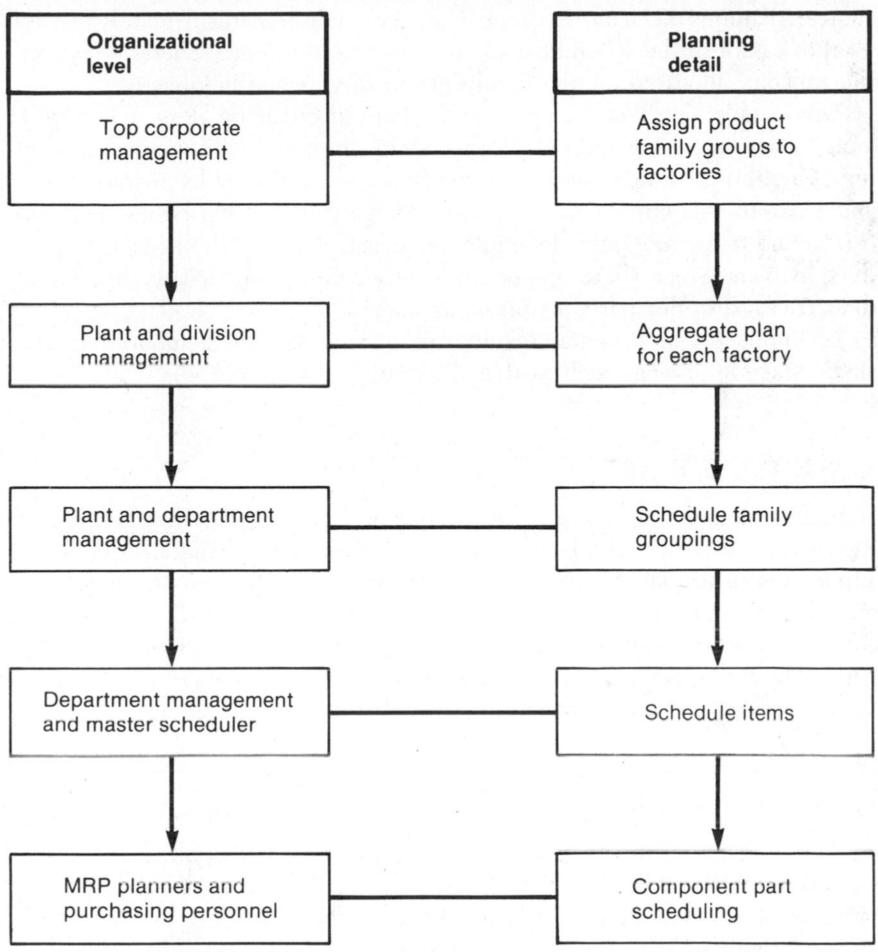

Source: G. D. Briton, R. A. Haas, and A. C. Hax, "Hierarchical Production Planning: A Two-Stage System," *Operations Research*, March–April 1982, pp. 232–51.

The next step in the disaggregation calls for scheduling the family groupings within the factory. The schedule is constrained by the aggregate production plan and takes into account any inventories that may exist for the group. The intention at this stage is to realize the economies of producing a family grouping together. The production lots (or share of the aggregate capacity) for the groups are determined and sequenced. If no major economies are achieved by scheduling the group as a unit, the procedure can move directly to the scheduling of individual items, the next stage shown in Figure 15.7.

The determination of the individual item schedule is analogous to making a master production schedule (MPS). In the HPP schema, the MPS is constrained by the previously scheduled family groupings and may cover a shorter planning horizon. In some instances, mathematical models can be used to establish the schedules. In all cases, the items are scheduled within the capacity allocated for the family group to which it belongs.

The detailed part and component scheduling can be done with MRP logic, order launching and inventory systems, or even mathematical modeling. An alternative approach has recently been suggested by Britan, Haas, and Hax. In this approach, both the aggregate finished product schedule (MPS) and *aggregate* parts schedule are constrained by the aggregate production plan. Since there are possible mix errors and capacity utilization differences, a buffer parts inventory is maintained.

Preliminary experimental results are quite favorable compared to the single-stage approach, such as that illustrated in Figure 15.5.

STATE OF THE ART

In this section, we consider the current situation regarding aggregate capacity analysis. We start by evaluating a rather disappointing history of the application of formal models. One of the limitations to applying modeling techniques is the data required, a topic we address, as well. The section concludes with a description of practice at the Ethan Allen Furniture Company. The description will show that many of the principles of formal techniques are applied with considerable management involvement.

Application of modeling techniques

The application of quantitative models has been disappointing at best; LDR is more than 25 years old, but has seen very limited application. Linear programming models have been used extensively, but only for firms that have relatively homogenous output measures and simple product structures, such as oil refineries and feed mixing plants. Hierarchical production planning, which is relatively new and parallels the managerial organization, has had few applications.

Most of the interest in modeling techniques has been academic. In firms where the aggregate capacity problem is treated, the approaches are often combined with the long-range planning and budgeting cycles using methods like the tabular method described earlier in the chapter. We maintain guarded optimism that theory and practice are converging. In the meantime, however, there are three key reasons for the lack of demonstrated applications of the theory.

A major reason is that few firms actually make aggregate decisions in the way implied by the models. For most firms, the aggregate is merely the sum of several lower-level decisions. Among these decisions are output rates for particular factories, product lines, or even work centers. Management guidance on some overall or aggregate basis tends to be of a general nature, rather than one of providing a fixed set of constraints within which a process of disaggregation can unambigously proceed. A related issue is the assumption of homogeneity. The existence of some uniform measure of output makes more sense in a paint factory than in a multiproduct, multiplant firm. Also, there are great differences among workers. The analytical models treat them as equivalent.

A second reason for the lack of application may be managerial understanding. It is difficult for many managers to understand the analytic underpinnings to LDR and other model forms. The increase in management background in formal techniques will improve the situation somewhat, but our experience has shown that the logic must be transparent to gain wide acceptance. This seems to be particularly true for aggregate planning models.

A final element inhibiting expanded application of the formal approaches is the data requirements. Often real-world data do not correspond to the model assumptions. In other cases, the data implied do not exist. This is an area where data bases like those developed for the manufacturing planning and control (MPC) system can help. The issues are important enough that we devote the next section to them.

Data issues

The existence of a high-quality data base for manufacturing, especially if it is linked to the cost accounting and financial analysis system, can help greatly in gathering data for aggregate capacity analysis. Even so, there remain many problems. Looking just at the data requirements for the XYZ company in Figure 15.4, or those required for the mathematical models raises several issues.

Although of limited applicability in some countries (or companies), one of the most difficult issues is the question of how one would estimate hiring and firing costs. Clearly, the most important aspects of these costs are not part of the accounting records. For determining the hiring costs, the more easily estimated components are those for recruiting, interviewing, and training. More difficult estimations are the length of time to become fully effective, the time to reach the quality levels required, and the ability to become assimilated into the social environment of the firm. Firing costs can be extremely difficult to assess, particularly in terms of the influence on morale.

In the analyses we presented earlier, we treated both hiring and firing costs as linear, with no constraints on the number of persons who could be hired or fired in a time period. In the XYZ company example, the pure strategy of hire/fire resulted in a labor force reduction of about one half in one month, followed by almost a tripling of the labor force the following month. This simply might not be possible in many firms. Moreover, the costs of small adjustments are almost surely different from those of large adjustments.

A somewhat similar problem relates to overtime/undertime costs. Overtime in modest amounts does represent a useful means for dealing with short-term capacity problems. However, to go from a 40-hour workweek to a 64-hour workweek is quite severe. Experience indicates that there is a reduction in hourly productivity when people work that many hours. The situation is aggravated when the number of weeks worked on overtime increases. Moreover, the ability to vary the workweek at will (23.9 to 64.4 hours per week in the XYZ company example) is clearly very limited. The costs of undertime are very difficult to measure, especially in terms of the long-term influence on worker morale, turnover, and loss of skill.

The inventory carrying costs might be linear over fairly wide ranges, but could change as capital resources are strained or new opportunities are developed. The selection of 2 percent per month for the XYZ company is presumed to include more than the interest charges from bank loans and direct storage costs. The risks of obsolescence, physical deterioration, and having the wrong items in finished goods also have to be considered.

Again we raise the issue of finding a single aggregate output measure. In the XYZ company analysis, we rather cavalierly converted sales dollars to labor-hours. The assumptions are that all sales dollars are equal, that any labor-hour can be used to make any sales dollar, and that any inventory is, in fact, useful to meet any marketplace demand. In fact, the existence of an overall single homogenous capacity measure is often not a meaningful concept in many firms. For example, the company with several different product lines, particularly if one product is highly labor intensive and another is capital intensive, will have difficulty finding a uniform capacity measure.

Aggregate capacity analysis at Ethan Allen

This example will trace aggregate planning, disaggregation, and control at the Case Goods Division of the Ethan Allen company. The process has been in effect for quite some time, so there is already an assignment of product to factory in place. The planning process reviews and adjusts the current assignment rather than making a new assignment, as was suggested in the HPP approach to aggregate capacity analysis.

Ethan Allen is a manufacturer of home furnishings. The annual sales are approximately $200 million, of which the Case Goods Division accounts for approximately $120 million. The division produces solid wood, as opposed to upholstered, furniture and manufactures in 14 plants located in the northeastern United States. The products move from the 14 factories to five consolidation warehouses that ship to field warehouses or directly to the 287 franchised Ethan Allen dealers who account for 90 percent of the sales volume.

Production planning is done on a monthly cycle, as illustrated in Figure 15.8. One of the key inputs to the process is the manual forecast. It is a

FIGURE 15.8 Monthly preparation cycle for forecasting, production planning, and MPS

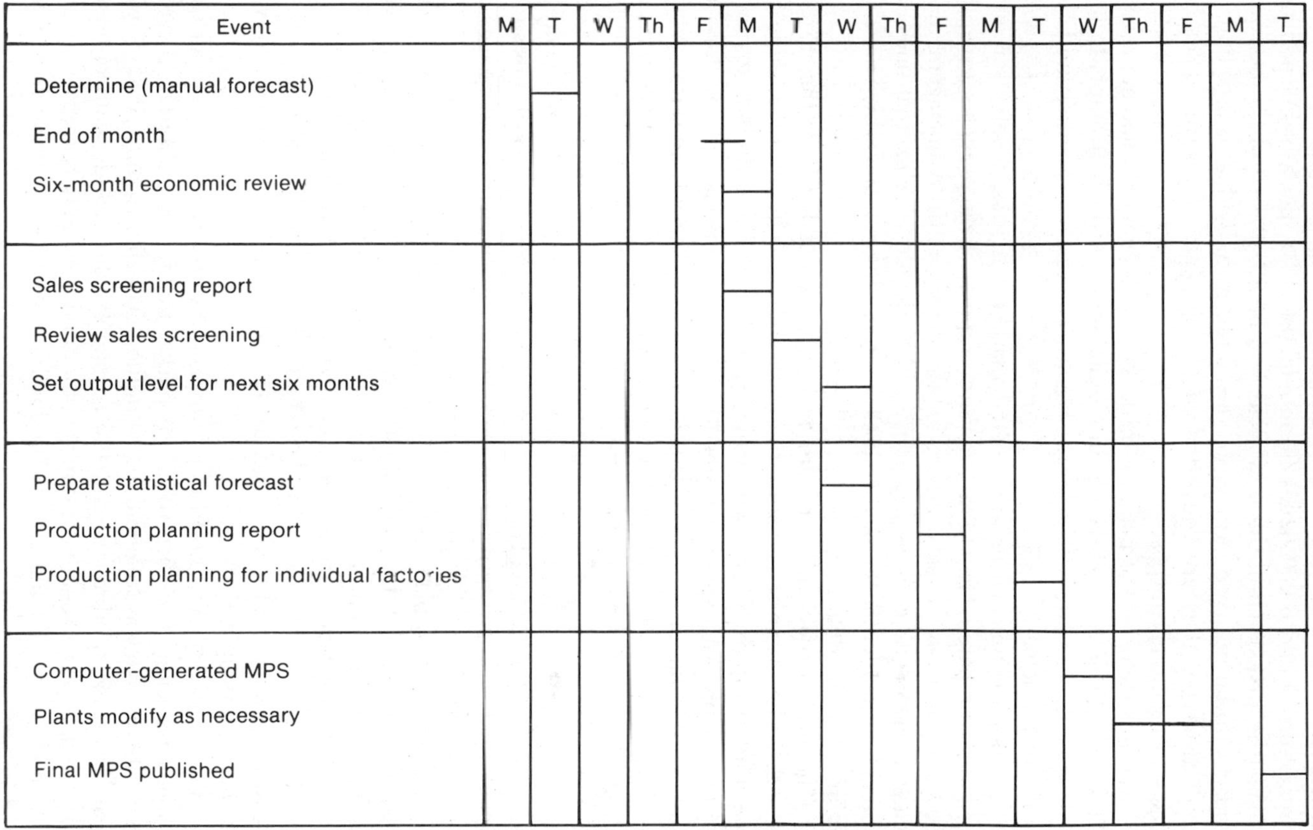

Event	M	T	W	Th	F	M	T	W	Th	F	M	T	W	Th	F	M	T
Determine (manual forecast)																	
End of month																	
Six-month economic review																	
Sales screening report																	
Review sales screening																	
Set output level for next six months																	
Prepare statistical forecast																	
Production planning report																	
Production planning for individual factories																	
Computer-generated MPS																	
Plants modify as necessary																	
Final MPS published																	

W. L. Berry, T. E. Vollmann, and D. C. Whybark, *Master Production Scheduling: Principles and Practice,* April 1979, p. 45.

determination of all demand that is not part of a routine forecast of customer orders. It includes contract sales (e.g., Holiday Inn wants 3,000 beds), sales promotions (build 5,000 tables in anticipation of a special sale), and new items (the first batch of the new chair will be 1,000). All of these require capacity to be reserved. Although considered as individual transactions by furniture type, they are converted to the aggregate measure—sales dollars—for planning purposes.

Another factor in the planning process is a six-month economic review. This is a consolidation of data from various sources which attempts to indicate what the changes will be for the furniture industry in general and Ethan Allen in particular.

To monitor unusual or unexpected market activities, a sales screening report is prepared. This is a computer report which provides exception codes for all unusual sales activity for the prior month. A management review of the sales screening report is used to decide which actual sales data are to be included in the next statistical forecasting run and which are to be excluded or modified.

The next activity is to set the aggregate output level for the next six months. This is the basic commitment to a production plan. It is done in a meeting of top executives who have as input data the economic review, a statistical forecast (exponential smoothing) of sales, the manual sales forecast, inventory balances, and order backlogs. They also have time series data on each of these items as well as any prior commitments to the six-month total production plans stemming from previous planning meetings. The result of the meeting is one number, in sales dollars, for the six-month period ahead. This number is the key to preparing the production planning report and the subsequent production planning for individual factories. It constrains subsequent decisions, but provision is made for feedback later in the disaggregation process.

The production plan, as set by the meeting of top management, is comprised of four items: the manual forecast, the statistical forecast, any inventory adjustments, and any backlog adjustments. The four categories must sum to the total specified by the executive group. The question is how to do it. Ethan Allen believes that of these four items, the statistical forecast is the least well known, so it is the residual. The others are set. Let us see this with a specific example.

Figure 15.9 shows the production-planning report for the overall Case Goods Division. For the six-month period beginning in March, the total production plan was set equal to $64 million. The first column (W/0 98) is for wholly owned production, and the second (W/99) includes subcontracted production. The executive group sets the total to include both; it is a manufacturing activity to allocate production between owned capacities and vendor capacities.

The inventory adjustment is based upon a target inventory of six weeks of sales. It is calculated from some of the other data in the report. The Inventory Item Status ($8,939) is the dollar value of all finished goods. The present

FIGURE 15.9 Production planning report for overall case goods operations

*Production requirement program**

	Total (000) W/O 98	*Total (000) W/ 99*
Inventory adjustment	$ 6,547	$ 6,480
Backlog adjustment	5,643	5,304
Forecast March report	40,938	42,401
Adjusted forecast	33,780	34,987
Adjusted forecast weekly rate	1,407.5	1,457.8
Transfers	2	(2)
April new items 60 percent	1,177	1,177
April market special	14,847	15,320
Remainder October Market Special	731	732
Total requirement	62,728	63,998
Eight-week production	19,678	20,523
Balance required as of 4/24	43,114	43,567
Production yield	2,476.9	2,569.8
Inventory item status	8,314	8,939
Backlog item status	25,458	25,862
Weeks of inventory	3.4	3.5
Weeks of backlog	10.3	10.1

* March through August eight-week backlog; $64 million grand total.
W. L. Berry, T. E. Vollmann, and D. C. Whybark, *Master Production Scheduling: Principles and Practice,* April 1979, p. 46.

weekly output rate is called Production Yield ($2,569.8). When the production yield is multiplied by 6 and the inventory item status is subtracted, the result ($6,480) is the Inventory Adjustment. The current Weeks of Inventory is 3.5; so the $6,480 is an addition to production to build up the inventory position.

The backlog adjustment involves a similar calculation. Ethan Allen has a target backlog position of eight weeks. The present backlog on an item basis is shown as Backlog Item Status ($25,862), which represents 10.1 weeks of backlog. When the production yield ($2,569.8) is multiplied by 8, the result is $20,558.4. The actual backlog is $5,304 (rounded) in excess of this target. Reducing the present backlog level to the desired level requires additional production.

Before considering the forecast section, we describe the manual forecast. The manual forecast is comprised of new items for April ($1,177), a market special for April ($15,320), and the remainder of an October market special ($732). This totals to $17,229. These are all agreed upon commitments to be met within the current production plan.

The statistical forecast prepared for March is based upon exponential smoothing of sales data that have been reviewed by management. It yields a total six-month forecast of $42,401. However, as noted above, this component of the production plan is the least well known. As a consequence, it is adjusted after the other components are accounted for. The result is as follows:

	Production plan	= $ 64,000
−	Manual forecast	(17,229)
−	Inventory adjustment	(6,480)
−	Backlog adjustment	(5,304)
=	Allocated to statistical forecast	= $ 34,987

We see then that although the exponential smoothing model predicts routine sales of $42,401,000 over the next six months, by approving the manual forecast, inventory, and backlog target levels, the executive group allocates to the statistical forecast only $34,987,000. In making this adjustment, the executives realize that the actual inventory and backlog conditions at the end of the next six months will not be at the target levels unless more capacity is provided (i.e., unless the production plan is increased). In fact, the routine sales will probably be closer to $42 million than the adjustment indicates, so at the end of the six-month period, the inventories may not be increased to the target levels, and the backlogs will probably still be higher than desired.

Ethan Allen uses 48 weeks of actual production per year for planning purposes. Thus, the amount shown as "Adjusted Forecast Weekly Rate ($1,457.8) is obtained by dividing the Adjusted Forecast ($34,987) by 24. The Transfers (2), indicate a shift from subcontractor to owned production. That is why the Total Requirement is $63,998 instead of $64,000. Ethan Allen has an eight-week frozen master production schedule (MPS). This represents current commitments against capacity. The Eight-Weeks Production ($20,523) is that portion of the MPS that is frozen. The Balance Required by the production plan ($43,567) must be produced in the last 16 weeks of the plan.

The next step is to disaggregate this overall Case Goods Division production plan to individual factories. In fact, it is broken down even further, by individual assembly lines in each factory. Figure 15.10 is the production planning report for one of the Case Goods production facilities, the Beecher Falls, Vermont factory. We will demonstrate the approach using the first column (Cases 06). The inventory and backlog adjustments are calculated for the line as they were for the overall Case Goods Division (six and eight-week targets, respectively). The manual forecast is based on only the specific items that are produced on this production line. The statistical forecast (4,016) is the sum of the forecasts for just the items made on this line.

The key to the disaggregation of the production plan to the individual lines is in the Adjusted Forecast (3,314). This is obtained by using the ratio of adjusted forecast to total forecast from the overall production plan. Since the

FIGURE 15.10 Production planning report for Beecher Falls Plant by assembly line

PRODUCTION REQUIREMENT PROGRAM
MARCH THROUGH AUGUST 8WK B/L $64M
BEECHER FALLS

	CASES	C/ HUTCH	HUTCH	BEDS	MISC	BKSTACK	DESKS	MIRRORS	RAILS
	06	07	08	20	21	22	24	26	30
INVENTORY ADJUSTMENT	605	60	22	292	5	148	30	48	(31)
BACKLOG ADJUSTMENT	1,590	(4)	180	277	(15)	152	1	104	
FORECAST MARCH RPT	4,016	171	251	1,416	62	467	142	301	4
ADJUSTED FORECAST	3,314	141	207	1,168	51	385	117	248	3
ADJ. FCST. WEEKLY RATE	138.1	5.9	8.6	48.7	2.1	16.1	4.9	10.3	0.1
TRANSFERS	45					(133)			
APRIL NEW ITEMS 60%			11	12				41	
APRIL MKT SPEC INCL REPL	524			383	37	290	54	128	
REM OCT MKT SPECIAL	5	3				78			
TOTAL REQUIREMENT	6,083	200	421	2,132	78	919	202	570	(28)
EIGHT WEEKS PRODUCTION	1,731	67	142	628	32	265	66	158	
BAL REQT AS OF 4/24/	4,352	133	279	1,504	46	654	136	412	
PRODUCTION YIELD	227.1	11.4	15.4	73.8	3.3	32.4	8.0	18.2	
INVENTORY ITEM STATUS	758	8	70	151	15	48	18	61	31
BACKLOG ITEM STATUS	3,407	87	303	867	11	411	65	250	
WEEKS OF INVENTORY	3.3	0.7	4.5	2.0	4.5	1.5	2.3	3.4	
WEEKS OF BACKLOG	15.0	7.6	19.7	11.7	3.3	12.7	8.1	13.7	

Note: All figures are in thousands (000).
W. L. Berry, T. E. Vollmann, and D. C. Whybark, *Master Production Scheduling: Principles and Practice*, April 1979, p. 47.

total forecast was 42,401 and the adjusted forecast was 34,987, the adjusted forecast amount for the 06 Case line is calculated as follows:

$$(34{,}987 / 42{,}401) \times 4016 = 3314$$

What this means is that Ethan Allen establishes the backlog and inventory levels on a line-by-line basis, thereby reflecting the actual inventory and backlog situations for each production line at each plant. The production that is to be allocated to the statistical forecast is spread proportionately across all of the lines by using the overall adjustment ratio. The result is an attempt to bring each line into a common inventory/backlog position so that uniform customer service is provided across all lines.

The Total Requirement (6,083) is now the sum of the inventory adjustment (605), the backlog adjustment (1,590), the manual forecast for the remaining October and April market specials (524 + 5), the statistical forecast (3,314), and the transfers (45).

The master production scheduling (MPS) process is the next step in the disaggregation of the plan. The first eight weeks of the MPS are frozen (as are any of the manual forecast items) using firm planned orders. The remainder of an 18-week MPS is developed using lot sizes for individual items and priorities that take into account demand, inventory (or backlog) position, and the time required to produce a lot. The lines are loaded to capacity for the 18 weeks, in priority sequence, using the priorities of the individual items.

The priority for any item at any point in time is calculated by dividing the expected inventory position by the weekly requirement, giving an estimate of the weeks of supply in inventory. Now, consider the priority associated with the first item scheduled on a particular line at the end of the MPS horizon (the 18th week). If that priority number were zero, the implication is that the match between line capacity and demand for the items made on this line was quite good. That is, the item which was needed in week 18 would, in fact, be scheduled for production in week 18. If the priority were +6, it means that using the line at its assigned balanced capacity will result in at least a 6-week inventory at the end of 18 weeks for the items built on that line. Another way of looking at a priority of +6 is that in week 18 the items that will be produced are not required until week 24.

A negative priority could also occur. If the priority for week 18 for a product on the line were −8, the inference is that there would be a backlog of 8 weeks of demand for items produced on this line. Goods desired by customers in week 10 would not be manufactured until week 18.

Ethan Allen constructs a matrix each month in which the rows are production lines and the columns are factories. Figure 15.11 is a simplified version of this matrix. For each cell in the matrix, two numbers are given. The upper number is the currently planned weekly capacity of the line taken from the reports like that shown in Figure 15.10. The lower number is the

FIGURE 15.11 Ethan Allen capacity analysis matrix

Line \ Factory	1	2	3	4	5	6	7
I	35 − 1	100 − 6		400 7			
II					250 − 1		180 1
III		75 − 9					
IV	75 12					155 − 4	
V		180 − 7					100 0
VI			300 − 1		175 − 1		

expected priority in week 18, as explained above. For example, line I in factory 1 has a priority of −1, and this line has 35 hours of weekly rated capacity.

Not all lines are in all factories. For example, line I might be for chairs, line II for beds, line III for tables, etc. This means that chairs are produced in factories 1, 2, and 4, beds are produced in factories 5 and 7, and tables are only produced in factory 2.

A perusal of Figure 15.11 leads to the conclusion that of all the factories, factory 2 has the least capacity relative to its demands. It has capacity shortage problems in all lines. Factories 3, 5, and 7 seem to be reasonably matched in terms of capacity and demand. Factory 1 has too much capacity on line IV, as does factory 4 on its only line. Factory 6 appears to have insufficient capacity.

By reviewing each line in terms of the match between its expected priority in week 18 and zero, a judgment can be made of the adequacy of capacity. For example, the −4 for line IV, factory 6 might lead to a query to that factory on how to increase its 155 hours of capacity. This also allows capital appropriation requests to be targeted to specific kinds of capacity. The executive group uses this matrix to monitor the disaggregation of the production plan.

The actions at the Ethan Allen monthly meeting include how to change line capacities. More importantly, however, are product shifts between factories. For example, can chairs now made at factory 2 on line I be shifted to factory 4 for manufacture? If so, there will be fewer products competing for the 100 hours of capacity in factory 2 and more products to use up the 400 hours of capacity in factory 4. A similar shift might be possible from factory 6 to factory 1 on line IV.

One primary objective of the monthly planning meeting is to reassign products to factories, and to make capacity adjustments on specific lines. In each case, the matrix only indicates desirable actions. There are constraints on what can indeed be achieved. For example, if factory 2 makes pine chairs and factory 4 works only with oak, a transfer of products may be very difficult.

Another capacity planning objective is to decide when to build new factories and what products should be made in them. This is equivalent to adding a column (factory 8) to Figure 15.11. If the two product shifts described above (2 to 4, 6 to 1) solved these problems, it would seem that factory 8 should have lines of type III and V.

Ethan Allen has some factories that cannot become any larger. For example, several are in small towns where additions to the labor force are virtually impossible. This means that as overall company sales grow, there will be a net outflow of products from these factories (e.g., factory 2) to new factories (e.g., factory 8). This reassignment is carefully planned to rationalize overall company production. In general, new factories are built with large capital investments to produce high-volume items. However, the skill needed to produce some items only exists in the older factories.

This system has worked well for planning the growth of capacity, but it has been more important during times when capacity has had to be reduced. Even when sales start to fall, the MPS approach will still be to load the lines to capacity. But when the monthly matrix is constructed, the priorities will all become greater than zero, indicating quickly the need to adjust and where to do it.

This is precisely what happened in 1974–75. But the matrix indicated the potential problem (i.e., 18 weeks in the future) before it became an actual problem. The result was a series of remedial actions, including the reduction of capacities. These actions were taken *before* the warehouses were full. The result allowed the company to come through a period of sharply reduced sales while maintaining profitable operations.

The Ethan Allen approach does not use many formal models, but does use many of the principles of HPP. The process clearly involves sequential disaggregation and executive constraints on action. It also involves detailed planning for shorter planning horizons than the horizons used for aggregate planning. Ethan Allen uses both a top-down approach (like HPP) to planning and a bottom-up approach to control from their MPC system. It will be interesting to watch future development to see whether formal approaches will be applied at Ethan Allen or if HPP can incorporate bottom-up feedback.

CONCLUDING PRINCIPLES

This chapter has primarily reviewed formal approaches to aggregate capacity analysis and disclosed a gap between theory and practice. We see the following principles as important:

- To be accepted, the logic of formal procedures must be made transparent.
- Data realities must be considered before formal techniques can be expected to have wide application.
- Provision for management review must be made in the planning process.
- Bottom-up feedback needs to be developed for monitoring aggregate plans.
- Simple models that are easily addressed on a what if basis are a good start for aggregate capacity analysis.
- Some of the aggregate planning models are logically consistent with the evolutionary approach now coming from practice.

REFERENCES

Bowman, E. H. "Consistency and Optimality in Managerial Decision Making." *Management Science*, January 1963.

Bitran, G. D., E. A. Haas and A. C. Hax. "Hierarchical Production Planning: A Two-Stage System." *Operations Research*, March-April, 1982, pp. 232–51.

Cooper, J. C. "A Capacity Planning Methodology." *IBM Systems Journal* 19, no. 1 (1980), pp. 28–45.

Conti, Robert E. "Living with Poor Capacity Planning Forecasts." *APICS Annual Conference Proceedings*, 1979, pp. 113–15.

Gordon, J. R. M. "A Multi-Model Analysis of an Aggregate Scheduling Decision." Unpublished Ph.D. dissertation, Sloan School of Management, M.I.T., 1966 (published in Elwood S. Buffa, *Production-Inventory Systems: Planning and Control*, Homewood, Ill.: Richard D. Irwin, 1968, pp. 168–69).

Hansman, W. H. and S. W. Hess, "A Linear Programming Approach to Production and Employment Scheduling," *Management Technology*, vol. 1, January 1960, pp. 46–52.

Holt, C. C., F. Modigliani, J. F. Muth, and H. A. Simon. *Planning Production, Inventories, and Workforce*. New York: Prentice-Hall, 1960, p. 16.

Nellemann, David O. "Production Planning and Master Scheduling: Management's Game Plan." *APICS 22d Annual Conference Proceedings*, 1979, pp. 166–68.

Skinner, C. W. "Manufacturing—The Missing Link in Corporate Strategy." *Harvard Business Review*, May-June, 1969, pp. 136–45.

Sule, Dileep R. "Simple Methods for Uncapacitated Facility Location/Allocation Problems." *Journal of Operations Management* 1, no. 4 (May 1981), pp. 215–24.

Taubert, W. H. "A Search Decision Rule for the Aggregate Scheduling Problem." *Management Science* 14, no. 6 (February 1968).

Vollmann, T. E. "Capacity Planning: The Missing Link." *Production and Inventory Management Journal*, 1st Quarter 1973.

16

Forecasting systems

Forecasts of demand are one important input to manufacturing planning and control (MPC) systems. In this chapter, we treat short-term forecasting for individual items. Applying effective forecasting systems will result in low-cost routine forecasts and a set of monitors to indicate when forecasting problems are incurred. These forecasts of end items, spare parts, and other independent demand should be a part of the front-end modules of the MPC system. A key objective is to provide one, and only one, source for forecast data; this source is to be unbiased and usable by all areas in the firm.

Forecasts used for production and resource planning can be of many types, including subjective estimates, econometric models, Delphi techniques, etc. A detailed exposition of all these is a book in itself. Although there are many techniques that could be applied to forecasting the demand for individual end items, we focus here on short-term forecasts based on observations of actual demand in the past. The chapter is organized around the following five topics:

- The forecasting problem: How is the forecasting problem defined for manufacturing planning and control purposes?
- Basic forecasting techniques: What are the basic techniques for forecasting short-term demand?

- Enhancing the basic exponential smoothing model: How can trend, seasonality, and other kinds of information be incorporated?
- Using the forecasting system: How does one select initial forecasting parameter values and monitor forecast results?
- Forecasting in industry: How have these techniques been put into practice?

This chapter has very close linkages to Chapter 10 on demand management. The forecasting activities are accomplished in the demand management module of the MPC system. In addition Chapters 17 and 18, covering the management of inventory, presume the existence of effective, routine forecasting procedures. Chapter 18 contains material on advanced forecasting systems.

THE FORECASTING PROBLEM

In this chapter, we deal primarily with short-term forecasting techniques of the type most useful to routine decision making in manufacturing planning and control. However, there are other decision problems both within manufacturing and in other functional areas of the firm which require different approaches to forecasting. We turn now to a brief discussion of these situations before delving more deeply into the development of short-term forecasting techniques for manufacturing. We also treat a vital forecasting question: how to evaluate the performance of a forecasting technique.

Forecasting perspectives

Managers need forecasts for a variety of decisions. Among these are long-run decisions involving such things as constructing a new plant, determining the type and size of aircraft for an airline fleet, extending the guest facilities of a hotel, or changing the curriculum requirements in a university. Generally, these longer-run decisions require forecasts of aggregate levels of demand, utilizing such measures as annual sales volume, expected passenger volume, number of guest nights, or total number of students enrolled. In a sense, this is fortunate, since aggregate levels of an activity can usually be forecast more accurately than individual activities. As an example, a university administration probably has a pretty good estimate of how many students will be enrolled next term, even though the forecast of enrollment for an elective course may be off by a considerable amount.

For aggregate forecasts, we may be able to use causal relationships and the statistical tools of regression and correlation to help us do the job. For example, sales of household fixtures are closely related to housing starts. The number of vacationers at resorts is related to the net disposable income level in the economy. In such instances, the relationship may be statistically modeled, thereby providing the basis for a forecasting procedure. Managerial insight and judgment are also used extensively in developing aggregate forecasts of future activities for long-run decisions. Both statistical and qualitative forecasting methods can also be applied for medium-run decisions, such as the annual budgeting process. It is tempting to classify forecasting techniques as long-run or short-run, but this misses the point of developing and using techniques appropriate to the decision and situation.

Throughout this chapter we will look at fairly mechanical procedures for making forecasts. Specifically, we will look at models for "casting forward" historical information to make this "fore cast." Implicit in this process is a belief that the conditions of the past which produced the historical data will not change. Although the procedures that will be developed are mechanical, one should not draw from this the impression that managers always rely exclusively on past information to make estimates of future activity. In the first place, in certain instances, we simply have no past data. This occurs, for example, when a new product is introduced. Several other examples may come to mind, but we certainly should not ignore plans for a future sales promotion, the appearance of a new competitor, or changes in legislation that will affect our business. These circumstances all illustrate the need for managerial review and modification of the forecast where there is special knowledge to take into account. This should not be lost sight of as we move into the technical aspects of the chapter.

We will largely focus our attention on techniques for converting past information into forecasts. These are often statistical techniques, and we will also use statistical methods for evaluating the quality of the forecasts. The procedures are often called statistical forecasting procedures.

Forecast evaluation

Ultimately, of course, the quality of any forecast is reflected in the quality of the decisions that are based on the forecast. This leads to the suggestion that the ideal comparison of forecasting procedures would be based on the costs of producing the forecast and the value of the forecast for the decision. From these data, the appropriate trade-off between the cost of developing and the cost of making decisions with forecasts of varying quality could be made. Unfortunately, as one can readily guess, neither of these costs is very easily measured. In addition, such a scheme suggests that a different forecasting procedure might be required for each decision, an undesirably complex possibility. As a result of these complications, we rely on some direct measures of forecast quality.

One important criterion for any forecast procedure would be a low cost per forecast. For many manufacturing planning and control problems, one needs to make forecasts for many thousands of items on a weekly or monthly basis; the result is the need for a procedure that is simple, effective, and low cost. Unlike the rare occasions when the decision is to add more factory capacity, routine short-term decisions are made frequently, for many items, and cannot require an expensive, time-consuming forecasting procedure. Moreover, since the resultant decisions are made frequently, any error made in one forecast can be compensated for in the decision made next time. However, the expenditure that an aggregate, long-term forecast might require may well be justified in making the factory capacity decision.

Of more general and increasing importance for computer-oriented decision systems are the storage requirements and computer time for producing forecasts. Since the forecasts may be needed for several thousands or tens of thousands of items on a relatively frequent basis, computer time and storage become an increasingly important aspect of forecast procedure evaluation. The procedures that we will focus on in this chapter all have the attribute of simplicity, are easy to use, and have low computer time/storage requirements.

For any forecasting procedure that one develops, an important characteristic is honesty, or lack of bias. That is, the procedure should produce forecasts that are neither consistently high nor consistently low. The forecasts cannot be overly optimistic or pessimistic, but rather should tell it like it is. Since we are dealing with projecting past data, lack of bias means smoothing out the randomness of the past data so that overforecasts are offset by underforecasts. To measure bias, we will use the mean error as defined by Equation (16.1). In this equation, the forecast error in each period is the actual demand in each period minus the forecast of demand for that period. Figure 16.1 shows an example calculation of bias.

$$\begin{array}{l}\text{Mean error}\\ \text{(bias)}\end{array} = \frac{\sum_{i=1}^{n} (\text{Actual demand}_i - \text{Forecast demand}_i)}{n} \tag{16.1}$$

where:

i = Period number.
n = Number of periods of data.

FIGURE 16.1 Example bias calculation

		Period (i)			
		1	*2*	*3*	*4*
(1)	Actual demand	1,500	1,400	1,700	1,200
(2)	Forecast demand	1,600	1,600	1,400	1,300
	Error (1) − (2)	−100	−200	300	−100

$$\text{Bias} = \sum_{i=1}^{4} \text{error}_i/4 = (-100 - 200 + 300 - 100)/4 = -100/4 = -25 \tag{16.1}$$

As can be seen from Figure 16.1, when the forecast errors tend to cancel one another out, the measure of bias tends to be low. The positive errors in some periods are offset by negative errors in others, which tends to produce an average error or bias near zero. In the example of Figure 16.1, there is a bias and the demand was overforecast by an average of 25 units per period for the four periods.

Having unbiased forecasts is important in manufacturing planning and control, since the estimates, on the average, are about right. But that is not enough. We still need to be concerned with the magnitude of the errors. Note that for the example in Figure 16.1, we would obtain the identical measure of bias if the actual demand for the four periods had been 100, 100, 5,500, and 100 respectively. However, the individual errors are much larger, and this difference would have to be reflected in buffer inventories if one were to maintain a consistent level of customer service.

Let us now turn to a widely used measure of forecast error, the mean absolute deviation (MAD). The formula is given as Equation (16.2), and example calculations are shown in Figure 16.2

$$\text{Mean absolute deviation (MAD)} = \frac{\sum_{i=1}^{n} \left| \text{Actual demand}_i - \text{Forecast demand}_i \right|}{n} \quad (16.2)$$

where:

i = Period number.
n = Number of periods of data.
$|x|$ = Absolute value of x.

The mean absolute deviation expresses the size of the average error irrespective of whether it is positive or negative. It is the combination of bias and MAD that allows one to evaluate forecasting results. Bias is perhaps the most critical, since forecast errors can be compensated for through safety stocks, expediting, faster delivery means, and other kinds of responses. MAD gives an indication of the size of the expected compensation (e.g., required safety stock). However, if a forecast is consistently lower than demand, the entire material-flow pipeline will run dry; it will be necessary to start over again with raw materials. Similar issues exist for a consistently high forecast. The great advantage of the techniques described in this chapter is that they tend to be unbiased. Moreover, routine monitoring techniques identify bias when it is present. Judgmental forecasts, such as those made by marketing groups, are often biased because the forecasting incorporates other goals (e.g., stimulate the sales force). The key is to clearly separate the *process* of forecasting from the *use* of forecasting. The goals for the process are no bias and minimum MAD. What is *done* with the forecast is another issue.

Before turning to the techniques, there is one other relationship that

FIGURE 16.2 Sample MAD calculation

		Period (i)			
		1	*2*	*3*	*4*
(1)	Actual demand	1,500	1,400	1,700	1,200
(2)	Forecast demand	1,600	1,600	1,400	1,300
	Error (1) − (2)	−100	−200	300	−100

$$\text{MAD} = \sum_{i=1} |\text{error}_i|/4 = (|-100| + |-200| + |300| + |-100|)/4 = 175 \tag{16.2}$$

		Period (i)			
		1	*2*	*3*	*4*
(1)	Actual demand	100	100	5,500	100
(2)	Forecast demand	1,600	1,600	1,400	1,300
	Error (1) − (2)	−1,500	−1,500	4,100	−1,200

$$\begin{aligned}\text{MAD} &= \sum_{i=1}^{4} |\text{error}_i|/4 \\ &= (|-1{,}500| + |-1{,}500| + |4{,}100| + |-1{,}200|)/4 \\ &= 8{,}300/4 = 2{,}075\end{aligned} \tag{16.2}$$

needs to be made. MAD is a measure of error or deviation from an expected result (the forecast). The best-known measure of deviation or dispersion from statistics is the standard deviation. When the errors are distributed normally, the standard deviation of the forecast errors is arithmetically related to MAD by Equation (16.3).

$$\begin{array}{l}\text{Standard deviation of} \\ \text{forecast errors}\end{array} = 1.25 \text{ MAD} \tag{16.3}$$

BASIC FORECASTING TECHNIQUES

Now that we have identified the objectives of forecasting procedures, let us turn to some procedures that meet the objectives. In this section, we will introduce some of the basic concepts that lie behind two very common short-term forecasting techniques: moving averages and exponential smoothing. Before we discuss these techniques, however, we present an example problem that allows us to continually relate the concepts and formulas to a real-world context.

Example forecasting situation

Enrique Martinez is manager of one of the restaurants located in a large hotel near the Loop in Chicago. The restaurant, Panchos, caters both to guests of the hotel and to local street traffic. Pancho's reputation has been growing, and a few months ago, the restaurant's capacity was expanded. Enrique was studying ways to improve and routinize his decisions for managing the restaurant operations, and he chose three situations to study in some detail: a new contract offer from his linen service, the trend in tequila-based drinks, and his twice weekly orders to the local wholesale grocery distributor. All of these decisions depended upon his ability to forecast demand. Although the decision in each situation involves placing orders, each presents quite a different forecasting problem. With the variety he had chosen, Enrique felt that he had a good basis for studying forecasting methods for Panchos.

The first situation involved a new contract proposal for tablecloths and napkins from the linen supply service with which the restaurant did business. The owner of the linen supply firm offered an attractive discount if Enrique would prespecify the quantity he wanted each week rather than continuing the current practice whereby the linen supply firm brought enough clean linen to replace whatever dirty linen there was each week. Enrique collected data on the number of tables served during the last few weeks as the basis for determining how to forecast his needs. These data are summarized in Figure 16.3.

Before going on to the forecasting techniques, it is worth reiterating a point: We are *not* presently dealing with the decision of how to order tablecloths, how many to hold as safety stock, or any other decision. We are simply trying to forecast demand. The premise is that a *good* forecast will allow for better decisions, but we are not combining the act of forecasting with any decision.

The orders for tequila-based drinks in the lounge had been growing rapidly, creating a problem in determining how much tequila to order from the supplier for delivery each week. The number of tequila-based drinks served in each of the last several weeks was collected by Enrique and is presented in Figure 16.4.

The final activity that Enrique chose to review was that of deciding how

FIGURE 16.3 Number of tables served during the last nine weeks

	Week number								
	24	*25*	*26*	*27*	*28*	*29*	*30*	*31*	*32*
Tables served	1,600	1,500	1,700	900	1,100	1,500	1,400	1,700	1,200

FIGURE 16.4 Number of tequila-based drinks served during the last nine weeks

	Week number								
	24	*25*	*26*	*27*	*28*	*29*	*30*	*31*	*32*
Number of drinks	16	71	40	85	196	351	254	261	364

much to order for the twice weekly delivery from the local wholesale grocery distributor. The distributor delivered on Tuesday (Panchos was closed on Mondays) and Friday mornings. The deliveries consisted of canned goods, staples, condiments, etc. for use during the next three days. There was a substantially smaller volume of business during the first three days of the business week than during the last three. To get an idea of what the pattern might be, Enrique kept track of the usage of number 10 cans of vegetables for each of six three-day periods. The data are shown in Figure 16.5.

Returning first to the tables served example, Figure 16.6 is a plot of the data given in Figure 16.3.

The number of tables served appears relatively stable (for the number of periods that we have data available) and seems to fluctuate randomly about some central value. If we were interested in using these past data to forecast the number of tables that would be served in future weeks, a tempting procedure would be to simply draw a line through the data points and use that line as our estimate for week 33 and subsequent weeks. This would produce an estimate of the average or expected demand in future weeks, and the process of drawing that line is an averaging or smoothing process. The process removes fluctuations around the line and focuses on the underlying average. It is this smoothing process that provides the basis for the techniques to which we now turn our attention.

Moving averages

Rather than draw a line through the points in Figure 16.6 to find the average, we could simply calculate the arithmetic average of the nine histori-

FIGURE 16.5 Number 10 cans of vegetables used during the last six three-day periods

	Period					
	F–S–Sun	*T–W–Th*	*F–S–Sun*	*T–W–Th*	*F–S–Sun*	*T–W–Th*
Week number	29	30	30	31	31	32
Number of cans	48	35	47	30	51	37

FIGURE 16.6 Number of tables served at Panchos during last nine weeks

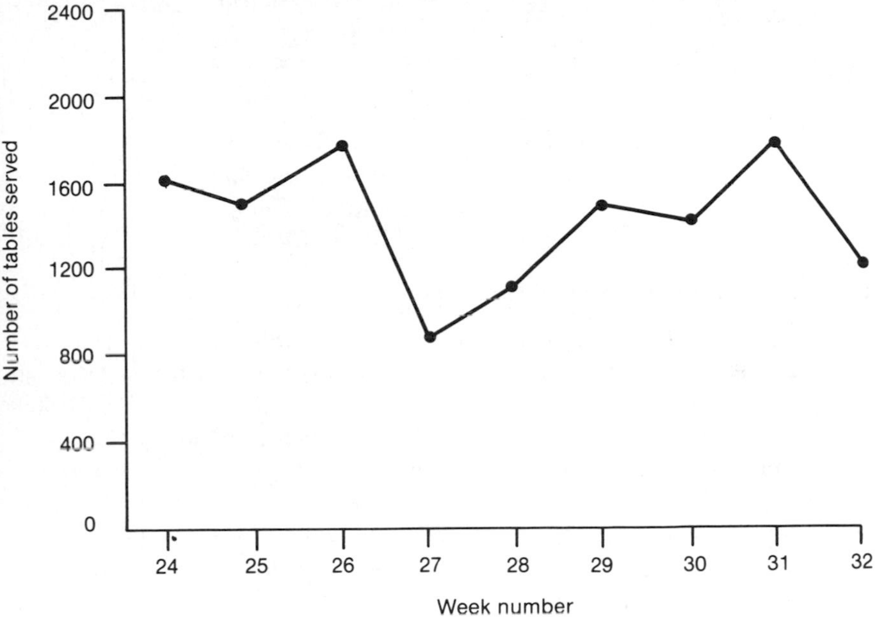

cal demand observations. Since we are interested in averaged past data to project into the future, we could use an average of all the past demand data that were available for forecasting purposes. There are several reasons, however, why this may not be a desirable way of smoothing. In the first place, there may be so many periods of past data that storing them all is an issue. Second, it is often true that the most recent history is of most relevance in forecasting the short-term demand in the near future. Recent data may reveal current conditions better than do data that are several months or years old. For these reasons, many firms use the concept of a moving average for forecasting demand.

The moving average model for smoothing historical demand proceeds, as the name implies, by averaging a selected number of past periods of data. The average moves because a new average can be calculated whenever a period's demand is determined. Whenever a forecast is needed, the most recent past history of demand will be used to do the averaging. The model for finding the moving average is shown in Equation (16.4). The equation shows that the moving average forecast always uses the most recent n periods of historical information available for developing the forecast. Notice that the moving average is the forecast of demand for the next and subsequent periods. Figure 16.7 shows sample calculations for the number of tables served.

$$\text{Moving average forecast (MAF) at the end of period } t\text{: MAF}_t = \sum_{i=t-n+1}^{t} \text{Actual demand}_i/n \quad (16.4)$$

where:

i = Period number.
t = Current period (the period for which the most recent actual demand is known).
n = Number of periods of moving average.

The basic exponential smoothing model

You will note that the moving average model does smooth the historical data, but does so with an equal weight on each piece of historical information. Thus, if one were at the end of period 29 with that demand (1,500) known, and the demands for periods 30 and beyond unknown, the three-period moving average forecast for period 30 would be (900 + 1,100 + 1,500/3) = 1,167. At the end of period 30, the forecast for period 31 would be (1,100 + 1,500 + 1,400/3) = 1,333. If one looks at a single period's demand, such as the 1,500 in period 29, it is used *only* for forecasts made at the end of periods 29, 30, and 31. In each case, the 1,500 has a weight in the forecast of one third. For forecasts made before the end of period 29 or after the end of period 32, this piece of demand data has no weight.

FIGURE 16.7 Example moving average calculations

	Period					
	27	*28*	*29*	*30*	*31*	*32*
Actual demand	900	1,100	1,500	1,400	1,700	1,200

$$\text{6-period MAF made at the end of period 32} = \sum_{27}^{32} \text{Actual demand}/6$$

$$= (900 + 1{,}100 + 1{,}500 + 1{,}400 + 1{,}700 + 1{,}200)/6 = 1{,}300 \quad (16.4)$$

$$\text{3-period MAF made at the end of period 32} = \sum_{30}^{32} \text{Actual demand}/3$$

$$= (1{,}400 + 1{,}700 + 1{,}200)/3 = 1{,}433 \quad (16.4)$$

The exponential smoothing model for forecasting does not eliminate *any* past datum, but adjusts the weights given to past data so that older data get increasingly less weight (hence the name exponential smoothing). The basic idea is a fairly simple one and has a great deal of intuitive appeal. Each forecast is based on an average which is corrected each time there is a forecast error. For example, if we forecast 90 units of demand for an item in a particular period and the actual demand for that item turns out to be 100 units, an appealing idea would be to increase our forecast by some portion of the 10-unit error in making the next period's forecast. In this way, if the error indicated that demand was changing, we could begin to change the forecast. We may not want to incorporate the entire error (i.e., add 10 units) since the error may have just been due to the random variations around the mean. The proportion of the error that will be incorporated into the forecast is called the exponential smoothing constant, and is identified as α. The model for computing the new average is shown in Equation (16.5) as we have just described it. The most common computational form of the exponentially smoothed average is given in Equation (16.6). The new exponentially smoothed average is again the forecast for the next and subsequent periods. Figure 16.8 shows example calculations for the number of tables served.

Exponential smoothing forecast (ESF) at the end of period t:

$$\text{ESF}_t = \text{ESF}_{t-1} + \alpha\,(\text{Actual demand}_t - \text{ESF}_{t-1}) \qquad (16.5)$$

$$= \alpha\,(\text{Actual demand}_t) + (1 - \alpha)\text{ESF}_{t-1} \qquad (16.6)$$

where:

α = The smoothing constant ($0 \leq \alpha \leq 1$).

t = Current period (the period for which the most recent actual demand is known.

ESF_{t-1} = Exponential smoothing forecast made one period previously (at the end of period $t - 1$).

FIGURE 16.8 Example exponential smoothing calculations

	Period	
	27	*28*
Actual demand	900	1,100

Assume: ESF_{26} = Exponential smoothing forecast made at the end of period 26 = 1,000, $\alpha = .1$

ESF_{27} (made at the end of period 27 when the actual demand for period 27 is known but the actual demand in period 28 is not known) =

1,000 + .1(900 − 1,000) = 990 (16.5)

1(900) + (1 − .1)1,000 = 990 (16.6)

ESF_{28} = .1(1,100) + (1 − .1)990 = 1001 (16.6)

A comparison of exponential smoothing and moving average forecasting procedures can be seen in an example. A five-period MAF is compared to an ESF with $\alpha = .3$ in Figure 16.9. In the preparation of the forecast for period 28, the five-period MAF would apply a 20 percent weight to each of the five most recent actual demands. The ESF model (with $\alpha = .3$) would apply a 30 percent weight to the actual demand of period 27 as seen here:

$$\begin{aligned} ESF_{27} = \text{Period 28 forecast} = &.3 \text{ (period 27 actual demand)} \\ &+ .7\ (ESF_{26}) \end{aligned}$$

By looking at the ESF made for period 27, at the end of period 26 (i.e., ESF_{26}), we see that it was determined as:

$$ESF_{26} = .3 \text{ (period 26 actual demand)} + .7\ (ESF_{25})$$

By substitution, ESF_{27} can be shown to be:

$$\begin{aligned} ESF_{27} = .3 \text{ (period 27 actual demand)} + .7\ [&.3 \text{ (period 26 actual demand)} \\ &+ .7\ (ESF_{25})] \end{aligned}$$

This results in a weight of .21 (.7 × .3) being applied to the actual demand in period 26 when the forecast for periods 28 and beyond is made at the end of period 27. By similar substitution, the entire line for the exponential smoothing weights in Figure 16.9 can be derived.

Figure 16.9 shows that for the forecast made at the end of period 27, 30 percent of the weight is attached to the actual demand in period 27, 21 percent for period 26, and 15 percent for period 25. The sum of these weights, 66 percent, is the weight placed on the last three periods of demand. The sum of all of the weights given for the ESF model in Figure 16.9 is 94 percent. If one continued to find the weights for periods 19, 18, etc., the sum for all weights is 1.0, which is what intuition would tell us. If the smoothing constant were .1 instead of .3, a table like Figure 16.9 would have values of .1, .09, and .081 for the weights of periods 27, 26, and 25 respectively. The sum of these three (27 percent) is the weight placed on the last three periods. Moreover, (1 − 27% = 73%) is the weight given to all actual data *more than* three periods old.

FIGURE 16.9 Relative weights given to past demand by a moving average and exponential smoothing model

	Period								
	20	*21*	*22*	*23*	*24*	*25*	*26*	*27**	*28*
5-period MAF weights	0%	0%	0%	20%	20%	20%	20%	20%	—
ESF weights ($\alpha = .3$)	2%	4%	5%	7%	10%	15%	21%	30%	—

* Forecast made at the end of period 27.

This result shows that larger values of α give more weight to recent demands and utilize older demand data less than is the case for smaller values of α. That is, larger values of α provide more responsive forecasts and smaller values produce more stable forecasts. The same argument can be made for the number of periods in an MAF model. More periods provide more stable but less responsive forecasts. This points out the basic trade-off in determining what smoothing constant (or length of moving average) to use in a forecasting procedure. The higher the smoothing constant or shorter the moving average, the more responsive the forecasts are to the changes in the underlying demand, but the more "nervous" they are in the presence of randomness. Similarly, smaller smoothing constants or longer moving averages provide stability in the face of randomness, but slow reactions to changes in the underlying demand.

ENHANCING THE BASIC EXPONENTIAL SMOOTHING MODEL

Thus far, the exponential smoothing model we have described assumes that the demand is essentially constant, with only random variations around an average. However, if we have any indication of a pattern underlying the randomness of demand, it is important that it be taken into account to improve our forecast accuracy. There are two broad categories of factors that might explain nonrandom patterns. The first category of factors includes characteristics of the marketplace, such as cycles and seasonal or trend patterns in demand. Note that these need not be natural, but could be induced by events like new model introductions or special shows. The second broad category of nonrandom patterns are results of plans we may have for future events which will influence demand. These events could consist of special product promotions, timing of a major customer's orders, special ordering requirements for customers, or new product announcements by either ourselves or our competitors. In this section, we will first look at the changes that can be made to an exponential smoothing model to incorporate market factors and will close with methods for taking into account plans or knowledge of events that will affect future demand.

Trend enhancement

The first market characteristic we will take into account is a trend in the demand for the product. This is represented by the increase in tequila-based drinks that Enrique Martinez faces. A cursory glance at the demand for tequila-based drinks (see Figure 16.4) indicates a substantial growth (trend) in demand. To take the trend into account explicitly, we need a method for making an estimate of the trend (i.e., the amount of change in basic demand from period to period). Thinking again of drawing a line through the data to make a smoothed estimate of the trend leads us to consider using smoothing procedures to make the estimate. As a first step in the process of developing the estimate of the trend, we use exponential smoothing to smooth out the random fluctuations and create a new base value. As was true with the basic model, we perform the calculations as soon as we find out what actual demand was during the period, i.e., at the end of the period. The method for computing the new base value is shown in Equation (16.7).

$$\text{Base value}_t = (\text{Actual demand}_t) + (1 - \alpha)(\text{Base value}_{t-1} + \text{Trend}_{t-1}) \tag{16.7}$$

where:

α = Base smoothing constant ($0 \leqslant \alpha \leqslant 1$).
t = Current period (the period for which the most recent actual demand is known).
Base value_{t-1} = Base value computed one period previously (at the end of period $t - 1$).
Trend_{t-1} = Trend value computed one period previously (at the end of period $t - 1$).

Once the new base value for this period is determined, we apply exponential smoothing to develop the most current estimate of the trend value. A second smoothing constant is introduced to do this, β, and is applied as shown in Equation (16.8).

$$\text{Trend}_t = \beta\ (\text{Base value}_t - \text{Base value}_{t-1}) + (1 - \beta)(\text{Trend}_{t-1}) \tag{16.8}$$

where:

β = Trend smoothing constant ($0 \leqslant \beta \leqslant 1$).
Base value_t = Base value computed at the end of period t.
Base value_{t-1} = Base value computed one period previously (at the end of period $t - 1$).
Trend_{t-1} = Trend value computed one period previously (at the end of period $t - 1$).

Once the most current trend value and the new base value have been determined, trend-enhanced forecasts of future demand can be made. The method for doing this is given as Equation (16.9). Notice that this equation can be used to forecast for more than one period in the future by multiplying the trend value by the number of periods in the future. Figure 16.10 provides sample calculations.

Trend-enhanced forecast (TEF) for X periods in the future at the end of period t:

$$\text{TEF}_{t+X} = \text{Base value}_t + X\ (\text{Trend}_t) \tag{16.9}$$

FIGURE 16.10 Example trend-enhanced forecast calculations

Data: $\alpha = .2$, $\beta = .1$, $\text{Trend}_{t-1} = 5$, $\text{Base value}_{t-1} = 100$

TEF_t (that is, the trend-enhanced forecast made at the end of period $t - 1$ before actual demand for period t was known) =

$$\text{TEF}_t = \text{Base value}_{t-1} + \text{Trend}_{t-1} = 100 + 5 = 105$$

At the end of period t, the demand for period t becomes known:
$\text{Actual demand}_t = 107$

We now produce forecasts using equations (16.7), (16.8), and (16.9).

$$\text{Base value}_t = .2(107) + (1 - .2)(100 + 5) = 105.4 \quad (16.7)$$

$$\text{Trend}_t = .1(105.4 - 100) + (1 - .1)(5) = 5.04 \quad (16.8)$$

$$\text{Forecast for next period (i.e., TEF}_{t+1}) = 105.4 + (1)5.04 = 110.44 \quad (16.9)$$

$$\text{Forecast for four periods from now (i.e., TEF}_{t+4}) = 105.4 + (4)5.04 = 125.56 \quad (16.9)$$

where:

X = Number of periods beyond period t for which the forecast is desired.
t = Current period for which actual demand is known.
Base value_t = Exponentially smoothed base value computed at the end of period t.
Trend_t = Exponentially smoothed estimate of trend per period computed at the end of period t.

An alternative to the TEF model might be to use the ESF with a high smoothing constant, since we noted how high values of the smoothing constant were responsive to changes in demand. In fact, this alternative will not produce results that are as good as the TEF when there is a definitive trend component in the demand. This can be seen in Figure 16.11, which compares an ESF with $\alpha = .8$ and a TEF ($\alpha = .2$, $\beta = .2$) for the tequila-based drink data. As noted, the TEF approach produces better measures of both bias and MAD. By looking at the graph, you will see that the ESF lags the actual demand which leads to a much higher bias.

Figure 16.11 clearly demonstrates the advantage of explicitly including information about patterns in demand when such patterns do, in fact, exist. However, the opposite statement is also true: If a pattern in demand does not clearly exist, then using a model that assumes such a pattern will lead to poor forecasts. For example, if the TEF model were applied to the data for tables served at Panchos (Figure 16.6), the result should be larger values for both bias and MAD than those obtained with an appropriate ESF.

Seasonal enhancement

Many products have a seasonal demand pattern. We can all think of examples like baseballs, skis, lawn furniture, antifreeze, holiday greeting cards,

FIGURE 16.11 Comparison of trend-enhanced and basic exponential smoothing models

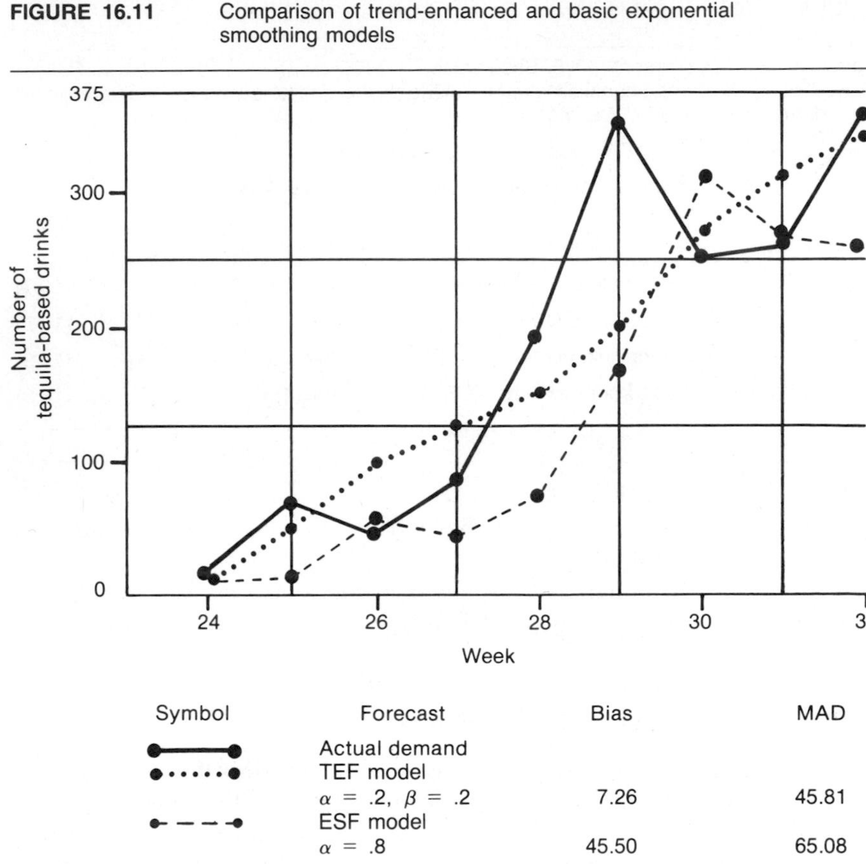

and so on. Perhaps less obvious are seasons for a product or service during a day, week, or month, like increased bank deposits on paydays, travel on the weekend (or mornings and evenings), mail deposits on Friday afternoons, or long-distance phone calls during the day. A useful indication of the degree of seasonal variation for a product is the seasonal index. This index is an estimate of how much the demand during a season will be above or below the average demand for the product. For example, a bathing-suit line may sell 100 units a month on the average, but 150 suits a month in peak season and 75 in the off-season. The index for peak season sales would be 1.50 and .75 for the off-season for bathing suits. The seasonal index is used to adjust forecasts for seasonal patterns.

Much the same kind of logic that was used for adjusting for the trend is applied in adjusting for the seasonality of a product. As before, we will use exponential smoothing to estimate the seasonal indexes of demand for a product. A seasonal pattern during the week is quite clear in the number 10 cans of vegetables used during three-day periods at Panchos (Figure 16.5). Demand is much less in the early part of the week than it is in the latter part of the week. Enrique's forecasting model should take this into account. The seasonally enhanced forecasting procedure (SEF) again involves updating some new base value at the end of some period t. Next, there is an updating of the seasonal index that applies to the period just past. Finally, there is a forecast of demand one or more periods in the future based upon the latest base value and the appropriate seasonal index for the period to be forecast. The formulas for updating the base value and seasonal index are shown as Equations (16.10) and (16.11). The first equation produces the new base by exponentially smoothing the "deseasonalized" demand data (i.e., the actual demand divided by the seasonal index), and the second equation uses another smoothing constant to produce an updated estimate of the seasonal index for the period just past.

$$\text{Base value}_t = \alpha\left(\frac{\text{Actual demand}_t}{\text{Old index}_s}\right) + (1 - \alpha)(\text{Base value}_{t-1}) \tag{16.10}$$

$$\text{New index}_s = \gamma\left(\frac{\text{Actual demand}_t}{\text{Base value}_t}\right) + (1 - \gamma)(\text{Old index}_s) \tag{16.11}$$

where:

α = Smoothing constant for base value.
γ = Smoothing constant for seasonal indexes.
s = Season indicator.
Base value_{t-1} = Base value computed one period previously (at the end of period_{t-1}).
Old index_s = Index value for season s, calculated one full cycle ago.

The updating of the base at the end of period t is similar to that done for the TEF model, except that the actual demand is first deseasonalized. A seasonal index is maintained and updated for however many periods are included in a cycle of demand. For the number 10 cans of vegetables, there would be two seasonal indexes, one for the three-day period of F–S–Sun, and the other for T–W–Th. For a monthly series in an annual cycle, there would be 12 seasonal indexes, each updated when that month's actual demand became available and used to forecast that month in the future whenever the forecast is desired.

The method for forecasting demand is to multiply the updated base value obtained using Equation (16.10) by the appropriate seasonal index. This is shown as Equation (16.12) and examples are given in Figure 16.12.

Seasonal enhanced forecast (SEC) for season s in the future at the end of period t:

$$\text{SEC}_s = \text{Base value}_t\ (\text{Index}_s) \tag{16.12}$$

FIGURE 16.12 Example seasonal enhanced forecast calculations

Data: $\alpha = .2$, $\gamma = .3$, old $\text{index}_{\text{F–S–Sun}} = 1.22$, old $\text{index}_{\text{T–W–Th}} = .77$

$\text{Base value}_4 = 40.2$, $\text{Actual demand}_5 = 51$ (this was a F–S–Sun)

$\text{Base value}_5 = .2(51/1.22) + (1 - .2)(40.2) = 40.5$ (16.10)

$\text{New index}_{\text{F–S–Sun}} = .3(51/40.5) + (1 - .3)1.22 = 1.23$ (16.11)

$\text{SEF}_6 = 40.5(.77) = 31.2$ (this was a T–W–Th) (16.12)

where:

Base value_t = most recent deseasonalized base value at the end of period t.

Index_s = seasonal index associated with the season s.

If Panchos wanted to forecast the demand for number 10 cans of vegetables for the next F–S–Sun period now (that is, at the end of period 5 before waiting until the actual demand for period 6 is known):

$$\text{SEF}_7 = 40.5(1.23) = 49.8 \quad (16.12)$$

Trend and seasonal enhancement. A logical extension of either trend enhancement or seasonal enhancement is a model which incorporates both patterns in demand. Without going into a detailed explanation, the approach is to first apply an expanded version of Equation (16.10) to update the base value; this is shown as Equation (16.13). Next, the seasonal index is computed with Equation (16.11) as before, and the trend component is updated with Equation (16.8). Finally, the forecast Equation (16.14) incorporates the trend enhancement from Equation (16.9) and the seasonal enhancement from Equation (16.12). The entire sequence would be:

$$\text{Base value}_t = \alpha \left(\frac{\text{Actual demand}_t}{\text{Old index}_s}\right) + (1 - \alpha)(\text{Base value}_{t-1} + \text{Trend}_{t-1}) \quad (16.13)$$

$$\text{New index}_s = \gamma \left(\frac{\text{Actual demand}_t}{\text{Base value}_t}\right) + (1 - \gamma)(\text{Old index}_s) \quad (16.11)$$

$$\text{Trend}_t = \beta\,(\text{Base value}_t - \text{Base value}_{t-1}) + (1 - \beta)(\text{Trend}_{t-1}) \quad (16.8)$$

Trend seasonal enhanced forecast (TSEF) for X periods in the future at the end of period t:

$$\text{TSEF}_{t+X} = (\text{Base value}_t + X\ \text{trend}_t)\ \text{Index}_{t+X-m} \quad (16.14)$$

where:

Base value_t = Most recent deseasonalized base value at the end of period t.

Index_s = Seasonal index for the season s.

Trend_t = Trend estimate per period calculated at the end of period_t.

X = Number of periods beyond period t for which the forecast is desired.

m = Number of periods in the seasonal cycle.

The subscript on the index in Equation (16.14) is worthy of an additional note. The forecast is made at the end of period t, for X periods into the future; hence, $t + X$. The subtraction of m moves the index subscript back to the seasonal value computed at the end of that last season in the cycle. For example, if at the end of month 5 (May) one wished to forecast for August, the index subscript would be $5 + 3 - 12$, or the seasonal index computed nine months previously at the end of the preceeding August.

Other enhancements

We have illustrated the use of multiplicative seasonal factors and additive trend factors. Other approaches have used additive seasonality and/or multiplicative trend. Still other approaches allow for acceleration, which would be applicable to fad products; others utilize the fitting of mathematical functions such as sine waves to past data. The point is, *if* a genuine pattern in the underlying demand exists, then a model that incorporates this pattern can produce better forecasts. We saw this in Figure 16.11 comparing a trend model and the basic exponential smoothing model for the tequila-based drink data. A similar comparison could be made for the vegetables, using models with and without seasonal enhancement. However, once again we caution against use of these enhanced models if the underlying data do not clearly support their application. We know of a firm which has a definitive seasonal sales pattern with growth—when one is talking about overall sales in dollars. However, the same demand pattern does not exist for many of the individual items in this company.

There are also other kinds of information that can and should be used to make good forecasts. For example, in a college town on the day of a football game, traffic around the stadium is an absolute mess. An intelligent forecaster adjusts travel plans on game days to avoid the stadium traffic, if possible. He or she modifies the forecast because of knowledge of the football game's impact on traffic. An exponential smoothing model based upon observations during the week would probably forecast very little traffic around the stadium. We certainly would not use the exponential smoothing forecast without adjusting it for game day. That simple principle is applicable to business forecasting as well, but it is surprising how often people fail to make these adjustments.

Examples of activities that will influence demand and perhaps invalidate the routine forecasting model are special promotions, product changes, competitors' actions, and economic changes. There are two primary ways that information about such future activities can be incorporated into the forecast. The first is to change the forecast directly and the second is to change the forecasting model. We might use the first method if we knew, for example, that there was to be a promotion of a product in the future, or that we were going to open more retail outlets, or that we were going to introduce a competing product. In these instances, we could adjust the forecast directly to account for the activities, just as we do for game day. By recognizing explicitly that future conditions will not reflect past conditions, we can modify the forecast directly to reflect our assessment of the future.

The second method for dealing with future activities would be to change the model itself. This might work best when we are unsure of what the effect of these activities will be. If, for example, we know that one of our competitors is going to introduce a new product, we suspect that the market will change, but may not be sure just what the direction or magnitude of the change will be. If the product is expensive, we may gain sales; if it is novel, we may lose sales. All we know is that there may be a change. In this instance, we could increase the smoothing constant, making the model more responsive to changes in the marketplace. In this way, we can incorporate changes into our forecasts more quickly. If we know something of what may happen, we could change both the forecast and the smoothing constant. Both of these methods help to incorporate information we have about the future into the forecasts before using the forecasts to make decisions.

USING THE FORECASTING SYSTEM

Two important problems in using forecasting models in practice involve determining the forecasting model parameters and monitoring the forecasting model results. It is not enough to determine the demand patterns and to select the forecasting model that appears to provide minimum bias and MAD. Before we can start making forecasts, it is necessary to choose the smoothing constants and establish the base value, trend value, and seasonal indexes. Once forecasting has started, these initial values are recalculated with each new piece of demand information. But we are not done. It is necessary to continue evaluating the quality of the forecasts to make sure that the model chosen is still appropriate, to determine whether market conditions have changed, and to find out quickly when something has gone awry. It is to the two issues of getting started and monitoring demand and forecast that we now turn our attention. Thereafter, we briefly raise some strategic issues relating to forecasting.

Getting started

When historical demand data are available, there is nothing like a plot of those data for getting started. If there is a pattern to the demand, it can be most easily seen from a plot. The plots also help one to set the initial values for doing the forecasting in a way that is consistent with the historical data. If, for example, the plots show that seasonal factors exist, the base value can be estimated by eyeballing the base value line (or by taking the average for at least one seasonal cycle).

The seasonal indexes can be found by averaging the indexes calculated for each of the seasonal peaks and valleys that exist in the data. Similarly, a plot of the values for trend data would enable one to draw in a trend line (or one could average the period-to-period changes) to get an estimate of the trend value. The plot would also help determine the base value to use for starting to make forecasts. In every instance (constant data, trend data, or seasonal data), the plots will help determine whether it is desirable to use the more recent data in setting the starting values.

Once starting values have been determined, one can also use relatively high smoothing constants for the early forecasts to quickly overcome any errors in the starting values. It is also desirable to make simulated forecasts of the last few periods of historical data as test data for the model. By using, say, 75 percent of the historical data to estimate initial values, and then simulating forecasts for the remaining quarter of the data, the values for starting the initial forecasts would already have been smoothed by the forecasting model.

The choice of smoothing constants for use in the models for forecasting is a matter of balancing responsiveness with stability. This is not an easy balance, however, and practice has provided some guidance. For smoothing the average or base value, an α of about .1 to .2 has been found useful in practice. The β value is generally held to less than the α value, about .05 to .1. The value for γ depends on how frequently the seasonal index is recalculated. If often, such as every few weeks, a low γ (.1) is acceptable. If less frequently (yearly), γ = .3 to .4 might be used. In practice, some simulation with past data can be useful. However, our opinion is that this approach is of limited value since the objective is to forecast well in the *future*. The issue always comes down to the stability-responsiveness trade-off, based on how stable the future environment is judged to be.

Demand filter monitoring

All of the smoothing models presented in this chapter incorporate actual demand data into the forecasts as soon as the information is available. Therefore, it is important that the actual demand data be correct. One way of helping ensure this is through demand filtering, i.e., checking the actual demand against a range of reasonable values. An approach that works well is to screen the actual demand values against some limit before calculating the updated forecasts, and to have some thinking person (not a computer) determine whether exceptions are correct or not. A common screening limit is four MADs in either direction of the forecast of demand for the period. Since

4 MADs correspond to 3.2 standard deviations, this limit provides a probability of less than .001 of the demand value being a random occurrence for normally distributed forecast errors. If an actual demand falls outside this limit, a manual review is applied.

Once the filter catches a value outside the limits, the review might consist of checking to make sure that there wasn't a clerical error in the recording of the demand, that there wasn't some explainable cause for the big change, or that conditions really have changed and demand will be changed significantly. If conditions are changing, the situation may call for using some of the techniques for modifying the forecasts that were discussed earlier.

The limits to use for filtering individual actual demand observations depend upon the costs of a manual review compared to the cost of an error. The probabilities of exceeding the limits can be determined from a normal table using the relationship between the number of standard deviations and MAD, given in Equation (16.3). This can provide some insight into setting the limits on the observations.

Tracking signal monitoring

The approach of exponential smoothing can also be used to compute a useful statistic called a *tracking signal*. The tracking signal helps in monitoring the quality of the forecast. We use the methods of exponential smoothing to make a smoothed average of the bias and MAD. The equations for doing this, (16.15) and (16.16), follow. These equations simply smooth the same error measures that we introduced in Equations (16.1) and (16.2) early in this chapter. By using exponential smoothing, the measures incorporate and weight most heavily the recent demand information. The smoothing constant, δ, is between 0 and 1, and has the same properties as the smoothing constant in the exponential smoothing forecasting model. The larger the δ, the more heavily weighted or responsive to the most recent forecast error. Figure 16.13 shows some sample calculations.

$$\text{Smoothed bias}_t = \delta(\text{Actual demand}_t - \text{Forecast}_t) + (1 - \delta)(\text{Smoothed Bias}_{t-1}) \quad (16.15)$$

$$\text{Smoothed MAD}_t = \delta|\text{Actual demand}_t - \text{Forecast}_t| + (1 - \delta)(\text{Smoothed MAD}_{t-1}) \quad (16.16)$$

where:

$$0 \leq \delta \leq 1.$$

$|\text{Actual demand}_t - \text{Forecast}_t|$ = Absolute value of the forecast error observed during period t.

The smoothed bias and smoothed MAD are combined to calculate the tracking signal. The formula for this is given in Equation (16.17). Note that the smoothed MAD provides an estimate of the expected error (i.e., the

FIGURE 16.13 Example smoothed bias and MAD calculations

Data: $\text{Forecast}_t = 100$, $\text{actual demand}_t = 90$, $\delta = .1$

$\text{Smoothed bias}_{t-1} = -1$, $\text{smoothed MAD}_{t-1} = 5$

$$\text{Smoothed bias}_t = .1(90 - 100) + (1 - .1)(-1) = -1.9 \quad (16.15)$$

$$\text{Smoothed MAD}_t = .1|90 - 100| + (1 - .1)(5) = 5.5 \quad (16.16)$$

average error) and the bias shows consistent over- or underforecasting. The tracking signal varies between -1 and $+1$. Either of these extreme values indicates that all of the forecast errors are of the same sign. If the forecast is unbiased, the tracking signal will be near zero, irrespective of the value of MAD. The tracking signal allows one to compute a measure of bias that is independent of MAD; one that will have the same numerical meaning for every item forecast. As the tracking signal deviates from zero in any significant way, manual review of the particular item is called for.

$$\text{Tracking signal}_t = \frac{\text{Smoothed bias}_t}{\text{Smoothed MAD}_t} \quad (16.17)$$

where:

$$-1 \leqslant \text{Tracking signal}_t \leqslant +1.$$

The tracking signal is an indicator of forecast bias that is consistent for all observations. Its use is essentially the same as that described for demand filtering. That is, by isolating those items for which the tracking signal is deviating significantly from the nominal value of zero, one can take corrective actions. For example, if an item were forecast with the basic exponential smoothing model (ESF), and an underlying trend existed in the data, the tracking signal would move away from zero.

The issue of what tracking signal value to use for initiating a review is essentially the same as that for demand filtering. The closer the limit is to zero, the sooner poor forecasts are discovered. On the other hand, with small limits, the number of times that a review will be necessary is increased. Also, the chance for reaching an erroneous conclusion from the review is increased. The appropriate value is also not independent of δ. Small values of the smoothing constant for MAD and bias result in more stability and less responsiveness in these measures. Stability means that it will take longer for the tracking signal to respond to an underlying change in conditions.

Strategic issues

There are a number of strategic and managerial questions about forecasting that we have passed over rather rapidly or have not discussed. Certainly we have not had the space to discuss all the possible forecasting models, and it would not be fair to leave this discussion without indicating that there are several more approaches to short-term forecasting than we have mentioned here.

Although it was not indicated for any of Pancho's restaurant problems, it is often necessary to make longer-term decisions for which the item-level, short-term forecasts simply are not adequate. Among these decisions are capital expansion projects, proposals to develop a new product line, and merger or acquisition opportunities. For these long-term decisions, forecasts based on causal or econometric models, or simply on managerial insight and judgment, can often produce improved results. Causal models are those that relate the business of the firm to indicators which are more easily forecast or are available as general information. Early in this chapter, we used the sales of household fixtures and their relation to housing starts as an indication of a causal relationship. A substantial amount of managerial judgment is required in reviewing the forecasts which form the basis for making long-term decisions. The general principle indicated here is that the nature of the forecast must be matched with the nature of the decision. The level of aggregation, the amount of management review time, the cost, and the quality of the forecast needed really depend upon the nature of the decision being made. Many short-term operating decisions do not warrant the use of expensive forecasting techniques, and that has been one reason for focusing on short-term projection techniques. For strategic decisions with more at risk than two extra bottles of tequila, the investment in more expensive procedures (more management involvement) is called for. A general schema of this is presented as Figure 16.14.

In the ongoing management of forecasts, strategic questions can also come about from a review triggered by forecast monitoring. For example, the forecasting model might be appropriate, but there are insufficient adjustments to account for known actions in the marketplace. The forecasting procedure must be managed to make sure that special knowledge is included in the forecasts.

A review might indicate that the model is no longer appropriate. There may be trend or seasonal effects that should now be included or dropped, or perhaps a compound model that has both trend and seasonal enhancements should be developed. In such cases, the model needs to be adjusted accordingly.

Yet another instance where the model may not be appropriate is where the demand is dependent upon other decisions in the firm. For example, the demand for tires in an automobile factory is dependent upon the number of cars being produced. That is quite a different forecasting problem from trying to determine how many cars the public wants to buy. A dependent demand relationship should always be looked for.

It is apparent that forecasting is a pervasive, central activity in the management of operations. To be effective, the forecasting system must be

FIGURE 16.14 Applicability of various forecast attributes to decision attributes*

Decision attributes

Level	Frequency	Money	Time
Mission	Rare	Much	Long-run
Strategic	Occasional	Some	Medium-run
Tactical	Often	Little	Short-run

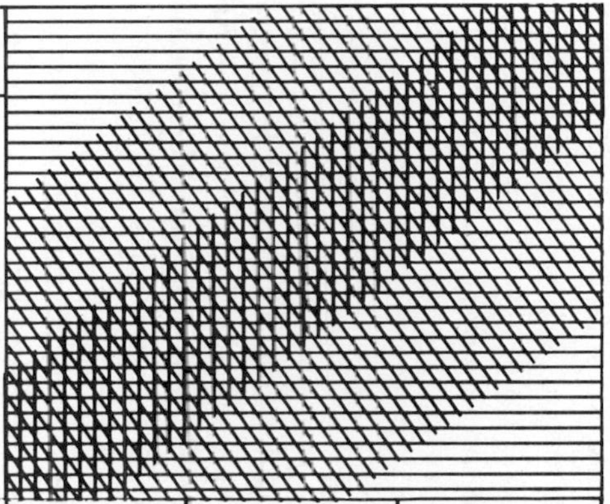

Forecast attribute

Increasing aggregation	Item level	Product family	Total sales or output
Cost/ forecast	Low	Medium	High
Degree of management involvement	Low	Medium	High
Nature of forecast model	Projection technique	Econometric causal	Management judgement

* The darker the area, the greater the applicability.

linked closely to a number of other systems. Certainly, those decisions requiring forecast information must be linked directly to the output of the forecasting system. Since all of the forecasting models presented in this chapter require demand data, there must be a close linkage between the order entry system and the forecasting system. Many firms will use sales data or shipment data instead of demand for adjusting their forecasts. In cases where demand information is not available, this may be warranted, but there is a difference between sales, shipments, and demand. Since it is demand that we are interested in forecasting, the link with the order entry system should be capable of picking up demand information. If we do not have the stock available to make the sale or shipment, this will affect our customer service, but not the fact that there was a demand.

FORECASTING IN INDUSTRY

We come now to the last of our five topical issues in forecasting. In this section we briefly describe the approach used by one firm, the Ethan Allen Furniture Company. They utilize an exponential-smoothing-based forecasting system to forecast the demand for their products. The forecasting models are part of an overall managerial system that provides for monitoring demand, developing the forecasts, reviewing and modifying forecasts, aggregating the information, producing sales history data, and developing a variety of other management reports. Figure 16.15 provides one example of the type of report that can be produced by the forecasting system. This particular report can be produced by request, for any product that management might wish to scrutinize. The forecasting model used to produce the forecasts shown in Figure 16.15 was a seasonally enhanced model, using a smoothing constant of .2. The monthly seasonal factors are shown on the report along with the forecasts, actual demand, errors, and percent errors. Note also that manual adjustments can be made and that MAD and the tracking signal can be reported.

The report shown as Figure 16.16 is one of the monitoring reports produced by the system whenever a manual review is indicated by the system. The first product shown in Figure 16.16, a governor's chair, has triggered a review because the error exceeds 50 percent of the forecast. The limit of tolerance is shown at the top of the report. This triggered the exclusion of this particular governor's chair on the sales screening report, which suggests possible manual correction. Information on the last three forecasts, actual demand, MAD, and other review data are also included in the report. Adjustments are made manually, if needed, and will appear in subsequent runs of the report if the actual demand continues to fall outside of the limits for review. The next two items in Figure 16.16 are included in the report because one individual customer order was larger than the stated percentage of the total forecast. The report shows any information on past changes to the forecast, as well. This keeps the entire process explicit to the reviewer. The

FIGURE 16.15 Ethan Allen Inc sales and forecasts

MIRROR FOR ITEM 11-9008- 225

AVG SALES 44.5

SEASONAL FACTORS	JAN	FEB	MAR	APR	MAY	JUN	JUL	AUG	SEP	OCT	NOV	DEC
	.74	1.12	1.39	.63	.72	.85	.79	1.17	1.73	1.01	.79	1.06

SALES	TOTAL FCST	ERROR	PCT ERROR	DATE	NUMBER OF UNITS FORECAST AND SOLD 0...20...40...60...80...100..120..140..160..180..200..220..240	ADJUSTMENTS TO AMOUNT FOR	ADJUSTMENTS TO AMOUNT FOR	MAD	TRACK SGNL
27				FEB					
70				MAR					
16				APR					
20				MAY					
28				JUN					
29				JUL					
66				AUG					
53				SEPT					
28				OCT					
38	26	+12	+46%	NOV					
53	37	+16	+43%	DEC					
38	25	+13	+52%	JAN					
52	38	+14	+36%	FEB					
71	48	+23	+47%	MAR					
	22			APR					
	24			MAY					
	29			JUN					
	27			JUL					
	40			AUG					
	59			SEPT					
	34			OCT					

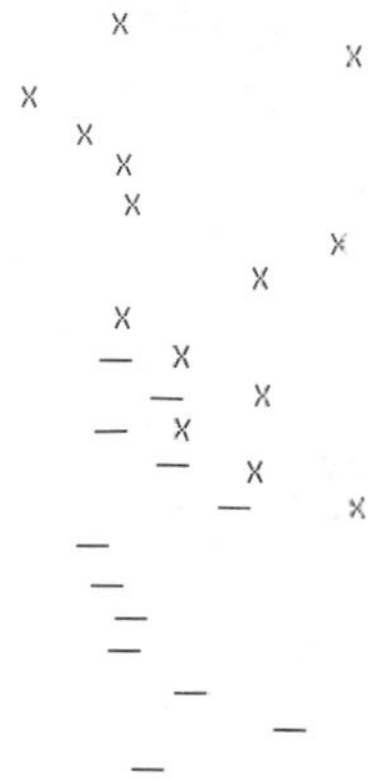

— TOTAL FORECAST

X SALES

FIGURE 16.16 Ethan Allen Inc. sales screening exception report

```
                                                       FOR MAY
                      UPPER LIMIT PERCENT = 50%   LOWER LIMIT PERCENT = 50%   NUMBER OF MADS = 2.5

PERCENT/MAD LIMITS EXCEEDED                 CHR GOV
 ADJUSTED   ACTUAL            PERCENT   MAD    SALES RANGE
 FORECAST   SALES   ERROR     ERROR    ERROR   FROM - TO         AV SLS   SEAS   FORECAST   ADJUSTMENT   REASON   MAD     MAD/AV
   268        84    -184      -68%      2.2     134    402        372.4   0.72     268                            81.7     21%
   232       282     +50      +21%               TWO MONTHS AGO                   232
   534       379    -155      -29%             THREE MONTHS AGO                   534
   434       236    -198      -45%              FOUR MONTHS AGO                   434
                            30-6050-A   218 R   CHR GOV CRVR                            CONSOLIDATION NO. 30-6050-A   218   FACTORY 018
LARGE INDIVIDUAL ORDER   CUST ACCT NO 17-4870-0   ORDER DATE  5/21       QUANTITY   12   AVERAGE SALES   97.9   ORDER % OF AV SLS  12%
PERCENTAGE LIMITS EXCEEDED
 ADJUSTED  ACTUAL             PERCENT   MAD    SALES RANGE                                                                 MAD   CUMUL   TRACK
 FORECAST  SALES    ERROR     ERROR    ERROR   FROM - TO         AV SLS   SEAS   FORECAST   ADJUSTMENT   REASON   MAD    MAD/AV  LIM   ERROR   SGNL
    70       34      -36      -51%      0.8     35     105        97.9    0.72      70                            40.8    41%   104%   +225   +5.5
    68       44      -24      -35%               TWO  MONTHS AGO                    68
   143      171      +28      +19%             THREE  MONTHS AGO                   143
   123       60      -63      -51%              FOUR  MONTHS AGO                   123
                            30-6052-   218 R   CHR CPTN                             CONSOLIDATION NO. 30-6052-   218   FACTORY 018
LARGE INDIVIDUAL ORDER   CUST ACCT NO 35-3595-0   ORDER DATE  5/01       QUANTITY   12   AVERAGE SALES   61.3   ORDER % OF AV SLS  19%
LARGE INDIVIDUAL ORDER   CUST ACCT NO 13-5448-0   ORDER DATE  5/24       QUANTITY   24   AVERAGE SALES   61.3   ORDER % OF AV SLS  39%
 ADJUSTED  ACTUAL             PERCENT   MAD    SALES RANGE                                                                 MAD   CUMUL   TRACK
 FORECAST  SALES    ERROR     ERROR    ERROR   FROM - TO         AV SLS   SEAS   FORECAST   ADJUSTMENT   REASON   MAD    MAD/AV  LIM   ERROR   SGNL
    44       42       -2       -4%      0.0      0      0         61.3    0.72      44                            28.4    46%   116%    +22   +0.7
    46       12      -34      -73%               TWO  MONTHS AGO                    46
    95      123      +28      +29%             THREE  MONTHS AGO                    95
    82       40      -42      -51%              FOUR  MONTHS AGO                    82
PERCENTAGE LIMITS EXCEEDED   30-6055-   218 R   DRY SINK                            CONSOLIDATION NO. 30-6055-   218   FACTORY 022
 ADJUSTED  ACTUAL             PERCENT   MAD    SALES RANGE                                                                 MAD   CUMUL   TRACK
 FORECAST  SALES    ERROR     ERROR    ERROR   FROM - TO         AV SLS   SEAS   FORECAST   ADJUSTMENT   REASON   MAD    MAD/AV  LIM   ERROR   SGNL
    30        9      -21      -70%      1.3     15     45         42.3    0.72      30                            16.0    37%    95%   +109   +6.8
    28       23       -5      -17%               TWO  MONTHS AGO                    28
    58       77      +19      +32%             THREE  MONTHS AGO                    58
    52       20      -32      -61%              FOUR  MONTHS AGO                    52
```

sales screening process ensures that the ultimate responsibility for forecasting rests with management.

CONCLUDING PRINCIPLES

Forecasts provide an important input to manufacturing planning and control systems. Although many kinds of forecasts are possible, this chapter has focused on short-term forecasts based on past data. We have shown how exponential smoothing models can be used to make these short-term forecasts and how routine forecast monitoring can be achieved.

We have tried to emphasize that forecasting is too important to leave to a forecasting model. Firms which use forecasting models wisely use them to support, not to supplant, managerial judgment. The importance of taking future information into account is one example. Another is the necessary judgment required in a review resulting from forecast monitoring. For example, a tracking signal can indicate a review. It takes a thinking person to decide precisely how to do the review, how (or whether) to change the model, and how to modify the forecasting model data.

The following basic concepts or principles are those we see as particularly important:

- Evaluative criteria must be chosen for the short-term forecasting system. The choices implied in this chapter are minimize bias, minimize MAD, lost cost, and simplicity.
- Controlling bias is the most critical problem. It is easier to live with larger errors (larger MAD) if that is what it takes to reduce bias.
- Use of short-term forecasts must be separated from the act of forecasting.
- Methods for monitoring forecasts over time must be installed.
- Forecasting needs to be embedded in a management structure.
- Forecasting is not a computer program, and the result should not be monitored by the computer department. A key user group must monitor.

REFERENCES

Box, G. E. P., and G. M. Jenkins. *Time Series Analysis: Forecasting and Control*, Holden-Day, 1970.

Brown, R. G. *Decision Rules for Inventory Management*. New York: Holt, Reinhart & Winston, 1967.

Chambers, J. C., S. K. Mullick, and D. D. Smith. "How to Choose the Right Forecasting Technique." *Harvard Business Review*, July-August 1971, pp. 45–74.

Fiedes, R., and D. Wood, *Forecasting and Planning*. Gower Publishing, 1978.

Forecasting Reprints. Falls Church, Va.: American Production and Inventory Control Society, 1979.

Groff, G. R. "Empirical Comparison of Models for Short-Range Forecasting." *Management Science*, September 1973, pp. 22–31.

Mabert, V. A. "An Introduction to Short-Term Forecasting Using the Box Jenkins Methodology." Atlanta: *AIIE Monograph*, 1975.

Mather, Hal. "Too Much Precision, Not Enough Accuracy." *APICS 22d Annual Conference Proceedings*, 1979, pp. 116–19.

Sickel, Walter F. "Integrating the Forecast into MRP." *APICS 22d Annual Conference Proceedings*, 1979, pp. 120–22.

Stratton, William B. "How to Design a Viable Forecasting System." *Production and Inventory Management*, 1st Quarter 1979, pp. 17–27.

Trigg, D. W., and A. G. Leach. "Exponential Smoothing with an Adaptive Response Rate." *Operations Research Quarterly*, March 1967, pp. 53–59.

Wheelwright, S. C., and S. Makridakis. *Forecasting Methods for Management*. New York: John Wiley, 1977.

Winters, P. R. "Forecasting Sales by Exponentially Weighted Moving Averages." *Management Science*, April 1960, pp. 324–42.

17

Independent demand inventory management

This chapter is devoted to the management of nonmanufacturing inventories. These include finished goods at the factory or in field warehouses, spare-part inventories, and nonproduction items such as supplies and maintenance materials. The techniques in this chapter are directed to determining the appropriate order quantities and when to place replenishment orders. If these basic decisions are made well, appropriate levels of customer service will be provided without excess levels of inventory.

This chapter is organized around five topics:

- Basic concepts: What types of inventory are there and why should funds be invested in inventories?
- Measuring inventory performance: What are the costs associated with inventory management?
- Routine inventory decisions: What are the day-to-day decisions for managing independent demand inventories?
- Order timing decisions: How does one buffer uncertainty in demand and how are desired customer-service levels maintained?
- Information systems for inventory control: What systems are in use for managing independent demand inventory items?

Chapter 17 is related to Chapters 2 and 12 in that lot-sizing and order-timing decisions are considered. However, those chapters are based on dependent demand. Chapter 17 is also linked to Chapter 3 in that data base integrity issues exist for *any* inventory control system. There is also a linkage with Chapter 16, in that the forecast is typically used as one input to an independent demand-based inventory system. Chapter 18 discusses advanced independent demand inventory systems.

BASIC CONCEPTS

The investment in inventory typically represents one of the largest single areas of capital in a business, often more than 25 percent of total assets. In this section, we discuss where this investment is made, noting the distinction between independent and dependent demand inventories, the functions served by inventories, movement inventories, organization inventories, cycle stock, safety stock, and anticipation stock.

Independent versus dependent demand items

This chapter is primarily concerned with the management of independent demand inventories. There are major differences between the methods for managing these inventories and manufacturing inventories. The differences occur mainly because of differences in the sources of demand for the items contained in independent demand inventories and those in manufacturing inventories. The demand for end-product items, such as those stocked in the field warehouses shown in Figure 17.1, is primarily influenced by factors which are independent of the company decisions. These external factors induce a certain amount of random variation in the demand for such items. As a result, forecasts of demand for these items are typically projections of historical demand patterns. These forecasts estimate the average usage rate and the pattern of random variation.

The demand for the items in the manufacturing inventories shown in Figure 17.1, e.g., the raw material and component items, is directly influenced by internal factors that are well within the control of the firm, such as the assembly and fabrication production schedule. That is, the demand for raw materials and component items is a derived demand which can be calculated exactly once the assembly and fabrication production schedules are determined. Therefore, the demand for end-product items is referred to as *independent* demand, while the demand for items contained in manufacturing inventories is referred to as *dependent* demand.

The concepts of independent and dependent demand are important in selecting appropriate inventory management techniques. The inventory management techniques described in this chapter are best suited for independent demand items such as those found in distribution inventories, while material requirements planning techniques are best suited for the dependent demand items found in manufacturing inventories.

FIGURE 17.1 Materials flow system

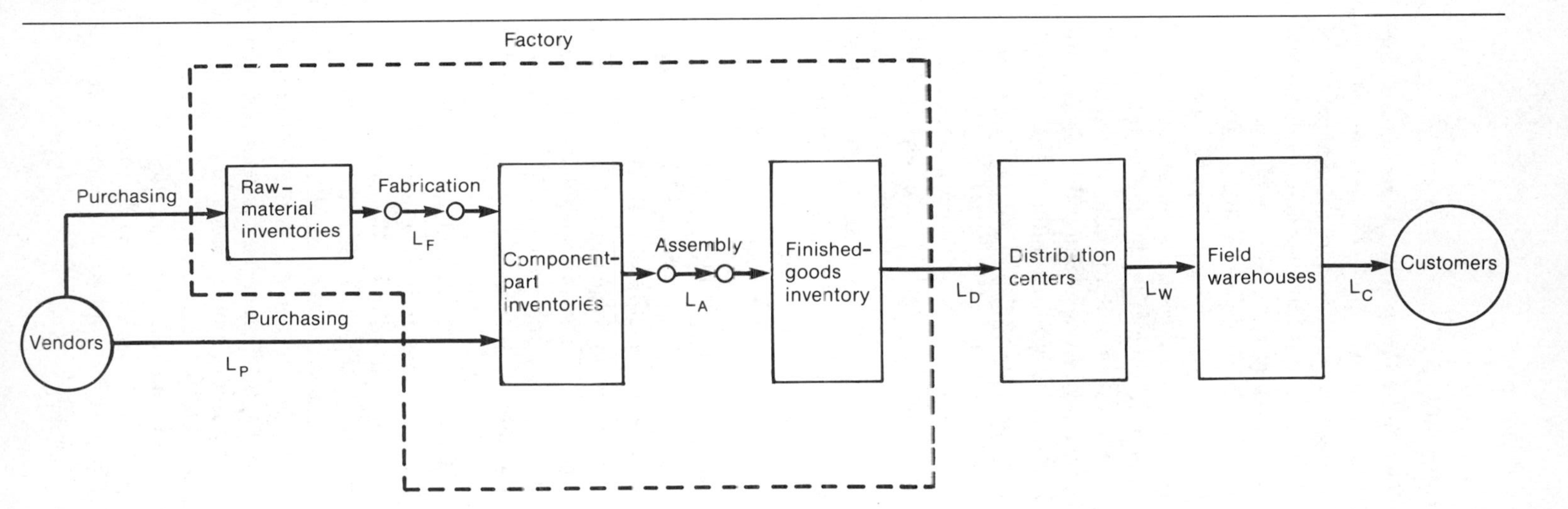

Functions of inventory

The questions "Why invest funds in inventory?" and "What benefits are derived by investing in inventories?" are frequently raised by industrial executives. An investment in inventory is made for one of two purposes. First, inventory makes it possible to produce goods at some distance from the actual consumer. Second, the existence of inventory provides management with the flexibility to decouple successive production and distribution operations. Therefore, two types of inventory can be found in production and distribution systems: *movement* and *organization* inventories. These two types of inventory are illustrated by the materials flow diagram shown in Figure 17.1. The arrows denote movement inventories, and the boxes indicated organization inventories. Since time is required to accomplish the production and transportation operations in Figure 17.1, a lead time (L) is associated with each of these steps, e.g., L_F represents the time required to fabricate a component item in the factory.

Movement inventories. Movement inventories exist because time is required to manufacture products or to transport goods from one location to another. Movement inventories for transportation purposes are also called in-transit or pipeline inventories. Movement inventories during the manufacturing process are called work-in-process (WIP) inventories. As an example, a WIP inventory is shown in Figure 17.1 between raw material and component part inventories. Since it takes fabrication time (LF) to convert raw materials into component items, work-in-process inventory is incurred. This inventory takes the form of orders waiting to be transported between machines or of orders waiting to be processed on a particular machine. Management can change the level of WIP by changing the manufacturing process, lot sizes, or production schedules.

Management can influence the magnitude of the movement inventories by changing the design of the production/distribution system. For example, the in-transit inventory between the raw material vendor and the factory can be reduced by: (1) changing the method of transportation, e.g., switching from rail to air freight, or (2) switching to a supplier located closer to the factory to reduce the transit time. These choices, however, involve cost and service trade-offs which need to be considered carefully. For example, shipping raw material by air freight instead of by rail may cut the transit time in half and therefore reduce the average pipeline inventory by 50 percent, but this might well involve an increase in the unit cost of the raw material because of higher transportation costs. Therefore, the consequences of changing suppliers or transport modes needs to be weighed against investing in more (or less) inventory.

Organization inventories. Organization inventories exist to decouple successive stages in the production and distribution systems. For example, in Figure 17.1, the factory operations are decoupled from the distribution system by the finished-goods inventory. This inventory makes it unnecessary to produce directly to meet the demands from the distribution centers. That is, demand from the distribution centers can be satisfied out of inventory, thereby permitting flexibility in scheduling assembly operations and in fabricating components. There are several types of organization inventory, each having a different purpose: cycle stock, safety stock, and anticipation stock.

Cycle stock. Cycle stock exists whenever one produces (or buys) in larger quantities than are needed to satisfy the immediate requirements. For example, a distribution center may order two units of a given end product weekly from the factory. However, because of the costs of setting up an assembly line and the productivity gained with larger production quantities, the plant might choose to produce a batch of eight units once each month. Thus, the investment in cycle stock provides more economical production costs. Similar savings in unit costs, e.g., transportation costs, purchase price reductions, and clerical costs, are gained by establishing cycle stocks at other points in Figure 17.1, e.g., for raw materials, component items, and in the distribution centers and field warehouses.

Safety stock. Safety stock exists to provide protection against irregularities or uncertainties in the demand or the supply of an item, i.e., when the demand exceeds what is forecast or when the resupply time is longer than anticipated. Safety stock provides insurance that customer demand can be satisfied immediately, and that the customers will not have to wait while their orders are backlogged. For example, a portion of the inventory held at the distribution centers may be safety stock. That is, for example, if the average demand for a given end product is 100 units a week with a restocking lead time of one week, on occasion the weekly demand might be as large as 150 units and the replenishment lead time as long as two weeks. Therefore, a safety stock of 100 units might be created to ensure meeting the maximum demand requirements.

Similar investments in safety stock can be made at other stocking points in Figure 17.1, e.g., for raw materials, component items, finished goods, or in the field warehouses. An important management question concerns the amount of safety stock that is actually required, i.e., how much protection is desirable? This question represents another inventory-investment trade-off, i.e., between protection against demand and supply uncertainties and the costs of investing in safety stock.

Anticipation stock. Anticipation stock is needed for products whose markets exhibit seasonal patterns of demand and whose production (or supply) is more uniform. Air-conditioner manufacturers, children's toy manufacturers, and calendar manufacturers all face peak demand conditions where the production facility is frequently unable to meet the demand on a period-by-period basis. Therefore, anticipation stocks are built up in advance and depleted during the peak demand periods.

Anticipation stock can be created at several points in Figure 17.1. For example, anticipation stocks may be built up in advance of the peak selling season in the factory warehouse. There are, however, trade-offs to be considered in investing in anticipation stocks. For example, an investment in additional factory capacity could be made, thereby reducing the need for anticipation stocks. It may be that operating the factory at a level production rate and allowing the finished-goods inventory level to fluctuate during the year costs less than investing in additional production facilities and varying the production rate.

MEASURING INVENTORY PERFORMANCE

While the benefits derived from inventory may be evident, the costs of inventory need to be clearly identified. These costs are often not reflected directly in a firm's financial statements. Therefore, inventory performance is sometimes measured in relation to sales volume, using inventory turnover as a surrogate measure, i.e., annual sales volume divided by the average inventory investment. For example, annual sales volume for an end product of $200,000 and an average inventory investment during the year of $50,000 produces an inventory turnover of 4.

High inventory turnovers suggest a large return on the inventory investment. Yet an analysis of the costs actually affected by inventory management decisions indicates that inventory turnover is not a comprehensive measure of inventory management performance. There are several pertinent inventory costs which are not reflected in the turnover measure. These include order preparation costs, the costs of carrying inventories, shortage costs, and other customer-service costs.

Order preparation costs

Order preparation costs are incurred in placing orders and are directly related to the frequency with which such orders are placed. These costs include clerical costs associated with writing and issuing replenishment orders and one-time costs incurred in setting up production equipment or in transporting goods between plants and warehouses. Work measurement techniques, such as time study methods, can be used to measure the labor content of order preparation activities. The measurement of other types of order preparation costs is sometimes much more subtle. For instance, in process industries a significant material waste is often incurred in changing from one product to another, e.g., an important paper loss is incurred in switching from one order to another on corregator machines in cardboard box manufacturing plants. Likewise, when the demand for a firm's products exceeds the production capacity, an opportunity cost, i.e., lost profit, is incurred during the production changeover time. In addition, the learning time is often significant in manual assembly operations, and large replenishment orders can have an important impact on the unit cost of production and, therefore, on a firm's labor productivity.

Inventory carrying cost

Inventory commits management to certain costs which are related to the size of inventories, the value of the items carried in the inventory, and the length of time the inventory is carried. By committing capital to inventory, a firm forgoes the use of these funds for other purposes, e.g., to acquire new equipment, to develop new products, or to invest in short-term securities. Therefore, a cost of capital, which is expressed as an annual interest rate, is incurred on the inventory investment.

The cost of capital may be based on the cost of obtaining bank loans to finance the inventory investment (e.g., 15 to 20 percent), the interest rate on short-term securities that could be earned if the funds were not invested in inventory (e.g., 10 to 15 percent), or the rate of return on capital investment projects which cannot be undertaken because the funds must be committed to inventory. For example, the cost of capital for inventory investment might be 25 percent in the case where a new machine would yield a 25 percent return on investment. In any case, the capital cost for inventory might be determined by alternative uses for funds. The cost of capital typically varies from 6 to 35 percent, but can be substantially higher in some circumstances.

Once the cost of capital is determined, several additional costs need to be considered. These typically include the costs of taxes and insurance on inventories, the costs of inventory obsolescence or product shelf-life limitations, and operating costs involved in storing inventory, e.g., either in the rental of public warehousing space or in the costs of owning and operating the warehouse facilities, such as heat, light, labor, etc.

As an example, if the capital cost is 10 percent, and the combined costs of renting warehouse space, product obsolescence, taxes, and insurance amounted to an additional 10 percent of the average value of the inventory investment, the total cost of carrying inventory would be 20 percent of the value of an inventory item. Therefore, a purchased item costing $1 per unit would have an inventory carrying cost of $.20/unit/year.

Shortage and customer-service costs

A final set of inventory-related costs are those incurred when the demand for product exceeds the available inventory for an item. This cost is more difficult to measure than the order preparation and inventory carrying costs. It may be negligible in cases where the customer is willing to have the order backlogged until a product becomes available.

In some cases, this cost may equal the contribution margin of the product when the customer can purchase the item from competing firms. Moreover, this cost may be even more substantial in cases where significant customer goodwill is lost. The major emphasis placed on meeting delivery requirements in many firms suggests that, while shortage and customer-service costs are difficult to measure, they are critical in measuring inventory performance.

One frequently used surrogate measure for inventory shortage costs is the level of customer service achieved in meeting product demand, i.e., the percentage of demand that is shipped from inventory directly upon demand. For example, if the annual demand for an item is 1000 units and 950 units are shipped directly from inventory, a 95 percent customer-service level is achieved.

The level of customer service can be measured in several ways, e.g., as the percentage of units (or of customer orders) shipped directly from inventory, the average length of time required to satisfy back orders, or the percentage of replenishment order cycles in which one or more units are back ordered. The level of customer service can also be translated into the level of inventory investment required to achieve a given level of customer service. As an example, a safety stock of 1,000 units (or $1,000 at a $1 per unit cost) may be required to achieve a 95 percent customer-service level, while 2,000 units of safety stock may be required to achieve a 99 percent customer-service level. Translating customer-service-level objectives into inventory investment dollars often is useful in determining customer-service level/ inventory trade-offs.

Incremental inventory costs

Two criteria are useful in determining which costs are relevant to a particular inventory management decision: (1) Does the cost represent an actual out-of-pocket expenditure either as a cash payment or as forgone profit? and (2) Does the cost actually vary with the decision being made? The determination of the item value used in calculating the inventory carrying cost is a good illustration of the application of these criteria.

The item value should represent the actual out-of-pocket cost of placing an item in inventory, i.e., the variable material, labor, and overhead cost of an item. An element of the overhead cost, such as a cost allocation for general administrative expenses, is not an actual out-of-pocket expenditure. Neither does this cost vary with the decision being made, i.e., the size of the inventory investments, and therefore it should not be included in the determination of the inventory carrying costs.

Another example involves the measurement of clerical costs incurred in preparing replenishment orders. If the size of the clerical staff remains constant throughout the year, regardless of the number of replenishment orders placed, this neither represents an out-of-pocket cost nor does it vary with the decision being made, i.e., the replenishment order quantity. These examples are not meant to be exhaustive, but rather illustrative of the careful analysis required in determining the costs to be considered in evaluating inventory management performance.

ROUTINE INVENTORY DECISIONS

Two types of routine decisions need to be made in managing inventories at any of the stocking points shown in Figure 17.1. These decisions are concerned with *how much should be ordered (size) and when these orders should be placed (timing).* Decisions regarding the size and timing of replenishment orders primarily affect the size of the cycle and safety stock inventories. These decisions are influenced by four main factors: the forecast of demand for an item, its replenishment lead time, the inventory related costs for the item, and management policies.

Inventory decision rules

Routine decisions on the size and timing of replenishment orders for independent demand items can be made using any one of the four inventory control decision rules shown in Figure 17.2. These decision rules are designed for use with routine item forecasting systems. The decision rules shown in Figure 17.2 involve placing orders for either a fixed or a variable order quantity, with either a fixed or a variable time between successive orders. For example, under the commonly used order point (Q,R) rule, an order for a fixed quantity (Q) is placed whenever the stock level reaches a reorder point (R). Likewise, under the S,T rule, an order is placed once every T periods for an amount equaling the difference between the current on-hand balance and a desired inventory level (S) upon the receipt of the replenishment order.

FIGURE 17.2 Inventory decision rules

	Order quantity	
Order frequency	*Fixed (Q)**	*Variable (S)†*
Variable (R)‡	Q,R	S,R
Fixed (T)§	Q,T	S,T

*Q = Order a fixed quantity (Q).
†S = Order up to a fixed expected opening inventory quantity (S).
‡R = Place an order when the inventory balance drops to (R).
§T = Place an order every (T) period.

The effective use of any of these decision rules involves the proper determination of the decision rule parameter values, e.g., Q, R, S, and T. Procedures for determining the order quantity (Q) and recorder point (R) parameters for the order point rule are given in this chapter, while references are provided concerning the determination of the parameter values for the other decision rules in Figure 17.2.

Order quantity decisions. Order quantity decisions primarily affect the amount of inventory held in cycle stocks at the various stocking points in Figure 17.1. Large order quantities enable orders to be placed infrequently and reduce the costs of preparing replenishment orders, but they also increase the cycle stock inventories and the costs of carrying inventory.

The determination of replenishment order quantities focuses on the question of what lot size provides the most economical trade-off between order preparation and inventory carrying costs. An example item stocked in the field warehouses in Figure 17.1 provides an illustration of this decision.

Example. The Model 100 movie camera is sold to several hundred retail stores in a surrounding three-state sales region. To avoid excessive inventories, these stores place orders for this item frequently and in small quantities. The resulting demand for the movie camera, measured from the historical records of warehouse sales, averages 5 units per weekday (or 1,250 units per year). The movie camera can be obtained within a one-day lead time from the distribution center (DC) serving the field warehouse. This requires the preparation of a DC order and the transmission of this order over the firm's TELEX system. The cost of preparing a replenishment order is estimated to be \$6.25. The firm's cost of carrying inventory is estimated at 25 percent of the item value per year, including the costs of capital, insurance, taxes, and obsolescence. Since the unit cost of the camera is \$100, the inventory carrying cost is \$25/unit/year.

Currently, the field warehouse orders the Model 100 movie camera on a daily basis in lots of five units. A plot showing the inventory level versus time for this decision rule is shown in Figure 17.3. This plot assumes that the demand rate is a constant 5 units per day, and the resulting average inventory level is 2.5 units. Since orders are placed daily, 250 orders are placed per year, costing a total of \$1562.50/year (\$6.25 × 250). The average inventory of 2.5 units represents an annual inventory carrying cost of \$62.5/year (2.5 × \$25), yielding an overall combined cost of \$1,625/year for placing orders and carrying inventory.

The inventory level plot for an alternative order quantity of 25 units, or placing orders weekly, is shown by the dashed line in Figure 17.3. In this case, the average inventory level is 12.5 units and 50 orders are placed annually. The larger order quantity in this case provides important savings in ordering costs (\$312.50 versus the previous \$1,562.50) with a small increase in the annual inventory costs (\$312.5 versus the previous \$62.50). Overall, a shift to a larger order quantity would produce a favorable trade-off between

FIGURE 17.3 Inventory level versus time for Model 100 movie camera

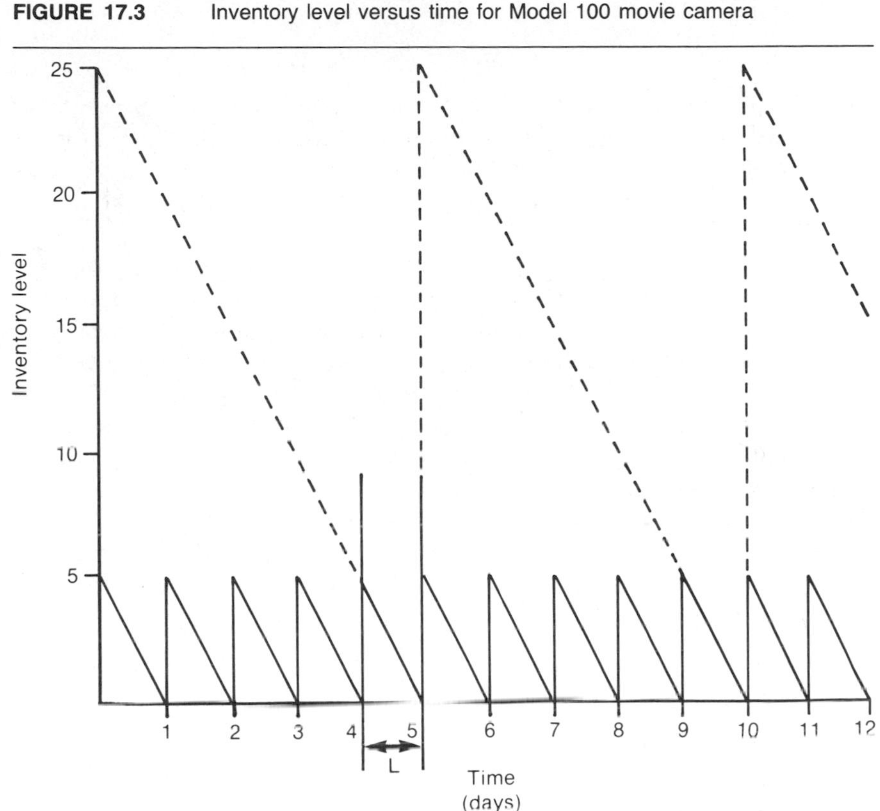

the ordering and inventory carrying costs, resulting in a reduction of the total annual costs to $625.

There are clearly a number of order quantities to be evaluated to determine the best trade-off between ordering and inventory carrying costs. The economic order quantity provides a means of determining the lowest-cost order quantity directly.

Economic order quantity model. The ordering decision is stated in formal terms in the economic order quantity (EOQ) model. This model is an equation which describes the relationship between the costs of placing orders, the costs of carrying inventory, and the order quantity. Several simplifying assumptions are made by this model, these include: the demand rate is constant, costs remain fixed, and production and inventory capacity are unlimited. Despite the fact that these assumptions seem restrictive, the EOQ model provides useful guidelines for ordering decisions even in operating situations that depart substantially from these assumptions.

The incremental total cost equation for the economic order quantity is shown as follows:

$$TC = (A/Q)\ C_p + (Q/2)\ C_H \tag{17.1}$$

This equation contains two terms. The first term, $(A/Q)\ C_p$, represents the annual ordering cost, where A is the annual demand for the item, Q is the order quantity, and C_p is the cost of order preparation. Therefore, the total ordering cost per year is proportional to the number of orders placed annually (A/Q).

The second term, $(Q/2)\ C_H$, represents the annual inventory carrying cost, where the average inventory is assumed to be one half of the order quantity (Q), and C_H is the inventory carrying cost per unit per year, i.e., the item value (v) times the annual percentage cost of carrying inventory (C_r).

The combined costs of ordering and carrying inventory are expressed as a function of the order quantity (Q) in Equation (17.1), enabling the total cost of any given order quantity to be evaluated.

Solving the EOQ model. One method of determining the lowest-cost ordering quantity is to plot the total cost equation for various order quantities on a graph. Figure 17.4 shows a plot of the total cost equation for the Model 100 Movie Camera, based on the following data:

$A = 1{,}250.$

$C_p = 6.25.$

$C_H = 25.$

$TC = (1{,}250/Q)625 + (Q/2)25.$

The total costs for several different order quantities have been plotted in Figure 17.4, and the minimum total cost can be found graphically to equal 25, i.e., placing orders weekly. Both terms of the total-cost equation have also been plotted.

Several facts should be noted in these graphs. First, the inventory carrying costs increase in a straight line as the order quantity is increased, while the ordering cost diminishes rapidly at first and then at a slower rate as the ordering cost is allocated over an increasing number of units. Second, in the EOQ model, the minimum cost solution exists where the ordering costs per year equals the annual inventory carrying cost. This fact is also used in developing lot-sizing decision rules for dependent demand items. Finally, the total cost is relatively flat around the minimum cost solution (of $Q = 25$ in this case), indicating that inventory management performance is relatively insensitive to small changes in the order quantity around the minimum-cost solution.

A second and more direct method of solving for the minimum cost order quantity is by using the EOQ formula shown in Equation (17.2):

$$EOQ = \sqrt{2C_pA/C_H} \tag{17.2}$$

FIGURE 17.4 Total inventory related costs versus order quantity for Model 100 movie camera

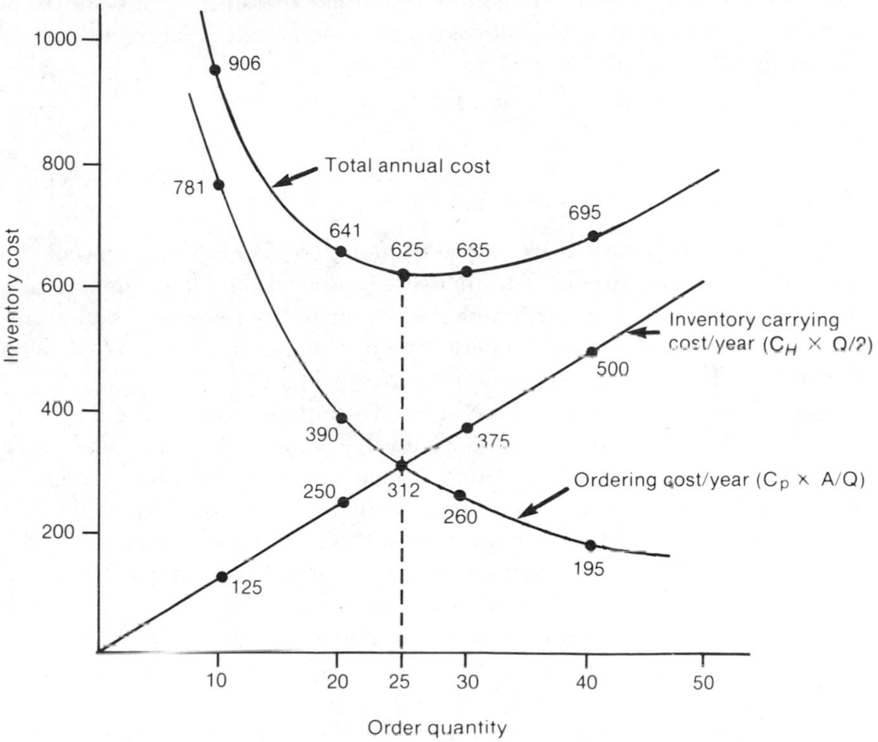

This formula is derived from the total-cost equation (17.1), using calculus. That is, Equation (17.1) is differentiated with respect to the decision variable Q and solved by setting the resulting equation equal to zero, as is shown in Equations (17.3) through (17.6):

$$dTC/dQ = -Cp(A/Q^2) + C_H/2 \quad (17.3)$$

$$C_pA/Q^2 = C_H/2 \quad (17.4)$$

$$Q^2 = 2\ C_pA/C_H \quad (17.5)$$

$$Q^* = \sqrt{2C_pA/C_H} \quad (17.6)$$

where:

Q^* = The optimal value of Q.

The use of the EOQ formula for the Model 100 movie camera produces a lot size of 25, i.e., $\sqrt{[(2)(6)(25)(1250)]/25}$. In using this expression, it is important to make sure that both the demand and the inventory carrying cost are measured in the same units, e.g., 1,250 units/year and $25/unit/year, in this case.

In addition to its use in determining order quantities, the EOQ formula can also be used to develop another important measure in the control of inventories—the economic time between orders (*TBO*). This measure is shown in Equation (17.7):

$$TBO = Q^*/W \tag{17.7}$$

where:

W = The average weekly usage rate.

In the case of the Model 100 movie camera, the *TBO* equals one week (25 units/order)/(25 units/week). This measure can be used to determine an economic ordering frequency or time between inventory reviews. As an example, in the case of the movie camera, one might consider using a Q,T decision rule, i.e., order an economic lot size weekly.

Quantity discount model. One of the assumptions underlying the EOQ model is that the unit cost, i.e., the item value, remains fixed over the range of order quantities considered. This frequently is not the case for purchased items where price discounts and transportation rate breaks are quoted when these items are ordered in large quantities. When discounts are possible, the trade-offs reflected in the decision model become more complex, and the solution procedures require more computations. The trade-offs involve a reduction in both the ordering cost and the item cost for an increase in the inventory carrying cost, when the order quantity is increased (and vice versa).

The total cost expression for the quantity discount model includes three terms: the annual purchase cost (vA), the annual ordering cost $(A/Q)C_p$, and the annual inventory carrying cost $(Q/2)C_H$. This expression, shown as Equation (17.8), is different in two respects from the EOQ total cost equation:

$$TAC = (v)A + (A/Q)C_p + (Q/2)C_H \tag{17.8}$$

The total annual cost of purchasing the item (CA) is a function of the item value (v); the inventory carrying cost (C_H) also depends on the item value ($C_H = vC_r$, where C_r is the annual percentage carrying cost). The item value, in turn, depends on the order quantity.

For example, the variable transportation cost for shipping the Model 100 movie camera from the distribution center to the field warehouse is $10 per unit for lot sizes of less than 40 units, and $5 per unit for lot sizes of 40 or more units. If we assume that the $100 unit cost for the movie camera was the delivered cost, based on the daily shipment quantities (5), this means that the item value is $100/unit ($v_1$) for order quantities of less than 40 units, and $95/unit ($v_2$) for larger order quantities.

Since the item value is not a continuous function of the order quantity, the quantity discount model cannot be solved for an exact solution using calculus, and the computational procedure involves several steps. Magee and Boodman suggest the following five-step method for the direct calculation of the minimum-cost order quantity:

1. Calculate the economic order quantity, using the minimum unit price; if this quantity falls within the range for which the vendor offers this price, it is a *valid* economic order quantity and will result in the minimum cost for the particular item.
2. If the EOQ calculated in 1 is not valid, find the total annual cost for each price-break quantity.
3. Calculate an EOQ for each unit price.
4. Calculate the total annual cost for each valid EOQ determined in 3.
5. The minimum-cost order quantity is that associated with the lowest cost found in either 2 or 4.

This procedure is illustrated, using the Model 100 movie camera and $v_1 = \$100$, $V_2 = \$95$, and a minimum order quantity (b) of 40 for the \$95 price. The calculations at each step are:

1. $EOQ = \sqrt{(2\ (1250)\ (6.25))/(.25)\ 95} = 26.$
   (This EOQ is *invalid* since it is less than the minimum order quantity of 40).
2. $TAC_b = (95)\ (1250) + (6.25)(1250/40) + (.25)(95)(40/2) = \$119{,}420.$
3. $EOQ = \sqrt{[(2)\ (1250)\ (625)]/(.25)\ (100)} = 25.$
4. $TAC_1 = (100)(1250) + (625)\ (1250/25) + (.25)(100)(25/2) = \$125{,}625.$
5. The minimum cost order quantity is therefore the break point $b = 40$.

We see then that the minimum cost order quantity is 40 units. Each step in this process is illustrated in Figure 17.5. Note that the EOQ of 26 on TAC_2 is not a feasible solution since it lies below the break point b, and that TAC_b is less than TAC_1.

ORDER TIMING DECISIONS

The timing of replenishment orders under the order point rule is determined by the use of a trigger level, i.e., the reorder point. The inventory level is assumed to be under continuous monitoring (review), and when the stock level reaches the reorder point, a replenishment order for a fixed quantity (Q) is issued. The setting of the reorder point is influenced by four factors: the demand rate, the lead time required to obtain replenishment inventory, the amount of uncertainty in the demand rate and the replenishment lead time, and the management policy regarding the acceptable level of inventory shortages.

When there is no uncertainty in either the demand rate or the lead time for an item, safety stock is not required, and the determination of the re-

FIGURE 17.5 Purchase discount cost curves

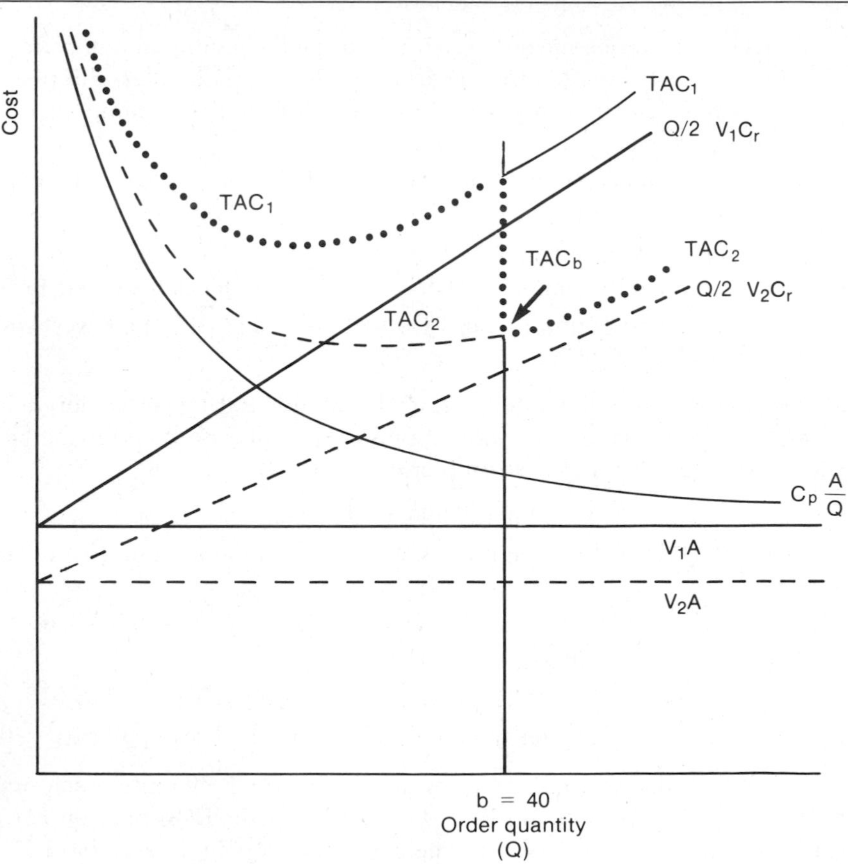

order point is straightforward. For example, the demand rate for the Model 100 movie camera is assumed to be exactly five units per day, and the replenishment lead time is exactly one day in Figure 17.3. In this case, a reorder point of five units provides sufficient inventory to cover the demand until the replenishment order is received.

Sources of demand and supply uncertainty

The assumption of a fixed demand rate and a constant replenishment lead time is rarely justified in actual operations. Random fluctuations in the demand for individual products occur because of variations in the timing of the purchase of the product by consumers. Likewise, variations often occur in the length of the replenishment lead time because of machine breakdowns, employee absenteeism, material shortages, or transportation delays in the factory and distribution operations.

The Model 100 movie camera illustrates the amount of uncertainty usually experienced in the demand for end-product items. An analysis of the warehouse sales and inventory records for this item indicates that the replenishment lead time is quite stable, primarily involving a one-day transit time from the distribution center to the field warehouse. However, the daily demand varies considerably for the camera. While the daily demand averages five units, variations of from one to nine units have been experienced, as indicated in Figure 17.6.

If the reorder point is set at five units to cover the average demand during the one-day replenishment lead time, inventory shortages of from one to four units can result when the daily demand exceeds the average of five units, i.e., when the demand equals six, seven, eight, or nine units. Therefore, if one is to provide protection against inventory shortages when there is uncertainty in demand, the reorder point needs to be increased beyond the average demand during the replenishment lead time, and some level of safety stock is required. Increasing the reorder point to nine units would provide a safety stock of four units. It would also prevent any stock-outs from occurring, given the historical pattern of demand for the Model 100 movie camera.

FIGURE 17.6 Model 100 movie camera demand

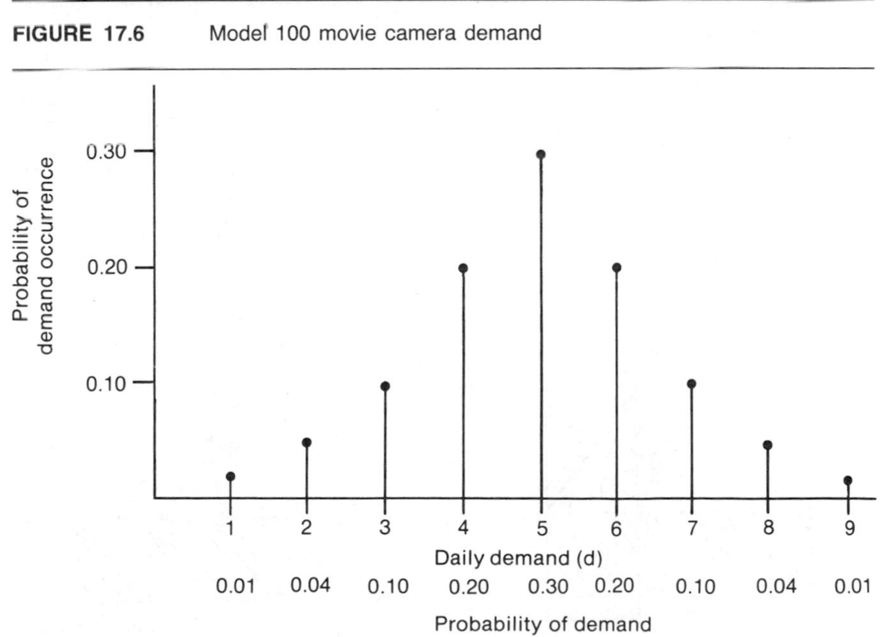

The introduction of safety stock

The introduction of safety stock into the reorder point setting is illustrated in Figure 17.7. The reorder point (R) in this diagram has two components: the safety stock level (S), and the level of inventory ($R - S$) required to satisfy the average demand (D) during the average replenishment lead time (L). The reorder point is the sum of these two, i.e., $R = D + S$. To simplify this explanation, the lead time in Figure 17.7 is assumed to be constant while the demand rate varies.

When a replenishment order is issued (at point a), variations in the demand during the replenishment lead time mean that the inventory level can drop to a point between b and d. In the case of the movie camera, the inventory level may drop by one to nine units (points b and d, respectively) before a replenishment order is received. When the demand equals the average rate of five units, or less, the inventory level reaches a point between b and c, and the safety stock is not needed. However, when the demand rate exceeds the average of five units and the inventory level drops to a point between c and d, a stock-out will occur unless safety stock is available. (A similar diagram can be constructed when both the demand rate and the lead time vary.)

Determining the safety stock level. Before the level of safety stock can be decided, a criterion must be established for determining how much pro-

FIGURE 17.7 Safety stock level

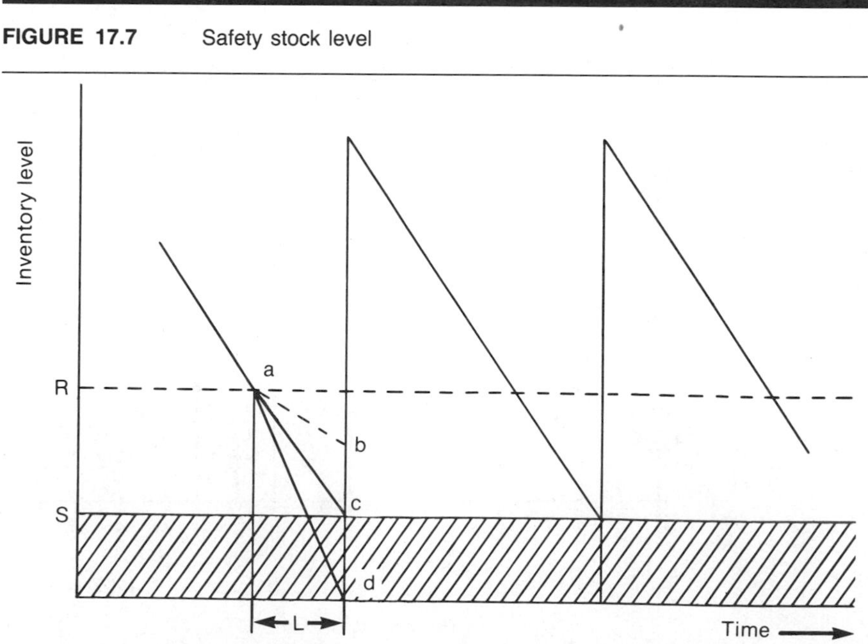

tection against inventory shortages is warranted. One of two different criteria is often used: the probability of stocking out in any given replenishment order cycle, or the desired level of customer service in satisfying the product demand immediately out of inventory. Both of these criteria are illustrated using the demand distribution for the Model 100 movie camera shown in Figure 17.6.

Stock-out probability. One method for determining the required level of safety stock is to specify an acceptable risk of stocking out during any given replenishment order cycle. The demand distribution data for this analysis for the Model 100 movie camera are shown in Figure 17.6. There is a .05 probability of the demand exceeding seven units, i.e., a demand of either eight or nine units occurring. A safety stock level of two units, which means a reorder point of seven units, would provide a risk of stocking out 5 percent of the time or in 1 out of 20 replenishment order cycles. This safety stock level provides a .95 probability of meeting the demand during any given replenishment order cycle, and a .05 probability of stocking out by either one or two units when the demand exceeds seven units.

The risk of stocking out can be reduced by making a larger investment in safety stock. That is, with a safety stock of three units, the probability of stocking out can be reduced to .01, and with four units of safety stock the risk of stocking out is 0, assuming that the demand distribution does not change. Thus, one method of determining the required level of safety stock is to specify an acceptable trade-off between the probability of stocking out during a replenishment order cycle and the investment of funds in inventory.

Customer service level. A second method for determining the required level of safety stock is to specify an acceptable level of customer service. For doing this, we define the customer-service level as the percentage of demand, measured in units, that can be supplied directly out of inventory during a stated time period. Data for doing the calculations are provided for the Model 100 movie camera in Figure 17.8. It shows that a safety stock of 1 unit enables 95.8 percent of the annual demand of 1,250 units for this item to be supplied directly out of inventory to the customer. The service level (SL) is computed using Equation (17.9):

$$SL = 100 - (100/Q) \sum_{D=R+1}^{D_{MAX}} P(D)(D - R) \qquad (17.9)$$

where:

Q = The order quantity.
D = The demand during the replenishment order cycle.
R = The reorder point.
$P(D)$ = The probability of a demand of D units during the replenishment order cycle.
D_{MAX} = The maximum demand during the replenishment order cycle.

FIGURE 17.8 Safety stock determination

Reorder point (R)	*Safety stock (B)*	*Demand probability (P(D) = R)*	*Probability of stocking out (P(D) > R)*	*Average number of shortages per replenishment order cycle**	*Service† level (SL)*
5	0	.30	.35	.56	88.8%
6	1	.20	.15	.21	95.8%
7	2	.10	.05	.06	98.8%
8	3	.04	.01	.01	99.8%
9	4	.01	.00	0	100.0%

*This is calculated by:

$$\sum_{D=R+1}^{D_{max}} P(D)(D-R)$$

†Assuming the replenishment order quantity is five units.

For example, when the safety stock is set at one unit in Figure 17.8, the service level is computed as shown in Equation (17.10):

$$SL = 95.8 = 100 - (100/5)\,[(.01)(3) + (.04)(2) + (.10)(1)] \quad (17.10)$$

A service level of 95.8 percent means that 4.2 percent of the annual demand, or (.042) (1,250) = 52.5 units, cannot be supplied directly out of inventory. Since the current lot size (Q) is 5 units and the item is ordered 250 times per year, the average number of stock-outs per reorder cycle is .21, i.e., 52.5/250, as is shown in Figure 17.8.

The impact of increasing the safety stock level on both the service level and the average number of shortages per replenishment order cycle are shown in Figure 17.8. The service level can be raised to 100 percent by increasing safety stock to four units. Again, as in the case of the stock-out probability method described previously, the choice of the required safety stock level depends on determining an acceptable trade-off between the customer service level and the inventory investment.

So far, the determination of the safety stock and the order quantity parameters for an order point system have been considered separately. These two parameters are, however, interdependent in their effect on customer-service-level performance. This interactive effect can be seen in Equation (17.9), since both the safety stock level and the size of the order quantity affect the level of customer service.

As an example, in the case of the Model 100 movie camera, a shift in order quantity from $Q = 5$ to $Q = 25$, raises the customer-service level from 95.8 percent to 99.16 percent when the safety stock equals one unit. This occurs because larger orders are placed less frequently, thereby reducing the number of times this item is exposed to inventory shortages during a year. This reduction in the average ordering frequency and the exposure to inventory shortages, in turn, reduces the average number of inventory shortages per year, effectively raising the level of customer service. Therefore, a change in the order quantity for an item can affect the level of safety stock required to meet a given customer-service-level objective in an order point system.

Continuous distributions

Two different criteria for determining the required level of safety stock and the reorder point have been described, i.e., the use of a stock-out probability and a desired level of customer service. In the discussion of both cases, a discrete distribution is used to describe the uncertainty in demand during the replenishment lead time. It is frequently convenient to approximate a discrete distribution with a continuous distribution to simplify safety stock and reorder point calculations. One distribution that often provides a close approximation to empirical data is the normal distribution. In this section, we indicate the changes that are required in the calculations when the normal distribution is used to describe the uncertainty in demand during the replenishment lead time.

The data in Figure 17.9 show a comparison of the empirically derived probability values for the Model 100 movie camera demand shown in Figure 17.6, with similar values derived by using the normal distribution as an approximation for this distribution. The comparison shows that the normal distribution closely approximates the empirical distribution, and can be used to determine the safety stock and reorder point levels.

FIGURE 17.9 Normal approximation to the empirical demand distribution*

Midpoint X	*Discrete distribution probability*	*Interval*	*Normal distribution probability*	*Probability of demand exceeding X − 0.5*	*Expected number of stock-outs when reorder point = X*†
1	.01	.5–1.5	.0085	.9902	4.0068
2	.04	1.5–2.5	.0380	.9522	3.0128
3	.11	2.5–3.5	.1109	.8413	2.0591
4	.20	3.5–4.5	.2108	.6305	1.2303
5	.30	4.5–5.5	.2610	.3695	.5983
6	.20	5.5–6.5	.2108	.1587	.2255
7	.10	6.5–7.5	.1109	.0478	.0641
8	.04	7.5–8.5	.0380	.0098	.0127
9	.01	8.5–9.5	.0085	.0013	.0018

*A χ^2 test indicates that these two distributions are not significantly different. ($\chi^2 = 8.75$ versus 20.09 at the 0.01 level of significance.)

†This is σ_D E(Z) based on the E(Z) values from R. G. Brown, *Decision Rules for Inventory Management* (New York: Holt, Rinehart & Winston, 1967), pp. 95–103.

When the probability of stocking out is used as the safety stock criterion, the required level of safety stock and the reorder point values are easily computed using the normal distribution. First, it is necessary to determine the mean and the standard deviation for the distribution of demand during the replenishment lead time. These values have been calculated using the empirical distribution data for the Model 100 movie camera in Figure 17.6 and are shown in Figure 17.10 along with examples of the area (probability) under the normal distribution.

Next, the safety stock (or reorder point) value can be calculated using a table of normal probability values. For example, suppose sufficient safety stock is desired for the Model 100 movie camera so that the probability of stocking out in any given replenishment order cycle is .05. The safety stock level and the reorder point are determined, using Equations (17.11) and (17.12), respectively:

$$\textit{Safety stock} = Z\sigma_D \tag{17.11}$$

$$\textit{Reorder point} = \text{Mean demand during the replenishment lead time} + Z\sigma_D \tag{17.12}$$

FIGURE 17.10 Daily demand distribution

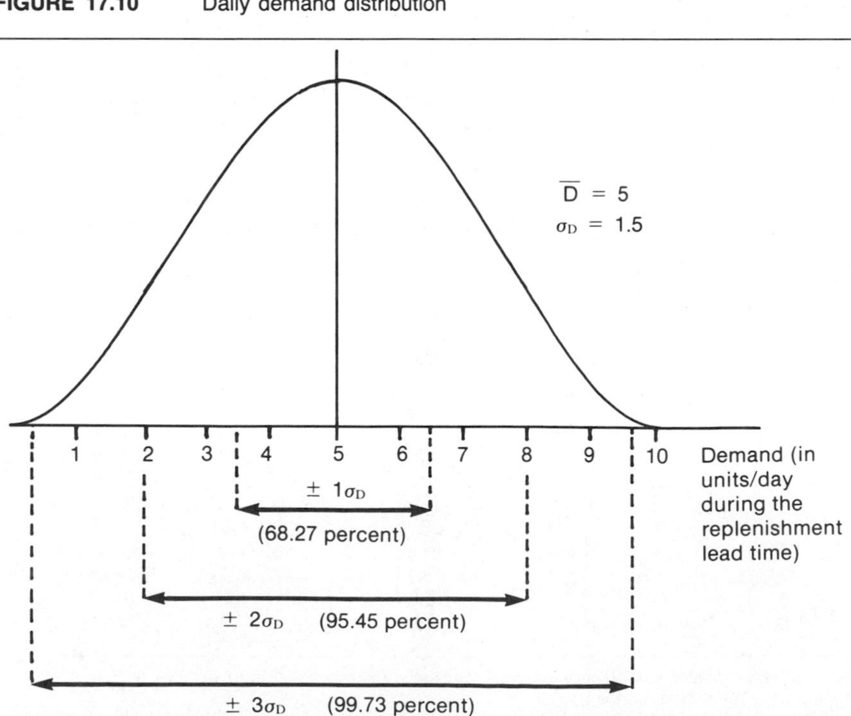

where:

Z = The appropriate value from a table of standard normal distribution probabilities.

σ_D = Demand during the replenishment lead time standard deviation.

The Z value for a .05 probability of stocking out is 1.645. The required level of safety stock therefore is 2.5 units, i.e., (1.645) (1.5), and the reorder point is 7.5 units. This can also be seen directly from the data in Figure 17.9 where the probability of demand exceeding 7.5 is shown to be .0478. In this example, the demand distribution is calculated for one day, the same as the replenishment lead time.

When this is not the case, an adjustment must be made as shown in Equation (17.13)

$$\text{Safety stock} = Z\,(\sigma_D \sqrt{m}) \qquad (17.13)$$

where:

m = The lead time expressed as a multiple of the time period used for the demand distribution.

If the lead time for the Model 100 movie camera were three days instead of one day, the required safety stock would be 4.3 units, i.e., (1.645) (1.5) $\sqrt{3}$, and the reorder point would be 19.3 units, i.e., (3 days)(5 units/day) + 4.3 units. Since the lead time in this example is three times the demand interval of one day, the $\sqrt{3}$ factor has been included in calculating the required safety stock. The resulting safety stock level increases for the three-day lead time to allow for the possible increase in variation in demand over the additional two days.

When the customer-service level is used as the safety stock criterion, the desired level of safety stock can also be determined, using the normal distribution approximation. For this case, we need the average number of stock-outs per replenishment order cycle. To get this, the quantity $\sum_{D=R+1}^{D_{MAX}} P(D)$ $(D - R)$ shown in Equations (17.9) and (17.10), is replaced by $\sigma_D\, E\,(Z)$. The σ_D still equals the standard deviation of the normal distribution being used to approximate the demand-during-lead-time distribution. The $E(Z)$ value is the partial expectation of the normal distribution called the service function. It is the expected *number* of stock-outs when Z units of safety stock are held in the standard normal curve. A graph of the service function, $E(Z)$, is plotted in Figure 17.11. Note that when Z is less than -1, the service function, $E(Z)$, is approximately linear.

The safety stock and reorder point calculations are similar to those shown earlier in Equations (17.9) and (17.10). As an illustration, suppose that we

FIGURE 17.11 Service function

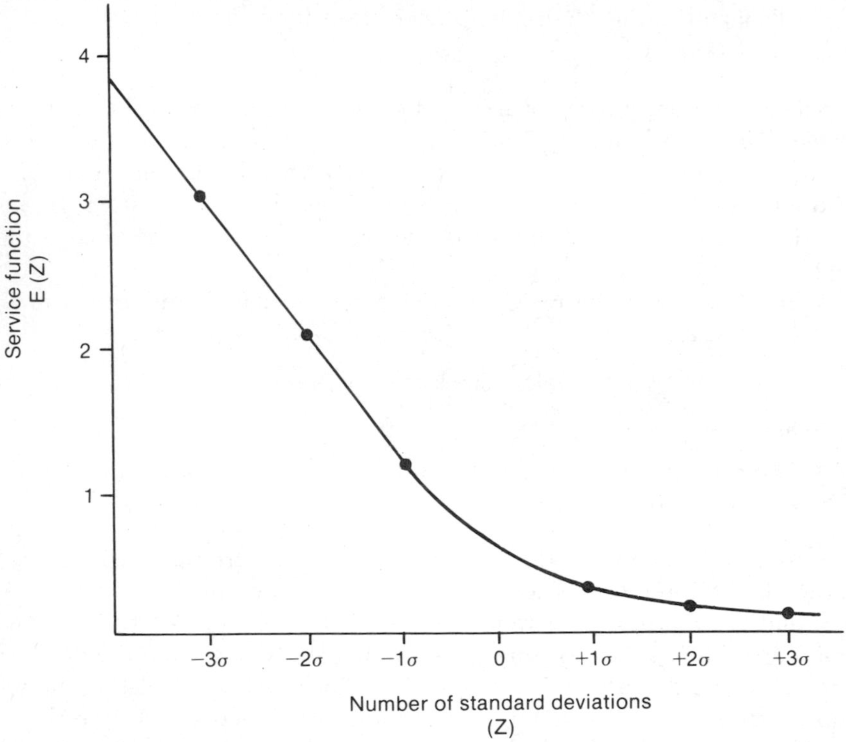

Source: R. G. Brown, *Decision Rules for Inventory Management* (New York: Holt Rinehart & Winston, 1967), pp. 95–103.

want a service level of 95 percent for the Model 100 movie camera, and we go back to the use of an order quantity of five units. The required value for $E(Z)$ is computed, using Equation (17.15) which is derived from Equation (17.14):

$$SL = 100 - (100/Q)\ (\sigma_D\ E\ (Z)) \qquad (17.14)$$

or

$$E\ (Z) = [(100 - SL)\ Q]/100\ \sigma_D \qquad (17.15)$$

In this case, the service function value, $E(Z)$, equals .167, i.e.:

$$[(100 - 95)\ (5)]\ /\ [(100)\ (1.5)]$$

and

$$\sigma_D E(Z) = 2.505$$

Using the service function graph in Figure 17.11, this represents a Z value of approximately $+.61\ \sigma_D$. The safety stock level therefore is $.92 = (.61)(1.5)$. The reorder point would be 5.92. Alternatively, from Figure 17.9, we find $R = 6$ when $\sigma_D\ E(Z) = .2255$. Note that this is the same result we got before using the empirical discrete distribution.

Forecast error distribution

In many inventory management software packages, the demand values for the economic order quantity and reorder point calculations are forecast, using statistical techniques such as exponential smoothing. When these forecasting techniques are used, the required safety stock level will depend upon the accuracy of the forecasting model, i.e., how much variation there is around the forecast. Very little safety stock will be required when the forecast errors are small, and vice versa, for a fixed level of customer service. One commonly used measure of forecasting model accuracy is the mean absolute deviation (MAD) of the forecast errors. This measure can be used directly in determining the required safety stock level.

The methods for determining the safety stock and reorder point levels described earlier in this chapter are also relevant when the product demand is forecast and a MAD value is maintained for the forecasting model. As an illustration, suppose that an exponential smoothing model is used to forecast the demand for the Model 100 movie camera, a .05 probability of stocking out during a reorder cycle is specified, and the forecast errors are normally distributed, as shown in Figure 17.12. The safety stock is calculated using Equation (17.16):

$$\text{Safety stock} = Z\sigma_E = Z\ (1.25\ \text{MAD}) \qquad (17.16)$$

where:

$Z =$ The appropriate value from a table of standard normal distribution probabilities.

$\sigma_E =$ Forecast error distribution standard deviation. (The value of σ_E is often approximated by 1.25 MAD when the forecast errors are normally distributed.)

Since the Z value is 1.645 for a .05 probability of stocking out and the MAD value equals 1.2 from Figure 17.12, in this example the required level of safety stock is 2.5 units, i.e., (1.645) (1.25) (1.2). The reorder point would be 7.5 units, as we found before. In this example, the forecast interval is the same as the replenishment lead time, i.e., one day. When this is not the case, an adjustment must be made to the MAD value in a manner analogous to equation (17.13). The adjustment is shown in Equation (17.17):

$$\text{Safety stock} = Z\ (1.25\ \text{MAD})\sqrt{m} \qquad (17.17)$$

where:

$m =$ The lead time expressed as a multiple of the forecast interval.

FIGURE 17.12 Model 100 movie camera forecast error distribution

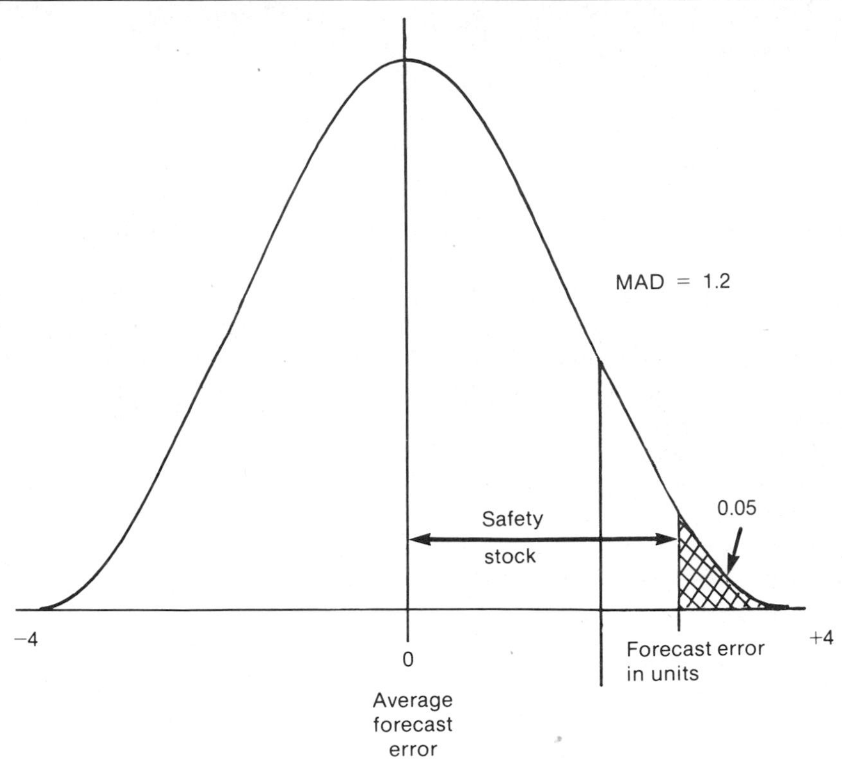

The safety stock can also be determined when customer-service level is used as the safety stock criterion and the product demand is forecast. In this case, Equation (17.15) is modified slightly, as shown in Equation (17.18):

$$E(Z) = [(100 - SL)\ Q] \ / \ [100\ (1.25\ \text{MAD})] \qquad (17.18)$$

After making this change, the safety stock and the reorder point calculations are similar to those involving $E(Z)$, shown earlier in this chapter.

INFORMATION SYSTEMS FOR INVENTORY CONTROL

Attention is focused on the decision-making aspects of the inventory management function for independent items in the previous sections. We discuss the development of routine decision rules for determining the timing and quantity of replenishment orders. The information system aspects of these decisions are, however, also critical in the effective management of inventories. Therefore, attention is now directed toward the information requirements of an effective inventory control system. This information consists of the basic inventory records, the handling of inventory transactions, the reporting of inventory performance, and computer software for managing the inventory system data base. We see these information needs by looking at a series of increasingly complex inventory control systems.

Bin reserve system

The bin reserve system is one of the simplest inventory control systems in terms of its information requirements. In fact, no records are necessary for this system to function. In this system, inventory is carried in two bins. Whenever the first bin is empty, a replenishment order is placed for additional material. The second bin contains sufficient material to last during the replenishment lead time, and serves as the reorder point quantity.

Although this system is simple to administer, it has several disadvantages. For example, the actual stock balance at any given time is unknown. One knows only whether the stock level is above or below the reorder point. In addition, there is no information available which can be used to estimate the current usage rate for an item. Furthermore, information is also unavailable for management purposes in evaluating inventory performance, e.g., in determining slow-moving and surplus material.

Perpetual inventory systems.

Perpetual inventory systems overcome many of the disadvantages inherent in a bin reserve system. A perpetual inventory system maintains a record of the current stock balance for each inventory item, and receipt and disbursement transactions are routinely processed to update the inventory balance, as well as to obtain historical usage data. An example stock status report for such a system is shown in Figure 17.13. This record contains information concerning the present on-hand balance, the quantity currently on order, the date of the last inventory transaction, an estimate of the item usage rate, etc. It also includes the inventory management parameters for each item, e.g., the order quantity, reorder point, safety stock, lead time, etc.

The inventory data base provided by a perpetual inventory system enables closer control to be exerted over inventory system performance. For example, the record of stock disbursements enables better estimation of the item usage rates to be prepared, thereby helping avoid excessive inventory levels and inventory shortages. Furthermore, special inventory reports can be prepared to analyze surplus or slow-moving items. Such reports can serve as the basis for inventory parameter changes, i.e., in the order quantities or safety stocks, and to initiate special programs to apply surplus inventory to other applications. These improvements in inventory performance are, however, obtained at the expense of the additional administrative effort required to maintain a perpetual inventory system. Using a report of the type shown in Figure 17.13, the records for several thousand items can be maintained on a small-scale computer system. Computer software packages for managing a perpetual inventory system data base are widely available from management consulting, computer, and software firms.

FIGURE 17.13 Perpetual inventory record

INVENTORY STOCK STATUS

XYZ COMPANY
REPORT NO. IC-340B
REQUESTED BY: YOUR NAME

①	SELECTION CRITERIA							
	PART NO	VALUE CLASS	TYPE CODE	COMM CODE	NEG ON-HAND	MINUS AVAIL	DATE LASTISS	SURPLUS
	BY REQUEST	XXX	X	XXX	X	X	XXXXX	X

PART NO DESCRIPTION	UM	TYP CDE	COM CDE	B A	V C	I C	② ORD POL	ORDER QTY	SAFTY STOCK	LEAD TIME	STOCK LOC	③ ON HAND	ON ORDER	ALLOC QTY	AVAIL QTY	GROSS REQMT	YTD USAGE	DATE LASTISS
AA-01 DOUBLE DOOR SET	EA	MFG	END	A	A	R	A/R	0	50	5	A0101	50	100	0	150	650	0	
AA-02 RIGHT DOOR	EA	MFG	ASY	A	A	R	F/T	2	0	5	A0102	250	0	100	150	600	0	
AA-03 LEFT DOOR	EA	MFG	ASY	A	A	R	F/T	2	0	5	A0103	200	0	100	100	600	0	
AA-04 COMMON DOOR	EA	MFG	ASY	A	A	R	F/Q	200	0	VAR	A0104	150	150	0	300	750	0	
AA-05 CENTER MEMBER	EA	PUR	PUR	B	B	R	EOQ	600	100 VENDOR NO	15	B0102 VEN075	600	0	450	150	1950	400	12/31/4

① **Stock status reports can be requested by part, value class, type (purchased/manufactured), or commodity to analyze negative-on hand, minus availability, date of last issue for obsolescence, or surplus conditions in any combination selected by user**

② **Order policies and quantities, safety stock, and leadtime information for order planning**

③ **Current inventory balances include availability, planned requirements, and year-to-date usage; on hand + on order − allocated = available**

Source: *MAC-PAC Manufacturing Planning and Control System General Description Manual* (Chicago: Arthur Andersen & Co., 1980), p. 11.

ABC analysis

In many firms, an ABC analysis is frequently prepared to determine the most economical method for controlling individual inventory items. Such an analysis can serve, for example, as the basis for determining which items should be controlled, using a perpetual inventory system and those best controlled by a bin reserve system. An ABC analysis consists of separating the inventory items into three groupings according to their annual cost volume usage (unit cost × annual usage). These groups are then divided into A items having a high dollar volume usage, B items having an intermediate dollar volume usage, and C items having a low dollar volume usage.

The results of a typical ABC analysis are shown in Figure 17.14. For this inventory, 20 percent of the items are A items which account for 65 percent of the annual cost volume usage. The B category comprises 30 percent of the items and 25 percent of the annual cost usage, while the remaining 50 percent of the items are C items accounting for only 10 percent of the annual

FIGURE 17.14 ABC analysis

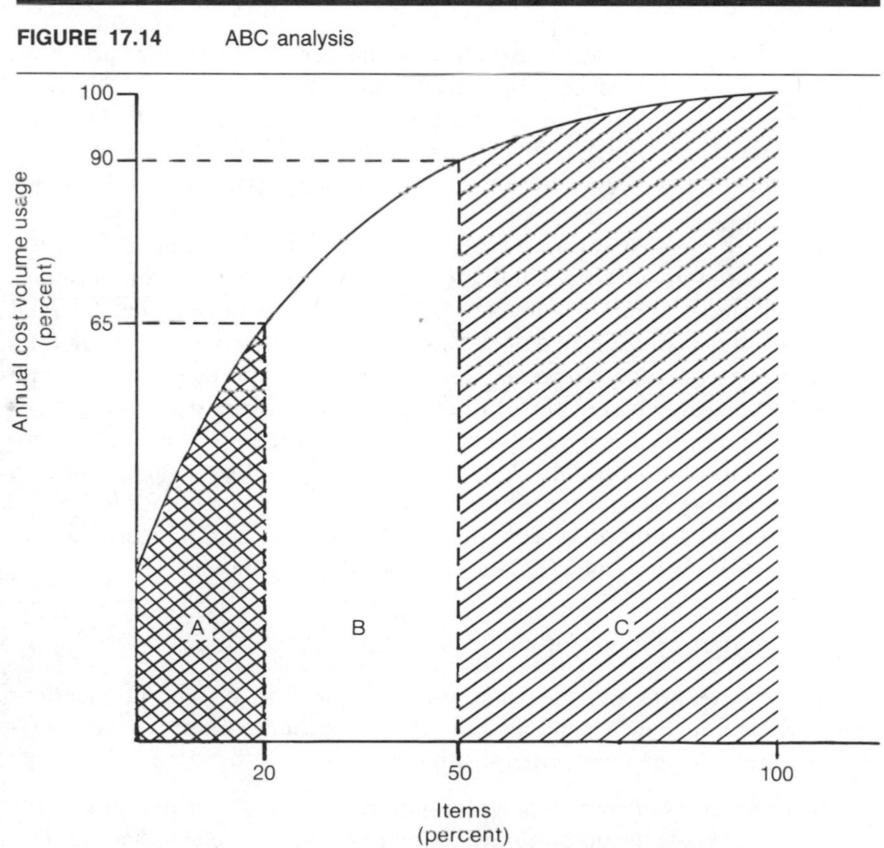

cost volume usage. While the percentage values vary from firm to firm, it is common to find that a small percentage of the items accounts for a large percentage of the annual cost volume usage.

An ABC analysis provides a tool for identifying those items that will make the largest impact on the firm's inventory performance when improved inventory control procedures are implemented. That is, the use of a perpetual inventory system, improvements in forecasting procedures, and a careful analysis of the order quantity and timing decisions for A items will provide a larger improvement in inventory performance than will similar efforts on the C items. Therefore, conducting an ABC analysis is often a useful first step in designing a program of action to improve inventory performance.

The report shown in Figure 17.15 is included to illustrate the results of conducting an ABC analysis. For this report, several additional criteria have been applied. These include lead time and unit cost as well as the annual usage value, as is shown in the block labeled Value Class Rules. The A items in each of these categories are clearly candidates for the application of improved inventory control procedures.

Management issues

Several issues have been raised in this chapter, which require action on the part of management for appropriate control of inventories. These include: the selection of the appropriate inventory management techniques, the evaluation of inventory management performance, and the proper use of inventories in managing operations. The material presented in this chapter is useful in analyzing these issues.

After all of the analyses have been completed, the critical element in the management of inventories is judgment as to when to take action in implementing changes to improve inventory performance. For example, informal procedures for managing inventories may be quite effective for a small-scale warehousing operation. However, as the business experiences growth and there are substantial increases in the number of products stocked and sales volume, more formal inventory control methods are needed to ensure continued business growth. The key to effective inventory management is, therefore, that of recognizing when to turn to the formal methods for inventory control presented in this chapter, to handle the routine decisions that must be made in managing day-to-day inventory operations.

CONCLUDING PRINCIPLES

This chapter presents a considerable amount of theory on independent demand inventory management. Despite the technical nature of the material, several management principles emerge:

- The difference between dependent and independent demand must serve as the first basis for determining the appropriate inventory management procedures.

FIGURE 17.15 ABC analysis

A B C I N V E N T O R Y C L A S S I F I C A T I O N

XYZ COMPANY
REPORT NO. IC-480A
REQUESTED BY - YOUR NAME

VALUE CLASS	LEAD TIME	UNIT COST	ANNUAL VALUE	PERCT VALUE	USAGE WEIGHT FACTORS		POST VALUE CLASS
A	20	100.00	100,000	25	YTD	50	N
B	15	50.00	50,000	50	GROSS	50	
C	10	5.00	5,000	80			
D	0	.00	0	100			

(VALUE CLASS RULES ①; USAGE WEIGHT FACTORS ②)

PART NO/ DESC	CODES TY	CODES AC	PART COUNT	PERCT TOTAL COUNT	ANNUAL USAGE	LEAD TIME DAYS		CURRENT UNIT COST		ANNUAL USAGE VALUE		CUMM USAGE VALUE	PERCT TOTAL VALUE		VALUE CLASS CURR	VALUE CLASS PREV
AA-05 CENTER MEMBER	1	3	1	14.3	11,000	15	B	10.00	C	110,000	A	110,000	24.5	A	A	A
AA-09 RAW MATERIAL	3	4	2	28.6	12,500	30	A	7.50	C	93,750	B	203,750	45.4	B	A	A
AA-11 KNOB & LOCK	1	3	3	42.8	20,000	15	B	4.50	D	90,000	B	293,750	65.5	C	B	B
AA-10 GLUE	3	4	4	57.1	15,000	10	C	5.00	C	75,000	B	368,750	82.2	D	B	C ③
AA-13 HINGE	1	3	5	71.4	240,000	10	C	.25	D	60,000	B	428,750	95.6	D	B	B
AA-12 LOCK CATCH	1	3	6	85.7	30,000	10	C	.50	D	15,000	C	443,750	98.9	D	C	C
AA-14 SCREW	1	3	7	100.0	480,000	5	D	.01	D	4,800	D	448,550	100.0	D	D	D

① **User specified ABC parameters for leadtime, unit cost, annual dollar value, and per cent total value determine value class rules**

② **Annual usage can be weighted by year-to-date and/or planned usage percentages for more effective ranking**

③ **Value class ranking based on highest value in accordance with specified parameters**

Source: *MAC-PAC Manufacturing Planning and Control System General Description Manual* (Chicago: Arthur Andersen & Co., 1980), p. 11.

- Order point procedures should be used for independent demand items.
- The organizational criteria must be clearly established before setting safety stock levels.
- The choice of decision rule to use for managing a particular item depends upon where it is in an ABC analysis.
- The performance of the inventory management procedure must be monitored.
- The procedures used to manage inventory should change as the company changes.

REFERENCES

Brown, R. G. *Statistical Forecasting for Inventory Control.* New York: McGraw-Hill, 1959.

———. *Decision Rules for Inventory Management.* New York: Holt, Rinehart & Winston, 1967.

Buchan, J., and E. Koenigsberg. *Scientific Inventory Management.* New York: Prentice-Hall, 1963.

Davis, E. W. and D. C. Whybark, "Inventory Management," *Small Business Bibliography 75,* Washington, D.C.: Small Business Administration, 1980.

Fogarty, D. W., and T. R. Hoffman. *Production and Inventory Control.* Falls Church, Va.: American Production and Inventory Control Society, 1983.

Greene, J. H., *Production and Inventory Control Handbook.* Falls Church, Va.: American Production and Inventory Control Society, 1970.

Inventory Planning Reprints. Falls Church, Va.: American Production and Inventory Control Society, 1978.

MAC-PAC Manufacturing Planning and Control System General Description Manual. Arthur Andersen & Co., Chicago, 1980.

Magee, J. F., and D. M. Boodman. *Production Planning and Inventory Control.* New York: McGraw-Hill, 1967.

Peterson, R., and E. A. Silver. *Decision Systems for Inventory Management and Production Planning.* New York: John Wiley, 1979.

Service Parts Management Reprints. Falls Church, Va.: American Production and Inventory Control Society, 1982.

Vandemark, Robert L. "The Case for the Combination Systems." *APICS 23d Annual Conference Proceedings,* 1980, pp. 125–27.

18

Advanced independent demand systems

In this chapter we present several approaches for improving the management of independent demand items. Most of the improvements derive from increasing the number of problem elements considered and explicitly recognizing interdependencies between problem elements. Applying these concepts to managing independent demand items requires an expanded system perspective but promises important improvements. In addition, a more knowledgeable software selection can be made since many of the ideas are incorporated in commercial software approaches. Applying the ideas presented in this chapter can lead to improved inventory and service performance in independent demand environments. Specifically we address the following topics:

- A perspective on advanced independent demand systems: How should the advanced concepts be viewed and what is required for their use?
- Order quantity and reorder point interactions: Why is it important to determine the order quantity and reorder point simultaneously, and what form does the analysis take?
- Inventory and transportation mode interactions: How should the impact of alternative transportation choices be incorporated into the analysis?
- Multiple items from a single source: What procedures exist for placing orders for many items from a single vendor?

- Advanced concepts in forecasting: What forecasting techniques work best, and how can they be made consistant throughout the organization?
- Living with advanced systems: How can the organization be prepared to use the advanced approaches wisely?

This chapter builds upon the material in Chapter 17 dealing with basic independent demand concepts. The forecasting material in this chapter assumes a basic understanding of exponential smoothing and the monitoring techniques presented in Chapter 16. The ideas in Chapter 11 on implementation are germane to installing advanced systems.

A PERSPECTIVE ON ADVANCED SYSTEMS

Throughout this chapter an overriding objective is to present an expanded viewpoint for managing independent demand items. A great deal of the writing on inventory techniques tends to be in watertight compartments. That is, the theoretical materials are based on assumptions that limit the system under study and the evaluative criteria for judging the value of problem solutions. In expanding the system perspective, we necessarily incorporate additional problem elements, break some of the barriers that force problems to be considered in isolation, and consider problems with a more realistic set of objectives or evaluative criteria. Such a viewpoint provides an enhanced understanding of inventory related problems. It also can lead to demonstrable improvements in certain problem environments.

Before turning to the technical issues of particular inventory and forecasting approaches, a caveat is in order. The ideas presented here depend upon having some of the basic system elements in place. These elements include accurate inventory and demand records, clear-cut reporting procedures and transaction controls, timely and effective forecasts of demand, and a managerial willingness to clearly address trade-offs between inventory levels and customer service measures.

In some cases, one needs to take an evolutionary point of view. One first implements a basic system even though it is flawed by the limited system view. With the basic system, the objectives are more straightforward, conformance to procedures can be more easily assessed, and operations of the firm are more easily brought into harmony with the dictates of the system. *Thereafter*, it may be desirable to consider some of the techniques presented here as enhancements.

We begin this chapter by considering advanced reorder point techniques. These techniques provide performance improvements by combining factors that interact in the determination of the reorder point and order quantity values. These factors include: the inventory required for satisfying customer service level objectives, the interaction between transportation mode and inventory system decisions, and joint ordering of multiple items from a single supplier. We then turn to considering advanced forecasting methods for independent demand items. We include techniques for coordinating the forecasts made for individual product items with those made by top management in preparing overall business plans and a discussion of recent research into forecasting techniques.

In addition to generating important cost savings, the enhancements considered in this chapter often provide major improvements in the productivity of inventory planners. This occurs because many of the clerical tasks performed by the inventory planners can be accomplished routinely using computerized logic. The substitution of routine procedures for manual efforts permits applying the limited personnel resources where they are best utilized in problem-solving activities. When this is done people can spend more time on decision making and coordinative activities and less time on clerical work.

ORDER QUANTITY AND REORDER POINT INTERACTIONS

In this section we look at the interaction between the reorder point and order quantity for a small example. We will then present two ways of jointly determining the reorder point and order quantity: a search procedure and an iterative procedure. We consider both service level and total cost criteria.

Service levels and order quantities

Figure 18.1 provides data for a single inventory item which will serve as our example. Note that both the lead time and the weekly demand are variable. This means that the process of determining the demand during lead time distribution is somewhat complicated. We use a tree diagram to illustrate all possible combinations of demand and lead time that can occur. These are then summarized to give the distribution of demand during lead time.

FIGURE 18.1 Data for single-item example

	Notation	
Item value	v	\$500 per unit
Average demand	A	35 units per year
Fixed ordering cost	C_p	\$45 per order
Shortage cost	C_s	\$60 per unit short
Inventory carrying cost rate	C_r	25% of value per year
Economic order quantity	*EOQ*	5 units
Replenishment lead time	*LT*	1 week, probability = .8
		2 weeks, probability = .2
		Average lead time = 1.2 weeks
Weekly demand distribution:		0 units, probability = .5
		1 unit, probability = .3
		2 units, probability = .2
		Average demand/week = .7 units

FIGURE 18.2 Tree diagram of possible occurrences of lead time and demand for example problem

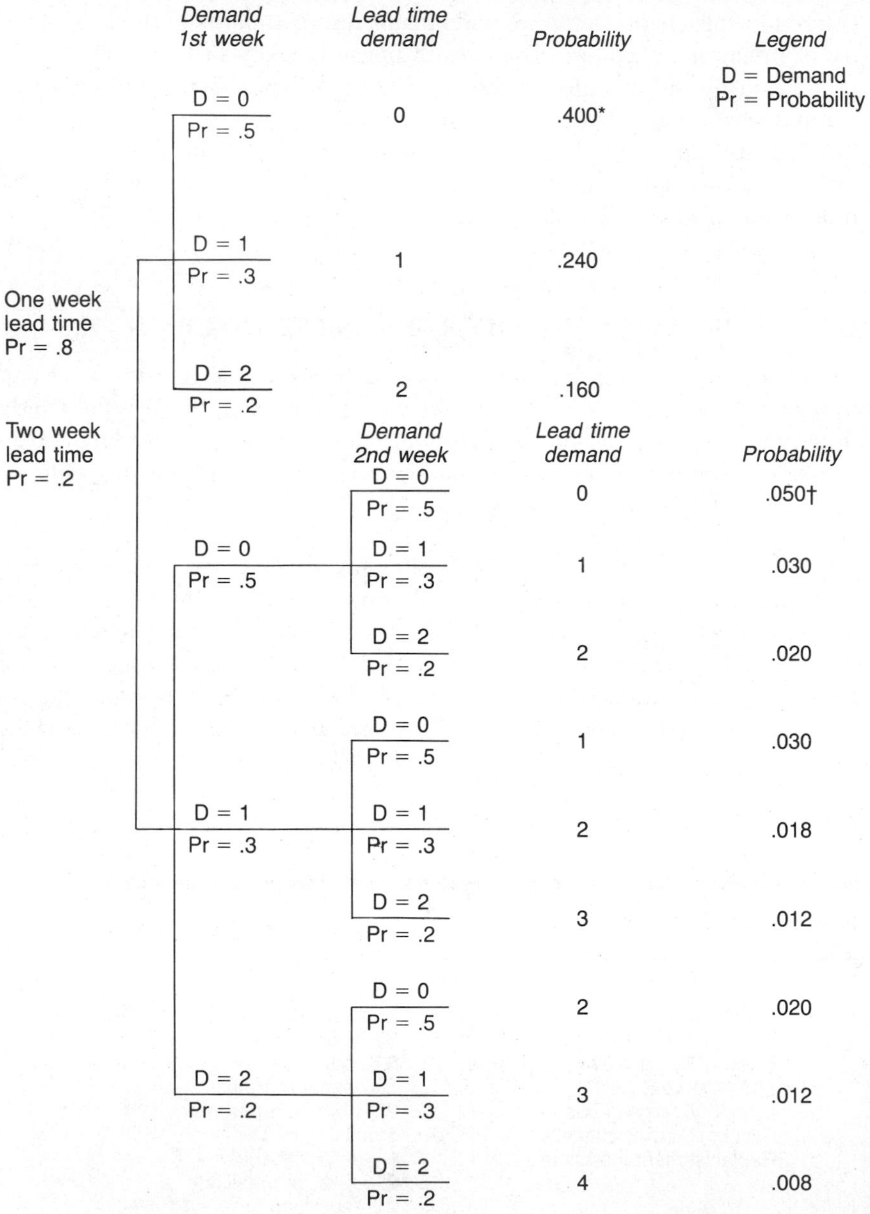

Legend: D = Demand; Pr = Probability

One week lead time Pr = .8

Demand 1st week	*Lead time demand*	*Probability*
D = 0, Pr = .5	0	.400*
D = 1, Pr = .3	1	.240
D = 2, Pr = .2	2	.160

Two week lead time Pr = .2

Demand 1st week	*Demand 2nd week*	*Lead time demand*	*Probability*
D = 0, Pr = .5	D = 0, Pr = .5	0	.050†
	D = 1, Pr = .3	1	.030
	D = 2, Pr = .2	2	.020
D = 1, Pr = .3	D = 0, Pr = .5	1	.030
	D = 1, Pr = .3	2	.018
	D = 2, Pr = .2	3	.012
D = 2, Pr = .2	D = 0, Pr = .5	2	.020
	D = 1, Pr = .3	3	.012
	D = 2, Pr = .2	4	.008

*LT = 1 week (Pr = .8) and D = 0 for that week (Pr = .5). Probability of both occurring is .4 = (.8 × .5)

†LT = 2 weeks (Pr = .2) and D = 0 (Pr = .5) for each week. Probability of all three occurring is .05 = (.2 × .5 × .5).

The lead time and the weekly demand distribution data shown in Figure 18.1 have been used to develop the tree diagram in Figure 18.2. As an example of the calculations, we will use the branch at the bottom of Figure 18.2. The 4-unit demand occurs during the replenishment lead time only when the lead time is 2 weeks and 2 units are demanded each week. The probability of these events occurring is: (.2)(.2)(.2) = .008. The remaining combinations of daily demand and lead time values are enumerated in Figure 18.2, and the results are summarized in the demand during lead time distribution, shown as Figure 18.3.

Also shown in Figure 18.3 are the expected number of units short for specified reorder points. A shortage can only occur when the demand exceeds the reorder point. So, for example, when the reorder point is 4, no shortages can occur. If the reorder point is 2, there is a one-unit shortage if the demand is 3 and a 2-unit-shortage if demand is 4. The probabilities of these demands occurring are .024 and .008, respectively. This means the expected number of stockouts are (.024 × 1) + (.008 × 2) = .040, when the reorder point is 2.

To show the interaction between reorder point and order quantity, we use the data in Figure 18.3. Suppose the item was currently ordered about five times per year in quantities of 7. If the reorder point was set to 1 unit, the expected number of units short *per reorder cycle* would be .29. This would mean, for the 5 cycles per year, that about 1.5 units would be out of stock in a year. This corresponds to a service level of about 95 percent [(35 − 1.5)/35].

If the order quantity is changed to 35, only 1 reorder cycle per year would occur. There would be an expected .29 units short in the cycle if the reorder point was 1, but that is now the expected number short for the year as well. This corresponds to a service level of 99 percent [(35 − .29)/35]. Even a reorder point of 0 would provide a level of service of about 97 percent [(35 − .84)/35] when 35 units are ordered at a time.

The order quantity of 35 provides more cycle stock than the order quantity of 7. For the larger order, the exposure to stockout is only once a year, as opposed to 5 times per year when the order quantity is 7. Thus the cycle

FIGURE 18.3 Demand during lead time distribution

Demand (D)	Probability of demand = D	Probability of demand > D	Reorder point (R)	Expected number of units short (E{s}) when reorder point = R
0	.450	.550	0	.840 units
1	.300	.250	1	.290 units
2	.218	.032	2	.040 units
3	.024	.008	3	.008 units
4	.008	0	4	0 units

Expected demand during lead time = .840

FIGURE 18.4 Inventory costs and service levels

Reorder point	*Order quantity*					
	4		*5*		*6*	
0	$643.75	79%	$627.50	83%	$637.50	86%
1	663.75	93%	647.50	94%	657.50	95%
2	788.75	99%	772.50	99%	782.50	99%

stock protects against demand fluctuations during the year—acting much like safety stock.

In many companies, the determination of shortage costs is very difficult and/or there is a preference to use a service criterion for inventory management. In these firms, the question of the trade-off between service level and inventory cost is still relevant but complicated because the order quantity and reorder point both affect sevice levels and inventory costs. One way of providing an explicit trade-off is to develop tables like that shown in Figure 18.4. In this table the inventory holding plus ordering costs and service levels are shown for various order quantities and reorder points using the example data.

To illustrate the calculations for Figure 18.4, consider a reorder point of 2 and an order quantity of 4. The annual ordering cost would be (35/4)(45) = $393.75. The cycle stock carrying cost would be (4/2)(.25)(500) = $250, while the cost of safety stock would be (2 − .84)(.25)(500) = $145. This totals $788.75.

Total cost equation

So far, our example has measured customer service levels as the percentage of the units ordered by the customers met from stock. In some cases, the costs of not having the units in stock (e.g., lost profits, penalty costs, and the loss of customer goodwill) can be quantified. This permits a more global examination of inventory decisions since the ordering, carrying, and inventory shortage costs can all be considered in determining the inventory parameters.

The equation for total cost per period (18.1) contains terms for the costs of placing orders, carrying inventory, and incurring inventory shortages. This equation requires estimates for all the costs, probably the most difficult of which is the cost of incurring inventory shortages; i.e., the shortage cost. Once the cost estimates are made, the expression can be used to find the lowest total cost set of order quantity (Q) and reorder point (R) parameter values. The equation is:

$$TC = A/Q\left[C_p + C_s\left(\sum_{D=R+1}^{D_{max}} (D - R)\, P(D)\right)\right] + C_H[Q/2 + (R - \bar{D})] \tag{18.1}$$

where:

A = Average demand per period.
Q = Order quantity.
C_p = Fixed ordering cost.
C_H = Inventory carrying cost per unit per period = v.
D = Demand during the replenishment lead time.
$\bar{D}$ = Average demand during the replenishment lead time.
$P(D)$ = Probability of demand during lead time equaling D.
R = Reorder point.
$(R - \bar{D})$ = Safety stock level.
C_s = Shortage cost.

The first part of Equation (18.1) includes the ordering cost and the stock-out cost. The number of reorder cycles per period is A/Q, and this can be used to convert the costs per cycle to period costs. The expression $(A/Q)C_p$ is the cost per period of placing orders. The expected number of units short ($E\{s\}$), for a reorder point of R is:

$$\left[\sum_{D=R+1}^{D_{max}} (D - R)\, P(D)\right]$$

Multiplying this by $(A/Q)C_s$ gives the cost per period of inventory shortages. The cost per period of carrying cycle stock is $(Q/2)C_H$, and the cost per period of carrying safety stock inventory is $C_H(R - \bar{D})$.

Any particular solution to Equation (18.1) provides the total cost per period for a given setting of the order quantity (Q) and the reorder point (R). If the unit cost of acquiring an item depends on the quantity ordered, additional terms would be required in this model. This can occur when volume or transportation discounts are available.

We shall present two methods for using Equation (18.1) to determine the least cost order point/order quantity values, a grid search approach, and an iterative approach. We will use the example problem to illustrate the approaches.

Grid search procedure

Using the example problem and Equation (18.1) gives an expression for total annual cost as a function of the order quantity Q and reorder point R. The expression is:

$$TC = (35/Q)[45 + 60\, E\{s\}] + 125[(Q/2) + (R - .84)]$$

FIGURE 18.5 Total costs for several reorder points and order quantities

Reorder point	Order quantity 4	5	6	7	8
0	979.75	875.30	826.50	809.50	812.38
1	816.00	769.30	759.00	769.50	793.00
2	790.85	789.30	796.50	808.70	852.38
3	917.95	899.18	910.30	934.90	967.93
4	1038.75	1022.50	1032.50	1057.50	1091.88

Evaluating this expression for several values of Q and R provides the results shown in Figure 18.5 which serve as the basis for a grid search.

Our strategy for performing the grid search is to start with Q equal to the economic order quantity (5 units). Next we search on the reorder point (starting at the maximum of $R = 4$) until the costs reach a minimum and start to increase. This occurs at $R = 1$ when $Q = 5$.

The next step is to vary Q around $Q = 5$, when $R = 0$, 1, and 2, to see if costs increase. Since they decrease for $Q = 6$, when $R = 0$ and 1, we continue on to $Q = 7$. At this point only the value at $R = 0$ is still decreasing, so we go on to $Q = 8$, where we finish. (We have underlined the additional values that were provided for completeness.) We have now identified the point of minimum total cost; $R = 1$, $Q = 6$.

Several observations can be made from Figure 18.5. The solution suggested is $Q = 6$, $R = 1$. It trades off some exposure to stockouts by increasing the order quantity over the economic order quantity. In some instances, the solution will reduce the reorder point as well. That is the reason for checking the costs at $R = 0$ and $Q = 8$. The economic order quantity (EOQ) provides a reasonable starting point for the search although the solution will be further from the EOQ the larger the stockout cost. We will use some of these observations in the iterative procedure.

The iterative (Q, R) procedure

The iterative procedure is summarized in Figure 18.6. The procedure starts with the EOQ, as we did with the grid search. The value of $P(D > R)$ at step 2 is found by equating the extra annual inventory carrying cost incurred by increasing the reorder point by 1 unit, C_H, to the savings in shortage costs that can be attributed to the additional unit of inventory; i.e., $C_H = (A/Q)C_s(E\{s\}_R - E\{s\}_{R+1})$. Since $(E\{s\}_R - E\{s\}_{R-1}) = P(D > R)$; $C_H = (A/Q)C_s \cdot P(D > R)$. The calculation of Q at step 4 is obtained by differentiating Equation (18.1) with respect to Q, setting the resulting expression equal to 0, and solving for Q.

FIGURE 18.6 The iterative procedure for finding Q and R

1. Compute the EOQ $= \sqrt{2AC_p/C_H}$
2. Compute $P(D > R) = QC_H/AC_S$ and determine the value of R by comparing the value of $P(D > R)$ with the cumulative demand during lead time distribution values.
3. Determine $E\{s\}$, the expected inventory shortages, using the value of R from step 2.
4. Compute $Q = \sqrt{2A[C_p + C_sE\{s\}_R]/C_H}$
5. Repeat steps 2 through 4 until convergence occurs; i.e., until sequential values for Q at step 4 and R at step 2 are equal.

Source: R. B. Felter and W. C. Dalleck, *Decision Models for Inventory Management* (Homewood, Ill.: Richard D. Irwin, 1961).

$$Q = \sqrt{\frac{2A[C_p + C_sE\{s\}_R]}{C_H}}$$

To illustrate the procedure, we will use the example problem. Since the procedure iterates from calculating Q to calculating R, it is sometimes called the Q, R procedure.

Step 1: $Q = \sqrt{(2)(35)(45)/(.25)(500)} = 5.$

Step 2: $P(D > R) = (5)(.25)(500)/(35)(60) = .30$

The closest value in Figure 18.3 is .250 at $R = 1$.

Step 3: $E\{s\} = .290$ (from Figure 18.3 when $R = 1$).

Step 4: $Q = \sqrt{2(35)[45 + (.29)(60)]/(.25)(500)} = 5.91 \approx 6.$

Step 5: $P(D > R) = (6)(.25)(500)/(35)(60) = .36.$ $R = 1.$

The five-step procedure converged quickly on the same Q, R value solution that was indicated earlier in Figure 18.5. Since the procedure considers the expected shortage cost in determining Q in step 4, and since the computation effort is minimal, it is often a very useful approach for determining the order quantity and reorder point values. In cases where the magnitude of the shortage cost, C_s, is large, this procedure will take it into account and adjust the order quantity and reorder point accordingly. This may mean that an increase in the order quantity over the EOQ and a reduction in reorder point is required in order to reduce the total costs. The five-step procedure explicitly accounts for the interaction between inventory shortages and ordering costs in solving for the minimum cost reorder point/order quantity values.

INVENTORY AND TRANSPORTATION MODE INTERACTIONS

In this section we continue to broaden the number of factors which might be included in determining how to order an independent demand inventory item. Specifically we include the costs of transporting the item from the supplier to the stock-keeping location. In effect, this broadening of the analysis treats the interaction between management of inventories and determination of transportation policy. These considerations interact when alternatives exist for transporting inventory, and each alternative has different inventory management implications. For example, differences in transit time variability could lead to different reorder points, and differences in transportation costs could lead to different order quantities.

Interactions between inventory parameters and transportation alternatives suggest that decisions for these two problem areas should be made simultaneously. This suggestion is rarely carried out in practice, but doing so can lead to important cost savings in some firms. In practice, the determination of a transportation alternative usually starts with the selection of a primary transportation mode (i.e., rail, truck, air, ship) by one group of people. This is often done on the basis of cost or transit time only. Once this decision is made, the selection of a specific transportation company or routing is based on an evaluation of that company's service. This evaluation may not even consider the variability of transportation time. In some instances, the transportation decision is not even made inside the firm (for example, when a vendor is requested to ship by the "best method"). The resultant transportation decisions are then accepted as givens by another group of people who determine the parameters for managing inventories. Clearly, artificial organizational boundaries will need to be reduced if an integrated approach is to be applied.

We illustrate the interaction between inventory and transportation decisions by considering one item in a reorder point system. The transportation alternatives involve several different modes, each characterized by three attributes: transportation cost, expected time in transit, and variability of the transit time. In many instances, all alternatives need not be considered since any alternative that is more costly, has a greater time in transit, and has more variability in transit time than another alternative can be eliminated a priori.

The global problem is to determine which transportation alternative and inventory parameters (reorder point and order quantity) lead to the lowest combined inventory and transportation cost. We begin by presenting a total cost expression that combines the transportation attributes and the inventory policy parameters. Next, two procedures are described for solving this cost model: an exact enumeration procedure and a heuristic procedure. Finally, we discuss experiments that evaluate the performance of these procedures and their application in practice.

Total cost equation

The approach taken here is to develop the total cost equation like that previously given as Equation (18.1). To incorporate the transportation considerations we substitute the expected transit time for the replenishment lead time, incorporate the transit time variance into the demand during lead time, and account for transportation cost. The total cost per period for a specific transportation alternative and set of inventory parameters is comprised of the following cost elements: transportation, in-transit inventory, stored inventory, ordering and shortage.

Equation (18.2) is:

$$TC = AC_t + C_i vTA + C_H[Q/2 + (R - \bar{D})] + A/Q\left[C_p + C_s\left(\sum_{D=R+1}^{D_{max}} (D - R)\, P(D)\right)\right] \tag{18.2}$$

where:

A = Average demand per period.
C_t = Transportation cost per unit.
C_i = In-transit inventory cost per dollar of value (can be different for each mode).
v = Item value prior to transport cost.
T = Expected transit time.
C_r = Inventory carrying cost rate per period (percentage).
C_H = $C_r(v + C_t)$.
Q = Order quantity.
R = Reorder point.
$\bar{D}$ = Average demand during lead time (expected transit time).
C_p = Fixed ordering cost.
C_s = Shortage cost.
$P(D)$ = Probability of demand equalling D.

This equation has two inventory parameters, Q and R, as unknowns and incorporates data for a single transportation alternative: C_i, C_t, $\bar{D}$ and $P(D)$. These last two terms are related to the expected time in transit and its variability. The in-transit inventory cost term depends on $\bar{D}$ and the shortage cost term depends on $P(D)$. Faster modes reduce $\bar{D}$, and more reliable modes reduce the variance of demand during lead time. Before illustrating procedures for determining the choice of transport mode and inventory parameters, we will present an example.

Transport mode decision example

An example to illustrate the combined choice of inventory parameters and transport mode is shown in Figure 18.7. Product-related data, including cost and demand information, are provided in the top third of the figure. Three different transportation alternatives for this item are shown in the middle of Figure 18.7. For the modes shown, the unit transportation cost for this product increases as the expected transit time and variability of the transit time decrease.

FIGURE 18.7 Example: Inventory-transportation mode problem

Product data

Item	*Notation*	*Value*
Inventory carrying cost rate	C_r	.000605 per day*
Shortage cost	C_s	\$1 per unit short
Order cost	C_p	\$10 per order
Item value before transportation cost	V	\$2 per unit
Average demand per day	A	6 units
Demand per day standard deviation	σ_A	1 unit
Demand per day distribution		Demand = 5, probability = .5 Demand = 7, probability = .5.

Transportation alternatives

		Transportation alternative		
Item	*Notation*	*1*	*2*	*3*
Transportation cost/unit	C_t	\$ .32	\$ .38	\$ .40
In-transit carrying rate/day	C_i	.001	.001	.001
Expected transit time (days)	T	2.20	1.60	1.40
Transit time standard deviation (days)	σ_T	1.00	.49	.49
Transit time distribution		(Prob. = .4, T = 1) (Prob. = .6, T = 3)	(Prob. = .4, T = 1) (Prob. = .6, T = 2)	(Prob. = .6, T = 1) (Prob. = .4, T = 2)

Lead time demand distribution

		Transportation alternative		
Item	*Notation*	*1*	*2*	*3*
Average demand during lead time (in units)	$\bar{D}$	13.20	9.60	8.40
Standard deviation of demand during lead time	σ_D	6.06	3.20	3.17
Demand during lead time distribution		(Pr = .20, D = 5 or 7) (Pr = .075, D = 15 or 21) (Pr = .225, D = 17 or 19)	(Pr = .20, D = 5 or 7) (Pr = .15, D = 10 or 14) (Pr = .30, D = 12)	(Pr = .30, D = 5 or 7) (Pr = .10, D = 10 or 14) (Pr = .20, D = 12)

*The period for this example is one day. This is consistent with the period used for describing transit time. The conversion from annual costs assumes a 365-day year.

The demand and the transit time distributions must be combined to develop the demand during lead time distribution for use with Equation (18.2). Since there are two discrete distributions in the example problem, the demand during lead time distribution can be developed using the tree diagramming approach to enumerate the possibilities. For example, since the transport time is either 1 or 3 days for alternative 1 in Figure 18.7, and demand is either 5 or 7 units, the only possibilities are demands of 5, 7, 15, 17, 19, or 21 during the lead time. Each possible demand during lead time and its probability is given for each of the three transport alternatives in the bottom part of Figure 18.7. In addition, the mean and the standard deviation (σ_D) for each demand during lead time distribution has been calculated.

Exact solution methods

The solution of the example problem requires choosing the transportation alternative (1, 2, or 3), order quantity, and reorder point that will minimize the total cost [Equation (18.2)]. In this section we describe exact methods; i.e., methods that guarantee minimum cost. One method would be to use the iterative procedure to find the optimal value of Q and R for each transportation alternative. Then Equation (18.2) could be used to calculate the total cost for each transportation alternative using the optimal Q and R. The alternative with the minimum cost is the transportation alternative to use along with the optimal Q and R for that alternative.

Another method is to use partial enumeration to determine the optimal Q and R for each transportation alternative. First, the reorder point, R, is set equal to the maximum demand during lead time, (e.g., 21 units in the case of transport method 1 in Figure 18.6). Next the optimal value of Q and its associated total cost are calculated. Then the value of R is reduced by one, and a new Q value (and its associated total cost) are determined. R is again reduced by 1 and the process repeated until reductions in R begin to increase the total cost. The Q and R that produce the lowest total cost are optimal for the transportation alternative.

The results of applying the exact procedures to the example problem are summarized in Figure 18.8. The final choice is to use the first transportation alternative with $R = 19$ and $Q = 277$. The differences in total annual costs between alternatives are an indication of the potential savings from making the transportation and inventory decisions jointly. When several alternatives exist or the demand and lead time distributions are more complex, the exact procedures require considerable computation time. The heuristic method described next was developed to reduce these computation time requirements.

FIGURE 18.8 Exact solution to the example problem

Transportation alternative	*Reorder point (R)*	*Order quantity (Q)*	*Safety stock ($R - \bar{D}$)*	*Total cost per year**
1	19	277	5.8	$ 874.34
2	14	271	4.4	1,003.26
3	14	270	5.6	1,047.60

*Assuming 365 days per year.

Heuristic method

The heuristic method uses an estimation process to first choose a transportation alternative. The method does not guarantee that the choice will provide the lowest total cost. However, once the transportation alternative has been selected, all that remains is the calculation of the inventory parameters for that alternative.

The approach involves three phases. First, the exact procedure is used to determine the Q and R values that provide the minimum expected total cost for any one of the transportation alternatives. Second, those Q and R values are used with Equation (18.2) to calculate a total cost for each of the transportation alternatives. The alternative with the lowest total cost at this stage is selected as the transportation alternative for the problem. Finally, the Q and R values that minimize the total cost are determined for the alternative selected in the second phase—if it differs from that used in the first phase.

One additional simplification used in the heuristic method is the use of the normal distribution to approximate the distribution of demand during lead time. This is done even for such "non-normal" distributions as those in the example problem. The steps to making this approximation involve determining the mean and standard deviation of the demand during lead time. The mean is calculated as:

$$\bar{D} = AT \qquad (18.3)$$

The standard deviation is found using:

$$\sigma_D = (T\,\sigma_A^2 + A^2\,\sigma_T^2) \qquad (18.4)$$

The example problem, using transportation alternative 2 for the phase one calculation, will illustrate the heuristic method. First the exact procedure is used to find the Q and R values for transportation alternative 2. Using the exact enumeration procedure, we start with a reorder point of 19.2. This is 3 standard deviations of safety stock (i.e., $AT + 3\sigma_D = 9.6 + 3(3.2)$. The application of the enumeration procedure continues by calculating the expected total cost for successive Q and R values as the value of R is decreased until the expected total cost starts to increase in value. This occurs at $R = 14$ and $Q = 273$ for transportation alternative number 2. The reorder point of 14 implies a safety stock of 4.4 units $(14 - 9.6)$ which is 1.38 standard deviations above the mean demand during lead time.

The value of 1.38 standard deviations is used in phase 2 to estimate the amount of safety stock required for the other two transportation alternatives. This enables us to calculate the reorder point for each alternative. These reorder points and the order quantity (Q), determined for the starting alternative in phase 1, are used to estimate the total costs for the remaining transportation alternatives. The estimates are \$875.48 and \$1,047.68 for alternatives 1 and 3, respectively. Since the cost of alternative 2 was \$1,003.26 (see Figure 18.8) alternative 1 provides the lowest total cost and is selected for use.

In the experiments performed by Constable and Whybark, the heuristic procedure never failed to choose the same transportation alternative as the exact procedure, and it did so at a considerable savings of computer time. The maximum total cost penalty incurred by the heuristic procedure was less than 0.2 percent, even with the normal approximation for the lead time demand distribution. Interestingly, in more than half the cases, the lowest cost transportation mode was optimal. This gives some support to choosing low-cost transportation when the transport cost represents an important part of the cost of the product.

MULTIPLE ITEMS FROM SINGLE SOURCE

In this section we consider the economies of jointly ordering several items from a single source. In many independent demand situations, the stocking point may receive different items from the same source. Examples include most wholesale inventories, inventories of spare parts held in a central facility, and indirect supply items being purchased from a single vendor. Placing orders for several of these items at the same time can result in very significant inventory cost savings. Moreover, timing the orders to different vendors so that receipt of shipments is smoothed out can reduce warehouse costs for restocking, shelf space, and demurrage.

We treat joint ordering by successively increasing the amount of interdependency among the items considered. The first approaches presented are based on triggering the release of a joint order from individual item reorder points. Several methods for determining how much to order in total and how much of each item to order are presented. The next approaches base the release of the joint order on a group reorder point. We conclude the section with some experimental evidence of the savings possible from applying joint ordering techniques.

The joint ordering circumstance is so common that many companies have developed software packages for managing single supplier items. The approaches differ from package to package. These differences can lead to different service levels and inventory cost performances. The techniques illustrated in this section illustrate the differences. As a specific example, the last technique presented in this section is a modification of the approach used by IBM in their IMPACT package.

Methods based on individual item reorder points

An example problem is presented in Figure 18.9 for five items from the same source. In the example, the price and weight per unit, the forecasts, and the order quantities and reorder points have been calculated for each item independently. If the inventory were to be managed item by item, the only item to order this period (based on the present problem status) would be item A since it is the only item below its reorder point. The annual inventory carrying costs and ordering costs for managing these five items

FIGURE 18.9 Example: Five items from same source

Item	Price	Weight (lbs)	Monthly forecast Units	Monthly forecast $	Monthly forecast Lbs	Individual EOQ	Individual ROP	Current on-hand plus on-order
A	$1.10	5	100	110	500	330	79	50
B	.40	1	80	32	80	490	67	200
C	3.80	10	200	760	2,000	250	168	400
D	.25	.5	25	6	13	350	16	75
E	.05	.1	70	4	7	1,300	58	60
			475	912	2,600			

Individual order cost = $10
Joint order cost = $10 + $2/item

Inventory carrying rate = 20%/year
Full truck load quantity = 10,000 lbs.

independently are about $330 (applying equation (18.1) and ignoring the stockout and safety stock costs).

One approach to joint ordering is to place a single order whenever any *one* item drops below its reorder point. How much of each item to order could be determined from the individual economic order quantities. These quantities would then be used to construct one consolidated order. The choice of which items to order could be determined by how close each is to its reorder point. After including any items below reorder point, others could be added using the ratio of the current on-hand plus on-order to the reorder point. This assures ordering those items that are most likely to run out first. Individual items could be added to the joint order until some minimum dollar amount or weight is attained.

Applying this logic to the example problem would mean adding 330 units of item A first, 1,300 units of item E next, item C next, and so on until the joint ordering criterion was met. Note that not all items need to be ordered with this approach although all could be ordered. Using this approach does not necessarily result in a regular timing of orders from the vendor. The next order is placed when the next item reaches the reorder point, and that depends upon how many items are ordered this time, variations in usage rates, etc.

A method that does produce a regular cycle of orders to the vendor is based on developing a joint economic order quantity. This can be done by treating all the items from a vendor as a whole and determining an economic time between orders or an economic dollar value order. In general, the expression for the economic dollar value order is:

$$Q = \sqrt{\frac{2(\sum_i v_i A_i)C_p}{C_r}} \tag{18.5}$$

where:

$\sum_i v_i A_i$ = The total dollar volume per period for all items from the vendor. (v_i is the value of item i and A_i is the demand per period for item i).

C_p = The cost of placing an order which includes any costs per individual item.

C_r = The inventory carrying cost rate per dollar of inventory.

The economic time between orders is:

$$TBO = Q / \sum_i v_i A_i \tag{18.6}$$

Applying Equation (18.5) to the data in Figure 18.9 gives the following:

$$Q = \sqrt{2(912 \times 12)20/.2} = \$1{,}479$$

Note that the dollar forecast has been annualized and that C_p is $20, the joint order cost of $10 plus $2 for each of the five items. Applying equation (6) to this result gives:

$$TBO = 1{,}479/912 = 1.62 \text{ months}$$

The individual order quantities now must be established. Using the economic dollar value order basis, we could order each item in 1.62-month supply quantities. The results of applying this logic are shown in the first three columns in Figure 18.10 for each of the five sample items.

FIGURE 18.10 Three joint ordering alternatives for example using individual item reorder points

	Economic dollar value order		*Simultaneous reorder point*		*Full truck load*		
Item	*$*	*Item order quantity**	*Months supply over reorder point*	*Item order quantity†*	*Pounds over reorder point*	*Pounds to be ordered*	*Item order quantity‡*
A	$ 178	162	−.29	191	−145.0	2,520	504
B	53	130	1.66	—	133.0	247	247
C	1,232	324	1.16	92	2,320.0	7,180	718
D	10	41	2.36	—	29.5	30	60
E	6	113	.03	111	.2	33	330
	$1,479				2,337.7	10,010	

*1.62 months supply (1.62 × monthly forecast).

†For items with less than a 1.62 months supply over reorder point, order = 1.62 months supply − (on-hand + on-order).

‡4.75 months supply − (on-hand + on-order) all values in pounds.

Ordering each item in a 1.62-month supply leads to different quantities than using the EOQ for each item but suffers the same limitation. It ignores the present inventory positions. An alternative would be to order individual quantities so as to bring each item up to a 1.62-month supply above its individual reorder point. This takes into account the current inventory position and would mean all items would reach their individual reorder points at the same time if the forecast was perfect.

To illustrate the concept, item A's current inventory position of 50 is 29 units below its reorder point of 79. Thus, the order quantity would be 162 + 29 = 191 units. The middle section of Figure 18.10 shows the present inventory position of each item in terms of the number of months supply in excess of the order point. Items B and D do not need to be ordered because they have more than a 1.62-month supply over their order points. The order quantities are shown for those items that should be ordered. Note that this procedure will result in a regular pattern of orders to a supplier if the forecasts are generally correct.

A third alternative that uses individual reorder points is to base the combined order on some quantity discount or low-cost transportation alternative. For our example, a full truckload quantity is 10,000 pounds. When an order is made, the question is how to allocate the 10,000 pounds appropriately to the individual items. The analysis starts by noting that a 10,000-pound order represents a 3.85-month supply using the combined demand of 26,000 pounds per month for all items. When the individual item current on-hand plus on-order values are converted to pounds, there is an "excess" of 2,337.7 pounds above the reorder point. This is shown in the last section of Figure 18.10. This represents approximately a 0.9-month supply. Thus, if a 10,000 pound order is to be placed now, it must be placed so as to bring the total inventory to 4.75 (3.85 + 0.9) months above the reorder point quantities.

Allocating the 10,000 pound order to the individual items can be illustrated with item A. The present inventory is 29 units or 145 pounds below the reorder point value for this item. A 4.75-month supply in pounds is 2,375 pounds. To account for the 145 pounds below reorder point, the need is to order 2,520 pounds or 504 units of item A. The pounds and quantities of each item to be ordered are shown in the last section of Figure 18.10. Note the small rounding error in the number of pounds to be ordered.

One weakness of all procedures based on individual reorder points has to do with the service levels attained relative to the service levels expected. In each of these procedures, only *one* item, say item A, needs to be below the reorder point for the combined order to be placed. This means that other items might be above their reorder points, thus providing *higher* service than expected for them. On the next order it might be another item that is below reorder point, raising the service level for item A as well as for others.

This provision of "over-service" and higher than necessary inventory is difficult to overcome with methods where the joint order is triggered by individual reorder points. One "fix" is to specify the reorder points for the individual items so that they represent the *minimum* service level for each item. Note that only the item which is below reorder point will be exposed to this low service possibility. In the next section we look at treating the group as a whole for deciding when to place an order.

Methods based on group reorder points

In using individual reorder points to trigger joint orders, we have argued that individual item and group service levels would be higher than those associated with the independent reorder points. One way to overcome this problem is to create a group reorder point which will provide a service level for the group in total. This can be done by basing the joint reorder point on the individual ones. Several ways of doing this for the example problem of Figure 18.9 are summarized in Figure 18.11. Shown are reorder points that use units, dollars, and months of supply on hand as the basis for reordering.

The first group reorder point in Figure 18.11 is simply the sum of the individual reorder points. A joint order would be triggered whenever the combined inventory positions of items A through E fell below 388 units. This approach can combine "apples and bananas" in summing the reorder points. The second approach converts the item reorder points into dollars and sums these to find a group reorder point based on the dollar value of the joint inventory. The third alternative shown in Figure 18.11 is based on the reorder point for each item expressed in months of supply (dividing the reorder point by the forecast). The group reorder point is the arithmetical average of the individual reorder points. The final approach is similar but weights the group reorder point by the individual reorder points. This is done by dividing the sum of the reorder points by the total item forecast to get a group month's of supply. These same measures can be used to set group service levels directly by using the demand during lead time distribution measured in the same units.

To determine when to place a joint order, the group reorder point values are compared to the inventory position for all items in the group. When the

FIGURE 18.11 Group reorder point alternatives

	Item					*Group reorder point*
	A	*B*	*C*	*D*	*E*	
Reorder point units	79	67	168	16	58	388
Reorder point	$86.90	$26.80	$638.40	$4.00	$2.90	$759.00
Average reorder point month's supply	.79	.84	.84	.64	.83	.79
Weighted month's supply		388/475				.82

units, dollars, or months of supply *in total* fall below the group reorder point, a group order is placed. In each case, other tests can be added which prevent a single item from accumulating too many stockouts, falling below some minimum point, or being responsible for creating unjustified orders for everything in the group.

Once a group order is triggered, any of the approaches illustrated in Figure 18.10 can be used to determine the individual order quantities. For the group order point policies, however, only the last two methods shown in Figure 18.10 will provide relative balancing between items.

An alternative approach to joint ordering is to place orders on a single vendor on a periodic basis, where the period is based upon the economic order frequency, Equation (18.6). The quantities ordered could bring the inventory levels for each item up to the level necessary to provide the service desired until the next order. The orders for different vendors could be spread to smooth warehouse labor requirements.

Modified IMPACT

The IMPACT system from IBM contains joint ordering logic. A modified version is presented here with an example. The approach uses a group reorder point, based on desired group service levels, to determine when to place an order. The logic used for determining individual order quantities is simultaneous reorder point. The basic flow diagram is presented in Figure 18.12 and the definition of terms is provided in Figure 18.13. After describing the procedure an example is given.

Periodically the inventory is reviewed to see if an order should be placed. The decision is based on calculating the expected number of stockouts that would occur for each item if no order was placed. This involves determining the variance of the demand during lead and review time (step 7, Figure 18.12). The variance is used to determine how many standard deviations of each item are currently on hand (step 2). Calculating the expected number of stockouts if no order is placed is done next (step 3).

The total expected number of stockouts is compared to the group level required to meet desired service levels. The allowable level of stockouts is derived from the economic time between orders and the service level in step 8. If the total projected stockouts is greater than the allowed number, an order is initiated.

The order is made at least equal to the economic dollar value order in step 6. It is allocated so that each item has an inventory that will provide its service level and will reach the group reorder point at the same time as the other items given the current forecasts. The allocation is the MRD_j value in steps 9 and 13. Note that not every item needs to be ordered (steps 5 and 14). This cycle is expected to repeat every T periods, so labor smoothing can be done by scheduling other vendors' shipments at other times.

A numerical example of this procedure is presented in Figures 18.14–18.16. A two-product example is shown in Figure 18.14. The calculations in

FIGURE 18.12 Group ordering logic

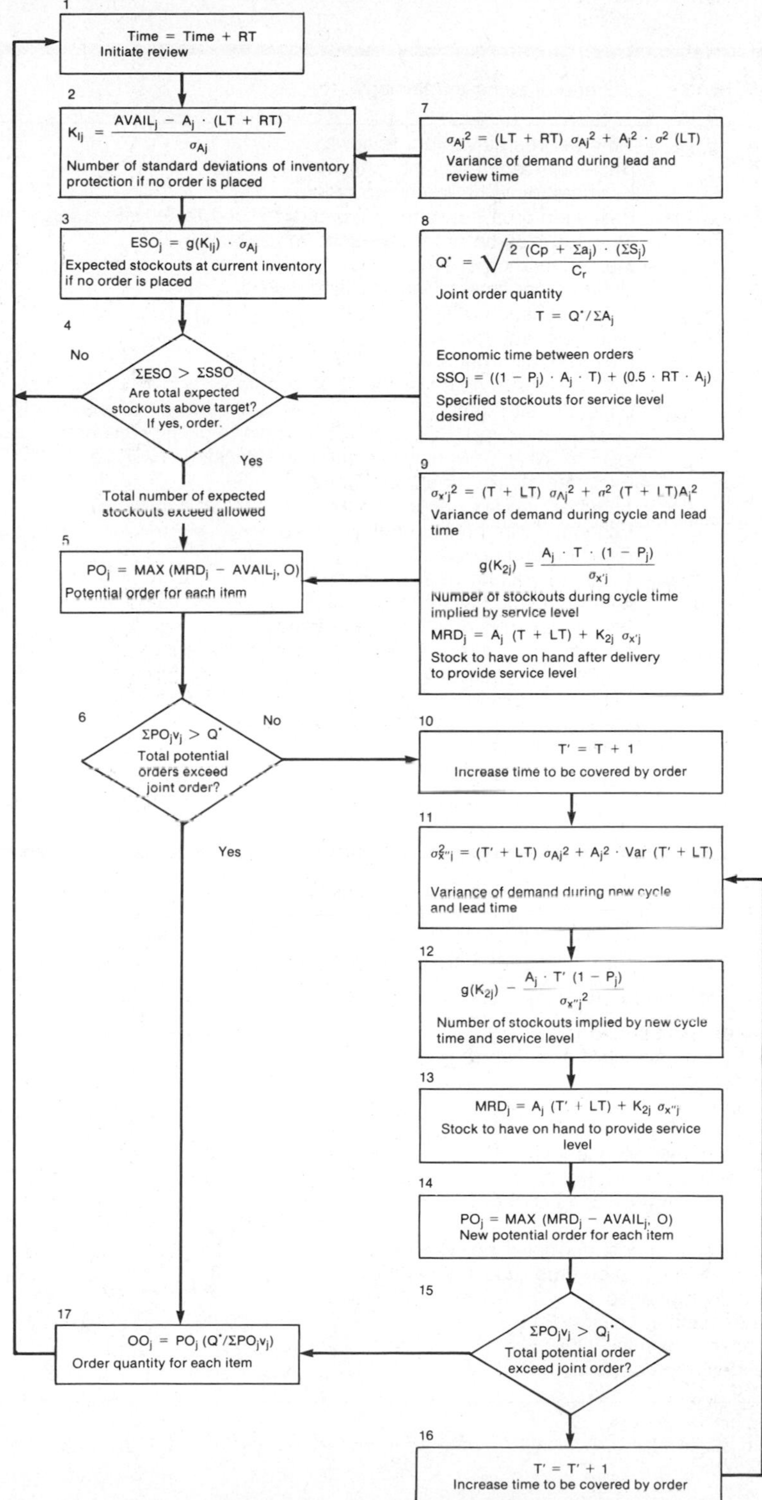

Source: Based on J. P. C. Kleijnen and P. J. Rens, "IMPACT Revisited: A Critical Analysis of IBM's Inventory Package—IMPACT," *Production and Inventory Management,* First Quarter, 1978.

FIGURE 18.13 Group ordering terminology

RT	= Time between inventory reviews
LT	= Replenishment lead time estimate
T	= Estimated time between two orders
T'	= Estimated time between two orders revised to provide a larger order
$AVAIL_j$	= On hand plus on order inventory (for item j)
A_j	= Mean demand per time period
σ_A	= Demand per time period standard deviation
X_j	= Mean demand during $LT + RT$
X_j'	= Mean demand during $LT + T$
X_j''	= Mean demand during $LT + T'$
K_{1j} and K_{2j}	= Number of standard deviations of inventory
$g(K_{1j})$ and $g(K_{2j})$	= Expected stockouts given K_1 and K_2 standard deviations of inventory [see, for example, R. G. Brown, *Decision Rules for Inventory Management* (New York: Holt, Rinehart and Winston, 1967), p. 179]
ESO_j	= Expected stockout amount during $LT + RT$
SSO_j	= Specified stockout amount during $LT + RT$ at service level P_j
Q^*	= Economic joint order quantity
C_p	= Fixed ordering cost
a_j	= Variable ordering cost (per item)
S_j	= Mean demand per period in dollars
C_r	= Inventory carrying cost rate per period
P_j	= Specified customer service level (percent of annual demand supplied directly from inventory)
MRD_j	= Maximum reasonable demand during $LT + T$ (or during $LT + T'$)
PO_j	= Preliminary order quantity in joint ordering
OO_j	= Final order quantity
v_j	= Value of item j

FIGURE 18.14 Example group ordering situation, period 1

	Product	
Parameter	*1*	*2*
Average demand period (A_j)	10	20 units
Demand period standard deviation (σ_j)	2	3 units
Annual demand*	2,600	5,200 units
Lead time (LT)	1	1 period (constant)
Review time (RT)	1	1 period
Desired customer service level (P_j)	.95	.98
Fixed ordering cost (C_p)	\$100	\$100
Variable (per item) ordering cost (a_j)	\$10	\$10
Unit cost	\$100	\$25
Inventory carrying cost per dollar per year (C_r)	.25	.25
Current on-hand plus on-order quantity ($AVAIL_j$)	8	50
Demand during period 1	2	26
Annual demand in dollars (S_j)	\$260,000	\$130,000
Independent ordering EOQ	151	428
Independent reorder point†	7	21

*260 periods per year.

†$[A_j(LT + .5RT)] + K_j\sigma_j$, with $\sigma_j^2 = (LT + .5RT)\sigma_{Aj}^2 + [(A_j^2\sigma^2(LT + .5RT)]$ and $g(K_{ij}) = [EOQ(1 - P_j)/P_j]/\sigma_j$.

Figure 18.15 show that no order is to be placed in period 1, even though there is a 12-unit stockout of item 1 expected. After demands of 2 and 26 units for items 1 and 2, respectively, an order needs to be placed in period 2. The calculations in Figure 18.16 shows how the economic dollar value order of $21,689 is allocated to the two products.

Simulation experiments

Kleijnen and Rens performed an extensive set of simulation experiments to evaluate the modified version of the IMPACT group ordering procedure. They studied this procedure in a wide variety of operating situations by varying the following factors:

The number of items per group.
The length of the review period (RT).
The ratio of the order interval to the review period (T/RT).
The ratio of the fixed to the variable ordering cost (C_p/a_j).
The ratio of the optimum to the actual joint order size (Q^*/Q).
The lead-time variance.
The variability of the desired customer service level values (P_j) in a group.

FIGURE 18.15 Example reorder calculations

Step	*Period 1*	*Period 2*
7	$\sigma_{A1}{}^2 = (1 + 1)(2)^2 + (10)^2(0)^2 = 8$	—
2	$K_{11} = \dfrac{9 \quad (10)(1 + 1)}{\sqrt{8}} = -4.24$	$K_{11} = \dfrac{6 - (10)(1 + 1)}{\sqrt{8}} = -4.95$
3	$ESO_1 = (4.24)(2.83) = 12.0$	$ESO_1 = (4.95)(2.83) = 14.0$
7	$\sigma_{A2}{}^2 = (1 + 1)(3)^2 + (20)^2(0)^2 = 18$	—
2	$K_{12} = \dfrac{50 - (20)(1 + 1)}{\sqrt{18}} = 2.36$	$K_{12} = \dfrac{24 - (20)(1 + 1)}{\sqrt{18}} = -3.77$
3	$ESO_2 = (.003)(4.24) = .013$	$ESO_2 = (3.77)(4.24) = 15.98$
8	$Q^* = \sqrt{\dfrac{2 \cdot 120 \cdot (260{,}000 + 130{,}000)}{.25}}$	—
	$= \$21{,}289$	
8	$T = 434/30 = 14.5$ periods	—
8	$SSO_1 = (1 - .95)(10)(14.5) + (.5)(1)(10)$ $= 12.25$	—
	$SSO_2 = (1 - .98)(20)(14.5) + (.5)(1)(20)$ $= 15.8$	—
4	$ESO_1 + ESO_2 < SSO_1 + SSO_2$ $12.013 < 28.05$	$ESO_1 + ESO_2 > SSO_1 + SSO_2$ $29.98 > 28.05$

FIGURE 18.16 Period 2 order quantity determination

Step	*Calculations*
9	$\sigma^2_{x'1} = (14.5 + 1)(2)^2 + (10)^2(0)^2 = 62$
9	$g(K_{21}) = \dfrac{10 \times (14.5)(.05)}{\sqrt{62}} = .92$
9	$MRD_1 = (10)(14.5 + 1) + (-.8)\sqrt{62} = 149$
5	$PO_1 = MAX\,(149 - 6, 0) = 143$
9	$\sigma^2_{x'2} = (14.5 + 1)(3)^2 + (20)(0)^2 = 130.5$
9	$g(K_{22}) = \dfrac{(20)(14.5)(.02)}{\sqrt{130.5}} = .51$
9	$MRD_2 = (20)(14.5 + 1) + (-.21)\sqrt{130.5} = 308$
5	$PO_2 = MAX\,(308 - 24, 0) = 284$
6	$\Sigma PO_j v_j > Q^*?$ $143(100) + 284(25) < 21{,}689$ $21{,}400 < 21{,}689$
10	$T' = T + 1 = 14.5 + 1 = 15.5$
11	$\sigma^2_{x''1} = (15.5 + 1)(2)^2 + (10)^2(0)^2 = 66$
12	$g(K_{21}) = \dfrac{(10)(15.5)(.05)}{\sqrt{66}} = .95$
13	$MRD_1 = (10)(15.5 + 1) + (-.84)\sqrt{66} = 158$
14	$PO_1 = \text{MAX}\,(158 - 6, 0) = 152$
11	$\sigma^2_{x''2} = (15.5 + 1)(3)^2 + (20)(0)^2 = 148.5$
12	$g(K_{22}) = \dfrac{(20)(15.5)(.02)}{\sqrt{148.5}} = .51$
13	$MRD_2 = (20)(15.5 + 1) + (-.21)\sqrt{148.5} - 327$
14	$PO_2 = MAX\,(327 - 24{,}0) = 303$
15	$\Sigma PO_j v_j > Q^*?$ $152(100) + 303(25) > 21{,}689$ $22{,}775 > 21{,}689$
17	$00_1 = 152(21{,}689/22{,}775) = 145$
17	$00_2 = 303(21{,}689/22{,}775) = 289$

The results of these experiments are summarized for four measures of performance (customer service, inventory carrying cost, ordering cost, and total cost) in Figure 18.17.

The experimental results indicate that the use of the joint ordering procedure can have a major effect on inventory system performance. The use of the joint ordering procedure reduced the total cost by nearly 50 percent in comparison with independent ordering. Much of this improvement came from the reduction in ordering costs, reflecting the objective of the joint ordering procedure. However, this procedure also dominates independent ordering in terms of inventory carrying cost due to the reduction in order quantities.

The modifications incorporated in the procedure provide actual customer service levels close to those obtained by independent ordering. Across all 16 experiments joint ordering averaged within .5 percent of the customer service level for independent ordering. Also, joint ordering is more effective than independent ordering when the actual customer service level is compared with the desired customer service level. The actual customer service level under joint ordering was less than the desired customer service level in half of the experiments, while under independent ordering this occurred in 10 out of the 16 experiments.

In this section we have evolved an ever expanding view of the "inventory" system and its objectives. First we looked at treating the reorder point and order quantity simultaneously. Next transportation considerations were added to provide a more global view. Finally we considered combined or-

FIGURE 18.17 Experimental results

Experiment number	*Customer service level ratio*[1]	*Inventory carrying cost ratio*[2]	*Ordering cost ratio*[3]	*Total cost ratio*[4]
1	.999	.489	.664	.555
2	1.041	.787	1.251	.896
3	.989	.452	1.649	.629
4	1.001	.337	.672	.423
5	1.015	.411	.441	.424
6	1.017	.400	.874	.579
7	.988	.599	.614	.605
8	.945	.269	.463	.339
9	.983	.558	.792	.630
10	.981	.361	.528	.430
11	.946	.351	.381	.364
12	.987	.525	.680	.592
13	1.012	.461	1.319	.686
14	1.015	.469	.651	.522
15	1.008	.179	.692	.348
16	1.000	.446	.864	.607
Average	.995	.443	.783	.539

Notes:

1. Average customer service level (group ordering)/average customer service level (independent ordering).
2. Average inventory carrying cost (group ordering)/average inventory carrying cost (independent ordering).
3. Average ordering cost (group ordering)/average ordering cost (independent ordering).
4. Average total cost (group ordering)/average total cost (independent ordering).

Source: J. P. C. Kleijnen and P. J. Rens, "IMPACT Revisited: A Critical Analysis of IBM's Inventory Package—IMPACT," *Production and Inventory Management,* First Quarter, 1978.

ders for individual items in a group. By achieving appropriate timing of these group orders, we can improve costs. This again is an expansion of the system view. The potential for improved cost performance that is possible using this expanded view should raise skepticism for single, narrow measures (e.g., 95 percent service level, order full carload only, etc.). The task is to determine what is really important and design the procedures accordingly.

ADVANCED CONCEPTS IN FORECASTING

At one time we planned to devote an entire chapter to advanced forecasting models. The reduction to a single section of this chapter is largely due to the recent research work of Spyros Makridakis and his colleagues. The research, which will be overviewed here, contains a key message for practice. It has been shown that simple forecasting models usually outperform more complex procedures, especially for short-term forecasting.

Our primary emphasis in this section, apart from overviewing the research, is on the *use* of forecasts. That is, how are data provided for forecasts and how are forecasts integrated into systems for the control of independent inventory items. One key organizational issue is consistency. The development of forecasts that are consistent across organizational entities and product groups is often more important than reducing the error produced by a particular forecasting method for a particular item. Thus we look at a method for providing consistency of the forecasts, pyramid forecasting.

Forecasts in independent demand inventory management

A great deal has been made of the idea of directly coupling a forecasting procedure to the calculation of the inventory parameters for managing independent demand inventories. Indeed, this concept has been applied in many software packages. For example, IBM's IMPACT package does contain a forecasting routine in addition to the inventory management modules. Research has shown that the suggested direct couplings of the forecasts to the inventory management shows great promise. There are great risks, however.

The laboratory environment doesn't have to contend with the data accuracy problems that industry does. Thus the "actual" demand used in a research experiment, for example, doesn't have clerical errors in it. The forecasts produced for the experiment come from a procedure that has been under the scrutiny of the experimenters and is probably used only by the experimenter. In contrast, human data errors, differences in people using the procedure, and surprises that can occur in industry argue for separating the forecasting function and the management of the inventories.

This is not an argument against the research. We must continue to create and test new ideas to improve forecasting performance in the long run. It is an argument to recognize the difference between the application world and the laboratory and to make the appropriate modifications to the theory to meet the application world's needs.

In preparing the forecasts, monitoring is a must, and some aspects of that can be routinized as a part of the system. Unexpectedly high or low demand should be screened and reviewed before being fed into the data base for making forecasts. Similarly, any "out-of-bound" forecasts should be reviewed. The techniques of demand and forecast monitoring should be incorporated into the system. The data fed to the forecast system can then be used with a relatively high level of confidence, and human skills can be devoted to the task of management.

Forecasting method comparison

A variety of forecasting techniques have been developed, and more are being created all the time. They range from very simple to mathematically complex, from aggregation oriented to stockkeeping-unit oriented, and from very costly to inexpensive. Among the techniques at the business planning level are those involving expert opinion and consensus, causal or regression approaches that link activities in one sector with those in another sector, and economic or business analysis approaches. For the more operations oriented forecasts the techniques range from attempts to characterize past data by using mathematical approaches (e.g., spectral analysis, Box-Jenkins or trigonometric patterns) to simple projections of past performance using moving averages or exponential smoothing.

Spyros Makridakis organized a forecasting competition in which seven experts evaluated 21 forecasting models. The competition was based on 1,001 different actual time series. Some of these were yearly, some quarterly, and still others monthly. Some of the series were micro data (e.g., for business firms, divisions, or subdivisions), and others were for macro data (e.g., GNP or its major components). Some series were comprised of seasonal data and others were not. Expert proponents of a variety of forecasting models analyzed the data, determined appropriate model parameters, and made forecasts of the series. The length of the forecasting horizon was varied from one to 18 periods into the future. Accuracy of the forecasts was determined with five different measures.

There was no one model that consistently outperformed all the others for all series, all measures, or all forecasting horizons. Some models do better than others on macro data while others are better for micro data. Similarly some models were better for monthly data than for quarterly or yearly data, and still others were good for longer forecasting horizons. Therefore, one conclusion that comes out of this work is that a forecast user can improve forecast accuracy by choosing a model that fits the criterion and the environment in which he or she is interested (e.g., micro versus macro data, short versus long horizon, and measure of accuracy).

Since managing the inventory of independent demand items involves short-term horizons, the general conclusion that simple methods do better than the more sophisticated models, especially over short horizons for micro data, is an important one. Techniques such as simple exponential smoothing tend to outperform sophisticated methods such as Box-Jenkins or econometric models.

A summary of the rankings for some of the procedures (for one period forecasting horizons) is given in Figure 18.18. For most of the criteria shown, the exponential smoothing models do quite well. Figure 18.18 is for all the 1,001 data series; the best techniques do even better for just the micro data. One of the surprises of the research is the performance of the combination technique. It indicates that the focused forecasting idea of selecting the *one* forecasting technique with the lowest error to make the forecast was partially right. It would be even better to average the forecasts from the several models that are used each period.

FIGURE 18.18 Performance rank for forecasting techniques among 21 methods for a 1 period planning horizon

	*Criterion**			
Method (all adjusted for seasonality)	MAPE (mean average percent error)	MSE (mean squared error)	Average ranking relative to all other techniques	Median APE (median value of percentage error)
Naive (forecast = current actual)	7	17	8	8
Moving average	15	20	10	11
Simple exponential smoothing	3	13	7	7
Exponential smoothing with trend	4	7	2	4
Exponential smoothing with trend and seasonal factors	4	7	2	2
Combination (an average of the forecasts from six methods)	1	10	1	1

*The best performance on the criterion is 1, the worst 21.

Source: Makridakis et al., "The Accuracy of Extrapolation (Time Series) Methods: Results of a Forecasting Competition," *Journal of Forecasting* 1, no. 2 (1982).

The important conclusion for practitioners is that more sophisticated and expensive is not necessarily better. It means that those who advocate the use of complex forecasting models need to justify their choice. They need to clearly demonstrate that they can provide better forecasts than the simpler procedures and that the error measures are consistent with the needs of the forecasts. This "show-me" attitude becomes even more important when one considers the preparation cost for using many of the sophisticated models. In addition to the computer and other costs one should also add the cost to the organization of using a procedure that is difficult for the non-expert to understand.

Forecasting consistency

Often forecasts are prepared for a variety of business decisions by many different people in a company. In addition to forecasts for *individual products* (units) used in scheduling operations, top managers utilize forecasts of *overall sales activity* (dollars) to plan and prepare budgets, and product managers frequently prepare forecasts for *groups of products*, e.g., by horsepower (units), package size (pounds), product brand (dollars), etc., in developing marketing plans for sales promotions, advertising, and distribution. The fact that sales forecasts are used for so many different decision-making purposes presents a significant coordination problem in many firms. Often these *independent* forecasts are never brought together within the organization to ensure that they are consistent and that the whole equals the sum of the parts.

One means of providing a consistency of forecasts for various purposes is through the bill of material (BOM). Using the BOM to pull together forecasts for different purposes may require special structuring of the bill. The "super bill" is one such example. The bill of materials forces a consistency to the forecasts by explicitly calling out the relationships. The constraint on forecasts for differing "levels" in the bill is a concept that lies behind other techniques for providing forecast consistency.

Another method of "constraining" the forecasts is pyramid forecasting. It provides a means of coordinating, integrating and forcing consistency between the forecasts prepared in different parts of the organization. These consistent forecasts can then be used to meet the needs in marketing, manufacturing, distribution, and so on. Implementation of techniques to constrain forecasting can be done in a number of ways, but we will focus on a specific example of pyramid forecasting.

The procedure used in implementing the pyramid forecasting approach begins with individual item forecasts at level 3 which are rolled up into forecasts for groupings of individual products shown as level 2 in the example in Figure 18.19. The forecasts for product groupings are then aggregated into a total dollar forecast at level 1 in the product structure. Once the individual item and product grouping forecasts have been rolled up and

FIGURE 18.19 Pyramid forecasting example

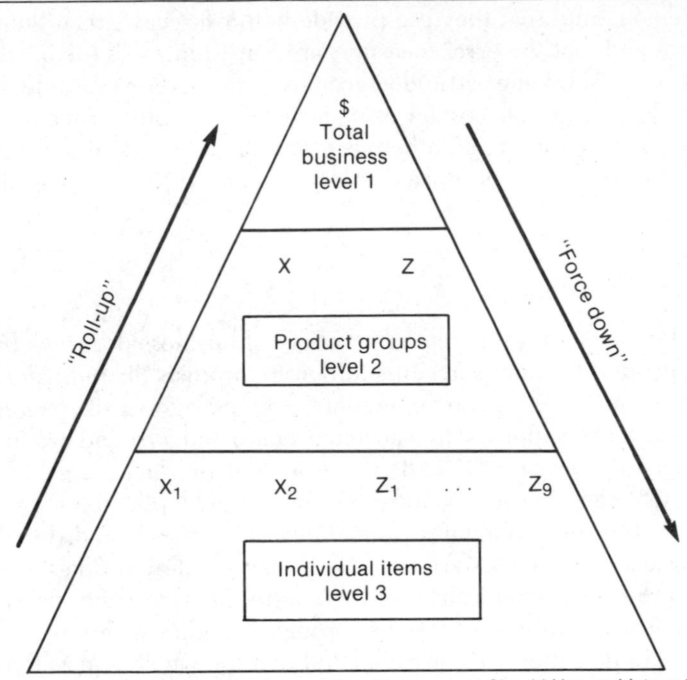

Source: T. L. Newberry and Carl D. Bhame, "How Management Should Use and Interact with Sales Forecasts," *Inventories & Production Magazine,* July–August 1981.

considered in finalizing the top management forecast (plan), the next step is to force down (constrain) the product grouping and individual item forecasts, so they are consistent with the plan.

In the example the 11 individual items are divided into two product groupings. Two of these items, X_1 and X_2, form product group X (which we will study in detail), while the remaining products, Z_1 through Z_9, are included in product group Z. These two product groups, X and Z, represent the entire line of products sold by the firm. The unit prices and initial forecasts for each level are shown in Figure 18.20.

The roll-up process starts by summing the individual item forecasts (level 3) to provide a total for each group (level 2). For the X group the roll-up forecast is 13,045 units (8,200 + 4,845). Note that this does not correspond to the independent group forecast of 15,000 units. If there is substantial disagreement at this stage a reconciliation could take place or an error might be discovered. If there is to be no reconciliation at this level, the independent forecasts for the groups need not be prepared. If dollar forecasts are required at level 2, the prices at level 3 can be used to calculate an average price. For our example the sum of the individual Z group items gives a forecast of 28,050 units for Z.

To roll up to the level 1 dollar forecasts, the average prices at the group level are combined with the group roll-up forecasts. The total of $778,460 (13,045 × 16.67) + (28,050 × 20.00) is less than the independent business forecast of $950,000. For illustrative purposes, we will assume that management has evaluated their business forecast *and* the roll-up forecast and has decided to use $900,000 as the forecast at level 1. The next task is to make the group and individual forecasts consistent with this amount.

The method for bringing about the consistencies is in the forcing-down process. The ratio between the roll-up forecast at level 1 ($778,460) and the management total ($900,000) is used to make the adjustment.

The forecasts at all levels are shown in Figure 18.21. The results are consistent forecasts throughout the organization, and the sum of the parts is forced to be equal to the whole. Note, however, that the process of forcing the consistency needs to be approached with caution. In the example, the forecasts at the lower levels are now higher than they were originally. Even though the sum of the parts equals the whole, there is a possibility that the people responsible for the forecast won't "own" the number. They must not be made to feel they are simply being given an allocation of someone elses wish list.

FIGURE 18.20 Initial and roll-up forecasts

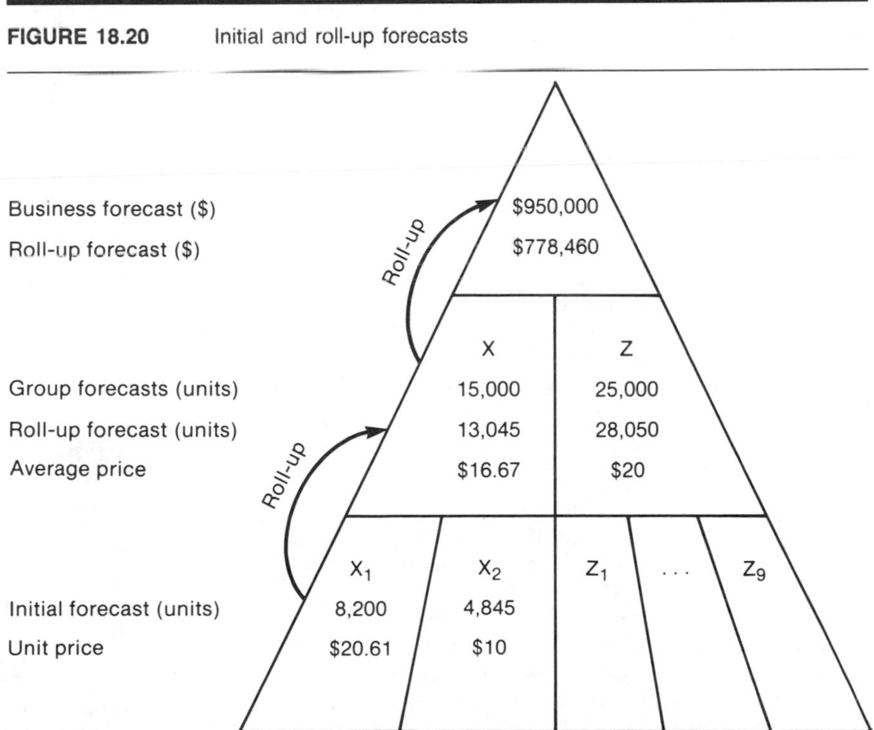

FIGURE 18.21 Forcing-down the management forecast of total sales

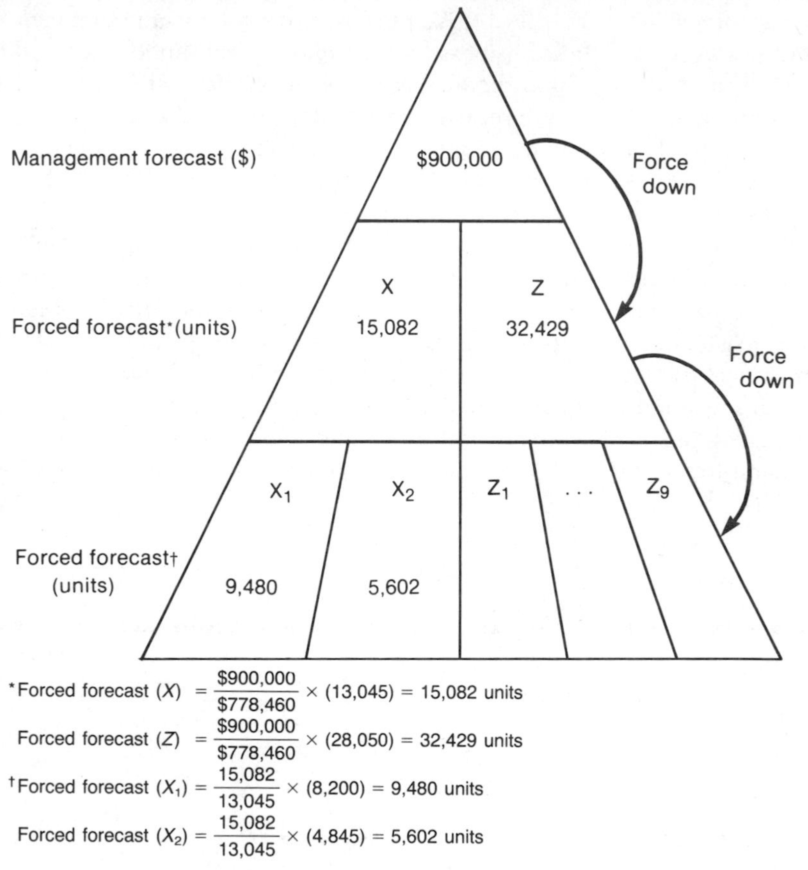

$$*\text{Forced forecast } (X) = \frac{\$900{,}000}{\$778{,}460} \times (13{,}045) = 15{,}082 \text{ units}$$

$$\text{Forced forecast } (Z) = \frac{\$900{,}000}{\$778{,}460} \times (28{,}050) = 32{,}429 \text{ units}$$

$$^{\dagger}\text{Forced forecast } (X_1) = \frac{15{,}082}{13{,}045} \times (8{,}200) = 9{,}480 \text{ units}$$

$$\text{Forced forecast } (X_2) = \frac{15{,}082}{13{,}045} \times (4{,}845) = 5{,}602 \text{ units}$$

LIVING WITH ADVANCED SYSTEMS

The installation of many of the advanced concepts discussed in this chapter depends upon having functioning basic systems and minds receptive to organizational change. Several managerial and technical notions are important in keeping the system from taking over. In this section, we will discuss some of these concerns.

The importance of organizational preparedness

The first and foremost concern in assessing the value of the advanced concepts for any organization is whether the basic systems are in place. Managers must have a clear understanding of fundamental relationships as well. If the service level reorder point trade-off is not understood *and* order quantities are not appropriately determined, the interaction between the two can not be well understood. Inventory accuracy, transaction procedures, systems for routine activities and effective warehouse, traffic, logistics and inventory groups must all be in place before advanced concepts should be implemented.

The concepts discussed in this chapter all require an expanded view of the system. For example, to incorporate the transportation dimension or to use procedures for group orders requires a non-provincial view of particular jobs. The implementation of some of these ideas change the roles of people in the organization. Flexibility and open-mindedness are required. The new coordination tasks may strain the capabilities of otherwise effective persons.

Once the organization is ready, these ideas can lead to improved performance and better response to problems. It depends upon whether the right rules and roles can be developed. Expectancies are important as well. A substantial number of small improvements over a large number of items can lead to large totals. But the payoff from any one inventory decision could be small and thus discouraging to the people.

Preparing the organization

Clearly one of the risks in systematizing the management of independent demand items, is that the system will take over; i.e., "it's the computer's fault." After one retail organization installed IMPACT, the buyers spent their time changing the suggested group orders because they were triggered by non-key items in the group. Their understanding of the system was insufficient to make it work *for* them. It is clear that one of the key elements in living successfully with advanced systems is training. If there is an insufficient understanding of the purposes, theory, and approach of the system, people will not use it effectively.

Training should be a continuous process. New people come into the organization, and trained ones move on to other tasks. Every now and then a thorough updating of the staff may be warranted. Training is important in monitoring the system outputs and inputs. Even though some of the technical monitoring approaches could be used, the key point is to not let silly things happen because someone doesn't understand.

To do routine things routinely means specifying the routine. This is a management task. With the routine things defined and systematized, the appropriate resources (information, training, authorities, etc.) need to be provided for solving the nonroutine problems. Again, this is the management task. The payoff from these efforts is increasing the productive use of human and system resources.

CONCLUDING PRINCIPLES

In this chapter we have presented advanced techniques for independent demand systems. Some of these techniques, such as ordering a group of items and pyramid forecasting, have already been implemented by manufacturing and distribution firms. They are presently enjoying the payoffs from these enhancements to their systems. In many other firms, however, the implementation of these advanced methods awaits the development of a properly functioning basic system; i.e., a system that is built on sound data and the timely handling of transactions. We conclude this chapter by summarizing several principles that we have observed concerning the methods presented in this chapter:

- A well-understood basic independent demand system must be in place before attempting to obtain further benefits from the advanced techniques presented here.
- Savings in inventory related costs can be achieved by a joint determination of the order point and order quantity parameters.
- Savings in firm-wide costs can be obtained by the joint consideration of decision-making activities that are often performed by different groups in an organization.
- Combined ordering of several inventory items obtained from a single source can provide important savings in inventory related costs.
- Simple forecasting techniques work better than sophisticated methodologies for short-term forecasts of micro data.
- The wide variety of demand forecasts prepared by an organization should be coordinated so that top management business plans and objectives are, in fact, reflected in the forecasts.
- Management must be sure their organization is prepared to take on advanced systems before attempting implementation.

REFERENCES

Ballou, Ronald H. "Estimating and Auditing Aggregate Inventory Levels at Multiple Stocking Points." *Journal of Operations Management* 1, no. 3 (February 1981), pp. 143–54.

Bryson, William L. "Profit-Oriented Inventory Management." *APICS 22d Annual Conference Proceedings*, 1979, pp. 88–91.

Constable, G. C., and D. C. Whybark. "The Interaction of Transportation and Inventory Decisions." *Decision Sciences* 9, no. 4 (October 1978), pp. 688–99.

Eilon, S., and J. Elmaleh. "An Evaluation of Alternative Inventory Control Policies." *International Journal of Production Research*, July 1968, p. 3–14.

Hadley, G., and T. M. Whitin. *Analysis of Inventory Systems*. New York: Prentice-Hall, 1963.

Johnson, L. A., and D. C. Montgomery. *Operations Research in Production Planning, Scheduling and Inventory Control*. New York: John Wiley & Sons, 1979, Chap. 2.

Kuehne, W. A., and P. Leach. "A Sales Forecasting Pyramid for Dow Corning's Planning Endeavors." *Production and Inventory Management Review*, August 1982.

Lewis, C. D., and A. L. Foo. "GIPSI—A General Purpose Inventory Policy Simulation Package." *International Journal of Production Research* 18, no. 1 (January/February 1980), pp. 73–82.

Silver, E. A. "Operations Research in Inventory Management: A Review and Critique." *Operations Research* 29, no. 4 (July/August 1981).

Smith, Bernard T. *Focus Forecasting Computer Techniques for Inventory Control*, CBI Publishing, 1978.

19

Logistics

Logistics encompasses all material flows, from the flows of purchased material into a facility, through the manufacturing processes, and out to the final customers. The primary emphasis in this chapter is on the outward flows of material through the physical distribution system. We are concerned with describing the elements of physical distribution systems and presenting some techniques for their management.

Improved management of logistics activities can lead to improvements in customer service. This can often be done while simultaneously reducing total inventory, transportation, and warehousing costs. Our attention has only recently been focused on improving productivity in logistics even though the potential has long been recognized. For example, logistics was described as the "Last Frontier for Profits" (by Peter Drucker in the 1950s) and "A 40 Billion Dollar Goldmine" (by the National Council of Physical Distribution Management and A. T. Kearney, Inc., in 1978).

The chapter is organized around the following six topics in logistics:

- A framework for logistics: What is the scope of logistics, and how do logistics decisions influence other manufacturing planning and control decisions?

- Physical distribution system elements: What are the primary activities and tasks in physical distribution?
- Distribution center (DC) replenishment system: How are systems for distribution center replenishment designed and operated?
- Distribution center location analysis: How are the number and locations of distribution centers determined?
- Vehicle scheduling analysis: How are vehicles used for delivery and/or pickup scheduled?
- Customer-service measurement: How are customer-service measures developed and used to evaluate logistics performance?

There are many linkages between this chapter on logistics and other chapters of the book. Since we treat purchasing material flows in Chapter 6 and much of the rest of the book is concerned with manufacturing material flows, we concentrate here on physical distribution. A closely related topic is demand management, covered in Chapter 10. Technical material on forecasting is found in Chapter 16, and on inventory management in Chapters 17 and 18.

A FRAMEWORK FOR LOGISTICS

We will soon turn to the detailed systems and models that are primarily oriented toward the flow of material outbound from manufacturing to the customers. Before doing so, however, it is useful to develop a context for logistics. In this section, we present an overview of the entire logistics activity, the need to look at overall costs, and the integrative viewpoint that should be taken by management.

The breadth of logistics

One definition of logistics encompasses all material-flow decisions, from raw materials to final consumption. Dealing with this entire spectrum at once is virtually impossible. However, when portions of the overall flow become rationalized, such as by component-part planning with MRP, it becomes more reasonable to increase the scope of study. Moreover, the materials management organization form applied in some companies fosters improved interactions among material-flow-related-problems.

Even when the area under study is only concerned with the more limited segment of the outward flows (i.e., physical distribution), the interactions with other manufacturing planning and control (MPC) systems are still of critical importance. The outward flow of materials from the factory is constrained by what is made available by the master production schedule (MPS). The replenishment of warehouse stocks can be considered (often erroneously) to be demand. Without proper system design, it is possible for chaotic factory conditions to be self-induced by physical distribution system decisions.

A framework for logistics recognizes the need for integrative thinking. We *know* that the MPS has to take into account the demands that are placed on manufacturing by physical distribution decisions. The need for coordinated design is clear. However, coordination should not stop at the boundary lines of the company. The final demand placed against physical distribution may be generated by customer purchasing systems. One firm's output can be the other firm's input. A proper view of logistics encompasses linking the decisions made in the firm with both those made by the firm's customers and those made by the suppliers.

The total cost concept

The basic idea in the total cost concept is that costs accrue and values are added by the various stages of product conversion and movement. That is, as raw materials become end products and are moved from manufacturing to the point of consumption, costs are added. The general goal is to minimize the total or overall cost while meeting customer-service goals. This is accomplished by reducing the suboptimization associated with treating each conversion or movement stage independently. If cost performance is improved by some action at one stage, at a more than offsetting cost disadvantage at another stage, the action is to be avoided. Further, if an action at one stage, although increasing costs at that stage, will provide a large cost savings elsewhere, it should be taken.

The total cost concept can be exemplified by a series of actions taken by Ethan Allen. A study of customer service provided by retail stores in the New York metropolitan area was undertaken. Each retailer maintained an inventory. In total, for the 40 retailers in the New York metropolitan area, the value of the inventory was about $3 million.

For an average customer order, the probability that all items desired would be in stock at a single retail store was approximately .25. This meant back ordering, long delivery times, etc. Ethan Allen created one large field warehouse that could be drawn upon by any of these 40 retailers. The retailers, in turn, would no longer carry separate inventories. The value of the inventory in this field warehouse was approximately $700,000, and the probability of filling an entire customer order from the warehouse stock increased to approximately .8. These actions required changes in delivered prices for the furniture, but the retailer no longer had inventory carrying costs. The total cost was clearly reduced. The key is to not permit parochial views of enterprise boundaries and accounting systems to impede progress.

Design, operation, and control decisions

It is clear that logistics decisions can be wide reaching. The impact of some decisions will be felt in more than one functional area of the firm, or even between firms. Making these decisions is not easy. In fact, the difficulties and potential payoffs are highly correlated.

The most basic logistic design decisions, such as the establishment of the Ethan Allen field warehouses, require top management action. This is also true for other basic logistics decisions, such as the number of warehouses, their locations, the type of replenishment planning system, and programs for interfirm cooperation.

The operation and control of logistics systems tend to be assigned to functional groups. In many companies, these functional groups are separated organizationally. In a growing few, there is a materials management form of organization that facilitates coordination.

A critical dimension of logistics management is to provide leadership for continued evolution. Once a subsystem is designed and operating, there is a natural tendency to feel that the problem is solved—forever. There is no ultimate weapon, and there is no ultimate logistics system. Improvements are always possible. As more and more subsystems become highly rationalized, transparent, and integrated through data bases, new improvement opportunities can be found. To do so, management must devote analytical resources to the study of logistics within the framework of the total cost concept.

An example of this evolutionary point of view is again provided by Ethan Allen. The New York field warehouse was an unqualified success. This led to the rapid establishment of 12 additional field warehouses in other metropolitan areas. All were successful. However, in a few years, most of the field warehouses were closed down. The reason is that the concept behind their success can be applied again. An even larger *regional* warehouse was established adjacent to one of the large Vermont factories. This warehouse provides one- to two-day deliveries to the entire eastern seaboard.

The most important aspect of this example is that Ethan Allen management was concentrating on the function of the warehouses—not the warehouses themselves. Some key issues are: How quickly must the delivery response be? Who are the customers? What do they really want? How do we reduce lead time variability? What are the costs of stock-outs? How do we measure customer service?

Many times the personal prestige of executives can impede evolution in logistics. The executives at Ethan Allen who were instrumental in the field warehouse program could not regard their closure as a personal failure. The program was a success, and it led the way to the achievement of even further progress.

An overall framework for logistics implies the need for evolution and integration. The management of manufacturing must necessarily be integrated with logistics material-flow decisions. So must many aspects of marketing. The objective is continuous and rapid evolution in the understanding and management of the total scope of logistics.

We now leave this overall focus and turn to some more detailed aspects of logistics. In particular, we will address some technical issues in physical distribution. We will provide some examples of application, as well. As we treat individual topics and recognize that each of the physical distribution issues is important, we do not, however, want to lose sight of the overall direction implied in the framework of logistics.

PHYSICAL DISTRIBUTION SYSTEM ELEMENTS

In this section, we provide general descriptions of some basic elements of physical distribution. We deal with the *physical attributes* of systems for distributing products to customers. The management and information system issues will be addressed in subsequent sections.

Specifically, we want to identify some of the key characteristics of transportation, warehouses (we will use the term *distribution centers*), and inventory. For each of these physical distribution system elements, the intent is to understand the functions performed. Basically, these elements deal with the place and time utility of the products. Manufacturing provides the form utility.

Transportation

Physical distribution is concerned with the movement and storage of products. Achieving the former requires some method of transportation. There are a variety of modes available, and technological change is fairly rapid. Evaluation of transportation alternatives is, therefore, an ongoing need.

For example, there are companies that now move coal and fish in pipelines, automobiles are moved by ship, and many finished and semifinished products are moved by air. The most common modes of transportation are air, rail, truck, pipe, and combinations of them. Among these modes, however, are alternative ownership/management forms. For example, there are private carriage, courier, common carrier, and contract services, cooperative arrangements and forwarding agents. Our purpose here is not to discuss these in detail, but to point out the need for having access to someone with expertise in this area. We also want to focus on the key transportation variables and their impact on physical distribution planning and control decisions.

One of the prime considerations in product movement is cost. There are substantial quantity discounts for shipping large volumes of products. Specifically, there are large cost differences between less than carload (LCL) or truckload quantities and full carload (CL) or truckload quantities. This does not literally mean that a "full" carload must be shipped to get the discount, but that more than some specific weight must be shipped. The extent of freight rate differences is illustrated by Figure 19.1.

Another major variable in the determination of transportation costs is the selection of routing. Several options usually exist for delivering products to multiple customers. Drop privileges, for example, may enable the manufac-

FIGURE 19.1 Example freight rates for trucks between Chicago and Los Angeles

Household effects		*Machine parts*	
Weight (lbs.)	*Rate (per cwt)**	*Weight (lbs.)*	*Rate (per cwt)**
7,000	$42	24,000	$17.78
10,000	$37	25,000	$ 9.99

*cwt = Hundredweight or 100 pounds.

turer to combine shipments to two or more customers, thereby gaining lower freight rates. Clever combinations of customers into shipping schedules can result in substantial savings. This is illustrated in Figure 19.2, which also shows how the number of alternatives to evaluate for even a simple example can be quite large.

In Figure 19.2, five alternatives are evaluated; the cost from lowest to highest is nearly double. Such extremes are not unusual at all. For companies with private fleets, the vehicle scheduling activities (about which more will be said later) are the equivalent of the routing activities. They can have an important impact on costs.

FIGURE 19.2 Alternative routing example to serve two customers

Locations and weights

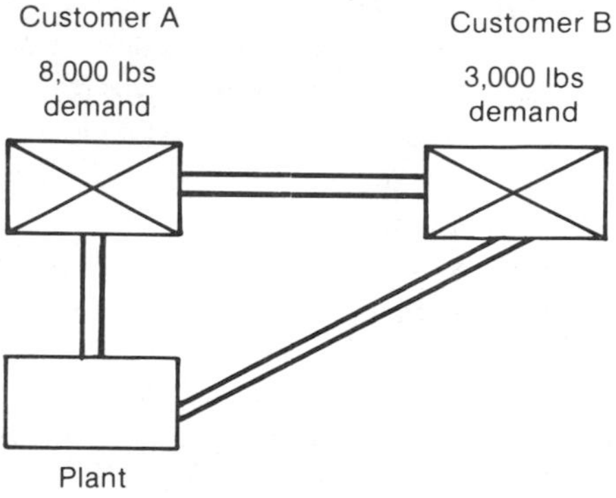

Customer A
8,000 lbs demand

Customer B
3,000 lbs demand

Plant

Rate schedules

Route	*Weight*	*Cost/cwt*
Plant to B	0–10,000 lbs	$ 8
Plant to B	>10,000 lbs	$ 6
Plant to B via A	0–10,000 lbs	$10
Plant to B via A	>10,000 lbs	$ 5
Plant to A	0–10,000 lbs	$ 7
Plant to A	>10,000 lbs	$ 5
Plant to A via B	0–10,000 lbs	$11
Plant to A via B	>10,000 lbs	$ 9
A to B	0–10,000 lbs	$ 5
A to B	>10,000 lbs	$ 3
B to A	0–10,000 lbs	$ 5
B to A	>10,000 lbs	$ 3

Alternative routes	*Costs*
Ship A to A and Ship B to B	($8,000/100) × 7 + ($3,000/100) × 8 = $ 800
Ship A and B to B and drop A	($11,000/100) × 5 + 20 = $ 570
Ship A and B to A and drop B	($11,000/100) × 9 + 20 = $1,010
Ship A and B to A and ship B to B	($11,000/100) × 5 + ($3,000/100) × 5 = $ 700
Ship A and B to B and ship A to A	($11,000/100) × 6 + ($8,000/100) × 5 = $1,060

Drop charge = $20/drop (any weight).

Another aspect of transportation is trade-offs between speed, price, and reliability. In general, the faster a mode, the more costly (e.g., airfreight is more costly than trucks). But a more subtle consideration is that of reliability or the variance around the average speed (lead time). Clearly, the greater the variance around the average lead time, the more safety stock or safety lead time is necessary. From a management point of view, safety stock levels are directly affected by the choice of transportation mode and routing, since these will offset the uncertainty in demand during lead time (DDLT).

Distribution centers (DCs)

We have been asked by very serious practitioners why a company should have warehouses (distribution centers) at all. Ethan Allen answered that question one way for the eastern seaboard. From the customer standpoint, though, the benefit is in time *and* place utility. That is, the warehouse locates the product closer to the customer in both distance and time. Whether this is worthwhile is a function of the market value of product proximity. Many executives have commented that there is a positive competitive advantage and market response to warehouses located near to the market. We dub this the "warm puppy effect." That is, having a distribution center nearby gives the customers a more comfortable feeling about service. Very little work has been done to quantify this effect, however, so the best that we can do at the moment is to calculate the costs of having warehouses and determine whether the value of proximity is likely to exceed these costs or not.

Distribution centers have other functions than the warm puppy effect. In multiplant operations, the distribution centers (DCs) can mix the products from several plants for shipment to customers or to other distribution centers. As an example, General Foods ships full car-/truckloads of unmixed quantities from plants to distribution centers, mixes the products from several plants, and reships full car-/truckloads to other distribution centers and customers. This allows them to take advantage of full carload rates *and* get the right mixture of products to locations.

Another function that can be performed at the DC is completing or packaging the product. Shipping in bulk and finishing the product at the distribution center permits the manufacturer to delay the addition of that value until the last possible moment. It is also possible that it can be done with less expensive labor and with better information on local product needs. Note that product completion and/or packaging at the warehouse necessitates additional MPC systems to plan and control these activities.

One final distribution center function is providing a point to break bulk. This is an opportunity to take partial advantage of the substantial difference between LCL (less than carload) rates and CL (carload) rates for shipping products. By putting a DC in a region, the product can be transported into that region at the CL rate, and then can be delivered to customers at the

FIGURE 19.3 Example cost comparison LTL versus full truckload Chicago to California

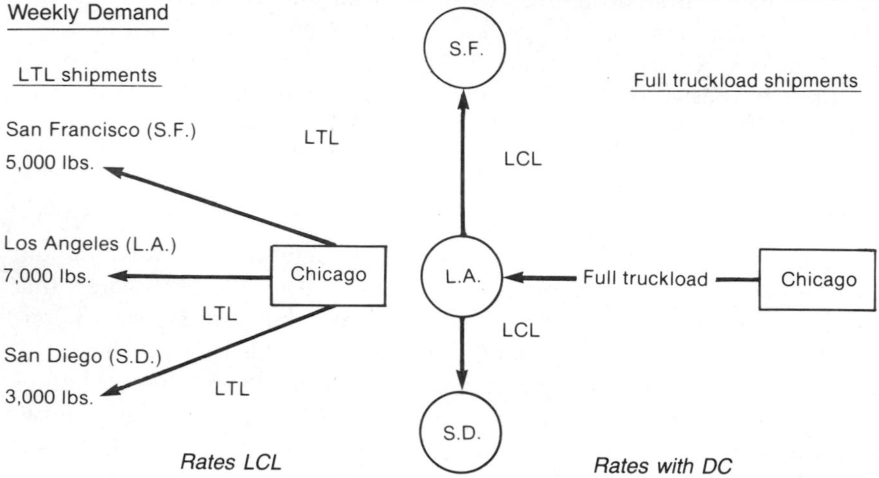

Weekly Demand

LTL shipments

San Francisco (S.F.) 5,000 lbs.

Los Angeles (L.A.) 7,000 lbs.

San Diego (S.D.) 3,000 lbs.

LTL

Chicago

LTL

LTL

S.F.

LCL

L.A.

LCL

S.D.

Full truckload shipments

Full truckload

Chicago

Rates LCL

Chicago–SF	\$15.00/cwt
Chicago–LA	\$16.00/cwt
Chicago–SD	\$16.00/cwt

Cost/week =	50 × 15 =	\$ 750
	70 × 16 =	1,120
	30 × 16 =	480
Total		\$2,350

Rates with DC

Chicago–LA	\$9.00/cwt
Local–LA	\$1.00/cwt
Local–SF	\$3.00/cwt
Local–SD	\$2.00/cwt

Cost/week =	150 × 9 =	\$1,350
	50 × 3 =	150
	70 × 1 =	70
	30 × 2 =	60
Total		\$1,630

LCL or local delivery rate. Consider, for example, shipment of products from Chicago to the Southern California region. An example of two alternatives is given in Figure 19.3. The example shows a potential cost savings of \$720 per week from a Los Angeles-based DC. This potential savings can be compared to the cost of operating the DC.

Inventory

Several functions of inventory will be mentioned before completing this section on the elements of the physical distribution system. Some of the marketing reasons for inventory are the maintenance of a full line of products, the provision of adequate display stock, or the provision of full inventory pipelines through the channels to each distribution center. Let us now turn to some key operational considerations of inventory in physical distribution.

Inventory performs a buffering role in physical distribution, but much confusion exists over the use of order quantities for buffering against uncertainty. Some firms incorrectly believe that order quantities should be increased when demand becomes less certain (i.e., the forecast error increases). In fact, it is safety stock that should be managed to buffer against increased uncertainty, not order quantities. In general, to increase safety stock, the order point needs to be raised, not the order quantity. Changes in the order quantity should be made as a result of changes in the inventory carrying cost, changes in the setup costs, changes in quantity discounts or transportation costs, etc.

Safety stock is a function of the demand during lead time. The uncertainty is influenced by the choice of transportation mode as well as the variability in demand rate. For each location, then, there is a possible need for safety stock. Each location will also have cycle stock, which is the result of shipping in economic quantities. Although safety stock and cycle stock interact, in this chapter we ignore the interaction in illustrating an important trade-off to be considered in designing the logistics system. This trade-off involves the pooling of safety stock at fewer locations to realize inventory savings.

The impact of pooling safety stocks must be evaluated against the possible advantage (product proximity) provided by a larger number of distribution centers. The potential savings in safety stocks are demonstrated in Figure 19.4, assuming a one-period lead time. Providing the service level of 95

FIGURE 19.4 Example safety stock savings from distribution center consolidation

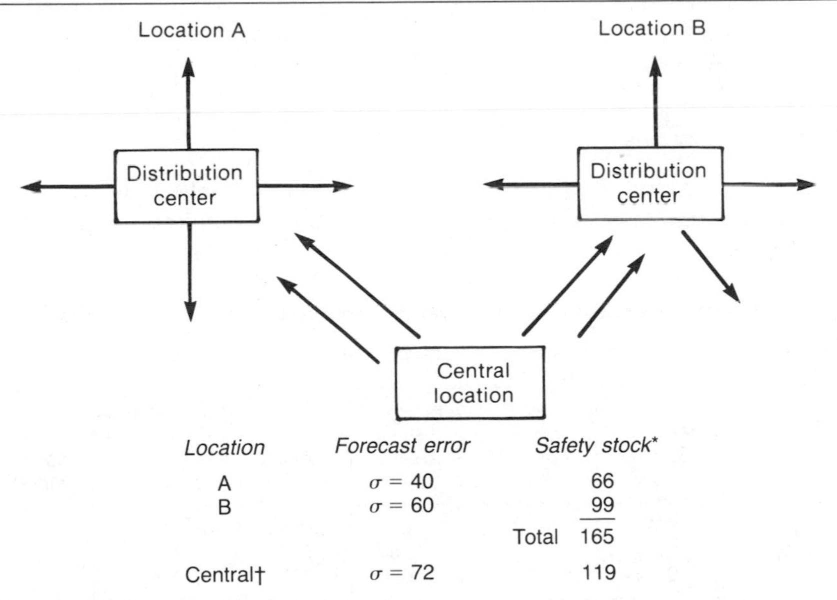

Location	*Forecast error*		*Safety stock**
A	$\sigma = 40$		66
B	$\sigma = 60$		99
		Total	165
Central†	$\sigma = 72$		119

*For 95 percent service level.

†Assuming independent forecast errors at A and B:

$$\sigma \text{ Central} = \sqrt{\sigma A^2 + \sigma B^2} = \sqrt{40^2 + 60^2} = 72$$

percent (the percent of demand that can be satisfied from stock at both A and B) requires 165 units of safety stock, while consolidation at a central location requires only 119 units. This is the same phenomenon that Ethan Allen capitalized on both in creating the New York warehouse, and later in creating the eastern seaboard regional warehouse.

The potential saving from distribution center consolidation of safety stock has led many firms to devise mixed service strategies. Since consolidation locates the inventory farther from the customers, delivery time may be increased. On the other hand, the savings from reduced safety stock may more than compensate for this reduction in service with some categories of products. The mixed service strategy provides different levels of service for different categories of products. Providing, for example, service levels of 95 percent for A items, 85 percent for B items, and 70 percent for C items, can lead to substantial savings in inventory, as shown in Figure 19.5.

Thus far, we have discussed the three basic elements of a physical distribution system: transportation, distribution centers, and inventory management. We now turn to the information system used to manage the routine replenishment of physical distribution inventories.

DISTRIBUTION CENTER (DC) REPLENISHMENT SYSTEM

In this section we describe three basic alternatives to distribution center replenishment: reorder point/economic order quantity (ROP/EOQ), base stock, and distribution requirements planning (DRP). We will concentrate on the operational differences between these three systems: the basis for deciding when to ship, how much to ship, which location makes the decision, and the information required. Figure 19.6 summarizes these issues.

ROP/EOQ systems

Historically, and perhaps currently, the dominant method for determining the amount to be shipped is the use of an economic order quantity, purchase quantity, or shipping quantity, and a reorder point to establish the

FIGURE 19.5 Example safety stock saving with mixed service level policy

	Constant service level			*Mixed service level*		
Item category	*Service level*	*Forecast error (σ)*	*Safety stock*	*Service level*	*Forecast error (σ)*	*Safety stock*
A	95%	100	165	95%	100	165
B	95%	100	165	85%	100	104
C	95%	100	165	70%	100	53
	Total		495	Total		322
Percent of saving in safety stock inventory = (495 − 322)/495 = 35%						

FIGURE 19.6 Three alternative DC replenishment systems

System	*When to order/ship*	*How much to ship*	*Where is decision made*	*Information system complexity*
Reorder point/ economic order quantity	DC actual inventory reaches reorder point	Economic lot size based on forecast or average usage	DC	Low
Base stock	Scheduled shipment dates	Actual usage in previous period	Central location	Medium
Distribution requirements planning	Projected on-hand balance offset by lead time	Economic shipment quantity based on projected time-phased usage	Central location	High

timing of the shipment. As seen in Figure 19.6, the actual inventory balance in the DC is used to determine when the inventory reaches the reorder point. At that point, an order is released by the DC and placed with the central resupply location. Order placement varies from mail forms to on-line communications. Any time delays between order placement by the DC and order receipt by the resupply point have to be compensated for with longer lead time.

The shipment quantities are determined, using economic order quantity methodology. The expected demand is assumed to be constant, and is based on past averages or a forecast of future demand. The quantity determination can incorporate quantity discounts and transportation economies, if necessary. Both are treated in the same analytical way. Other practical considerations such as full-case, full-pallet, or mixed-product carloads can also be taken into account.

A key aspect of ROP/EOQ replenishment systems is that the decisions are made at the DC level. From an information point of view, this means that the central location does not have to maintain inventory records or process detailed DC transactions. The complexity of the information system is low. Information handling and decision making are decentralized.

A fundamental disadvantage in the classic ROP/EOQ replenishment system is that the information received by central has been filtered by the individual decision processes at each of the DCs. That is, the demand being expressed by customers is seen by the DCs individually. The way in which this demand is transmitted to central is influenced by the parameters of the ROP/EOQ system in use at each DC. The problem is often compounded by the fact that the selection and modification of the system parameters are also done by DC personnel. There is a natural tendency for amplification. As end-customer demand grows, for example, adjustment of parameters often results in a larger growth in the orders being placed by the DCs on the central inventory.

Still another problem with the pull orientation of ROP/EOQ systems occurs when the demand on central in a particular time period exceeds the available supply. Some form of allocation is necessary, but without detailed DC information, the allocation will necessarily be somewhat arbitrary. In a similar vein, phased withdrawals of products will tend to be uneven at different DCs. Also, the ability to cross-ship between DCs will be reduced. The implication is that centralized information can yield more effective distribution inventory management.

Base stock systems

There are two distinguishing features of the base stock system. The first is the separation of the information flow on end-item demand from replenishment order data. That is, information on actual end-item demand is fed back to all stages in the logistics chain, including the factory. This feedback allows certain key decisions to be based on data that have had no amplification. The data can be transmitted as received at the DC with on-line communication systems or batched for daily or longer time period processing. The second distinguishing feature of the base stock system is the establishment of a routine replenishment cycle. In its simplest form, the base stock system uses a direct replacement system. That is, the exact amount sold by a warehouse during a fixed time cycle is replenished at the next shipment time.

The base stock quantities for each DC are set to cover the maximum expected demand for each item during the lead time necessary to replenish the DC. When the next delivery is scheduled to leave for a DC, the quantity shipped for each item is the quantity sold since the last delivery plus any adjustments to the base stock level. If, for example, a truck goes to a DC on a weekly basis, the quantity shipment would replenish the actual usage in the previous week (if there were no information-processing delays).

The base stock system is predicated on the determination of a shipping frequency to each distribution center. This is seen in Figure 19.6 as the when to order/ship decision. In determining this frequency, a major tradeoff is larger shipments made with less frequency, which can reduce transportation costs, versus smaller shipments made more frequently, which can reduce DC inventory carrying costs.

Although Figure 19.6 shows the base stock system shipment quantities as equal to the actual usage in the previous period, convenient shipping sizes can also be accommodated. For distribution center replenishment, there will almost always be the issue of pack sizes, full pallet quantities, etc. This is accommodated by measuring actual demand in the pack or pallet sizes and providing some gross to netting at the DC.

The base stock system incorporates centralized decision making. Rather than having DCs determine when and how much to ship, these decisions are routinized with centrally determined parameters and monitoring. The result is better coordination of central inventory resources and multilocation demands. The cost is increased information handling.

A recent application of the base stock system is the Kanban system which is being used in many Japanese manufacturing companies. It is a base stock system—applied in a manufacturing environment. As a user department actually uses parts provided by a supplier department, the information is passed back to the supplier department. The form of information is empty containers to be refilled with parts by the supplier department and passed on to the user department. In other words, the system is designed to have the supplier department replace the parts the user department just used.

The Kanban system *inside* the factory is based upon a fixed lot size (the number of items in a container). The periodicity or timing of the replenishment order varies, but lots are so small that, in general, several lots are made in a single day. When the system is applied to vendors, it is more like the distribution base stock system. The vendor brings in a variable number of items on a fixed delivery cycle. The number of items in a batch is essentially what was just used in production.

Distribution requirements planning

The primary distinguishing feature of distribution requirements planning (DRP) is the use of time-phased projected future usage. This means that the determination of when to ship an order is based on a projected inventory position and the shipment is made in anticipation of inventory availability as opposed to reacting to an actual inventory position. The determination of the shipping quantity is similarly made from time-phased projected usage information. This means that replenishment can be based on the best estimates of future needs, with possibilities of combining future requirements to fill trucks or railcars for shipment to the distribution centers.

The distribution requirements planning process logically begins at the field location, which we will continue to call a distribution center, although it could be a warehouse, dealer, or even a customer location. Note, however, that the *decisions* are not made at the field location. The first step is the development of a forecast of the *independent* demand for each stockkeeping unit at the distribution center. The forecast can be produced by judgment, by allocating some global forecast by percentages, by using any of the statistical techniques, or by some combination of methods. An example of a DC time-phased record appears in Figure 19.7.

In Figure 19.7, the forecast appears as the gross requirements would in an MRP record. As can be seen, the forecast for the first four weeks is for 20 units, and 30 units for the next three. The difference in forecasts can come about because of seasonal factors in an exponential smoothing model, planned promotions for a product, timing preferences of customers in the particular distribution center, or a host of other reasons. In practice, it is

FIGURE 19.7 Distribution center DRP record

		Period						
		1	2	3	4	5	6	7
Forecast requirements		20	20	20	20	30	30	30
Scheduled receipts			60					
Projected available balance	45	25	65	45	25	55	25	55
Planned shipments				60		60		

Safety stock = 20, shipping quantity = 60, lead time = 2.

critical to have an evaluation of the forecast made by both marketing and distribution center people. This is particularly important if the forecast is machine generated. The people can take into account the nonrecurring intangibles such as promotions, customer timing preferences, introductions of new products, competitive actions in the distribution center region, and the need for the sum of DC forecasts to be synchronized with overall forecast levels.

Once the forecast has been determined and put into the records, MRP logic applies for determining the planned shipping releases (equivalent to planned order releases in the manufacturing environment). Whenever forecast information is used as the gross requirements, and a time-phased MRP approach is used to develop the planned shipments, it is called *time-phased order point (TPOP)*. The planned shipping quantities typically are heavily influenced by carload, truckload, and palletload considerations.

There are advantages to using the time-phased order point (TPOP) approach, even when the best forecast of future requirements is for some constant average usage. Since the constant usage assumption is incorporated into the reorder point/economic order quantities (ROP/EOQ) model, an alternative to TPOP is ROP/EOQ. To show the advantages of TPOP, we use Figure 19.8.

If an ROP/EOQ system were used, the reorder point for the situation depicted in Figure 19.8 would be the safety stock (10) plus the demand during lead time (15, assuming continuous review of inventory balances), or 25 units. Note that the planned shipments are in periods 1, 3, and 6. The *beginning* inventories for these periods are 22, 32, and 27 respectively. Thus, the timing of the orders in the record shown in Figure 19.8 does *not* exactly match the timing of orders using ROP/EOQ, e.g., when the inventory level reaches 25 units.

The results are, however, very close. The differences are primarily due to the fact that ROP/EOQ assumes continuous review, whereas MRP logic is based on periodic (i.e., each bucket) review. Also, the TPOP approach is based on the MRP logic of triggering (planning) an order so that the ending balance in the period when the order arrives will not be below the safety stock level.

One advantage of TPOP over ROP/EOQ is that the TPOP record shows the *planned* shipment data. These are not a part of ROP/EOQ. Moreover, these data are not a part of the base stock system either. By generating all the planned shipment data, actual shipments can be based on this enhanced information.

TPOP is not limited to the use of constant requirement assumptions. When forecast usages vary, the differences between TPOP and ROP/EOQ will be much larger than those shown in Figure 19.8 (see, for example, Figure 19.7).

Of even more importance is the concept of demand management. Forecast sales requirements are only one source of demand input. DRP can use TPOP, plus actual order data, plus service-part requirements, plus interplant demands. *All* of these demand sources can be integrated into the demand data driving DRP.

Another advantage of the TPOP record with MRP logic is the gross to net capability. As actual demands occur, the inventory is adjusted and the entire time-phased record is regenerated to reflect up-to-date actual results. For example, suppose that the actual withdrawals during period 1 were 5 instead of the 15 forecast for the DC shown in Figure 19.8. The planned shipment of 40 currently in week 3 would appear in week 4 after the record is regenerated at the end of week 1. The result of these changes is a constant adaptation to actual conditions.

FIGURE 19.8 Example distribution requirements planning TPOP record

		Period						
		1	*2*	*3*	*4*	*5*	*6*	*7*
Forecast requirements		15	15	15	15	15	15	15
Scheduled receipts								
Projected available balance	22	7	32	17	42	27	12	37
Planned shipments		40		40			40	

Safety stock = 10, shipping quantities = 40, lead time = 1.

Once the planned shipping schedule has been determined for each DRP record for each distribution center, these data are combined for the central warehouse. This process is illustrated in Figure 19.9. Distribution center number 1 is the one that is detailed in Figure 19.7 and DC number 2 in Figure 19.8. The combined planned shipments for both DCs become the gross requirements at the plant or central warehouse level. The usual MRP logic determines the planned order releases at this level, except that we have shown a zero lead time. This is a convenient device for creating a record which becomes the basis for master production scheduling.

The MPS is treated as a set of firm planned orders. The planned order releases shown in Figure 19.9 would be reviewed and firm planned by the master scheduler. That is, he or she would change their timing and quantities to utilize capacity fully, etc. Thereafter, they would only be changed by master scheduler intervention.

Once the records have been completed for all distribution centers and all stockkeeping units, the time-phased information can be used for planning actual shipments. Summarizing the planned shipments to each warehouse for each product in each time period provides the basis for estimating the total weight and volume destined for each distribution center. If the total is not a full carload or truckload, future planned shipments can be reviewed to

FIGURE 19.9 Distribution center to plant warehouse records for DRP

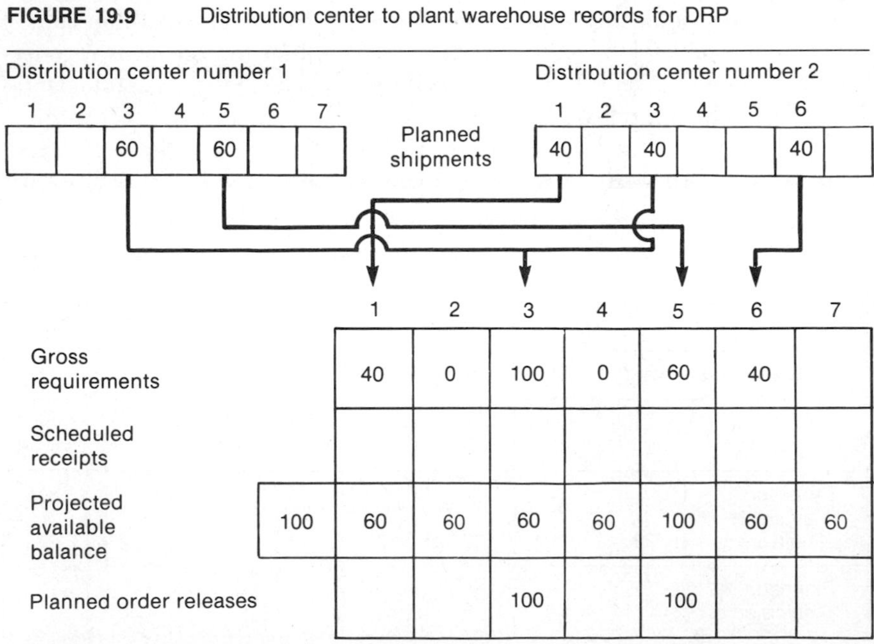

		1	2	3	4	5	6	7
Gross requirements		40	0	100	0	60	40	
Scheduled receipts								
Projected available balance	100	60	60	60	60	100	60	60
Planned order releases				100		100		

Safety stock = 50, order quantity = 100, lead time = 0.

determine which would be the best addition to make up a full carload. An analysis of weight/volume per time period can help determine shipment frequencies. In addition, if there are shortages, the information can be used to determine allocations and promise dates for future shipments.

A final difference between DRP and MRP should be pointed out. It is very difficult to reassign priorities for the scheduled receipts in a distribution system, since it is different from material flowing through work centers of a factory. The 60 units for period 2 in Figure 19.7 are an example. Once a shipment is loaded on a train or truck and is destined for a distribution center, the ability to slow down or speed up that shipment is very limited. The choice of transportation mode can be made at the time of shipment, but once material is shipped, changes in timing are usually not possible.

DRP at Abbott Laboratories. Abbott Laboratories, Ltd. of Canada produces health-care products. Three lines, pharmaceuticals, hospital products, and infant nutrition products are produced in three plants. About 750 end items are distributed through DCs to customers throughout Canada.

Abbott Laboratories uses the DRP approach described above. Detailed DC forecast data are input to MRP records. These records are represented as the zero level of the bill of materials (BOM). Figure 19.10 illustrates these records for two DCs, Vancouver and Montreal. The forecast data are entered as the gross requirements rows. The first 20 weeks are displayed in weekly time periods (buckets). Thereafter, monthly buckets are used for a total planning horizon of two years.

In the Montreal record, there is an entry of 120 in the week of 8/7, in a row labeled Customer Orders. This row allows the inclusion of specific advance order information. However, the information does not affect the MRP record calculations. It is there for the detailed planning of shipments and to recognize advanced special orders.

The lead time shown in the Vancouver record is 35 days, or five weeks. This includes safety lead time. The MRP time-phased records are produced using these parameters. For example, the projected on-hand balance at the end of week 9/4 for Vancouver is insufficient to meet the gross requirements of 9/11. The result is a planned order for a quantity of 24, five weeks earlier in the week of 8/7.

Figure 19.11 shows the MRP records for the central warehouse and the bulk item used to make the end-item product B. The gross requirements for central are based on the planned orders from all the DCs. For example, in the week of 8/7, the gross requirement of 1,908 is comprised of 24 from Vancouver, 1,872 from Montreal, and 12 from some other DC.

The batch size shown for central in Figure 19.11 is 7,619. In fact, this is the number of product Bs yielded from a batch of 4,000 in the unit of measure for the bulk product. That is, the 7,619 shown as a firm planned order in 9/11 becomes a gross requirement of 4,000 for bulk in that week.

The master production scheduler works with the MRP record for central. This person's job is to convert planned orders into firm planned orders, and

FIGURE 19.10 Abbott DRP records for Vancouver and Montreal

Description	Size	um	Std bactr	FC	BY	PL	IT	C	Scrap	Total landed costs	OP	Life	O-LT	P-LT	O-LT	QA-LT	T-LT	On hand	OA inventory	Allocated	Safety stock
Product-B	200		24			08	F	C	1.00	0.000		1095	35		0	0	35	36.0	0.0	0.0	0.0

03-VANCOUVER

	PAST DUE	7/24	7/31	08/07	08/14	08/21	08/28	09/04	09/11	09/18	09/25	10/02	10/09	10/16
CUSTOMER ORDERS														
GROSS REQUIREMENTS		5	5	5	5	5	5	5	5	5	5	5	5	5
SCHEDULED RECEIPTS														
ON HAND	36	31	26	21	16	11	6	1	20	15	10	5	24	19
FIRM PLANNED ORDERS														
PLANNED ORDERS				24					24			24		

MONTHLY

	10/23	10/30	11/06	11/13	11/20	11/27	12/04	01/01	01/29	02/26	03/26	04/23	05/21	06/18
CUSTOMER ORDERS														
GROSS REQUIREMENTS	7	7	7	7	5	4	17	21	23	20	20	20	20	20
SCHEDULED RECEIPTS														
ON HAND	12	5	22	15	10	6	13	16	17	21	1	5	9	13
FIRM PLANNED ORDERS														
PLANNED ORDERS			24				24	24	24	24		24	24	24

	07/16	08/13	09/10	10/08	11/05	12/03	12/31	01/28	02/25	03/24	04/21	05/19	06/16	TOTAL
CUSTOMER ORDERS														
GROSS REQUIREMENTS	20	20	20	24	23	17	20	20	20	20	20	20	26	533
SCHEDULED RECEIPTS														
ON HAND	17	21	1	1	2	9	13	17	21	1	5	9	7	
FIRM PLANNED ORDERS														
PLANNED ORDERS	24	24	24	24		24	24	24	24		24	24		504

NOTES & COMMENTS

Comm list no.
List xyz

Description	Size	um	Std bactr	FC	BY	PL	IT	C	Scrap	Total landed costs	OP	Life	O-LT	P-LT	C-LT	QA-LT	T-LT	On hand	OA inventory	Allocated	Safety stock
Product-B	200	BL	1872	A2		08		C	1.0			1095	14		0	0	14	2520.0	0.0	0.0	0.0

21-MONTREAL

	PAST DUE	7/24	7/31	08/07	08/14	08/21	08/28	09/04	09/11	09/18	09/25	10/02	10/09	10/16
CUSTOMER ORDERS				120										
GROSS REQUIREMENTS		601	601	601	601	576	556	556	556	578	633	633	633	633
SCHEDULED RECEIPTS														
ON HAND	2520	1919	1318	717	116	1412	856	300	1616	1038	405	1644	1011	378
FIRM PLANNED ORDERS														
PLANNED ORDERS				1872			1872			1872			1872	

MONTHLY

	10/23	10/30	11/06	11/13	11/20	11/27	12/04	01/01	01/29	02/26	03/26	04/23	05/21	06/18
CUSTOMER ORDERS														
GROSS REQUIREMENTS	777	801	801	801	633	507	2100	2386	2744	2167	2356	2404	2479	2212
SCHEDULED RECEIPTS														
ON HAND	1473	672	1743	942	309	1674	1446	932	60	1637	1153	621	14	1546
FIRM PLANNED ORDERS														
PLANNED ORDERS	1872			1872			1872	3744	1872	1872	3744	1872	1872	1872

	07/16	08/13	09/10	10/08	11/05	12/03	12/31	01/28	02/25	03/24	04/21	05/19	06/16	TOTAL
CUSTOMER ORDERS														
GROSS REQUIREMENTS	2418	2289	2400	2844	2742	2100	2323	2480	2285	2356	2280	2348	2944	62735
SCHEDULED RECEIPTS														
ON HAND	1000	583	55	955	85	1729	1278	670	257	1645	1237	761	1561	
FIRM PLANNED ORDERS														
PLANNED ORDERS	3744	1872	1872	3744	1872	1872	1872	3744	1872	1872	1872	3744	1872	61776

NOTES & COMMENTS

Comm list no.
List xyz

Source: W. L. Berry, T. E. Vollmann, and D. C. Whybark, *Master Production Scheduling: Principles and Practice* (Falls Church, Va.: American Production and Inventory Control Society, 1979), p. 87.

FIGURE 19.11 Abbott DRP records for central and bulk

Description	Size	um	Std bactr	FC	BY	PL	IT	C	Scrap	Total landed costs	OP	Life	O-LT	P-LT	O-LT	QA-LT	T-LT	On hand	OA inventory	Allocated	Safety stock
Product-B	200	BL	7619	A2	00	03	C	0	1.07			1095		12	0	11	23	5220.0	0.0	144.0	1000.0

01-CENTRAL

	PAST DUE	7/24	7/31	08/07	08/14	08/21	08/28	09/04	09/11	09/18	09/25	10/02	10/09	10/16
CUSTOMER ORDERS	0	0	0	0	0	0	0	0	0	0	0	0	0	0
GROSS REQUIREMENTS	204	12	12	1908	12	12	2916	156	36	1884	12	1104	1980	12
SCHEDULED RECEIPTS	0	0	0	7619	0	0	0	0	0	0	0	0	0	0
ON HAND	4872	4860	4848	10078	10066	10054	7138	6982	6946	5062	5050	3946	9104	9092
FIRM PLANNED ORDERS	0	0	0	0	0	0	0	0	7619	0	0	0	0	0
PLANNED ORDERS	0	0	0	0	0	0	0	0	0	0	0	0	0	0

MONTHLY

	10/23	10/30	11/06	11/13	11/20	11/27	12/04	01/01	01/29	02/26	03/26	04/23	05/21	06/18
CUSTOMER ORDERS	0	0	0	0	0	0	0	0	0	0	0	0	0	0
GROSS REQUIREMENTS	2952	12	36	1884	96	1092	1944	4968	3108	3012	4968	3108	2076	3108
SCHEDULED RECEIPTS	0	0	0	0	0	0	0	0	0	0	0	0	0	0
ON HAND	6140	6128	6092	4208	4112	3020	8214	10384	7276	4264	6434	3326	8388	5280
FIRM PLANNED ORDERS	0	0	0	0	7619	0	7619	0	0	7619	0	7619	0	7619
PLANNED ORDERS	0	0	0	0	0	0	0	0	0	0	0	0	0	0

	07/16	08/13	09/10	10/08	11/05	12/03	12/31	01/28	02/25	03/24	04/21	05/19	06/16	TOTAL
CUSTOMER ORDERS	0	0	0	0	0	0	0	0	0	0	0	0	0	0
GROSS REQUIREMENTS	4740	3120	3108	4980	2052	3108	3012	4980	2964	2052	3108	4956	2808	87612
SCHEDULED RECEIPTS	0	0	0	0	0	0	0	0	0	0	0	0	0	7619
ON HAND	7678	4558	8588	10746	8694	5586	2574	4732	1768	6854	3746	5928	3120	0
FIRM PLANNED ORDERS	0	7619	7619	0	0	0	0	0	0	0	0	0	0	60952
PLANNED ORDERS	0	0	0	0	0	0	7619	0	7619	0	7619	0	0	22857

NOTES & COMMENTS

Comm list no.
List xyz

Description	Size	um	Std bactr	FC	BY	PL	IT	C	Scrap	Total landed costs	OP	Life	O-LT	P-LT	O-LT	QA-LT	T-LT	On hand	OA inventory	Allocated	Safety stock
Product-B	200	L	4000			00	B	C	1.00		N						0	0	0	0	0

84-Bulk

	PAST DUE	7/24	7/31	08/07	08/14	08/21	08/28	09/04	09/11	09/18	09/25	10/02	10/09	10/16
CUSTOMER ORDERS									4000					
GROSS REQUIREMENTS														
SCHEDULED RECEIPTS														
ON HAND														
FIRM PLANNED ORDERS														
PLANNED ORDERS									4000					

MONTHLY

	10/23	10/30	11/06	11/13	11/20	11/27	12/04	01/01	01/29	02/26	03/26	04/23	05/21	06/18
CUSTOMER ORDERS														
GROSS REQUIREMENTS					4000		4000			4000		4000		4000
SCHEDULED RECEIPTS														
ON HAND														
FIRM PLANNED ORDERS														
PLANNED ORDERS					4000		4000			4000		4000		4000

	07/16	08/13	09/10	10/08	11/05	12/03	12/31	01/28	02/25	03/24	04/21	05/19	06/16	TOTAL
CUSTOMER ORDERS														
GROSS REQUIREMENTS		4000	4000				4000		4000		4000			44000
SCHEDULED RECEIPTS														
ON HAND														
FIRM PLANNED ORDERS														
PLANNED ORDERS		4000	4000				4000		4000		4000			44000

NOTES & COMMENTS

Comm list no.
List xyz

Source: W. L. Berry, T. E. Vollmann, and D. C. Whybark, *Master Production Scheduling: Principles and Practice* (Falls Church, Va.: American Production and Inventory Control Society, 1979), p. 88.

to manage the timing of the firm planned orders. For example, all of the orders at central are firm planned in Figure 19.11 until 12/31 in the last row. The last three orders (12/31, 2/25, and 4/21) are only planned orders. MRP logic can replan these as needed. Only the master production scheduler can move the firm planned orders that appear early in the record. The result is a stable MPS for the bulk production.

Figure 19.12 illustrates the information available for actual shipment planning. The requirements due to be shipped this week or in the next two weeks (also any past-due shipments) are summarized by distribution center and product type. This enables the planner to look at the current requirements or future planned shipments in making up carloads destined for a distribution center. Since the information is available in terms of cube, weight, and pallet load, the planner can use the resource that is most limited in making a shipment decision. This flexibility enables planners to efficiently use transportation resources to meet product needs.

DISTRIBUTION CENTER LOCATION ANALYSIS

One of the key elements in managing the logistics activities of a firm is the determination of how many warehouses or distribution centers to have and where they should be located. We will consider several approaches to that problem in this section. The basic approach we will take is to choose among a set of predetermined alternative locations.

To illustrate the problem and solution approaches, let us assume that some staff group has developed the information (perhaps with regression analysis estimates) shown as Figure 19.13. This figure shows the annual fixed cost of using each of the possible DCs plus the variable costs associated with serving the customers in particular locations from each distribution center.

Simulation

A useful approach to determining the number and locations of distribution centers is simulation. One way to do this is to specify a number of DCs to evaluate, say two, and randomly choose several examples of two distribution centers. Once a particular set of DCs is chosen, customers are assigned to specific DCs on the basis of minimum cost, and total annual costs are calculated. For example, a Hammond/Indianapolis set of DCs would be calculated as follows (in $1,000 of cost):

$$\text{Fixed costs} = 8 + 7 = 15$$

$$\text{Variable costs (Hammond)} = 10 + 22 = 32$$

(for serving only Gary and Michigan City)

$$\text{Variable costs (Indianapolis)} = 20 + 5 + 3 + 14 + 8 + 4 + 11 + 19 + 18 = 102$$

$$\text{Total costs} = 15 + 32 + 102 = 149$$

FIGURE 19.12 Abbott short-term shipping information

MPDR0030 DISTRIBUTION REQUIREMENTS PLAN PAGE 206

DC 21 - MONTREAL

DIVISION 2

LIST/SIZE	QUANTITY	PALLET	WEIGHT	CUBE	QUANTITY	PALLET	WEIGHT	CUBE
	PAST DUE				WEEK 1			
XYZ-200 PRODUCT B	0	0.0	0.0	0.0	0	0.0	0.0	0.0
	WEEK 2				WEEK 3			
	0	0.0	0.0	0.0	1872	2.0	3744.0	112.3

PRIORITY 96: 5076 AVAILABLE IN CENTRAL

DC 03 VANCOUVER

LIST/SIZE	QUANTITY	PALLET	WEIGHT	CUBE	QUANTITY	PALLET	WEIGHT	CUBE
	PAST DUE				WEEK 1			
XYZ - 3 PRODUCT B	0	0.0	0.0	0.0	0	0.0	0.0	0.0
	WEEK 2				WEEK 3			
	0	0.0	0.0	0.0	24	0.0	48.0	1.4

PRIORITY 96: 5076 AVAILABLE IN CENTRAL

Source: W. L. Berry, T. E. Vollmann, and D. C. Whybark, *Master Production Scheduling: Principles and Practice* (Falls Church, Va.: American Production and Inventory Control Society, 1979), p. 90.

FIGURE 19.13 Costs for alternative DC locations

Potential distribution center location	Fixed cost per year	Customer locations										
		Michigan City	Gary	Indianapolis	Lafayette	Kokomo	Columbus	Richmond	Vincennes	Evansville	Louisville	Terre Haute
Hammond	8	10*	22	25	7	4	17	11	5	15	25	22
Indianapolis	7	13	30	20	5	3	14	8	4	11	19	18
Columbus	6	15	32	22	7	4	12	9	3	11	19	17
Terre Haute	5	13	30	22	8	5	17	10	2	12	20	15
New Albany	5	18	40	24	10	7	15	10	4	10	17	17

*Variable cost (in $000) per year for serving all Michigan City customers from a Hammond DC.

Many pairs of DCs would be similarly evaluated to find a good (but not optimal) set. Next, a different number of DCs is investigated in the same way, say three, with random sets of three DCs chosen for analysis. The end result would be the ability to plot the total annual expected costs as a function of the number of DCs. Figure 19.14 is an example of such a plot. Once the interesting range of the number of DCs is determined, more detailed analysis can be made, both in terms of the number of DCs and location. At this point, management/subjective considerations can also be taken into account.

Heuristic procedures

Several heuristic procedures have been developed to permit rapid determination of good DC location patterns. Among these are the *add* and *drop* procedures. The add procedure will be illustrated with the data from Figure 19.15. The procedure starts by considering which single DC would serve all the customer locations at the least cost if used *alone*. Once this DC is found, the least-cost DC to *add* to the first one is chosen. Next, the third best DC to add to the first two is determined, and so on, until the addition of another distribution center increases total costs. In the example shown in Figure

FIGURE 19.14 Total annual cost for varying numbers of DCs

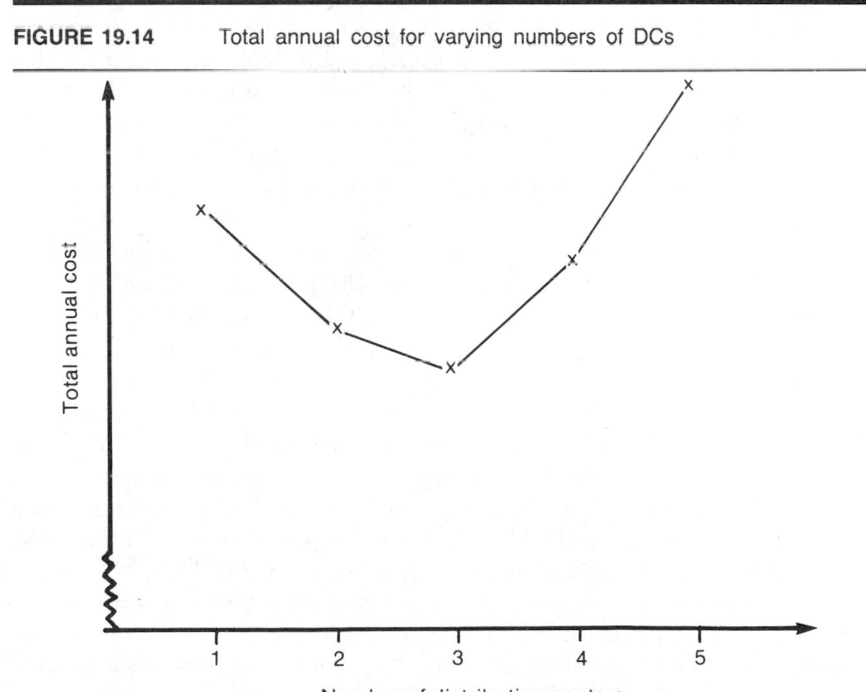

FIGURE 19.15 The add procedure for determining DC location

	Step	*DC(s)*	*Cost*	*Choice*
1	DC	Hammond	171	
		Indianapolis	152*	
		Columbus	157	Indianapolis
		Terre Haute	160	
		New Albany	177	
2	DCs	Hammond	149*	
	Indianapolis +	Columbus	155	Hammond
		Terre Haute	154	
		New Albany	157	
3	DCs	Columbus	152	
	Indianapolis +	Terre Haute	151	No choice: costs are increasing
	Hammond +	New Albany	151	

*Final choice: Indianapolis and Hammond.

19.15, the addition of a third warehouse to the combination of DCs in Indianapolis and Hammond increases costs, so the procedure stops with the two suggested.

Programming procedures

Neither simulation nor the heuristic procedures guarantee an optimal solution to the selection of distribution centers. It is tempting to suggest that all combinations be examined, that is, to completely enumerate all possible DC-customer combinations to find the best. However, for a typical problem of 100 potential DC locations and customers throughout the United States, enumeration would take approximately one year of computer central processing unit time.

Exact procedures do exist for optimally solving the DC location problem. Branch and bound techniques have been made quite efficient, and are now feasible for problems of 100 to 200 potential DCs. The general approach of the branch and bound technique is to use the transportation method of linear programming sequentially to bound the solution space. Linear programming techniques alone cannot be applied because of the fixed costs associated with each DC. The first step in the procedure is to treat all the fixed costs as variable and solve a transportation linear programming (TLP) problem. The cost of this solution represents a lower bound on costs in that no solution accounting for the fixed costs can be better. If the solution to the TLP problem assigns all customers fully to some of the DCs, that is the solution. If some are only partially assigned, the procedure continues.

The next step is to select one DC that is to be constrained as open. This adds the full fixed costs of that DC. All other fixed costs are still assumed to be variable. The TLP produces a lower bound to this condition. Next, the same DC is constrained to be closed and the TLP solved. Another lower bound is thereby obtained.

The branch with the lowest bound of the two branches (first DC open or closed) is then selected for further analysis. Another DC is added and again constrained as both open and closed. Lower bounds are obtained with TLP, as before. Again the smaller lower bound path is chosen. The process is repeated until a terminal solution is obtained. A terminal solution is one where all DCs are either open or closed. The cost of this terminal solution now becomes an upper bound. That is, it is a feasible solution—any other solution with a greater cost can be ignored.

All branches for which lower bounds were calculated but not explored en route to obtaining the first terminal solution can now be compared to the upper bound. Any branches that have a lower bound greater than the upper bound can be omitted from further consideration. Those that are lower have to be evaluated. The evaluation proceeds either until lower bounds are achieved for the branches that exceed the current upper bound or until a terminal solution is reached. If the cost of the terminal solution is lower than the current upper bound, it becomes the new upper bound.

This basic approach has been augmented to reduce the computational effort. For example, in the problem shown in Figure 19.13, it is possible to quickly determine that the optimal solution will use the Hammond DC. This is so since Hammond can most cheaply serve Michigan City and Gary. The next best alternative to serve these two customers would add $3,000 and $8,000 respectively. This is more than the fixed costs of the Hammond DC.

The Heinz Company simulation. We turn now to an actual DC location problem. One of the pioneering efforts in distribution center location analysis was at the H. J. Heinz Company. Heinz has factories geographically located near major growing areas, with DCs located nationally. In the 1950s, major changes in customer buying patterns took place. The primary cause of the changes was the rapid growth of independent grocery wholesaling firms which took the place of direct store deliveries from firms such as Heinz.

Heinz reduced the number of DCs from 68 to 43 between 1957 and 1959. At that time, Shycon and Maffei were called in as consultants to consider further changes. A simulation model was constructed to evaluate DCs, some in existing locations and some in new locations. The annual cost savings were estimated to be $250,000.

The initial model evaluated 10 alternative location patterns, which were user specified. Sequential runs of the model led users to what if questions which would be analyzed with further runs of the model. The preparation of the simulation model required extensive data collection. The consultants spent a great deal of their time coordinating the collection of customer order data (pattern, frequency, product mix), and delivery mode, warehousing costs, and transportation costs.

Management found the model very useful, but it was necessary to make certain adjustments for unique considerations not included in the model.

These involved things like finding inadequate transportation service in one location, special tax and labor constraints, and a few cases where actual transport costs differed substantially from those assumed for the initial model.

The Heinz Company study was the first of many carried out by Harvey Shycon and others. The underlying model has evolved steadily and is now called LOGISTEK. The most fundamental change has been to make the model adaptive. Rather than evaluating a fixed set of location choices input by users, the LOGISTEK model iterates in an adaptive fashion to find good location choices. That is, in the terms of this section, it is no longer purely a simulator, but a heuristic model, suggesting location choices for management consideration.

VEHICLE SCHEDULING ANALYSIS

In this section we treat vehicle scheduling. We assume a given system for DC replenishment and a given set of DCs, and ask: How should vehicles be best scheduled to achieve logistics objectives? The problem, as typically formulated, is to determine the order in which customers will be visited by delivery/pickup vehicles, often called the route. Other questions include determination of the proper number of vehicles, the frequency with which each customer should be visited, and the times to be associated with the stops along the route.

Our approach to vehicle scheduling is to first present a discussion of the *traveling salesmen* problem. This provides an analytical framework. We then consider solution methodologies, and thereafter examine some actual operating problems.

Traveling salesman problem

The traveling salesman problem is one of those easily stated but difficult to solve problems on which mathematicians thrive. The statement is: given a set of cities (DCs) to be visited, what is the least-cost method of visiting each of them, starting from and returning to a given point (the central facility)? An example is shown in Figure 19.16, where there are five DCs to be visited from a central plant.

Solution methodologies

The traveling salesman problem can be formulated as a zero-one integer programming problem. Optimal solution approaches include branch and bound procedures similar to those discussed for the DC location problem, and dynamic programming. Producing optimal procedures becomes computationally costly as the size of the problem goes up. That is, as the number of DCs to visit in a schedule increases, the computational costs rise geometrically.

FIGURE 19.16 Traveling salesman example

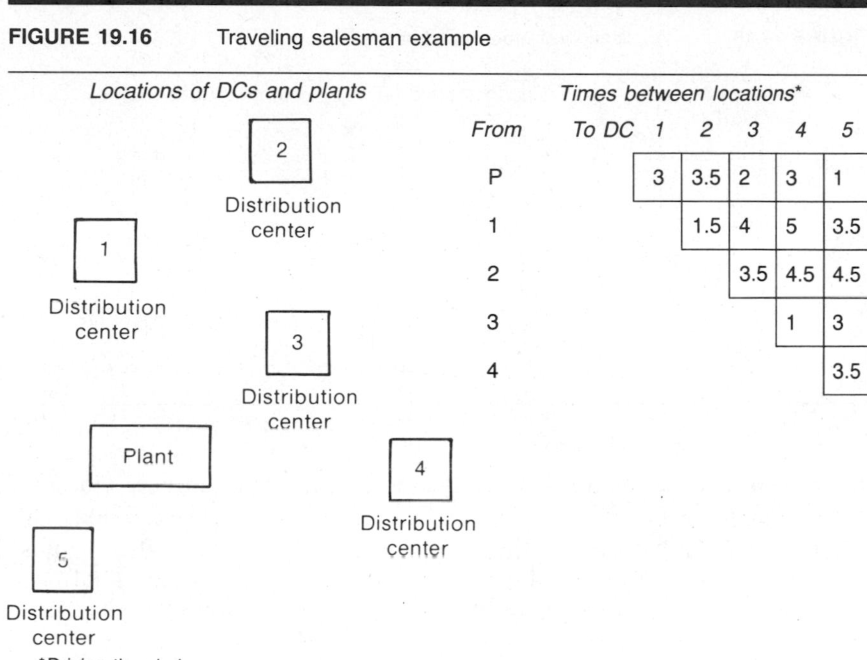

*Times between locations**

From	To DC 1	2	3	4	5
P	3	3.5	2	3	1
1		1.5	4	5	3.5
2			3.5	4.5	4.5
3				1	3
4					3.5

*Driving time in hours.

Heuristic procedures have been devised for this problem that produce reasonably good results in far less time than the optimal procedures. One widely used heuristic is based on the *time-saved* concept. The basic consideration is the time or distance that would be saved if two DCs were visited in a single tour, as opposed to visiting each separately. For the example shown in Figure 19.16, a matrix of time saved can be constructed. Figure 19.17 provides this information.

The time-saved matrix can be utilized for several purposes. But let us first start with the determination of the route. The most desirable combinations

FIGURE 19.17 Time-saved matrix and formula

Time saved

	2	3	4	5
1	5*	1	1	.5
2		2	2	0
3			4	0
4				.5

Formula and example

Time saved $x - y =$
time (P to x) + time (P to y) − time (x to y)
Time saved (1 − 2) = 3 + 3.5 − 1.5 = 5*
Time saved (3 − 4) = 2 + 3 − 1 = 4

*Time saved by traveling from P–1–2–P instead of P–1–P and P–2–P.

FIGURE 19.18 Application of time-saved heuristic

Rank of pairing by time saved		*Unconstrained route*	*Eight-hour constraint route*	
1–2	5	1–2	P–1–2–P	8 hrs
3–4	4	3–4	P–3–4–P	6 hrs
2–3	2	1–2–3–4		
2–4	2			
1–3	1			
1–4	1			
1–5	.5	5–1–2–3–4		
4–5	.5		P–3–4–5–P	7.5 hours
2–5	0			
3–5	0	P–5–1–2–3–4–P	P–1–2–P, P–3–4–5–P	

to put on a route are those that save the most time. Since a route that goes from 1 to 2 (or vice versa) would save the most time, it is selected first. The application of the heuristic to the entire set of data in Figure 19.17 is illustrated in Figure 19.18. Also shown are two resultant routes; one if all DCs are visited in one route, and another if a truck has to return to the plant within an eight-hour shift.

If no restrictions on time capacity exist, the time-saved procedure suggests first pairing 1–2, next 3–4, and then 2–3. These three pairs lead to the partial route 1–2–3–4. The next pair that can be used is the 1–5 pair, which suggests a complete route would join 5–1 so that the complete route would be P–5–1–2–3–4.

The addition of the eight-hour time constraint is readily included in the time-saved heuristic. In Figure 19.18, pairs would be combined until the constraint was reached, and then a new route would be started. The first route would be P–1–2–P using eight hours (there is no distribution center that can be visited from DC 1 or 2 with return made to the plant within eight hours). The second vehicle would then be routed P–3–4–5–P to complete the deliveries.

Other heuristics have also been applied to the traveling salesman problem. One approach is to take any feasible tour and try to improve it. A feasible tour could be generated randomly or produced with the time-saved heuristic. One improvement procedure would be to examine pair exchanges. For example, 2–3 and 3–4 could be exchanged for 2–4 and 4–3. If the result would be a time saving, the exchange would be made.

Vehicle scheduling at Ohio National Bank

The procedures described here are not exclusively manufacturing procedures. We will use the Ohio National Bank (ONB) as an example of an application of vehicle scheduling. The problem facing ONB and many other banks is how to schedule the pickups of checks at branch bank locations. The problem is made more complex by the need to provide a flow of work to the central bank processing (encoding) facility. A further complication is the desire to process as many checks as possible by the transfer deadlines imposed for closing the checks through the Federal Reserve system. That is, all banks desire to minimize the checks held, the so-called "float."

The buildup of checks at the branches often depends upon the particular branch: location, clientele, etc. Moreover, this buildup can vary significantly from day to day because of conditions such as paydays or holidays. If a branch bank is visited early in the day, work can be generated earlier for the central processing facility. However, a later visit to the branch means more checks have accumulated, which will generate a larger volume of work. But later visits also decrease the available time until the transfer deadline. More frequent pickups help keep work in the central facility, but at an increase in pickup vehicle costs. The trade-off is between the number of banks on a route, the timing of the pickups, and the size of the vehicle fleet.

ONB uses a special vehicle scheduling program developed by Arthur Hill, called CHEXPEDITE. It schedules a specified number of vehicles so that travel cost is minimized, subject to the constraint of maintaining a check supply so as to meet the required check-processing schedule. Travel cost is based on the variable costs per hour to operate a vehicle. CHEXPEDITE uses a four-step heuristic process to produce a set of routings. The program also produces a series of other output reports. Figure 19.19 is a sample report showing the expected arrival pattern of check volume at the central processing facility.

The benefits achieved by ONB from this program were significant. A total savings of $30,000 in annual costs were realized by reducing the vehicle fleet from eight to five. Work now arrives at a better rate for central processing. The float has been substantially reduced by the program. Finally, a routine response mechanism is now in place to deal with evaluating changing banking conditions.

The work described here at ONB is not unique to banking. The same conditions exist for any business that has central equipment which depends upon decentralized pickups of input materials. Examples include food processors, mineral concentrators, and post offices. Less obvious examples include high-speed repetitive manufacturers of products like automobiles and appliances. Deliveries need to be scheduled with much the same set of criteria.

Efficient vehicle scheduling has become important not only because of rising vehicle operating costs. The relationships to inventory levels, customer service, and other operating performance measures have also become important. For example, by holding DC (or customer) delivery orders until more have been received, fewer miles need be driven per delivered order. The trade-off, of course, is that some DCs or customers will wait longer for service. It is to this issue that we now turn our attention.

FIGURE 19.19 ONB vehicle arrival schedule

Dispatch	Vehicle	Begins	Ends	Travel time	Check volume
1	1	1014 hrs	1100 hrs	0.65 hrs	6,022. cks
2	2	1012 hrs	1112 hrs	0.88 hrs	7,005. cks
3	3	1048 hrs	1126 hrs	0.50 hrs	3,734. cks
4	4	1025 hrs	1133 hrs	1.02 hrs	8,937. cks
5	5	1046 hrs	1151 hrs	0.96 hrs	8,069. cks
6	1	1100 hrs	1207 hrs	0.99 hrs	8,530. cks
7	2	1125 hrs	1224 hrs	0.86 hrs	6,389. cks
8	3	1140 hrs	1237 hrs	0.83 hrs	8,615. cks
9	4	1147 hrs	1254 hrs	1.00 hrs	9,210. cks
10	5	1236 hrs	1313 hrs	0.49 hrs	4,092. cks
11	1	1244 hrs	1321 hrs	0.50 hrs	3,881. cks
12	2	1236 hrs	1328 hrs	0.76 hrs	5,432. cks
13	3	1240 hrs	1339 hrs	0.88 hrs	7,710. cks
14	4	1255 hrs	1355 hrs	0.88 hrs	7,135. cks
15	5	1308 hrs	1409 hrs	0.90 hrs	7,821. cks
16	1	1324 hrs	1425 hrs	0.89 hrs	7,515. cks
17	2	1323 hrs	1440 hrs	1.17 hrs	9,454. cks
18	3	1333 hrs	1459 hrs	1.31 hrs	9,475. cks
19	4	1447 hrs	1527 hrs	0.53 hrs	2,742. cks
20	5	1445 hrs	1536 hrs	0.75 hrs	4,493. cks
21	1	1451 hrs	1547 hrs	0.81 hrs	4,706. cks
22	2	1446 hrs	1557 hrs	1.07 hrs	7,485. cks
23	3	1452 hrs	1617 hrs	1.31 hrs	9,805. cks
24	4	1520 hrs	1656 hrs	1.49 hrs	10,532. cks
25	5	1529 hrs	1721 hrs	1.74 hrs	18,727. cks
26	1	1540 hrs	1755 hrs	2.14 hrs	3,750. cks
Totals				25.31 hrs	191,265. cks
Branch bank 806 check volume					39,748. cks
Total incoming check volume for day					231,012. cks

Source: V. A. Mabert and J. P. McKenzie, "Improving Bank Operations: A Case Study at Banc Ohio/Ohio National Bank," *Omega,* 8, no. 3 (pp. 345–53).

CUSTOMER-SERVICE MEASUREMENT

The last of our topics in logistics concerns the measurement of customer service. This is included for a very simple reason: Without some objective measure of customer service, it is extremely difficult to compare, measure, and control many logistics alternatives. We divide the discussion of customer service into make-to-stock firms and make-to-order firms. However, many of the principles are the same in both cases.

Make-to-stock companies

In this section, we consider firms that ship from an inventory to customers (or provide an inventory for customers). We look at the difficulty of defining and measuring customer service.

A major issue in measuring customer service for the make-to-stock firm concerns delivery timing. Among firms shipping from factory inventories to retail centers, warehouses, or DCs, many feel that customer service should be assessed in terms of the speed of delivery. That is, after a customer places an order, how soon is it delivered? This leads to policies like one-week or overnight delivery. This fixed delivery time implies levels of inventory and/or capacity that should be thought through carefully before setting the policy.

An alternative measure of customer service is the consistency of delivery. This is related to available-to-promise logic. Make an honest promise—then keep it. This is not common, but the emergence of manufacturing planning and control systems is making it more possible. It still is not as popular as the fixed response ideas—such as next-day delivery.

Our experience indicates that there is no one best measure. *All* firms state that they are very concerned about customer service, but we find firms falling into two major groups. The key difference is whether they have unambiguously defined and measured customer service. One group of firms does not systematically measure and does not have unambiguous definitions of customer service. Among the second group, those who do have definitions and measures, there tend to be very different measurements.

Once the issue of when (promise date or response time) has been resolved, there is still the issue of how to measure service in terms of *what* is delivered. Again, there are a number of different measurements used for this aspect of customer service. One common measurement is the percent of the items demanded in any period (i.e., a year) actually supplied from stock when demanded. A related measure is the percent of demand satisfied from stock during the reorder cycle. This measure reflects the notion that the exposure to stock-outs occurs between the time the replenishment order has been placed and the time the delivery arrives in inventory. Another measure is the percent of the line items in an individual customer order that have been filled out of inventory. Still another measure is the percent of the customers for whom all line items were filled from inventory.

One has to be a bit careful in selecting among these measures. The objective is to provide customer service—to measure how well one is doing and to continually look for improvement, both in the service provided and in the measurement used. If a completely responsive production facility were available, no customer-service issue would ever arise. All orders would be shipped upon order receipt. While clearly unrealistic for most products, there are some instances where it is competitively necessary to provide such service. For example, some firms have a customer-service policy of "immediate" delivery of spare parts. Again, one must recognize that this measure is going to fail for some customers unless the normal demand can be postponed, so the manufacturing facility can literally make the spare part immediately.

All of these measures signify different aspects of trying to satisfy customer demand. It is not always possible (or even desirable) to satisfy all demands. Moreover, many actual delivery requirements vary. For this reason, variable specifications may be in order, depending upon the customer served. The General Foods Company has recognized this. They have written customer-service contracts with their most important customers that reflect terms of delivery, tolerable levels of customer service (based upon a mutually satisfactory measure), and a methodology for ensuring that the customer service contract is lived up to. Although this requires substantially more information and management control, it is a legitimate method for tailoring a company's activities to the needs of its customers.

The final point we want to make in this regard comes back to the total cost concept. The relation of General Foods to its major customers and the appropriate measures of customer service depend upon *customer* inventories and logistics. Benefits are to be obtained by finding the best measures for end-item customer service from both the customer and the General Foods standpoint. Particular DC locations, transport means, and vehicle schedules should all be evaluated on the basis of this agreed upon measure.

Make-to-order companies

The primary customer service consideration in a make-to-order (or assemble-to-order) firm is the ability to meet promised delivery dates. Thus, measuring performance against these promises is as important in the make-to-order as it is in the make-to-stock firm. The timing issue is also critical in the make-to-order firm. One key dimension of timing is the time from order placement until delivery. An important element of this is the manufacturing lead time. If insufficient time exists, some promises will have to be made on the basis of previously forecast volumes. Managing that requires an effective MPC system.

Customer-service measurement in the make-to-order firm is somewhat complicated by the fact that customers often change desired delivery dates. In measurement then, one issue is whether the change was made by the customer or the manufacturer. Should performance be measured against the assigned date or the revised date? Against both? The Tennant Company (assemble-to-order) tracks performance against the original due date assigned, even if it was later changed by the customer, because that is where they assigned the capacity. Whether this makes sense or not depends upon the business and relationships with customers.

The implications of the necessity to control and measure against delivery promise dates underscores the need for close coordination between order entry and master production scheduling. Many make-to-order firms have a simple policy of six weeks (or some other such period) delivery for every order. If this were correct on the average, it means that in 50 percent of the cases delivery could have been sooner, and in 50 percent of the cases delivery will be late. It is the function of the master production scheduling activity to monitor the capability of the shop to deliver. This ability to monitor the customer promising capability through the available-to-promise logic means that the delivery date can be specified on the basis of actual shop capability and the logistics function can deliver to the customer against a date that was feasible from the shop's standpoint and agreeable to the customer.

We see then that customer-service measurement is critical to assess logistics system design choices. It is also intertwined with other manufacturing planning and control (MPC) systems. Good master production scheduling makes for better customer service. Good execution systems make for an attainable master production schedule. MPC system strengths can support new and exciting changes in physical distribution.

CONCLUDING PRINCIPLES

Several technical principles are expounded in the chapter; here, we concentrate on managerial principles:

- The role and contributions of each element of a physical distribution system must be determined and managed.
- Management must provide the integration for the elements of these systems and evaluate alternatives in terms of total cost.
- The information from distribution requirements planning systems should be used for planning product deliveries.
- The design of warehouse systems should incorporate the locational (warm puppy) effect on sales.
- The vehicle scheduling activities must be coordinated with customer-service requirements.
- Customer-service objectives and standards must be set and monitored. These should reflect the types and classes of customers and products.

REFERENCES

Aggarwal, S., and D. G. Dhavale. "Simulation Analysis of a Multi-Product Multi-Echelon Inventory Distribution System." *Academy of Management Journal*, March 1975, pp. 41–54.

Baumol, W. J., and P. Wolfe. "A Warehouse Location Problem." *Operations Research*, April-May 1958, pp. 252–63.

Berry, W. L., T. E. Vollmann, and D. C. Whybark. *Master Production Scheduling: Principles and Practice*. Falls Church, Va.: American Production and Inventory Control Society, Inc., 1979, p. 87.

Carroll, Thomas M., and Robert D. Dean. "A Baysian Approach to Plant-Location Decisions." *Decision Sciences* 11, no. 1 (January 1980), pp. 81–89.

DuBois, Rudolph, Jr. "Increasing Capacity Utilization to Improve Return on Investment in Logistics Facilities." *Annual Conference Proceedings, NCPDM*, 1979, pp. 65–74.

Efroymson, M. A., and T. L. Ray. "A Branch Bound Algorithm for Plant Location." *Operations Research*, May-June 1966, pp. 361–69.

Eilon, S., G. D. T. Watson-Gandy, and N. Christofides. *Distribution Management: Mathematical Modelling and Practical Analysis*. New York: Hafner, 1971.

Friedman, W. F. "Physical Distribution: The Concept of Shared Services." *Harvard Business Review*, March-April 1975.

Geoffrin, A. M. "A Guide to Computer-Assisted Methods for Distribution Systems Planning." *Sloan Management Review*, Winter 1975, pp. 17–41.

Glover, F., G. Jones, D. Karney, D. Klingman, and J. Mote. "An Integrated Production Distribution and Inventory Planning System." *Interfaces*, November 1979, pp. 21–35.

H. J. Heinz Company Simulation (ICH9M78), Intercollegiate Case Clearing House, Boston.

Heskett, J. L. "Sweeping Changes in Distribution." *Harvard Business Review*, March-April 1973.

Hill, A., and D. C. Whybark. "Chexpedit: A Computer-Based Approach to the Bank Courier Problem." *Decision Sciences*, April 1982.

Khumawala, B. "An Efficient Branch and Bound Algorithm Procedure for the Uncapacitated Warehouse Location Problem." *Management Sciences*, August 1972, pp. 718–33.

Khumawala, B., and D. C. Whybark. "A Comparison of Some Recent Warehouse Location Techniques." *The Logistics Review*, Spring, 1979, pp. 3–19.

Kuehn, A. A., and M. J. Hamberger. "A Heuristic Program for Locating Warehouses." *Management Science*, July 1963, pp. 643–66.

Little, J. D. C., K. G. Murty, D. W. Sweeney, and G. Karel, "An Algorithm for the Travelling Salesman Problem," *Operations Research*, vol. 11, pp. 979–89, 1963.

Mabert, V. A. and J. P. McKenzie. "Improving Bank Operations: A Case Study at Banc Ohio/Ohio National Bank." *Omega* 8, no. 3, 1980.

Magee, J. F. *Industrial Logistics*. New York: McGraw-Hill, 1968.

Martin, A. "Distribution Resource Planning (DRP II)." *1980 APICS Conference Proceedings*, pp. 161–65.

________. *Distribution Resource Planning*. Newburg, N.H.: Oliver Wight Publications, 1983.

Mole, R. H. "A Survey of Local Delivery Vehicle Routing Methodology." *Journal of Operations Research*, March 1979, pp. 245–52.

O'Neil, B. F., and D. C. Whybark. "Vehicle Routing From Central Facilities." *International Journal of Physical Distribution*, February 1972, pp. 93–97.

Schuldenfrei, R. L., and J. M. Shapiro. "Inbound Collection of Goods: The Reverse Distribution Problem." *Interfaces*, August 1980, pp. 30–33.

Schwarz, L. B. "Physical Distribution: The Analysis of Inventory and Location." *AIIE Transactions* 13, no. 2 (June 1981).

Shycon, H. N., and R. B. Maffei. "Simulation—Tool for Better Distribution." *Harvard Business Review*, November-December 1960, pp. 65–75.

Shycon, H. N. "Site Location Analysis, Cost and Customer Service Considerations." *1974 APICS Conference Procedings*, pp. 335–47.

Stenger, A. J., and J. L. Cavinato. "Adapting MRP to the Outbound Side—Distribution Requirements Planning." *Production and Inventory Management*, 4th Quarter 1979, pp. 1–14.

Vollmann, T. E. *Operations Management*. Reading, Mass.: Addison-Wesley, 1973, pp. 393–97.

20

Other MPC approaches

In this chapter we describe three somewhat different approaches to manufacturing planning and control (MPC). The objective is to provide some basic knowledge of these approaches, as well as to put them into the perspective developed in this book. That is, we want to explain what these systems are and how they work; we also want to provide a context for thinking about new MPC systems and approaches. The three approaches have all been successfully applied. Impressive results have been achieved, and we will describe them. Achieving the results has required significant managerial and organizational changes in every case. The firm contemplating these systems must assess this dimension of the job.

The chapter is organized around the following five topics:

- The MPC system schematic: How can our general model of a manufacturing planning and control system be used to assess new systems?
- The optimized production technology (OPT) system: What is this approach? How does it work? What have been the results?
- The Kanban system: What is the Japanese Kanban system, and how does it contribute to productivity?
- The periodic control system at Kumera Oy: How did a European firm quickly improve manufacturing performance?
- Observations on the systems: What generalizations and conclusions can be drawn from these new MPC approaches?

Chapter 20 is related to many other chapters. The comparison of the three approaches utilizes some of the ideas in Chapter 1. The OPT system uses finite loading (Chapter 6). Finally, the issues encountered in implementation of all these systems are discussed in Chapter 11.

THE MANUFACTURING PLANNING AND CONTROL (MPC) SYSTEM SCHEMATIC

In this section, we relate our general model for manufacturing planning and control (MPC) systems to other systems and approaches. The MPC system schematic is presented as Figure 20.1. We first discuss the concept of a standard for MPC systems and then turn to the question of using the schematic.

The "standard" for MPC systems

It is tempting to say that the MPC system shown in Figure 20.1 is the standard for evaluating and comparing alternative systems. This is accurate in a limited but important sense. The schematic presents a set of functions that must be performed, coordinated, and managed. It does not dictate *how* the functions are to be performed. The standard is that each of these functions must be accomplished in any firm. That is, there must be front-end, engine, and back-end activities.

What is not captured in Figure 20.1 is the emphasis or importance that each module will have in a particular company. For example, firms that have only a limited number of suppliers would have a very different emphasis on the purchasing module than a company that has many vendors.

The differences between firms are not only manifested in different emphases; different systems or techniques will be used as well. Moreover, all of this needs to be viewed from an evolutionary point of view. *No* system is incapable of improvement. Once a fairly complete integrated (and transparent) system is in place, it is easier to evaluate new items and to implement them.

In summary, we see the MPC system schematic as the standard for the general functions to be performed. The specific procedures that are applied to accomplish these functions must be evaluated on an ongoing basis, both in terms of alternatives and in terms of what is currently viewed as important. In some instances, activities can be combined, performed less frequently, or reduced in importance.

Beyond the schematic

Figure 20.1 can be used as a checklist for auditing an MPC system. The crucial questions are whether each of the activities is performed, how well they are integrated, and how well each of the subsystems works. As noted above, there can always be improvements made in the subsystems.

FIGURE 20.1 Manufacturing planning and control system

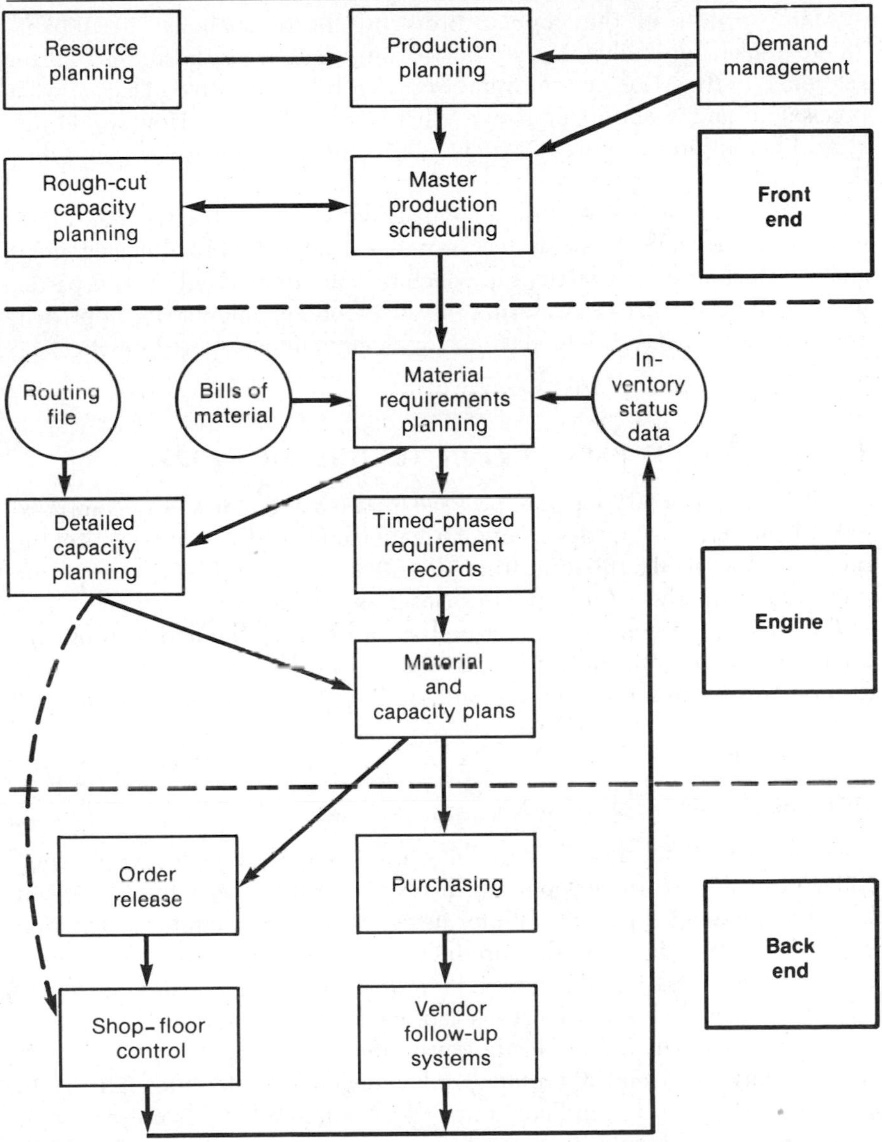

Of perhaps more fundamental importance is the role played by the MPC system in meeting the goals of the firm and supporting the management philosophy of the company. It is from this perspective that some of the latest MPC system approaches should be viewed. For example, Kanban can be viewed as an alternative to some of the techniques presented in this book. It is also appropriate to consider Kanban as it relates to high quality, the minimization of uncertainty in manufacturing, and the Japanese style of management.

Many articles in the popular press use terms such as "MRP-like," "Kanban-like," or "fully integrated." To understand what the authors mean, reference to the MPC system framework can be informative. That is, what precisely is and is not done? How? What is the data base? How would this system be put into practice? (Who would be the users and what would they do?)

For many of the approaches, a comparison with the MPC system frameworks is not enough. It is also necessary to consider the broad management and sociotechnical environment in which they are embedded. This is particularly true for the firm considering the adaptation of a new MPC approach. Sometimes it is necessary to make major changes in managerial practice and policies.

THE OPTIMIZED PRODUCTION TECHNOLOGY (OPT)

OPT is a proprietary software package from Israel that has been compared to MRP and Kanban. Little direct information on the technical aspects of the program is available. Reports from the OPT user group and some of the publications on the system provide insights into how the system works.

OPT has been generally described as utilizing mathematical programming, simulation, and network procedures. The objective is to provide a general capability for modeling complex interdependent flows through a network of production processes.

OPT and the MPC framework

OPT is sometimes described as being a complete manufacturing planning and control system. In our opinion, this is not justified. OPT has no explicit front-end module. A prerequisite for using OPT is that a master production schedule (MPS) exists, and that production planning and resource planning have been done. OPT could be used for customer order promising, since one output is a schedule for when each job will be completed.

OPT is essentially a finite loading procedure. As such, it is perhaps best thought of as a back-end system for producing detailed schedules. That is, to some extent OPT is a shop-floor control procedure. What this means is that the disaggregation (explosion of the MPS into component part plans) will still have to be done with a system such as MRP.

A fundamental principle of OPT is that only the bottleneck operations (resources) are of critical scheduling concern. The argument is that production output is limited by the bottleneck operations, and that increased throughput can only come via better capacity utilization of the bottleneck facilities.

To maximize output from bottleneck operations, larger lot sizes are run. The result is to reduce the percentage of nonproductive time devoted to setups in these work centers. For nonbottleneck work centers, the opposite lot-sizing approach is taken. Smaller batches can be made at these work centers, since the only result is to reduce the time these work centers would stand idle. Calculation of the batch sizes is a part of the OPT procedure.

We then see that OPT produces different batch sizes throughout the plant, depending upon whether a work center is or is not a bottleneck. This has several MPC connotations. In Figure 20.1, the lot sizes are produced as a part of the MRP explosion process. In typical finite loading procedures, the batch size is fixed. Such is not the case with OPT. It also follows that a batch size for one operation on a part could be different from other operations on the same part. This implies that special treatment will be required for any paperwork that travels with shop orders. In fact, OPT is designed to do order splitting. In usual practice, order splitting is done on backlogged (bottleneck) machines; it is precisely in this situation that OPT would do the opposite.

The key to lot sizing in OPT is distinguishing between a *transfer* batch (that lot size which moves from operation to operation) and a *process* batch (the total lot size released to the shop). Any differences are held in work-in-process inventories in the shop. In essence, no operation can start until at least a transfer batch is built up behind it. Also, whatever the buildup behind the work center, it *only* produces a transfer batch unless the finite scheduling routine calls for multiple batches.

To some extent, OPT is considerably broader than a finite loading system. Some users claim great abilities to do what if analysis. Several firms feel that OPT is quite useful in group technology design projects. Other MPC areas where OPT could play a role might be in the development of better master production schedules. Since OPT is a networking model, it could also be applied to the make-to-order (project) environment.

Results

OPT is a fairly recent development, and there has not been much published about it. A users group has been formed, but well-documented success stories are rare. One application was at the M & M/Mars Candy Company. M & M/Mars produces a broad line of candy products including candy bars (e.g., Snickers, Mars, Milky Way) and candy bits, including M & Ms plain and peanut chocolate candies. In an application of OPT to the production of M & Ms peanut chocolate candies, a 15 percent increase in output was realized in peanut spraying. (Overall output increased only 5 percent, however, because of bottlenecks in subsequent operations.)

A General Electric engine plant was studied with OPT as a GE corporate consulting project. The assignment took six weeks (four in data collection). The result was a production schedule which predicted a reduction of work-in-process inventories of 30 percent in three months. A 28 percent reduction was, in fact, achieved in three months.

The Prime Computer Company and Timex both intend to use OPT for worldwide planning activities. In each case, the objective is to use OPT to model the flows of materials between different geographical locations to study sourcing issues and international materials planning.

A final "result" of OPT use should be mentioned. Several OPT users have chosen OPT over MRP because they see it as a quicker, less costly way to achieve results. The final word is not yet in on the success of this strategy. The speed with which OPT can be applied has been shown. Whether it is a substitute for MRP remains to be seen.

Implementation

Since OPT is a finite loader, there are several special problems that apply to implementation. Two of these are key. The first is the general idea of believability on the shop floor and transparency of the system. OPT is a "black box" that no one on the shop floor can really understand. This might cause behavioral problems and is clearly an issue in implementation.

There is always a difficulty of implementation if the basis for the schedule is not clear to the shop-floor people who are responsible for its execution. This is aggravated when the performance evaluation of the shop-floor people is not directly related to schedule execution. Some evidence of these problems was expressed by members of the OPT users group who talked about the time required to get schedule adherence among foremen on the floor.

The second key problem of OPT is the certainty assumptions used in processing. To the extent that data are incorrect on capacities, batch time requirements, etc., the system will produce imperfect results. Use of techniques such as input/output could help in this regard.

OPT buffers the schedules by using both safety stocks and safety lead time. In scheduling a sequence of jobs on the same machine, safety timing can be introduced between subsequent batches. This provides a cushion against variations adversely affecting the flow of jobs through this same operation.

To protect against having these variations affect subsequent operations on the same job, safety time is again employed. In this case, the start of the next operation on the same job is not scheduled immediately after completion of the current operation. A delay is introduced to perform the buffering here. Note that there can be another job in process during the delay; its completion will affect the actual start date for the arriving job. Each of these allowances means that actual conditions will vary from the OPT schedule. The question for the foremen at some point could easily be *which* job to run next.

To ensure that there is always work at the bottleneck operation (to provide maximum output) there are safety stocks in front of these work centers.

Thus, whenever one job is completed, there is another ready to go on the bottleneck machine.

To protect the assembly schedule against shortages that could severely cut output, a safety stock of completed parts from the bottleneck operations are held before assembly. The idea is that disruptions of the bottleneck operation to produce a part that is short will cause reduced output. Part shortages that can be made up by going through operations that are not bottlenecks, will not cut capacity.

Finally, management factors enter into the OPT scheduling system. These help make realistic schedules that meet management criteria. Factors involving the levels of work-in-process inventory, the capacity utilization that is attainable, degree of schedule protection, and batch size controls can all be applied to the procedure. These help take into account the company culture as the procedure is implemented.

THE KANBAN SYSTEM

The Japanese have made enormous productivity gains over the last decade, and much of this has been attributed to the *Kanban* system. The Japanese word *kanban* means *card*, and a Kanban card is used to control material flows in the system. Consequently, we tend to think of the Kanban system as being a material planning and control system. The Japanese, however, think quite differently about it. To them, it is a philosophy of improving *all* manufacturing practices which leads to improved material-flow systems, as well. This is clearly the attitude at Toyota; we base much of this discussion on their systems and approach.

The Kanban philosophy

Some evidence of the breadth of the Kanban system can be seen in Figure 20.2. This is the Toyota production system. One aspect of this approach that has been widely publicized is the *just-in-time* system. Kanban is a part of the information system that supports just-in-time. Just-in-time, in turn, is but one part of the Toyota approach to providing smooth production flows.

The philosophical basis for these systems in Japan is substantially broader than material planning and control. The overall goal is to attempt to make continued improvements in the process or product. The production people at Toyota take as a desirable objective lot sizes of one piece, finished just in time to be used on the next higher level item. This would reduce in-process inventory to an absolute minimum.

The reduction of inventories and improvements in all other manufacturing activities is a continual goal for the Japanese. They draw an analogy between inventory and water in a lake full of rocks (Figure 20.3). The inventory hides the problems as the water hides the rocks. If the inventory is systematically reduced, the problems are disclosed, and attention can be

FIGURE 20.2 Toyota production system

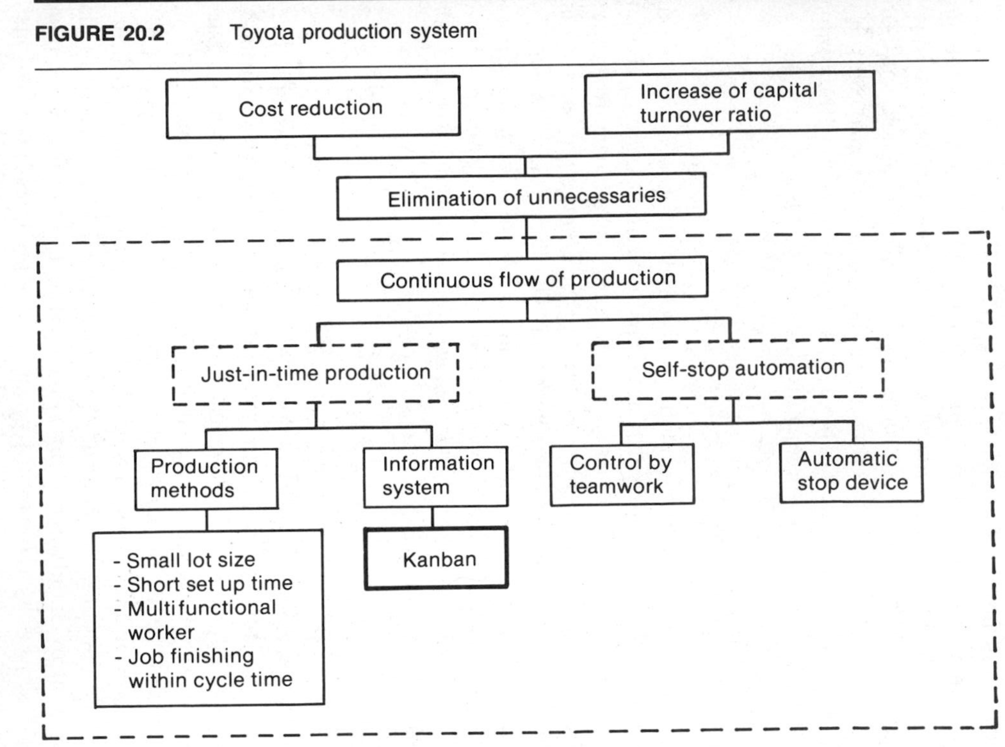

Source: European Working Group for Production Planning and Inventory Control, Lausanne, Switzerland, July, 1982.

FIGURE 20.3 Japanese view of inventory

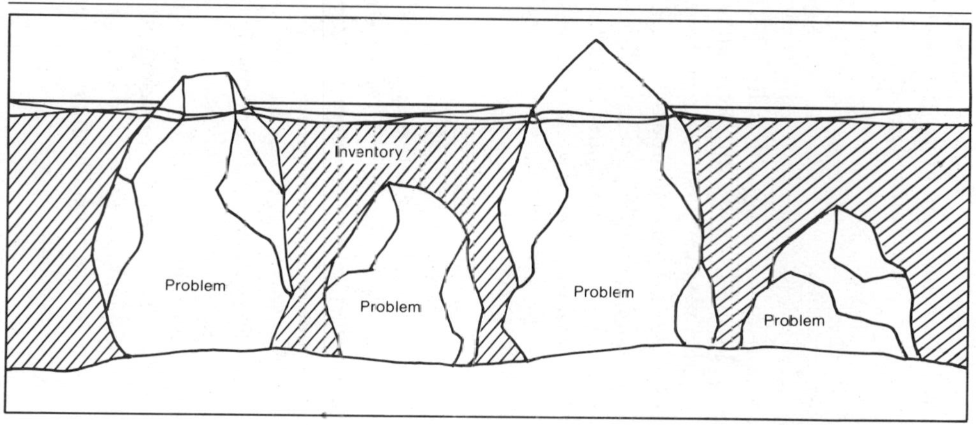

paid to solving them. Problems that are simply covered over with inventory still remain.

All this does not come free, however. A great deal of management discipline, organizational change, and capital investment is required to carry out the improvements. Moreover, the Kanban card control system is only suited to very stable production schedules. (Toyota says plus or minus 10 percent.) Thus far, the applications of Kanban have only been in repetitive manufacturing.

We first discuss the Kanban system in the perspective of the MPC framework. We then describe results of installations in Japan and Europe.

The front end

The Kanban system requires very stable schedules as a prerequisite. The preparation of these schedules starts with the production-planning process. At Toyota, the production plan has a one-year horizon. This plan is updated monthly with a marketing and finance input. The game-planning activity is very important in developing coordinated marketing/production plans.

Cooperation with marketing at Toyota is important because the master production schedule is frozen for one month. The master production schedule *is* the final assembly for the month. The next two months specify the master production schedule (MPS) by model family. All three months of the MPS are in daily buckets.

An important feature of the daily schedule is that it is identical for each day of the month. The daily rates are determined by dividing the number of units required for the month by the number of working days in the month. This gives the same production for each item in the MPS each day. This is critical to the use of Kanban.

One benefit of the daily level load is that the parts requirement explosion is made very simple. It is necessary only to explode one day's requirement for each of the three months, since it is the same for all days in the month. The parts requirements for each of the three months are distributed to each work center and supplier. The number of model/option choices at Toyota is *far* less than that for European and U.S. producers. A part of this reduction is achieved by putting several options together in an option group so there is still considerable variety possible.

The engine

The explosion process takes place each time the master production schedule gets updated. The first month's requirements at each work center or supplier are firm. They represent the schedule of need for each day. The schedules for the next two months are derived from the model families that are planned for production in each month. This gives advance capacity planning information. Each work center can assess the capacity implications of the planned schedules. If there are problems, they can be resolved before the plans are firm. The feedback is through the MPS.

Another major task performed in the engine is the determination of the number of Kanban cards to issue for each part and each work center. This calculation is performed every time the MPS is changed. The Kanban cards needed for the next month are issued to the work centers and suppliers. The process is repeated the next month. Whenever there is a change needed in the number of cards, it can be executed by production control or foremen on the shop floor.

The back end

In this section, the discussion will be phrased in terms of work centers in the factory, but Toyota treats a large number of their suppliers just as work centers. They refer to these vendors as *coproducers*. Indeed, many of the vendors use the Kanban system in their plants as well, although it is not required.

The heart of the shop-floor activities is the Kanban card. We will describe a system with two types of Kanban cards: a transport (conveyance) card and a production card. An example is shown in Figure 20.4. The transport card

FIGURE 20.4 Kanban cards

Conveyance Kanban

Part number: 33311-3501
Container capacity: 50
No. of Kanban released: 7 of 12

Following work center: K123
Stock location no.: A-12

Stock location no.: A-07
Preceding work center: Y321

Production Kanban

Work center no.: Y321
Part number to be produced: 33311-3501
Container capacity: 50 units
Stock capacity at which to store: A-07
Materials required:
Material no. 33311-3504
Stock location: A-05
Part no. 33825-2474
Stock location: B-03

Source: R. W. Hall, *Driving the Productivity Machine: Production Planning and Control in Japan* (Falls Church, Va.: American Production and Inventory Control Society, 1981), p. 37, Reprinted with permission, American Production and Inventory Control Society, Inc.

FIGURE 20.5 Flow of Kanban cards

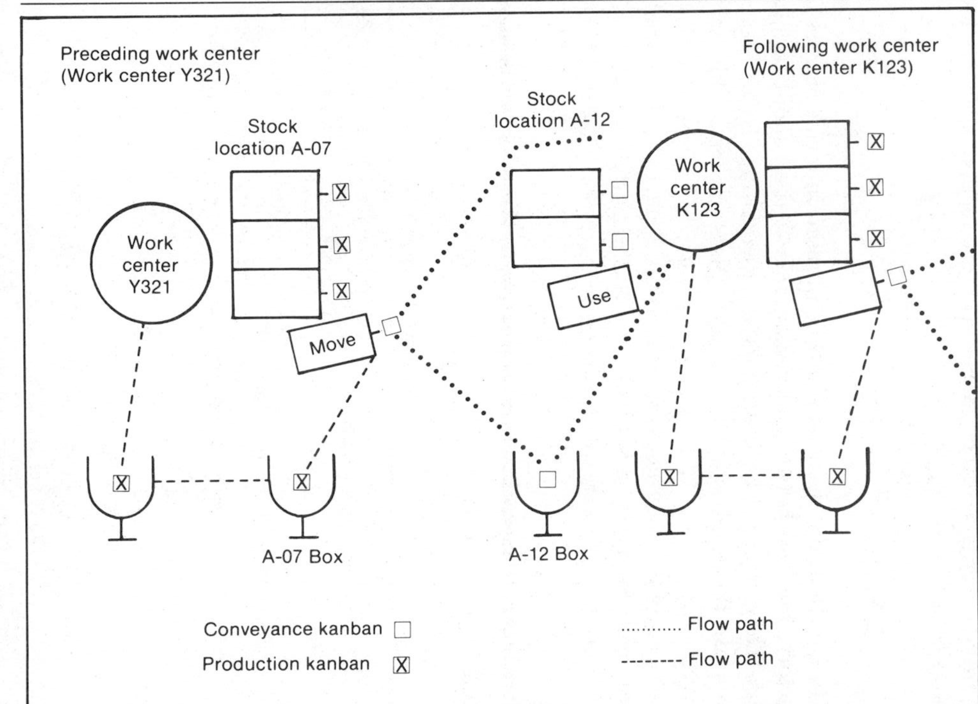

Source: R. W. Hall, *Driving the Productivity Machine: Production Planning and Control in Japan* (Falls Church, Va.: American Production and Inventory Control Society, 1981), p. 38.

need only contain information on from where to where, part number, and quantity. There may be other information, as well (e.g., which of how many Kanbans is this, special instructions, etc.). The production Kanban may also have information relating to lot sizes, materials required, and standard times. The Kanban cards replace all work orders, dispatch sheets, move tickets, etc. Routing sheets may be used for some complex parts *inside* a work center.

The exchange of Kanban cards for all shop paper is a *very* important attribute of the Kanban system. Kanban works with small lot sizes (just-in-time concept). One could think of doing this with MRP, perhaps based on hourly buckets. However, the process of opening and closing a shop order in MRP takes time and effort. It is precisely this time and effort that is avoided by Kanban. Moreover, the lead time required to open and close orders has to be reflected in inventories. These are also reduced with Kanban.

The flow of the Kanban cards is illustrated in Figure 20.5. The system simply replaces what was used in a subsequent operation. When a worker on the assembly line removes a container from inventory, the transport Kanban is removed. It is used to authorize the materials handler to bring another container to replace the one just used. This replacement aspect makes the system very much like a base stock system.

As soon as a material handler moves a container from inventory at the work center that produces the part, the production Kanban is removed and placed where the foremen of the work center can see that it is necessary to produce another full container. This chain of Kanban cards can extend all the way back to the suppliers.

The Kanbans control the flow of materials by authorizing production and product movement. No additional paper is required. Since the daily schedules are the same, no priority systems are necessary. Notice also that the number of Kanbans directly affects the level of work-in-process inventory. The more Kanban cards, the more containers filled and waiting to be used at a work center.

The formula that is used to calculate the number of Kanbans needed is given in Figure 20.6. In this formula, there is a factor for introducing safety

FIGURE 20.6 Calculating the number of Kanbans

$$y = \frac{DL(1 + \alpha)}{a}$$

where:
y = Number of kanbans.
D = Demand per unit of time.
L = Lead time.
a = Container capacity.
α = Policy variable (safety stock).

stock, which Toyota says should be less than 10 percent. Using the formula, no safety stock, and a container size of 1, we can see the philosophy of the system. If a work center required eight units a day (one per hour) and it took one hour to make and deliver one unit, only one Kanban card would be theoretically necessary. That is, just as a unit was finished, it would be needed at the subsequent operation.

The container sizes are kept small and standard. Toyota feels no container should have more than 10 percent of a day's requirements. Since everything revolves around these containers and the flow of cards, a great deal of discipline is necessary. The following rules are used to keep the system operating:

1. Each container of parts must have a Kanban card.
2. The parts are always pulled. That is, the using department must come to the providing department for parts and not vice versa.
3. No parts may be obtained without a Kanban card.
4. All containers contain their standard quantities and *only* the standard container for the part can be used.
5. No extra production is permitted.

These rules keep the shop floor under control. The execution effort is to keep all parts moving according to the schedule in the Kanban card dictated quantities.

Using the Kanban system

It is important to recall Figure 20.2, where Kanban is shown as only one part of the Toyota production system. The concept of just-in-time is of higher importance than Kanban, which is one tool to make this happen. The objective is to lower the water, or reduce the inventory. This means a constant attack on how to reduce lead times, work in process, and setup times. The result is fewer Kanban cards and smaller quantities in the containers.

One beauty of the Kanban system is its simplicity. It is largely a manual system, and we can readily see the relation between Kanban cards, work orders, and work in process. Moreover, it is possible to understand *why* reducing Kanban cards is of importance—and exactly what will be the result. It is also possible to not use a card for a few days to see whether it could be eliminated. Again, the workers can feel that they are in charge while trying to improve production in a recognized way.

The simplicity of Kanban allows workers to concentrate on solving the problems revealed by lowering the water. The rocks (problems) can be too-large lot sizes (how to cut setup times), vendor problems, scrap losses, etc. *Solving* those problems is a participative process. The firm uses quality control circles as one key means to find and solve problems. These quality circles generate a large number of improvement suggestions. Since the workers are also instrumental in *implementing* the suggestions, the implementation process goes well. Implementation also involves change at the direct-labor worker level. Because of the participative aspects of the quality circles, there is less resistance to change and more interest in upgrading skills required to do the best job—as that job keeps being redefined.

A reduction in the number of Kanban cards is directly analogous to reducing lead time as it is done in some shop-floor control systems. However, the emphasis in the Kanban system is much more strongly on the direct labor workers to do this. In more usual shop-floor scheduling systems, lead-time reduction is more the job of supervisors or even staff persons in materials management. With Kanban, lead time reduction is *everyone's* job.

Not all of the parts to make a Toyota are planned and controlled with Kanban. The system is only used for about 60 to 70 percent of the part numbers. The rest fall into two categories. Large items such as engines and chassis are scheduled directly. The other class of items not scheduled/controlled with Kanban are options. However, the number and variety of options at Toyota is carefully managed. The net result is that Kanban does *not* do everything. What it does do is provide a simple routine mechanism to plan and control the shop—one that is highly transparent.

The results of Toyota's system are found on the highways of the world. Their systems took about 15 years to reach the stage of maturity at which it was drawing worldwide attention. Many other Japanese firms have developed similar systems, and some Western firms are now experimenting with such approaches.

Results from two Japanese firms are typical of results from diligent users in Japan. One firm reported labor productivity increased 40 percent in four years, inventory dropped 80 percent in two years, and the quality reject percentage dropped to 10 percent of its value four years previously. The second firm experienced a 30 percent improvement in labor productivity in two years, a 60 percent reduction in work in process in two years, and a 15 percent reduction in plant space in three years. In both cases, it took several years to prepare the plant and work force to reap the benefits reported.

The L.M. Ericsson Company in Sweden installed a Kanban system in a relay assembly plant. Their results have been impressive, as can be seen in Figure 20.7. They have not done all the things that Toyota has done, yet they have made good progress. After L.M. Ericsson had embarked upon their Kanban installation, several Swedish managers studied their approach. One summarized his views in Figure 20.8. Note that the Kanbans are just about the last thing in the implementation schedule.

A variant of Kanban installed by the Yamaha Motor Company is called Synchro MRP. It is, in essence, a system that combines attributes of Kanban and MRP. A major issue at Yamaha is that the company cannot level its MPS for one month. (They try to level it for 10 days.) Moreover, they have many model and engineering changes. Yamaha felt the Kanban system would not work well in this dynamic environment. As a consequence, they use MRP to

FIGURE 20.7 Kanban at L. M. Ericsson

	Toyota	*Ericsson, Sweden*
Job rotation	Yes	Yes—partly
Group wage incentive	Yes	Yes—partly
Balancing	Yes	No
Self-stop automation	Yes	Yes—partly
Quality control circles	Yes	No
Kanbans	Yes	Yes
α Less than 10 percent	Yes	No
α Less than 10 percent of daily requirements	Yes	Yes—partly
Product-oriented layout	Yes	Yes—partly
Smoothing of production	Yes	No

Results:		
	Throughput time	56 → 12 days
	Turnover rate	4 → 15 times per year
	Raw material and work-in-process inventories	1.2 → 0.2 million Swedish kroner

Source: European Working Group for Production Planning and Inventory Control, Lausanne, Switzerland, July, 1982.

FIGURE 20.8 Kanban implementation schedule at L. M. Ericcson

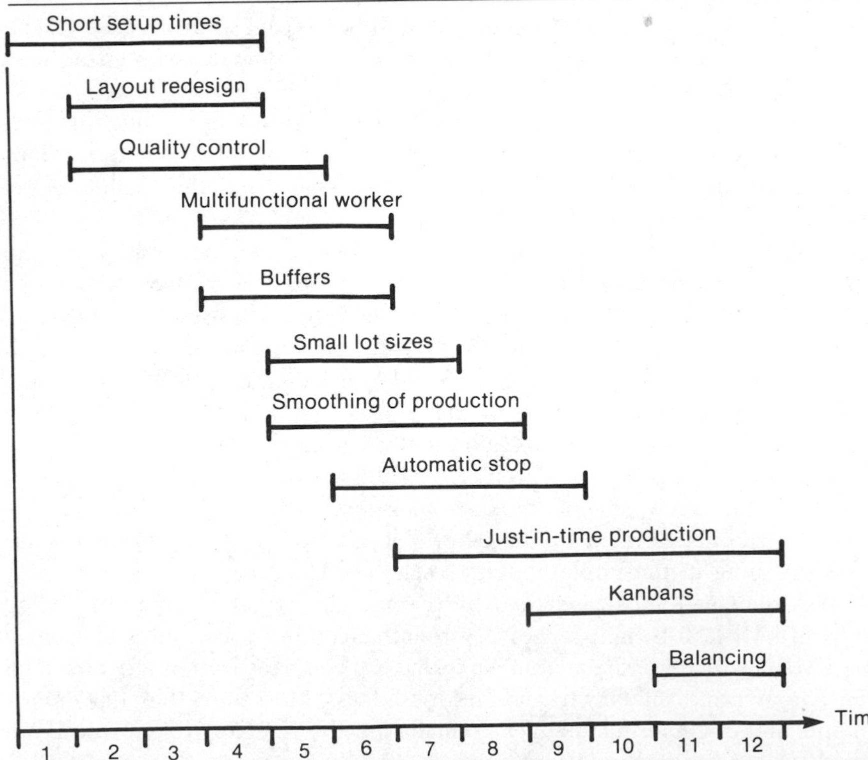

Source: European Working Group for Production Planning and Inventory Control, Lausanne, Switzerland, July, 1982.

schedule their *synchro* cards. This permits them to manage the changes explicitly. The system is very complex, however; perhaps more so than a comparable U.S. MRP system.

The use of synchro MRP is designed to achieve the major benefits we have seen with Kanban. Synchro MRP also uses cards like Kanban cards to reduce paper flow times and to work with small batch sizes. At Toyota, Kanban is only used for 60 to 70 percent of the parts—those that can be made repetitively. This separation concept is even more critical for Yamaha. They divide their work centers into repetitive centers and job-shop centers. Within the 10-day frozen MPS, the repetitive centers function very much as they would under Kanban. A new 10-day schedule allows for all engineering changes to be reflected in the product structure data base, and to thereafter be exploded into the synchro cards. Operating the system requires the same discipline and interest in continual improvements that are described for the basic Kanban system.

THE PERIODIC CONTROL SYSTEM AT KUMERA OY

Kumera Oy is headquartered about 40 miles north of Helsinki in Riihimäki, Finland. The company produces a broad range of gear-driven, speed-reducing power transmissions. They engage in all phases of manufacturing, from engineering to parts fabrication and assembly. Kumera employs about 450 people in four manufacturing plants and two sales affiliates located in four countries. The periodic control system has been installed in all plants except one.

A typical product would consist of a housing, mounting devices, shafts, gears, assembly hardware, and perhaps a motor. Some 50 different part numbers would be usual, with 100 or more individual pieces. Of the 50 part numbers one third to one half would be manufactured (generally the large items such as gears, shafts, housings, etc.), and the rest purchased. Under usual conditions, the lead times for some of the items would exceed two months, though most are within five weeks. The large number of potential end items possible means virtually no finished-goods inventory can be carried, but competitive pressures require short delivery times to customers. The periodic control system has helped resolve this basic conflict between sales and production.

The system

To describe the periodic control system, we use the manufacturing planning and control system shown in Figure 20.1. The description of the system will start with the front-end activities, pass to the engine, and will conclude with the back end. The production planning part of the front end is an intimate part of the company game planning. The resultant commitment to an integrated plan provides direction to the specific production-planning and control activities.

The first step in the installation of the periodic control system was the designation of production product groups. The planning and scheduling activities could not be based on specific end items since the number is too large, and the company must quote delivery times less than total product lead times. Five product groups have been formed on the basis of production process similarities. Within each group, divisions exist for product options. The groupings do not exactly conform to the catalogue product families, but it is easy to translate from customer orders to the groups for order entry purposes.

The groupings facilitate front-end activities. Forecasts are made at the main option level and are aggregated by product group as the basis for demand management, budgeting, profit and cash planning, and production planning. Production and resource planning specify the overall production rate and any capacity expansion that the company will undertake. The resulting plan (which reflects sales, finance, and engineering objectives, as well) is a one-year plan, by week, in units, for each of the five product groups.

The product groups provide the basis for master production scheduling. The basic process will be illustrated using an example with the five groups, shown in Figure 20.9. To start, rough-cut capacity planning ensures that capacity at key machines will be available to produce the forecast product group mix before going forward with master production scheduling.

The master production schedule is based on the period of the periodic control system. It is determined by dividing the year into equal periods. Each of the groups of products will be scheduled *once* during a period.

FIGURE 20.9 Group forecasts, capacity allocation, and periodic quantities

Product group	*Annual forecast*	*Share of available labor (percent)*	*Capacity of key machine (percent)*	*Period quantities*
A	500	15	25	50
B	100	20	5	10
C	1,000	10	30	100
D	2,000	25	20	200
E	1,500	30	10	150

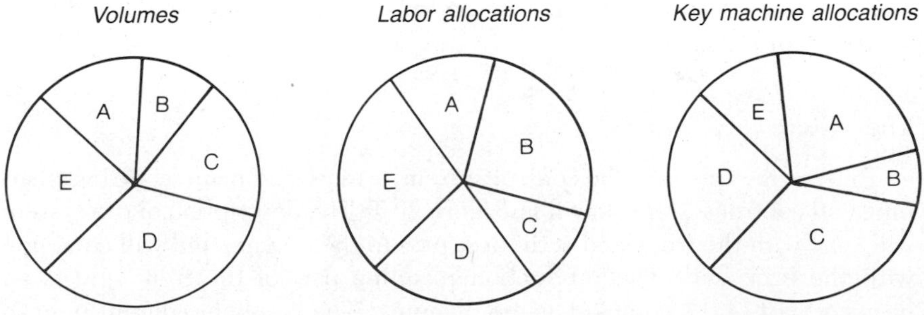

Volumes *Labor allocations* *Key machine allocations*

Source: D. C. Whybark, "Production Planning and Control at Kumera Oy," Proceedings of the National AIDS Conference, San Francisco, 1982.

FIGURE 20.10 Sequence for releasing production orders for groups

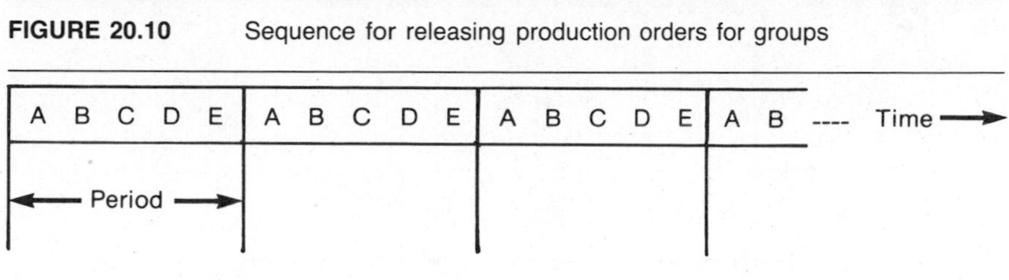

Period length trade-offs

Longer period	Shorter period
Manufacturing efficiency	Quicker customer response
Larger purchase quantities	Lower inventories (cyle stock)
Fewer setups	Higher potential market share

Source: D. C. Whybark, "Production Planning and Control of Kumera Oy," Proceedings of the National AIDS Conference, San Francisco, 1982.

Kumera calls the specific products to be produced a *production set*. Actual customer orders are assigned to the production set in a period, using available-to-promise concepts. That is, actual orders replace the period quantities used for planning. The shop orders for production of all of the components necessary to produce the actual customer orders in particular production sets are released at one time. In general, the components are *only* for those specific items in the production set. The sequence of production sets within a period is based on manufacturing efficiencies in changing from one group to another.

The choice of a repetitive cycle of production aids control and coordinates the release dates of production orders. The length of period determines how many units of each group will be made in a production set. The quantity effects the manufacturing costs. The length of period also affects how much of the production can be made strictly to order and how much to forecast. These and other factors which influence the length of the period are indicated in Figure 20.10. The final decision requires managerial assessment of the trade-offs between all these factors.

For the example in Figure 20.9, a period of five weeks was chosen. This means each group will be scheduled 10 times per year (using a 50-week year). Once the period length is chosen, forecasts are used to calculate the number of products to be produced in each production set each period. Figure 20.11 shows the master production schedule for the example. The manufacturing objective is to have completed, by the fifth week of the period, all materials required for assembly of the actual products in each production set. This means that, as the next group A is launched, the previous group A is being scheduled into assembly (see the top of the schedule). Kumera thinks in terms of the launch date for each production set (see the bottom of the schedule). They provide wide dissemination of the timing table data to customers and vendors, and within the company.

FIGURE 20.11 Master production schedule (the timing table)

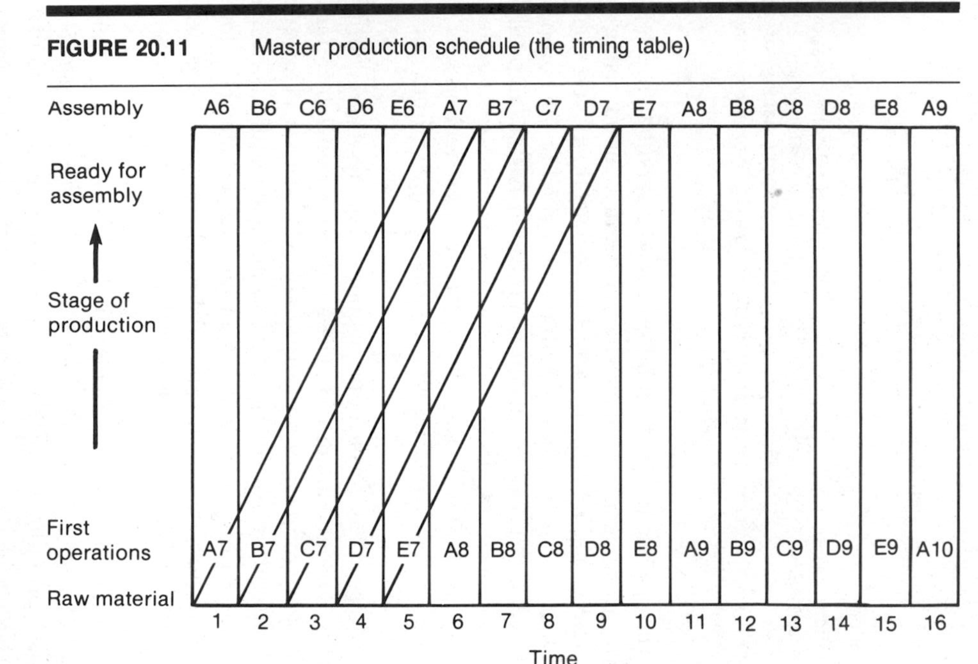

Source: D. C. Whybark, "Production Planning and Control of Kumera Oy," Proceedings of the National AIDS Conference, San Francisco, 1982.

To specify material requirements, the exact customer orders to be produced in a production set must be determined. This is the job of order entry in demand management. An attempt is made to assign each order to the production schedule that will meet the delivery date requested by the customer. For example, a request for an item from the B product group for delivery in week 14 would be assigned to B_8 if possible (see Figure 20.11).

The order promising is done in accordance with the commitment between marketing and manufacturing. No more orders may be entered into a production set than the period quantity (e.g., 10 units for B in each production set). Once the period quantity is reached, the next customer order must be delayed until a later production set, or the order must be exchanged for one that is in an earlier set. Kumera looks at the timing table as a train schedule. When the launch date arrives, the production orders for the set are released (the train leaves). The sales department can make any allocation of schedule dates among customers until the train leaves for the factory. After that no more changes, they have to wait for the next train. No release is made for any order that does not have the engineering completed, thereby avoiding potential mix-ups in manufacturing. If the launch date arrives and the "train is not full," sales can decide to make some orders in anticipation (i.e., against a forecast), but this is very dangerous in this firm since almost all orders are custom-made. The alternative is to pull up an order from a production set scheduled for a later release. At the date of launch, the train *leaves*—sometimes with empty seats! That is, if the production set is not up to the period quantity, the company only makes to order. In the words of one Kumera manager, "If there are empty beds in the hospital, you don't go out and make people sick just to fill the beds."

When the release date has arrived, a composite bill of material is prepared for the actual set of customer orders in the production set. The composite bill is built up from the separate bills for each of the actual orders in the set. Actual inventories and allocations are checked against the computer records (Kumera runs well over 95 percent accuracy) before calculation of the net requirements and release to the shop.

Lot sizing is performed for selected items. The bill of material processor can look ahead to the actual orders in the next and subsequent production sets for end items that use the same parts. Subject to parameters on how far ahead to look, some aggregation of order demands can be used to justify the production of more than the net requirements.

Once the quantities have been determined, items are released to the factory floor and the shop-floor control system carries them through to completion. The purchased items are scheduled to be received as needed on the week before the staging week. (This provides one week of safety lead time.) They are collected into an assembly storage area where they are joined by the manufactured parts.

Purchase and shop orders are released at the same time. Shop orders have an implicit due date at assembly staging time (five weeks hence in the example). Purchased raw materials are due as needed during the five weeks, and purchased assembly components are due prior to the assembly staging week. Kumera numbers the production sets in release date sequence. The sequence numbers are displayed conspicuously on all shop papers associated with the production set. They provide a very simple shop-floor priority rule: "Always work on the lowest-numbered item next."

The production set sequence numbers are also used for other circumstances. For example, emergency production of pieces not required in assembly (e.g., a part needed because a customer's machine is down) can be accomplished by assigning a low number. The scheme can also be used for producing low-priority items as capacity is available (e.g., service parts not immediately required). The assembly foreman schedules the assembly sequence to make an efficient progression through the products in the production set. If any products are still awaiting parts, their assembly can be delayed until the latter part of the week. The late parts will have the lowest number (highest priority) on the shop floor, and so will go through as quickly as possible.

Not all purchase orders can be delayed until the release date for the production set because of long lead times. In these cases, the purchase quantities are calculated to provide just enough inventory to produce the period quantities scheduled for future production. Kumera works at keeping the parts and raw materials that are ordered this way highly common. The commonality and gross to net logic used in calculating the production quantities help keep the residual inventories low. To help key vendors plan their production, Kumera provides them with the timing table data. Vendor follow-up is done from this information or the staged inventories for assembly.

Using the system

The simplicity of the periodic control system enabled Kumera to do the implementation in about six months. The initial system was totally manual. It was converted to the computer two years later. The system required certain disciplines and induced others. Some were necessary to use the system effectively, while others provided the opportunity for later improvements.

Inventory accuracy is essential at the time of net requirement calculation. The physical check at the time the bill of material is processed ensures correct counts. At Kumera, the required accuracy is maintained even though not all inventory is locked up. The short period helps maintain accuracy since there is less time for shrinkage; short periods also result in smaller production lots and lower inventory quantities.

The marketing disciplines were the most difficult—no more maximization of sales or arbitrary delivery promises. There were to be no more orders in a given production set than the period quantities. The customers were to be told honestly when delivery could be expected and, if it was not good enough, exchanges with previously scheduled customers would have to be worked out or the order lost. There would be no more "we'll try" answers.

At the management level, the adherence to the game plan and a willingness to back the order entry function when difficult decisions were being made was required. Management integrated the budget and profit-planning activities with the periodic control concept. That way, all the management activities were keyed to the same basic information and control reports.

In production, the required disciplines were not as difficult, but some major changes were required. The new priorities had to be followed and reliance on "hot" or shortage lists had to stop. The quantities indicated on the shop orders would be the quantities produced. (No more running a "few extra" since the machine is set up.) The short period meant more setups and lower inventories.

One of the reactions to Kumera's improved delivery capacity was a shift in customer behavior. As they recognized that the promised delivery dates were honest, customers began to rely on them. The distribution of the timing table data to customers shifted their ordering patterns to correspond more closely with Kumera's schedules.

Much the same thing happened with vendors. As vendors realized that the timing table really was used for purchasing, they found they could make better plans. The distribution of the data to key vendors reinforced this. As Kumera reduced the amount of "panic" buying, the utility of the schedule for the vendors was further reinforced.

Internal changes evolved, as well. Engineering was added to the order entry checks. No customer order is released to the shop without complete engineering. This means that order entry must check before promising a delivery date (assignment to a production set) for any product on which there is a substantial amount of engineering. The same is true for orders needing long-lead-time items that are not part of the common items purchased prior to release. Purchasing is consulted before a promise date is given.

Payoffs

There have been many tangible benefits from the installation of the periodic control system and some intangible ones, as well. Principal among the tangible benefits have been the reduction in inventories, improvement in margins and customer service, and reduction in the number of expeditors. These are summarized in Figure 20.12.

The development of the production groupings has greatly facilitated the forecasting task and helped focus marketing on meeting their sales objectives for the groups. The scheduling and priority systems have routinized management of the production and assembly activities. The problems are very visible. This focuses management attention on them quickly, very much as the Japanese approach does.

FIGURE 20.12 Some payoffs from periodic control

	Before periodic control	*After implementation*	*Currently*
Inventory turns	2.5	9.2	10.1
Late deliveries	50%	10%	0%
Gross margin (percent)	10	27	30
People: Production control	4	1	1
People: Expediting	2	1	0

Source: D. C. Whybark, "Production Planning and Control at Kumera Oy," Proceedings of the National AIDS Conference, San Francisco, 1982.

The simplicity of the system makes it easy to work with. The system is transparent to everyone in the company, so they can make well-informed decisions. No one guesses at priorities, changes instructions on work in process, or shifts the schedule around. This has improved all working relationships and further enhances the attitude of working together to solve problems as they appear.

Engineering changes are much easier to implement and manage. They are always tied to a particular production set, in a way similar to that done by Yamaha. With very low inventories in the shop and actual customer orders in every production set, the effectivity dates for engineering changes are much easier to determine and control.

One strong test of the system and its benefits was the recession in Finland. Kumera managed to expand business during the period, largely due to their customer-service capability. At the same time, they have vertically integrated. The periodic control system has been installed in their new acquisitions (except the foundry) as a first step in improving the operations.

The periodic control system at Kumera is more than a technique for planning and controlling production. It is a management tool and state of mind, like the Kanban system at Toyota. The application of sound management principles at the front end of the system is key to the successful application of the engine and back-end techniques. A great deal of attention is focused on the timing table at Kumera. But the timing table is just one aspect of the entire process.

OBSERVATIONS ON THE SYSTEMS

In this chapter we have examined three quite different approaches to manufacturing planning and control. In each case, we conclude that it is necessary to have a front end, an engine, and a back end. It is tempting to focus attention on engine/back-end activities, losing sight of the need for the front end. It is also tempting to focus on techniques, losing sight of managerial dimensions.

OPT can be seen as a finite loading/scheduling system. More broadly, it can be seen as a simulation model to configure work stations, capacities, and flows. Implementation of OPT raises some interesting questions. As a black box, it is almost the antithesis of Kanban.

Kanban needs to be seen less as a technique than as one single piece of a mosaic. Kanban is a very transparent system to support just-in-time production, that is designed to clearly point out all problems, which, in turn, are to be identified and worked on in a participative way (quality circles)—part of the basic philosophy of Japanese management.

Periodic control is a transparent system that can be visualized as the timing table to coordinate production sets. Again, this view is shortsighted. Periodic control has allowed the company to shorten lead times, make accurate promises, and truly coordinate their operations with those of customers and suppliers. Achievement of these objectives was less a technical matter than one of management.

The message from each of these approaches is clear. The system may be less important than the management. The Bell Telephone Company did us a disservice when they came up with the slogan, "The system is the answer." In fact, the system is not the answer; management is the answer. The system is the tool that improves the answer.

CONCLUDING PRINCIPLES

- There is no "ultimate weapon" in MPC system. Firms should continually be evaluating improvements.
- Use of the MPC framework is useful in assessing where a particular approach or system fits into the firm.
- Once a working MPC system is in place, improvements can often be made more easily.
- Improvements in the MPC system must be integrated with the management and direction of the company.
- Management commitment is more important to installing new MPC systems than is technical expertise.

REFERENCES

Bolander, S. F., R. C. Heard, S. M. Seward, and S. G. Taylor. *Manufacturing Planning and Control in the Process Industries.* Falls Church, Va.: American Production and Inventory Control Society, 1981.

Goldratt, E. M. "Optimized Production Timetable (OPT): A Revolutionary Program for Industry." *APICS Annual Conference Proceedings*, 1980, pp. 172–176.

Hall, R. W. "What Can Americans Copy From Japan?" *APICS Repetitive Manufacturing Seminar Proceedings*, Las Vegas, April 1981.

________. *Kawasaki U.S.A.: Transferring Japanese Production Methods to the United States.* Falls Church, Va.: American Production and Inventory Control Society, 1982.

________. *Driving the Productivity Machine.* Falls Church, Va.: American Production and Inventory Control Society, 1981.

Kumpulainen, Vesa. *Periodic Production Control,* 11100 Rühimaki 10, Finland, Kumera Oy, 1983.

Mattila, Veli-Pekka. *Periodic Control System,* 11100 Rühimaki 10, Finland, Kumera Oy, 1983.

Monden, Yasuhiro. "Adaptable Kanban System Helps Toyota Maintain Just-In-Time Production." *Journal of Industrial Engineering,* May 1981, pp. 29–46.

Nakane, J., and R. W. Hall. "Management Specs for Stockless Production." *Harvard Business Review,* May/June 1983, pp. 84–91.

Nellemann, David O., and Roy L. Harmon. "MRP vs Kanban: Combining the Best of the East and West." *APICS Planning and Control Seminar Proceedings,* Las Vegas, March 1982, pp. 49–58.

Powell, Cash. "Systems Planning/Systems Control." *Production and Inventory Management,* 1st Quarter 1977.

Schonberger, R. J. *Japanese Manufacturing Techniques.* New York: Free Press, 1982.

APPENDIX

Self-testing questions

This appendix contains questions similar to those found on the certification examinations of professional societies in this field. The questions are organized by chapter, beginning with Chapter 2. The answers for all of the questions may be found on the last three pages of the Appendix.

Chapter 2

1. The following *input* data are required by an MRP system:
  a. Lead time estimates, inventory balances, bill of materials.
  b. Planned orders, reorder points, critical ratios.
  c. Both *a* and *b*.
  d. Neither *a* nor *b*.

2. The following information shows product and MRP records relating to part A.

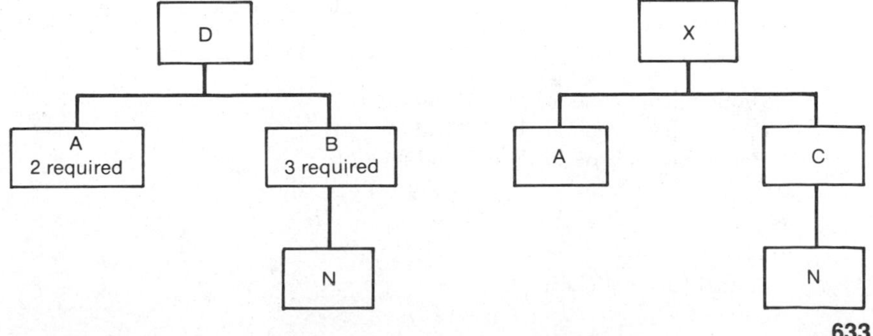

Part A		1	2	3	4	5	6
Gross requirements		15	10	30	10	20	10
Scheduled receipts		35					
Projected available balance	28						
Planned order releases							

Lead time = 2
Order quantity = 35
Safety stock = 20

In what weeks should there be planned order releases for part A?

a. 1 and 4.
b. 2 and 3.
c. 1 and 3.
d. 1, 2, and 3.
e. Some other combination.

3. The XYZ company manufactures three products X, Y, and Z. The product structures are shown below.

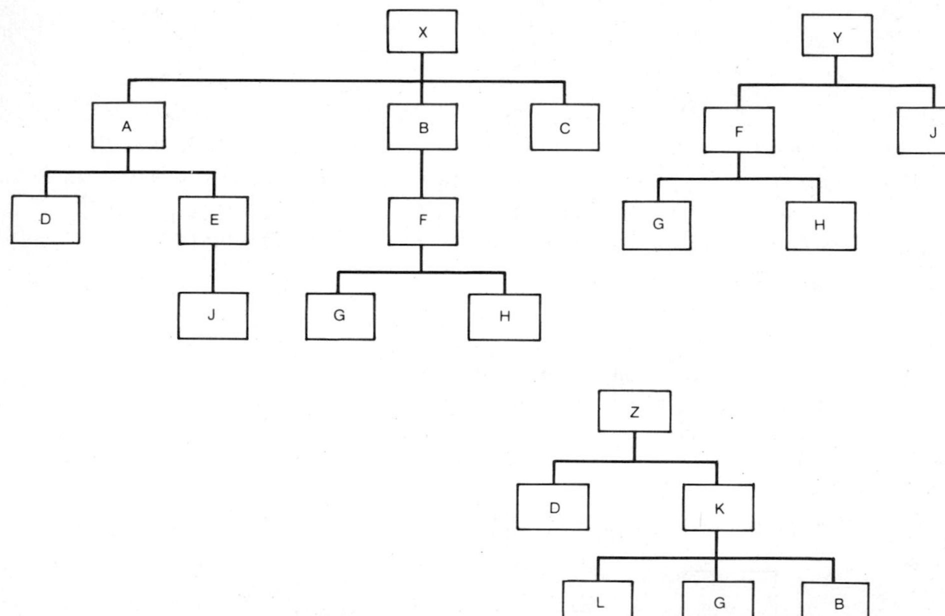

I. The low level code for D is 1 and for K is 1.
II. The low level code for H is 2 and for G is 3.
III. The low level code for K is 1 and for G is 3.

a. I only.
b. II only.
c. III only.
d. II and III are both correct.
e. None of the above statements are true.

4. The product structure and schedule of planned order release data for two products of the Ajax Company are as follows:

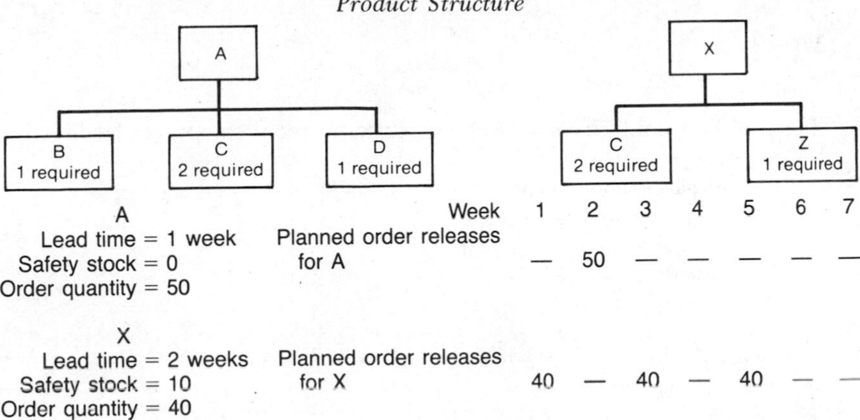

If there is also an independent demand for 100 units of C in week 3, the total gross requirements for C over the 7 weeks is:

a. Less than or equal to 150.
b. Greater than 150 but less than or equal to 250.
c. Greater than 250 but less than or equal to 350.
d. Greater than 350 but less than or equal to 450.
e. Greater than 450.

Answer questions 5 and 6 using the time-phased record for item A below.

		1	2	3	4	5	6
Gross requirements		50	50	50	50	50	50
Scheduled receipts							
Projected available balance	75						
Planned order releases							

Item A
Lead time = 1
Order quantity = 75

5. Using the MRP record for item A, in what weeks should there be planned order releases (assuming no safety stock)?

a. 1, 3, and 4.
b. 2, 4, and 5.
c. 1, 2, 4, and 5.
d. 1, 2, 3, 4, and 5.
e. None of the above.

6. Using the MRP record for item A, in what weeks should there be planned order releases (assuming a safety stock of 25 units)?

a. 1, 3, and 4.
b. 2, 4, and 5.
c. 1, 2, 4, and 5.
d. 1, 2, 3, 4, and 5.
e. None of the above.

7. A regeneration of the MRP records is generally done every:
   a. Hour.
   b. Day.
   c. Week.
   d. Month.
   e. Quarter.

8. In an MRP record for a component part, the gross requirements can be directly related to:
   a. Parent part planned orders.
   b. Parent part scheduled receipts.
   c. Parent part gross requirements.
   d. Both *a* and *b*.
   e. Both *b* and *c*.

9. For Sears Roebuck, independent demand would be for:
   a. Bicycle baskets.
   b. Bicycle spare parts.
   c. Unassembled bicycles.
   d. Assembled bicycles.
   e. All of the above.

Week		1	2	3	4	5	6	7	8	9	10	11	12	13	14	15
Gross requirements		5	0	10	25	10	20	10	10	10	5	5	5	10	20	30
Scheduled receipts				55												
Planned receipts							30				15		60			
Projected available balance	20	15	15	60	35	25	35	25	15	5	15	10	65	55	35	5
Planned order releases					30				15		60					

10. The above record is for part Q.

    If there is no safety stock required for part Q, the record shows a safety lead time of:
   a. 0 weeks.
   b. 1 week.
   c. 2 weeks.
   d. 3 weeks.
   e. 4 weeks or more.

Chapter 3

1. If a scheduled receipt for part N has been changed by an inventory planner from week 5 to week 6, the influence on the shop floor control system should be to:
   a. Change the due date on the appropriate shop order from week 5 to week 6.
   b. Change the due date on the appropriate shop order from week 6 to week 5.
   c. Change the due date on the appropriate shop order from week 5 to week 4.
   d. Leave the due date on the shop order unchanged.
2. A key requirement for an effective MRP system is:
   a. Accurate lot sizing based on the EOQ formula.
   b. Accurate forecasts.
   c. Accurate inventory records.
   d. Accurate cost estimates.
   e. Both *a* and *b*.
3. All of the following are correct except:
   a. Scheduled receipts are directly tied to entries in the planned order release row.
   b. Scheduled receipts are created as the actual work is commenced.
   c. Scheduled receipts account for open shop orders.
   d. Scheduled receipts account for open purchase orders.
   e. Scheduled receipts are an integral part of time phased records.
4. Which of the following is *not* true with regard to MRP?
   a. MRP provides a central focus for production planning and inventory control in the manufacturing environment.
   b. The stockroom is the nerve center in MRP-oriented manufacturing.
   c. Inventories exist primarily to support production schedules.
   d. Once an order is launched, its date of need, quantity, and relative priority will not change.
   e. The combination of time phasing and gross to net explosions is the heart of MRP.

The following MRP record for part N was generated at the beginning of period 1. It will be used for questions 5, 6 and 7.

		Period				
		1	2	3	4	5
Gross requirements		40	0	10	15	75
Scheduled receipts		40				
Projected available balance	25	25	25	15	10	10
Planned order releases		0	10	75		

Lead time = 2
Safety stock = 10
Order quantity = Lot-for-lot

The following transactions occur during period 1:
a. 5 units of the scheduled receipt of 40 in period 1 are scrapped.
b. 40 units of part N are disbursed in period 1.

5. After regeneration in period 2, the record would show that all of the following are true except:
   a. The planned order release for period 2 will be 10.
   b. The planned order for period 4 will be exactly equal to the gross requirements for period 6.
   c. There will be 10 units of inventory at the end of period 3.
   d. The 10-unit gross requirement in period 3 can be met.
   e. The 15-unit gross requirement in period 4 can be met.

6. Assume that the worker did not tell anyone about the scrap, and no transaction for scrap was processed. After processing the record for period 2, it would show all the following as true except:
   a. The planned order release for period 2 will be 10.
   b. The planned release for period 4 will be exactly equal to the gross requirement for period 6.
   c. There will be 10 units of inventory at the end of period 3.
   d. The 10-unit gross requirement in period 3 can be met.
   e. The 15-unit gross requirement in period 4 can be met.

7. Assume the 5 units of scrap was recorded properly *and* that a cycle count found 8 more parts in inventory than shown by the records. When the MRP record is updated at the beginning of period 2, the projected available balance for period 3 would be:
   a. Less than or equal to 5.
   b. Greater than 5 but less than or equal to 10.
   c. Greater than 10 but less than or equal to 15.
   d. Greater than 15 but less than or equal to 20.
   e. Greater than 20.

8. Data base integrity requires all of the following except:
   a. No informal systems can be tolerated.
   b. No action is worth a mismatch between a record and reality.
   c. Transactions must be processed within 24 hours.
   d. Responsibility for transaction processing must be assigned to accounting.
   e. Transactions should be integrated with shop–floor-based systems; e.g., payroll.

9. Creation of a shop order involves all of the following except:
   a. Deleting a planned order release.
   b. Allocation.
   c. Availability checking.
   d. Creation of a scheduled receipt.
   e. Rescheduling.

10. An effective cycle counting program utilizes all of the following except:
   a. Continuous counting of on hand-balances.
   b. More frequent counting of C items than B items.
   c. Tight control over all "ins" and "outs"
   d. Controlled access to the stockrooms.
   e. Tolerance limits on errors.

Chapter 4

The following data are to be used for questions 1, 2, and 3:

Products	*Production last year*	*Standard hours/unit*	*MPS*	
			Jan.	*Feb.*
A	100	1	10	15
B	150	2	20	15
C	200	3	10	15

Work center	*Historical percentage of total labor hours*	*Bill of capacity in standard hours/unit*		
		A	*B*	*C*
100	65%	.4	1.4	1.8
200	35%	.6	1.6	1.2

Resource profile

Standard hours required by month for one end product to be completed in February

	January	*February*
End product A		
Work center 100	.1	.3
Work center 200	0	.6
End product B		
Work center 100	.9	.5
Work center 200	0	.6
End product C		
Work center 100	1.4	.4
Work center 200	1.2	0

1. The expected capacity load (in standard hours) for work center 100 in January using CPOF (capacity planning using overall factors) is:
a. Less than or equal to 50.
b. Greater than 50 but less than or equal to 70.
c. Greater than 70 but less than or equal to 90.
d. Greater than 90 but less than or equal to 110.
e. Greater than 110.

2. The expected capacity load (in standard hours) for work center 100 in January using bills of capacity is:
a. Less than or equal to 50.
b. Greater than 50 but less than or equal to 70.
c. Greater than 70 but less than or equal to 90.
d. Greater than 90 but less than or equal to 110.
e. Greater than 110.

3. If the production of products A, B, and C is on schedule, the expected capacity load (in hours) for work center 100 in January using resource profiles is:
   a. Less than or equal to 50.
   b. Greater than 50 but less than or equal to 70.
   c. Greater than 70 but less than or equal to 90.
   d. Greater than 90 but less than or equal to 110.
   e. Greater than 110.

4. Work center 48B has the following two jobs:

Job	*Part*	*Order quantity*	*Quantity remaining*	*Started*
1011	X	40	30	Yes
1172	Y	20	20	No

Standard time data

Set-up hours		*Run time per piece*
X	2 hrs.	1.0 min.
Y	1 hr.	5.0 min.

The capacity required at work center 48B to complete these two jobs is:
   a. Less than or equal to 100 minutes.
   b. Greater than 100 but less than or equal to 200 minutes.
   c. Greater than 200 but less than or equal to 300 minutes.
   d. Greater than 300 but less than or equal to 400 minutes.
   e. Greater than 400 minutes.

The following data are to be used for questions 5, 6, and 7.

	Week		
	Start	*1*	*2*
Planned input		5	6
Actual input		7	7
Cumulative deviation	0		
Planned output		8	8
Actual output		6	7
Cumulative deviation	0		
Backlog	15		

5. The cumulative input deviation for week 2 is:
   a. Less than or equal to −3.
   b. Greater than −3 but less than or equal to 0.
   c. Greater than 0 but less than or equal to 3.
   d. Greater than 3 but less than or equal to 6.
   e. Greater than 6.

6. The cumulative output deviation for week 2 is:
   a. Less than or equal to −3.
   b. Greater than −3 but less than or equal to 0.

c. Greater than 0 but less than or equal to 3.
d. Greater than 3 but less than or equal to 6.
e. Greater than 6.

7. The actual backlog for week 2 is:
   a. Less than or equal to 5.
   b. Greater than 5 but less than or equal to 10.
   c. Greater than 10 but less than or equal to 15.
   d. Greater than 15 but less than or equal to 20.
   e. Greater than 20.

8. Which of the following procedures requires the most extensive data base?
   a. Capacity planning using overall factors.
   b. Capacity planning using resource profiles.
   c. Capacity planning using bills of capacity.
   d. Capacity requirements planning.
   e. Shop floor control.

9. In input/output analysis, the capacity planning procedure provides:
   a. The planned input.
   b. The actual input.
   c. The planned output.
   d. The actual output.
   e. The actual backlog.

10. Alterations planning is a procedure which examines the impact of changes in timing or quantity of selected values of the:
   a. Bills of capacity.
   b. Resource profiles.
   c. Capacity requirements planning.
   d. Master production schedule.
   e. Shop floor control.

Chapter 5

The following data are to be used for questions 1, 2, 3, and 4.

Part XYZ, lot size = 100, shop order 1234, due date = at the end of 20 days.

Operation	*Work center*	*Set-up*	*Run time per piece**	*Run time for 100**	*Queue time + move time**
1	100	3	.1	10	25
2	200	5	.2	20	25
3	300	9	.3	30	33
Total		17		+ 60	+ 83 = 160 hours†

* In hours
† 160 hours = 4 weeks = 20 days

Shop order 1234 was issued on Monday morning of week 1. It is now Friday morning of week 1 and operation 1 has been completed.

1. The order slack for shop order 1234 is:
   a. Less than or equal to 20 hours.
   b. Greater than 20 but less than or equal to 40 hours.
   c. Greater than 40 but less than or equal to 60 hours.
   d. Greater than 60 but less than or equal to 80 hours.
   e. Greater than 80 hours.

2. The slack per operation for shop order 1234 is:
   a. Less than or equal to 20 hours.
   b. Greater than 20 but less than or equal to 40 hours.
   c. Greater than 40 but less than or equal to 60 hours.
   d. Greater than 60 but less than or equal to 80 hours.
   e. Greater than 80 hours.

3. The critical ratio for shop order 1234 is:
   a. Less than or equal to 0.5.
   b. Greater than 0.5 but less than or equal to 1.0.
   c. Greater than 1.0 but less than or equal to 1.5.
   d. Greater than 1.5 but less than or equal to 2.0.
   e. Greater than 2.0.

4. The value used by the shortest operation next sequencing rule for shop order 1234 is:
   a. Less than or equal to 20 hours.
   b. Greater than 20 but less than or equal to 40 hours.
   c. Greater than 40 but less than or equal to 60 hours.
   d. Greater than 60 but less than or equal to 80 hours.
   e. Greater than 80 hours.

5. One main goal of a shop floor control system is to:
   a. Establish shop order priorities.
   b. Establish shop order due dates.
   c. Both *a* and *b*.
   d. Neither *a* nor *b*.

6. In critical ratio scheduling, when the (due date-now) is a negative value, the due date
   a. Can be met by reducing run times.
   b. Can be met by reducing set up times.
   c. Can be met by reducing either queue or move times.
   d. Cannot be met.

7. Most finite loading systems in practice use:
   a. Horizontal loading.
   b. Vertical loading.
   c. Both *a* and *b*.
   d. Neither *a* nor *b*.

8. Lead time management is best accomplished by:
   a. Reducing set-up times.
   b. Reducing run times.
   c. Reducing queue times.
   d. Reducing move times.

9. The Twin Disc priority scheduling system rule is:
   a. Schedule jobs by critical ratio.
   b. Schedule jobs by critical ratio for (PO) orders before (PI) orders.
   c. Schedule jobs by critical ratio for (PI) orders before (PO) orders.
   d. Schedule jobs by shortest operation next for (PO) before (PI) orders.
   e. Schedule jobs by slack per operation for (PI) before (PO).

10. A work center scheduled with critical ratio has all jobs with priorities greater than 1.0.
   a. All jobs are ahead of schedule.
   b. All jobs are behind schedule.
   c. Capacity needs to be increased.
   d. Both *b* and *c*.

Chapter 6

1. In the Twin Disc open P.O. Buyer Fail-Safe Report, the F Week is the week to which at least some quantity of a present purchase order:
   a. Must be expedited.
   b. Can be deexpedited.
   c. Both *a* and *b*.
   d. Neither *a* nor *b*.

2. In the Twin Disc open P.O. Buyer Fail-Safe Report, the F Quantity is the quantity:
   a. To be expedited.
   b. Of the projected shortage.
   c. Both *a* and *b*.
   d. Neither *a* nor *b*.

3. In the Twin Disc open P.O. Buyer Fail-Safe Report, a purchase order might appear in the F Week column for any of the following reasons except:
   a. Cycle counting.
   b. Increase in gross requirements.
   c. Customer order cancellation.
   d. Scrap.
   e. Service part demand.

4. Providing planned order data to vendors allows them to improve all of their MPC systems except:
   a. Master production schedule.
   b. Material requirements planning.
   c. Shop floor control.
   d. Capacity planning.
   e. Cycle counting.

5. A state of the art purchasing package should allow one to perform analyses on all of the following bases except:
   a. Part.
   b. Operation.
   c. Vendor.
   d. Buyer.
   e. Commodity.

6. A state of the art purchasing package should allow one to evaluate all of the following except:
   a. Cost.
   b. Delivery.
   c. Storage.
   d. Scrap.
   e. Rework.
7. At Steelcase, buying has been separated from all of the following activities except:
   a. Planning order quantities.
   b. Issuing purchase orders.
   c. Scheduling delivery dates.
   d. Prioritizing orders.
   e. Performing value analysis.
8. The materials management concept provides a common organizational focus for all of the following except:
   a. Purchase orders.
   b. Shop orders.
   c. Bills of material.
   d. On-hand balances.
   e. Transactions.
9. The interaction between Twin Disc and Neenah Foundry is analogous to that between Steelcase and Cannon Mills.
   a. The analog for the molds at Neena is the cotton cloth at Cannon.
   b. The analog for the castings at Twin Disc is the colored cloth at Steelcase.
   c. Both *a* and *b* are correct.
   d. Neither *a* nor *b* is correct.
10. Purchasing in an MPC framework includes all of the following activities except:
    a. Buying materials.
    b. Releasing orders.
    c. Following up orders.
    d. Maintaining backup files.
    e. Analyzing performance.

Chapter 7

The following data are to be used for questions 1 and 2

The Alaskan Fertilizer Cooperative has recently developed a cumulative charting model in order to coordinate its urea fertilizer production with its barge shipments of fertilizer to customers in the Matanuska Valley. The cumulative charting model is shown below:

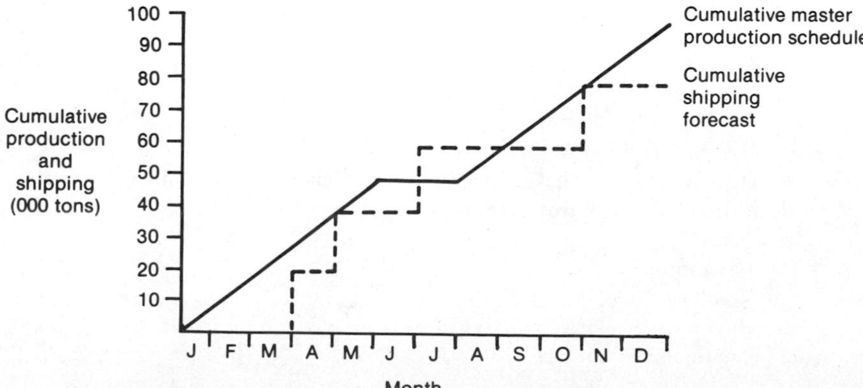

Notes:

I. There are no barge shipments after December 15 nor before April 1 because of heavy ice conditions in the Cook Inlet.

II. Monthly production is 10,000 tons except for June and July when the plant is shut down for maintenance.

III. Each barge shipment is 20,000 tons when fully loaded.

1. Based upon the existing shipping schedule, which barge shipment will not be a full load?
   a. April 1 *b.* May 1 *c.* July 1 *d.* November 1 *e.* None of the above

2. If the barge shipments are rescheduled for every two months beginning April 1, which is the first shipment that will not have a full load?
   a. April 1.
   b. June 1.
   c. August 1.
   d. October 1.
   e. December 1.

3. The cumulative chart below depicts two alternative production plans.

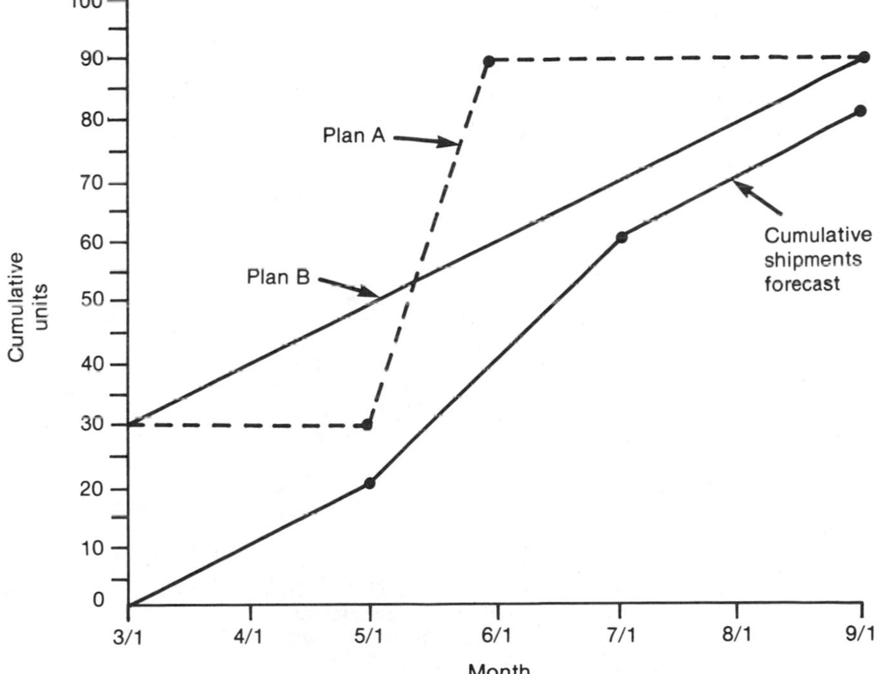

The average additional monthly inventory that will be held if plan A is followed instead of plan B over the 6-month period indicated is:
a. Less than or equal to 0 units.
b. Greater than 0 units but less than or equal to 5 units.
c. Greater than 5 units but less than or equal to 10 units.
d. Greater than 10 units but less than or equal to 15 units.
e. Greater than 15 units.

4. The purpose of Master Production Scheduling is to:
   a. Specify the planned output in terms of production.
   b. Sequence jobs at individual machines in a machine shop.
   c. Schedule individual orders at all of the machines in a department.
   d. Schedule end product items in an assemble-to-order company.
   e. Construct the bills of material for component parts.

5. All of the following statements concerning the Master Production Schedule (MPS) are true except:
   a. The MPS is an anticipated production schedule.
   b. The MPS drives MRP and shop floor control.
   c. The MPS is a detailed plan for control of materials.
   d. The MPS on a cumulative basis must never be less than the cumulative planned shipments.
   e. The MPS is the disaggregation of the aggregate or production plan.

The following data are to be used for questions 6 and 7.

	Week					
	1	*2*	*3*	*4*	*5*	*6*
Forecast	25	25	25	25	25	25
Orders	30	20	10			
Available						
Available to promise						
Master production schedule	75			75		

On-hand = 50

6. The available to promise in week 1 is:
   a. Less than or equal to 0.
   b. Greater than 0 but less than or equal to 40.
   c. Greater than 40 but less than or equal to 60.
   d. Greater than 60 but less than or equal to 80.
   e. Greater than 80.

7. The available in week 3 is:
   a. Less than or equal to 0.
   b. Greater than 0 but less than or equal to 40.
   c. Greater than 40 but less than or equal to 60.
   d. Greater than 60 but less than or equal to 80.
   e. Greater than 80.

	Period									
	1	2	3	4	5	6	7	8	9	10
Forecast	10	5		10	10		20	20		
Orders	10		12		60	20			10	
Available	60	55	43	83	23	3	33	13	3	53
Available to promise										
Master production schedule	50			50			50			50

On-hand = 20

8. The Mighty Zapper has the above partially completed time-phased MPS record:

   The available to promise in period 1 for the Zapper is:
   a. Less than or equal to 20 units.
   b. Greater than 20 units but less than or equal to 30 units.
   c. Greater than 30 units but less than or equal to 40 units.
   d. Greater than 40 units but less than or equal to 50 units.
   e. Greater than 50 units.

9. Product B is made in batches of 50 units at a time. At the beginning of month 1 there are no units of product B in inventory. The sales forecast for Product B over the next 6 months is as follows:

Month	*Forecast sales (units)*
1	30
2	30
3	30
4	50
5	50
6	50

   In which months will the master production schedule indicate that a batch of product B should be made assuming that demand must be satisfied in each month and that inventory levels are to be kept to a minimum?
   a. Months 1, 2, 3, 4, and 5.
   b. Months 1, 3, 4, 5, and 6.
   c. Months 1, 2, 4, 5, and 6.
   d. Months 1, 2, 3, 5, and 6.
   e. Months 1, 2, 3, 4, and 6.

10. The Drake Manufacturing Company produces three products, and all three use the same production equipment. Thus, it is not possible to produce the products simultaneously. The equipment has a rated capacity of 25 hours per week. The following data have been compiled on the three products.

	Product	Inventory	Weekly forecast	Lot size	Hours required per lot size
A.	Shipley Shotglasses	10	4	40	15
B.	Hillside Beer Mugs	30	30	60	10
C.	The Lounge Ashtrays	20	10	60	15

What product(s) should be scheduled to start during week 1?

a. A then B.
b. B then A.
c. C then A.
d. A then C.
e. B then C.

Chapter 8

1. The Paintyur Wagon Company sells wagons in either red, white, or blue, with mud flaps of either silver, gold, jewels, or fur. The number of end items is:
   a. Less than or equal to 3.
   b. Greater than 3 but less than or equal to 6.
   c. Greater than 6 but less than or equal to 9.
   d. Greater than 9 but less than or equal to 12.
   e. Greater than 12.

The following super bill has been constructed for the Paintyur Wagon Company. Use the data to answer questions 2, 3, and 4.

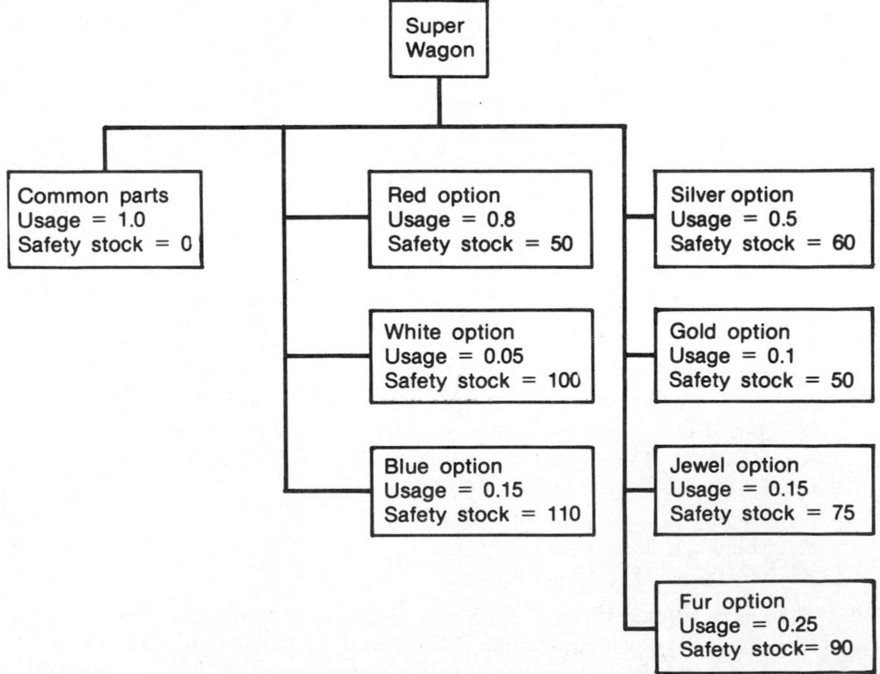

2. The master scheduler releases an order for 500 super wagons. This results in a gross requirement for red options of:

a. Less than or equal to 350.
b. Greater than 350 but less than or equal to 400.
c. Greater than 400 but less than or equal to 450.
d. Greater than 450 but less than or equal to 500.
e. Greater than 500.

3. If 50 red wagons are in inventory and 20 have been promised to customers when the 500 units released in question 2 become available, the available to promise for red options is:
a. Less than or equal to 350.
b. Greater than 350 but less than or equal to 400.
c. Greater than 400 but less than or equal to 450.
d. Greater than 450 but less than or equal to 500.
e. Greater than 500.

4. The available to promise for common parts is:
a. Less than or equal to 350.
b. Greater than 350 but less than or equal to 400.
c. Greater than 400 but less than or equal to 450.
d. Greater than 450 but less than or equal to 500.
e. Greater than 500.

5. The final assembly schedule is most critical in a firm that:
a. Makes to stock.
b. Makes to order.
c. Assembles to stock.
d. Assembles to order.

6. All of the following statements about the demand time fence time period are correct except:
a. It is the point of last commitment to an end item.
b. It is equal to the final assembly schedule lead time.
c. It is less than the planning time fence period.
d. It is the point where all MPS quantities become firm planned orders.
e. It is the point where decisions result in the firm becoming either make-to-stock or make-to-order.

7. All of the following about option over planning are correct except:
a. One objective is to get expensive parts into common parts.
b. Common parts have a usage less than one.
c. Safety stocks are utilized.
d. Gross to netting replenishes safety stocks.
e. Safety stocks are not utilized for common parts.

8. In the Ethan Allen approach to master production scheduling, the firm planned order is used for all of the following except:
a. Market specials.
b. New items.
c. TPOP orders.
d. Customer orders.
e. Frozen schedule.

9. Volume hedging is based upon:
a. Safety stocks for each option.
b. Buffers kept just beyond the planning time fence.
c. Commitment to end items at the demand time fence.
d. Product mix variations.
e. Small value parts.

10. An overstated master production schedule results in all of the following except:
    a. A mismatch between budget and MPS.
    b. Poor capacity utilization.
    c. Erosion of the formal system.
    d. Poor customer service.
    e. Past due MPS.

Chapter 9

1. A production plan might be stated in any of the following units except:
    a. Dollars.
    b. Aggregate units.
    c. End items.
    d. Strategic business units outputs.
    e. Tons.

2. Production planning has a direct interaction with all of the following except:
    a. Resource planning.
    b. Demand management.
    c. Game planning.
    d. Master production scheduling.
    e. Material requirements planning.

3. The production plan is:
    a. A forecast of demand.
    b. A statement of production output.
    c. Both *a* and *b* are correct.
    d. Neither *a* nor *b* is correct.

4. The Ethan Allen monthly cycle for the production planning process includes all of the following activities except:
    a. Sales screening.
    b. Six-month economic review.
    c. Statistical forecast.
    d. Master production schedule (MPS).
    e. Material requirements planning (MRP).

5. The cumulative chart below is for Sagging Zugs.

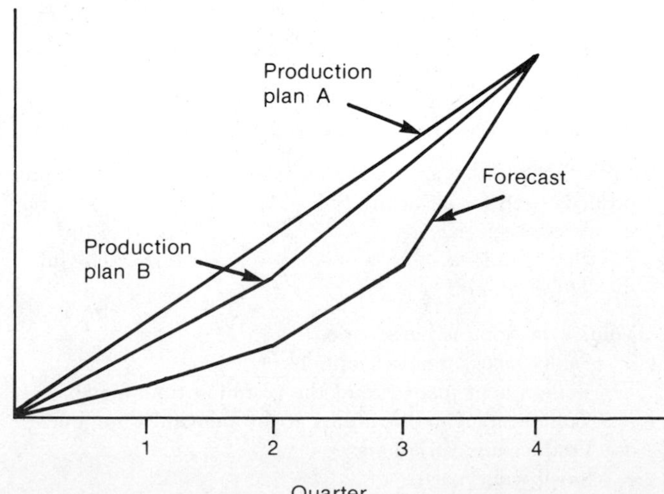

Based on the cumulative chart for Sagging Zugs, all of the following statements are correct except:

a. The forecast increases for each quarter.
b. Plan A will result in more average inventory than plan B.
c. Plan B will result in a change in output rate at mid-year.
d. Plan A will result in more level production than plan B.
e. Plan B will result in better protection against stockouts than plan A.

The following data are to be used to answer questions 6, 7, and 8:

Quarter	*Demand (units)*
I	10,000
II	19,000
III	17,000
IV	10,000

Beginning inventory (beginning of quarter I)	= 0 units
Beginning work force	= 120 workers
Hiring cost	= $100 per worker hired
Firing cost	= $500 per worker fired
Wages	= $2,700 per worker per quarter
Overtime payroll cost	= Two times base wage
Productivity	= 100 units per worker per quarter on regular time
Inventory carrying cost	= $10 per unit per quarter
Backorder cost	= $50 per unit per quarter

6. Assume that the firm decides to produce just enough to meet the demand each quarter, operates with zero ending inventory for each quarter, and does not use overtime or undertime. The total annual cost of an aggregate schedule based on this approach would be:
   a. Less than or equal to $1,450,000.
   b. Greater than $1,450,000 but less than or equal to $1,550,000.
   c. Greater than $1,550,000 but less than or equal to $1,650,000.
   d. Greater than $1,650,000 but less than or equal to $1,750,000.
   e. Greater than $1,750,000.

7. The total annual cost of an aggregate schedule based on a constant rate of output per quarter, using no overtime, permitting backorders between quarters; and completing the year with zero inventory is:
   a. Less than or equal to $1,450,000.
   b. Greater than $1,450,000 but less than or equal to $1,550,000.
   c. Greater than $1,550,000 but less than or equal to $1,650,000.
   d. Greater than $1,650,000 but less than or equal to $1,750,000.
   e. Greater than $1,750,000.

8. For the aggregate schedule based on the approach to question 7, ending inventory will exist in:
   a. Quarter I.
   b. Quarter II.
   c. Quarters I and II.
   d. Quarters I, II, and III.
   e. None of the above.

9. In preparing the production plan at Mohawk (called the "delivery plan"), all of the following are considered except:
   a. Cash requirements.
   b. Component part requirements.
   c. Sales forecasts.
   d. Desired inventory changes.
   e. Personnel availabilities.

10. The Hill-Rom planning bill of material:
   a. Is established so as to utilize the same units as those used in strategic planning.
   b. Derives the planning for minor products such as overbed tables from the planning of major products such as beds.
   c. Both *a* and *b* are correct.
   d. Neither *a* nor *b* is correct.

Chapter 10

1. Demand management deals with all of the following except:
   a. Order entry.
   b: Order delivery date promising.
   c. Service part demands.
   d. Raw material planning.
   e. Intra-company requirements.

2. Which of the following forecasts will be subject to the largest percentage error?
   a. End items by week.
   b. End items by month.
   c. Product family by week.
   d. Product family by month.
   e. Annual sales in monetary units.

3. Percentage forecasting:
   a. Derives the total or aggregate forecast from the individual item forecasts.
   b. Results in a reduced number of end item forecasts.
   c. Both *a* and *b* are correct.
   d. Neither *a* nor *b* is correct.

4. In distribution requirements planning (DRP), the zero level in the bill of material is typically:
   a. The end item.
   b. Major subassemblies.
   c. Product options.
   d. The end item in the central warehouse.
   e. The end item in a distribution warehouse.

The following data are to be used to answer questions 5, 6, and 7.

Warehouse A
(Lead time = 1 period, shipping quantity = 20, safety stock = 12)

Period		1	2	3	4	5
Forecast		10	10	10	10	10
Scheduled receipts		20				
Projected available balance	15					
Planned shipments						

Warehouse B
(Lead time = 2 periods, shipping quantity = 50, safety stock = 10)

Period		1	2	3	4	5
Forecast		25	25	25	25	25
Scheduled receipts						
Projected available balance	90					
Planned shipments						

5. The planned shipments for warehouse A are in periods:
   a. 3 and 4.
   b. 3.
   c. 2 and 3.
   d. 2.
   e. 1 and 3.
6. The planned shipments for warehouse B are in periods:
   a. 3 and 4.
   b. 3.
   c. 2 and 3.
   d. 2.
   e. 1 and 3.
7. Assuming no other distribution warehouses, the gross requirements at the central warehouse in period 1 are:
   a. Zero.
   b. Greater than zero but less than or equal to 20.
   c. Greater than 20 but less than or equal to 40.
   d. Greater than 40 but less than or equal to 60.
   e. Greater than 60.
8. In DRP, the firm planned shipment is used to stabilize:
   a. Demand at central.
   b. Demand at distribution centers.
   c. Both *a* and *b*.
   d. Neither *a* nor *b*.

9. Distribution centers A and B have exponential smoothing forecasts of 10 and 25 per period, respectively, for some product. An overall forecast for this product is 30 units per period for the next 2 periods and 50 units thereafter. Using the approach of Abbott Laboratories, North Chicago, the forecast for distribution center A in period 1 would be:
   a. Less than or equal to 7.
   b. Greater than 7 but less than or equal to 8.
   c. Greater than 8 but less than or equal to 9.
   d. Greater than 9 but less than or equal to 10.
   e. Greater than 10.

10. Using the data and approach in question 9, the forecast for distribution center B in period 3 would be:
   a. Less than or equal to 30.
   b. Greater than 30 but less than or equal to 33.
   c. Greater than 33 but less than or equal to 36.
   d. Greater than 36 but less than or equal to 39.
   e. Greater than 39.

Chapter 11

1. A class "A" MPC system includes all of the following except:
   a. Shop floor dispatching.
   b. Vendor scheduling.
   c. Shortage lists.
   d. Game planning.
   e. Capacity planning and control.

2. Which of the following is true:
   a. A class "D" MPC system only works in the data processing department.
   b. It costs as much to be a class "D" user as it does to be a class "A" user.
   c. Both *a* and *b* are correct.
   d. Neither *a* nor *b* is correct.

3. All of the following data elements must be accurate to high levels except:
   a. Forecasts.
   b. Open orders.
   c. Inventory records.
   d. Bills of material.
   e. Routing records.

4. In order to achieve data accuracy, it is imperative that tight control be exercised over all of the following transaction procedures except:
   a. Item master changes.
   b. Backup file maintenance.
   c. Engineering changes.
   d. Scrap reporting.
   e. Rejected materials.

5. In the Swissair approach to project management the primary project leader (called a "system planner") is:
   a. A professional project manager whose career path is to become ever better at project management.
   b. An expert in systems and data processing.
   c. Both *a* and *b* are correct.
   d. Neither *a* nor *b* is correct.

6. The primary MPC project team should include representatives from:
   a. Marketing.
   b. Engineering.
   c. Both *a* and *b*.
   d. Neither *a* nor *b*.

7. The MPC system implementation should be divided into subprojects that each have definite goals. A reasonable maximum expected time for each subproject is:
   a. Six months.
   b. One year.
   c. Two years.
   d. Three years.
   e. Four years.

8. Education for first-line managers and other system users must include:
   a. Training in the way the new systems will impact the person's individual area.
   b. Broad based education to provide a new set of frameworks and understanding.
   c. Both *a* and *b*.
   d. Neither *a* nor *b*.

9. All of the following queries should be used to evaluate an MPC system except:
   a. Are the time buckets no longer than one month?
   b. Is there a defined measure of customer service?
   c. Are machine center outputs compared with expectations?
   d. Is a cycle counting system in place?
   e. Is there a well functioning approach to engineering change control?

10. Implementation of an MPC system includes all of the following costs except:
   a. Computer hardware.
   b. Computer software.
   c. Finished goods inventory.
   d. Consultants.
   e. Project team personnel.

Chapter 12

1. A firm has estimated annual requirements of 9,000 and an economic order quantity of 700. If the firm uses the period order quantity, orders will be placed every:
   a. Week.
   b. Two weeks.
   c. Three weeks.
   d. Four weeks.
   e. Five weeks or longer.

2. Which of the following lot sizing procedures uses dynamic programming?
   a. Economic order quantity.
   b. Period order quantity.
   c. Part period balancing.
   d. Wagner Whitin.
   e. McLaren's order moment.

3. In comparing McLaren's order moment and part period balancing
   a. Part period balancing out performs McLaren's order moment in conditions of certainty.
   b. It is hard to distinguish the performance of lot sizing procedures when uncertainty grows above some value.
   c. Both *a* and *b* are correct.
   d. Neither *a* nor *b* is correct.

4. The following record is for battering rams:

Period:		*1*	*2*	*3*	*4*	*5*	*6*	*7*	*8*	*9*	*10*	*11*	*12*
Requirements		20	80	0	40	5	1100	100	0	75	25	400	200
Scheduled receipts													
Planned receipts					1145			175			625		
Projected available balance	100	80	0	0	1105	1100	0	75	75	0	600	200	0
Planned order releases				1145				175		625			

   The order quantity for the rams appears to be based on:
   a. Economic order quantity.
   b. Period order quantity.
   c. Part period balancing.
   d. Wagner-Whitin.
   e. McLaren's order moment.

5. A product T, which is assembled in batches of 400, has 3 component parts: A, B, and C.

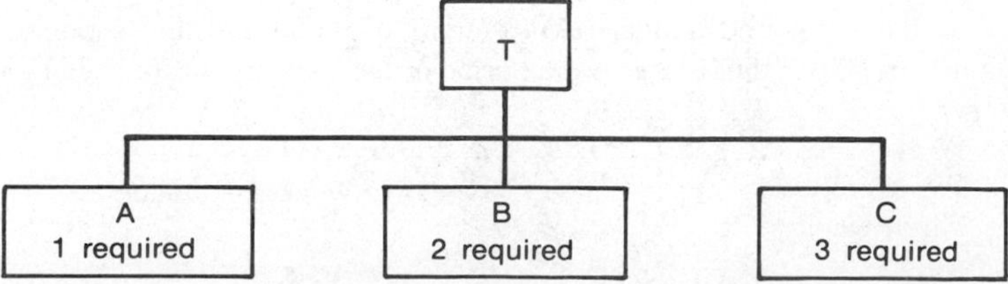

	Calculated EOQ
T....	400
A....	447
B....	730
C ...	120

a. The best lot size for A is 447.
b. The best lot size for B is 800.
c. The best lot size for C is 400.
d. The best lot size for B is 730.
e. Both *a* and *d* are correct.

6. All of the following procedures can take into account a purchase discount in lot sizing problems except:
a. Period order quantity.
b. Least unit cost.
c. Least period cost.
d. McLaren's order moment.
e. Least unit cost with look ahead.

7. The following information has been compiled for a part:

Period	1	2	3	4	5
Projected requirements	0	0	150	170	65
Actual requirements	150	170	0	65	0

The information illustrates uncertainty in:

a. Demand timing.
b. Supply timing.
c. Demand quantity.
d. Supply quantity.

8. In dealing with uncertainty in MRP systems:
a. Safety stock is the preferred technique for dealing with conditions of uncertainty in timing.
b. Safety lead time is the preferred technique for dealing with conditions of uncertainty in quantity.
c. Both *a* and *b* are correct.
d. Neither *a* nor *b* is correct.

9. All of the following are useful in reducing MRP system nervousness except:
a. Freezing the master production schedule.
b. Setting time fences for the master production schedule.
c. Incorporating forecasts for spare parts into MRP records.
d. Following MRP plans with regard to planned order releases.
e. Updating parameter changes in planned lead times rapidly.

10. A bucketless MRP system:
a. Specifies the exact quantities and due dates for each requirement, scheduled receipt, and planned order.
b. Can be used to print reports with any desired bucket size.
c. Both *a* and *b* are correct.
d. Neither *a* nor *b* is correct.

Chapter 13

1. All of the following are important objectives in scheduling except:
a. Maximizing delivery performance.
b. Minimizing late orders.
c. Maximizing work center utilization.
d. Minimizing lateness variance.
e. Maximizing time in the system.

The following data on five jobs in queue at a work center are to be used to answer questions 2, 3, 4, and 5 (1 day = 8 hours).

Job	*Due date–now (days)*	*Processing time in this work center (hours)*	*Processing time in all remaining work centers (hours)*	*Operations remaining*
A	2	3	12	3
B	2	4	6	2
C	1	2	3	1
D	3	5	6	1
E	3	1	5	2

2. The first job to process, using the earliest due date rule is:
a. A.
b. B.
c. C.
d. D.
e. E.

3. The first job to process, using the shortest processing time rule is:
a. A.
b. B.
c. C.
d. D.
e. E.

4. The first job to process, using the slack time per operation rule is:
a. A.
b. B.
c. C.
d. D.
e. E.

5. The first job to process, using the critical ratio rule is:
a. A.
b. B.
c. C.
d. D.
e. E.

6. The shortest processing time rule works well for all of the following criteria except:
a. Minimize the maximum number of jobs in the system.
b. Minimize the average number of jobs in the system.
c. Minimize the maximum job lateness.

d. Minimize the average job lateness.
e. Minimize the average flow true.

7. In the static problem approach to scheduling research:
a. A fixed set of jobs is run.
b. At the end of the problem all machine centers are empty.
c. Both *a* and *b* are correct.
d. Neither *a* nor *b* is correct.

8. In labor limited scheduling, the following have been found to provide additional benefits beyond those obtained using different sequencing rules:
a. Flexibility in assigning jobs to machines.
b. Flexibility in assigning workers to machines.
c. Both *a* and *b* are correct.
d. Neither *a* nor *b* is correct.

9. The potential advantage of a hybrid scheduling rule such as shortest processing time-critical ratio, is to improve:
a. Lateness measures.
b. Flow time measures.
c. Work-in-process measures.
d. Both lateness and flow time measures.
e. Both flow time and work-in-process measures.

10. The scheduling research on due date setting offers the potential to provide better estimates of:
a. Lead time offset data for MRP.
b. Customer order promise dates.
c. Queue lengths of work centers.
d. Work center utilization.
e. Work force utilization.

Chapter 14

The following data are to be used for questions 1, 2, 3, and 4.

A project consists of the following activities:

Activity	*Preceding activity*	*Time*
A	—	2
B	A	6
C	A	3
D	B,C	4
E	B	5
F	D,E	3

1. Which of the following statements is correct?
a. Activities A and B can be started at the same time.
b. Activities B and C can be performed concurrently.
c. Activity D can be started immediately after C is completed.
d. Activity F can be started immediately after D is completed.
e. All of the above are correct.

2. Which activity will *not* be on the critical path?
a. Activity A.
b. Activity B.
c. Activity D.
d. Activity E.
e. Activity F.

3. The time to complete the project will be:
a. 12 days or less.
b. 13 days.
c. 14 days.
d. 15 days.
e. 16 days or more.

4. The early finish time F_E and late finish time F_L for activity D would be:
a. $F_E = 5$, $F_L = 7$.
b. $F_E = 9$, $F_L = 10$.
c. $F_E = 9$, $F_L = 13$.
d. $F_E = 12$, $F_L = 13$.
e. None of the above is correct.

5. Resource leveling may involve
a. Reducing the time for activities.
b. Setting the start time for a noncritical activity between its early start time and late start time.
c. Both *a* and *b*.
d. Neither *a* nor *b*.

6. The time chart permits greater flexibility in scheduling:
a. Critical path activities.
b. Noncritical path activities.
c. Both *a* and *b*.
d. Neither *a* nor *b*.

7. In utilizing the manufacturing planning and control (MPC) system approach for project planning and control, the primary system used is:
a. Demand management.
b. Master production scheduling.
c. Material requirements planning.
d. Capacity requirements planning.
e. Shop floor control.

8. The MPC system approach to project planning and control utilizes all of the following except:
a. Low-level coding.
b. Available to promise logic.
c. Project bills of material.
d. Part numbers as activities.
e. Shop floor control for non-shop oriented activities.

9. In the Ethan Allen example, the primary benefits were obtained from:
a. Resource loading for managerial resources.
b. Incorporating soft activities such as training.
c. Both *a* and *b*.
d. Neither *a* nor *b*.

10. In the Elliott Company example, the MPC system was utilized to plan and control all of the following except:
    a. Order processing.
    b. Design engineering.
    c. Finished goods inventory.
    d. Manufacturing.
    e. Purchasing.

Chapter 15

The following data are to be used to answer questions 1, 2, 3, and 4.

A company manufactures axle housings. Management is currently attempting to establish an aggregate capacity plan for the next year. As of December 31, the following information is available:

Demand forecast	January–June = 7,000/month July–December = 12,000/month
Number of employees	400
Present inventory	0
Available working hours per month per employee	160 regular, paid at \$6 per hour; 40 overtime, paid at \$9 per hour
Axle housings/employee/month	16
Inventory carrying cost	\$35 per axle housing at the end of the month
Hiring cost	\$600 per employee hired
Firing cost	\$1,500 per employee fired
Backorder cost	\$35 per axle housing
Desired inventory at end of year	0

1. If the company adopts a chase strategy without use of overtime the inventory carrying cost for the month of February will be:
    a. Less than or equal to \$100,000.
    b. Greater than \$100,000 but less than or equal to \$200,000.
    c. Greater than \$200,000 but less than or equal to \$300,000.
    d. Greater than \$300,000 but less than or equal to \$400,000.
    e. Greater than \$400,000.

2. If the company produces just enough to meet demand without overtime, the hiring cost plus firing cost for January will be:
    a. Less than or equal to \$5,000.
    b. Greater than \$5,000 but less than or equal to \$10,000.
    c. Greater than \$10,000 but less than or equal to \$15,000.
    d. Greater than \$15,000 but less than or equal to \$20,000.
    e. Greater than \$20,000.

3. If the company maintains 400 employees, producing without overtime, the backorder cost for January will be:
    a. Less than or equal to \$5,000.
    b. Greater than \$5,000 but less than or equal to \$10,000.
    c. Greater than \$10,000 but less than or equal to \$15,000.
    d. Greater than \$15,000 but less than or equal to \$20,000.
    e. Greater than \$20,000.

4. If in any period one more axle housing were needed beyond the regular time capacity, the company is best advised to:

a. Produce the housing with overtime labor.
b. Produce the housing in the previous period and carry it in inventory to this period.
c. Produce the housing two periods earlier and carry it in inventory to this period.
d. Backorder the housing and produce in the next period.
e. Backorder the housing and produce it two periods later.

5. Aggregate planning models typically involve decisions regarding:

a. The scheduling of machine operations at the departmental level.
b. The size of the labor force.
c. The size of the shop work load aggregated across several machines.
d. The accumulation or depletion of inventories for individual component items.
e. All of the above.

6. Pick the correct statement about the Linear Decision Rule (LDR) and Linear Programming (LP).

a. LDR assumes linear cost functions, LP assumes quadratic cost functions.
b. Both LDR and LP assume linear cost functions.
c. Both LDR and LP assume quadratic cost functions.
d. LDR assumes quadratic cost functions, LP assumes linear cost functions.
e. None of the above.

7. A "Chase" strategy:

a. Is named after Richard B. Chase.
b. Maintains production at a uniform rate.
c. Maintains inventory at a uniform level.
d. Minimizes hiring/firing costs.
e. Minimizes the maximum number of employees.

8. Hierarchical production planning is:

a. An aggregation of factory plans to determine the overall production plan.
b. Consistent with decision making levels in the organization.
c. Both *a* and *b* are correct.
d. Neither *a* nor *b* is correct.

9. Aggregate planning models have had very limited application for all of the following reasons except:

a. Few firms make decisions in the ways indicated by the models.
b. The limited existence of some uniform measure of output.
c. Few firms face the tradeoffs implied in the models.
d. The limited ability of managers to understand the analytical underpinnings of the models.
e. Few firms have data that correspond to those required by the models.

10. For the Ethan Allen approach to aggregate capacity analysis, all of the following statements are correct except:

a. The approach is similar to that utilized by the linear decision rule.
b. The approach plans capacity at an overall level as well as at the factory level.

c. The approach allows for capacity to be allocated to special sales and new products.
d. The approach incorporates an overall analysis of economic conditions.
e. The approach is updated on a regular cycle.

Chapter 16

The following data are to be used for questions 1, 2, 3, 4, 5, and 6.

Period	*Sales*
1	26
2	32
3	39
4	40
5	38
6	47
7	50
8	59
9	56

1. The three-period moving average forecast for period 8 made at the end of period 7 is:
   a. Less than or equal to 35.
   b. Greater than 35 but less than or equal to 40.
   c. Greater than 40 but less than or equal to 45.
   d. Greater than 45 but less than or equal to 50.
   e. Greater than 50.
2. The three-period moving average forecast for period 9 made at the end of period 7 is:
   a. Less than or equal to 35.
   b. Greater than 35 but less than or equal to 40.
   c. Greater than 40 but less than or equal to 45.
   d. Greater than 45 but less than or equal to 50.
   e. Greater than 50.
3. If the forecast for period 3 was 33, the forecast for period 4 made at the end of period 3 (with $\alpha = 0.2$) is:
   a. Less than or equal to 35.
   b. Greater than 35 but less than or equal to 40.
   c. Greater than 40 but less than or equal to 45.
   d. Greater than 45 but less than or equal to 50.
   e. Greater than 50.
4. If the base at the end of period 6 is 45 and the trend per period at the end of period 6 is 4 ($\alpha = 0.2$ and $\beta = 0.4$), the forecast for period 7 made at the end of period 6 is:
   a. Less than or equal to 35.
   b. Greater than 35 but less than or equal to 40.
   c. Greater than 40 but less than or equal to 45.
   d. Greater than 45 but less than or equal to 50.
   e. Greater than 50.

5. Continuing with the data given in question 4, the forecast for period 8 made at the end of period 7 is:
   a. Less than or equal to 35.
   b. Greater than 35 but less than or equal to 40.
   c. Greater than 40 but less than or equal to 45.
   d. Greater than 45 but less than or equal to 50.
   e. Greater than 50.

6. Suppose the forecasts for periods 1, 2, and 3 are 30, 31, and 35, respectively. The MAD for those periods is:
   a. Less than or equal to 1.5.
   b. Greater than 1.5 but less than or equal to 2.0.
   c. Greater than 2.0 but less than or equal to 2.5.
   d. Greater than 2.5 but less than or equal to 3.0.
   e. Greater than 3.0.

7. Increasing the smoothing constant α:
   a. Increases stability of the forecast.
   b. Reduces responsiveness of the forecast.
   c. Both *a* and *b* are correct.
   d. Neither *a* nor *b* is correct.

8. MAD is:
   a. A measure of forecast error.
   b. A measure of forecast bias.
   c. Both *a* and *b* are correct.
   d. Neither *a* nor *b* is correct.

9. A local bar sells 4 kegs of beer per day on the average. Friday sales are 25 percent higher than average, Monday sales are 15 percent lower than average, and Tuesday sales are 10 percent lower than average. In forecasting daily beer requirements, the bar would be best advised to use:
   a. 3-period moving average.
   b. 5-period moving average.
   c. Basic exponential smoothing.
   d. Exponential smoothing with trend.
   e. Exponential smoothing with seasonality.

10. If the value of the tracking signal is zero:
    a. The value of the smoothed MAD must be equal to zero.
    b. The value of the smoothed BIAS must be equal to zero.
    c. Both *a* and *b* are correct.
    d. Neither *a* nor *b* is correct.

Chapter 17

1. The use of the economic lot size leads to creation of the following type of inventories:
   a. Cycle stocks.
   b. Safety stocks.
   c. Transit stocks.
   d. Anticipation stocks.
   e. All of the above.

2. The economic order quantity is doubled when:
   a. The cost of preparing an order doubles.
   b. The annual order requirements double.
   c. The annual order requirements quadruple.
   d. The inventory carrying costs double.
   e. The inventory carrying costs quadruple.

3. The total cost for various discounts are shown below:

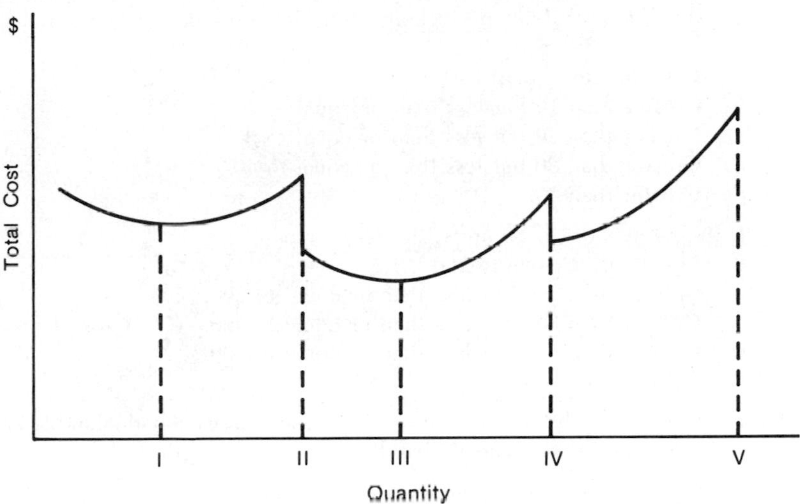

   For the above total cost function, the best order quantity is at:
   a. Point I.
   b. Point II.
   c. Point III.
   d. Point IV.
   e. Point V.

The following data for one purchased item are to be used in answering questions 4, 5, 6, and 7.

Weekly forecast of demand	=	250
Standard deviation of weekly demand	=	20
Ordering cost	=	$60
Annual holding rate	=	20 percent
Unit value	=	$5
Lead time	=	2 weeks
1 year	=	50 weeks

4. The economic order quantity is:
   a. Less than or equal to 950.
   b. Greater than 950 but less than or equal to 1,050.
   c. Greater than 1,050 but less than or equal to 1,150.
   d. Greater than 1,150 but less than or equal to 1,250.
   e. Greater than 1,250.

5. If the firm now orders in quantities of 1,000, the expected time between orders is:
   a. Less than or equal to 4.5 weeks.
   b. Greater than 4.5 weeks but less than or equal to 5.5 weeks.
   c. Greater than 5.5 weeks but less than or equal to 6.5 weeks.
   d. Greater than 6.5 weeks but less than or equal to 7.5 weeks.
   e. Greater than 7.5 weeks.

6. If the demand during lead time distribution is normally distributed and the firm accepts a .05 probability of stocking out during a reorder cycle, the safety stock is:
   a. Less than or equal to 10.
   b. Greater than 10 but less than or equal to 20.
   c. Greater than 20 but less than or equal to 30.
   d. Greater than 30 but less than or equal to 40.
   e. Greater than 40.

7. If the safety stock is 30 units, the reorder point is:
   a. Less than or equal to 200.
   b. Greater than 200 but less than or equal to 300.
   c. Greater than 300 but less than or equal to 400.
   d. Greater than 400 but less than or equal to 500.
   e. Greater than 500.

8. For one item at the XYZ Company, the forecast of weekly demand is 12 units, and the following demand probabilities have been estimated:

Demand	*Probability*
10	.1
11	.2
12	.4
13	.2
14	.1

   If the lead time is one week, the probability of stocking out during a reorder cycle with a reorder point of 13 units is:
   a. Less than or equal to .05.
   b. Greater than .05 but less than or equal to .15.
   c. Greater than .15 but less than or equal to .25.
   d. Greater than .25 but less than or equal to .35.
   e. Greater than .35.

9. Companies 1 and 2 each sell five products. The distribution of sales by product are as follows:

Company 1		*Company 2*	
Product	*Sales*	*Product*	*Sales*
A	$120,000	K	$60,000
B	60,000	L	58,000
C	20,000	M	54,000
D	15,000	N	50,000
E	8,000	O	46,000

a. ABC analysis is more appropriate for Company 1 than 2.
b. ABC analysis is more appropriate for Company 2 than 1.
c. ABC analysis is equally appropriate for Companies 1 and 2.
d. ABC analysis for managing the inventory of the products is not appropriate for Company 1 or 2.

10. If a company has done an ABC analysis, which items would be best managed with a bin reserve system?
a. A items.
b. B items.
c. C items.
d. Both A and B items.
e. Both B and C items.

Chapter 18

1. The Fetter and Daleck procedure jointly determines the order quantity and:
a. The reorder point.
b. The service level.
c. Both *a* and *b*.
d. Neither *a* nor *b*.

2. All of the following statements about simultaneous inventory and transportation decisions are true except:
a. The costs of transporting items from suppliers to stockkeeping locations are to be minimized.
b. Variability in transit times can lead to different reorder points.
c. Differences in transportation costs can lead to different order quantities.
d. Any transportation alternative that is more costly, has a greater transit time, and more variability in transit time than another alternative can be eliminated from consideration.
e. Simultaneous inventory/transportation decisions are usually not made in practice.

3. An Impact system would be appropriate for:
a. A wholesale druggist.
b. A machine tool manufacturer.
c. Both *a* and *b*.
d. Neither *a* nor *b*.

4. A firm is considering making simultaneous inventory/transportation decisions, and has calculated the ratio of the average transportation cost per unit to product value per unit.
a. When the ratio is low, savings through integrated decisions are more likely than when the ratio is high.
b. When the ratio is high, savings through integrated decision are more likely than when the ratio is low.
c. The ratio needs to be adjusted for variability in lead time.
d. When the ratio is low, heuristic methods produce results similar to those obtained with exact methods.
e. When the ratio is high, exact methods produce results that are significantly better than the heuristic methods.

The following data for two items purchased jointly from the same vendor are to be used in answering questions 5, 6, and 7.

Item	Monthly forecast	Standard deviation of forecast	Unit weight	On-hand balance	Lead time (months)
A	100	20	5	50	1
B	80	30	1	200	1

5. What is the order point for item A if a 2.5 percent chance of stocking out in the reorder cycle is the criterion?
a. Less than or equal to 100.
b. More than 100 but less than or equal to 115.
c. More than 115 but less than or equal to 130.
d. More than 130 but less than or equal to 145.
e. More than 145.

6. If the order points for items A and B are 150 and 120, respectively, and the combined purchase quantity is 2,000 lbs., the amount of item A to be purchased is:
a. Less than or equal to 100 units.
b. More than 100 but less than or equal to 200 units.
c. More than 200 but less than or equal to 300 units.
d. More than 300 but less than or equal to 400 units.
e. More than 400 units.

7. Continuing problem 6, the amount of item B to be purchased is:
a. Less than or equal to 100 units.
b. More than 100 but less than or equal to 200 units.
c. More than 200 but less than or equal to 300 units.
d. More than 300 but less than or equal to 400 units.
e. More than 400 units.

8. All of the following statements about pyramid forecasting are correct except:
a. At the top management level, judgmental factors are included.
b. The lower-level forecasts are made for individual products.
c. Lower-level forecasts are "rolled up" into higher-level forecasts.
d. The first step is to "force down" the high-level forecast.
e. The overall objective is to eliminate inconsistencies among independently produced forecasts.

9. The sales forecasts for groups I and II are $18,000 and $15,000, respectively. The agreed-upon total sales forecast is $35,000. The forced down forecast for group I is:
a. Less than or equal to $18,000.
b. Greater than $18,000 but less than or equal to $19,000.

c. Greater than $19,000 but less than or equal to $20,000.
d. Greater than $20,000 but less than or equal to $21,000.
e. Greater than $21,000.

10. In the research by Makridakis, all of the following statements apply except:
a. Simple models outperform more complex models.
b. Some models perform better for longer forecasting horizons.
c. The Box-Jenkins model is a consistently good performer.
d. Seasonal and nonseasonal data series were studied.
e. Forecast accuracy was measured in several different ways.

Chapter 19

1. The total cost concept for logistics involves all of the following except:
a. Overall cost minimization from raw materials to consumption.
b. Cooperative efforts between manufacturers and retailers.
c. Improved coordination among supplying firms.
d. An evolutionary approach to problem definition and solution.
e. A focus on customers needs.

2. Reorder point/economic order quantity systems for replenishing distribution centers:
a. Base the decision of when to ship on the inventory balance at the central warehouse.
b. Are based on high information system complexity.
c. Base the shipment quantity on the actual usage in the prior period.
d. Base the decision of when to ship on planned shipment data.
e. Base the decision of how much to ship on forecast or past average usage.

3. Distribution centers provide all of the following except:
a. Place utility.
b. Time utility.
c. Customer information.
d. Supplier information.
e. A mixing function.

4. The base stock system has the following distinguishing features:
a. The quantity shipped to a distribution center (DC) in some period is directly related to the quantity sold from that DC in an earlier period.
b. Establishment of a fixed order replenishment quantity.
c. Both *a* and *b*.
d. Neither *a* nor *b*.

5. In distribution requirements planning, a shipment decision is made:
a. In anticipation of an inventory need.
b. At the distribution center.
c. When the distribution center inventory reaches the reorder point.
d. On a fixed time cycle.

The following data are to be used to answer questions 6, 7, and 8.

Distribution center A

Period		1	2	3	4	5
Forecast		10	10	10	20	20
Sched. receipts						
Projected available balance	25	15	35	25		
Planned shipments		30		30		

Safety stock = 10, shipping quantity = 30, lead time = 1

Distribution center B

Period		1	2	3	4	5
Forecast		25	25	30	30	30
Sched. receipts		50				
Projected available balance	35	60	35	55		
Planned shipments		50				

Safety stock = 20, shipping quantity = 50, lead time = 2

6. The planned shipments for distribution center "A" in week 4 are:
a. Zero.
b. Greater than zero but less than or equal to 20.
c. Greater than 20 but less than or equal to 40.
d. Greater than 40 but less than or equal to 60.
e. Greater than 60.

7. The gross requirements in week 1 at the central warehouse that replenishes distribution centers A and B are:
a. Zero.
b. Greater than zero but less than or equal to 20.
c. Greater than 20 but less than or equal to 40.
d. Greater than 40 but less than or equal to 60.
e. Greater than 60.

8. The gross requirements in week 2 at the central warehouse that replenishes distribution centers A and B are:
a. Zero.
b. Greater than zero but less than or equal to 20.
c. Greater than 20 but less than or equal to 40.
d. Greater than 40 but less than or equal to 60.
e. Greater than 60.

9. In the Abbott Canada approach to distribution requirements planning, the "zero level" in the bill of materials is:
a. The end item in transit to a customer.
b. The end item in a distribution center.
c. The end item at the central warehouse.
d. The end item at the factory warehouse.
e. The end item in the final assembly schedule.

10. All of the following solution methodologies have been applied to the traveling salesman problem except:
a. Linear programming.
b. Zero-one integer programming.
c. Dynamic programming.
d. Branch and bound.
e. Heuristic procedures.

Chapter 20

1. OPT makes use of all of the following except:
   a. Network models.
   b. Simulation.
   c. Mathematical programming.
   d. Infinite loading.
   e. Order splitting.

2. OPT:
   a. Provides a master production schedule (MPS).
   b. Reduces lot sizes for bottleneck operations.
   c. Both *a* and *b* are correct.
   d. Neither *a* nor *b* is correct.

3. Kanban:
   a. Is a philosophy of improving *all* manufacturing procedures not just material planning and control systems.
   b. Is based on a stable flow of production.
   c. Both *a* and *b* are correct.
   d. Neither *a* nor *b* is correct.

4. All of the following statements about Kanban at Toyota are correct except:
   a. Daily time buckets are used.
   b. The monthly explosion produces the same results for each time bucket.
   c. New Kanban cards are issued each day.
   d. Kanban cards replace all other shop papers.
   e. The chain of Kanban cards extends all the way back to the suppliers.

5. The number of Kanbans for a particular part with the following data is:

   Daily demand = 10 units
   Lead time = 2 days
   Container capacity = 3 units
   Policy factor for safety stock = 10 percent

   a. Less than or equal to 2.
   b. Greater than 2 but less than or equal to 4.
   c. Greater than 4 but less than or equal to 6.
   d. Greater than 6 but less than or equal to 8.
   e. Greater than 8.

6. All of the following statements about Kanban cards are correct except:
   a. The objective is to develop a level flow of parts.
   b. Fewer cards results in less work-in-process inventory.
   c. Set-up time has a direct influence on the number of cards.
   d. All cards must be used.
   e. Kanban cards are not used for every part at Toyota.

7. In implementing Kanban at the L. M. Ericsson plant in Sweden, which of the following was to be implemented last?
   a. Reduced set-up time.
   b. Kanban cards.
   c. Layout redesigns.
   d. Multifunctional workers.
   e. Small lot sizes.

8. The periodic control system at Kumera Oy is based upon:

a. Product groups rather than end items.
b. Critical ratio shop-floor dispatching.
c. Both *a* and *b*.
d. Neither *a* nor *b*.

9. All of the following statements about the periodic control system at Kumera Oy are true except:

a. Each product group is scheduled only once in a production period.
b. Forecasts are used to calculate the number of products to schedule in each production set.
c. Customer orders are assigned to a specific production set.
d. Actual orders replace forecast quantities in each production set.
e. The final production set usually includes a mixture of forecast orders and actual customer orders.

10. All of the following principles are important in evaluating improvements to MPC systems except:

a. There is no "ultimate weapon" in the MPC system. Firms should continually be evaluating improvements.
b. Use of the MPC framework is useful in assessing where a particular approach or system fits into the firm.
c. Once a working MPC system is in place, improvements can often be made more easily.
d. Improvements in MPC systems must be integrated with the management and direction of the company.
e. Technical expertise is the most important attribute for implementing new MPC systems.

Solutions key

Chapter 2

1a, 2c, 3c, 4d, 5a, 6c, 7c, 8a, 9e, 10b

Chapter 3

1a, 2c, 3b, 4d, 5a, 6c, 7d, 8d, 9e, 10b

Chapter 4

1b, 2a, 3b, 4b, 5c, 6a, 7d, 8d, 9a, 10d

Chapter 5

1d, 2b, 3d, 4b, 5a, 6d, 7a, 8c, 9b, 10a

Chapter 6

1a, 2c, 3c, 4e, 5b, 6c, 7e, 8c, 9c, 10d

Chapter 7

1c, 2c, 3b, 4a, 5c, 6d, 7c, 8a, 9c, 10e

Chapter 8

1d, 2b, 3c, 4d, 5d, 6d, 7b, 8c, 9b, 10b

Chapter 9

1c, 2e, 3b, 4e, 5e, 6c, 7e, 8a, 9a, 10c

Chapter 10

1d, 2a, 3d, 4e, 5c, 6d, 7a, 8a, 9c, 10c

Chapter 11

1c, 2c, 3a, 4b, 5d, 6c, 7b, 8c, 9a, 10c

Chapter 12

1d, 2d, 3b, 4b, 5b, 6a, 7a, 8d, 9e, 10c

Chapter 13

1e, 2c, 3e, 4a, 5a, 6c, 7c, 8b, 9d, 10a

Chapter 14

1b, 2c, 3e, 4d, 5c, 6b, 7c, 8b, 9c, 10c

Chapter 15

1a, 2e, 3e, 4a, 5b, 6d, 7c, 8b, 9c, 10a

Chapter 16

1c, 2c, 3a, 4d, 5e, 6d, 7d, 8a, 9e, 10b

Chapter 17

1a, 2c, 3c, 4d, 5a, 6d, 7e, 8b, 9a, 10c

Chapter 18

1a, 2a, 3a, 4b, 5d, 6d, 7c, 8d, 9c, 10c

Chapter 19

1c, 2e, 3d, 4a, 5a, 6a, 7e, 8a, 9b, 10a

Chapter 20

1d, 2d, 3c, 4c, 5d, 6d, 7b, 8a, 9e, 10e

Index

Q

R

U

V

W

X–Y